Clayton P. Coates
668-2709 home
225-8525 work

Lotus 123
dbase ~~III~~
Wordstar 2000

Principles of Real Estate Decisions

SECOND EDITION

Donald R. Epley
Robert Warren Chair of Real Estate
Mississippi State University

Joseph Rabianski
Professor, Department of Real Estate and Urban Affairs
Georgia State University

Prentice-Hall, Englewood Cliffs, New Jersey 07632

Library of Congress Cataloging-in-Publication Data

Epley, Donald R.
  Principles of real estate decisions.

  Includes bibliographies and index.
    1. Real Estate business.   I. Rabianski, Joseph.
II. Title.
HD1375.E36 1986b   333.33   85-28091
ISBN 0-13-709791-3

To Amy, Sara, and Sue;
and Stanley, Mary, and Rose

Editorial/production supervision and
    interior design: Eve Mossman and Allison DeFren
Cover design: Wanda Lubelska Design
Manufacturing buyer: Carol Bystrom

© 1986, 1981 by Prentice-Hall
A Division of Simon & Schuster, Inc.
Englewood Cliffs, New Jersey 07632

Printed in the United States of America

10 9 8 7 6 5 4 3 2 1

ISBN 0-13-709791-3 01

Prentice-Hall International (UK) Limited, *London*
Prentice-Hall of Australia Pty. Limited, *Sydney*
Prentice-Hall Canada Inc., *Toronto*
Prentice-Hall Hispanoamericana, S.A., *Mexico*
Prentice-Hall of India Private Limited, *New Delhi*
Prentice-Hall of Japan, Inc., *Tokyo*
Prentice-Hall of Southeast Asia Pte. Ltd., *Singapore*
Editora Prentice-Hall do Brasil, Ltda., *Rio de Janeiro*
Whitehall Books Limited, *Wellington, New Zealand*

Contents

PART II
The Decision to Estimate Market Value

PART III
The Decision to Invest

PART IV
The Decision to Buy or Sell

PART V
The Decision to Manage the Property and Seek Information about the Lease

PART VI
The Decision to Finance the Transaction

PART VII
The Decision to Transfer the Title

Estate Settlement Procedures Act requirements; Truth-In-Lending; Supervision of the closing; Recommendations to the buyer, seller, and agent; Chapter summary

22 The Closing, 624

Introduction; Relationship of closing to the listing contract and the sales contract; Documents required at closing; Prorating; Expenses; Settlement statement; Completion of the title transfer; Default of closing; Real Estate Settlement Procedures Act; License law and rules and regulations; Chapter summary

Preface

This text makes several unique contributions. First, the material is presented in a "need to know" order that a prospective agent, buyer, or seller would require for real estate decision making. Most texts are organized around *topics;* this book, however, is organized around *decisions* and the flow of the decision-making process. Thus, the material is arranged in the order that information is required by the typical consumer for decision making in a typical real estate transaction.

The viewpoint taken is that of the *consumer* who is the prospective buyer, seller, or agent. The underlying question addressed is, What does the consumer need to know to make decisions in various steps of the typical real estate transaction? We suggest that prospective agents need to know the same information as consumers to represent adequately the needs of their clients.

For example, the first question typically asked by a potential buyer or seller is, What is the real estate business, and why should I become involved with any aspect of it? To answer this question, Part I of the text explores the consumer's "Decision to Acquire Knowledge about the Real Estate Business." Chapter 1, "The Real Estate Commodity and the Business," introduces the reader to the nature of the real estate commodity, the real estate business, and the specialities of the individuals and firms that provide services. Chapter 2, "Public Controls, Private Restrictions, and the Concept of Value," covers the limitations placed upon the use of property by the public and private owners. In addition, Chapter 2 provides an introduction to the factors causing some parcels of real estate to have value. Chapter 3 extends the discussion of public limits and controls on the rights of ownership into the topic of land development procedures and urban growth.

Another question asked by the typical consumer at an early stage of the transaction is, How much is the property worth? Consequently, Part II, covering the next five chapters of the text, discusses the various aspects of estimating property values. In addition to the traditional appraisal chapters, unique chapters in this section are Chapter 7, "Housing Market Analysis," which gives basic information necessary to understand local and regional housing trends, and Chapter 8, "Real Estate Market Analysis and Feasibility Study," which introduces the techniques to understand and estimate market and site specific value determinants.

This section is followed by Part III, two chapters on "The Decision to Invest"; Part IV, three chapters on "The Decision to Buy or Sell"; Part V, two chapters on "The Decision to Manage the Property and Seek Information about the Lease"; Part VI, four chapters on "The Decision to Finance the Transaction"; and Part VII, two chapters on "The Decision to Transfer the Title." Thus, in addition to seven chapters that identify the real estate commodity, the business, the buying and selling process, and the transfer of the title, the book covers appraisal, investment, management, and finance in twelve chapters, giving adequate background and the proper tools for decision making.

A second unique contribution of the book is the fact that legal concepts are integrated into the subject matter rather than studied as a separate topic. We view real estate law as only a tool to assist in the successful completion of a transaction. For example, deeds are discussed in Chapter 21, "Preparing for the Closing," to provide the agent or consumer with the information necessary to ascertain whether the deed is the one requested in the sales contract. Any problems should be rightfully referred to an attorney for an opinion. Consequently, the reader is given only enough information to protect his or her interests instead of a detailed description of the deed's clauses and their ramifications.

We have included a description of many detailed points within the sales contract and the lease because we view them as "decision" documents. Many of the clauses within both can be adapted to the needs and wishes of the parties involved. The deed is not in the same class of decision documents because its components are typically predetermined and not negotiable.

The third contribution is that the theoretical concepts are oriented toward decision making rather than presented in a descriptive manner only. For example, students are shown in Part II, "The Decision to Estimate Market Value," how the theory of value can be applied to their benefit and why they need to know it.

Fourth, new material and several new approaches are included. The information in Chapter 7, "Housing Market Analysis," is not generally presented in similar books, yet it is critical to estimating market value because it describes the factors that influence the housing market. Chapters 11 and 12, "The Listing Motive and Contract" and "Methods of Marketing and Persuasion," respectively, are not typical in a text of this kind, and the approach used here is unique. The consumer is actually shown techniques taught to prospective agents in their Graduate REALTORS Institute courses. Thus, a prospective seller or buyer knows in advance the agent's motives and the approach that could be taken with the potential buyer and seller. All parties need to know this information as a basis for responding to the actions of the other parties in the transaction. Also, Chapter 21, "Preparing for the Closing," is new; most texts concentrate on the closing process only. However, any practitioner will confirm that the preparation for the closing is actually more important than the closing itself. For example, a prospective buyer and all agents should know to call the county tax collector and ask for verification that the last year's property taxes have been paid. What is the proper course of action if they have or have not been paid? Answers to these questions provide information on which to base the settlement statements.

Fifth, an attempt is made to achieve an appropriate balance between theoretical concepts and applied material. Our hope is that a student who finishes this text will understand *why* the concept exists, *how* it works, and the *motives* of the participants in the market.

This text is designed for a one-semester course in the Principles of Real Estate. We do not presume that the students have completed any prerequisites. Each chapter is a separate entity containing the information needed to make the decision at hand. Certain material is reiterated among sections as needed. For example, liens are introduced in Chapter 1, "Real Estate Commodity and the Business," are mentioned in Chapter 13, "The Real Estate Sales Contract," and are noted again in Chapter 21, "Preparing for the Closing."

Each chapter contains good teaching aids. Learning objectives are listed to guide the reader. A list of important terms is provided to identify key terms. Review questions are given at the end of each chapter to test the student's reading comprehension. Discussion questions follow, which give the instructor a starting point for open-end class discussion. A list of additional readings inform the reader of sources that can be used to acquire more detail and information.

The text will meet the needs of courses that are offered in a semester with 45 class periods of 50 minutes each. It can also be used in courses that are offered on a quarter basis with 20 class periods of 120 minutes each. Following is a schedule of appropriate assignments.

TOPIC	CLASS PERIODS 15-week semester	CLASS PERIODS 10-week quarter
PART I: The Decision to Acquire Knowledge about the Real Estate Business		
1. The Real Estate Commodity and the Business	$1\frac{1}{2}$	$\frac{1}{3}$
2. Public Controls, Private Restrictions, and the Concept of Value	$1\frac{1}{2}$	$\frac{1}{3}$
3. Land Development, Zoning and Environmental Regulations	1	$\frac{1}{3}$
PART II: The Decision to Estimate Market Value		
4. The Property Appraisal Process and Determinants of Value	1	$\frac{1}{2}$
5. Residential Property Appraisal	2	1
6. Income Property Appraisal	2	1
7. Housing Market Analysis	2	$\frac{3}{4}$
8. Real Estate Market Analysis and Feasibility Study	2	$\frac{3}{4}$
EXAM I	1	$\frac{1}{2}$
	14	$5\frac{1}{2}$

TOPIC	CLASS PERIODS 15-week semester	CLASS PERIODS 10-week quarter
PART III: The Decision to Invest		
9. Real Estate Equity Investment	3	1½
10. Taxation of the Real Estate Investment	3	1½
PART IV: The Decision to Buy or Sell		
11. The Listing Motive and Contract	2	½
12. Methods of Marketing and Persuasion	2	½
13. The Real Estate Sales Contract	2	1
EXAM II	1	½
	13	5½
PART V: The Decision to Manage the Property and Seek Information about the Lease		
14. Property Management and the Residential Lease	2	1
15. The Commercial and Industrial Lease	2	1
PART VI: The Decision to Finance the Transaction		
16. The Residential Mortgage and the Application Process	3	1½
17. The Commercial Loan	2	1
18. Creative Financing	2	1
19. The Lenders and the Secondary Mortgage Market	1½	1
20. Title Insurance, Property Insurance, and the Homeowner's Warranty	½	½
EXAM III	1	½
	14	7
PART VII: The Decision to Transfer the Title		
21. Preparing for the Closing	1½	½
22. The Closing	2	1
Total Class Periods	45	20
FINAL EXAM		

Any new entrant into the textbook market must pass three tests to be successful; it must be *well organized, easily teachable,* and *pedagogically sound.* We think that our text fills all three requirements. Our intention is to offer the marketplace a good alternative, and we feel we have accomplished that objective.

We intend for this material to be used for educational purposes only. Some terminology is defined as we have encountered it in our activities and may not coincide exactly with the standard legal literature. We emphasize that this material is supplementary to and not a substitute for legal advice.

A number of colleagues made valuable contributions to the manuscript at various times. Special thanks goes to Jay Butler, Arizona State University; Gerard Halpern, University of Arkansas; Kenneth Lusht, Pennsylvania State University; Ronald Racster, Ohio State University; and Barry Diskin, Florida State University. Several organizations gave permission to use their material. These include the American Institute of Real Estate Appraisers, the Arkansas REALTORS Association, Federal National Mortgage Association, Mortgage Bankers Association, and the Mortgage Corporation.

State University, Mississippi   D.R.E.
Atlanta, Georgia   J.R.

1 | The Real Estate Commodity and the Business

QUESTIONS TO BE ANSWERED

1. What is real estate?
2. What is the nature of the real estate business?
3. What is the relationship among its participants?
4. What do the participants have to offer a potential buyer? or seller?

OBJECTIVES

When a student finishes the chapter, he or she should be able to

1. Explain the nature of real estate by analyzing its physical and ownership components.
2. Identify the economic characteristics of real estate.
3. Describe the various services an agent can offer to a client.

4. Explain the differences among an agent, a REALTOR, a REALTOR-ASSOCIATE, and an agent who holds a designation in a specialty.

5. Explain the differences among the Real Estate Commission, the National Association of REALTORS, the State Association of REALTORS, and the local board.

6. Identify the other professionals who contribute to the real estate business and explain the services that each offers to a prospective buyer or seller.

7. Describe how public agencies influence the real estate business.

8. Identify the future characteristics of the real estate business.

IMPORTANT TERMS

Air Rights
Appraiser
Environment
Estate for Years
Estate from Year to Year
Estate in Expectancy
Estate in Possession
Estate *Pur Autre Vie*
Fee Simple
Fixture
Freehold Estate
Freehold Estate of Inheritance
Freehold Estate Not-of-
  Inheritance
General Agent
General Contractor
Improvement
Improvements-on-the-Land
Improvements-to-the-Land
Joint Tenancy
Land
Leasehold
Less-than-Freehold Estate
Life Estate
Local Board

Mineral Rights
National Association of
  REALTORS
Property Manager
Real Estate
Real Estate Agent
Real Estate Business
Real Estate Commission
Real Estate Counselor
Real Estate Developer
Real Estate Lender
Real Rroperty
REALTOR
REALTOR-ASSOCIATE
Rights of Ownership
Situs
Special Agent
State Association of
  REALTORS
Tenancy at Will
Tenancy by Sufferance
Tenancy in Common
Title Company
Waste

NATURE AND PURPOSE OF THE TEXT

Most real estate texts are topic-oriented. Typically, each chapter covers one topic in detail without much discussion of the reasons for studying one topic before or after another. For example, why are deeds examined prior to the settlement statements?

Why are property taxes examined after a discussion of estimating the market value of a parcel? Why are license laws examined in the first chapter of the book?

This text presents topics on a need-to-know basis; that is, topics are presented and discussed in the order in which a typical normal consumer would encounter the need to use this information in a real estate transaction. In addition, information is presented in a decision-making framework that the reader can use to make decisions. Thus, the purpose of the text is to present the topics in a need-to-know framework, in order that a typical consumer can use the information to understand a typical real estate transaction and to make intelligent decisions.

The consumer may be a buyer, seller, interested citizen, potential agent, or an actual agent. The typical transaction is basically the same for all. The same questions arise and must be answered in approximately the same order. Exceptions may exist in the order of the topics encountered for a particular transaction, but the steps remain essentially the same for the majority of the transactions.

Typical Steps in the Real Estate Transaction

A summarization of the typical steps in a normal real estate transaction appears in the contents as Parts I through VII. These steps are repeated and expanded upon in the following paragraphs.

I. *The Decision to Acquire knowledge about the Real Estate Business*

The consumer must understand the nature of real estate by first examining both the definition and meaning of real estate as a commodity. What characteristics does it have? What restrictions are placed upon its use? In addition, the consumer must decide whether there are any benefits to be gained from asking for help from one or several of the many individuals and firms that provide services. What services are provided? Who provides them? What are the advantages and disadvantages of asking for help, and should I? What is the role of the government in land-use development, and what are the tools commonly used? How do land-use controls influence business development and metropolitan growth? This material is covered in the first three chapters.

II. *The Decision to Estimate Market Value*

A question that the typical consumer asks very early is, What is my property worth? Immediately, he or she is expected to interpret local housing trends and understand the mechanics and concepts of income-property appraisal and residential appraisal. If this task is too time-consuming, the consumer may use the services of an appraiser (identified in Chapter 1). This material is covered in Chapters 4 through 8.

III. *The Decision to Invest*

A typical consumer will inquire early about the chance of receiving a capital gain and will ask whether the property is a good buy. In addition, a typical consumer may be interested in investment real estate in order to receive a tax shelter or a capital gain from either price appreciation or mortgage reduction. Chapters 9 and 10 cover the basics of real estate investment and real estate taxation.

IV. *The Decision to Buy or Sell*

If an agent is involved, the typical buyer or seller needs to know the economic motivations behind the agent's actions in order to evaluate the circumstances. Chapters 11 and 12 are written from the viewpoint of the agent. Chapter 11 covers the basics of listing property and explains that the agent may be motivated more by listing than by selling. Chapter 12 covers the basics of showing property and counseling the seller. Chapter 13 covers the components of the sales contract, so that a buyer, seller, or agent is made aware of the commitments made by all involved parties.

V. *The Decision to Manage the Property and Seek Information about the Lease*

Another decision the typical consumer may need to make is whether to lease the property and use a property manager. Chapters 14 and 15 cover the residential and commercial lease and the basics of property management.

VI. *The Decision to Finance the Transaction*

All of the earlier decisions assume the buyer is able to raise the necessary cash to pay the negotiated purchase price. Chapter 16 covers the residential loan application process and presents the types of information that the consumer will need to know to evaluate the loan application process and the contracts used in residential financing. Chapter 17 considers the commercial loan. Chapter 18 discusses other types of financing arrangements and instruments that may be used in special financial circumstances. Chapter 19 is a discussion of the forces of supply and demand for credit that will determine the terms of the financing the consumer can obtain at any given time.

VII. *The Decision to Transfer the Title*

The final three chapters cover the preparation for the closing when the title is transferred. Chapter 20 discusses title insurance, property insurance, and the homeowner's warranty. Chapter 21 includes a discussion of the steps that may be followed to prepare for the closing, and Chapter 22 covers the preparation of the buyer's, seller's, and broker's settlement statements. Every party should be able to verify the accuracy of the settlement statements.

In sum, every chapter contains the information the authors think the typical buyers, sellers, or agents need to know about that step of a real estate transaction. In addition, the steps follow a central theme of *need-to-know* that presents information to the consumer as he or she would encounter it. When the text is finished, the topics and presentation should allow the consumer to make decisions about the particular set of circumstances in a particular transaction.

THE REAL ESTATE COMMODITY

Real estate is a commodity in the same sense that an automobile and a television set are commodities. Each of these items is useful to an individual and each one is bought and sold in its own specialized market. Moreover, each product is complex. Automobiles can be classified by their obviously different external characteristics such as luxury versus compact, new versus used, four-door sedan versus sports car, domestic versus foreign, red versus blue. Less obvious, but also important, are such components as an eight-cylinder versus a four-cylinder engine, automatic versus standard transmission, and disc versus drum brakes. An analysis of television sets would reveal that they also could be categorized by external characteristics and on the basis of major components.

To understand the nature of a complex commodity, the consumer must identify and closely examine its components. Before buying an automobile, the consumer must know about the engine, the transmission, the brake system, and so on. These components are just as important as the external features of the commodity. The greater the consumer's knowledge about the component parts, the greater will be his or her understanding of the nature and the functions of the product.

This section presents a discussion of the commodity known as **real estate.** The public and private controls that affect its use and the basis for its value are discussed in Chapter 2. The role of government in land-use development and the tools commonly used are discussed in Chapter 3.

The real estate commodity has two major physical components—the land and the improvements—and a legal dimension consisting of a bundle of legal rights. The consumer must analyze each of the components and the legal aspects in detail in order to understand the nature and function of the commodity as a whole.

The Components of Real Estate

Legal concept of land   When the term *land* is used, it typically refers to thoughts of the solid surface of the earth. It is the ground upon which individuals live and build things. It is the dirt in which vegetation grows. An examination of any dictionary definition of the term reveals that this concept underlies the major part of the meaning of the word *land* in the sense of its being a physical entity or commodity.

The legal concept of **land,** however, includes more than just the visible solid surface of the earth. The legal definition of land contains two additional, less visible components. When the consumer buys a parcel of land, that person legally buys whatever is below ground, the mineral rights, whatever is above ground, and the air rights. The term *rights* is used in this sense to identify the claim or the interest to which the owner is justly entitled under law or custom. The term *mineral rights* denotes the legal claim of the owner of land to the minerals under the surface. The term *air rights* denotes the owner's claim in the space above the surface area of the property.

Mineral rights apply to a legally specified, three-dimensional, subterranean space. The surface area of the parcel forms the base of the three-dimensional figure.

For simplicity, assume that the land area is a square. In this case, the three dimensional figure is an inverted pyramid with a square base and a depth that is the distance from the surface to the center of the earth—roughly 4,000 miles.

Under the legal concept of land, the owner has an automatic claim to all minerals enclosed within the geometric shape formed by the surface area and the center of the earth. The minerals belong to the owner unless the owner and the seller agreed that mineral rights did not transfer when the property sold. Even though the legal extent of the mineral rights reaches to the center of earth, the current state of technology establishes a practical limit to the extent of these mineral rights. Mine shafts and oil wells can go down to a depth of several miles; they do not descend for tens or hundreds of miles. The technology of the extractive industry determines the feasible quantity of mineral rights, and the law defines the full extent of these rights within the American system of laws and customs.

Air rights also apply to a legally defined, three-dimensional space. In this case, the surface area or shape of the parcel defines the air space. If the three-dimensional figure used to define the mineral rights were to be extended above the surface of the land parcel, the base and the sides of the air-rights space could be outlined. The height of this space, or the upward extent of the air rights, must still be defined. Typically, the height dimension is expressed as extending "to the sky" or "to the heavens."

These statements could lead to an esoteric debate about the exact location of the sky and whether celestial bodies belong to the owners of land parcels. However, two considerations eliminate the need for such discussion: (1) The state of construction technology limits the feasible height of the landowner's air rights. Currently, the height of most commercial structures does not exceed 1,400 feet above the surface. The tallest buildings are only slightly higher than1,400 feet. (2) The federal government limits the height of air rights by establishing the airways above a stated height as public property for use by aircraft. Local governments also limit the upward extent of air rights by enacting building-height restrictions.

Due to the technological and governmental restrictions, the space in which a person has air and mineral rights, for all practical purposes, extends no more than 50,000 feet below the ground and no more than 1,500 feet above the ground, and the boundaries are established by the size and the shape of the land parcel.

Exhibit 1-1 shows the legal concept of land. Notice the distinction between legal dimensions and feasible/permissible range.

Improvements and fixtures   The second obvious component of real estate is any building or structure on the land. The term **improvement** is used to denote these buildings and structures, as well as other man-made additions such as fences, driveways, and retaining walls. The general term used to represent all types of permanently erected man-made structures is **improvements-on-the-land.** (See Exhibit 1-2.)

Another kind of improvement, called **improvements-to-the-land,** denotes such changes to the land as improving drainage, grading, and filling; providing utilities in the form of water and sewage laterals to the water and sewer mains, natural

EXHIBIT 1-1 The legal concept of land

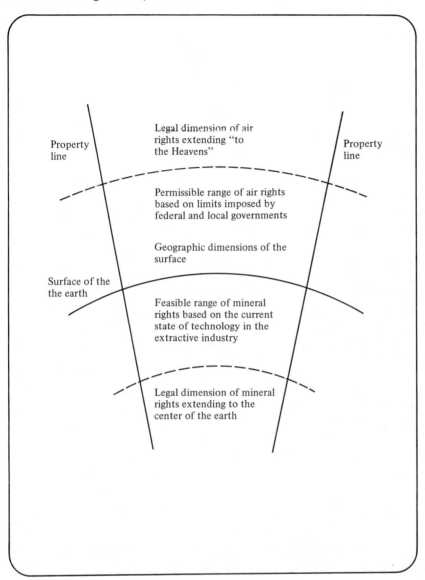

Property
line

Legal dimension of air
rights extending "to
the Heavens"

Property
line

Permissible range of air rights
based on limits imposed by
federal and local governments

Geographic dimensions of the
surface

Surface of the
the earth

Feasible range of mineral
rights based on the current
state of technology in the
extractive industry

Legal dimension of mineral
rights extending to the
center of the earth

gas lines, electricity and telephone lines and construction of access roads to main
arterial streets and highways. These changes make the land suitable for some form of
economic or public use, such as homes, stores, industries, schools, and parks.

Improvements-on-the-land and improvements-to-the-land, taken together,
are referred to as *on-site improvements*. Thus, the second major physical component

of the commodity known as real estate is the entire complex of man-made additions known as on-site improvements.

A **fixture** is personal property that is legally considered real estate because it is attached to the land or to an improvement, which is itself permanently attached to the land. Examples show the difference between fixtures and personal property: (1) "Stone, in its natural condition in the earth's crust, is real estate; but when it is severed from the earth's crust—quarried—it becomes personal property, and is bought and sold as such. When the quarried stone is fashioned into a building, it becomes real estate, and is bought and sold as such along with the land on which the structure has been erected."[1] (2) A microwave oven installed in the counter space of a kitchen is a fixture whereas the same oven, as a freestanding mobile appliance, is personal property.

Attachment is only one criterion used to identify a fixture. Other factors that must be considered are the method of attachment, the intention of the party making the attachment, and the purpose for which the personal property is to be used. In terms of the method of attachment, if the item of personal property is firmly attached so that its removal would injure the property, the item is considered to be a fixture. However, an item can be attached in such a way that it can be removed without injury to the property; in this case, the item is considered to be personal property.[2] In a residential structure, a dishwasher that is built into the counter would be a fixture but a dishwasher fastened to the floor in an open space next to the counter can be considered as personal property.

The intention of the person making the attachment is another criterion. When an owner builds an appliance into the counter, the courts view the appliance as a fixture because, by building it in, the owner has expressed an intent to make the appliance a fixture. In another situation, the owner of a parcel of residential real estate may offer to sell the house with a fully equipped kitchen. In this case, the court may well interpret the unattached refrigerator and the dishwasher fastened to the floor in an open space next to the counter as fixtures. This view can be substantiated because the intent of the seller was to sell a "fully equipped kitchen."

Finally, the purpose for which the personal property is used also is important. If the item is used to promote the purpose for which the real estate is owned, the presumption is that the owner intended the item to be a fixture regardless of the manner of the attachment.[3] An example of this situation is the sale of a retail store as a clothes store to a buyer who expresses an intention to use the property in the same way. In this example, the display cases and the clothes racks are presumed to be fixtures. If, however, the retail space is sold merely as square footage and the buyer expresses an intention to change the use from a clothing store to an appliance store, the display cases and the clothes racks are presumed to be the personal property of the seller, unless some express agreement to the contrary is reached by the buyer and the seller.

The question of whether an item of personal property is a fixture arises only if the property to which the item is attached changes owners, or if the property has been rented to a tenant and is subsequently returned to the owner, or if the property is used as security for a loan. If the object does not change hands or if it is not used

THE DECISION TO ACQUIRE KNOWLEDGE ABOUT THE REAL ESTATE BUSINESS

as collateral for a loan, the character of the item as personal property or a fixture is immaterial because it belongs to the owner in any event (see Exhibit 1-2).

The Legal Dimension of Real Estate

The legal dimension of the commodity known as real estate is a package called **rights of ownership.** These rights include the right to use the commodity, the right to possess the commodity, the right to exclude others from using it, and the right to dispose of the commodity by selling it or by giving it away as a gift. These rights are intangible factors that exist in law and pertain to the physical or tangible aspects of real estate—land and on-site improvements.

When the ownership dimension is added to the two physical components, a change occurs in the term designating the commodity. Real estate becomes **real property** when the rights of ownership are considered. However, in the generally accepted use of the term *real estate,* most people imply these intangible rights of ownership. In popular usage, the term *real estate,* which denotes only the physical aspect of the commodity, and the term *real property,* which denotes the physical entity and the ownership rights in the commodity, are used as synonyms. The term *realty* is also used by many people. Realty typically refers to the physical components of the property and is thereby a synonym for real estate.

Any classification of ownership must be based on the degree to which the rights of use, possession, exclusion, and disposition are held by the owner of the real estate. In other words, the owner of real estate can use the property, but only within limits established by the government. The owner can have the property in his or her possession. The owner can exclude others from the property, and, finally, the owner can choose the means of disposing of the property—i.e., by sale or gift. The material in this section will be presented by analyzing these four rights. However, these same rights can be presented as a classification system of more than four items. For example, the right to dispose of the property could be subdivided into the rights to sell, the

EXHIBIT 1-2 The concept of real estate (a physical entity)

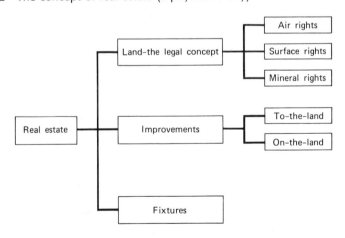

right to give away, and the right to lease. The discussion in this section will focus on the four rights identified. Of these four rights, the most significant in real estate law are the right of disposition and the right of possession. These two rights are closely intertwined in the body of real estate law (see Exhibit 1-3).

The freehold and less-than-freehold estates   Ownership can be broken down into freehold and less-than-freehold (leasehold) estates. The **freehold estate** is a package of the rights of ownership possessed by the owner for the duration of a lifetime, a time period that must be recognized as indefinite because it can last from a day to many decades. The **less-than-freehold estate** is a package of the rights of ownership obtained by a tenant from an owner; it can last for either a definite period or an indefinite period, depending on the expressed wishes of the landlord and the tenant.

The owner of a freehold estate may or may not have the right of disposition along with the right of possession. A **freehold estate of inheritance** is the situation in which the owner has all four rights of ownership—to use the land, to possess the land, to exclude others from that land, and to dispose of the land according to his or her wishes. This is the highest form of ownership and is often called a *fee simple estate.*[4]

A **freehold estate not-of-inheritance** is an estate in which the owner has the rights of use, possession, and exclusion, but does not have the right of disposition. The most common form of this type of estate is the **life estate.** The rights of ownership are limited to a lifetime, in this case the lifetime of the owner. As an example of this form of estate, consider the following case.

Your parents retire to Hawaii and give you the family home for as long as you live, an estate based on the duration of your lifetime. Upon your death, the home goes to your younger sister. Your parents owned the home as a freehold estate of inheritance; they have the right to dispose of it. The fact that they gave it to you as a life estate allows you to use, possess, and exclude others from the property for as long as you are alive. However, they did not give you the right of disposition. Regardless of your wishes, your younger sister will receive that property upon your death.

An interesting sidelight of this example is that the creation of the life estate by your parents created two ownership packages. You received an **estate in posses-**

EXHIBIT 1-3   The concept of real property

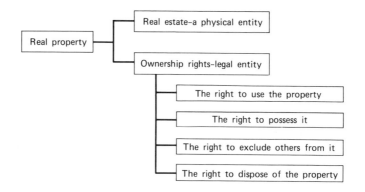

THE DECISION TO ACQUIRE KNOWLEDGE ABOUT THE REAL ESTATE BUSINESS

sion. Your younger sister received an **estate in expectancy.** You have the right of possession; your sister has an ownership interest that is expected to materialize in the indefinite future. Each of you has a clearly defined package of rights. You can live in the house or rent it out; your sister can sell the property with a delivery date to the new owner that occurs upon or slightly after your death. In this example, you are known as the owner and your sister's estate is legally referred to as a *remainder* while you are alive.

Alternatively, your parents may have arranged to give you the family home for as long as you live and to have it returned to them upon your death. Such an arrangement might be used if your life expectancy, due to illness, is shorter than theirs. In this case, your parents' interest in the property is known legally as the *reversion.*

A second form of freehold estate not-of-inheritance is an **estate *pur autre vie.*** A loose translation of this phrase is "an estate for another's life." An example of this estate is the case in which your parents give you the family home for as long as your younger sister's husband is alive. Upon his death, the home goes to your sister. You have an estate of possession; your sister has a remainder. Both estates are based on your brother-in-law's lifetime.

The person in possession of a freehold estate not-of-inheritance has certain obligations to the owner of a remainder or the reversion. The owner of a life estate cannot commit **waste.** The legal term *waste* refers to an act that does permanent injury to the real estate that is owned as a life estate.[5] Examples of waste are the destruction of a building without agreement by the owner of the remainder, failure to make ordinary repairs and to provide necessary maintenance, and failure to pay all of the property taxes and other charges imposed by the local government upon the property. The first two examples are readily identifiable as waste because they affect the physical condition of the real estate. The last example is waste because the estate in possession and the estate in expectancy can both be taken away by the local government for nonpayment of property taxes.

In addition to the life estate and the estate *pur autre vie,* some states maintain legal life estates known as *dower* and *curtesy.* Dower, in common law, is the wife's life estate in the real property of her deceased husband. The common-law provision generally held that the wife was given a life estate equal to one third of all of the real estate that the husband owned at the time of his death. Curtesy is the reciprocal of dower; it is the legal life estate created, in common law, for the husband out of the wife's property at her death. Some states still maintain this life estate concept of dower and curtesy. Other states have altered these common-law rights by establishing a freehold estate of inheritance for the surviving member in some portion of the deceased person's real property. Some states define the dower or curtesy right in the real property held at the time of the death, whereas other states hold that the dower and curtesy right exists for all the real estate held by the deceased person during his or her lifetime, provided that the surviving member had not joined the deceased in selling or giving the property away in any manner.[6] Dower and curtesy rights are complicated, and this brief discussion does not cover their full legal ramifications.

The less-than-freehold estates are a specified package of the rights of ownership that last for less than a lifetime and do not include the right of disposition. In other words, the owner of a less-than-freehold estate possesses it for a prescribed period of time, and has no right to sell or give away the property. This form of estate is more commonly known as a **leasehold.**

Stated in positive terms, the rights of the holder of a leasehold are the rights to possess and use the property; the right to exclude others from the property, except that the owner has the right of entry in certain situations; and the right to transfer the use and possession of the property to others through the process of subletting with the consent of the owner.

The body of real estate law defines four categories of leasehold estates. An **estate for years** is a leasehold that continues for a definite period of time. The duration of the leasehold can be for one year (as in a residential lease), for more than a year (as in the case of a commercial or industrial lease), or for a definite period of time that is less than a year.

The second type of leasehold is an **estate from year to year;** it is often referred to as an *estate from period to period.* This estate comes into effect when a tenant maintains possession of the property after an estate for years expires and the owner agrees to the tenant's continued possession of the property by accepting a payment of rent. In this case, the terms of the original, but expired, lease are reestablished for a maximum period of one year if the original lease was for one year or more. If the original lease was for less than one year, the same shorter period of time is reestablished.[7]

The third type of leasehold is the **tenancy at will.** Under the provisions of this leasehold, the duration is not definitely specified. The agreement between the owner and the tenant exists for as long as both are in agreement. If either party chooses to negate the agreement, the lease arrangement is terminated. The only limitation imposed on the owner and the tenant is that they must give legal notice of their intent. As a general rule, the notice is in the order of magnitude of thirty or sixty days. Finally, the death of either party terminates the lease under the tenancy at will agreement.

The last type of leasehold is the **tenancy by sufferance.** This form of leasehold comes into existence when a tenant's rights under one of the other leaseholds expires and the tenant retains possession against the owner's wishes. In common usage the tenant at sufferance is called a *holdover tenant.* This situation generally culminates in an eviction of the tenant by the owner of the property. The property owner's right of eviction varies from state to state. At times, the holdover tenant pays the rent, which is accepted by the landlord. In this instance, the tenancy at sufferance usually becomes a tenancy from period to period (see Exhibit 1-4).

Co-ownership   The rights of ownership to a parcel of real estate can be held by one person or organization or can be owned by more than one entity. When the rights are held by more than one entity, the persons or organizations are known as *co-owners* of the property. The principal forms of co-ownership are joint tenancy, tenancy in common, tenancy by the entirety, and community property. They differ in terms of the right of disposition.

The first form of co-ownership, **joint tenancy,** requires the existence of four

EXHIBIT 1-4 The rights of ownership

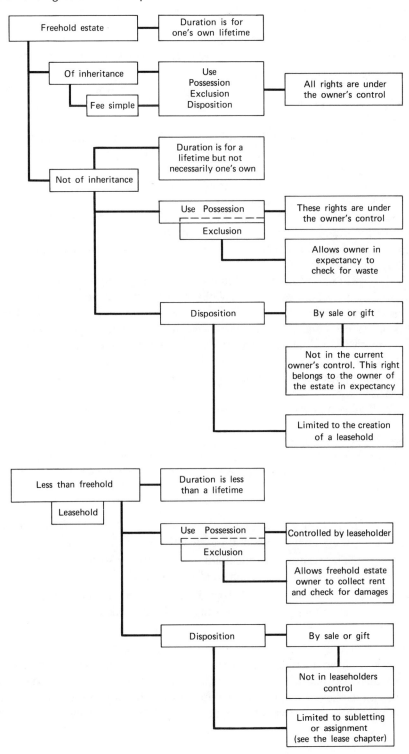

unities—the unities of title, time, possession, and interest.[8] The *unity of title* implies that individual owners in the joint-tenancy arrangement do not have the right of disposition of the entire property. It can only be sold when the co-owners all agree to the sale. Furthermore, upon the death of one of the co-owners, the total number of owners is reduced by one and the deceased person's ownership rights revert to the surviving owners.[9] In other words, the co-owners have the right of survivorship; that is, they take over the legal interests of the deceased co-owner. When all the other co-owners have died, the last surviving member of the joint tenancy owns the property completely.

Related to the unity of title discussed in the preceding paragraph is the *unity of time;* the joint tenants must receive title to the property at the same point in time. Moreover, the joint tenants take possession of the property as though they were a single individual. This is the fact implied by the *unity of possession.* Finally, the joint tenants have a *unity of interest.* They hold an undivided interest in the property; no separate components are identified as the portions of the property owned and possessed by any one of the co-owners. They own equal shares in the entire property, their individual shares cannot be divided, and they all have the same right of possession.

In terms of each individual's right of disposition, the joint tenancy can be viewed as a freehold estate not-of-inheritance that is owned by two or more people. The individual cannot sell the property, give it away, or leave it as an inheritance for his or her heirs and have this new owner incorporated into the joint tenancy. However, each individual joint tenant can sell his or her undivided interest. The new owner does not become a member of the joint tenancy, but becomes a tenant in common. (The concept of tenancy in common is the next form of co-ownership to be discussed.)

A joint tenancy can be dissolved when any of the individuals so chooses. Each joint tenant has the right to destroy the agreement upon desire. All that is required is "a simple written, signed and recorded declaration by one joint tenant."[10] In addition to this intentional act, other acts can break the joint tenancy even against the wishes of the owners, and possibly without their knowledge. The most common actions of this type are

☐ The conveyance or transfer of one joint tenant's ownership rights to an individual who is not a joint tenant

☐ The transfer of one joint tenant's ownership rights involuntarily to a trustee because of personal bankruptcy

☐ The signing of a mortgage by one joint tenant without the other joint tenant's signature appearing on the document[11]

In the second form of co-ownership, **tenancy in common,** the individual owners do have the right of disposition within the form of co-ownership and do have separate, identifiable interests, which need not be equal. Each tenant in common owns an explicit percentage of the undivided total interest. The tenants in common can pass their respective interests on to their heirs or can sell their own interest. In other words, tenancy in common is a freehold estate of inheritance among several persons or organizations.

The tenancy in common also differs from the joint tenancy in the way the property passes from a deceased tenant in common. Under a joint tenancy arrangement the surviving tenant(s) receives the deceased member's interest. Under a tenancy in common, the surviving tenant(s) in common does not automatically receive the interest held by the deceased member. In a tenancy in common, each member can dispose of his or her undivided share by will—i.e., leave the property interest to an heir.

Co-owners often do not agree on the use or management of the property. Sometimes one of the co-owners does not fulfill the financial obligations required to operate the property. In these circumstances, a court-ordered partition of the property can be requested. The court can divide the property into distinct portions, if it is possible, so that each co-owner can own a share as a joint owner, or the court can order the sale of the property and specify the distribution of the proceeds from the sale.

The other two forms of co-ownership are ways in which property is owned under the institution of marriage. The form known as *tenancy by the entirety* is a joint estate between married people. It is thereby a freehold estate not-of-inheritance; it is an estate in which the marriage partners do not have individual rights of disposition. They can only dispose of the property jointly. Neither the husband nor the wife is able to dispose of the property or any part of it without the consent of the other person.

The other marriage-oriented form of co-ownership is *community property* that is property jointly acquired and owned by a husband and wife. Each individual may own property separately, but this property is typically property acquired before the marriage. The legalities of the community-property concept come into effect when a divorce or a death occurs. In the event of an amicable, no-fault divorce, each spouse receives 50 percent of the common property. However, in cases of adultery, extreme cruelty, abandonment, or other such action, the courts may award more than 50 percent of the common property to the aggrieved spouse.[12]

Nonpossessionary rights   The freehold estates and the leaseholds discussed in the preceding sections are all estates of possession. The only exceptions are the remainder and the reversion interests, which are estates in expectancy, and even these estates in expectancy are estates of future possession. In contrast to such estates of ownership, which include the rights of use, possession, exclusion, and disposition, certain nonpossessionary rights of use and exclusion can be held by one person in real estate owned by another person. The two types of nonpossessionary rights in real estate are *easements* and *liens,* which are discussed in the next chapter under private restrictions to the use of property.

The Bundle-of-Rights Theory

In the discussion of the components of real estate, several rights are identified. Some rights are related to the physical commodity (e.g., surface rights, mineral rights, and air rights). Other rights are the intangible rights of ownership such as the several estates based on the right of disposition (e.g., freehold estates of inheritance, freehold estates not-of-inheritance, and leasehold estates). These various rights can be held as either estates in possession or estates in expectancy. If the right of disposition is defined, the separate estates in possession can be disposed of by several methods—sale, gift, or lease.

The usually accepted analogy is that these various rights in real estate are like a bundle of sticks, each stick representing an identifiable right. Each stick can be disposed of as a separate entity. If an individual holds a freehold estate of inheritance, that individual owns the whole bundle of rights. The owner can dispose of these rights in a variety of ways. The use of the surface and the mineral rights can be leased to one person and the air rights can be leased to someone else. At the same time, an easement or several easements can be created and sold to third parties. Then, even while these leaseholds and easements are in force, the entire estate could be sold in expectancy with a delivery date ten, fifteen, or twenty years in the future.

CHARACTERISTICS OF REAL ESTATE

The characteristics of the real estate commodity are of two types: physical and economic. The physical characteristics are related to the land itself and to the on-site improvements. The economic characteristics are different in certain respects from those of other commodities.

The Physical Characteristics

The physical characteristics of land are its immobility, indestructibility, and non-homogeneity. Once the size and shape of a parcel of land are established, the legal nature of the land is also established with respect to mineral and air rights. Knowledge of the legal concept of land is important for making an analysis of its physical characteristics. Land in its legal sense is immobile because it cannot be moved from one place to another. The property owner can spend years moving the earth on the surface, as in the case of a strip mine, but such activity does not move the rights to the minerals in the deeper strata or move the rights to the air above the newly created surface. This point can be reemphasized by saying that the location of the mineral rights and the air rights cannot be moved even if the surface is moved.

Land is indestructible in the sense that movement of the surface does not destroy the full package of rights. Moreover, other deliberate human acts, as well as the acts of nature, are not capable of destroying land in its legal sense. Fire can char the land. Wind and rain can erode the surface. Earthquakes can rearrange the sub-surface strata and cause the surface to rise or fall. Nuclear bombs can dissipate part of the surface. However, in none of these instances is the land destroyed in the legal sense. The land cannot be destroyed because its location cannot be destroyed.

Land is nonhomogeneous. Each parcel of land can be distinguished from all other parcels of land on the basis of several physical characteristics. The size and shape can differ. The geological features of elevation, slope, drainage capacity, mineral composition, soil fertility, and bedrock characteristics can be different. However, even if all of these characteristics are perfectly identical, each parcel of land is unique because of its location. No two parcels of land occupy the same space on the earth's surface. The physical feature of location is a very important issue because it is a dominant physical attribute of any property.

The physical characteristics of the on-site improvements are similar to the physical characteristics of the land. First, the improvements are *economically immobile.* The cost of moving a structure is a high percentage of that structure's value and could even be a multiple of the structure's value. For this reason, houses, retail stores, and other buildings are very seldom moved even though to do so is physically possible. Second, the improvements are destructible, but they have the *attribute of durability.* Unless a destructive human act or an act of natural violence occurs, the structure will stand for a very long period of time. In other words, the structure has a long physical life. Third, the improvements are *nonhomogeneous.* Even two structures that serve the same purpose, such as residential units, are different in many ways; for example, in style, shape, size, design, quality, and number of rooms. If by chance these features are identical, other attributes of the structure can be different, such as the type and color of the exterior and interior covering (brick or frame, paint or wallpaper).

The Economic Characteristics

The economic features or characteristics of the real estate commodity are somewhat different from those of other commodities. Real estate is the only commodity that the typical consumer buys that is measured in multiples of that individual's or household's income. The home is usually valued at two or three times the household's yearly income, whereas all other commodities—even the automobile—are measured in fractions of the household's yearly income. Because of this first economic characteristic of real estate, *its high price,* the purchase of real estate is generally undertaken with *borrowed funds.* This second characteristic of real estate is shared with many other commodities that the consumer buys. Typically, the household borrows money or, similarly, pays on the installment plan, for almost all of the consumer durable goods it purchases. However, the method of borrowing to purchase real estate is different from other purchases. The mortgage will be discussed in detail in Chapter 16.

The third economic characteristic of real estate arises from its physical characteristics of immobility, nonhomogeneity, and location. The *search costs,* or *information-gathering costs,* associated with comparison shopping are greater for real estate than for any other product. Each parcel is unique in its location and cannot be moved. Consequently, unless the properties are adjacent, side-by-side comparison is not possible. The purchaser must expend money and time to examine the many different units that are being considered for possible purchase or rental.

The fourth economic characteristic of real estate is *scarcity.* Real estate in both its components of land and improvements is not available in sufficient quantities to meet the desires that all individuals have for them. At any point in time, the total amount of land available is limited. For example, if a local geographic area is defined, within that area there is only a limited amount of available land. Moreover, within that same geographic area, there is a limited number of structures. Even if a specific use such as residential activity is postulated, within that geographic area there is still only a limited amount of land that is in residential use, and a limited number of structures that are in residential use at that point in time. Consequently, individuals within that geographic area cannot fulfill all the needs and desires that they may have for residential land and structures.

Analyzing the concept of scarcity over a period of time, instead of at a single point in time, leads to the same conclusion. Land and structures are still scarce. Over a period of time, only a limited number of new residential sites can be developed either from raw land or through conversion from other land uses. In addition, over that same period of time only a limited number of additional housing units can be created given the economic scarcity of productive resources.

A fifth economic characteristic is the concept of *situs,* which represents the economic location of a parcel of real estate. Each parcel is immobile—a physical characteristic. Therefore, each parcel is affected by changes in economic and demographic factors in the surrounding area. This topic will be discussed in greater detail in Chapter 2 in the section entitled "Attributes of the Location." For present purposes favorable changes in the economic factors, such as an increase in the income level of the surrounding area, will favorably affect the value of the property in question.

A sixth economic characteristic is the influence that the quantity and the quality of *surrounding structures* and other off-site improvements-to-the-land have on the property in question. As the quantity of desirable improvements increases, or, as their physical quality improves, there is a favorable impact on the value of the subject property. The reverse situation can and does happen if the physical surroundings deteriorate. Many refer to this sixth economic characteristic as "modification" on value caused by adjacent parcels of property.

Finally, the concept of *fixity* is often introduced as an economic characteristic. As land is improved by the addition of on-site improvements (buildings, driveways, water lines, etc.) the investment is fixed. It cannot be moved or easily altered, and it has a long physical and economic life. This topic is seen by the authors as more of an economic limit than an economic characteristic, so it is discussed in greater detail in Chapter 2. However, the reader should realize that fixity of the investment is an economic characteristic (see Exhibit 1-5).

THE REAL ESTATE BUSINESS

The purpose of this section is to explore the nature of the **real estate business.** The participants are identified, their relationships to each other are explained, and the services that each offers to a potential buyer, seller, and the public in general are described. This information is important to the potential consumer (buyer or seller) for the following reasons:

1. It can eliminate any misconceptions about the real estate business.
2. It can assist either the buyer or seller in deciding whether to handle

certain steps of a transaction by using personal knowledge or training or to seek assistance from a real estate specialist.

3. It identifies the specialists from whom the consumer can solicit assistance.

4. It helps to illustrate that a real estate transaction can be a very detailed process and could require the services of several individuals within the real estate business to ensure that the needs of all parties are satisfied and protected.

The real estate business encompasses all individuals and organizations who receive compensation for providing a service. It includes the carpenter who frames a new structure as well as a life insurance company that loans several million dollars for the construction of a new shopping center. It encompasses the real estate agent, the financial lender, the attorney, the title company, the appraiser, the counselor, the insurance agent, the developer, the contractor, and the property manager. Each plays a specific role by providing a service to, and satisfying a need of, the buyer, seller, or the public in a real estate transaction.

One government report views the real estate business as composed of four phases geared for the production of housing, as shown in Exhibit 1-6. The various components of the economy that can influence each phase are listed. Phase 1, the Preparation Phase, consists of land acquisitions, planning, and zoning amendments if needed. The individuals participating in this phase range from the developer to persons who prepare the public master plan. Phase 2, the Production Phase, includes site preparation, construction, and financing. Individuals who can become involved in this phase range from the developer to persons influencing the laws controlling the transportation of materials. Phase 3, the Distribution Phase, consists of the sale of the property and its financing. A range of individuals can become involved including

EXHIBIT 1-5 Physical and economic characteristics of real estate

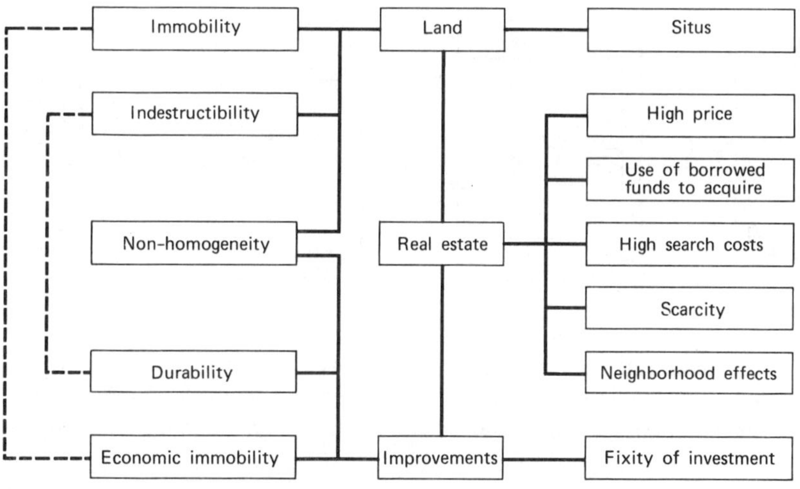

EXHIBIT 1-6 The housing process: Major participants and influences

Developer	Developer	Developer	Owner
Land owner	Lending institutions (interim and permanent)	Real estate brokers	Maintenance firms and employees
Lawyers	FHA, VA or private mortgage insurance company	Lawyers	Property management firms
Real estate brokers	Contractors	Lending institutions	Insurance companies
Title companies	Subcontractors	Title companies	Utility companies
Architects and engineers	Craftsmen and their unions	FHA, VA, or private mortgage insurance company	Tax assessors
Surveyor	Material manufacturers and distributors		Repairmen, craftsmen and their unions
Planners and consultants	Building code officials		Lending institutions
Zoning and planning officials	Insurance companies		Architects and engineers
	Architects and engineers		Contractors
			Subcontractors
			Material manufacturers and distributors
			Local zoning officials
			Local building officials

1 **PREPARATION PHASE**	**2** **PRODUCTION PHASE**	**3** **DISTRIBUTION PHASE**	**4** **SERVICE PHASE**
A. Land acquisitions B. Planning C. Zoning amendments	A. Site preparation B. Construction C. Financing	A. Sale (and subsequent resale or refinancing)	A. Maintenance and management B. Repairs C. Improvements and additions

			Property taxes
			Income taxes
	Banking laws		Housing and health codes
	Building and mechanical codes		Insurance laws
	Subdivision regulations		Utility regulations
Real estate law	Utility regulations		Banking laws
Recording regulations and fees	Union rules	Recording regulations and fees	Union rules
Banking laws	Rules of trade and professional associations	Real estate law	Rules of trade and professional association
Zoning	Insurance laws	Transfer taxes	Zoning
Subdivision regulations	Laws controlling transportation of materials	Banking laws	Building and mechanical codes
Private deed restrictions		Rules of professional association	Laws controlling transportation of materials
Public Master plans			

the broker, the developer, lawyers, title company personnel, bankers, and individuals designated as specialists by various professional associations. Finally, Phase 4, the Service Phase, includes maintenance and management, repairs, and improvements and additions.

As the exhibit shows, the real estate and housing business is very large, involves many people and organizations, and can be very complex. For example, the real estate broker is identified in Phase 1, Preparation, and Phase 3, Distribution. Real estate law services also may be needed in Phase 1 and Phase 3. Banking laws, insurance law, and real estate law may be needed in all phases. The following sections describe selected activities of the individuals and organizations whose services typically are used by consumers in real estate transactions.

The Real Estate Agent

A **real estate agent** is licensed by the state to enter into a contractual relationship with a client for the purchase or sale of real estate in the expectation of a commission. Typically, the agent must satisfy a series of prerequisites prior to receiving a license. Although these differ among states, they typically include requirements for education and/or experience, recommendations from property owners, references covering high morals and good character, and a passing score on an examination.

Real Estate Commission   In every state a **Real Estate Commission** or, in some cases, a Real Estate Commissioner is charged with the responsibility of enforcing the state license law. The commission issues licenses to real estate agents, holds hearings on complaints, issues penalties such as suspensions and revocations against the license, and passes rules and regulations governing the operation of the real estate business.

All license laws contain a description of the activities that characterize a broker and a salesperson. Typically, there are two essential distinctions of a broker. A broker may (1) name the firm after himself or herself and advertise the firm in his or her name, and (2) employ salespeople as independent contractors or employees. The salesperson may not.

Other requirements also affect the broker and the salesperson. For example, every yard sign typically must show the name of the firm with the name of the salesperson. In addition, some license laws require the broker to supervise the activities of the salesperson. Further, a broker must maintain a trust account for all monies coming into his or her possession that belong to other people.

Some states require other participants in the real estate business to obtain a real estate license to ensure that they have a knowledge of the real estate transaction even though they may not be involved in selling. For example, Mississippi requires all real estate appraisers to hold a broker's license, and Arkansas requires all auctioneers to be licensed.

National, state, and local boards   The **National Association of REALTORS** (NAR) acts as a parent trade organization for the **State Association of REALTORS** and **local boards.** The purpose of these organizations is to promote the business, offer education, express the members' views politically, and support a code of ethics. Any agent has the option of joining all three groups. A principal, partner, or corporate officer who is a member is called a *REALTOR* and may use the symbol "R" in advertising. A salesperson, independent contractor, or certain affiliate members who are affiliated with a member firm is called a *REALTOR-ASSOCIATE.*

Several institutes affiliated with the NAR award a number of designations to members to indicate completion of a prescribed course of education and the presentation of satisfactory experience in specialized areas. For example, a member may become a Certified Residential Broker (CRB) to indicate a specialty in the brokerage of residential properties. A member may pursue a "CCIM" designation to indicate a specialty in commercial and industrial property brokerage and management. Other specialties are available through affiliate programs such as in appraising (Member of the Appraisal Institute and Residential Member) and in property management (Certified Property Manager) known respectively as MAI, RM, and CPM.

Typically, a buyer or seller would have good reason to expect a high level of professionalism and performance from an agent who is a REALTOR and holds a designation in the appropriate specialty. For example, a person buying or selling a home would expect a high level of competence from an agent who is a REALTOR and a CRB.

General agent versus special agent[13]   The term **agent** denotes an arrangement whereby a licensed individual or firm is authorized by the client, called the "principal," to accomplish a specific objective for compensation. The agent has the right to exercise his or her judgment about the best methods to accomplish the objective. The typical special agency arrangement is created when a seller contracts with a firm to locate a buyer who is ready, willing, and able to purchase the property. The agent has the right to contact potential buyers by mail, newspaper, direct solicitation, sign, radio, TV, or other alternatives that are within the firm's budget.

Services offered   What services can a prospective buyer or seller expect from a real estate agent?

The agent can *advertise the property* in the proper places to ensure that the property receives maximum exposure. The agent can *screen all inquiries* to ensure that the property is described correctly to interested buyers. The agent can *make suggestions for improvement* to the property that will cause it to be presented in the best condition. The agent can *show* the property. The agent can *save the buyer time* by showing only those properties that satisfy the buyer's needs. The agent can *educate both the seller and the buyer about local market trends* to ensure that the property is offered for sale at a reasonable price and that the buyer makes a *reasonable offer*.

In addition, the agent provides the buyer with *free transportation* to look at property. A buyer who finds a property through the services of an agent can expect the agent to assist in *locating adequate and reasonable financing*. The agent should know which financial institutions currently have money available to loan or what terms are available in the market. In providing such information, the agent saves the buyer's time by eliminating the need to visit numerous financial institutions. As a result, the buyer has the *prospect of taking possession* of the property soon. Also, the buyer or seller can expect an agent to assist in *ordering the abstract brought up to date, ordering a survey* of the land, if necessary, *contacting the County Health Department* to request an inspection of the water and septic tank, if applicable, and *ordering a termite inspection* of the property. The agent in some states performs another service for the buyer and seller—*supervision and preparation of the closing forms.* When the closing date is set, the buyer simply appears at the closing with required funds. The seller simply appears at the closing to sign the necessary documents and receive the funds from the transaction.

The agent, whether general or special, is committed to absolute loyalty to the client. This *fiduciary relationship* is expected in all services that the agent provides for the principal.

Example The services provided by an agent are illustrated in the following example of a family's decision to buy a home in another town.

Bill Reeves, an employee of Sears, has just been transferred to El Paso, Texas. Bill desperately needs to find a residence because his family will be joining him within a short time. Bill knows his wife's preferences, but he must trust his own judgment in selecting a house because she cannot journey to El Paso to house-hunt. He knows nothing of the real estate market in the El Paso area, and decides to depend on the expertise of a local REALTOR. Being unfamiliar with the real estate companies in the community, Bill decides to consult with Quik-Sale, a national chain, because he has seen their advertisements on TV and several of his friends have had good experiences with transactions conducted by a Quik-Sale office at home.

Bill goes to the El Paso Quik-Sale agent, Louise Bourquin, and discusses his need for a residence. Louise questions Bill about house preferences, price range, available down payment, income, schools preferred, and other desires and needs of the Reeves family. Using this information, Louise surveys the available houses for sale and narrows the choice of houses to three neighborhoods. Since Bill knows nothing of preferable locations within the community, he relies on Louise's recommendations on areas that will most likely increase in value rapidly and that exhibit pride of ownership among the residents. Finally, three houses are selected that seem to fit the Reeves family's needs.

Louise takes Bill to see the houses, and they discuss the characteristics of each in detail. House A is priced at $85,000, house B at $87,000, and house C at $88,000. All of the houses are similarly constructed and have comparable square footage. All are in different neighborhoods. Bill likes all three houses but cannot decide which is the best purchase because houses B and C are both located in slightly better neighborhoods than house A. Soliciting Louise's opinion, Bill concludes that houses B and C are very acceptable but are $5,000–$6,000 overpriced. Also, the fact that the local community appears to be growing toward the neighborhood of house A would cause property values to increase faster in that neighborhood than in the others. And so, Bill decides to write an offer on property A.

Because Bill is just moving to the community, he has no knowledge of the best loan terms. Louise provides the needed information about required down payments, mortgage interest rates, prepayment penalties, grace periods, and points. She drives Bill to Superior Federal Savings and Loan and introduces him to Jay Dutton, a loan officer. Bill submits a loan application, which is later approved.

Bill must rejoin his family prior to their move, and he is assured by Louise that closing will be held on June 1, the day on which Bill and his family will arrive back in El Paso.

Real Estate Lenders[14]

Real estate lenders provide *equity* and *debt* funds to investors and borrowers who do not have sufficient cash to pay the full purchase price of property. These lenders serve a valuable function in the economy by competing with other markets for the investment dollar in order that it can be loaned into real estate. Thus, they serve as a valuable conduit of money into the real estate market and provide loans to potential buyers who otherwise would be unable to purchase real estate.

Equity and debt funds   Typically, a lender loans either equity funds or debt funds for the purchase of real estate. Equity funds come from the assets of the potential buyer. If the buyer provides this money from his or her own resources, it is expressed on that person's balance sheet as an asset. Debt funds are supplied from the assets of other people and are added to the equity funds to equal the purchase price of the property. This additional amount is usually in the form of a mortgage, which enters the buyer's balance sheet as a liability because it is a debt that he or she owes with interest. A buyer usually cannot borrow 100 percent of a property's purchase price. If the buyer does not have enough cash for the down payment (the difference between the purchase price and the mortgage amount), he or she can sometimes borrow the needed funds.

Services offered   The real estate lender typically offers additional services to the borrower. The lender obtains a *credit report* on the borrower's credit record to ensure that the borrower is a good credit risk and will not become overextended. Neither the lender nor the borrower wants to commit to a loan that carries a very high probability of early default on the monthly payment. Also, the lender *arranges for the property to be appraised* to determine that the appraised value is greater than the requested loan. This procedure protects the lender from lending more than the normal amount for a similarly priced property, and it protects the buyer from paying a price higher than the appraised market value.

The lender typically conducts an *employment verification* to determine that the borrower's employment and income prospects are sufficient to justify the loan. Since borrowers are usually optimistic about their ability to make monthly payments, the lender is providing a service by ensuring that the borrower is capable of repaying the loan.

The lender can offer other services that are necessary to the closing, such as *ordering the abstract, obtaining an opinion of title* from an attorney, *ordering the deed, ordering any other legal documents* that are necessary to the transaction, and, if asked, *conducting the closing* in some states.[15]

Example The real estate lender's services to a buyer are illustrated by the following example of a person's decision to borrow funds to buy a home.

Janet Nichols has just sold her home in Mountain Home, Arkansas, because she intends to purchase an existing single-family home just east of Mountain Home near Norfork Lake. Janet has always admired this house because of its unique construction, contemporary style, and location overlooking the lake. The selling price of Janet's home is $65,000 and she receives $10,000 after paying her current mortgage. The asking price of the new home is $75,000 and it has no current mortgage. The sellers of the lake home are not willing to extend credit to Janet by owner financing. Therefore, Janet visits Guaranty Savings and Loan and discusses the intended purchase with Rhoda Barrett.

Rhoda tells Janet that the most Guaranty can loan is 80 percent of the appraised value because of the unavailability of loan funds. She asks Janet to submit a loan application to enable the savings and loan to request a credit check and appraise the house. Within five days, Rhoda calls Janet to tell her that the credit check and income report are good and that the house is appraised for $75,000, which means that Guaranty will loan $60,000. Since Janet has only $10,000 cash, she needs an additional $5,000 to purchase the house. Therefore, she goes to the First National Bank in Mountain Home and consults with her banker, Joel Tabor.

Janet explains her problem to Joel and asks whether the bank can help. Joel tells Janet that the bank can loan her $5,000 if she has something of equivalent value to pledge as collateral. Janet's income is sufficient, and she would have no problem making the house and the bank payments. Janet has a 1985 Chevrolet that she owns with no debt. She gives the bank the title to the Chevrolet and the bank in turn loans Janet $5,000 at 10 percent interest, which she must pay in monthly installments over a three-year period.

Janet returns to Guaranty and tells Rhoda what has transpired. Rhoda says that if Janet purchases the house, Guaranty will make her a $60,000 loan at 12 percent interest for thirty years with payments to be made monthly. Janet makes an offer on the house, it is accepted, and the transaction is closed. Janet makes a $15,000 down-payment and the remainder ($60,000) of the $75,000 selling price is financed by Guaranty Savings and Loan.

The Appraiser

The job of the appraiser is to provide an independent estimate of the value of property. The appraiser inspects the premises, gathers data on the local market and trends, and applies a professional approach to determining the property value.

Several states, such as Mississippi, require the appraiser to be licensed by the state for the protection of the public. Typically, the appraiser must pass a state exam or present evidence of successful completion of a course of study conducted by a professional appraisal organization. Other states, such as Arkansas, impose no professional competency requirements on the appraiser.

In addition, the appraiser may be designated by one of the professional appraisal organizations. For example, the appraiser may be a Residential Member (RM) or a Member of the Appraisal Institute (MAI), which means that he or she has successfully completed a course of instruction and satisfied an experience requirement prescribed by the American Institute of Real Estate Appraisers. The Senior Residential Appraiser (SRA), Senior Real Property Appraiser (SRPA), and Senior Real Estate Analyst (SREA) designations are conferred by the Society of Real Estate Appraisers. An appraiser also may complete the requirements for an American Society of Appraisers (ASA) designation with a specialty in real- or personal-property appraising. Other organizations offer designations to appraisers specializing in review appraising and determining market value for tax rolls.

State licensing requirements for appraisers establish minimum educational and/or experience levels for the protection of the public. The purpose of these requirements is to ensure that all individuals who attempt to estimate the value of property for a client have at least the minimum qualifications.

The professional groups that award designations attempt to establish educational and experience requirements commensurate with the type of assignment. For example, appraisers holding the RM and SRA designations are expected to provide estimates on residential properties and one- to four-family units only. Clients desiring an opinion of value on property that produces an income stream should consult with an appraiser holding the SRPA, SREA, MAI, or ASA designation.

Services offered   The seller can benefit from an appraisal because it helps to *establish limits on the listing price* of the property. The seller could not reasonably expect to receive more than the appraised value unless he or she wanted to raise the price artificially for additional negotiation room. The buyer can benefit from an appraisal because it *determines the limit of the offering price.* The buyer may want to offer less than the appraised value but can always raise subsequent offers.

Example The appraiser's services are illustrated in the following example of an individual's problem of deciding how much to offer for a house.

Joe Kidd, living in Eugene, Oregon, has sold his home and is looking into the prospects of buying a new one. Joe visits with a friend in the real estate business, John Brooks, who shows Joe several houses that he has listed for sale. Joe likes one of the houses very much but is not sure about the price. The seller is asking $100,000 and even though Joe knows very little about the real estate market in the neighborhood, he believes the house might be overpriced. Not wanting to give more for the house than it is worth, Joe decides to ask Edith Berry, an independent real estate appraiser in Eugene, to appraise the property. Joe is thus relying on an expert in the field instead of his own judgment. Edith has been in the real estate appraisal business for several years and is regarded as a very competent appraiser in residential, commercial, and rural property. Joe will have to pay Edith a fee of $225, but he feels that the expenditure is worthwhile to prevent the possibility of making a large financial mistake.

Edith appraises the house using the market-comparison approach based on comparable recent sales in the area. On the basis of the comparable sales, Edith appraises the property at $95,000. Therefore, Joe decides that the maximum amount he will offer for the house is the amount of the appraisal. The seller first refuses Joe's offer, but he reconsiders and accepts after Joe shows him the appraisal. As a result, Joe does not make a $5,000 mistake.

The Title Company

The **title company** prepares an abstract (chain of title) containing the complete history of a parcel of real estate. This history includes all title transfers and all encumbrances against the property, including mortgage releases and outstanding liens. The title company compiles this history by searching the public records to locate all recorded documents that pertain to the subject property.

Services offered   The abstract is very valuable to the buyer in that it *gives the buyer and his or her attorney the facts* from which to determine whether the seller actually owns all of the property rights. Also, it *informs the buyer of any outstanding encumbrances* and *shows whether any other parties have interests in the property.* Therefore, the title company, by preparing the abstract, is giving the buyer the opportunity to determine whether good title can be acquired from the seller. The abstract is usually sent to the buyer's attorney for an opinion on the seller's ownership rights. It thus protects the buyer.

In addition, *the title company could issue title insurance* at the buyer's request, which would *protect the buyer in case the abstract company or the attorney makes a mistake* in preparing and examining the abstract. Also, *it would protect the buyer if documents previously recorded for the property were fraudulent* or contained errors.

Before issuing the insurance, the title company would diligently search all public records of the property and would have its attorney give an opinion covering the present owner's rights. This two-step process yields a *title report* upon which the title company bases its insurance decision. Therefore, if a buyer purchases title insurance and goes through with the purchase of the real estate, the buyer can be reimbursed for damages if a mistake discovered in a later abstract examination indicates that another party has interest in the land. The buyer can be reimbursed for damages up to the purchase price of the property or the amount of the policy, whichever is less. Typically, a title insurance company will include an exception in the policy whereby it will not be liable for unrecorded liens and easements on the property.

Title insurance assures the buyer that he or she is protected from loss if the title received on the property contains errors or is fraudulent. The homeowner will be compensated not only for a negligent abstract but also for any of the unknown defects in the title, subject to any exceptions in the title policy, for which an attorney is not ordinarily liable.

Example The services of an abstract company are illustrated in the following example of a person's decision to buy a home.

Wendell Fleming, a resident of Wichita, Kansas, is considering buying a home. Wendell graduated from college two years ago, has a good job, and is tired of renting. He has saved enough money and believes that he can afford to purchase a $125,000 home. A former classmate tells Wendell about a one-year-old home that has just come on the market for sale because the owner is being transferred. Wendell goes to see the house and finds it to be very appealing. The house is priced at $115,000 and seems to have the features Wendell needs. Wendell wants to buy the house on the spot but hesitates because he remembers a very important item he learned in a Real Estate Principles class in college—always request that the condition of the title be examined or insured. He tells the seller that he needs to examine several documents on the property and will be back shortly. The seller tries to push the sale, but Wendell does not budge on his decision. Wendell contacts a local abstract company and requests that history of title be sent to Ellen Burns, his attorney. This service will cost Wendell $200, but it will be worthwhile to prevent a possible mistake. After reviewing the abstract, Ellen calls Wendell and informs him that the seller of the property built the house one year earlier than advertised. Furthermore, Ellen has discovered from the abstract two very important conditions that the seller did not disclose. First, the seller does not have a fee simple title. Second, a mechanic's lien has been filed against the property for an unpaid $5,000 bill for building materials. By employing a title company to prepare the abstract and an attorney to examine it, Wendall avoids a large financial mistake. He does not purchase the property because the owner cannot pay the $5,000 lien and will not lower the asking price by that amount.

The Real Estate Attorney

A **real estate attorney** specializes in real estate matters. Typically, his or her training includes at least two courses in property and one course in mortgages in law school. Usually, an attorney can buy and sell real estate for a client without being licensed if the transaction is conducted in the normal course of an attorney–client relationship.

Services offered   A real estate attorney can provide a number of services to the buyer and seller. The attorney can *write a contract of sale* if the buyer requests assistance. Normally, a real estate agent will fill in a preprinted contract, but *a buyer who is concerned with the legal aspects of the transaction can hire an attorney.* The attorney *gives opinions about the validity of the present owner's rights of ownership and any outstanding encumbrances.* Also, the attorney *prepares the deed and any other necessary legal documents.*

A real estate attorney can perform numerous other services for a buyer or seller that consist of *legal advice or service related to problems with the subject property.*

Example In the preceding example, Wendell sends the abstract to an attorney for an opinion on the condition of the title because the attorney is able to read the abstract much more accurately that Wendell can read it. Thus, the attorney advices Wendell on the legal ramifications of going ahead with the purchase.

A real estate attorney's services are also illustrated in the following example of a farmer's decision to buy land directly from the owner without an agent.

Jim Long, a resident of Tempe, Arizona, has been a successful farmer all of his life. He feels the need to expand his current farm operation by adding more acreage. An eighty-acre parcel that joins Jim's land on the west is currently for sale. This land is cleared, unimproved pasture and is just what Jim needs. Jim goes to the owner of the land (the property is not listed with a REALTOR) and discusses the possibility of purchasing the property. The two men agree on a price of $80,000 payable as follows: $23,200 down and the balance of $56,800 at 12 percent interest payable in equal monthly installments over twenty years. Everything sounds fine to Jim but, to make sure, he asks his attorney to write the contract for sale.

Jim's attorney writes the contract and the seller's attorney approves the conditions. Both attorneys advise their clients on all the legal conditions and problems involved. Both buyer and seller sign the contract and the transaction is closed. By bringing attorneys into the matter before any contract is signed, both parties are informed on legal matters that could arise as a result of the sale.

The Property Manager

A **property manager** is a specialist in the management of real estate. Typically, the property is income-producing, and the manager is needed to collect rents, negotiate leases, supervise maintenance, reduce expenses, and advise the investors. Property managers generally are not required to be licensed by the state, although resident managers living on the premises may be required to hold a real estate agent's license.

A property manager may be designated or nondesignated. He or she may be an Accredited Residential Manager (ARM) or a Certified Property Manager (CPM). To obtain either of these designations the candidate must complete a course of study and satisfy an experience requirement administered by the Institute of Real Estate Management.

Services offered   The property manager *collects the rents, rents the vacant units, pays the mortgage payments for the investor, supervises the maintenance,* and *solves any problems pertaining to the property.* A property manager *provides the client an income and expense statement periodically.*

The obvious advantage to an owner is that the *property is managed by a professional.* Also, the owner is not bothered by the problems of the tenants.

Example The services of a property manager are illustrated in the following example of a person's decision to buy income property in another city.

Gus Rusher, a resident of Dallas, is considering investing a large amount of money in an eight-unit apartment complex in Fort Worth. Gus has had considerable experience with investment properties and believes the price of $168,000 to be fair. The property gross income is $24,000 per year and expenses have been typical for an apartment complex. One issue bothering Gus is the question of who will take care of the property because Gus will be in Dallas and he doesn't want to commute to Fort Worth. He considers hiring a resident manager and leaving him in charge of everything but decides that it would be difficult to find an individual with the property knowledge.

A friend in the Dallas area informs Gus about a property management firm in Fort Worth that manages apartment complexes for several nonresident owners. Gus visits the firm to discuss their services. He finds that the firm will rent units, collect rents, pay bills, supervise the maintenance, and advertise the property for 6.5 percent of the effective gross income. In addition, Gus will receive a monthly income and expense statement and an annual report for his tax return. Gus can stay in Dallas and allow his investment to be managed by competent, experienced people in Fort Worth. Therefore, Gus purchases the apartment complex and hires the property management firm to manage it.

The Real Estate Counselor

A **real estate counselor** is any individual who offers advice about real estate for a fee. A commission is not charged. Any individual can serve as a counselor to a buyer or seller if the client believes the advice is useful and is willing to pay the fee.

The counselor may be designated by the American Society of Real Estate Counselors. Upon reaching age thirty-five and acquiring acceptable experience, he or she may be invited to apply for a Counselor of Real Estate (CRE) designation.

Services offered   The counselor is essentially *a problem solver* who *provides independent advice* to the buyer or seller. The counselor *may provide advice as a guide to action* when the alternatives are not clear, *may suggest the proper use and development of property* when the owner is unsure, and *may advise the buyers and owners of the effect of real estate economics on their enterprises and of the real estate implications of proposed undertakings.* In addition, a counselor *may give the client confidence,* which promotes rational decision making.

The real estate counselor offers *competent, impartial, and professional advice to a buyer or seller who may be uncertain of the alternatives.*

Example The services of a real estate counselor are illustrated in the following example of a person's evaluation of real estate investment alternatives.

Pat Norvell, a resident of Mobile, Alabama, recently inherited $50,000. Pat does not want to deposit the money in a savings account and earn between 9 and 10 percent—she wants to speculate and take a chance on earning more. Pat has always been fascinated by the real estate business but has never been involved in buying and selling real estate except for the purchase of her home. Knowing little about investing in real estate, she calls a local real estate broker, Roger Turner, and asks for information about investments. This particular broker is also a CRE and tells Pat that he is willing to discuss the alternatives. During their conference the next day, Pat tells Roger that she has $50,000 to invest and would like to receive at least a 15 percent return on her investment. Roger knows of several investment properties that would return 12 percent to the owner, but some are more risky than others. Pat replies that risk does not matter because she wants the investment that has the possibility of the greatest return. Seeing that Pat lacks experience in real estate investments, Roger recommends that Pat purchase a duplex requiring only a small down payment, showing a good stable income, and yielding approximately a 12 percent return. At first, Pat is reluctant but eventually realizes her lack of experience and buys the property. She decides that she can acquire more risky properties later if this one is successful.

The Insurance Company

Any improvements on property that have a value should be covered by insurance against loss from common hazards. If the improvements have been mortgaged, the lender will require an insurance policy protecting their interests. The insurance is purchased from a property and casualty insurance company through an agent who has been licensed by the State Insurance Department.

Services offered   The service provided by an insurance company is *giving protection to the lender and the buyer in the event of a financial loss to the property from a hazard.* A typical homeowner's policy covers a home, home fixtures, and garages on the premises, as well as furniture, clothing, appliances, and most other family personal property. The policy specifically identifies the hazards against which the property is insured; for example, fire, lightning, explosion, smoke, vandalism, riot damage, hail, windstorm, vehicle damage, and glass breakage. The policy also lists certain hazards to which the insurance does not apply; for example, acts of war, rebellion, and revolution. No payment is made for damage caused by unlisted hazards.

Additional coverage can include protection against claims by other people for accidental injury or damage to their property on or off the insured's premises, protection against theft hazards not otherwise specified in the policy, and protection (in most states) for second homes such as seasonal dwellings located in or out of the insured's home state. Earthquake coverage can be provided as additional coverage, and flood insurance may be available through the National Flood Insurance Association.

By means of insurance, the *risk of any financial loss is transferred from the lender and the homeowner to the insurance company.* The lender and the owner can be assured that they will not face the possibility of bankruptcy if damage occurs to a property that is covered by insurance.

Example An insurance company may require a homeowner to take certain precautions in order to obtain a homeowner's insurance policy, as shown in the following example.

Barbara Brandon has just purchased a house in Omaha. Barbara was left an inheritance and was able to pay cash for the house. The selling price of the house was $60,000, which included the lot valued at $12,000. Barbara has lived in the house for one week and now suddenly realizes that she has not insured the house or her personal belongings. Therefore, Barbara goes to the local Safety Insurance Agent, Gerri Danenhauer, for a policy.

During their discussion, Barbara learns that her house is in an area that is approximately a twenty-minute drive from the nearest fire station. The station is only three miles away, but the house is on a side road that is not well maintained and is sometimes difficult to travel in bad weather. A fire truck carrying water would have great difficulty driving over the road. Gerri informs Barbara that, to obtain a policy, she will have to improve the access road to her property significantly or change it to another location. In addition, she wants Barbara to purchase several types of fire extinguishers for placement in the house at strategic locations. This would enable Barbara and her family to fight any fire with the proper equipment until a fire truck could arrive. Gerri tells Barbara that any future remodeling or additions would need to be approved by her in advance to ensure that the building materials are the nonflammable type. Gerri's company requires these precautions to minimize the possibility of a major loss.

If Barbara had purchased the house with a loan, the financial institution making the loan would have required her to present a homeowner's policy before the loan was issued.

The Real Estate Developer

A **real estate developer** is any person or firm that transforms property from one stage of use to another. Developers typically start with raw acreage. They have the property subdivided and plotted by an engineer. They solicit and receive the necessary permits from the city, county, state, and federal agencies to erect a structure on the site. The developer may be a real estate agent who is involved in marketing the properties. Thus, the property is transformed from raw acreage to a site ready for construction, to a potentially inhabitable structure, to an inhabited structure.

Anyone can develop property who can bear the financial burden and has the knowledge. There are no licensing requirements unless the developer acts as a broker by employing other people to sell the property for a commission and thus becomes subject to the real estate license law.

Services offered   A developer can offer *the same services as any real estate company.* For example, the developer can *sell vacant lots* that have been approved either by the city or county for proper zoning, street requirements, and utility requirements. Also, the developer can *sell finished buildings.* The development company can *arrange for financing* of the transaction. A developer can *serve as a counselor* to the potential buyer. Because the developer must work with all phases of the development process, he or she *is familiar with local trends* in market demand, building and environmental codes, building costs, financing, and sales.

Example A real estate developer's services are illustrated in the following example of a person's decision to buy raw land for development.

Phil Travis, a resident of Lexington, Kentucky, is considering the purchase of a ten-acre tract of land just inside the city limits. The tract consists entirely of cleared, unimproved pasture. City water and sewer lines are located only a short distance to the east. The problem with the tract is that it has no road frontage. At one location, however, a road could be constructed without much trouble. Phil believes the property has tremendous residential potential because of its location and the small supply of development property left within the Lexington city limits. The owner is asking $5,000 per acre, and Phil feels the price is fair on the basis of sales of properties in the immediate area. However, to be sure, Phil decides to consult a local developer. Phil has never developed land and realizes that he needs help from an expert in the field.

Phil asks Al Davis of the Al Davis Development Company to look at the property. After viewing the property and considering the possibilities, Al tells Phil that all surrounding houses are worth about $70,000, and that he should conform with the neighborhood. Al recommends that the lot prices be 15 percent of the overall selling price, or $10,500 ($70,000 × 0.15). To achieve conformity with the neighborhood, only two lots per acre could be developed. Because of a large drainage ditch and the single entry and exit into the subdivision, a large cul-de-sac would have to be constructed to permit a fire truck to turn around. In addition, bridges would have to be built over the drainage ditch. Phil has not considered such factors and he realizes that the construction costs to develop the land will be higher than normal. The comparable developments that Phil has examined are adjacent to higher priced residential areas and are generally problem-free. Al advises Phil, on the basis of his experience, that a developer would not pay more than $1,300 per acre for the land. Phil offers the seller this amount, and the offer is refused. Phil decides not to buy the property because he cannot raise additional cash and the project would require more time than he anticipated.

The Escrow Agent

An **escrow agent** is a neutral, independent third party who agrees to execute the escrow agreement. The agreement typically allows the deed to be given to the buyer and the funds to be paid to the seller once certain predetermined conditions of the sale arc satisfied. The essential purpose in using the escrow agent is to assure that the terms negotiated within the contract of sale are satisfied.

Services offered   The escrow agent provides a convenient method of *assuring that the terms of the escrow agreement are fulfilled.* Essentially, this means that the *terms negotiated within the contract of sale are satisfied.* This can include providing an abstract and opinion of title, title insurance, warranty deed, paid utility receipts, evidence of liens that have been paid, completion of construction, predetermined repairs, recording of the deed, and so on. The agent serves as a depository who has the authority to transfer, dispose, and execute according to the predetermined escrow agreement.

Example A simplified example of the services provided by an escrow agent would show the advantages of using their services.

Beth Buyer agrees to purchase a parcel from Susie Speed for $45,000 once the terms of the escrow agreement are satisfied. The escrow agreement is written between them and given to First National Bank, the agent. The agreement says that Susie must provide current paid utility receipts, a warranty deed supported by an abstract and an attorney's opinion that the title is free and clear of encumbrances, and a key showing that the property has been vacated by February 16. Once this material has been provided to the agent, the money may be paid to Susie. Following the terms of the agreement, Susie provides the required material and receives the $45,000.

Unique Features of the Real Estate Transaction

A typical real estate transaction involves several parties working together to ensure that the purchase (or sale) progresses smoothly and everyone's interests are protected. Thus, the transaction is not similar to that carried out by a consumer in purchasing a suit of clothes or a new automobile. In the latter cases, the consumer enters a retail outlet that carries the product, examines the item, and, if it meets his or her needs, pays for it and takes it home. In a real estate transaction, the buyer must find a seller who possesses the product that he or she desires or vice versa. A tremendous search cost may be incurred before the two parties find each other. An agent's services can be used to lower this search cost and to enable one or both parties to save time. Once the buyer finds a seller with acceptable property, a considerable amount of negotiation may transpire before an acceptable selling price is reached. An agent can be asked to help with the negotiations or an attorney can be employed to review and/or write the contracts. Next, appropriate financing needs to be arranged and at this point the local lending institutions become involved. The lender may insist that an appraiser be hired to estimate the market value of the property and in addition may require an abstract with an attorney's opinion or title insurance. A survey may be needed, and an attorney may be called upon to solve any legal problems. The agent can handle the closing or it can be conducted by the title company or the financial institution.

Thus, a typical real estate transaction involves several specialists who are asked by the buyer or seller to give their service or who are involved because one of the participants requires their service. It is different from a routine retail transaction because it requires a prolonged search, complex negotiations, the services of numerous specialists, and hence more time to complete successfully.

OTHER BUSINESSES THAT SERVICE REAL ESTATE

Numerous other individuals and firms service the real estate business, especially in the construction sector. For example, when a structure is built, one contractor is hired to excavate, another contractor lays the sewer pipe, a lumber company supplies the lumber, a carpenter performs the labor, an appliance store provides appliances and fixtures, a cabinet shop makes the cabinets, a paint store supplies the paint, a painter contracts for the painting, and so on through a wide range of specialists from the architect who designs the structure to the new custodian who is hired to maintain it. A new structure involves a large number of people who sell their supplies or services.

All of these suppliers of products and labor are brought together to build one structure by the **general contractor.** This individual enters into a contract with a prospective occupant to build a structure by supervising all of the individual suppliers of products and services. The general contractor negotiates a fee that is typically a percentage of the cost of construction. This individual can be the future owner, a developer, or someone in business as a general contractor.

Multiplier Impact

Since so many individuals supply products and labor to the real estate business, the effect of one person's decision to buy or build a structure is multiplied by the number of people involved directly and indirectly in the project. Moreover, the effect is multiplied by the number of individuals who are making the decision to buy or build at any given time. Thus, a change in demand for real estate can have a tremendous impact on both employment and incomes in a city, a region, or the nation. A change in economic conditions, such as a rapid increase in the interest rate, that dampens the demand for ownership and/or new construction can have a severe and widespread effect. Many products would remain unsold, contractors and laborers would be unable to find work, and the demand for many services would decline. Conversely, a change in economic conditions that increases the demand for real estate can produce a similarly broad effect, stimulating the sale of goods and services and expanding job opportunities.

FUTURE CHARACTERISTICS OF THE REAL ESTATE BUSINESS

Several trends appear to be developing that should influence the structure of the real estate business in the future.

1. *The real estate transaction for a purchase or a sale is becoming more complex.* Numerous lawsuits have shown that any real estate specialists involved in a transaction need a high level of knowledge and competence and must perform their services honestly. Common types of suits are those against agents for misrepresenting the property characteristics, against the buyer for breach of contract, against the seller for breach of contract, against an attorney for an error in rendering an opinion on an abstract, against lenders for discrimination in their lending practices, against an appraiser for overestimating the value of property, against agents for discriminating in the showing of properties to minorities, and against local real estate boards for fixing commissions.

2. *The level of knowledge required by the public to evaluate their own interest is increasing.* In the area of real estate finance, for example, several new types of mortgages are appearing on the market. The public will need a certain minimum level of education about them as a basis for selecting the most suitable alternative.

3. *Prospective agents will find entrance requirements to the profession to be much more stringent because of rising educational requirements.* In addition, *continuing education requirements for maintaining the license are increasing.*

4. *The small local firm will have more competition from the growing number of franchises and larger national or regional firms.*

5. *Lenders probably will be giving a lower percentage of the purchase price in a loan and hence the new buyer will need more cash.* In addition, *higher interest rates will take a higher proportion of the family budget than the typical 25 percent used for housing in the past.*

6. *Federal and state intervention in real estate transactions will continue to increase.*

CHAPTER SUMMARY

Real estate is a physical entity consisting of land in its legal definition and the man-made improvements permanently affixed to that land. The legal concept of land includes the surface area of the earth, plus the mineral and air rights that extend below and above the surface. The improvements are the structures put on the land as well as changes or additions that are made to the land itself, such as grading, clearing, and landscaping. Fixtures are also a component of real estate. They are items of personal property that are either attached to or intended to be part of the land or the improvement. They are items of personal property that are viewed as part of real property.

The legal dimension of real estate involves several legal rights—the rights to use, to possess, to exclude other people from, and to dispose of real estate. When the legal dimension is considered in conjunction with land, improvements, and fixtures, the term *real property* is used.

In addition to these components, real estate has the physical characteristics of immobility, indestructibility (or durability), and nonhomogeneity, as well as several economic characteristics. Its purchase price is typically a multiple of the consumer's yearly income, its purchase is almost always facilitated by the use of borrowed money, and the decision to buy necessitates large expenditures of time, effort, and money in gathering relevant information about the product.

The real estate business may be viewed as composed of four phases geared for the production of housing. The *Preparation Phase* consists of land acquisition, planning, and zoning amendments if needed. The individuals and firms participating in this phase range from the developer to individuals who prepare the master deed. The *Production Phase* includes site preparation, construction, and financing. Individuals who participate in this phase range from the developer to persons influencing the laws controlling the transportation of materials. The *Distribution Phase* consists of the sale of the property and its financing. A range of individuals can become involved including the broker, developer, lawyer, title company personnel, lenders, bankers, and individuals designated as specialists by various professional associations. Finally, the *Service Phase* includes maintenance and management, repairs, and improvements and additions. The real estate and housing business is very large, involves many people and organizations, and is very complex.

Various individuals, firms, and organizations provide services to the buyer, the seller, and/or the agent. Examples include the appraiser, title company, real estate attorney, surveyor, lender, real estate agency, and the National Association of REALTORS.

An agent has the option of joining the local board, the State Association of REALTORS, and the National Association of REALTORS. A principal, partner, or corporate office who joins is called a REALTOR, and a salesperson, independent contractor, or certain affiliated members affiliated with member firms are called a REALTOR-ASSOCIATE. Membership means that the agent subscribes to a code of ethics. In addition, an agent may hold a designation, such as a CRB or CCIM, that shows he or she has completed a prescribed course of study and acquired satisfactory experience. A buyer or seller could expect a high level of professionalism from an agent who is a REALTOR and who holds a designation in the appropriate speciality.

Review Questions

1. What is real estate? As part of your definition, be certain to explain the legal concept of land, as well as the nature of improvements-to-the-land and improvements-on-the-land.

2. What are fixtures and how are they determined?

3. Distinguish between freehold and leasehold estates.

4. Distinguish between freehold estates of inheritance and freehold estates not-of-inheritance (fee simple estate).

5. Identify and describe the four types of leaseholds.

6. Define and distinguish between joint tenancy and tenancy in common.

7. What are the economic characteristics of real estate?

8. What does the phrase "real estate business" mean?

9. Contrast the roles of the National Association of REALTORS and the State Real Estate Commission.

10. Are all agents REALTORS? Why not?

11. What is the difference between a general agent and a special agent?

12. Explain the services offered by each of the following that a potential buyer or seller might use:

agent	real estate insurance company
appraiser	property manager
title company	real estate attorney
developer	

13. Describe the multiplier effect of the real estate business.

14. Discuss the trends that could influence the real estate business in the future.

Discussion Questions

1. The bundle of rights held by the owner of a freehold estate of inheritance can be manipulated in a variety of ways. Devise at least three different alternatives by which this landowner can sell and rent out the several rights that he or she possesses.

2. Should a prospective buyer or seller always use an agent who is a REALTOR? Why?

3. What are the merits of using an agent?

4. Should all of the services described in this chapter be used in a typical real estate transaction? Why or why not?

5. Should all prospective candidates for a real estate license be required to pass a *national* exam? Should they be given a *national* license?

6. Are the public controls applied equally to all private property? If you answer no, give examples.

7. Since the real estate business is tied into the economy through many related businesses, should the federal government give increased financial support and regulation to minimize the impact of adverse fluctuations in the business cycle?

Notes

1. Harold F. Lusk and William B. French, *Law of the Real Estate Business* (Homewood, Ill.: Richard D. Irwin, Inc., 1975), p. 51.

2. Ibid., p. 54.

3. Ibid., p. 56.

4. Ibid., p. 26.

5. Ibid., p. 33.

6. Ibid., p. 39.

7. Ibid., pp. 390–391.

8. Robert Kratovil and Raymond J. Werner, *Real Estate Law* (Prentice-Hall Series in Real Estate, Englewood Cliffs, N.J.: Prentice-Hall, Inc., 1979), p. 193.

9. Lusk and French, *Law of the Real Estate Business,* p. 89.

10. Kratovil and Werner, *Real Estate Law,* p. 196.

11. Ibid., pp. 194–195. The last point is true for states in which the title theory of the mortgage is used. The rulings by the courts do not agree about this occurrence in states where the lien theory of the mortgage is used.

12. Lusk and French, *Law of the Real Estate Business,* p. 101.

13. This distinction between a general agent and a special agent is discussed in Chapter 12 in terms of the agent's contractual relationship with the client.

14. Real estate lenders are discussed fully in Chapter 16.

15. These steps are discussed in other chapters.

Additional Readings

BORDESSA, RONALD. "Rhetoric vs. Reality in Residential Real Estate Brokerage." *Real Estate Review* 8 (Winter 1979): 98–101.

BOYCE, BYRL N., ed. *Real Estate Appraisal Terminology.* Cambridge, Mass.: Ballinger Publishing Co., 1975.

CLAURETIE, TERRENCE. "New Opportunities for Collegiate Real Estate Programs." *Journal of Real Estate Education* (Winter/Spring, 1985): 4–6.

DOWNO, ANTHONY. "Public Policy and the Rising Cost of Housing." *Real Estate Review* 8, 1 (Spring 1978): 27–38.

GALLAGHER, THOMAS. "Who Will Own Our Homes in 2000 A.D.?" *Real Estate Review* 6, 1 (Summer 1976): 108–111.

GRAASKAMP, JAMES A. *A Guide to Feasibility Analysis.* Chicago, Ill.: Society of Real Estate Appraisers, 1970. Chapters 3, 5, and 6.

HENSLEY, BENJAMIN N., and RONALD M. FRIEDMAN. *Real Estate Law.* New York: Warren, Gorham and Lamont, 1979. Chapters 1–3.

KLAMAN, SAUL B. "Maintaining Deposit Inflows When Interest Rates Rise: The Impossible Dream?" *The Mortgage Banker* 38 (April 1978): 46–50.

KRATOVIL, ROBERT, and RAYMOND J. WERNER. *Real Estate Law.* Englewood Cliffs, N.J.: Prentice-Hall, Inc., 1983.

LUSK, HAROLD F., and WILLIAM B. FRENCH. *Law of the Real Estate Business.* Homewood, Ill.: Richard D. Irwin, Inc., 1984.

MCMAHAN, JOHN. "America Urbanizes: The Twentieth Century Transition." *Real Estate Review* 6, 1 (Spring 1976): 86–93.

_____. "The Postwar Development Boom: Real Estate Rides High." *Real Estate Review* 6, 2 (Summer 1976): 89–94.

_____. "The Future of the Real Estate Industry: Changing Supply Patterns." *Real Estate Review* 7, 1 (Spring 1977): 68–72.

_____. "The Future of the Real Estate Industry: New Directions and New Roles." *Real Estate Review* 7, 2 (Summer 1977): 91–96.

MILLER, NORMAN G. "The Changing Structure of Residential Brokerage." *Real Estate Review* 8 (Fall 1978): 46–51.

NEISH, DAVID R. M. "The One-Person Office: All Alone." *Real Estate Today* (August 1975): 28–31.

REILLY, JOHN W. *The Language of Real Estate.* Chicago, Ill.: Real Estate Education Co., 1977.

SCHOEFFLER, WILLIAM. "The Secret Ingredient for Successful Syndication." *Real Estate Review* 5, 3 (Fall 1975): 125–131.

SMITH, DAVID L. "Regional Impact of Disintermediation." *Federal Home Loan Bank Board Journal* 10 (June 1977): 20–24.

"Staying Small." *Real Estate Today* 9 (May/June 1976): 22–31.

STEVENSON, HOWARD. "The Reasons Behind the Real Estate Crash: A Case Study." *Real Estate Review* 6, 2 (Summer 1976): 35–46.

2 | Public Controls, Private Restrictions, and the Concept of Value

1. What public controls and private restrictions may be placed on the ownership rights of property?

2. What factors play an important role in determining value?

OBJECTIVES

When a student finishes the chapter, he or she should be able to

1. Identify and explain the public controls and private restrictions on real estate.

2. Explain the difference between value-in-use and value-in-exchange.

3. Identify and discuss determinants of value.

IMPORTANT TERMS

Attribute Analysis
Building Code
Construction Code
Easement
Easement Appurtenant
Easement-in-Gross
Eminent Domain
Escheat
General Lien
Highest and Best Use
Housing Code
Lien

Market Value
Most Probable Selling Price
Occupancy Code
Police Powers of the State
Restrictive Covenant
Rights of Ownership
Specific Lien
Subdivision Regulation
Value-in-Exchange
Value-in-Use
Zoning Ordinance

INTRODUCTION

Chapter 1 discussed the nature and characteristics of the real estate commodity. In addition, it contained an explanation of the real estate business and the various individuals and firms that comprise the business and offer services that assist in solving the real problems and satisfying the needs of a buyer, seller, or agent. The consumer has not been introduced to the public controls and private restrictions on real estate ownership. Consequently, the purpose of this chapter is to explain these controls and typical restrictions. The chapter concludes with an introduction to forces that determine the property's value.

PUBLIC CONTROLS AND LIMITS ON REAL ESTATE

The rights of ownership described in the preceding chapter are not absolute rights because there are constraints on the owner's ability to use the property. The controls and limits are of two major kinds: public and private. In this section, the public controls that affect a property owner are considered. One category of these controls is known as the **police powers of the state.** These powers are provided in the federal and state constitutions to enable governments to protect the public by regulating factors that can adversely affect the public health, morals, safety, and general welfare.

Four types of police power can be instituted by a local government under the approval of the state legislative body: (1) the zoning ordinance, (2) the subdivision regulations, (3) the building code, and (4) the housing code. In the following sections, each of these controls is described and the impact on an owner's use of property is examined.

Zoning Ordinance

The **zoning ordinance** initiated by a local community usually contains three distinct elements: (1) land-use restrictions, (2) height restrictions, and (3) area or bulk restrictions.

In the land-use restriction section of the zoning ordinance, all parcels of property in a community are classified or zoned into four general categories: industrial, commercial, residential, and agricultural. This section of the ordinance establishes a geographic distribution of the land uses in the local community. Once this pattern of land use is stipulated, the land-use restrictions may legally allow only the use specified and exclude all other land uses (exclusive zoning), or the land-use restriction may legally allow the stated use and all other compatible or suitable land uses, such as residential activity in a commercial zone (inclusive zoning). The land-use categories may contain more specific subcategories, such as single-family detached residences on large lots, single-family detached residences on small lots, duplexes, or multifamily units. Commercial and industrial land-use categories may also be broken down into more detailed subclasses.

The height restrictions in the zoning ordinance specify the legal height of structures by land-use category and by geographic area. They could state a maximum height for apartment buildings in the multifamily residential land-use category and a different maximum height for the structures in the single-family detached residential category. The height restrictions could also differ by geographic area. Tall structures could be prohibited near municipal airports but allowed in the central business district.

The area regulations of the zoning ordinance specify the relationship between the structure and the land components on individual parcels of property. In the case of residential property, the area regulations could contain setback rules that establish the minimum distance between the street and the location of the structure. The size of side yards and the minimum size of the building lot could also be established. For commercial property, area regulations could dictate whether the structure is situated at the front or at the rear of the property. They could also regulate the location of parking areas by dictating that parking be provided in front of or behind the building.

The zoning ordinance in general and each of the three categories in particular limit a property owner's right to use property. The property owner is told what activity is allowed on the property, how tall a structure can be, the legally allowable minimum distance that must be provided between the structure and the front, side, and back lines, and finally the position of the building and its relationship to the land surface. These restrictions can influence either the income derived from the property or the value of the property itself. The zoning ordinance could legally rule out commercial activity; it could thereby reduce the income-generating capabilities of the property. The height-restriction component of the zoning ordinance could reduce the square footage of office space or commercial space available on a parcel of property and, thus, reduce the income and the value of the real estate for its owner.

Once the zoning regulations are established, the property owner can try to change their impact in either of two ways. One way is to obtain a variance. In this case, the owner is asking permission to deviate from the current land-use regulation in some way. A request might be made to establish a different setback or a slightly different allowable height. Usually, the argument made by the owner must be based on the fact that a hardship will be incurred if the variance is not granted. The second procedure is the rezoning application. In this case, the owner is asking for a change in the ordinance to allow a different land use on a specific piece of property. For example, a request can be made to change the zoning from single-family detached to townhouse, to multifamily, or even to commercial use.

If the local government decides not to grant the request for a variance or a rezoning, it thereby sustains the legally allowable use imposed by the zoning ordinance. Consequently, the zoning ordinance is a limitation on the individual's right to use the property. The property could be less valuable in the permitted use than it would be in a use that is not allowed.

The zoning ordinance is imposed to protect the health, safety, morals, and general welfare of the community. The benefits derived by the community may greatly exceed the cost imposed on the property owners by the restriction of their land use. Moreover, the zoning ordinance might even encourage the stability of use for surrounding property and minimize the uncertainty about the future, thereby enhancing the value of the individual owner's property.

When the zoning ordinance is established for the public benefit, the local government must act to protect the interests of property owners. The legislation establishing the zoning ordinance must be reasonable, clear and specific, free from discrimination, and not arbitrary in its application. Moreover, any changes in the zoning ordinance, especially those in response to rezoning applications, must fulfill the same requirements. When such a change is made, it must be justified on the basis of a current need that has arisen due to changes in economic and social factors, or due to the recognition of newly discovered facts.

When a zoning ordinance is imposed, or when circumstances require a restructuring of the land-use restrictions, certain property may not conform with surrounding property under the new zoning ordinance. For example, there may be a single-family detached housing unit in an expanded commercial section, or there may be an apartment building or convenience store in a newly created single-family residential zone. These properties are known as *nonconforming uses*. As a general rule, the owner can continue using the property as before and can maintain it in good repair. However, unless given express permission, the owner cannot enlarge the structure or undertake an alteration that will lengthen the physical life of that structure. Moreover, if the property is damaged or destroyed, it cannot be repaired or reconstructed unless the zoning ordinance expressly allows such action.

Subdivision Regulations

Subdivision regulations are another type of police power imposed by the local government to promote and protect the health, safety, and general welfare of the community. These goals are accomplished by having a local agency, such as a planning body, review and approve builders' plans for new residential developments within the local jurisdiction. The regulations are generally designed to prevent construction in floodplains, on land with poor or inadequate drainage capabilities, and on land parcels that have unacceptably steep slopes coupled with soil conditions that could cause land and mud slides.

In addition to requiring an analysis of the geological features of the development site, subdivision regulations require the developer to meet locally acceptable standards for street systems, building-lot specifications, and block size. The street system standards include the street layout, the design and frequency of intersections, street widths, maximum slopes and grades, and minimum construction standards for the roadway.

By means of building-lot specifications, the subdivision regulations can discourage the creation of building lots and residential blocks that are inefficient in size and shape; for example, lots that are very deep but also very narrow and lots that have a very irregular shape. Building lots are generally designed as squares, rectangles, and other four-sided shapes, such as trapezoids or parallelograms. In some situations, a five-sided lot may be acceptable, but building lots whose sides number six or more are typically viewed as being inefficient.

Block size is closely related to the street system. Subdivision regulations can be used to discourage the creation of long blocks with few street intersections and blocks that are so narrow that housing units cannot be built back-to-back facing different streets. In addition, long dead-end streets can be prohibited. As a rule, a dead-end street less than 500 feet long is viewed as acceptable.

The subdivision regulations are imposed by requiring the prospective developer to file a plat map for approval. The plat map is a graphic representation of the subdivision's relative size and shape. It includes the street system, blocks, and building lots, all represented in scale. If the plat map is approved, it is recorded and becomes part of the public domain. Prospective buyers of a lot can examine the plat map to verify the shape and the dimensions of the land parcel.

Building, or Construction Code

The third police power is the **building, or construction code** imposed by local government. This code is designed to establish the minimum acceptable standards for construction within the local jurisdiction. It specifies the type and positioning of structural members in the floors, walls, ceiling, and roof of a building (i.e., 2 × 4's every 16″ on center in the walls, 2 × 8 × 12's as floor joists, etc.). Another section of the construction code specifies the minimally acceptable standards for plumbing systems with respect to water-supply lines and waste-disposal lines. Still another section of the code specifies the minimum gauge of electric wires and the positioning of outlets and switches.

Finally, the local community's building code can require the installation of fire-protection devices in buildings. In this area of the code, contractors can be required to provide multiple exits, fire escapes in multiple-story units, sprinkler systems, and exit signs. Moreover, the code can prohibit dead-end corridors and structural obstacles that could impede the steady flow of traffic in case of a fire.

Compliance to the specifications of the building code can be checked by requiring that the contractor apply for a building permit with the local government's department of building or construction. In order to complete the application for a building permit, the contractor must submit copies of the construction specifications for examination by local authorities. If the application is approved, the authorities issue a building permit. While the work is under way, inspectors from the building department check the work to see that the contractor is complying with the construction specifications. When the job is completed, a final inspection is performed. If the work is done according to the specifications of the building code, a *certificate of occupancy* is issued and the structure can then be occupied and used.

Housing, or Occupancy Code

The fourth police power is the **housing, or occupancy code.** This code is designed to establish socially acceptable minimum standards for safe and healthy occupancy of existing and newly constructed buildings. One aspect of the housing code is related to the structural quality and physical condition of existing units. Any building that needs major repairs is generally considered in violation of the local housing code. Moreover, any structure that is lacking certain plumbing facilities, such as hot running water and/or private toilet facilities for individual dwelling units, is considered in violation of the housing code.

The housing code can also cover such items as unprotected stairways, improper lighting in hallways, falling plaster, exposed electrical wiring, and the use of lead-base paints. The owner of a building that has any of these safety or health defects can be fined and required to pay the cost of repair. Depending on the extent of repairs, a building permit may have to be obtained at the outset of the repair work and a certificate of occupancy issued upon completion of the job.

Police Powers as Public Limits on the Use of Property

Knowing the specific features of the four police powers, a person can easily see that they are indeed limits on the use of individual property. The zoning ordinance limits the use of the site and the height of the structure. The building code specifies the minimal acceptable construction standards for the structure. The housing code specifies the necessary levels of structural quality as well as health and safety features. The property owner must conform to these ordinances, and in so doing loses the total control or absolute freedom to use the property as he or she desires.

However, the reasons for the legislation enacted under the police-power provisions are also easy to understand. The local government is concerned with the health, safety, morals, and general well-being of the community. The basic premise underlying the regulations is that the benefits derived by the community exceed the sum of the losses incurred by the individual property owners from the restrictions placed upon them. In theory, this issue is debatable and for the most part it eludes quantification. Social or communal benefits cannot be stated easily in dollar terms. These losses are the difference between the property's most profitable, but not allowed, use and its legally allowable use.

The various state and federal courts in the United States have supported the legal foundations of the police-power techniques. However, there have been, are, and always will be challenges to the manner in which these powers are used by the local community.

Eminent Domain

Another public limitation on the rights of property owners is the legal concept of **eminent domain.** Eminent domain is a *right* vested in the state government and given to a local government, and at times, even to private agencies, to acquire possession of (to take) private property. The *act* of converting private property to public property by using eminent domain is called *condemnation.* The property must be acquired for public uses or public purposes, and fair or *just compensation* must be paid to the owner. Moreover, the property owner must be allowed due process of law. Thus, three important factors limit the local government's ability to acquire private property under eminent domain: (1) public use or public purpose, (2) fair or just compensation, and (3) due process of law.

The determination of public use or purpose can be made either by legislation that declares a use to be public or by the courts. In the case of judicial action, the courts can pass judgment on an existing law with its specific statement on public use and purpose, or the courts might be asked to decide on the legality of some specific public purpose. To date, the legal system in this country has found the following activities to be acceptable public purposes:

☐ Establishment of public transportation systems
☐ Establishment of a community water system
☐ Slum-clearance project
☐ Construction of off-street parking
☐ Construction of public facilities, such as municipal and state offices, public schools and institutions of higher learning, public parks and recreation centers
☐ Preservation of historic sites
☐ Irrigation projects, erection of dams, and the establishment of flowage areas for the generation of water power
☐ Construction of canals, widening of streams, and construction of piers and docks[1]

In the law, fair or just compensation means full remuneration for any loss that the property owner sustains as a result of the eminent-domain process. Generally, the standard applied is the market value of the real property that is taken.[2] Three methods can be used for estimating market value or the potential selling price. One method is to examine the sales prices of comparable properties that have been sold in the immediate past. Another method is to calculate the present value of future net income that could be derived from the property. In the third method, the construction cost of a comparable structure is used as the focal point for estimating market value. (These three methods are explained in detail in Chapters 4, 5, and 6.)

Other dimensions to the question of compensation must be considered in addition to the market value of the property. Certain losses sustained by the property owner are not reflected in the market value of the real property taken. Some of these losses may require compensation over and above the market value. Such losses could be

- An increase in commuting costs or the costs of doing business at a new location due to the forced move
- Loss of the business because of an inability to find a suitable or comparable alternate site
- Loss of access to a better street system or pedestrian flow when only part of the property is taken[3]

Another compensation problem arises when only part of the property is condemned. Two approaches are used to determine the compensation. One is to attempt to discover the market value of only that part of the property that is taken under eminent-domain proceedings. Generally, this approach is used if the property is unimproved land. The other approach is to attempt to discover and quantify the impact of the taking on the remaining portion of the property. Will the market value of the remaining property increase because it is adjacent to the public use? Or will the market value of the remaining portion be depressed because of proximity to the public use? For example, part of Mr. Smith's property might be taken to construct a public park, green belt, or public golf course, or it might be taken to construct a municipal dump or a landfill. The former action could have a positive effect on Smith's remaining property, whereas the latter could be very detrimental.

The third requirement in eminent-domain proceedings, due process, is guaranteed by the United States Constitution. The state constitutions also provide that no person shall be deprived of the rights to life, liberty, or property without due process of law. In the context of eminent domain, this provision simply means that the property owner must be given every legal opportunity to plead his or her case before the courts if the level of compensation offered is not satisfactory or if there is doubt about the public nature of the proposed use of the property.

The government's right of eminent domain is more than a limit on the rights of ownership because the government can deny the individual's property rights of use, possession, and disposition. This denial of rights imposed under eminent domain is more severe than the restrictions imposed under the police-power provisions, whereby the right of use is limited but not denied, and the owner retains the right of disposition. The impact of eminent domain gives rise to the need for compensation, but such compensation is currently not given under the zoning ordinance or other police powers.

Taxation and Assessment Powers

The power of the local jurisdiction to tax real property for the provision of public services is coupled with a legal remedy if this property tax is not paid. This legally sanctioned remedy is a limit or control on ownership rights. If the property tax is not paid, the local government has a specific lien, the property tax lien, against the delinquent property. As previously explained, the local government can force the sale of the property to obtain the delinquent taxes. This forced tax sale overrides the property owner's rights of possession and disposition.

Special assessments are charges that a local government levies against property owners for public services such as streets, storm-drain systems, and water and sewage disposal systems. These charges directly affect the value of the individual parcels. The major difference between assessment charges and the general property tax is that the services provided and paid for under the assessment are viewed as value-enhancers for specific properties, whereas the services provided and paid for under the property tax enhance the value of all property in the community. If the assessments are not paid, a specific lien is established against the property, which can then be sold to obtain the delinquent assessment payments. This forced sale to obtain delinquent assessment payments overrides the property owner's rights of possession and disposition.

Escheat

The last public limit on private ownership rights is the legal concept of **escheat.** When a property owner dies without leaving a will and legal heirs cannot be found for the property, the real estate tentatively belongs to no one. In this event, the state government can use the power of escheat to claim the land for the state. In this sense, the power of escheat is not really a limit but it is a control on ownership rights. When the possession and disposition of property are uncertain because of the lack of heirs, the state assumes possession and all other rights of ownership of the property (see Exhibit 2-1).

PUBLIC AGENCIES THAT INFLUENCE THE REAL ESTATE BUSINESS

The types of controls used by the local government to restrict the use of property are explained in the preceding section. All decisions involving purchases, sales, or use are subject to those controls. The purpose of this section is to describe briefly the emphasis of each level of government that can influence the real estate business.

Federal Government

The U.S. Justice Department has a long history of *antitrust litigation* against Boards of REALTORS and multilist organizations for price-fixing of the sales commission. These cases have resulted in decrees that the Boards of REALTORS may not establish recommended commission rates, may not discuss the setting of price commissions in groups, may not discriminate against any agent because he or she will not charge the desired amount, may not use multilist to exclude certain properties, and may not use any educational devices to train members on commission schedules. In

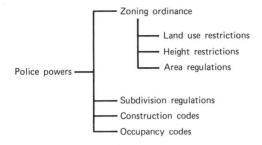

Police powers
- Zoning ordinance
  - Land use restrictions
  - Height restrictions
  - Area regulations
- Subdivision regulations
- Construction codes
- Occupancy codes

Eminent domain

Taxation and assessment power

Escheat

EXHIBIT 2-1 Public controls on the rights of ownership

one recent case,[4] the judge ruled that the listing contract must include a statement, printed on the front in bold letters, and that the commission is negotiable between the agent and the owner.

The federal government has attempted to regulate the *mortgage-application procedure* to inform the consumer about the details of the transaction and to ensure that the lender does not discriminate. The Real Estate Settlement Procedures Act (RESPA), the Equal Credit Opportunity Act (ECOA), the Truth-in-Lending Act, and the Mortgage Disclosure Act pertain to interest-rate charges, settlement costs, discrimination, and the region into which loans are originated. All are designed to inform consumers and protect their rights. These acts are implemented through such agencies as the Federal Reserve Board and the Department of Housing and Urban Development.

The federal government also has the right of *eminent domain.* Congress gives this right to federal agencies to convert private property into public property for the public good. The right is generally used to acquire land for national parks, military installations, and federal office buildings.

The federal government has attempted to establish *air and water controls* on property through such agencies as the Environmental Protection Agency (EPA). This agency can establish standards regulating the amount of air and water pollutants discharged into the atmosphere and streams.

The Federal Trade Commission has recently investigated several cities in the United States to determine whether unfair trade practices are in use. The investigations have been related mainly to the ability of minority group members to earn a living as real estate professionals and the ability of the consumer to buy and sell property without using a real estate agent.

The federal government has a long history of intervention in the real estate business through the *financing* sector. The government has provided special loan funds to promote housing for low and moderate income families. It has created such agencies as the Federal Housing Administration, the Veterans Administration, and the Farmers Home Administration to promote standards of quality for the construction of residences and to administer programs to fulfill the housing needs of certain special groups of consumers. The government has created other institutions such as the Federal National Mortgage Association, the Government National Mortgage Association, and the Mortgage Corporation to establish an orderly secondary mortgage market for the lenders who deal directly with the public. These local lenders who make loans to the public may, under certain conditions, sell the mortgages to institutions in the secondary mortgage market and thus recover their funds to loan again. Also, Congress has created the Department of Housing and Urban Affairs to sponsor solutions to the housing needs of the nation.

The federal government's long-standing influence on the real estate business undoubtedly will continue into the future.

State Government

A large majority of the controls influencing the uses of property are established by the state and local governments because real estate is localized. The state legislature and the state courts influence a wide range of real estate uses and decisions. For example, the state legislature recognizes various types of estates that contain bundles of rights that are transferred from the owner to the buyer. The system of recording title documents is determined by the state legislature. The legislature approves the legal descriptions used to identify the unique location of each property. The property owner's protection from creditors and the creditor's right to place a claim on the value of property for unpaid debts are created by the state legislature. Also, the state retains the right through the *doctrine of escheat* to claim the property of an owner who dies intestate (no will) and has no heirs.

Local Government

Local governments are any entities below the state level that have the authority to levy property taxes. The state legislature may also give these governments the right to impose other types of controls on property uses. For example, the county can levy a property tax and also may be able to regulate health standards on property and to control land use through a county planning department. The city can levy taxes; can, and usually does, impose zoning requirements to restrict certain land uses to specific locations; and can enforce building codes to maintain a minimum quality of construction, safety, and health standards. These controls over real estate transactions, uses, and decisions are called *police powers.* Other local governments, such as the school districts, special improvement districts, and townships, typically have authority only to levy taxes.

PRIVATE CONTROLS AND LIMITS ON REAL ESTATE

In addition to the public limits on the rights of ownership, two classes of private limits can affect the use of private property—legal limits and economic limits. The legal limits are absolute because they deny the right to dispose of, or to use, the property. The economic limits are not absolute because they do not deny a right; they just identify some use as inefficient or uneconomic.

Legal Limits

The legal limits in the private sector are the **easement,** the **lien,** and the **restrictive covenant.** The easement and the lien are nonpossessionary rights of use and exclusion held by a person who is not the owner of the property. The easement limits an owner's ability to use a predetermined and identified portion of the property. The lien limits the owner's right of possession and disposition because nonpayment of a debt secured by the property will give rise to a forced sale indicated by the creditor.

Easements   An **easement** is the right of one person to use the property of another for a specified purpose and under certain conditions that specify the extent of the allowable usage. The person holding the easement does not possess the property nor does that person have the right to dispose of that property. However, under certain circumstances, the holder of the easement can dispose of the nonpossessionary right by selling it or giving it away.

Two types of easements must be explained to clarify the last point. One type of easement "runs with the land"; that is, possession of the easement passes from one owner to the next. The best example of this form of easement is the **easement appurtenant.** It exists when there are at least two parcels of land and one of those parcels (the dominant estate) receives benefits that derive from the use of the other parcel of land (the servient estate). An example of an easement appurtenant is the right of the owner of parcel A to use an access that was created across parcel B. In this case, the owner of parcel A holds the easement and parcel A is the estate that receives the benefits from the access road. Parcel B is the servient estate, the estate that provides the benefit or service.

The right of special usage, which the owner of parcel A has in the land described as parcel B, cannot be revoked by the owner of parcel B once the easement is established and it is used and maintained. Thus, the easement "runs with the land." This type of easement can be passed from one owner of parcel A to successive owners of parcel A. When parcel B is sold, the successive owners of that parcel take possession of the real estate with the full realization that there is an easement against the property.

The second type of easement does not "run with the land"; it involves only one parcel of real estate. This type of easement is called an **easement-in-gross,** and it conveys only a personal right that cannot be sold or passed on to another person.[5] For example, a farmer may own a parcel of property that is adjacent to a highway. An advertising agency asks the farmer for permission to construct a billboard on the property near the highway. The agency will construct and maintain the billboard, and will provide a modest yearly payment to the farmer for the use of the space. In exchange, the agency wishes the right to change the signs periodically. The agency does not wish to rent the land, nor does it claim ownership of the billboard. This agreement provides the agency with an easement to get to the sign (easement by implication). The important point is that the advertising agency does not have the right to sell its easement to another agency because the easement is personal in nature. It applies only to the advertising agency.

Some easements-in-gross, however, are not personal in nature, do "run with the land," and involve only one parcel of property. They are *commercial easements-in-gross,* which can be sold or transferred to another individual. Examples of this type of easement are the rights-of-way that private corporations, such as railroad companies, pipeline companies, and public utilities, have across an individual parcel of land.[6]

Easements can be created in a variety of ways. The most common way is by express agreement between the persons involved. In this situation, the persons involved strike an acceptable agreement about the nature of the use and, in some cases, even the duration of the right to use the property. A second way in which an easement is created is by necessity or implication. In this case, the easement is created if the circumstances of a real estate transaction indicate that the prudent buyer would require special use that was not expressly stated because of some error, such as an oversight. For example, Mr. Jones sells Mr. Smith the back forty acres of his farm. The land that Smith buys is bounded on all sides by land holdings of other people, and there is no access to a road. In this case, the courts would recognize that Smith had an easement across Jones's land by implication or necessity. The courts would recognize that prudent individuals would have decided on the need for such an easement and would have created it.[7]

The easement carries certain rights and duties for each of the parties involved. The easement holder has a limited right of use, and the owner of the parcel against which the easement is held cannot interfere with the easement. The easement holder, however, cannot use the land in a manner that is not allowed. Moreover, the easement holder must maintain the physical part of the servient estate affected by the easement. To do this, the easement holder has the right to enter the property and to do the necessary maintenance and repair work. For example, if the servient estate contains an underground drainage system serving the dominant estate, the owner of the dominant estate, who is the easement holder, has the duty to maintain the drainage system and the right to enter the property to do so.[8]

Lien   The second type of nonpossessionary right in real estate is the **lien.** In general, the lien is the right of a creditor to petition the courts to force the sale of a debtor's property in order to obtain payment. This right is invoked only when the debtor does not fulfill contractual arrangements for the debt's repayment. When the creditor's right to petition to force a sale affects a certain identified parcel of real estate, the lien is referred to as a **specific lien.** When the right affects the asset holdings of an individual without specific reference to a certain piece of property, the lien is known as a **general lien.**

In real estate, specific liens are the most important type of lien. The tax lien and the mechanic's lien are the specific liens that are most often incurred. If a landowner fails to pay the property tax bill against a property, the local government has the right to force the sale of that specific piece of property to obtain the unpaid taxes. If the property sells for more than the amount of the unpaid tax, the former owner receives a cash settlement from the local government that is the difference between the sale price and the unpaid tax bill.

The laws providing for a mechanic's lien protect the contractor who improves another person's property by the application of labor services and materials. If the work is performed as specified in the contract and the quality of work conforms to the general standards of the community, the mechanic's lien will be granted by the courts if the property owner fails to pay the contractor. However, even if the work is not performed according to the contract and it is not up to community standards of acceptability, but the construction is structurally sound and it meets the needs of the property owner, the work must be accepted and paid for. The mechanic's lien will be granted by the courts if payment is not made.[9]

Restrictive covenant The **restrictive covenant,** sometimes called a deed restriction, is a statement placed in a deed (a legal instrument that passes ownership; discussed in Chapter 21) by the current owner when the property is being sold or given to a prospective owner. Since the owner of the property has control of that property subject to public limits, the owner can sell the property on whatever terms he or she chooses. One of these terms could be the restriction of the future use of the land. However, the owner must be reasonable about such restrictions because they can affect the marketability of the property.

Two major categories of restrictive covenants are used: (1) Restrictions can be imposed on the use of the land by an owner who will sell one parcel but will retain possession of adjacent parcels. In this situation, the owner may not want an industrial site next to his or her property, so the individual places a restrictive covenant into the deed that expressly forbids the use of the land for industrial purposes. (2) Restrictions can be imposed by a land developer to make a residential subdivision more attractive. In this case, the restrictions could limit the type of dwelling units constructed and the type of nondwelling structures, such as storage buildings or fences, that are allowed on each parcel of land.

The second class of restriction is often referred to as the *general plan restriction.* Under the subdivision-regulation provisions of the local government, the developer must file a plat, or map, of the subdivision's street layout and building lots. At this point, the developer can also file and record a *declaration of restrictions* that is referenced to the subdivision map. As the building lots are sold, the respective deed for each lot contains clauses stating that the parcel of land is purchased subject to the restrictions that are recorded for the subdivision.

The purpose of these general plan restrictions is to create a rule that any landowner can enforce against any other landowner in the subdivision. The enforceability of these restrictions arises from the fact that each individual landowner buys the parcel with knowledge of the restrictions and, through the act of purchase, agrees to abide by the subdivision's plan and its declaration of restrictions. To enforce the restrictions, all that needs to be shown is that the violator purchased a lot and received either notice of the restrictions or some evidence of their existence in the deed.[10]

One other type of legal limitation on the use of land is imposed in the various contracts used in real estate transactions. The two most common real estate contracts are the mortgage (Chapter 16) and the lease (Chapters 14 and 15). Both of these contracts contain clauses that restrict the owner's right to alter, remove, or demolish portions of the real estate as well as requirements to keep the property in good repair. These clauses thus limit the owner's or tenant's freedom to destroy or ignore the condition of the physical real estate.

Economic Limits

The economic controls and limits on the use of land in the private sector are (1) the inflexibility of the fixed investment in improvements, and (2) the concept of highest and best possible use.

The first of these economic factors is easy to conceptualize. When an improvement is constructed on the land, that improvement is designed to perform a certain service or to accomplish a specific task. If the improvement happened to be a structure designed to serve as a single-family residence, its use as a commercial or industrial property probably would not be efficient. The rooms could be too small for display areas and the ceilings could be too low for storage areas. The use of a commercial structure as a residential unit could present similar problems of inefficiency. Consequently, there is very little flexibility of usage for a structure and the land upon which it stands once the improvement is constructed for a specific use. Adaptation is not impossible—many old housing units have been converted to apartments and even commercial operations, but they are the exceptions, not the general rule.

The **highest and best possible use** is that legally permissible land use that generates the highest residual income to the parcel of land. The legally permissible use is the use permitted by the local zoning ordinance. The idea of residual income is based on the fact that real estate, when used for any purpose, generates a stream of benefits to its owner. These benefits could be psychic benefits in the case of a self-owned, single-family residence, or the benefits could be an income stream from ownership of an apartment building or retail store. A parcel of income-earning property could be used for several types of legally permissible land uses that generate a different income stream and a different level of costs to operate the property. However, the highest and best possible use is not simply the activity that produces the highest total income. The *residual income* to the land must be determined in order to determine the highest and best use.

To obtain an estimate of the residual income to the land, the owner of the land must estimate both the costs of operating the property and the revenues to be derived from alternative land uses. When the operating costs are subtracted from the income that is generated, the residual is obtained. The highest and best use is the legally permissible land use that generates the highest residual income value.

One other factor must be considered in determining the highest and best possible use—the residual income must be estimated not only for the current period but also for a reasonable length of time into the future. Typically, such projections are made for ten to twenty years. These projections are difficult to make if the analyst tries to achieve a high degree of conceptual reliability, that is, a realistic estimate of the income flows and the levels of all costs in each future period. Even after such efforts, the accuracy of the estimates may not be great when viewed with hindsight.

The value of the real estate at the end of the ten- to twenty-year period must be considered along with the estimated stream of net income. This estimate of the future worth of the real estate is as difficult to establish as the income and cost estimates. Finally, the analyst must establish the present value of the stream of net income figures plus the present value of the future worth of the real estate. (The techniques used to determine the present value of future payments are discussed in Chapter 9.)

The economically rational property owner must realize that there is a highest and best possible use, or perhaps there are several uses whose present value is in the same order of magnitude. In addition, the owner must realize that once a structure is built, the physical features of that structure will greatly influence the use of the property (see Exhibit 2-2).

THE CONCEPT OF VALUE

The discussion of real estate as a commodity, which appeared in Chapter 1, should leave the consumer or potential owner with an understanding of the nature of the commodity. The consumer should realize what factors influence his or her capability to use the product, and what circumstances can arise to affect his or her possession of the product. In addition, the explanation of public and private limits on the rights of ownership should show the scope of the consumer's authority or control over the commodity. Finally, the discussion of the components and legal dimensions of the commodity are a logical starting point for the following discussion of the aspects of the commodity that give it value, and the market in which it is exchanged.

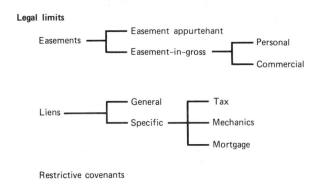

Legal limits

Easements ──┬── Easement appurtenant
            └── Easement-in-gross ──┬── Personal
                                    └── Commercial

Liens ──┬── General
        └── Specific ──┬── Tax
                       ├── Mechanics
                       └── Mortgage

Restrictive covenants

Economic limits

Fixity of investment

Highest and best use limitation
(created by zoning ordinance)

EXHIBIT 2-2 Private controls and limits on real estate

The Nature of Value

The term *value* typically is defined as a commodity's worth, which arises from its utility to an individual, or as its ability to command other commodities in exchange. This definition means that a commodity can have a **value-in-use** and a **value-in-exchange.** Value-in-use arises from an individual's ability to obtain satisfaction or utility from the consumption of the product. In this sense, the commodity is valuable even if no other person desires it or recognizes its worth.

Value-in-exchange arises when at least two people recognize the value-in-use or utility of the commodity. The owner of the commodity can then ask for something in exchange for the commodity if he or she chooses to trade with the other individual. However, for a commodity to have value-in-exchange, two conditions must be met: (1) The commodity must be transferable; it must be capable of being passed to another person. Without this quality, the exchange is impossible. (2) The commodity must not be a free good. It must be relatively scarce so that it is not in everyone's possession, as are air and sunlight.

Determinants of Value

Certain physical and economic features of the commodity give rise to its value-in-use and its value-in-exchange. These determinants of value are different from the physical and economic characteristics of the commodity. The characteristics of the commodity are inherent attributes that describe the commodity or the circumstances surrounding its purchase. They are not features that in themselves make the product useful and thereby valuable. For example, the indestructibility of the land does not make it useful; the durability of an improvement does not make it useful; the homogeneity of the land and the improvement does not make land useful in and of itself. If they did, then even the most arid land in the most inhospitable climates would have value-in-use and value-in-exchange.

The determinants of value are attributes of the commodity that make it useful to someone and desirable to other people. They are the attributes that give rise to the value-in-use and the value-in-exchange that a commodity possesses.

Attribute Analysis: An Analysis of Determinants of Value

Attribute analysis is directed to the intrinsic geological features of the site, the structural and design features of its improvements, and the relationship of these on-site features with their environment.[11] In this sense, the term *environment* is used to describe "the social, physical, political, and economic characteristics of the area surrounding a property which have an effect on its value."[12] The urban environment surrounding the property includes the economy, the financial institutions, the social structure, and the physical features and design of the urban area. Because of the varied dimensions of the concept of the urban environment, many specific categories of factors must be analyzed when the urban environment is considered.

Attributes of the site   An analysis of the attributes of the site examines the geological features of the land and the physical features of the improvement. The geological features of the site consist of the soil, bedrock, drainage, and topographic characteristics of the parcel. These site-specific features are important value determinants because they can affect the owner's ability to use the site to its highest and best use. The soil and bedrock characteristics can determine the height of a structure. The drainage features could make the land undevelopable, especially if it is in a floodplain. The topography, specifically the slope of the land, might render the site unsuitable for some forms of use.

Every improvement is constructed, or was constructed, to meet a specific need. If the improvement fulfills that need, it is considered to be "functionally efficient."[13] In addition to this immediate requirement, every improvement is expected to meet new needs that arise due to changing circumstances in its environment. The ability of the improvement to adapt to changing needs is the second aspect of functional efficiency. The change can occur in the use of the structure or in the attitudes of people toward the correct use. As a general rule, the greater the degree of functional efficiency, the greater the value of the structure. If two structures are currently meeting the same need in an adequate manner, but if one structure can be easily adapted to a new use and the other is adaptable only with difficulty and great expense, the structure that can be easily adapted should be more valuable to its owner.

Two examples illustrate the adaptability of structures to changing needs: First, many modern production techniques require single-story industrial plants. Technological change has made multistory industrial plants, which are typically located in the central cities, functionally inefficient as production facilities. Some of these buildings have been adapted for storage and warehousing functions or to industrial space for small manufacturing plants whose volume of production does not require large amounts of space. However, a large portion of these old industrial buildings are vacant—a sign of either their functional inefficiency or lack of demand for their services. Second, changing tastes and preferences in housing made the multistory house with several dwelling units, situated on a small lot in the central city, less desirable than a single-family house on a large lot in a suburban area. However, rapid increases in the cost of transportation, heating, and cooling, due to the energy crisis, have caused a growing trend in several cities to renovate these multistory houses on small lots. These older structures in the central cities, which did not fill the needs of housing consumers in the 1950s and 1960s, have begun to fill the needs of many families in the 1980s.

Another factor in the category of site-specific determinants of value is the quality of the improvement. Each structure or improvement is durable. However, durability or long physical life does not impart value-in-use or value-in-exchange. The aspect of durability that is important is the quality of the material and workmanship that were used both in construction and in the maintenance and repair routines. If two similar improvements or structures are productive—that is, they render similar services, the structure with the higher quality of construction will be more valuable because the repair and maintenance expenses on a year-to-year basis will be less. In other words, given the same level of maintenance and repair, the higher quality structure could have a longer physical life.

The final site-specific determinant of value for on-site improvements is the attractiveness of the building. The external measures of attractiveness are typically factors of structural design, positioning of the structure on the lot, landscaping, and the covering of exterior surfaces. The internal measures of attractiveness are room size and shape, placement of windows and doors, orientation of sunlight and natural ventilation, the floor plan, wall coverings, fixtures, and the degree of privacy and quiet provided. Because the standards of attractiveness differ among people and also change over time, the influence of this factor is difficult to measure. However, it does affect an individual's decision about the value of a structure.

Attributes of the off-site improvements   The second group of attributes or determinants of value consists of off-site improvements to a particular site. One set of these off-site improvements is the public improvements-to-the-land that are not on, but are adjacent to, the site—the street and sidewalk network, the utility lines, and the storm-drain system that serves the property. This category typically includes improvements provided through special assessments by the local government. These public improvements-to-the-land unquestionably affect the value of the individual parcels they serve.

The second set of off-site improvements that affects a particular site's value is the neighboring improvements-on-the-land. This category includes the neighboring structures and the types of land use nearby. If the quality of the neighborhood is deteriorating because little, if any, repair and maintenance work is done on the surrounding structures, the value of the subject property will be lower than it would be in a neighborhood that is not deteriorating. The proximity of dissimilar and/or incompatible land uses also has an adverse effect on the subject property. If an industrial district is adjacent to a residential area, the proximity of the dissimilar use could have a value-depressing effect on the residential units. However, a prestigious commercial area could have a value-enhancing effect on an adjacent residential area and the individual parcels of real estate.

The third off-site improvement category consists of the public services that are typically provided through the general revenue or property-tax base of the community. The value of a particular site is affected by the availability and quality of instruction in community schools, the level of fire and police protection, the availability of community parks and recreational areas, as well as the existence of community-sponsored cultural and recreational activities. The availability of these public services should enhance the value of a parcel of real estate if the potential homeowners view these features as desirable.

Attributes of the location   In a geographic sense, every parcel of real estate is located in a unique place on the face of the earth. However, each parcel of real estate is also economically and socially located in a unique place with respect to every other parcel of real estate. These economic and social relationships between the land use on one parcel and the land uses on all the other parcels are known as the *linkage pattern* of the parcel in question. As an example, a residential user of land is linked economically with employment centers where the husband and wife might work, and with commercial areas where all types of products and services are bought and sold. The residential land user is also linked socially with the school system, the local church, various social organizations, and recreational centers.

Maintenance of these linkages requires the household to move through space. The adults in the household must travel to do their jobs and in so doing they incur travel or transportation costs. Traditionally, these job-oriented transportation costs are known as *commuter costs*. Other transportation costs are incurred to maintain each of the linkages. Such costs, because they depend on the household's linkage pattern, are part of a rational household's decision about its dwelling site. Consequently, the composition of these transportation costs in general and the commuter costs in particular should be understood.

Each household has money costs and nonmoney costs of transportation. The money costs of moving through space are generally obvious—they include the price of gasoline, oil, tires, tune-ups, repairs, replacement of parts, depreciation, insurance, parking, and licenses for automobiles, and the price of fares for public transportation. The nonmoney costs of moving through space are less obvious. The time involved in travel is a nonmoney cost; however, the anxiety and aggravation associated with travel on congested highways must also be considered a nonmoney or psychic cost.[14] Because the nonmoney costs cannot be quantified directly into dollar terms, they cannot be easily measured. Researchers in the area of commuting costs have typically used the commuter's income level as a proxy for the time cost of travel. The higher the income level of the commuter, the higher the value of leisure time, and the higher the commuting cost. The dollar value of freedom from aggravation is also difficult to establish and few resources have been spent to measure it.

Another nonmoney aspect of transportation costs is the environment of the transportation route between the linkages. The route environment must be examined by analyzing the structural characteristics of the transportation system, the aesthetics of the route, and the health and safety features of the route.[15] The structural features include the width of the street and its lanes, the quality of the surface, the frequency of intersections, the system of lighting, and demarcation. The aesthetics of the route can heighten or ameliorate the aggravation factor of commuting. Driving on a tree-lined highway with greenery and attractive structures can be less aggravating than driving through a congested industrial district flanked by a railroad line on one side and dilapidated industrial structures on the other side. The health of the commuter can also be affected if the industrial district poses an air pollution threat. Finally, the safety factor is included because an irritable driver is a careless, inconsiderate driver who is more prone to irrational and negligent acts behind the wheel. The level of driver irritation is possibly a function of the aesthetics, but it is most assuredly a function of the traffic congestion and time delays.

Trip frequency is the multiplier that greatly affects the costs of transportation. Commuter costs are the most frequent travel costs and they are usually high in both money and nonmoney elements. The value of a real estate parcel is affected by the linkage pattern and the cost of transportation to maintain the linkages. If all other things are equal, the site that is most conveniently located to minimize the costs of transportation, especially the commuter costs, is the site that will be considered most valuable.

The dynamic nature of the attributes   With the exception of the attributes of the site itself (such as the geological features), the attributes of the location, the off-site improvements, and to a lesser extent the on-site improvements are susceptible to change over time. Linkage patterns can change as employment opportunities shift and commercial enterprises change sites. The cost of transportation can change as gasoline prices change and as new highways and alternate modes of transportation are initiated. The quality of public services and the neighborhood structures can change. Standards of attractiveness change. Consequently, the value of a parcel of real estate can change over time as its attributes change. For these reasons, real estate analysts must understand the changing locational patterns and physical characteristics of the urban area.

Relationship of the Market to Value

The term **market** represents the willingness and ability of two distinct entities to interact and to exchange one item for another. One entity expresses a need for real estate. The other entity is willing to exchange real estate for something of value. The two entities are identified by the terms *demand* and *supply*. The demand side of the market is composed of the potential buyers. The supply side of the market is composed of the current owners or producers of the commodity—that is, the potential sellers. In this context, a market can be defined as an economic environment in which a commodity is exchanged.

The demand side of the market is governed by the value-in-use that arises from the property's physical and economic attributes that each potential buyer envisions in the commodity. In other words, the demand side is influenced by the concept of utility, which is the inherent quality of the product to provide some form of satisfaction to the buyer. Value-in-exchange is based on the existence of value-in-use for a group of potential buyers. The desire for the commodity must be accompanied by the ability to provide some valuable item in exchange for the product. This ability is known as *purchasing power.* Finally, the demand for the commodity is affected by the number of individuals who want the product and who can purchase it.

The supply side of the market is also governed by the property's value-in-use and the resultant value-in-exchange of parcel of real estate. Value-in-exchange is influenced by the utility of the commodity—the value-in-use as perceived by the buyers. In addition, value-in-exchange is influenced by the availability of the commodity. Real estate in general is not infinitely available; it is economically scarce. No matter what aspect of real estate is examined, only a finite number of units of the commodity exist. For example, consider the following quantities: the number of acres of land in the United States, the number of building sites in a state, and the amount of land zoned for residential purposes in an urban area. Each of these land parcels is limited in quantity. An analysis of the structures on land would yield the same result. For example, consider the number of existing housing units in an urban area and the number of new housing units that can be built in a given period of time. Each of these categories of housing units is represented by a finite number.

Thus, the value of real estate is affected by the value-in-use and the resultant value-in-exchange that determine the willingness and ability of individuals to buy and sell property. In this way, value-in-use and value-in-exchange as perceived by groups of individuals underlie demand and supply in the market. In turn, demand and supply determine the selling price or market value of a parcel of real property. However, a more thorough understanding of the concepts of market value and selling price is required, especially when the consumer is dealing with a real estate appraiser.

Market Value and Most Probable Selling Price

When the term *market value* is used by a real estate appraiser, it implies that the exchange of the property is carried out under certain market conditions. These conditions have been defined in real estate appraisal literature in several ways. A frequently used definition of **market value** consists of the following six necessary conditions:

1. Buyer and seller are typically motivated.
2. Both parties are well informed or well advised, and each is acting in what he or she considers his or her own best interest.
3. A reasonable time is allowed for exposure in the open market.
4. Payment is made in cash or its equivalent.
5. Financing, if any, is on terms generally available in the community at the specified date and typical for the property type in its locale.
6. The price represents a normal consideration for the property sold, unaffected by special financing amounts and/or terms, services, fees, costs or credits incurred in the transaction.[16]

Market value is obtained when these necessary conditions are reflected in the market. However, all of these conditions rarely exist at the same time in any given market. Therefore, the appraisers use a less rigorous theoretical concept known as **most probable selling price.** It is

> The price at which a transaction is most likely to occur under actually existing market conditions and actually prevailing levels of information on the part of buyers and sellers. Most probable selling price is somewhat less rigid and idealistic a concept than market value. . . . The buyer or user is expected to produce the best return he can under the conditions of existing market information, but not necessarily with the full knowledge stipulated as part of the market value. The estimation of the most probable selling price does not require that the prospective buyer search out every possible alternative type and intensity of use for the property before rationally selecting the best one.[17]

When real estate markets are analyzed by the appraiser or by an investment analyst, the value-in-exchange concept that is typically obtained is the most probable selling price and not market value, because participants in the real estate market are not fully knowledgeable due to inexperience and the high costs to obtain information about alternative properties as well as alternative uses of a piece of property. In addition, market participants differ in their relative ability to obtain financing in order to purchase the property. For at least these two reasons, the concept of value generated in the market for any piece of real property is the most probable selling price of the property, which happens to be a reasonably good estimate of the property's true market value.

COMMON FALLACIES ABOUT VALUE

There are two fallacies about the value of real estate. One is that all real estate is valuable. As extreme examples, consider parcels of land in the Sahara Desert and Antarctica that have neither value-in-use nor value-in-exchange. If a building were erected on these parcels, it could have value-in-use to the owner but may have no value-in-exchange because no one else would be willing to make a trade for it. The fallacy that all real estate is valuable was probably an underlying factor in the land frauds that took place in the 1960s in Florida and Arizona. People bought such land "site" unseen with the belief that the land was, and would continue to be, valuable.

The second fallacy is that all urban real estate increases in value. Each parcel of urban real estate does have a market value, but that value can be high or low, and it can increase, decrease, or stay constant over time. The potential buyer should realize that market value is established by demand and supply factors in the market. The fallacy arises when the consumer assumes that urban real estate will always have an increasing market value and that when it is time to sell, an able and willing buyer will be in the market and will pay the original price plus a significant number of additional dollars as profit to the owner. The visual proof of this mistaken assumption can be seen in every urban area in the form of vacant land and vacant buildings. The owners of some of these parcels of urban real estate chose to give up their rights of ownership through tax foreclosure when they decided not to pay taxes on a structure they could not sell. Other owners pay the tax with the hope that, sometime in the future, an individual will appear who has a value-in-use for that parcel and will make a reasonable offer. Still other owners of other vacant land parcels are holding land off the market voluntarily with the expectation of a gain in the future. They expect to obtain an increase in the market value because of the location of the property in a sector that should be undergoing growth. However, they do not know with certainty whether that gain will be large or small, or whether there will be a gain at all.

The knowledgeable real estate purchaser should not make unwarranted assumptions about the market value of real estate in general or urban real estate in particular. These properties have value-in-exchange only when there are potential buyers.

CHAPTER SUMMARY

The right to use property is not an absolute right, because it can be limited by both public and private controls. The primary public controls and limits are the police powers of the state and eminent domain. The private limits are legal, such as restrictive covenants, and economic, such as highest and best use.

A variety of public agencies at the federal, state, and local level of government impose restrictions on the private use of property and influence real estate transactions and decisions.

The main determinants of real estate value are the specific attributes that give rise to value-in-use and, thereby, give rise to value-in-exchange. However, for the product to have value-in-exchange, more than one person must be able to derive value-in-use from the commodity. A market is established if one or more individuals are willing and able to sell a property (supply) and if one or more individuals are willing and able to buy it (demand).

Review Questions

1. What is an easement? What is the difference between an easement appurtenant and an easement-in-gross?
2. What is a lien? What is the difference between a specific lien and a general lien?
3. Define and explain the concept of police power.
4. Define and explain the concept of eminent domain.
5. What are the private restrictions on the use of real estate?
6. Define and explain the concepts of value-in-use and value-in-exchange.
7. What is attribute analysis? Describe the attributes of the site, the off-site improvements, and the location.
8. Define *market*. Describe the demand side and the supply side.

Discussion Questions

1. Based on your understanding of police powers and eminent domain, argue the case of a landowner who owns residentially zoned land that is either adjacent to or across the street from commercial land. The basis for the argument is that the landowner wants compensation for the limitation on his right to use his property.
2. Assume that the landowner in question (1) files a petition in civil court against the municipality. You are the city attorney; how would you argue the case so that the city need not pay compensation?
3. Discuss how increasing gasoline prices and increasing traffic congestion are affecting the relative value of parcels of land close to centers of economic activity versus parcels of land at the fringe of the area surrounding the center of economic activity.

Notes

1. Harold F. Lusk and William B. French, *Law of the Real Estate Business* (Homewood, Ill.: Richard D. Irwin, Inc., 1975), pp. 462–63.
2. Ibid., p. 468.

3. Ibid.

4. Donald Epley and Cameron Parsons, "Real Estate Transactions and the Sherman Act: How to Approach an Antitrust Suit," *Real Estate Law Journal,* Vol. 5 (Summer 1976), pp. 3–14.

5. Lusk and French, *Law of the Real Estate Business,* p. 44.

6. Ibid., pp. 44–45.

7. Robert Kratovil and Raymond J. Werner, *Real Estate Law* (Prentice-Hall Series in Real Estate, Englewood Cliffs, N. J.: Prentice-Hall, Inc., 1979), p. 24.

8. Lusk and French, *Law of the Real Estate Business,* p. 47.

9. Ibid., p. 362.

10. Kratovil and Werner, *Real Estate Law,* pp. 287–88.

11. James A. Graaskamp, A *Guide to Feasibility Analysis* (Chicago, Ill.: Society of Real Estate Appraisers, 1970), pp. 67–72.

12. Byrl N. Boyce (ed.), *Real Estate Appraisal Terminology* (Cambridge, Mass.: Ballinger Publishing Co., 1975), p. 77.

13. Richard U. Ratcliff, *Real Estate Analysis* (New York: McGraw-Hill Book Company, 1961), p. 58.

14. Graaskamp, *A Guide to Feasibility Analysis,* p. 77.

15. Richard B. Andrews, *Urban Land Economics and Public Policy* (New York: The Free Press, 1971), pp. 46–47.

16. Boyce, *Real Estate Appraisal Terminology,* p. 137.

17. William N. Kinnard, Jr., *Income Property Valuation: Principles and Techniques of Appraising Income-Producing Real Estate* (Lexington, Mass.: D. C. Heath and Co., 1971), p. 13.

Additional Readings

American Institute of Real Estate Appraisers. *The Dictionary of Real Estate Appraisal.* Chicago, Ill.: National Association of Realtors, 1984.

GRAASKAMP, JAMES A. *A Guide to Feasibility Analysis.* Chicago, Ill.: Society of Real Estate Appraisers, 1970. Chapters 3, 5, and 6.

HENSLEY, BENJAMIN N., and RONALD M. FRIEDMAN. *Real Estate Law.* New York: Warren, Gorham and Lamont, 1979. Chapters 1–3.

HINDS, DUDLEY S., NEIL G. CARN, and O. NICHOLAS ORDWAY. *Winning at Zoning.* New York: McGraw-Hill Book Co., 1979. Chapters 2, 4, and 5.

KRATOVIL, ROBERT, and RAYMOND J. WERNER. *Real Estate Law.* Englewood Cliffs, N.J.: Prentice-Hall, Inc., 1983.

LISTOKIN, DAVID, ed. *Land Use Controls: Present Problems and Future Reform.* New Brunswick, N.J.: Center for Urban Policy Research, 1974.

LUSK, HAROLD F., and WILLIAM B. FRENCH. *Law of the Real Estate Business.* Homewood, Ill.: Richard D. Irwin, Inc., 1984.

NATIONAL ASSOCIATION OF HOME BUILDERS. *Land Development Manual.* Washington, D.C.: National Association of Home Builders, 1974.

REILLY, JOHN W. *The Language of Real Estate.* Chicago, Ill.: Real Estate Education Company, 1982.

3 Land Development, Zoning, and Environmental Regulations

QUESTIONS TO BE ANSWERED: _____

1. What is the role of the government in land-use development and what tools are commonly used?
2. What are the recent trends in land-use regulation?
3. How do land-use controls influence business development and metropolitan growth?

OBJECTIVES: _____

When a student finishes the chapter, she or he should be able to

1. Discuss the role of the government in land-use control.
2. Explain the tools typically used by the government in land-use regulation.

3. Discuss recent trends in the use of government regulations.

4. Explain the influence of regulations on business development.

5. Explain the influence of regulations on metropolitan development.

IMPORTANT TERMS

Concentric Zone Model	Occupancy Code
Construction Code	Planning Commission
Direct Regulations	Police Power
Economic Base Model	Proprietary Power
Eminent Domain	Pyramid Zoning
Escheat	Site Development Standards
Exclusive Use Zoning	Sector Model
Indirect Regulations	Spending Power
Multiple Nuclei Model	Taxing Power
Negative Externalities	Use Regulations (Zoning)
Nonconforming Zoning	Zoning

ROLE OF THE GOVERNMENT

Reasons for Regulation*

Real estate development in the United States is basically a function of private enterprise. Although government has long been a participant in the process, through the disposition of public lands and through the construction of supporting facilities such as highways, utilities, and schools, an overwhelming majority of the space used for living, manufacturing, and trade has been provided by private developers. Government may coax, assist, entice, limit, or discourage, but the basic decision to develop is a private one.

The specific reasons for a particular development regulation may differ from community to community and even within a community in the minds of various supporters and administrators. As is the case with many laws, development regulations are often the result of compromises reflecting differing points of view. Generally, however, the basic reasons for regulation can be condensed into two categories: *protection* and *planning.* The oldest known regulation of development, apparently motivated by a concern for *consumer protection,* is contained in the code of laws decreed by King Hammurabi of Babylon, whose rule extended from 2285 B.C. to 2242 B.C.:

*Some of the material in this section has been obtained with permission from Dudley Hinds, N. Carn, and N. Ordway, *Winning at Zoning* (New York: McGraw-Hill Book Company, 1979). Other material in this section has been extracted by permission from material written by Dudley S. Hinds who reserves the right to use it.

If a builder has built a house for a man and has not made strong his work, and the house he built has fallen, and he has caused the death of the owner of the house, that builder shall be put to death.

If he has caused the son of the owner of the house to die, one shall put to death the son of that builder.

Another way of explaining the reasons for controls is to point to the imperfect condition of the real estate market. If the market were perfect, then, theoretically at least, all of the participants, being both fully informed and willing to act, would put their respective holdings to the "highest and best" use, thereby maximizing the aggregate return to all owners. In reality, the market is not perfect. Many participants are poorly informed, and many are unwilling or unable to act upon the information that they do have. Furthermore, those who are both willing and informed will be tempted to slough some of their costs off upon neighboring properties or upon the community as a whole. For example, a builder might erect a tall structure right on the property line and impair the access of his neighbor to sunlight and natural ventilation. He also might provide insufficient parking, thereby causing tenants and visitors to park on nearby streets. Another developer might denude an area of its natural vegetation, replace it with excess coverage of buildings and pavement, and consequently cause flooding and silting on land downstream.

Costs that are passed off in this way are called *negative externalities.* When they are borne by the community as a whole, they are sometimes called *social costs.* The function of development regulations is to minimize negative externalities by forcing developers to *internalize* their costs. The developers can do this by absorbing the costs themselves, by passing them on to their users, or by compensating those damaged by the externalities.

Regulatory Powers

The developer is affected by both *direct* and *indirect* regulations. The *direct* regulations—zoning, subdivision regulations, building codes, other codes, FHA standards—are intended to affect his development (although the actual effects may not be exactly the same as those intended). The *indirect* regulations—public improvements, availability of water and sewer services, public land acquisition, control of highway access, and the local property tax—can have serious effects, but the effects are not usually intended. The regulatory effects are incidental to the main purpose of the actions or policies.

Regulations may also be categorized according to the powers on which they are based. There are five powers of government used to regulate development: *police power, proprietary power, taxing power, spending power* and *power of eminent domain.* (The *power of escheat* is not used to regulate development.)

The *police power* is an inherent power of government to regulate the conduct of people within its borders and to punish violators by fines or imprisonment. In the United States, this power basically rests with the states, but the states have delegated some of this power to the cities, counties, towns, and townships. Thus, enabling legislation permits local governments to adopt zoning ordinances, subdivision regulations, building codes, and occupancy codes. Compliance with regulations is compulsory if the developers wish to do anything at all with their property. Occupancy codes (for example, a lot-clearance ordinance) may apply even if developers do nothing with it. A violation is a matter of criminal law.

Unlike the police power, the *proprietary power* is not compulsory in its application. When using its proprietary power, government is acting a role similar to that of a private corporation—buying and selling land, making contracts, and leasing property. Thus, if a developer does not wish to comply with FHA Minimum Property Standards, the federal government, acting in a proprietary role, may refuse to insure the mortgage loan. If a developer does not wish to construct a street to a city's specifications, the city, acting in a proprietary role, can refuse to accept the street for city maintenance. Although in theory the developer has an alternative, in practice, the use of the proprietary power can be almost as compulsory as the use of the police power.

The *taxing power* of government is used primarily to raise revenue, but some uses of it can stimulate or suppress certain kinds of development. For example, the federal income tax code permits, as incentives for developers and investors of new business realty, deductions for interest during construction and accelerated depreciation allowances. New York City offers property tax reductions for those who construct new apartments if savings are passed on to tenants. Vermont heavily taxes short-term capital gains on land to discourage speculation. At the local level, the *ad valorem* property tax is influential. *Ad valorem* is a Latin term meaning "on the value of," and the property tax is just that. It is a tax levied annually on the assessed value of real property and, in many localities, personal property as well. Differing tax rates in different jurisdictions, varying ratios of assessed value to market value, and exemptions or concessions can discourage building and renovation in some locations and encourage them in others.

The *spending power* is used to buy land and rights in land for public use and to provide public facilities, such as roads, water and sewer systems, schools, and recreation facilities, without which development would be limited. It also is used to provide services such as police protection, without which development would be more risky.

The power of *eminent domain* is the power to take private property for a public purpose against the wishes of the owner, but it may not be exercised without the payment of just compensation to the property owner. The use of this power is often called "condemnation," which may be confusing because the same term is also used to mean an action under the police power to require a substandard building to be vacated or demolished without compensation.

Sources of Authority

The federal government has considerable influence over development through the administration of the Clean Air Act, Clean Water Act, Endangered Species Act, Coastal Zone Management program, and the Environmental Protection Administration. The latter agency has the authority to oversee all federal regulatory programs which cover air pollution, solid waste disposal, water pollution, pesticide regulation, environmental regulation, and noise pollution.

Each state administers its regulations over land development through the state constitution, police power, the power of eminent domain, and the power to tax. The right of the local government to zone, to tax, and to condemn property are given by the state legislature. Also, the state may have its own specific acts aimed toward clean air or water, which typically are administered by separate state departments. In addition, many states have established state housing agencies and state development agencies to become focal points for development in specific areas.

Local governments administer their land-use regulatory authority mainly through the city and county governments. Many have combined resources to form metropolitan or regional planning authorities that develop, oversee, and recommend comprehensive plans and policies to the appropriate groups for implementation. In addition, the local city and county often have the authority to implement local ordinances and building codes under their police power to influence the well-being of their citizens.

LOCAL REGULATIONS

The *planning* motivation for regulation has grown from a desire to decide, well in advance of development, the uses of land, building intensities, and spatial arrangements of those uses and intensities that a community or region wishes to have. In order to translate these objectives into a harmonious pattern of development, a community will frequently prepare a *comprehensive plan* stating how the community should develop over a specified period of time and what public facilities should be provided. The plan might also state a desired sequence and rate of growth. In order for the *comprehensive plan* to be implemented, some regulation of the activities of private developers is necessary.

Police Power

Of the five powers of government used to regulate development, the most direct impact is made by the regulations based on the police power. These regulations include: zoning, building codes, electrical codes, plumbing codes, housing codes, health and sanitation codes, fire prevention codes, off-street parking ordinances, tree-cutting ordinances, sign controls, and subdivision regulations.

Zoning. From the point of view of the property owner, zoning is an ordinance that regulates the use of a specific piece of property. The property owner can find out what the regulations are by consulting (1) the official zoning map to ascertain the zone (usually called *districts*) to which the property has been assigned and (2) the text of the ordinance to discover what regulations apply to properties in that particular district. Both map and text come in many varieties. The map might be in the form of one original, marked-up sheet, thumb-tacked to the back side of the door to the town clerk's supply closet, or it might be available for public distribution in the form of glossy, three-color, offset prints. Still others might be in atlas form with precise zoning boundaries indicated on a base that shows property lines and street rights-of-way to scale. Seldom are any of these maps up to date. The typical zoning map is amended so frequently that no map can be depended upon to contain the latest changes. Thus, to be certain of the designation of a particular parcel, the property owner must pursue all amendments not reflected on the map. The zoning text, like the map, is frequently amended, but less often.

District provisions fall into two separate categories: *use regulations,* which specify the uses to be permitted, and *site-development standards,* which specify permitted heights, bulk, and lot coverage of buildings, and required lot area, lot width, lot frontage, yards, setbacks, open space, buffers, and off-street parking and loading. There are three basic groups of districts: residential, commercial, and industrial. Many ordinances also contain special districts, some of which, such as airport-approach districts or floodplain districts, are superimposed on the others. In older ordinances, the districts are arranged in a heirachy beginning with the more restricted (in terms of uses allowed), usually a single-family category, and proceeding in a step-by-step fashion to the least restricted, usually a heavy industrial category. Each district permits all uses allowed in the preceding, more restricted districts plus one or more additional uses. Under this arrangement, called *cumulative use* or *pyramid* zoning, industry is not permitted in residential districts, but residences are permitted in industrial districts. In recent years, this approach has been altered by the introduction of a modified *exclusive-use* concept so that the uses permitted in the preceding, more restricted districts are not necessarily permitted in the "less restricted" ones.

Site development standards are more complex than use regulations. The most simple standards are those found in the districts designed for one/and two family homes. Typically, they include

☐ Minimum area of lot expressed in square feet or acres

☐ Minimum yard setbacks, front, rear, and side in feet

☐ Minimum lot width at front building line in feet

☐ Maximum height of building in stories

☐ Maximum percentage coverage of lot by buildings

Some ordinances also contain minimum requirements for floor area, and many contain off-street parking requirements.

A zoning ordinance represents a compromise between a desired pattern of land use and the need to accommodate a substantial investment already in existence. In order to comply with the constitutional prohibition against taking private property without just compensation, some allowances must be made for the retention, at least temporarily, of uses and structures existing at the effective date of the ordinance, but no longer permitted by the ordinance.

Some ordinances permit *nonconforming uses and structures* to remain indefinitely unless the structure is destroyed to the extent of a specified proportion of its replacement cost—i.e., 60 percent. They generally do not, however, permit the nonconforming use to be increased in extent by substantially altering the structure. Nor is the nonconforming use allowed to be reestablished after having been discontinued for a specified period of time (usually either six months or one year).

Every zoning ordinance contains provisions for amendments to it, and the typical ordinance is amended frequently. Amendments to the map, which are much more common than amendments to the text, provide the frequent public contacts with zoning in most communities and are the greatest source of controversies. Amendments may be originated by the local governing body, the planning commission (board), the planning department, or by property owners. Most are originated by applications of property owners to the *planning commission*. This body (also variously called the planning board or zoning commission) is made up of citizens who are appointed by the governing body and who usually serve without compensation. They are responsible for holding a public hearing on each application, after due notice of such hearing has been published. The commission then makes a recommendation to the governing body based on the findings made at the public hearings and the commission's evaluation of the amendment's ostensible relation to the community's "comprehensive plan." In many communities, they are assisted by a staff of professional planners, sometimes representing a *planning department*. In larger communities, the *planning department* may actually substitute for the *planning commission*.

Construction and Occupancy Codes   Construction and occupancy codes are a group of regulations governing the original construction of buildings, subsequent additions and alterations, and the manner in which both buildings and sites may continue to be occupied. Building, electrical, and plumbing codes tend to deal more with construction than with occupancy, while fire prevention, sanitation, and housing codes tend to deal more with occupancy requirements. However, there is considerable overlap.

Construction Codes   The term *building code,* like the term *construction code,* is not a precise one. In its strictest meaning, it includes those requirements pertaining to the structural soundness of a building, its resistance to fire, and its ability to withstand earthquakes, high winds, and heavy loads of snow. In its broadest meaning, it also includes requirements for wiring, plumbing, mechanical equipment, safe occupancy, and demolition.

In a community with a building code, no construction may be initiated on a site unless a permit is posted conspicuously at the front of the site. To obtain a permit, the contractor must first submit plans to the office of the *building official,* who also is the administrator of the electrical and plumbing codes, and in some localities, the zoning ordinance. Copies of the plans are referred to the structural, electrical, plumbing, and zoning division for review. If the plans are in compliance with the codes, then a permit is issued, and work may begin. At various stages along the way—for example, when the foundations have been completed—work must be stopped until an inspection has been made. Once the inspectors have given their approval, building may be resumed. Similar interim inspections are made under the electrical and plumbing codes. When the entire structure is finished, a final inspection is made, and if everything is in order, a *certificate of occupancy* is issued permitting the building to be used. Disagreements with the inspectors may be appealed to a board of adjustment that is separate from the one set up to consider zoning appeals.

Occupancy Codes   Occupancy codes are basically concerned with how a building is used and maintained after completion. A developer who retains ownership of a building will find that these codes will affect the management of the property even if no permits are sought. Inspectors may periodically require him or her to make various improvements for reasons of health or safety, especially if the building is an old one. *Fire prevention* codes are concerned with the adequacy of exits, maintenance of fire extinguishers, storage of flammable materials, and similar safety matters. *Health* and *sanitation* codes are concerned with the control of rodents, flies, mosquitoes, garbage handling, and other matters pertaining to environmental health. *Housing* codes are usually catchall regulations covering all matters of import to housing that are not covered by other codes. Included may be provisions having to do with heating, hot water, illumination in corridors, ventilation, cubic space per person in bedrooms, and privacy. Inspections are either part of a systematic program or in response to complaints. In either case, the resultant orders for compliance may be contested before a board of appeals.

Spending Power

In contrast to the use of the police power, which is a negative sanction, a use of the spending power is a positive sanction. An incentive is offered in the form of public facilities and services that may be provided if the developer helps to achieve community goals through his development. If a real estate entrepreneur wishes to develop, then he must go where facilities and services are available and where they will support the intensity of development contemplated. Many communities still wait for developers to set the basic direction, sequence and rate of development, and then respond by providing facilities and services where and when needed and to the capacity required. Others, however, no longer content to serve in a passive role, have found that the spending power can be used to influence the location, sequence, rate and intensity of development with results more acceptable to the community.

Taxing Power

Like the spending power, the taxing power provides local government with an opportunity to influence development through the use of public money. Instead of a direct outlay, however, it makes possible concessions in the form of lower taxes for developers or property owners who act in ways considered to be in the public interest. The taxing power can be used either to stimulate development or to discourage it. Examples of the former are exemptions from the property tax of new buildings and of improvements to existing buildings for a certain number of years, as an incentive for developers to build those facilities deemed desirable for the public interest. Examples of the latter include reductions in assessed valuations for undeveloped land of scenic value and of developed property containing buildings of historical or architectural significance if the owners agree to preserve them.

Power of Eminent Domain

The power of eminent domain, like the taxing and spending powers, involves the use of money, but, unlike them, it does not involve money used as an enticement to developmental actions. Indeed, its use carries with it a force similar to that of a police-power regulation, for the exercise of eminent domain represents a *compulsory taking* of property rights. The money paid to property owners is in *compensation* for the compulsory taking. Thus, eminent domain presents the possibility of a strong and direct control over development, but with a monetary "sweetener" lacking in the police power.

Proprietary Power

We have already mentioned that subdivision regulations were based, in part, on the proprietary power in so far as they involved reliance upon a local government's right to accept, or refuse to accept, streets and utilities for public maintenance. The only other extensive use of this power at the local level has been in the disposition of urban renewal land subject to deed restrictions. By means of these restrictions, governments could impose more flexible controls than permitted under zoning or other police-power regulations. From time to time, communities find themselves in possession of large tracts of surplus land without resort to urban renewal, and similar action can be taken in their disposition. Local governments also sell or lease *air rights* over or under public property with appropriate restrictions attached.

RECENT TRENDS

In June 1983, the Urban Land Institute sponsored a group discussion of experts on regulations and policies influencing land use. The participants reached a consensus that the recent trend of comprehensive growth planning appears to be ending. In its place, local governments are attempting to update and streamline their regulations and policies to better serve the local needs of their populace.

The summary opinions covering recent trends is contained in Exhibit 3-1. In general, the recent debate among federal agencies concerning funding and their appropriate role has curtailed the overall role of the federal government in housing programs and economic development. State and local governments have become much more active in initiating programs in affordable housing and environmental concerns such as hazardous waste. States have developed programs in farmland protection, enterprise zones, and innovative financing programs. Communities have been curtailing innovative programs in favor of restructuring and streamlining old programs.

EXHIBIT 3-1 ULI roundtable on regulatory trends

Source: Urban Land Institute, *Development Review and Outlook,* 1983, p. 338.

□ The three states that will host 60 percent of the growth to occur in the 1980s—Florida, Texas, and California—will continue to set the tone for the regulation of development in the rest of the nation.

□ Negotiated understandings on agreements for approval of development are more and more common, which may subvert the concept of overall planning and omit key interest groups (such as future consumers and neighborhood groups) from decisions about development.

□ Problems with financing infrastructure are driving more communities to arrange deals with developers to provide infrastructure, with one result being an increased desire by developers for greater assurance that development can proceed unaffected by future changes in policy or regulations, thereby protecting their investment.

□ Public officials are more aware than ever before that regulations may adversely affect development and that streamlining and reform are necessary.

□ "Standard" planning and zoning are still being practiced in many areas of the country, although often with ideas selectively borrowed from innovative techniques being used elsewhere.

□ Many "innovative" regulatory techniques, such as transfer of development rights and performance zoning, have not taken hold.

□ Communities have found ways to closely control development without running afoul of the courts on the "taking" issue, although courts are now beginning to consider interim damages to compensate for unlawful takings affected by regulations. The courts are beginning to accept solid planning studies demonstrating a public need as the basis for stricter regulation.

□ State and regional planning and regulatory programs are active, but they focus on specific regional issues such as wetlands or hazardous waste rather than on comprehensive land use control.

In 1983, the Urban Land Institute conducted a survey of planning agencies in sixty-one cities across the United States. Each was asked to identify any changes in regulations or plans regulating development and the purpose of the change. The highlights are contained in Exhibit 3-2 on pages 76 and 77.

The results show that forty-seven of the sixty-one cities made changes primarily in their zoning ordinances. In order of the frequency of the changes, these were

□ To provide affordable housing
□ To make development requirements more flexible
□ To encourage economic development
□ To streamline regulations
□ To contain or direct growth
□ To finance the infrastructure
□ To protect the environment
□ To preserve the farmland

LAND-USE CONTROL AND BUSINESS DEVELOPMENT

The recent survey shown earlier by the Urban Land Institute revealed that the most frequent changes in zoning ordinances occurred to provide affordable housing, to make development requirements more flexible, to encourage economic development, and to streamline regulations. All of these reflect government attempts to promote a favorable environment for private business to locate, develop, or expand within a specific area. For a private business to do any of these, it must detect that a new or streamlined land use control will create a favorable economic environment for it.

Expansion and Retention of Existing Firms

In order for a firm to expand its operation at its current location, or for the firm to make the decision to stay at its current location and not move out, it must generate a level of revenues to cover its costs and make a return that is at least comparable to what it could obtain if it produced at its next best alternative location. For the firm considering an expansion of its plant, there must be an initiating expansion in its sales, or at least a high probability that such an expansion of sales will occur. For the firm considering a possible relocation, an expansion of sales would be beneficial, but cost control or even cost reductions might be necessary.

In both of these cases, the firm would favor any change in land-use regulations, programs, or policies that would favorably affect its demand curve. For example, a change in the city's master plan for the location of sewer lines or an extension of existing roadways or an improvement of existing roads could have a large impact on the existing firm. The sewer extension could increase the number of customers in close proximity to the firm that sells to local customers. Either of the road improvements could bring more customers to the site of the firm by extending the trade area or making travel easier for the consumer.

The decision to expand or relocate also is dependent upon transportation costs for the materials and the finished products as well as the production costs. Changes in land-use regulations, programs, or policies can affect the transportation costs by improving road conditions and access to the firm's location. Such changes can affect the production costs by making access to the site more convenient and easier for the worker; these changes may translate into a reduced employee journey-to-work cost and thereby lower nominal wages than would have to be paid otherwise. The extension of sewer and water lines can also affect the production costs of the firm. Property tax reductions in any form can also lower the costs of production.

Promotion of Commercial and Industrial Development

The promotion of business development necessitates the same actions that are required for the expansion and retention of existing firms. However, in addition, the land-use regulations, programs, and policies can also favorably affect the development costs of the potential incoming firm. The local government can provide a series

EXHIBIT 3-2 Local development policies and regulations: A ULI survey

Source: Urban Land Institute, *Development Review and Outlook,* 1983, p. 367.

☐ Forty-seven of the 61 cities and counties had made some changes.

☐ Most changes (51 percent) were made in zoning ordinances, followed by changes in comprehensive plans and subdivision regulations (each 19 percent).

☐ Jurisdictions (number in parentheses) made changes for the following purposes:

    To provide more affordable housing (34)

    To make development requirements more flexible (34)

    To encourage economic development (25)

    To streamline regulations (25)

    To contain or direct growth (19)

    To finance infrastructure (8)

    To protect the environment (6)

    To preserve farmland (3)

    For other purposes (16).

What is interesting about this list is the extent to which most jurisdictions expected policy and regulatory changes to encourage and support development rather than to restrict or constrain it. Even more interesting are the means selected to achieve those ends.

To provide more affordable housing, jurisdictions (number in parentheses) made the following changes:

    Increased allowable densities (18)

    Allowed more flexible design and uses—clustering, planned unit development, mixed-use development (9)

    Allowed more manufactured housing (9)

    Streamlined approval procedures (7)

    Reduced site development standards (6)

    Required low-income housing—inclusionary housing (5)

    Allowed more varied housing types (5).

To make development requirements more flexible, jurisdictions (number in parentheses) made the following changes:

    Allowed a greater mix of uses or more types of uses (22)

    Allowed changes in densities or other standards (14)

    Streamlined approval procedures (5)

    Provided performance standards (4)

    Adopted other regulations or procedures (7).

To encourage economic development, jurisdictions (number in parentheses) made the following changes:

    Expanded number of uses (11)

    Allowed more flexible design (8)

    Expanded zoning for commercial and industrial uses (5)

    Reduced standards (4)

    Increased densities of development (4)

    Provided financial incentives or financing for infrastructure (3).

To streamline regulations, jurisdictions (number in parentheses) made the following changes:

    Clarified requirements and procedures (20)

    Reduced number of steps or agencies in the approval process (15)

    Speeded up review time (14)

    Offered improved staff assistance to applicants (7)

    Reduced the amount of application material (4)

    Took other steps (5).

To contain or direct growth, jurisdictions (number in parentheses) made the following changes:

    Created agricultural or open space districts (5)
    Scheduled public improvements (5)
    Encouraged infill or higher densities (3)
    Discouraged growth in certain areas (2)
    Established an urban boundary (2)
    Adopted other regulations or procedures (3).

To finance infrastructure, jurisdictions (number in parentheses) made the following changes:

    Required development or impact fees (3)
    Created tax increment finance districts (3)
    Established special taxing or assessment districts (1)
    Required contributions from developers (1).

To preserve farmland, jurisdictions (number in parentheses) made the following changes:

    Zoned for large lots (1)
    Encouraged cluster development (1)
    Related commercial development to agriculture (1).

(Note: detailed data were not collected for the categories of environmental protection and "other purposes.")

Many responses overlapped as to the purposes served and means employed. That is, one new program in a zoning ordinance could serve more than one purpose, and several means could be employed to meet one purpose. The purposes themselves are overlapping: streamlining, for example, can be both an end and a means, and financing infrastructure can support economic development or affordable housing. Nevertheless, the heavy responses to certain items tell something about what is going on in local policies and regulations:

☐ Almost one-third of the communities contacted are promoting more affordable housing by increasing allowable densities and allowing more flexible design, and one-fifth are permitting more varied housing types, including manufactured housing.

☐ Over one-third of the communities contacted are expanding the types of uses permitted in some districts to encourage affordable housing or economic development.

☐ Relatively few communities are adopting provisions that constrain development by restricting areas of growth or requiring development fees.

    Finally, each respondent was asked what local development issue he or she regards as most serious at this time. The answers reveal current concerns in local planning. How they relate to the regulatory actions described in this chapter will be left to the reader to decide. The most important issues (with the number of respondents who identified them in parentheses) are as follows:

    Capacity and expansion of utilities (18)
    Transportation (16)
    Shortages of municipal revenue (12)
    Quality and quantity of growth (10)
    Environmental quality (5)
    Housing shortages (5)
    Economic development (4)
    Other (4).

of inducements to attract the firms to the desired location in the metropolitan area. These inducements mostly focus on property tax reduction, local public services, and possibly the training of workers to meet the skill needs of the prospective employer. These are uses of the local governments taxing and spending powers.

In addition the local government can use its power of eminent domain to obtain the necessary site for the new firm. In this instance, the local community aids the potential migrant in its land acquisition and clearing tasks. The local government might even provide the structure for the firm by building the structure to suit the firm and then leasing the space at favorable rates for some predetermined time.

Land-Use Controls, Metropolitan Growth, and Development Patterns

Land-use regulations, programs, and policies can also have an impact on the direction and intensity of growth in a metropolitan area. The extension and provision of utilities and streets can cause growth to progress in a certain section of the urban area, or to procede along a certain direction. Zoning can open up new land for certain uses where it never existed before. Property tax reductions can attract industry to certain portions of the urban area. Sales tax differentials can encourage retail establishments in certain sections of the area at the expense of other areas.

Since the economic aspect is of paramount importance in the location of commercial and industrial firms, land-use controls should be applied with an understanding of how they can affect the profits of the firms and their desire to locate at a certain point in space. Since access and its linkages (economic variables) are important to the residential land user, land-use controls must also be applied with these factors in mind.

Descriptive Models of Metropolitan Spatial Development and Growth[1]

Early attempts at describing the growth/development patterns examined these economic factors because they were seen as the causes for long-term growth. These theories are presented in the following paragraphs.

Three classic spatial models of urban structure describe the land use pattern in the traditional North American city. Every student of urban studies encounters at least one or two of these conceptualizations because they are so widely accepted by all social science disciplines. Only one of the models can be credited to geographers, the others having been developed by sociologists and economists (see Exhibit 3-3).

Concentric-Zone Model   The earliest of these models, the *concentric ring* model, emerged from the study of Chicago by sociologists at the University of Chicago in the early 1900s and is attributed to the work of Burgess.[2] That model positioned a central business district (CBD) at the center (zone 1) around which all other uses formed. Surrounding the CBD, a factory, slum, and ethnic community zone existed (zone 2). This area became known as a *transition zone* or *gray zone* between the

THE DECISION TO ACQUIRE KNOWLEDGE ABOUT THE REAL ESTATE BUSINESS

EXHIBIT 3-3 Generalized explanations of the land-use patterns of cities

Source: Truman Hartshorn, *Interpreting the City* (New York: John Wiley & Sons, 1980).

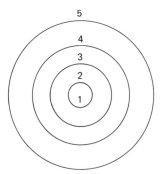

Concentric Ring Model

1. Central business district (CBD)
2. Transition area (manufacturing, warehousing, commercial)
3. Low income residential
4. Moderate income residential
5. High income residential (commuter zone)
6. Manufacturing/industrial parks
7. Commercial districts/shopping areas
8. Office/business parks.

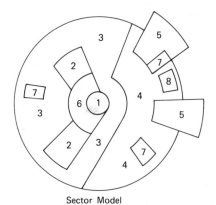

Sector Model

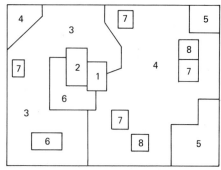

Multiple Nuclei Model

commercial core and residential communities farther out. The transition concept refers to the tendency for older residential areas to be converted to commercial uses as the business district grew. Such an area often attracted immigrants and was generally run-down and a center of crime and vice. Frequently the land is held by speculators, and the housing function is only an interim use. Zone 3 consisted of lower-income working people's homes. Other successive zones consisted of higher-income residences, with a commuter zone lying on the periphery.

The ring model has several deficiencies but its elegance and simplicity have stood the test of time. It evolved at the University of Chicago at the same time as a new field of *human ecology,* which had roots in the field of plant ecology and social Darwinism.[3] The concepts of *dominance, specialization,* and *succession,* taken from the biological community, helped account for rings of specialized land use.

The concentric ring model inadequately accounted for the development of specialized clusters of industrial uses. It also failed to explain the impact of transportation routes of land use. Some later students of the ring model did adjust it to meet these deficiencies by superimposing a radial highway system on it, which had the effect of stretching the rings outward where they intersected transportation corridors, creating a starlike rather than a circular urban form.

Sector Model   A land economist, Hoyt, published a landmark article setting forth the notion of a *sector model* of urban land uses in 1939 after an exhaustive study of patterns in over 100 cities.[4] He suggested that once similar uses emerged around the CBD (at the center of the city), activities would remain in that particular area and extend outward over time in the same direction as the city grew. The intuitive appeal of this argument is strong because similar uses do in fact grow in specific directions, often following rail or highway arteries, high or low ground, or simply clustering on the same side of the city.

High-income residential areas are notorious for being in high, rolling, or wooded ground, and low-income areas being in less-desirable low-lying valleys and industrial basins. Hoyt's model also easily accommodates growth because it allows new activities to be added to the periphery rather than requiring redevelopment of existing areas as the ring model implies. The model is also consistent with the observation that cities grow more rapidly in the direction of the high-income sector as entrepreneurs seek business sites near the affluent market.

The wedges that form the basis of the sector model have particular relevance to the residential function. The distribution of families by income in a metropolitan area is highly differentiated by neighborhood, conforming to a zonal pattern. Even with the random mobility afforded by the automobile, and the locational flexibility it promotes, land use areas have remained relatively distinctive. Particular uses continue to cluster together and grow along specific axes.

Multiple Nuclei Model   Two geographers, Harris and Ullman, are responsible for the *multiple nuclei model.*[5] It provides an alternative conceptualization of urban form, one based on the premise that uses do not evolve around a single core, but at several nodes or focal points. The CBD is not necessarily at the center of the city in this situation. The model recognizes that different activities have varying accessibility requirements. For example, a commercial area could develop around a government complex, a cultural center such as a university, or a theater district. The airport could also induce commercial or industrial uses. Each of these areas could develop its own satellite residential communities.

The multiple nuclei model acknowledges not only that specific functions have unique locational and functional needs, but also that some activities are detrimental to one another and need widely separated locations. Historical inertia that maintains relatively unique districts can also be an important factor as cities grow and envelop existing industrial and commercial nodes.

Harris and Ullman philosophized that none of the three models just discussed were universally applicable and that all cities exhibited patterns identifying with aspects of one or more of the models.

Economic Base: A Descriptive Model of Economic Growth

The concept of economic base is discussed in detail in Chapter 8 on market analysis and feasibility studies. At this point, recognize that the historical and current period data can serve two functions. First, the historical data can show how the economy grew in terms of employment, population, income, retail sales, and how the economy changed with regard to its industrial structure, the occupational composition of its labor force, its age distribution, income distribution, and the structure of retail expenditures. In addition, the current period data provide a snapshot of the economy as it exists today with regard to these same variables.

Inferences from the Descriptive Models

These descriptive models point out the importance of several in the urban growth process. The ones that will be singled out for discussion are transportation networks, land use succession, clustering of compatible land users, and multiple centers of economic activity.

Transportation played a part in each of these descriptive models. The axial pattern of transport routes was superimposed on the concentric zone model and the growth occurred initially at the intersections of the transport routes and the fringe of the city. Each sector in the sector model was served by at least one main aterial that was extended out to the fringe to enable growth to progress in that direction. Each of the centers of economic activity in the multiple nuclei model was connected to the others and to its surrounding areas by transport routes. Consequently, the land-use controls imposed by the local government must rely upon additional transport facilities and their maintainance at high-quality levels as an important development factor.

Each model, especially the concentric zone and the sector models, recognized the occurrence of land-use changes. In the concentric zone model, the land-use succession occurred at the border of each zone. In the sector model, the changes in land use took place in the inner segment of each sector where it met the central business district. Consequently, the local land-use controls must recognize that there are economic factors that cause land-use succession. Land-use planners must recognize these factors and then act to encourage the changes that are necessary to keep the local economy functioning and that generate favorable effects, while trying to stop or at least reduce the adverse changes.

Since land users tend to form clusters of similar uses in both the residential and commercial sectors of the local economy, the zoning ordinance should not stand in the way of these economic realities. The zoning ordinance should aid in the process as long as the action does not harm any individual (i.e., discriminatory housing provision).

Finally, multiple centers of economic activity will arise in an urban area due to the economic reality of the situation. Land-use controls should not be used as an impediment to these changes, which reflect the necessities of the market. Whether the cluster is retail shops, office buildings, industrial plants or residences, the land-use planners should first try to understand why these clusters are occurring. Then they should evaluate their private and social benefits and costs before imposing restrictions or permitting their occurrence.

CHAPTER SUMMARY

Real estate development within the United States is a private function that operates within the land-use rules established by the government. The government uses direct and indirect regulations that include the five powers of taxing, spending, police, proprietary, and eminent domain.

Recent trends reveal that the federal government has curtailed its overall role in housing and economic development which has been given to the states. Recently, states have developed programs in farmland protection, enterprise zones, and innovative financing. Communities have been curtailing innovative programs in favor of restructuring and streamlining old programs.

Land-use regulations can be used to influence business location, expansion, and residential growth. Government regulations and the demand for local services interact to create growth patterns that often are measured and explained by concepts such as the economic base model, concentric zones, sectors, and multiple nuclei.

Review Questions

1. What are the reasons for the regulation of land use?
2. Name several regulatory powers that the government can use.
3. What is the government's authority for land-use control?
4. Discuss local regulation and the various tools used by the government.
5. What are the recent trends in land-use regulation?
6. How does government control of the land influence business development and metropolitan growth?
7. Outline the differences among the models described as the economic base, sector, concentric zone, and multiple nuclei.

Discussion Questions

1. In your opinion, what would be the success of private business development if no government regulations existed? Can you think of any cities in which this is the case?

THE DECISION TO ACQUIRE KNOWLEDGE ABOUT THE REAL ESTATE BUSINESS

2. Can you think of any situations in which government regulations and controls have been more harmful than helpful?

3. Can you think of any situations in which government zoning is not sufficient?

Notes

1. The material in this section was taken from Truman A. Hartshorn, *Interpreting the City: An Urban Geography* (New York: John Wiley & Sons, 1980), pp. 218–21.

2. R. E. Park, E. W. Burgess, and R. D. McKenzie, *The City* (Chicago, Ill.: University of Chicago Press, 1925), pp. 47–62.

3. James Hughes, "Social Area Analysis," in *Urban Economics and Spatial Patterns,* ed. by M. Goldbarn (New Brunswick, N.J.: Rutgers University Press, 1974), pp. 41–45.

4. Homer Hoyt, *The Structure and Growth of Residential Neighborhoods in American Cities* (Washington, D.C.: U.S. Government Printing Office, 1939).

5. C. D. Harris and E. G. Ullman, "The Nature of Cities," *The Annals of the American Academy of Political and Social Science,* Vol. LLXLII (1945), pp. 7–17.

Additional Readings

President's Housing Commission. *The Report of the President's 1982 Commission.* Washington, D.C.: President's Housing Commission, 1982.

_____. *The President's National Urban Policy Report, 1982.* Washington, D.C.: U.S. Department of Housing and Urban Development, 1982.

4 | The Property Appraisal Process and Determinants of Value

QUESTIONS TO BE ANSWERED

1. What is an appraisal and what is the appraisal process?
2. What are the factors that affect the market value of real estate?

OBJECTIVES

When a student finishes the chapter, he or she should be able to

1. Explain the appraisal process used by professionally designated appraisers.
2. Describe the impact of economic, physical, social, and governmental factors in the urban area, the region, and the nation on the value of a parcel of property.
3. Describe the impact of neighborhood and site-specific factors on the value of a parcel of property.

IMPORTANT TERMS

Appraisal
Appraisal Process
Area Analysis
Cost Approach
General Data
Government Survey
Highest and Best Use
Income Approach

Legal Description
Lot and Block
Metes-and-Bounds System
Neighborhood
Neighborhood Analysis
Plat-Map System
Sales Comparison Approach
Specific Data

DEFINITION OF AN APPRAISAL

A real estate **appraisal** is an estimate of the value of real estate.[1] In this definition, the term *real estate* denotes real property—the legal as well as the physical aspects of real estate. Thus, an appraisal of real estate is an estimate of the value of the physical property and the rights of ownership associated with that property.

The value estimates obtained from an appraisal can be of several different types. Market value is perhaps the most familiar concept and the value most often desired. However, most probable selling price is the proxy for market value which is obtained. Other types of value that can be estimated by appraisal are

- □ *Assessed value:* a dollar amount assigned to taxable property, both real and personal, by the assessor for the purpose of taxation.
- □ *Insurable interest value:* the amount of insurance that may be, or should be, carried on destructible portions of a property to indemnify the owner in the event of loss.
- □ *Investment value:* value to a particular investor based on individual investment requirements, as distinguished from market value, which is impersonal and detached.[2]

This chapter explores the appraisal process used to estimate market value (most probable selling price)—specifically, the market value of single-family residential property. The need for such an estimate arises for many reasons. A partial list of the uses of this type of estimate follows:

1. Transfer of ownership: (a) to help prospective buyers decide on offering prices, (b) to help prospective sellers determine acceptable selling prices, (c) to establish a basis for exchange of real property, (d) to establish a basis for reorganization or for merging the ownership of multiple properties, (e) to distribute the assets of an estate.
2. Financing and credit: (a) to arrive at the essential security offered for a proposed mortgage loan, (b) to provide an investor with a sound basis for deciding whether to purchase real estate mortgages, (c) to establish a

basis for a decision about the insuring or underwriting of a loan on real property.

3. Just compensation in condemnation proceedings: (a) to estimate market value of property as a whole, that is, before the taking, (b) to estimate value after the taking, (c) to allocate market values between the part taken and damage to the remainder.

4. A basis for taxation: (a) to separate assets into depreciable items, such as buildings, and nondepreciable items, such as land, and to estimate applicable depreciation rates, (b) to determine gift or inheritance taxes.

5. A basis for rental schedules and lease provisions.[3]

Thus, the need for a real estate appraisal arises for many reasons pertaining to a decision to purchase or sell real estate, a decision to offer funding for such a purpose, and the decision to insure a structure against casualty losses.

THE REAL ESTATE APPRAISAL PROCESS

The **appraisal process** for estimating the market value (most probable selling price) of a parcel of real property is a logical and concise step-by-step process. "This process is an orderly program by which the problem is defined; the work necessary to solve the problem is planned; and the data involved is acquired, classified, analyzed, interpreted, and translated into an estimate of value."[4] Exhibit 4-1 is a diagram of the appraisal process.

Definition of the Appraisal Problem

The first step in the appraisal process is definitional. Before the appraiser can start any task, the client's needs must be ascertained. The physical entity to be appraised must be identified first in terms of the land parcel and the structures. Then the bundle of rights must be analyzed. The mineral and air rights must be identified. Then the legal rights of ownership pertaining to the physical property must be specified: Does the owner have the right of disposition and possession (freehold estate of inheritance) or does the owner only possess the property without the right of disposition (life estate)? Is it an estate in possession or an estate in expectancy? Are there easements and restrictive covenants that affect the owner's ability to develop portions of the property? These types of questions must be answered by the client.

The concept of value also must be specified. Typically the client wants to know the market value of the property but may be interested in some other type of value, such as insurance value.

The next important step in defining the assignment is specification of the date of the value estimate. In most cases, the appraiser is expected to estimate the current market value on the date the property is inspected. However, in some situations the appraiser might be requested to estimate the market value in some past

EXHIBIT 4-1 The valuation process

Source: Reprinted from *The Appraisal of Real Estate* (8th edition), copyright 1983 by American Institute of Real Estate Appraisers. All Rights Reserved.

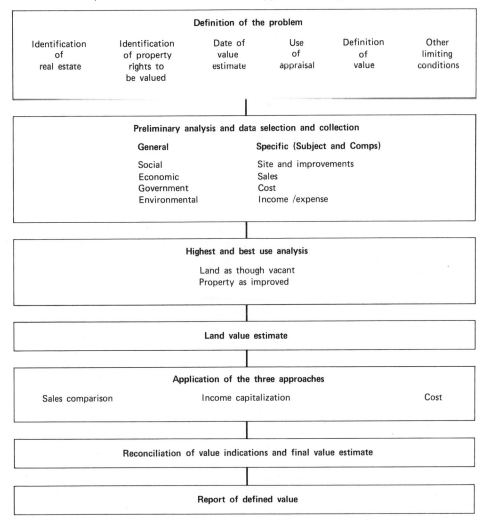

period. For example, assume that an individual is given a piece of property as an inheritance, but does not receive it until after a prolonged probate process. This property was given to the heir upon the relative's death last year, but it is legally received today. The inheritance tax must be paid. The heir would like to know the market value of the property as of the date the gift was made because property values have been rising. As a second example, consider the case of a condemnation trial in which the local government is taking property under eminent domain. The trial date is set four months in the future. The value estimate required is the market value of the property at that future date, specifically on the day of the trial.

Preliminary Analysis and Data Selection and Collection

Once the appraiser has clearly defined the assignment, the next step is the establishment of an execution plan for the assignment. In this step, the appraiser identifies the data required to complete the assignment; the public and private sources of the data; the type of personnel required to research the data, analyze the data, and produce the report; and the time requirements for each of the individuals involved in the project. The final task in this step is to make a fee proposal to the client. This fee is quoted as a lump sum charge that reflects the dollar per hour or dollar per day charges for the personnel and for overhead and expenses.

If the client accepts the stated fee for the specified estimate of value, the next step in the appraisal process is the actual gathering of data pertinent to the assignment. Two main categories of data must be gathered—general data and specific data. The **general data** include information about the overall economy that affects the site or property under analysis. For residential real estate appraisal, the local economic base of the community as reflected in market analysis for the residential submarkets is germaine. In addition, general data include information about the neighborhood in which the site is located. The **specific data** are factors that pertain to the property under consideration, such as information about the rights of ownership, the attributes of the site and its improvements, and the highest and best use of the site.

Highest and best use analysis and the land value estimate   The next step in the process requires the appraiser to evaluate the highest and best use of the subject property. An initial discussion of this topic was presented in Chapter 2. Based on that discussion the appraiser is required to find the legally permissible use of the land that produces the highest residual income to the land. Later in this chapter, the distinction between highest and best use as though the land were vacant and highest and best use of the property as improved will be discussed.

After the highest and best use is evaluated, the appraiser must establish the value of the land. This is a crucial and separate step in the cost approach so the methods of obtaining a land value estimate will be discussed in that section of Chapter 5. However, it may be necessary for the appraiser to obtain land value in the sales comparison and income approaches in order to fully understand the contribution of the two components, land and improvements, to the total value of the subject property.

The Three Appraisal Techniques

The next step in the appraisal process is the application of the appropriate appraisal technique to the assignment. Three techniques are available to the appraiser. They are traditionally known as the income approach, the cost approach, and the sales comparison approach. The purpose of this section is to identify each of these appraisal approaches by describing the format and the underlying principles involved. An appraiser should attempt all three approaches when undertaking an appraisal. However, if data are not available to support an approach, the appraiser can emphasize the others.

The sales comparison approach   In the **sales comparison approach,** the appraiser verifies the existence of a market for the type of property being analyzed. This means that the appraiser verifies the existence of buyers and sellers who are reasonably well informed about the properties in the market, discerns the state of the market in terms of vacancies, and verifies that the property would be exposed in the market for a reasonable period of time.

After establishing that a market does exist for the subject property, the appraiser undertakes the following activities:

1. Seeks similar or comparable properties for which pertinent sales data are available
2. Analyzes the conditions of the sale with regard to the date of sale, the transaction price, financial terms, and underlying motivations and bargaining advantages of the parties
3. Analyzes the attributes of the comparable properties and estimates the probable effect on sales price that would result if the comparable property had the same attributes as the subject property
4. Formulates an estimate of the market value of the subject property based on the analysis of the comparable properties

The underlying principle for this appraisal technique is the principle of substitution. This valuation principle is defined in the following statement: ". . . a prudent purchaser would pay no more for real property than the cost of acquiring an equally desirable substitute on the open market. The principle of substitution presumes that the purchaser will consider the alternatives available to him and that he will act rationally or prudently on the basis of his information about these alternatives, and that time is not a significant factor."[5]

The cost approach   In the **cost approach,** the appraiser separates the physical entity of real estate into the two components of land and improvements. Then the appraiser estimates the current market value of the land and approximates the value of the improvement. The two components are added to obtain the estimate of value of the entire property. The cost approach includes the following steps:

1. Obtaining the market value of the land by means of a market data approach under the assumption that the land is vacant
2. Calculating the current cost of constructing a reproduction of the existing improvements
3. Estimating the amount of accrued depreciation and subtracting its dollar value from the current construction cost of the improvements
4. Adding the market value of the land to the depreciated value of the construction to obtain the estimate of market value

The fundamental underlying principle for the cost approach is also the principle of substitution but restated in the following manner: "No rational person will pay more for a property than the amount at which a property of equal desirability and utility can be obtained, through purchase of a site and construction of a building, without undue delay."[6]

The income approach   To use the **income approach,** the appraiser starts with the realization that the parcel of real estate generates a stream of future benefits to its owner. The benefits are in the form of money received for allowing others to use and possess part or all of the physical property. The appraiser estimates the value of the current and the future revenues that can accrue to the owner and then estimates the costs incurred to operate the property. From these figures, the appraiser calculates the value for net operating income that the property could generate for a typical owner. By means of a discounting or capitalizing technique, which is essentially dividing the net operating income value by an interest rate, the appraiser obtains an estimate of the market value.

In more precise terms, the appraiser undertakes the following activities in using the income approach to obtain market value for an income-earning property. The appraiser

1. Calculates the revenues that the property can generate from rents on space and from other services that the owner of the building could provide
2. Estimates the probable vacancies that will occur in the structure
3. Gathers information about expenses incurred to operate the property
4. Calculates a value for net operating income and estimates the probable duration of time over which this net operating income stream will be positive. In other words, the appraiser estimates the period of time over which the building will generate revenues that exceed costs
5. Selects an appropriate capitalization rate and uses it to obtain the market value estimate

The underlying principle for the income approach is known as the principle of anticipation. This principle is merely the recognition that "value is created by the expectation of benefits to be derived in the future."[7] The principle of substitution also is applicable for the income approach. "Value tends to be set by the effective investment necessary to acquire, without undue delay, a comparable substitute income-producing property offering an equally desirable net operating income return."[8]

An alternative form of the income approach is the gross rent multiplier technique. The underlying assumption is that the revenue from comparable income earning properties and their recent sales prices can indicate the current market value of the subject property. To use this approach, the appraiser identifies several comparable properties and divides their sales price by monthly or yearly rent revenues to get a "multiplier" that is representative of the comparable properties. Then the revenue to be derived from the subject property is multiplied by this number to obtain an estimate of the current market value of the subject property. This income technique is often used to estimate value for residential properties that produce income. (A more thorough discussion of the gross rent multiplier technique is given in Chapter 6.)

In summary, the appraisal process is a logical sequencing of activities, which starts with a definition of the task. Once the task is defined, the type of general and specific data required to make the value estimate can be identified. These data then are used as inputs into the three appraisal techniques. If possible, the appraiser obtains an estimate of market value by each technique, then reconciles the three (or at least two) value estimates and presents the final estimate to the client.

The remainder of this chapter describes the data and their use. In Chapter 5, the sales comparison approach and the cost approach to appraisal, and their application to the valuation of residential property, are examined. The income approach and the reconciliation process are explained in Chapter 6.

THE ENVIRONMENTAL DETERMINANTS OF VALUE (GENERAL DATA)

Two types of value determinants must be analyzed in a thorough appraisal. One type consists of features of the environment of which the property is a part. The data required to analyze the environment are the general data on the local economy, as expressed by the economic base of the community, and on the neighborhood in which the parcel of residential real estate is located. The second type of value determinant consists of on-site features of the property itself. The specific data needed for analysis are the rights of ownership, the attributes of the site and its improvements, and the highest and best use.

General data consist of information about the economic, social, demographic, physical, and government/political environments that affects the property being appraised. One broad category of general data covers the environmental factors in the nation, the region, and the local community. The effect of these environmental factors on the value of the subject property is determined by analyzing their effect on the market in which the property is traded. The other broad category of general data covers the environmental factors that affect the immediate or surrounding area of the subject property and thereby affect the value of that property.

Area Analysis

The first category of general data is used in **area analysis**[9] or community analysis.[10] The general focus of area analysis is the impact on the urban area as a whole, or on a major sector of the urban area such as the northern suburbs, brought about by the environmental factors. The specific focus of area analysis is the impact of these environmental factors on the property being appraised.

Economic factors   The economic factors are "by far the most significant and numerous."[11] They include all the factors identified as part of the economic base of the community (as discussed in Chapter 7). Changes in the community's economic base indicate either growth or decline of the local economy. More importantly, change in the economic base is translated into change in the level of demand and supply in the market to which the subject property belongs. The appraiser must analyze past trends in the housing market that are reflected in the economic base of the community. With the aid of these past trends, the appraiser can estimate future levels of households by size and age, future levels of disposable income, future credit conditions, the supply of existing housing, and future levels of construction. The appraiser should not merely assume that the past trends will continue unabated or unchanged into the future. From the estimates of future levels of the factors affecting demand and supply, the appraiser can estimate the future trend of market value in the housing market for the subject property.

The forecast of the market factors is clearly important when the appraiser is estimating market value at some point in the future. For example, assume that a new plant will open in eighteen months. This plant opening should attract new households and thus should increase the demand for existing housing units in the future. Over the next eighteen months, some or all of this demand for existing units can be shifted to newly constructed units as the supply side of the market adjusts. However, the influx of people could eliminate vacancies, giving future owners of existing units a stronger bargaining position and thereby increasing future selling prices. Who obtains this increase in market value? Is it the current owner who is selling today, or the future owner, or could the total increase be split between the current and future owners? If the current market does contain well-informed buyers, they will pay prices that are higher than those offered before the plant opening was announced because these buyers fully expect appreciation of the property's value in the future. Thus, information about the future should affect current market values.

The process of forecasting the probable changes in the economic base of the community is a complex topic that cannot be explored in detail in this text. However, any forecasting technique must start with an analysis of the changes in external market factors. Some of the variables that need to be examined are

1. The impact of increased real income and different preference patterns of nonlocal consumers on the demand for locally produced goods and services
2. The desirability of the local community as a location for new firms that are looking for industrial or commercial sites
3. The ability of the local community to retain present industrial and commercial enterprises
4. The desirability of the local community as a place of residence
5. The impact of nonlocal competitors on the demand for locally produced goods and services

As these factors work in favor of the local economy, economic growth will occur and will enhance market value—or at least will inhibit a decline in market value—of the local community's housing units.

Social factors   Certain social and demographic factors are considered in economic base analysis; for example, the employment level and the occupational composition of the labor force, household and population size, age structure, and income structure. However, the social factors examined in area analysis are the preferences of people for material goods; the population density (the degree of crowding or congestion in dwelling units, as well as the crowding of the dwelling units themselves); and the social attitudes of the population toward such matters as marriage, divorce, birth control, integration, and the use of leisure time.

Changes in these social and demographic variables can affect the market value of the subject property. First, an increase in the absolute number of households can increase demand in several submarkets. Second, a change in the household's attitude toward the desirability of single-family detached housing units can change the level of demand in several different submarkets. For example, demand could decrease in the single-family detached submarket and increase in the townhouse and apartment submarkets if consumer preferences shifted away from single-family detached housing units. Changes in household attitudes toward city versus suburban lifestyles can cause a change in intra-urban locational preferences. In-town living could become a more popular lifestyle; such a change is occurring in many cities today. Finally, the postponement of marriage and the decision to have fewer children can affect the demand in different residential submarkets; demand for apartments and smaller houses could increase and the demand for large houses with four or more bedrooms could decline.

Physical factors   The physical features to be considered are those that make the local urban area attractive to households. Two such features are climate and scenery. A favorable climate and picturesque scenery can attract households and thus increase demand in the housing market. In addition, certain features affect the ability of the area to support residential units as well as places of employment. For example, the availability of water, the topography, soil and subsoil conditions such as drainage, and bedrock characteristics of the geographic area can affect industrial relocation into the area. An increase in job opportunities can increase the number of households through migration and thereby increase the demand in the housing market. On the supply side of the market, the availability of water affects the size of the stock of housing that can exist in the area. Drainage characteristics can limit the number of buildable sites if much of the land in the area is classified as floodplain.

Governmental and political factors   The local government's use of its police powers and eminent domain legislation, its provision of public services, and its taxation powers (described in Chapter 1) also affect the value of a residential unit through the market. The zoning ordinance affects the supply of land that can be used for new residential construction as well as the ability of a contractor to make conversions of existing structures from one form of residential use to another. The construction code affects the supply of new construction because it places a minimum supply price on the new unit.

Eminent domain can be used to reduce the stock of one type of housing unit, such as the old low-quality apartments in the central city. This action could increase the market value of the remaining units if the level of demand stays constant. In addition, the process of eminent domain can increase the supply of new construction in a geographic area after the older structures are demolished, the land is cleared, and the new units are built.

The provision of public services in the form of utilities such as water, sewerage, and street systems affects the supply of land that can be used for residential units. If such utilities are not extended into new areas, the supply of land for new-housing construction will become restricted; the price of both new and existing housing will rise dramatically if demand increases because additional housing units cannot be built. On the demand side of the market, the provision of public services such as high-quality schools, fire and police protection, trash collection, and street cleaning can make housing more desirable than similar housing in an area that does not provide high-quality public services. The last statement is especially relevant if households in both areas are paying the same level of property tax.

Where the quality of public services is high, households generally pay high property tax bills. However, if the tax level increases in an area without a commensurate improvement in the quality of services, the demand for housing in that area may decline. This decline in demand will occur only if there is another area in which the quantity and quality of public services per property tax dollar are higher.

Neighborhood Analysis

In **neighborhood analysis,** the environmental factors that affect the area surrounding the subject property are examined. First, an understanding of the concept of the neighborhood is needed. Then the features of the neighborhood are identified and their impact on the subject property is evaluated.

Definition of a neighborhood   The definition of a neighborhood used for many years by the appraisal profession follows:

> A portion of a larger community, or an entire community, in which there is a homogeneous grouping of inhabitants, buildings, or business enterprises. Inhabitants of a neighborhood usually have more than casual community of interest and a similarity of economic level or cultural background.[12]

Currently, the question of homogeneity is being examined more closely and a reformulation of this traditional definition is presented in the following series of statements:

> A neighborhood . . . may be more specifically defined as a grouping of similar or complementary land uses . . . residential neighborhoods . . . are sometimes composed of a narrow range of income levels and social groupings, but there is a growing preference for heterogeneity within neighborhoods. [13]

The currently acceptable definition of a **neighborhood** emphasizes the homogeneity of land uses; homogeneity of cultural, civic, and moral interests; homogeneity in the family structure and the attitude toward children and child rearing; but heterogeneity in economic, ethnic, racial, and religious status.

THE DECISION TO ESTIMATE MARKET VALUE

Any attempt to define the exact boundary of a neighborhood is subject to great difficulty. The two definitions indicate that several factors are used to define a neighborhood. One factor is the land uses on each site. The others are social and economic factors, such as the income level, age of household head, size of the household. Each of these social and economic factors has a small range of variation within a defined neighborhood. It is very improbable that homogeneity of land use and homogeneity of household income or household age would be present at the same points in space. Consequently, many areas could be considered to belong in either of two adjoining neighborhoods. For example, an area may have the income level of one neighborhood and the architectural style and land use of the other. In such situations, the appraiser's judgment and knowledge of the local community are important factors in determining what constitutes the neighborhood of the subject property. One such judgmental definition is

> A neighborhood is the area around a lot to a point where changes in land use have no direct effect on the value of the lot.[14]

However, for practical purposes, neighborhood boundaries are frequently defined in terms of political boundaries, zoning districts, planning areas, school districts, subdivision boundaries, or some other similar concept. At this point, the appraiser's experience in the community and knowledge of the population's perceptions about neighborhoods become the major determining factor in the definition of a neighborhood.

Neighborhood analysis versus area analysis   Once the boundaries of the subject-property's neighborhood are identified, the appraiser must analyze the impacts of the neighborhood's features on the value of the property being appraised. These neighborhood features are typically categorized as the physical, social, economic, and governmental factors.[15] They are the same factors used in area analysis but are examined in reference to the neighborhood rather than to a larger region.

Physical features   One set of neighborhood features that can have an impact on the value of the subject property are the physical features of the immediate environment. The typical features categorized as physical are

1. Age, condition, and appearance of residences and other improvements in proximity to the subject property
2. Conformity of structural style
3. Availability and quality of public services and utilities
4. Pattern of the surrounding land uses and the size and shape of the lots. This factor includes the physical density of the structures—that is, the number of lots per acre
5. Street patterns, width, and quality of construction
6. Quality of supporting facilities, such as public transportation, schools, commercial establishments, and social, cultural, and recreational activities

7. Proximity to the supporting facilities
8. Proximity to employment opportunities
9. Visual factors, such as topographic features, proximity to lakes and rivers, and the climate
10. Geological factors, such as drainage capacity of the soil and other soil conditions
11. The presence of nuisances and hazards, such as smog, smoke, odors, and pollution (air, water, noise, and visual)[16]

This list of physical factors consists primarily of the items previously described (Chapter 2) as the attributes of location, geographic/geological considerations, environmental aspects, and off-site improvements. The value of the subject property is affected by each of these physical factors. The best way to visualize their impact is to imagine a parcel of real estate, the subject property, as being situated in two different neighborhoods having different physical features. For example, view neighborhood A as consisting of ten- to fifteen-year-old houses in excellent condition both internally and externally, and neighborhood B as consisting of ten- to fifteen-year-old houses of the same size, style, and so on, that are in poor physical condition. If all other neighborhood factors are the same, the subject property located in neighborhood A would be valued more highly than the identical property located in neighborhood B.

The appraiser must evaluate each of the physical features in the same manner. In addition, the appraiser must be cognizant of the general public's reactions or tastes and preferences about these physical features. The preceding example is straightforward because it is generally correct to assume that the vast majority of people prefer to live in neighborhoods where the surrounding structures are well maintained. Similarly, it is reasonable to assume that people wish to live in neighborhoods that have a high quality of public services and utilities, a high quality of supporting facilities such as public transportation and schools, pleasant visual features, and few nuisances and hazards.

No such general assumptions can be made about other physical features. Their presence could enhance the value of the subject property or have no effect on value at all, because they might not be universally preferred. For example, some people might prefer conformity of structural style. They would like a neighborhood that consists of all brick split-level houses. Other people, however, might like diversity of architectural styles in the neighborhood. The appraiser's task is to analyze such physical features and determine how the typical purchaser would react to them. In other words, the appraiser must understand the public's preference patterns toward housing. Moreover, these patterns change over time, and the appraiser must stay in tune with these changes.

Social features   A second set of neighborhood features consists of the social factors that identify the neighborhood's residents. These social factors are listed below:

1. Demographic traits of the neighborhood's population; for example, age, household size, marital status, race, and religion

2. Social attitudes of the population toward child-rearing, cleanliness of property, respect for the private property of others, and general interpersonal social conduct

3. Existence and level of involvement of neighborhood organizations, community associations, and religious groups

4. The occupancy level (the number of people per room) of the structure

5. Extent of crime or the level of safety in the neighborhood[17]

As in the case of the physical features, certain social features generally are viewed as desirable in a neighborhood. A clean, crime-free neighborhood in which all landowners have respect for the property of others and where interpersonal contact is pleasant should enhance the value of a house.

However, the value-enhancing effect of population density and communal attitudes depends on the potential homebuyer's preferences about population homogeneity and interaction. If these traits are viewed as important by the potential buyers in the submarket for such housing, the house in the neighborhood that has these social features will be valued more highly.

Economic features   The third set of neighborhood features consists of the economic factors that identify the residents and the surrounding improvements. A list of these economic factors follows:

1. Economic profile of the neighborhood's residents, which includes such factors as the income level, the occupational status, and the employment status

2. Proportion of resident owners to renters in the neighborhood

3. Turnover and vacancy levels of the properties

4. Degree of land utilization—that is, the amount of vacant land and the amount of new construction

5. Relationship of the neighborhood to the growth path and development pattern of the urban area

6. Attitude of financial institutions toward the issuance of mortgages in the neighborhood[18]

The economic features of the neighborhood's residents and the surrounding improvements affect the value of the subject property. To analyze the impact of some of these factors, the appraiser must be a market analyst; to analyze the impact of the other factors, the appraiser must keep abreast of public attitudes. In examining the economic profile of the neighborhood's residents, the appraiser must consider the economic homogeneity of the neighborhood. Many people view such homogeneity as an important factor. In addition, the appraiser must consider the economic circumstances of the inhabitants in relation to the value of the structures and the level of maintenance and operating costs, which can determine the eventual physical condition of the improvements. The income level or employment pattern of the residents may be such that they are unable to expend a sufficient portion of their income to either maintain or renovate their homes.

The proportion of owners to tenants residing in a neighborhood also is related to the present appearance and future condition of the improvements. For a neighborhood that contains single-family detached housing, the common belief is that owners will maintain their homes at higher levels of exterior cleanliness and repair than will the renters of such housing. Restated, the belief is that residences occupied by their owners receive better care than residences owned by absentee owners and occupied by tenants. As a rule, this generalization is true. Therefore, a high proportion of owners to tenants in a neighborhood has an enhancing effect on the subject property.

However, if the neighborhood in question is a mixed residential-use neighborhood with single-family detached housing units and low-rise apartments, the proportion of owners to tenants is meaningless. A low ratio of owners to tenants in this type of neighborhood does not signal declining values. Tenants as a group are not unclean, destructive, and a public nuisance. Owners as a group do not always expend funds to keep their property in good repair. In this type of neighborhood, the appraiser must analyze the past trend and estimate the future trend with regard to expenditures for upkeep by both the owners of the single-family detached units and the owners of the apartment units.

Generalizations about the turnover rate and the vacancy level must be made with care. A neighborhood can have many houses for sale, but the houses may be on the market for only a short period of time. Such a neighborhood could be inhabited by very mobile people and it could be in great demand as a residential site. In this case, high turnover does not have a value-depressing effect. In contrast, a neighborhood with many houses for sale that stay on the market for long periods of time could be a neighborhood with problems. If the high levels of vacancies are due primarily to a relatively low level of demand for the properties, the values in this neighborhood should decline in the future.

The degree of land utilization in the neighborhood is also a difficult factor to analyze. Often, this information is presented as the amount of vacant land in the neighborhood. Potential buyers may fear that this vacant land will be used in such a way that property values in the neighborhood will be reduced. If inharmonious or incompatible uses actually do enter the neighborhood, property values will decline. However, for several reasons the amount of vacant land should not be considered a proxy for the possibility of invasion by value-depressing land uses. First, some of the vacant land is not suitable for development (land with excessively steep slopes or land that is in a floodplain). Such land will not be improved and will have no value-depressing or value-enhancing effect on the subject property. Second, some of the vacant land is voluntarily held off the market by private owners for the sake of increased privacy. This vacant land could be developed ultimately by its owner in a way that could depress or enhance the value of the subject property. Finally, the local zoning ordinance controls the types of development for which vacant land can be used. The specifications of the land-use restrictions could prohibit value-depressing land uses. Moreover, the community may have a history of being value-conscious when allowing variances and rezoning. To analyze the impact of vacant land on neighborhood values, the appraiser should know the zoning ordinance and the probability of rezoning to an inharmonious or nonconforming use.

THE DECISION TO ESTIMATE MARKET VALUE

The growth path of the urban area can also have a major impact on property values in the neighborhood. As decentralization of employment opportunities occurs in an urban area, some neighborhoods become more convenient and others become less convenient in relation to jobs. As decentralization of population continues, newer neighborhoods at the fringe become increasingly popular at the expense of most central city neighborhoods. (In some cities, revitalization of downtown as an employment center has led to rehabilitation of neighborhoods in the central city.) As the transport system is changed to accommodate decentralization, some neighborhoods become more accessible and others become less accessible. A neighborhood that is receiving the benefits of decentralization has a value-enhancing effect on a subject property.

Finally, the willingness of financial institutions to issue mortgages for the purchase of property in a neighborhood can affect property values. The term *redlining* is used to refer to a practice whereby financial institutions delineate certain areas or neighborhoods in which they do not issue mortgage loans. If the redlining practice exists in a community, it is justified on the basis that the financial institution has a responsibility to its depositors to invest in safe assets that retain their value. So, the financial institutions attempt to make loans on properties whose collateral value will exceed the mortgage balance at all times until the loan is repaid. Therefore, they try to identify and avoid properties and neighborhoods that might not maintain their collateral value at sufficiently high levels in the future. Legally, neither racial, ethnic, religious, nor sex characteristics of the neighbors can be used by the financial institutions to determine the future value of such properties. If the redlining does exist and the financial institutions do not issue mortgages in a neighborhood, the unavailability of mortgage funds has a depressing impact on the demand for properties there. Consequently, the value of the subject property falls because of the inability of potential buyers to obtain mortgages.

Governmental features   The fourth set of neighborhood features is related to local governmental activity. This category consists of the following factors:

1. Quantity and quality of public improvements and services
2. Property taxation and special assessments
3. Public restrictions and regulations

The most significant governmental factors affecting the value of the subject property are the off-site public improvements and public services available in the neighborhood. These features have a quantitative and qualitative component. In neighborhoods that offer high-quality and high-quantity levels of public improvements and services, the demand for houses is higher and hence their value is greater than in neighborhoods lacking such facilities.

All public services and improvements must be bought and paid for by the consumer through the property tax and the special assessment. The special assessment should reflect the dollar value of the adjoining public improvement, and the value of the newly constructed adjoining improvement should have a corresponding positive impact on the value of the subject property. The property tax, in contrast, does not have an impact that is directly identifiable. Generally, the property tax is a cost of home ownership. As the total level of this cost increases, the demand for housing would decline unless the higher tax were offset by improved or expanded public services. For example, if two neighborhoods have the same quantity and quality of public services but the tax bill in neighborhood A is greater than the tax bill in neighborhood B, the value of the subject property would be lower in neighborhood A.

The third governmental feature is the full complement of public restrictions and regulations embodied in the zoning ordinance, the subdivision regulations, the construction code, and the occupancy code. Each of these regulations (discussed in detail in Chapter 1) affects the neighborhood and hence the value of the subject property.

Assume that the subdivision regulations imposed on the development of neighborhood A provide that neighborhood with features consumers desire: wide curvilinear streets that heighten the aesthetic quality of the neighborhood and cul-de-sacs that reduce traffic and thereby reduce the noise level, increase the safety of children, and provide a building-block arrangement to maximize privacy without the need for fencing. Assume that neighborhood B does not have such features. If all other neighborhood features were the same, the value of the subject property would be higher in neighborhood A than in neighborhood B because of consumer preferences.

In terms of zoning, assume that neighborhood A has land-use restrictions that are incompatible with low-density, single-family, detached housing, such as high-density apartment complexes, commercial activity that generates a high volume of vehicular traffic (sports arenas, race tracks, large discount stores, etc.) and noisy, dirty industrial plants. Moreover, the planning department operates to maintain this feature of the neighborhood by carefully scrutinizing all requests for variances and rezoning. Assume that neighborhood B does not have a land-use plan that is as well prepared and well maintained as that of neighborhood A. If all other features of the two neighborhoods are the same, neighborhood A will be more desirable given consumer preferences, and thus, the subject property would be worth more if it were located in neighborhood A instead of neighborhood B.

The impact of construction codes and occupancy codes on the value of property is transmitted through the quality of the adjoining structures. If improvements in a neighborhood are well maintained because of the occupancy code, and if maintenance is relatively easy because of high-quality construction standards imposed in the past by the construction code, any specific property in that neighborhood is more valuable than it would be in a neighborhood of poorly maintained improvements.

THE SITE-SPECIFIC DETERMINANTS OF VALUE
(SPECIFIC DATA)

The site-specific determinants of value that the appraiser must analyze consist of the on-site features of specific parcels of real property. The purpose of the analysis is to identify the impact of on-site features on the value of the subject property. Specific data relevant to both the site and the improvements are gathered. Then the use of the property is analyzed to determine whether a change in the use could generate a higher value than that generated by the parcel in its present usage. Thus, the specific data gathered for parcels of real property are used for site analysis, improvement analysis, and highest-and-best-use analysis.

Site Data and Analysis

The specific data needed for site analysis include legal, physical, and economic features of the site. Each of these three types of data is described in the following paragraphs.

Legal information   The category of legal data consists of the rights of ownership that are held in the property, and the public and private limits on those rights. A prospective buyer obviously would pay more for an estate in possession than for an estate in expectancy, if all other aspects of the property were the same. Similarly, the buyer would pay more for a property that does not have an easement than for a property on which an easement eliminates the owner's ability to use all of the site.

Restrictive covenants in the deed also affect the value of the parcel of real estate. The typical prospective buyer will offer less for a property having this type of private land-use restriction than for a property that is not restricted as to use. For this reason, the person initially establishing the restrictive covenant must understand the impact of the covenant on prospective buyers.

Public limits on the rights of ownership in the form of the zoning ordinance also affect the value of the parcel of property. The most obvious examples are the land-use restriction, which disallows a particular land use; the height restriction, which limits the number of floors or stories that can be constructed on a given site; and the area regulations, which limit the amount of the land surface that can be utilized for the improvement. Other things being similar, the typical buyer will pay less for property that has the more severe restrictions.

Construction and occupancy codes are also limits on the rights of ownership. These codes affect the property owner because they directly affect the level of construction costs and maintenance/repair costs, respectively. The prudent buyer will pay more for a property that is subject to less demanding occupancy codes because the maintenance and repair costs will probably be lower. However, the prudent buyer will pay less for a property that was subject to less demanding construction codes because the maintenance and repair costs will probably be higher.

Legal description of the site   There is an obvious need to be able to describe the amount of land surface that is owned. Typically, the larger the surface, the more valuable the property. Three techniques of **legal description** currently are used to describe the extent of the land surface: the lot-and-block or plat-map system, the metes-and-bounds system, and the government survey system. In a sense, each of these techniques draws a picture of the land surface that is owned.

The **lot-and-block** or **plat-map** system for describing land is based on the use of publicly recorded maps. Most urban communities require developers to have their tracts surveyed and platted into building lots and blocks. This information is displayed on a map in which each building lot is identified by its size, shape, and location in the tract. The map is placed on file with the local government's records office. The requirements that establish this system are related to the community's subdivision regulations. Under this system, the legal description of a parcel of land would contain the following kind of information: the property is Lot #11 in the Chestnut Ridge Development as shown on page 412 of Volume 3 of the Plat Maps for Liberty County.

The **metes-and-bounds** system for describing land is based on the use of a well-known permanent beginning point and on the ability to describe a geometric shape using directions, distances, and a means to describe changes in directions. Monuments or any landmarks that are easily identified can also be used in the metes-and-bounds system. They can be man-made objects (fences, markers) or natural features such as distinct rock outcropping, a stream, or even a tree. First, a beginning point is described, for example, as the intersection of two roads. Then property is defined by describing the perimeter in the following manner: Starting at the northeast corner of the intersection of Avenue A and First Street (the beginning point), proceed due north for 520 feet, then turn 90° due east for 650 feet, then proceed 90° due south for 520 feet and 90° due west for 650 feet.

The metes-and-bounds description identifies a rectangular piece of property. The size, shape, and location of the property are all given and easily recorded. By use of more sophisticated angular measurements (i.e., degrees, minutes, and seconds), any irregularly shaped piece of property can be identified with the metes-and-bounds system.

The third legal description technique is the **government survey** method in which *base lines* and *principal meridians* are used to identify tracts of land. The base lines are latitude lines running east and west across the face of the earth. The principal meridians are longitude lines running north and south. At intervals of twenty-four miles north and south of the predetermined and recorded base line are *standard parallels*. At intervals of twenty-four miles east and west of the principal meridians are *guide meridians*. This system of base lines, standard parallels, principal meridians, and guide meridians is used to mark out plots of land that are twenty-four miles long and twenty-four miles wide. Within each of these twenty-four-mile-square plots of land, there are sixteen subdivisions called *townships*. (The term *township* in this sense should not be confused with any type of political designation.) The townships are plots of land that are six miles long and six miles wide. They are identified by reference to the base line and the principal meridian. The townships are arrayed in tiers (rows) and ranges (columns) and are referred to by their location. Thus, a township that is in the second tier north of the base line and second range west of the principal meridian is easy to identify and to distinguish from the township that is in the third tier south of the base line and the second range east of the principal meridian. This distinction is shown in Exhibit 4-2.

Each of the townships is in turn subdivided into 36 plots of land that are each one mile long and one mile wide. These one-square-mile parcels are called *sections*. Within the township, the sections are numbered from 1 through 36. The convention established for numbering these sections starts with the first section in the northeasternmost corner of the township. The numbers of the sections then run

THE DECISION TO ESTIMATE MARKET VALUE

EXHIBIT 4-2 Correction lines and guide meridians with division of townships in sections

Source: Kratovil and Werner, *Real Estate Law,* 8th Edition, © 1983, p. 54. Reprinted by permission of Prentice-Hall, Inc., Englewood Cliffs, New Jersey.

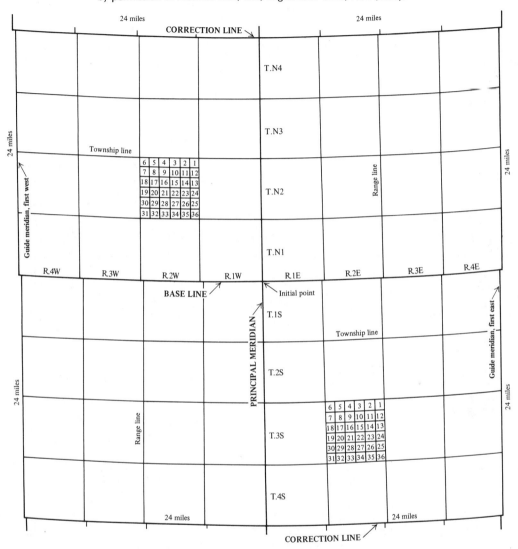

in the order depicted in Exhibit 4-2. The final section, #36, is in the southeastern-most corner of the township. These sections can be subdivided further by identifying the quarter sections, and the quarter sections also can be divided into quarters. These finer subdivision procedures are shown in Exhibit 4-3, as are the distances represented as rods, chains, and furlongs, and area measures such as acres and quarter sections. In many parts of the country, the government survey is used to describe the beginning point for the metes-and-bounds system.

EXHIBIT 4-3 Section of land divided into quarters and showing acreage and distances

Source: Kratovil and Werner, *Real Estate Law,* 8th Edition, © 1983, p. 55. Reprinted by permission of Prentice-Hall, Inc., Englewood Cliffs, New Jersey.

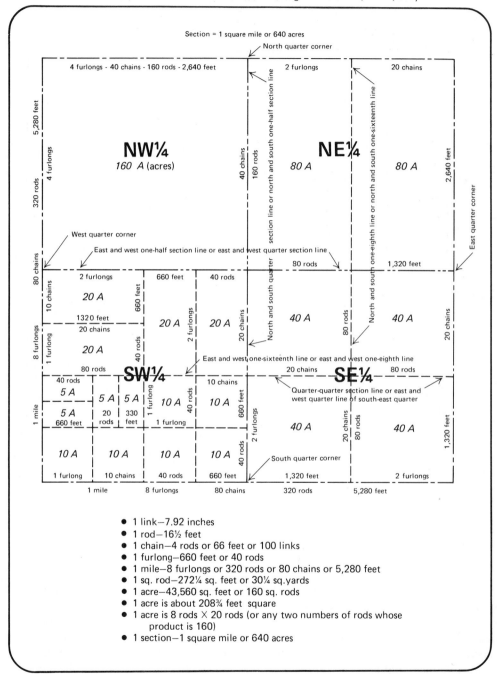

- 1 link—7.92 inches
- 1 rod—16½ feet
- 1 chain—4 rods or 66 feet or 100 links
- 1 furlong—660 feet or 40 rods
- 1 mile—8 furlongs or 320 rods or 80 chains or 5,280 feet
- 1 sq. rod—272¼ sq. feet or 30¼ sq.yards
- 1 acre—43,560 sq. feet or 160 sq. rods
- 1 acre is about 208¾ feet square
- 1 acre is 8 rods × 20 rods (or any two numbers of rods whose product is 160)
- 1 section—1 square mile or 640 acres

Physical data and analysis   This category of site-specific data is related to the geological and geographical features of the site. The geographical features include

- ☐ Width and frontage
- ☐ Depth
- ☐ Shape
- ☐ Size
- ☐ Corner and cul-de-sac influences

The geological features of the site include

- ☐ Topography
- ☐ Surface-soil quality and landscaping
- ☐ Subsoil and bedrock characteristics
- ☐ Drainage and runoff characteristics
- ☐ Availability of potable water

The purpose of this analysis is to examine the impact of each one of these physical features on the value of a residential property.

Width and frontage The width and frontage of a site measure the same physical dimension, but at different points on the site. Frontage is the width of the site where it is adjacent to an access road. Along the road, frontage and width are always the same. If the site is a rectangle or square, then the width of the lot is equal to the frontage at all points. However, for a nonrectangular-shaped lot, the width will differ from the frontage at all points except along the frontage road. The impact of frontage on value is readily identified. Other things being equal, the more front feet, the more valuable the site, especially in commercial areas. Similarly, the impact of width on value is readily apparent. The wider the site, the more valuable it is, given the same frontage because more square feet of space exist. In other words, two irregularly shaped lots with the same front footage wll have different values if the lots have different widths. The wider lot is typically more valuable.

Depth The depth of a site is the measurement from the frontage to the back property line. If other aspects of the site are the same, the deeper the site, the more valuable it is. However, appraisers realize that a few extra feet of depth are not as valuable as the first few feet of depth. The addition of a foot of depth increases the total value, but by smaller and smaller increments because the major improvement on most sites is constructed as near to the front of the site as permitted by the area regulations of the zoning ordinance. In this instance, the first 100 feet of depth should be worth more than the next 100 feet of depth, which in turn should be worth more than the next 100 feet of depth. In other words, the first feet of depth are worth more than the last feet of depth.

Shape The impact of the shape of a lot is not as easily determined. If the lot is irregular in shape but large enough to accommodate the planned improvement, the shape does not affect the value in relation to that of a regular rectangular lot if the two lots are approximately the same otherwise. However, a very irregular lot in a neighborhood of regularly shaped lots may be valued less than the other lots.

Size The size of a site has a direct impact on the value of that site. Size is determined by width and depth of the lot. For a rectangular lot, the product of these measures of distance is the square footage of the site. As a general rule, the larger the lot in square feet, the greater the value. Size, however, is only one of the major physical determinants of value. Frontage is generally more significant as a value determinant than sheer size of the lot. For example, consider two sites. Site A has a 100-foot frontage and a 200-foot depth; therefore it contains 20,000 square feet. Site B has an 80-foot frontage, a 250-foot depth, and also contains 20,000 square feet. All other things being equal, the lot with the greater frontage is more valuable as commercial property. However, it is difficult to generalize about the impact on residential value because the lots are the same size. If the lot is wide enough at 80 feet to provide privacy from the adjacent neighbors, the additional 50 feet of depth can provide an added degree of privacy from the street.

A problem arises for the appraiser when the frontage and the square footage both differ. For example, consider site A with its 100-foot frontage and 200-foot depth, containing 20,000 square feet, and site C, with its 99-foot frontage and 210-foot depth, containing 20,790 square feet. Site A has 1 percent more frontage. Site C is 5 percent deeper. Which site is worth more if all other things are equal? The answer depends on the type of land use and the standards for lot width and depth in the surrounding neighborhood. More specifically, the answer depends both on the appraiser's knowledge of the neighborhood's land-use pattern and on the appraiser's experience with consumer preferences about the issue.

A special aspect of size is *plottage value.* It "is the increase in unit value resulting from improved utility when smaller plots are combined to form a larger one. . . . For plottage value to be realized, there must be the potential of a higher and more profitable use. Otherwise, the whole could not be worth more than the sum of its parts . . ."[19] In other words, when several small adjacent lots are purchased and assembled into one large lot, the value of the large lot exceeds the sum of the values of the small lots. However, plottage value occurs only when the large lot can be used to generate a residual income from a highest and best use that exceeds the residual income obtained from the highest and best use of each individual lot summed together.

Corner and cul-de-sac influences The influence of a corner location on the value of a site depends on the type of land use for that site and the manner in which the improvement is related to the space provided on the site. In urban residential neighborhoods of the past, corner lots were considered more valuable because they were viewed as providing more light and air than lots in the interior of the block. The additional exposure provided a positive value increment to residences on corners. However, growth of cities brought about increased vehicular and pedestrian traffic along the street network and hence, more noise, air pollution, and litter. In addition, corner lots generally are subject to higher public improvement assessments because they front on two streets, and they may also be subject to higher property tax bills.

THE DECISION TO ESTIMATE MARKET VALUE

Finally, corner lots tend to have less privacy because the backyard is exposed to one of the streets. These adverse impacts counterbalance the positive impacts of sunlight and breezes. The appraiser must consider both the positive and the negative aspects in determining the influence of a corner location on a residential site. The impact of corner locations for commercial property is typically positive because the property faces pedestrian and vehicular traffic on two streets. Consequently, the volume of potential customers passing a corner location is greater than the volume passing an interior location. Moreover, interior lots can benefit from proximity to a corner. The interior lots closer to a corner receive a positive premium that is not credited to interior lots in midblock. The magnitude of the value premium declines quickly as the lot's distance from the corner increases.

A cul-de-sac is a street that has one entry point and a dead end that is a circular turnaround area bordered by houses. The increased prominence of cul-de-sac development patterns in new residential neighborhoods has been caused by the desire to reduce the negative impacts of vehicular traffic, as well as to provide safety for children at play and greater backyard privacy.

Topography The impact of a site's topography on value is not readily identifiable. This physical feature needs to be closely scrutinized for the benefits provided and the costs that must be incurred. According to present consumer preferences, a desirable residential lot is one that gently rises from the street level so that the house can be situated at a slight elevation above the street. At the back of the lot, consumers like a contour that allows for a patio at the back of the house and flat ground for a play area and possibly a swimming pool. A site having these features should be valued more highly than a flat site.

However, "a lot (that is) higher or lower than the abutting street level may create additional costs to correct poor drainage, erosion, or accessibility problems."[20] "Land tends to have a lower value if it is costly to improve because of topographical conditions."[21] Therefore, the appraiser must balance the extra costs for on-site improvements against the additional benefits derived from desirable topographic characteristics of the site.

Surface-soil quality and landscaping One geological feature that affects a site's value is the quality of the topsoil. "The soil's ability to support a lawn and landscaping is an important factor in the marketability of the property."[22] The soil supports the life of indigenous trees on the site as well as the man-made improvement called *landscaping,* which includes the lawn, shrubbery, and gardens. In general, this vegetation improves the appearance and the desirability of residential properties. Soil quality is a relative factor, however. If the soil quality of the site is inferior to that of the neighboring sites, it will have a value-depressing effect. If all the sites in the neighborhood or area have uniformly poor soil quality, there should not be a value-depressing effect on any one specific site due to poor soil quality.

Subsoil and bedrock characteristics The nature of the subsoil can affect the costs of building an improvement. It can also affect the height of the major improvement. If the soil is unstable, piles must be sunk to the bedrock to support a structure. The depth of the unstable soil greatly affects construction costs. If the subsurface is solid rock, great expense is incurred to dig foundations. Consequently, a site having geological features that increase construction costs above their level on neighboring properties will command a lower price.

Drainage and runoff characteristics The ability of the site's surface contour and subsurface soil to remove storm water greatly affects the value of that site. If the site is flat or slightly sloped and if it is composed of porous, stable subsurface soil, there is no problem of standing water after a rainstorm or after snow melts. However, if the site is below the level of abutting property and the soil is nonporous as, for example, is clay, the site will experience standing water and flooding. In the latter situation, the developer must incur additional site preparation costs to correct the problem. For example, porous tile pipe might have to be installed from the area of flooding on the site to a point where the water can run off. This project might necessitate digging a trench one foot wide and 12 to 18 inches deep for a distance of 100 or more feet and would clearly add to the site's improvement costs.

Therefore, a site that has good natural drainage and runoff characteristics should be more valuable—that is, have a higher selling price, than a site that does not have these physical characteristics, all other things being equal. The difference between the selling prices of the two plots of land represents the cost of the improvements needed to rectify the problem.

If the site with poor natural drainage is also not served with public sewers, the cost of residential construction is increased further. Any site that is not served by public sewers must have a septic tank and leach lines to disperse waste material. On a site with poor drainage, a layer of crushed rock must be placed below the tile pipe and leach lines to increase the drainage capability. In addition, the length of the leach line or the size of the leach field may have to be increased if drainage is poor. These requirements increase the cost of improvements and thus reduce the value of the site. At the extreme, local health ordinances may prohibit the construction of septic tanks and leach lines on sites that have extremely poor drainage capabilities. Such a prohibition would have an obvious detrimental impact on the value of the site.

Availability of potable water The term *potable water* simply means drinkable water. If a site is not served by a municipal water system, a well must be drilled to obtain water. In most counties, a site cannot be developed until potable water is discovered on that site. The site must have a natural water supply that meets minimum standards of purity imposed by the county health department. A site that is not served by a water system and that does not have a potable water supply is less valuable than a site that is similar in all respects but does have a supply of drinkable natural water. The reason for this value difference is that the latter site can be improved and the former cannot.

Economic and locational factors The third category of site data represents the site's relative economic and spatial position in comparison with other sites nearby. One economic factor the appraiser must consider is the price of nearby lots that are similar to the subject property. The principal of substitution implies that the selling price of the similar lots sets an upper limit on the most probable selling price of the subject property. A second economic factor is the tax burden imposed on the subject property. If it is higher than that imposed on similar lots in proximity to the subject property, and if all of the lots are receiving the same level of services, the lot with the excessive tax burden is depressed in value by the additional tax payment required. In other words, the subject property may be overassessed in comparison with comparable properties; or, if the assessments are the same, the subject property is overtaxed. Overassessment causes a reduction in market value. Conversely, if the subject property is underassessed or undertaxed, its market value will be greater than that of similar properties receiving the same quantity and quality of public services.

The locational factors of site analysis are the "attributes of location" (discussed in Chapter 2). The location of the site in relation to employment centers and other establishments has a significant impact on the market value of the site. The more accessible the site is to economic activities—that is, the shorter the linkages and the lower the cost of transportation—the more valuable the site.

Another locational factor is the site's position in space in relation to scenic views and other preferred natural features. The lakeside lot is more valuable than an identical interior lot. The hillside lot that overlooks a valley is more valuable than a similar lot on a flat plain or in an area without a view.

In addition, hazards and nuisances can affect the value of a site. Hazards may be large volumes of high-speed vehicular traffic, floods, earthslides, avalanches, steep cliffs, and fire danger. Typically, these hazards depress the value of a site. Nuisances include noisy highways, industry, and playgrounds full of noisy children. These nuisances in proximity to a site can have a value-depressing effect.

Improvement Analysis

The second phase of analyzing site-specific determinants of value is improvement analysis. It focuses on the man-made construction on the physical site. Both improvements-on-the-land and some of the improvements-to-the-land (described in Chapter 1) must be analyzed for their quantitative and qualitative features. Improvements-to-the-land, such as landscaping, access roads or driveways, utility connections, water wells, and septic tanks, can have a major effect on the value of a specific property.

Placement of the structure on the site   Two aspects of a structure's placement on the site are conceptually important in an analysis of the subject property's value. One aspect is the arrangement of public and private zones on the property. The public zone is the portion of the property that is visible from the street. By good site planning, this zone can be minimized within the area regulations or setback regulations of the local zoning ordinance. The private zone is the area of the property used for household activity. It includes playgrounds, patios, and gardens. This area on the site should be made as large as possible.[23] Other aspects being equal, people will view a house with a larger private zone as more desirable.

The second aspect of the structure's placement on the site is the positioning of the structure in relation to the sun and wind patterns. The structure and its windows should be positioned to catch the maximum amount of sunlight and breezes. Window space on the south side of a house provides sunlight in the winter months. Window space on the west side of a structure catches the maximum amount of breeze. Residential units that are naturally bright and airy tend to be more desirable.

The positioning of trees in relation to the structure can also affect the desirability of the property. If the northern and western portions of the lot contain trees, the house will be protected from winter winds and the glare of the summer sun as it sets. Protection from the wind can lower heating bills and thereby make the property more valuable than similar properties without trees. Protection from the setting sun can lower air-conditioning expenses and possibly enhance the usefulness of a patio, making the house more desirable and consequently more valuable.

Physical description of the improvements   The physical description of the improvements includes information on the following three factors:

1. The construction details of the exterior and interior of the structure
2. The description of the interior space
3. An analysis of the mechanical systems

When the construction details of the interior and exterior of the structure are examined, the appraiser analyzes the quantity and the quality of the materials and workmanship used in the construction of the unit. In general, the greater the quantity and quality of the materials, and the higher the quality of workmanship, the greater the value of the structure.

The description of the interior space of the structure specifies the size of the dwelling unit in square feet; the number, type, and size of the rooms; the amount of storage space in attics and/or basements; the quality of surface coverings such as tile, wallpaper, and paint; and the quantity and quality of fixtures. The more of these items in the structure and the higher their quality, the more valuable the property.

In an analysis of the mechanical systems, the appraiser examines the heating, cooling, plumbing, electrical, and other such systems in the structure. These systems are identified by their type and capacity. For example, heating systems might be forced hot air, forced hot water, or electric. The fuel might be natural gas, oil, or electricity. The heating capacity may be large or small. Similar analyses can be performed for the cooling system (central air conditioning versus window units), plumbing system (the size of hot water heaters), and the electrical system (110-volt circuits versus 220-volt circuits, number of circuits, number of wall plugs). Any miscellaneous systems (burglar alarms, fire alarms, intercoms, and central vacuum cleaners) also are evaluated. In general, the larger the number of mechanical systems and the higher their quality, the greater the value of the residential unit.

Physical condition of the improvements While gathering data on the quality and quantity of materials and workmanship, the magnitude and type of interior space, and the features of various mechanical systems, the appraiser also gathers information about the condition of these improvements. The need for repairs and/or replacements is noted. An opinion is formed about whether the repairs should be made now or deferred. If the repair or replacement adds more to the value of the property than the cost of that repair, the repair should be undertaken.

Functional description of the improvements Functional efficiency (explained in Chapter 2) is the ability of a structure to meet its current intended use and to be adapted to changing needs. In this sense, a house is functionally efficient if it meets the current and future needs of typical residents. The degree of efficiency depends on the services provided by the house and the desires of typical buyers in that housing submarket today and in the future. For example, assume that two houses are identical in every detail except that house A has 8-foot ceilings and house B has 12-foot ceilings. Although both houses meet the needs of the current owners, house A is more functionally efficient because it is less expensive to heat and cool. As a second example, assume that a tall couple built a customized house to meet their needs. They installed a kitchen counter, with a built-in range and a sink, that is six or eight inches higher than normal. This kitchen feature is functionally efficient in its current use for the tall couple. It probably will not be functionally efficient in the future, however, because the typical buyer is shorter and requires a house with a counter top of normal height. In both cases, the functionally efficient house is the more desirable.

The physical design and layout of the house and its rooms are another important aspect of functional efficiency. Like the lot, the house is divided into public and private zones. The working/service zone is composed of the kitchen, pantry, utility room, and other areas set aside for household-related work. The living/social zone is composed of the living room, dining room, family room, den, recreation room, and porch. The private/sleeping zone is composed of the bedrooms, bathrooms, and other rooms where quiet and privacy are desired. According to current preferences, these zones should be in separate and distinct parts of the residential unit. Such an arrangement is most desirable to current housebuyers and should be a value-enhancing factor.

Highest and Best Use

The third phase of analyzing site-specific determinants of value is the estimation of the **highest and best use** of the subject property. In Chapter 1, "highest and best use" is defined as the legally permissible use that generates the highest residual income over a reasonable period of time, such as the next ten to twenty years. To determine the highest and best use, the appraiser must examine four factors related to the site. One factor of concern is the land-use restrictions established in the zoning ordinances. Another concern is the physical capability of the site to support the improvement. In other words, in a legal and geological sense, what restrictions are placed on the construction of the improvement? The third factor is the market for each legally permitted and physically possible land use. Market analysis establishes the level of total revenue to be generated by the permitted project over each of the next several years. Finally, the appraiser estimates the highest and best use by subtracting the expenses from the revenue estimate to obtain the use with the highest residual income figure.

Highest-and-best-use analysis is applied in two steps. First, the site is analyzed as though it were vacant. In this phase of analysis, the investigator can examine all legally permitted and physically feasible land uses that the site can accommodate. By searching through these probable uses, the appraiser can find a highest and best use for the site "as if vacant." Then the site is analyzed as it is improved. In this phase of the analysis, the investigator can examine all the legal uses of the improved site to determine a highest and best use for the site "as it is improved." This highest and best use "as improved" is the dominant consideration because it prevails even if the highest and best use "as if vacant" yields a higher residual income level. The reason is that the highest and best use "as if vacant" cannot be realized until the existing improvement is demolished and the site is cleared for construction of the highest and best use identified for the vacant lot. Therefore, the highest and best use "as improved" dominates until the difference between the two residual income streams is great enough to pay for the demolition and clearing of the old improvement. The residual income generated by the highest and best use "as if vacant" must be larger than the residual generated by the highest and best use of the improved site plus the costs of demolition, clearing, and construction.

CHAPTER SUMMARY

An appraisal is defined as an estimate of value. The value that is most often sought is current market value, and a real estate appraisal is typically defined as an estimate of the current market value of a parcel of real property. To provide this estimate, the appraiser utilizes an orderly, logical, step-by-step process known as the appraisal process. As part of this process, the appraiser obtains a definition of the task, estimates data and manpower requirements to accomplish the task, gathers data relevant to the subject property, and utilizes the three appraisal techniques—the market data approach, the cost approach, and the income approach.

As part of the appraisal process, the appraiser must gather and analyze two broad categories of data, general data and site-specific data. The appraiser obtains these data by means of area analysis, neighborhood analysis, site analysis, improvement analysis, and highest-and-best-use analysis. Once this information has been acquired, the appraiser can apply the three appraisal techniques.

Review Questions

1. What issues does the appraiser consider in the definitional stage of the appraisal process?
2. What are the two classes of data that the appraiser collects and how do they differ?
3. Briefly describe the three appraisal techniques that the appraiser can use.
4. Distinguish between area analysis and neighborhood analysis.
5. Identify and explain the three methods by which a parcel of land can be legally described.

6. Define the concept of highest and best use, and describe the thought process used by the appraiser in determining the highest and best use for an improved parcel of real estate.

Discussion Questions

1. How could changes in the national economy affect the value of your home? Consider situations such as
   (a) a recession in which income levels decline and unemployment increases;
   (b) abnormally high levels of inflation for food, transportation, and shelter;
   (c) high interest rates that will continue to rise in the future.

2. How could changes in the city's economy affect the value of your home? Consider situations where
   (a) a new major industrial firm moves into the area;
   (b) the town's major employer suffers a significant reduction in the volume of output sold;
   (c) a decline in the population of the area occurs because of out-migration of the young and middle-aged individuals.

3. How could the following changes in the neighborhood affect the value of your home?
   (a) A deterioration in the physical appearance of surrounding housing units.
   (b) An increase of the crime rate due to increased levels of vandalism, robbery, and muggings.
   (c) An upgrading in the quality and quantity of public services such as schools, streets, police and fire protection.

4. Is the highest and best use for a property the use that places the most expensive improvement on the property? Please explain.

Notes

1. William N. Kinnard, Jr., *Income Property Valuation: Principles and Techniques of Appraising Income-Producing Real Estate* (Lexington, Mass.: D.C. Heath and Co., 1971), p. 9.
2. Byrl N. Boyce (ed.), *Real Estate Appraisal Terminology* (Cambridge, Mass.: Ballinger Publishing Co., 1975), pp. 16, 116, 119, 182.
3. *The Appraisal of Real Estate,* 8th ed., Textbook Revision Subcommittee (Chicago, Ill.: American Institute of Real Estate Appraisers, 1983), p. 13.
4. Ibid., p. 51.
5. Boyce, *Real Estate Appraisal Terminology,* p. 201.
6. *The Appraisal of Real Estate,* p. 33.

7. Ibid., p. 32.

8. Ibid., p. 33.

9. *A Guide to Appraising Residences,* 3d ed., prepared by H. Grady Stebbins, Jr., ·for the Education Committee, Society of Real Estate Appraisers (Chicago, Ill.: Society of Real Estate Appraisers, 1976), pp. 10–13.

10. William M. Shenkel, *Modern Real Estate Appraisal* (New York: McGraw-Hill Book Co., 1978), pp. 67–80.

11. *A Guide to Appraising Residences,* p. 11.

12. Boyce, *Real Estate Appraisal Terminology,* p. 147.

13. *The Appraisal of Real Estate,* pp. 90–91.

14. Robert O. Harvey, SREA Course Instruction Manual, Real Estate Certification Program, Indiana University, revised edition, August 1977, cited by George F. Bloom and Henry S. Harrison, *Appraising the Single Family Residence* (Chicago, Ill.: American Institute of Real Estate Appraisers, 1978), p. 86.

15. George F. Bloom and Henry S. Harrison, *Appraising the Single Family Residence* (Chicago, Ill.: American Institute of Real Estate Appraisers, 1978), pp. 90–100.

16. Ibid., p. 90; *The Appraisal of Real Estate,* pp. 94–104.

17. Bloom and Harrison, *Appraising the Single Family Residence,* p. 90.

18. Ibid.; *The Appraisal of Real Estate,* pp. 95–96.

19. Bloom and Harrison, *Appraising the Single Family Residence,* p. 120.

20. Ibid., p. 121.

21. *The Appraisal of Real Estate,* p. 133.

22. Bloom and Harrison, *Appraising the Single Family Residence,* p. 121.

23. Ibid., p. 156.

Additional Readings

BLOOM, GEORGE F., and HENRY S. HARRISON. *Appraising the Single Family Residence.* Chicago, Ill.: American Institute of Real Estate Appraisers, 1978. Chapters 3–8 and 10.

BOYCE, BRYL N., and WILLIAM N. KINNARD, JR. *Appraising Real Property.* Lexington, Mass.: Lexington Books, 1984. Chapters 1–6.

The Dictionary of Real Estate Appraisal. Chicago, Ill.: American Institute of Real Estate Appraisers, 1984.

KAHN, SANDERS A., and FREDERICK E. CASE. *Real Estate Appraisal and Investment.* New York: The Ronald Press Co., 1977. Chapters 3–5.

RING, ALFRED A. *The Valuation of Real Estate.* Englewood Cliffs, N.J.: Prentice-Hall, Inc., 1970. Chapters 5–9.

SHENKEL, WILLIAM M. *Modern Real Estate Appraisal.* New York: McGraw-Hill Book Co., 1978. Chapters 1–6.

SMITH, HALBERT C. *Real Estate Appraisal.* Columbus, Oh.: Grid, Inc., 1976. Chapters 1 and 2.

STEBBINS, GRADY H., JR. *A Guide to Appraising Residences.* Chicago, Ill.: Society of Real Estate Appraisers, 1976: 10–26.

Textbook Revision Committee. *The Appraisal of Real Estate,* 8th ed. Chicago, Ill.: American Institute of Real Estate Appraisers, 1983. Chapters 1–11.

5 | Residential Appraisal Property

QUESTION TO BE ANSWERED _____

How does the appraiser estimate the current market value of a single-family residence?

OBJECTIVES _____

When a student finishes the chapter, he or she should be able to

1. Explain the nature and structure of the sales comparison approach as it is used by the appraiser to estimate the current market value of residential property.
2. Explain the nature and structure of the cost approach as it is used by the appraiser to estimate the current market value of residential property.

IMPORTANT TERMS _____

Accrued Depreciation
Comparable Property
Comparative Method
Cost Approach
Economic Obsolescence
Functional Obsolescence
Physical Deterioration

Quantity Survey Method
Replacement Cost
Reproduction Cost
Sales Comparison
Subject Property
Unit-in-Place Method

INTRODUCTION

Chapter 4 described the process used by an appraiser to estimate market value for a specific parcel of real property and identifies the kinds of information the appraiser requires. The information consists of general data on the environmental conditions that surround the subject property, as well as specific data on the particular site and its improvements.

A large appraisal company may do appraisal work in an entire urban region, whereas an individual appraiser may work only within a certain portion of that region. Some appraisers do both residential and commercial work, and others focus exclusively on the appraisal of single-family residences. Regardless of the scope of the appraiser's work, it requires a data base that is more than adequate to provide current, relevant information about the economic, social, physical, and governmental factors in area analysis and neighborhood analysis, as well as such site-specific factors as the geographical and geological features of the land and the physical and functional features of the improvement.

The purpose of this chapter is to explore the principal methods used to estimate current market value of a single-family residence. The underlying assumption of the methods is that the owner-occupied, single-family residence is not used as an income-earning asset. In other words, the dwelling unit is inhabited by its owner, who does not intend to rent the premises. The two techniques used to appraise such property are the sales comparison (market data) approach and the cost approach.

THE SALES COMPARISON APPROACH

Once the general and specific data have been gathered, the appraiser can start the analysis of market value for a single-family residence, also referred to as the **subject property.** The most commonly used technique is the **sales comparison approach;** it is also known as the market comparison approach. The fundamental concept of this approach is that "market data usually provides the best indication of market value for a house."[1] The appraiser's task is "to discover what competitive properties have sold for recently on the local market and, through an appropriate adjustment process, to develop indications of what they would have sold for, if they had possessed

THE DECISION TO ESTIMATE MARKET VALUE

all basic and pertinent physical and economic characteristics of the subject property."[2]

The key terms in the last quotation are *competitive properties* and *adjustment process.* They are explained in the following sections.

The Selection of Comparable Properties

The selection of **comparable** (competitive) **properties** to use in the market data approach is based on an analysis of various aspects of the subject property and of the whole profile of properties that have sold in the recent past. From this very heterogeneous group of previously traded properties, the appraiser finds the ones that are comparable to the subject property in terms of physical features, neighborhood features, time of sale, financial terms of sale, bundle of rights, and conditions of sale.

Physical features of the site and the improvement   The comparable properties should be as similar as possible to the subject property in site-specific factors. There should be little, if any, difference in the physical characteristics of the sites as typified by geological and geographical features. The improvements should match closely in physical features, physical condition, and structural description. Moreover, there should be virtually no difference in the quality of construction between the subject property and the comparable properties. Any minor differences in physical features between the subject property and the comparable properties are recognized by an adjustment to the sales price of the comparable property. (The adjustment process is described in detail later in this chapter.)

Neighborhood features   Ideally, the comparable properties should be adjacent to the subject property. Realistically, the comparable properties should be drawn from the same neighborhood or if this is not possible from another neighborhood that is very similar to that of the subject property in all of the pertinent components of neighborhood analysis.

Time of sale   The date of the comparable property's sale is an indication of the market circumstances under which the comparable property sold. Ideally, the comparable properties should have been sold within the current market period—that is, the last sixty days or so.

If the comparable properties did sell in the last few months, there should be little need for an adjustment in their sales prices. However, if comparable properties must be chosen that were sold several months to one year in the past, an adjustment could be made for changes in the economic and demographic conditions that affect both the demand and the supply side of the market.

Typically, a time adjustment is used to reflect inflation. If the prices of construction inputs such as labor, construction loans, and building materials increase, market analysis reveals that the supply of new construction decreases and causes the price of new housing to rise. This price change for new housing units is reflected in a price rise for existing units, because these two markets are interrelated. As the price of the new unit increases, the demand for existing units increases.

Inflation is not the only economic change that must be recognized. Assume, for example, that two months ago a major employer announced a plant closing. When the plant closes in the very near future, 400 household heads will be out of work. Assume that all 400 people own similar houses in the community and that only 300 of these people will be able to find alternative employment in the general area. The other 100 households must migrate to other localities. The supply of existing houses for sale will increase. If demand is constant or (more realistically) declining, increased supply will cause the price of the existing units in the market to fall.

If the subject property is being appraised after the plant closing and if the comparable properties all sold before the plant closing was announced, an adjustment must be made to their sales prices. To make the comparable properties similar to the subject property, their sales prices must be reduced to reflect the negative market impact generated by the out-migration of formerly employed workers. Thus, the time of the sale is important because it allows the appraiser to analyze the economic and demographic changes that may have taken place between the comparable property's date of sale and the date for which the subject property's market value is to be estimated.

Because the vast majority of properties are purchased with borrowed funds, and because the interest rate and degree of credit availability affect the level of demand, changes in financial terms over time are an important aspect of comparability. To analyze this factor, the appraiser must know the financial conditions both in the present market and in the market when the comparable properties were sold. The adjustment process involves an understanding of the impact of mortgage interest charges on the demand for housing in the submarket. As interest rates drop, demand increases and, other things being equal, the price of housing increases.

If the mortgage interest rate in the past period was higher than the rate today, the sales price of the comparable property is adjusted upward. The reason for this adjustment is that the lower current mortgage interest rate would have increased demand if it existed in the past period. In contrast, if the mortgage interest rate in the past period was lower than it is today, the sales price of the comparable property is adjusted downward. As mortgage interest rates rise, the number of households able and willing to buy housing in the specific submarket declines. As the level of demand drops, the price of housing also drops if other economic and demographic factors stay constant. Therefore, if the interest rate has increased between the date of sale of the comparable property and the date for which market value is being estimated, a negative adjustment is incorporated into the appraiser's analysis.

The preceding adjustments reflect the financial terms that are available to the typical investor. If the appraiser learns that a sale took place under atypical or unusual financial terms—that is, at a time when the interest rate was significantly below the market rate—the adjustment becomes more complicated. In this case, the financial terms involved in the sale of the comparable property do not reflect the market in which the housing unit sold. Adjustments for market differences in financial terms are difficult to make. "It is difficult to estimate how much more the buyer paid for a given property because of a comparatively low down payment"[3] or a below-market interest rate.

Financial terms of the sale   This aspect of the search for comparable properties does not involve changes in the mortgage interest rate over time. The financial terms to be considered are the characteristics of the financing arrangement. "When comparing and contrasting comparable sales with the property being appraised, if the latter can be purchased with a conventional mortgage, the comparable properties should be those that have been purchased with the same type of financing."[4] (The various forms of financial arrangements are discussed in Part VI.) The type of financial arrangement the buyer can obtain can affect the sales price of the property. Therefore, to avoid inconsistencies, the subject and the comparable properties should be financed under the same arrangements, for example, conventional mortgage, FHA/VA mortgage, purchase money mortgage.

If the financial arrangements are generally the same, minor variations in the mortgage interest rate, in the length of the loan, or in the amount of the downpayment required can be reconciled by the adjustment process. As a general rule, if the actual mortgage interest rate on the comparable property is greater than the typical market rate, if the required down payment is higher than typical in the market, or if the maturity of the loan is shorter than typical in the market, the comparable property's sales price is adjusted upward. In essence, these conditions reduce the buyer's ability to pay a high sales price. Without these stringent conditions, the buyer would be able to pay more for the unit; in other words, the sales price would be higher.

The bundle of rights   The rights of ownership purchased in the sales price of the comparable properties and offered for sale with the subject property must be analyzed. The appraiser commonly finds that an easement has been placed on one property, but not on the others. If one of the comparable properties has an easement and the subject property has none, an adjustment must be made to the sales price of the comparable property. The sales price of the comparable property is adjusted upward to overcome the value-depressing effect of a diminished bundle of rights.

Conditions of the sale   Five necessary conditions define a competitive market. They are the following:

1. The buyer and seller are typically motivated and free of any undue pressure.
2. Both parties to the transaction must be informed about the market in which they are dealing.
3. Given this information, both parties must act rationally and their actions should be in their own self-interest.
4. The property must have been on the market for a reasonable amount of time.
5. Financing is on terms generally available and typical for the property type.[5]

If these market conditions did not apply in the sale of a certain property, that property must be rejected for use as a comparable property, even if it is similar in all other respects to the property being appraised. For example, an appraiser would reject from a list of comparable properties the ones that sold with unusually low down payments and below-market interest rates.[6]

The Adjustment Process

In the ideal situation, the subject property and all the comparable properties are identical in every detail. This situation could arise only if recent (i.e., yesterday's) market sales occurred for units that were all newly constructed units in a residential subdivision that contained identical structures on identical lots adjacent to each other, all financed by the same financial institution under identical terms. In this case, there should be no need for adjustments because the selling prices of the units would almost assuredly be the same. Consequently, the estimated selling price of the subject property would be equal to the selling price of the comparable properties.

However, this ideal situation is very unlikely. Generally, the comparable properties differ in some way from the subject property, and adjustments must be made to their sales prices to compensate for the differences. The process for making these adjustments is simple. First, the appraiser asks the following question: What effect does the presence or absence of a property feature or characteristic have on the probable sales price of the property? If the subject property contains an item or a characteristic that the comparable property does not have, the sales price of the comparable property is adjusted upward. In this case, the appraiser is asking the following question: What would have been the comparable property's sales price if it had possessed this additional factor? If the comparable property contains a feature that the subject property does not have, the sales price of the comparable property is scaled down by the dollar value of that feature.

Since one of the physical characteristics of real estate is heterogeneity, it is not surprising that perfect substitutes are difficult to find. There are always some differences in physical features of the on-site improvements. If the physical features are similar, there are differences in locational and neighborhood features. Finally, if the locational and neighborhood features are similar, there are differences in the time of sale.

As an operational principle, the appraiser should understand which features are most amenable to the adjustment process and thereby yield accurate results, and which features are difficult to measure and thus difficult to specify as a dollar adjustment. One of the factors most difficult to measure in dollar terms is the impact on value of neighborhood and locational features. Consequently, the appraiser should be diligent in choosing comparable properties that are in the same neighborhood as the subject property. Use of such properties eliminates the need for adjustments to overcome differences in the quality of the physical environment around the subject property, the safety of the area, and other variables discussed in the section on neighborhood analysis.

Another factor difficult to measure in dollar terms is the difference in the economic and demographic variables of the markets in which the subject and comparable properties sell. To eliminate the need for adjustment, the appraiser attempts to find comparable properties that sold in the immediate past. The close temporal

THE DECISION TO ESTIMATE MARKET VALUE

relationship validates the assumption that the subject property will sell in the same market as the comparable properties.

If the appraiser can control the neighborhood factors and date-of-sale considerations and thereby minimize, or totally eliminate, differences in these categories, the adjustment process can be limited to features that are much easier to measure in dollar terms. Consequently, the accuracy of the adjustments is increased and the adjustment process is subject to fewer criticisms. The adjustments that the appraiser can document and justify most easily are those representing differences in the physical features of the lot and the improvement. The documentation and justification are accomplished by referring to cost data or market evidence in the form of sales-price differences for houses with different features.

Exhibit 5-1 is a numerical example of the adjustment process. The items listed along the left side of the table are items of comparability. This list of items can be made very specific by identifying all subcategories of site, improvement, and neighborhood features, or the list can be made very general by including only the major topic headings such as physical features of the lot, physical features of the improvements, and neighborhood features. The example in Exhibit 5-1 represents a middle approach between the very specific and the very general.

The appraiser usually is commissioned to estimate current market value for the subject property. The appraisal problem is defined, and the general and specific data for the subject property are identified. The results of this analysis of the subject property are presented in the second column in Exhibit 5-1. The physical features of the subject property are the size of the lot, the shape of the lot, landscaping, square feet of livable space in the structure, structural condition, the age of the structure, and the age of the mechanical systems. In addition, the subject property has two special features, a cement block patio and attic storage space.

The neighborhood features of the subject property are stated in general terms, "Good, Average, and Fair" in descending order. The neighborhood is served by a school system that is considered to be of good quality. Other public services provided by the local government are also considered to be good. The neighborhood contains off-site improvements that are in good physical condition. Finally, the neighborhood's location in the urban area provides an average level of accessibility to employment opportunities.

The subject property is owned as a freehold estate of inheritance and there are no easements against the property. When the property sells, it will probably be financed under a conventional mortgage at an interest rate of 12 percent per year, a loan maturity of twenty-five years, and a down payment of 20 percent. Finally, the appraisal assignment is to place a current market value on the property and its fixtures, but no personal property will be included.

Having this information about the subject property, the appraiser can search for comparable properties. From a large pool of properties that have been sold, the appraiser first checks for sales that have taken place in the recent past in either the same or a similar neighborhood. Three such sales are found. One sale took place a week ago, a second took place a month ago, and a third took place four months ago. In addition, the three properties all sold under conventional financing with roughly the same interest rate and exactly the same loan maturity and downpayment require-

EXHIBIT 5-1   Comparative sales data for the market data approach

Item	Subject property
1. Sales price	?
2. Physical features of the lot	
a) Size	100 × 250
b) Shape	Regular
c) Other features (i.e., landscaping)	Average
3. Physical features of the improvement	
a) Size (in square feet)	2000
b) Condition and age of improvement	Average & 5 yr
c) Mechanical systems	5 yr old
d) Special features (1) Patio (cement block)	Yes
(2) Attic storage area	Yes
4. Neighborhood features	
a) Quality of schools + other public services	Good
b) Proximity to employment	Average
c) Physical condition of adjacent structures	Good
5. Time of sale	Current
6. Financial terms of sale (conventional mortgage)	12%, 25 yr, 20% down
7. Bundle of rights	No easement
8. Condition of sale	No personal property
Total adjustments	
Adjusted sales prices	
Value estimate of subject	$75,500

ments. They are all freehold estates of inheritance with no easements against the property. All three properties are the same physical size in terms of lot size and square footage in the improvement. Finally, the condition and the age of the improvements are roughly the same as those of the subject property. The appraiser has found the comparable properties required for the market data approach.

The appraiser now begins the analysis phase of the sales comparison approach. First, the physical comparability of property 1 with the subject property is checked. The two properties are the same size in terms of square feet of livable space. The condition of both structures is discovered to be average, but comparable property 1 is ten years old and the subject property is only five years old. This difference in age establishes a need for the first adjustment. The appraiser asks, "What would comparable property 1 have sold for if it were five years old and not ten years old?" Comparable property 1 has five additional years of wear and tear on its structural members, its fixtures, and its mechanical systems. This additional wear and tear is evaluated at $1,000 and the appraiser adds $1,000 as the adjustment to the sales price of property 1. The underlying assumption is that comparable property 1 would have sold for $1,000 more if it had been five years old instead of ten.

Next, the appraiser notices that comparable property 1 contains the same mechanical systems as the subject property but that a new furnace was recently

Comparable property 1		Comparable property 2		Comparable property 3	
$72,750		$77,250		$74,500	
100 × 250	0	100 × 275	−$500	100 × 250	0
Regular	0	Regular	0	Regular	0
Average	0	Good	−250	Fair	+$500
2000	0	2100	−2,000	2000	0
Average & 10 yr	+$1,000	Good & 5 yr	−1,000	Average & 6 yr	0
New furnace	−750			6 yr old	+200
No patio	+500			No patio	+500
Yes				No	+500
Average	+1,000	Average	+1,000	Good	0
Fair	+1,000	Average	0	Average	0
Average	+1,000	Good	0	Good	0
1 month ago	0	4 months ago	+750	1 week ago	0
12%, 25 yr, 20% down		11¾%, 25 yr, 20% down	−250	12%, 25 yr, 20% down	
No easement	0	No easement	0	No easement	0
No personal property	0	No personal property	0	Riding lawnmower	−400
+$3,750		−$2,250		+$1,300	
$76,500		$75,000		$75,800	

installed. The new furnace has an expected life of ten years and the cost was $1,500. The dollar adjustment, to be deducted in this case, is $750, half the value of the furnace, because the subject property's five-year-old furnace still has five years of expected life. Then the appraiser notices that comparable property 1 does not have a concrete block patio and the subject property does. If comparable property 1 did have a concrete block patio, and its installation cost had been $500, the sales price of the property would have been $500 more.

Next, the appraiser analyzes the neighborhood features and finds that the neighborhood surrounding comparable property 1 is inferior to the neighborhood surrounding the subject property. The quality of the school system is only average, there is only fair accessibility to employment opportunities, and the physical condition of adjacent structures is average. For each of these three features, the appraiser adds a $1,000 adjustment to the sales price of comparable property 1. These three adjustments each imply that comparable property 1 would have sold for more if it were located in the neighborhood surrounding the subject property.

In all other respects, comparable property 1 is identical to the subject property. Because comparable property 1 sold a month ago, the appraiser makes the judgment that the economic relationships in the market today are exactly the same as they were then. Comparable property 1 sold under conventional mortgage financing at the interest rate that prevails in the current market. Comparable property 1 has no easements and no personal property was exchanged in the sale.

The absolute value of the adjustments to comparable property 1 yields a positive adjustment of $3,750. By adding this figure to the actual price of $72,750, the appraiser obtains an adjusted sales price for comparable property 1 of $76,500. This adjusted sales price is interpreted as the current sales price of comparable property 1 under the condition that it is identical to the subject property in all respects.

The appraiser then goes through a similar analysis for comparable property 2 and the subject property. The necessary dollar adjustments are made in a similar manner. Briefly, comparable property 2 has a bigger lot with better landscaping than the subject property, so a negative dollar adjustment is needed for the physical features of the lot. The structure on comparable property 2 is larger and its condition is better, so a negative dollar adjustment is made for the physical features of the improvement. Comparable property 2 is in a neighborhood where the quality of schools is inferior to the quality of schools in the neighborhood surrounding the subject property. Therefore, a positive dollar adjustment is made to the sales price of comparable property 2 to reflect this feature. Comparable property 2 sold four months ago and the appraiser's best estimate is that the current and past markets are the same with the exception of inflation in building materials over time. Finally, comparable property 2 sold under conventional mortgage financing but the mortgage interest rate was $1/4$ of a percentage point lower. If comparable property 2 had sold under the current financial arrangement of a 12 percent mortgage interest rate, the buyer could have bid $250 more for that property. These adjustments result in a negative $2,250 adjustment. Subtracting this adjustment from the actual sales price of comparable property 2 gives an adjusted sales price of $75,000.

The appraiser then turns to an analysis of comparable property 3. This property is the same size and shape as the subject property, but the quality and the quantity of its landscaping are inferior. The structure is the same size as that of the subject property, and it is in approximately the same physical condition, but it is one year older. Due to the one-year age difference, the mechanical systems in comparable property 3 are a year older and a small positive dollar adjustment is required. Since comparable property 3 does not have a patio and does not have attic storage space, a dollar adjustment is required for each of these two special features.

Comparable property 3 is in the same neighborhood as the subject property, and no adjustment is required for neighborhood features. In addition, comparable property 3 sold one week ago under exactly the same financial terms as would apply to the subject property. The bundle of rights involved in the sale of comparable property 3 is the same as that for the subject property. However, comparable property 3 sold with a riding lawnmower valued at $400; the appraiser subtracts the $400 from the sales price of comparable property 3. Combining all of these dollar adjustments yields a positive adjustment of $1,300, which is added to the actual sales price of comparable property 3 for an adjusted sales price of $75,800.

After making these adjustments, the appraiser has three adjusted sales prices for the three comparable properties. The sales price of the subject property is now estimated from the adjusted sales prices of the comparable properties. Several methods can be used to obtain an estimate of value for the client. One method is to take the simple average of the three adjusted values. However, this practice is not viewed as acceptable because averaging a small group of numbers will produce a measure that may not reflect actual market value.[7] "The accepted procedure is to review each sale and judge its comparability to the property being appraised. Generally, the fewer and smaller the adjustments used on a comparable sale to produce the indicated value estimate, the more weight the sale is given in the final reconciliation. . . . The final value selected is a judgment made by the appraiser based on all the information available."[8] In the example, comparable property 3 requires the smallest adjustment and is also the most similar to the subject property in terms of the time of sale, the financial terms of the sale, and neighborhood features. The second most similar property is comparable property 2. Given these facts the appraiser could establish the market value as a single estimate between $75,000 and $75,800. For example, the single estimate of value could be $75,500. This figure is close to the adjusted sales price of comparable property 3, which is the most similar to the subject property, and is relatively close to the adjusted sales price of comparable property 2.

Some appraisers do not select a single figure but choose to present their client with a range of values. For the example shown in Exhibit 5-1, that range would be established from a low of $75,000 to a high of $76,500. The most probable selling price would be within this range but not at the end points.

The Applicability of the Sales Comparison Approach

The sales comparison approach for estimating the current market value of a piece of residential real estate is subject to certain limiting conditions that affect its applicability. The cornerstone of this valuation approach is the existence of comparable properties. If comparable properties can be found that are very similar to the subject property, the sales comparison approach is applicable. However, if comparable properties cannot be found, the sales comparison approach is inapplicable. An example of a property for which the sales comparison approach is not applicable is a property that is unique and does not sell frequently in the market. In this case, the comparable properties may have to be found among a limited number of nonlocal properties that may have sold several years in the past. Rather large adjustments would be needed to reflect differences in the economic and demographic features of the temporal and spatial markets.

The sales comparison approach is not applicable if the subject property and the potential comparable properties have some features that are very similar and some features that are very different. For example, the physical features of the lots and the improvements may be the same but the neighborhood features, the bundle of rights exchanged, or the financial terms of the sale may be very dissimilar. In this situation, the adjustments would be so severe that the accuracy of the value estimate would be suspect.

The sales comparison approach is also not applicable when the sale is not based on competitive market conditions (well-informed participants, no undue pressures on the participants, a reasonable exposure time for the property in the market, etc.). Finally, the sales comparison approach is not applicable when the financial arrangements surrounding the sale are highly dissimilar because different types of mortgages are used to facilitate the purchases.

THE COST APPROACH

The **cost approach** for estimating current market value is based on the recognition that a parcel of real estate is composed of two parts—the land and the improvements. The appraiser separates these two components of the real estate commodity and attempts to place a dollar value on each. To obtain a dollar estimate of market value for a specific residential site, the appraiser must analyze the market for residential land sales. To the value of the land, the appraiser adds the cost of constructing a building that is an exact replica or at least a close substitute for the subject property. Finally, if the subject property is not new, the cost of constructing the replica must be reduced by an estimate of the depreciation that the subject property has undergone. Each of these steps is described in the following sections.

Estimation of Site Value

Two basic procedures can be used for estimating the market value of the residential site; both rely on market data. One technique is the comparative procedure whereby comparable sites are compared with the land component of the subject property. The second technique is the allocation procedure that requires an initial estimation of the market value of the full residential property and then the division of the overall market value between land value and the value of the improvements on the site.[9]

The market comparison procedure   The market comparison procedure is similar to the sales comparison appraisal approach. The only difference is that there is no analysis of the physical features of an improvement in the market comparison procedure for estimating the value of land. The elements of this procedure are the analysis of the physical features of the lot, analysis of the locational attributes of the site, and neighborhood analysis. The geological features of the site, the location of the site, the availability of public services, and the quality of adjacent improvements can affect the market value of the site.

Once the appraiser finds comparable sites that are very similar to the subject property with respect to physical, locational, and neighborhood features, an adjustment process can be undertaken to compensate for any differences. Then the appraiser can examine the other aspects of comparability—the market conditions under which the comparable properties were purchased, the financing used in the purchase, and the bundle of rights that was transferred in each of the sales.

The allocation procedure   The allocation procedure is based on an analysis of parcels of real estate that have sold in the recent past. The land component of the comparable property must be very similar to the land component of the parcel that is being appraised. The sales price of the comparable parcel of real estate is then separated into the value of the land and the value of the improvement in the following way. The appraiser estimates the depreciated construction cost of the improvement and subtracts this figure from the actual sales price of the whole property. The difference between these two figures is the value of the land. If the subject property, viewed as a vacant parcel of land, is similar to the land component of this recently sold property, the appraiser has an estimate of the value of the subject land. To use this procedure effectively, the appraiser must analyze several comparable properties.

In actual practice, the market comparison method is used more extensively than the allocation procedure to estimate the value of the site in the cost approach. The market comparison method requires less time and effort. However, if comparable sales data are missing, the allocation procedure is useful as an aid to the comparative method.

Estimation of the Improvement Value

In the cost approach, the estimation process used to obtain a value for the structure is based on the cost to construct an exact replica of the subject property or at least a close substitute for it. A distinction must be made between *an exact replica* and *a close substitute* for the subject property. The key to this distinction is an understanding of the difference between reproduction cost and replacement cost.

The reproduction or replacement cost of new improvements   The **reproduction cost** is the current cost to construct a building that is exactly the same as the subject property in all respects. In the physical sense, reproduction denotes the fact that the replica is built with the same materials, workmanship, and technology as were used in the original construction of the subject property. Reproduction cost is the dollar outlay required to create the replica of the subject property based on current prices of building materials and construction labor. Conceptually, the materials and the workmanship should be exactly the same as those used originally in the construction of the subject property. However, some appraisers only require a high degree of similarity in materials and workmanship.[10]

The **replacement cost** is the current cost to construct a new improvement that serves the same purpose as the subject property and that is as useful as the subject property in meeting the needs of the owner. However, the new building is constructed with currently available building materials, workmanship, and technology. In addition, current standards, design, and layout are assumed in estimating the construction cost of the structure.[11] Replacement cost is the dollar amount that must be paid for labor and materials at current prices.

If the subject property is relatively new, reproduction cost should be used in estimating the construction cost of that property. The quality of building materials, the type of materials used, the workmanship involved in the construction process, and the techniques used in construction do not change drastically in short periods of time. A problem arises if the subject property is not relatively new. In this case, an alternative form of reproduction cost can be utilized; the appraiser can estimate the cost to construct the subject property to its actual physical specifications but with current materials, workmanship, and construction techniques. For example, if the house has 10-foot ceilings instead of 8-foot ceilings, the alternative reproduction cost would include the dollar expenditure of making the ceilings in all rooms ten feet high. Moreover, if the subject property has solid concrete foundation walls instead of cement block foundation walls, the alternative reproduction cost figure would estimate the dollar expenditure to reproduce the poured concrete foundation walls using current materials, workmanship, and standards of construction.

In the case of an old residential structure, the appraiser would use the replacement cost approach to estimate the cost of constructing a similar building that meets the needs of the owner. However, in this situation the appraiser would not estimate the construction cost for a building with 10-foot ceilings. The construction cost would be estimated for a building that meets current standards, design, and layout; it would have 8-foot ceilings and a concrete block foundation.

Reproduction cost is generally agreed to be the conceptual foundation for the cost approach to estimating value.[12] The decision to use reproduction cost is based on the notion that replacement cost, as a concept, "fails in practice because what is 'equal utility' cannot be measured directly, and the utility ends up being defined in terms of itself. . . . Because of the practical difficulties inherent in estimating Replacement Cost New, the cost approach and cost analysis almost always start measuring the present worth of improvements with an estimate of Reproduction Cost New."[13]

In summary, the cost approach is based on the estimation of reproduction cost for a new building. If the subject property is relatively new, the exact reproduction cost is estimated because the materials, workmanship, and techniques of construction have not changed since the subject property was initially constructed. If the subject property is not new, an alternative form of reproduction cost is used. In this case, the cost of constructing an exact replica is still estimated, but current standards of materials, workmanship, and construction technology are utilized in the cost estimate. The following section describes the methods that can be used to estimate the reproduction cost of a new improvement.

Methods of estimating reproduction cost   Three methods can be used by the appraiser to estimate the reproduction cost of a new structure—the quantity survey method, the unit-in-place method, and the comparative method.

The quantity survey method The **quantity survey method** is the most comprehensive of the three methods used to estimate construction cost. It is based on the premise that an appraiser can identify the quantities of all materials and labor used in the construction process. The appraiser must identify the units and the quantities of all materials used—for example, the number of cubic yards of concrete and/or the number of cement blocks used to construct the foundation. The number of 2 × 4 × 8 boards used in the construction of the structural frame must be specified. The number of plywood panels used to construct the exterior walls and the flooring must be identified. In essence, the appraiser identifies all the major and minor material items that go into the construction of the residential unit. In addition, the appraiser enumerates the labor required to assemble these materials. The appraiser ascertains the number of hours that concrete masons, brick masons, carpenters, plumbers, and electricians work to construct the finished product. When all of the material and labor inputs have been enumerated, they are multiplied by the current input price (i.e., each 2 × 4 × 8 costs $1.35, and each hour of a carpenter's time costs $11.25) to give the appraiser an estimate of the major direct costs incurred in the construction of the residential unit.

In addition to the direct costs of construction, the appraiser must estimate a dollar value for the indirect costs of construction. The components of indirect costs are fees for professional services of architects, engineers, surveyors, and lawyers; overhead expenditures of the developer; the cost of building permits and licenses; insurance premiums and property tax outlays during the construction process; the interest payments on the construction loan; and selling expenditures if the developer undertakes the marketing process. When these indirect costs of construction are added to the direct costs of construction on a per unit basis, the appraiser has a detailed estimate of the reproduction cost of a structure that is a replica of the subject property.

Because of the enormous degree of specificity required, and the need to know construction techniques, the quantity survey technique is rarely used in actual practice. However, an understanding of its structure does set the basis for an understanding of what the appraiser is attempting to accomplish in the estimation process to obtain the value of the improvement.

The unit-in-place method The **unit-in-place method** (also called the "subcontractors method"[14]) of estimating the reproduction cost of a new improvement is based on the realization that a structure consists of major components. The reproduction cost for the new improvement is estimated by calculating the cost of constructing each of the major components of the structure (the foundation, the frame and exterior walls, the flooring, the plumbing system, the electrical system, the roof, etc.). Each of these major components is installed by a construction firm that specializes in the installation of one or two of these structural members. When requested to perform such a service, each specialized construction firm or subcontractor calculates the full cost to construct or install the structural component. Each subcontractor estimates the cost of materials, the cost of labor, and the cost of equipment, as well as all the indirect costs. Upon completion of the direct and indirect cost estimates, the subcontractor specifies a price to install the component.

From the prices quoted by each of the subcontractors, the appraiser can obtain an estimate of the reproduction cost for a new improvement by simple addition. The unit-in-place method measures or estimates the same quantities as are estimated in the quantity survey method. The difference between these techniques is in their underlying assumptions. The quantity survey method is based on the supposition that a single entity constructs the house from beginning to end, whereas the unit-in-place method is based on the premise that the house is constructed by a group of specialists whose individual inputs are integrated in the completed structure.

The comparative method The **comparative method** for deriving the reproduction cost of a new structure is based on the availability of published data on construction costs for standard residential units, and the appraiser's knowledge of local costs of construction. For example, assume that a four-bedroom brick ranch house with 2,000 square feet of livable space and a two-car attached garage can be constructed for $38 per square foot. If the subject property is a similar type of residence with the same quality of materials, but containing only 1,900 square feet of livable space, a rough approximation of its construction cost can be obtained by multiplying 1,900 square feet by $38 per square foot. This multiplication yields a reproduction cost for the new structure of $72,200. If $38 per square foot accurately represents current prices, and if the construction techniques and materials used to build a 1,900-square-foot house are approximately the same as those used to construct a 2,000-square-foot house, then $72,200 is a fairly accurate estimate.

The appraiser can draw upon various data sources that provide construction costs per square foot for various sizes and types of residential structures.[15] In addition, data services provide figures on changes in the prices of building material and in the wage rates of construction labor. By using these data sources and local information, the appraiser can quickly estimate the reproduction cost of a residential structure in the local market. Conceptually, the comparative technique is the least accurate of the three cost estimating techniques because the appraiser must adjust the cost-per-square-foot figure to compensate for quality and quantity differences between the standard house and the subject property. However, in practice, the comparative technique may be the most accurate because the appraiser's expertise is not in the area of construction techniques that are required for the quantity survey and unit-in-place methods. The appraiser is probably more adept at making the adjustments required by the comparative method.

Estimation of Accrued Depreciation

When the reproduction cost has been estimated for a new structure, the appraiser recognizes that there are differences between the new structure and the subject property (which is not a newly constructed unit). These differences require an adjustment to account for all of the possible value-reducing phenomena that have affected the subject property. The dollar adjustment made to account for the value reduction is known as the **accrued depreciation**. As a background for the estimation of accrued depreciation, the appraiser examines three categories of value-reducing factors—physical deterioration, functional obsolescence, and economic obsolescence.

Physical deterioration **Physical deterioration** is defined as the reduction in value caused by wear and tear and/or disintegration of the structural components and fixtures of the building. Examples of physical deterioration are doors and windows that are difficult to open and close, cracks in plaster or wallboard caused by unusual amounts of settling, deterioration of roof shingles causing leaks and discoloration of ceilings, cracks in concrete foundations due to uneven settling, and a general wearing out of mechanical systems in the house due to continued use over time.

Physical deterioration is either curable or incurable, depending on the costs of repairing or replacing the deteriorating items in the structure. If the repair cost is less than or equal to the increase in the structure's value after the repairs are made, the physical deterioration is considered curable. However, if repair cost exceeds the increase in value consequent upon that repair, the physical deterioration is incurable.

The dollar estimate of physical deterioration is simply the cost to repair or replace the deteriorated component of the structure. Regardless of whether physical deterioration is curable or incurable, the appraiser must take note of it and estimate its value-reducing impact on the market value of the structure.

Functional obsolescence **Functional obsolescence** is defined as the reduction in value generated by inherent defects in the design of the structure or by changes in consumer attitudes toward the design of the structure and its fixtures. Regardless of the cause, functional obsolescence reduces the utility or satisfaction that the typical consumer derives from the property. Examples of functional obsolescence are 10-foot ceiling heights instead of the 8-foot ceiling heights now used to reduce heating and cooling costs, small room sizes and irregular room layout that make it difficult to use currently desirable sizes and styles of furniture, and antiquated fixtures (bathroom, lighting, etc.) that are not considered desirable by current standards.

Functional obsolescence is also subdivided into curable and incurable aspects. As in the case of physical deterioration, the distinction between the curable and incurable categories depends on the relation between the cost to replace and the value-enhancing effect that the replacement may have on the market value of the structure. If the replacement or addition of a factor in the house adds more to the market value than the cost of the change, the functionally obsolescent factor is considered curable. If the cost to replace, remove, or add exceeds the value-enhancing impact on market value, the functionally obsolescent factor is considered incurable.

The following quotation provides an excellent list of factors that are classified as curable functional obsolescence versus those that are classified as incurable functional obsolescence:

> Curable functional obsolescence usually includes such items as an insufficient number of electrical outlets, insufficient closet or cabinet space, too few doors or windows, and inadequate water heating capacity. Items of incurable functional obsolescence usually pertain to a structure's basic design and layout. Ceilings that are too high; inefficient traffic patterns; inadequate heating, electrical, plumbing, and air conditioning systems; and an insufficient number of bathrooms are good candidates for functional incurable obsolescence.[16]

Placing a dollar value on curable and incurable functional obsolescence is not as straightforward as it is in the case of physical deterioration. To establish a dollar value for functional obsolescence, the appraiser must ascertain three facts:

1. The cost to replace, remove, or add the feature to the structure as it is today
2. The cost to remove or add the feature when the structure was originally built
3. The increase in property value that results from the removal, addition, or replacement of the functionally obsolescent feature

Once these pieces of information are known, an estimate of functional obsolescence can be made. The dollar estimate of curable functional obsolescence is the difference between points 1 and 2 in the preceding list. It is the difference between (1) the construction cost of adding a missing factor, or removing a factor, in the house as it is today and (2) the construction cost of adding or removing this factor when the house was originally constructed. The underlying premise is that additions or removals after the initial construction are more expensive than inclusion or exclusion during the original construction phase.[17]

To estimate the dollar value of incurable functional obsolescence, the appraiser must determine the difference between points 3 and 2. The dollar estimate of incurable functional obsolescence is the difference between the value-enhancing aspect of the feature and the cost to include that feature in the original construction of the house.[18] For example, suppose the appraiser knows from experience that four-bedroom houses of a certain size, style, and quality located in a certain neighborhood typically sell for $2,500 more than three-bedroom houses of the same style and in the same neighborhood. This information reveals that the value enhancement created by the fourth bedroom is $2,500. Suppose that the appraiser also knows that the reproduction cost of that fourth bedroom is $3,500; in other words, there is a $3,500 difference in the construction costs of the four-bedroom and the three-bedroom residences. Given these two facts, the appraiser knows that the dollar value of incurable functional obsolescence in this case is $1,000, the difference between the $3,500 reproduction cost and the $2,500 market premium that is attached to a fourth bedroom.

Economic or locational obsolescence **Economic** or **locational obsolescence** is the value-reducing effect of changes in economic, demographic, or locational influences outside the property itself. It can be caused by changes in the economic, social, physical, and governmental factors of neighborhood analysis; by changes in the locational attributes of the site; and by changes in the economic and social factors of area analysis. "In an appraisal analysis of the property, economic obsolescence is not considered curable since the source is not inherent in the property."[19] The dollar value of incurable economic obsolescence is determined by an analysis of the market. The appraiser should identify comparable properties that are *not* affected by the value-reducing economic or locational obsolescence features and obtain the market value of such properties. Then comparable properties must be found that *are* affected by value-reducing economic or locational features and the market value of these properties must be ascertained. The dollar estimate of economic obsolescence is the difference between the market values of these two sets of comparable properties. For example, assume that the factor causing economic obsolescence is deterioration in the quality of adjacent structures. If comparable properties in the neighborhood are selling for $35,000, whereas comparable properties in a neighborhood that does not contain deteriorating structures are selling for $42,000, the dollar estimate of economic obsolescence is $7,000. This figure is subtracted from the reproduction cost of the new improvement to represent incurable economic or locational obsolescence.

In the case of an income-earning property, the value reduction can be established by examining the difference between rents of properties in a good neighborhood and those in a poor neighborhood. The difference in rent revenues between comparable properties serves as an indication of the value-depressing factors operating in the poor neighborhood. To calculate the value reduction, the appraiser determines the present worth of the difference in rent revenues.

Applicability of the Cost Approach

The cost approach for estimating market value requires three pieces of information—the market value of the site, the reproduction cost of a new improvement, and a dollar value for accrued depreciation. Once these three figures are known, the reproduction cost of the new unit is reduced by the dollar estimate for accrued depreciation and then the estimated market value of the site is added. The resultant figure is the estimate of the subject property's market value based on the cost approach.

The applicability and the accuracy of the cost approach depend on the following factors:

☐ The availability of market data for estimating site value

☐ The accuracy of the reproduction cost estimate

☐ The availability of data on repair costs to estimate physical deterioration

☐ The availability of market data and the accuracy of cost data for the calculation of dollar values for functional and economic obsolescence

The applicability and the accuracy of the cost approach also are influenced by the age of the subject property. The estimate for accrued depreciation is less accurate for an older structure. It is more difficult to calculate functional and economic obsolescence for an older structure that was built using different standards of construction and different construction materials.

THE RESIDENTIAL APPRAISAL FORM

The financial sector of the real estate business has adopted a uniform residential appraisal form. This form was initiated by the Federal Home Loan Mortgage Corporation (FHLMC) and the Federal National Mortgage Association (FNMA). These two organizations purchase mortgages from lending institutions such as savings and loan associations.

The structure of the uniform residential appraisal report reflects the data used by the appraiser as described in this chapter. Exhibit 5-2 is an example of the form. Side 1 of the form requires information about the neighborhood. It includes questions about the physical, economic, governmental, and social factors of neighborhood analysis.

Following the section on the neighborhood, there is a section on the site, which requires information about the size of the lot, the shape of the lot, its topography, the existence of a view, and its drainage capabilities. Information about current zoning, on-site utilities, and the availability of off-site improvements also is required.

The third section on side 1 of the residential appraisal form covers the improvements on the property. This section has four specific headings, "Improvements," "Room List," "Interior Finish and Equipment," and "Property Rating." The information requested is quantitative and qualitative and relates to the physical and functional aspects of improvement analysis.

EXHIBIT 5-2 Side 1

VALUATION SECTION

COST APPROACH

Purpose of Appraisal is to estimate Market Value as defined in Certification & Statement of Limiting Conditions (FHLMC Form 439/FNMA Form 1004B). If submitted for FNMA, the appraiser must attach (1) sketch or map showing location of subject, street names, distance from nearest intersection, and any detrimental conditions and (2) exterior building sketch of improvements showing dimensions

Measurements		No. Stories	Sq. Ft.
___ x ___	x ___	= ___	
___ x ___	x ___	= ___	
___ x ___	x ___	= ___	
___ x ___	x ___	= ___	
___ x ___	x ___	= ___	

Total Gross Living Area (List in Market Data Analysis below) _____

Comment on functional and economic obsolescence: _____

ESTIMATED REPRODUCTION COST – NEW – OF IMPROVEMENTS:

Dwelling _____ Sq. Ft. @ $ _____ = $ _____

_____ Sq. Ft. @ $ _____ = _____

Extras _____ = _____

Special Energy Efficient Items _____ = _____

Porches, Patios, etc. _____ = _____

Garage/Car Port _____ Sq. Ft. @ $ _____ = _____

Site Improvements (driveway, landscaping, etc.) = _____

Total Estimated Cost New . . . . = $ _____

Less   Physical | Functional | Economic

Depreciation $ ___ | $ ___ | $ ___ = $ (___)

Depreciated value of improvements . . . . . . = $ _____

ESTIMATED LAND VALUE . . . . = $ _____
(If leasehold, show only leasehold value)

INDICATED VALUE BY COST APPROACH . . . . $ _____

MARKET DATA ANALYSIS

The undersigned has recited three recent sales of properties most similar and proximate to subject and has considered these in the market analysis. The description includes a dollar adjustment, reflecting market reaction to those items of significant variation between the subject and comparable properties. If a significant item in the comparable property is superior to, or more favorable than, the subject property, a minus (-) adjustment is made, thus reducing the indicated value of subject; if a significant item in the comparable is inferior to, or less favorable than, the subject property, a plus (+) adjustment is made, thus increasing the indicated value of the subject.

ITEM	Subject Property	COMPARABLE NO. 1		COMPARABLE NO. 2		COMPARABLE NO. 3	
Address							
Proximity to Subj.							
Sales Price	$	$		$		$	
Price/Living area	$	$		$		$	
Data Source							
Date of Sale and Time Adjustment	DESCRIPTION	DESCRIPTION	+(–)$ Adjustment	DESCRIPTION	+(–)$ Adjustment	DESCRIPTION	+(–)$ Adjustment
Location							
Site/View							
Design and Appeal							
Quality of Const.							
Age							
Condition							
Living Area Room Count and Total	Total | B-rms | Baths	Total | B-rms | Baths		Total | B-rms | Baths		Total | B-rms | Baths	
Gross Living Area	Sq.Ft.	Sq.Ft.		Sq.Ft.		Sq.Ft.	
Basement & Bsmt. Finished Rooms							
Functional Utility							
Air Conditioning							
Garage/Car Port							
Porches, Patio, Pools, etc.							
Special Energy Efficient Items							
Other (e.g. fireplaces, kitchen equip., remodeling)							
Sales or Financing Concessions							
Net Adj. (Total)		☐ Plus; ☐ Minus $		☐ Plus; ☐ Minus $		☐ Plus; ☐ Minus $	
Indicated Value of Subject		$		$		$	

Comments on Market Data _____

INDICATED VALUE BY MARKET DATA APPROACH . . . . $ _____

INDICATED VALUE BY INCOME APPROACH   (If applicable) Economic Market Rent $ _____ /Mo. x Gross Rent Multiplier _____ = $ _____

This appraisal is made ☐ "as is" ☐ subject to the repairs, alterations, or conditions listed below ☐ completion per plans and specifications.

Comments and Conditions of Appraisal: _____

Final Reconciliation: _____

Construction Warranty ☐ Yes ☐ No   Name of Warranty Program _____ Warranty Coverage Expires _____

This appraisal is based upon the above requirements, the certification, contingent and limiting conditions, and Market Value definition that are stated in

☐ FHLMC Form 439 (Rev. 10/78)/FNMA Form 1004B (Rev. 10/78) filed with client _____ 19 ___ ☐ attached.

I ESTIMATE THE MARKET VALUE, AS DEFINED, OF SUBJECT PROPERTY AS OF _____ 19 ___ to be $ _____

Appraiser(s) _____   Review Appraiser (If applicable) _____

☐ Did   ☐ Did Not Physically Inspect Property

EXHIBIT 5-2 Side 2

RESIDENTIAL APPRAISAL REPORT

File No. _____

To be completed by Lender

Borrower	Census Tract _____ Map Reference _____
Property Address	
City _____ County _____	State _____ Zip Code _____
Legal Description	
Sale Price $ _____ Date of Sale _____ Loan Term _____ yrs	Property Rights Appraised ☐ Fee ☐ Leasehold ☐ DeMinimis PUD
Actual Real Estate Taxes $ _____ (yr) Loan charges to be paid by seller $ _____	Other sales concessions _____
Lender/Client _____	Address _____
Occupant _____ Appraiser _____	Instructions to Appraiser _____

NEIGHBORHOOD

Location	☐ Urban	☐ Suburban	☐ Rural
Built Up	☐ Over 75%	☐ 25% to 75%	☐ Under 25%
Growth Rate ☐ Fully Dev.	☐ Rapid	☐ Steady	☐ Slow
Property Values	☐ Increasing	☐ Stable	☐ Declining
Demand/Supply	☐ Shortage	☐ In Balance	☐ Over Supply
Marketing Time	☐ Under 3 Mos.	☐ 4–6 Mos.	☐ Over 6 Mos.

Present Land Use ___% 1 Family ___% 2–4 Family ___% Apts. ___% Condo ___% Commercial ___% Industrial ___% Vacant ___%

Change in Present Land Use ☐ Not Likely ☐ Likely (*) ☐ Taking Place (*)
(*) From _____ To _____

Predominant Occupancy ☐ Owner ☐ Tenant ___% Vacant
Single Family Price Range $ _____ to $ _____ Predominant Value $ _____
Single Family Age _____ yrs to _____ yrs Predominant Age _____ yrs

	Good	Avg.	Fair	Poor
Employment Stability	☐	☐	☐	☐
Convenience to Employment	☐	☐	☐	☐
Convenience to Shopping	☐	☐	☐	☐
Convenience to Schools	☐	☐	☐	☐
Adequacy of Public Transportation	☐	☐	☐	☐
Recreational Facilities	☐	☐	☐	☐
Adequacy of Utilities	☐	☐	☐	☐
Property Compatibility	☐	☐	☐	☐
Protection from Detrimental Conditions	☐	☐	☐	☐
Police and Fire Protection	☐	☐	☐	☐
General Appearance of Properties	☐	☐	☐	☐
Appeal to Market	☐	☐	☐	☐

Note: FHLMC/FNMA do not consider race or the racial composition of the neighborhood to be reliable appraisal factors.

Comments including those factors, favorable or unfavorable, affecting marketability (e.g. public parks, schools, view, noise) _____

SITE

Dimensions _____ = _____ Sq. Ft. or Acres ☐ Corner Lot
Zoning classification _____ Present improvements ☐ do ☐ do not conform to zoning regulations
Highest and best use: ☐ Present use ☐ Other (specify) _____

	Public	Other (Describe)	OFF SITE IMPROVEMENTS		
Elec.	☐	_____	Street Access: ☐ Public ☐ Private	Topo _____
Gas	☐	_____	Surface _____	Size _____
Water	☐	_____	Maintenance: ☐ Public ☐ Private	Shape _____
San. Sewer	☐		☐ Storm Sewer ☐ Curb/Gutter	View _____
☐ Underground Elect. & Tel			☐ Sidewalk ☐ Street Lights	Drainage _____

Is the property located in a HUD Identified Special Flood Hazard Area? ☐ No ☐ Yes

Comments (favorable or unfavorable including any apparent adverse easements, encroachments or other adverse conditions) _____

IMPROVEMENTS

☐ Existing ☐ Proposed ☐ Under Constr. No. Units _____ Type (det, duplex, semi-det., etc.) _____ Design (rambler, split level, etc.) _____ Exterior Walls _____
Yrs. Age: Actual _____ Effective _____ to _____ No. Stories _____
Roof Material _____ Gutters & Downspouts ☐ None Window (Type): _____ ☐ Storm Sash ☐ Screens ☐ Combination Insulation ☐ None ☐ Floor ☐ Ceiling ☐ Roof ☐ Walls

☐ Manufactured Housing
Foundation Walls _____

BSMT. ___% Basement ☐ Floor Drain Finished Ceiling _____
☐ Outside Entrance ☐ Sump Pump Finished Walls _____
☐ Concrete Floor ___% Finished Finished Floor _____
Evidence of: ☐ Dampness ☐ Termites ☐ Settlement

☐ Slab on Grade ☐ Crawl Space
Comments _____

ROOM LIST

Room List	Foyer	Living	Dining	Kitchen	Den	Family Rm.	Rec. Rm.	Bedrooms	No. Baths	Laundry	Other
Basement											
1st Level											
2nd Level											

Finished area above grade contains a total of _____ rooms _____ bedrooms _____ baths. Gross Living Area _____ sq. ft. Bsmt Area _____ sq. ft.

INTERIOR FINISH & EQUIPMENT

Kitchen Equipment: ☐ Refrigerator ☐ Range/Oven ☐ Disposal ☐ Dishwasher ☐ Fan/Hood ☐ Compactor ☐ Washer ☐ Dryer ☐
HEAT: Type _____ Fuel _____ Cond. _____ AIR COND: ☐ Central ☐ Other _____ ☐ Adequate ☐ Inadequate

Floors	☐ Hardwood ☐ Carpet Over	☐ _____
Walls	☐ Drywall ☐ Plaster	☐ _____
Trim/Finish	☐ Good ☐ Average ☐ Fair ☐ Poor	
Bath Floor	☐ Ceramic	☐ _____
Bath Wainscot	☐ Ceramic	☐ _____

Special Features (including energy efficient items) _____

ATTIC: ☐ Yes ☐ No ☐ Stairway ☐ Drop-stair ☐ Scuttle ☐ Floored ☐ Heated
Finished (Describe) _____
CAR STORAGE: ☐ Garage ☐ Built-in ☐ Attached ☐ Detached ☐ Car Port
No. Cars _____ ☐ Adequate ☐ Inadequate Condition _____

PROPERTY RATING

	Good	Avg.	Fair	Poor
Quality of Construction (Materials & Finish)	☐	☐	☐	☐
Condition of Improvements	☐	☐	☐	☐
Room sizes and layout	☐	☐	☐	☐
Closets and Storage	☐	☐	☐	☐
Insulation—adequacy	☐	☐	☐	☐
Plumbing—adequacy and condition	☐	☐	☐	☐
Electrical—adequacy and condition	☐	☐	☐	☐
Kitchen Cabinets—adequacy and condition	☐	☐	☐	☐
Compatibility to Neighborhood	☐	☐	☐	☐
Overall Livability	☐	☐	☐	☐
Appeal and Marketability	☐	☐	☐	☐

Yrs Est Remaining Economic Life _____ to _____ Explain if less than Loan Term _____

FIREPLACES, PATIOS, POOL, FENCES, etc. (describe) _____

COMMENTS (including functional or physical inadequacies, repairs needed, modernization, etc.) _____

Side 2 of the appraisal report is known as the valuation section. The appraisal approaches that appear on the form are the cost approach and the market data approach. For the cost approach, only the comparative method is used in estimating reproduction costs of the improvements. The appraiser can insert estimates for physical, functional, and economic obsolescence and an estimated land value to find the indicated market value by the cost approach.

For the market data analysis, the appraiser is required to examine the relationship between the subject property and three comparable properties in terms of the time, location, and site features. The next items considered are the design and appeal characteristics of the structure, the quality of construction, the age and the condition of the improvements, the size and number of rooms, the existence of a basement, and the functional utility or functional efficiency of the structure, as well as such features as air conditioning, garages, porches, patios, pools, fireplaces, and kitchen equipment. Finally, the appraiser analyzes any differences in the sale or financing aspects of the transactions. Once this information has been gathered and analyzed, the appraiser makes an estimate of the current market value by means of the sales comparison approach and states an opinion in the last section on side 2 of the form.

CHAPTER SUMMARY

To estimate the current market value of a single-family residential unit occupied by its owner, the appraiser generally relies on the sales comparison approach and the cost approach. To use the sales comparison approach, the appraiser identifies at least three recently sold comparable properties and examines them in relation to the subject property. Adjustments are made to the sales prices of the comparable properties to compensate for any differences from the subject property. The appraiser thus estimates current market value on the basis of information about the recent sales prices of very similar properties.

In the cost approach, the appraiser first estimates the land value by using a sales comparison approach. The reproduction cost of the structure then is obtained by either the quantity survey method, the unit-in-place method, or the comparison method. Typically, the comparative method is used. Once the reproduction cost of a new structure similar to the subject property is obtained, the appraiser adjusts it to reflect the value-reducing impact of the factors causing accrued depreciation of the subject property. These factors are physical deterioration, functional obsolescence, and economic obsolescence and may be curable or incurable. The dollar value of these factors is estimated and subtracted from reproduction cost. Finally, the appraiser adds the value of the land to this figure to estimate the current market value of the property.

Review Questions

1. List the elements of comparison that the appraiser uses to find properties comparable to the subject property.

2. After the comparable properties are selected, the appraiser uses an adjustment process in the sales comparison approach. Explain the purpose of the adjustment process and the manner in which the adjustments are made.

3. How does the appraiser obtain a value for the land when using the cost approach?

4. Differentiate between reproduction cost and replacement cost. Which does the appraiser typically use in the cost approach?

5. What is the relationship between the quantity survey method and the unit-in-place method for estimating reproduction costs?

6. What is accrued depreciation? What three elements does the appraiser consider in determining the value-reducing impact of accrued appreciation?

Discussion Questions

1. How does the appraiser estimate the market value of a unique residential unit? (The term *unique* implies that there are no comparable properties.)

2. What adjustments might the appraiser make when using the comparative method for estimating reproduction costs?

3. What are the most difficult types of adjustments needed in the sales comparison approach?

4. If the appraiser is using the cost approach, can the original sales price of the building lot be used as an estimate for the value of the land?

Notes

1. George F. Bloom and Henry S. Harrison, *Appraising the Single Family Residence* (Chicago, Ill.: American Institute of Real Estate Appraisers, 1978), p. 241.

2. *A Guide to Appraising Residences,* 3d ed., prepared by H. Grady Stebbins, Jr., for the Education Committee, Society of Real Estate Appraisers (Chicago, Ill.: Society of Real Estate Appraisers, 1976), p. 33.

3. William M. Shenkel, *Modern Real Estate Appraisal* (New York: McGraw-Hill Book Co., 1978), p. 139.

4. Bloom and Harrison, *Appraising the Single Family Residence,* p. 275.

5. Byrl N. Boyce (ed.), *Real Estate Appraisal Terminology* (Cambridge, Mass.: Ballinger Publishing Co., 1975), p. 137.

6. Shenkel, *Modern Real Estate Appraisal,* p. 139.

7. Bloom and Harrison, *Appraising the Single Family Residence,* p. 264.

8. Ibid., pp. 264–65.

9. Ibid., p. 137. Other methods exist but they aren't discussed here.

10. Ibid., pp. 212–13.

11. Boyce, *Real Estate Appraisal Terminology,* p. 176.

12. Bloom and Harrison, *Appraising the Single Family Residence,* p. 213.

13. William N. Kinnard, Jr., *An Introduction to Appraising Real Property* (Chicago, Ill.: Society of Real Estate Appraisers, 1975), p. 350.

14. Bloom and Harrison, *Appraising the Single Family Residence,* p. 217.

15. *Residential Cost Handbook* (Los Angeles, Calif.: Marshall and Swift Publishing Company); and *Boeckh Building Valuation Manual* (Milwaukee, Wis.: American Appraisal Co.).

16. Halbert C. Smith, *Real Estate Appraisal* (Grid Series in Finance and Real Estate; Columbus, Oh.: Grid, Inc., 1976), p. 115.

17. Ibid., p. 115.

18. Ibid.

19. Textbook Revision Subcommittee, *The Appraisal of Real Estate,* 7th ed. (Chicago, Ill.: American Institute of Real Estate Appraisers, 1978), p. 252.

Additional Readings

BLOOM, GEORGE F., and HENRY S. HARRISON. *Appraising the Single Family Residence.* Chicago, Ill.: American Institute of Real Estate Appraisers, 1978. Chapters 11–14.

BOYCE, BYRL, N., and WILLIAM N. KINNARD. *Appraising Real Property.* Lexington, Mass.: Lexington Books, 1984. Chapters 7, 8, 10, and 11.

DILMORE, GENE. "Appraising Homes." *The Real Estate Appraiser* (July–August 1974).

EPLEY, DONALD R. and JAMES H. BOYKIN. *Basic Income Property Appraisal.* Reading, Mass.: Addison-Wesley Publishing Co., 1983. Chapters 4 and 5.

KAHN, SANDERS A., and FREDERICK E. CASE. *Real Estate Appraisal and Investment.* New York: The Ronald Press Co., 1977. Chapters 7, 12, and 13.

KINNARD, WILLIAM N., JR. *An Introduction to Appraising Real Property.* Chicago, Ill.: Society of Real Estate Appraisers, 1975.

RING, ALFRED A. *The Valuation of Real Estate.* Englewood Cliffs, N.J.: Prentice-Hall, Inc., 1970. Chapters 10–13.

SHENKEL, WILLIAM M. *Modern Real Estate Appraisal.* New York: McGraw-Hill Book Co., 1978. Chapters 7–9 and 18.

SMITH, HALBERT C. *Real Estate Appraisal.* Columbus, Oh.: Grid, Inc., 1976. Chapters 3, 4, and 7.

STEBBINS, GRADY H., JR. *A Guide to Appraising Residences,* 3d ed. Chicago, Ill.: Society of Real Estate Appraisers, 1976: 33–68.

Textbook Revision Committee. *The Appraisal of Real Estate,* 8th ed. Chicago, Ill.: American Institute of Real Estate Appraisers, 1983. Chapters 13, 18–20.

WENDT, PAUL. *Real Estate Appraisal Review and Outlook.* Athens, Ga.: University of Georgia Press, 1974. Chapters 5 and 8.

6 | Income Property Appraisal

How does the appraiser use the income approach to estimate the current market value of a property that is an income-earning investment?

OBJECTIVES

When a student finishes the chapter, he or she should be able to

1. Identify the revenue sources and the operating expenses of an income-earning property.
2. Explain the structure and derivation of the capitalization rate.
3. Explain how the capitalization rate is used in the income approach to generate an estimate of market value.

IMPORTANT TERMS

Actual Gross Income
Band-of-Investment Technique
Basic Rate of Interest
Capital Improvement Expenditures
Capital Recovery Rate
Capitalization Rate
Contract Rent
Debt Service

Economic Life
Effective Gross Income
Ellwood Method
Gross Income Multiplier
Market Rent
Net Operating Income (NOI)
Operating Expense Ratio
Operating Expenses
Potential Gross Income
Sinking Fund Factor

AN OVERVIEW OF THE INCOME PROPERTY APPRAISAL PROCESS

The income property appraisal process is designed to estimate market value for a piece of property that generates an income payment to its owner. The typical income-earning properties are residential real estate in the form of apartment buildings, and commercial real estate in the form of offices and retail space in office buildings, shopping centers, and commercial districts. The owner of such a property negotiates a lease with another person for a portion, or in some cases all, of the parcel of real estate. The owner retains the right of disposition of the property and the leaseholder obtains the rights of possession and use and, to a limited extent, the right to exclude others (as discussed in Chapter 1). In return for giving away the rights of possession and use, the owner receives a payment known as *rent*.

The rent payment is the basis for estimating market value by the income property appraisal approach. As a very brief overview of the income property appraisal process, consider the following steps that the appraiser follows. First, the appraiser obtains an estimate of the rent revenues that the owner receives from the subject property. This income received by the owner is reduced by the expenses that the owner incurs in operating the property. The resultant dollar figure is known as **net operating income.** It is the number of dollars that the income property generates after meeting its expenses of operation.

The appraiser now needs a technique to convert net operating income into an estimate of value. The traditional technique is borrowed from the valuation of fixed income securities in the bond market. The value of a bond that has a very long maturity (usually considered to be many decades but conceptually considered as perpetuity) is estimated by using the following formula:

$$V = \frac{I}{r}$$

where

V = the value estimate,

I = a periodic income payment that is the number of dollars received by the owner of the asset less any expenses of ownership or operation, and

r = a discounting interest rate

As applied to real estate, this equation simply states the following relationship: the value of the income-generating parcel of real property is equal to the periodic income generated by the property divided by a discounting interest rate appropriate for that period of time. In appraisal literature, the discount rate is known as the **capitalization rate.** By this formula, if a parcel of real estate generates a periodic income payment of $10,000 per year, and the appraiser uses a capitalization rate of 10 percent per year, the value of the real property is $100,000.

The appraiser must consider many factors in determining the level of the periodic income payment that the investor would receive and the actual value of the capitalization rate that should be used. First, the rent payments and the expenses of operation associated with the property must be determined and analyzed. From these data, the appraiser calculates the property's periodic income (net operating income). Second, the appraiser must use a capitalization rate that adequately reflects the following three factors:

1. The typical owner's expectations about the financial benefits from this type of property

2. The nature and level of income that can be expected from other investment opportunities available to the typical investor, such as other real estate investments and nonreal estate investments (e.g., common stocks, preferred stocks, and corporate bonds)

3. The financial considerations involved in the purchase of the income-earning property

Although the concept of income property appraising is relatively simple, the actual process is very complex. The purpose of this chapter is to consider the many factors that must be analyzed in the process of identifying the property's income sources, its operating expenses, and the selection of the appropriate capitization rate.

INCOME ANALYSIS

An appraisal of income property starts with income analysis, which is the process of identifying the sources of revenue and level of income that will be earned by the property. Income analysis must be based on an understanding of three income concepts—actual gross income, potential gross income, and effective gross income.

Actual gross income is the total number of dollars actually generated by the property in the form of revenues from current rents. **Potential gross income** is the total number of dollars that the income-producing property *could* generate in the form of revenue if the rent prevailing in the market were charged. **Effective gross income** is an estimate of the number of dollars that might be received by the property owner after reducing potential gross income by an estimate of vacancy and rent collection losses.

The Concept of Potential Gross Income

The distinction between actual and potential gross income is based on the use of two different rent concepts—contract rent and market rent. **Contract rent** is "that rental income ascribable to the property as a result of contractual commitments which bind owners and tenants for a stipulated future time."[1] Contract rent is the rent payment actually being paid by the tenant and received by the property owner. The property's actual gross income is obtained by adding the contract rent revenues per unit of space for all units that are actually occupied.

In contrast, **market rent** is "the rental income that a property would most probably command on the open market as indicated by current rentals being paid for comparable space."[2] Market rent is the payment the property owner would receive if a tenant were found for the property in the current market. The property's potential gross income is the sum of the market rents for each of the rentable units contained in the property. To estimate the current market value of an income-producing property, the appraiser must estimate potential gross income for that property by using current market rent.

At any point in time, market rent and contract rent need not be the same. The current market rent can be greater than, equal to, or less than the contract rent, which may have been established one, two, or even ten years ago. At the time the contract rent was established, the economic circumstances in the market were more than likely different from those at the present time. The level of contract rent based on market circumstances two years ago should be different from the current market rent level.

If the appraiser is commissioned by the client to estimate the current market value of the income-producing property, the appraiser must seek one further clarification. This clarification involves a decision on the part of the client. Should the appraiser reflect only market conditions? Or should the appraisal also contain an analysis of the impact of the contract rents on the estimate of market value? The answer to both questions starts with market rent data used to generate potential gross income for the property. However, the second question requires an additional step in which the contract rents are used to adjust potential gross income. The adjustment can be positive or negative depending on whether contract rent is higher or lower than market rent.

The appraiser's responsibilities in this situation are indicated in the following statement:

> The property, too, must be considered in the light of its earning capacity in conformity with the principle of highest and best use. After value under these normal condi-

THE DECISION TO ESTIMATE MARKET VALUE

tions has been established, appropriate adjustments should be made to reflect economic advantages or disadvantages ascribable to limited contractual agreements or temporary managerial operating policies.[3]

In other words, the appraiser must always use market rent to project potential gross income. Then, at the client's request, the appraiser can make adjustments for the current contract rents for the space in the building.

Revenue Sources

To determine the level of potential gross income that a property can generate, the appraiser must identify all rentable space in that structure. This space, whether it is the number of apartment units or the floor area in square feet, must be priced at the prevailing market rate for similar space in competitive properties. In addition to the rentable space in the structure, the appraiser must identify other sources of potential gross income such as parking facilities for the tenants of the building. If the structure is an apartment building, the tenants may receive one parking space as part of the package of services they buy with their rental payment. However, a second parking space for the household's second car or a covered parking space may cost an additional $15 per month.

Another source of revenue that can add to potential gross income is the provision of other services such as washing machines and dryers in apartment buildings, and vending machines in office buildings and in commercial retail facilities. The owner of the property can receive such revenue in either of two ways. The fixtures can be purchased and operated by the owner, or the owner can sell the right to provide these services to some other person. In either case, the owner receives additional income. However, additional expenses are also incurred when the owner decides to purchase the equipment and provide the services. These additional expenses must be considered and in some way charged against the revenues that they generate.

When market rent is multiplied by the rentable space in the building, and when other sources of revenue are added to this figure, a quantitative measure of potential gross income is obtained. In addition to this quantitative aspect of the income stream, the appraiser must consider a qualitative aspect. The major factor that affects the quality of the potential gross income generated by the property is the uncertainty surrounding the actual receipt of rent payments. The owner and the appraiser are always uncertain about the exact level of future potential gross income that the property will generate. Market rents can change unexpectedly. They may actually decline when expectations are that they will increase, or rents may increase but not as much as anticipated. In addition, tenants might default on their agreement and not pay the stipulated contract rent. The degree of uncertainty determines the quality of the income stream. The higher the level of uncertainty, the lower the quality of the potential gross income generated by the property.

These quantitative and qualitative aspects of potential gross income are examined in greater detail in the next two sections.

Revenue Characteristics and Patterns that Affect the Quantity of Potential Gross Income

Several characteristics of an income stream affect the absolute number of dollars that the income-producing property generates. An income-producing property generates potential gross income for the current year *and for many years into the future*. To estimate the market value of an income-producing property, the appraiser must take both current and future potential gross income into account. For the most part, the revenue characteristics described in this section are related to this time element.

Duration of the Income Stream   The duration of the potential gross income stream of a property is related directly to the remaining economic life of the structure or improvement on the parcel of real property. The **economic life** of a structure can be defined in two ways. First, it is the number of years that the structure is expected to provide useful service. (Sometimes it is called *useful life*.) In terms of income or revenue, economic life is the number of years over which a positive net operating income (gross income minus expenses) will be realized.[4] Another definition of economic life involves the generation of a competitive level of net operating income (gross income minus expenses) instead of a positive net operating income. Here the economic life would be the number of years during which the property generates financial returns to its owner that are competitive or comparable to the returns generated by similar types of income-earning property. Whichever definition is chosen in order to predict the economic life to the improvement, the appraiser must consider the physical and functional features of the building, as well as the economic and demographic factors that affect the market in which the building's services are sold. If the building provides space for several uses, such as apartments and office space, then the economic factors in each market must be analyzed.

The physical characteristics of the improvement determine the physical life of the improvement, which is defined as "the period over which an improved property may be expected to remain in existence and to be capable of generating any gross income through services produced."[5] The physical life of the improvement establishes an upper limit to the economic life of the structure; the economic life of the improvement cannot exceed the physical life of the improvement. Therefore, a discussion of the duration of the potential gross income stream is in fact a discussion of the economic life of the improvement on the property. The appraiser is concerned with the length of time over which the property will generate an income that is sufficiently large to cover the costs associated with the building if the first definition of economic life is used or, alternatively, with the time required to provide a competitive return on the investment if the second definition of economic life is used.

The factors that affect economic life, whichever way it is defined, are the economic and demographic variables that affect the market in which the services of the building are sold. The economic life of the improvement can come to an end if the demand for its services declines while the number of buildings providing space for those services remains constant. In this situation, the market rent must decline, causing a decline in gross potential income. When the income level falls to the point where it just barely covers the costs of operating the building, or even falls below the

THE DECISION TO ESTIMATE MARKET VALUE

level of those costs, the economic life of that improvement has ended. The same result can occur if the demand for the improvement's services is constant but the number of buildings providing the services increases. In this situation, market rent may fall or vacancy rates may rise to the point where potential gross income does not exceed the costs of operating the structure. Clearly, a prediction of economic life must be based on an analysis of the dynamic aspects of the market.

An improvement can have several economic lives within the span of its physical life. As one economic life ends, another economic life may start. The ability of the structure to adapt to changes in demand for its use is a functional characteristic of that structure. The greater the building's adaptability to change (functional efficiency), the greater the possibilities of lengthening the total economic life of the structure by establishing a second or a third economic use. The structure's ability to adapt to changing demands for its services depends on its design and space layout.

The longer the total economic life of the improvement, the greater the potential gross income that can be generated. A building that generates positive or competitive returns for thirty years should generate more total potential gross income than a building that receives the same market rent but has an economic life of only twenty-five years.

The timing and pattern of the rental payments   If a building has a given economic life, and if a dollar received today is worth a little more than a dollar received next year, the pattern by which the rental payments are received becomes an important consideration in estimating potential gross income. For example, assume that the economic life of the building is one year and the owner can use one of two rent payment patterns:

1. An annual payment made by the tenant at the beginning of the year, or
2. An annual payment made by the tenant at the end of the year.

These two rent payment schemes generate two different levels of potential gross income. To calculate the levels of potential gross income, assume that the annual rental payment is $1,200, which can be paid in monthly installments of $100, and that the current interest rate is 10 percent (chosen only for simplicity of arithmetic). Under payment pattern 1, when the owner receives the $1,200 on January 1, he or she places that $1,200 in the bank for the full year. On December 31, the potential gross income generated is $1,200 plus 10 percent of $1,200, a total potential gross income of $1,320. Under payment pattern 2, the tenant delivers $1,200 to the landlord on December 31. In this case, potential gross income is $1,200 because no interest is earned. The timing of the payment between the start of the period and the end of the period affects the level of potential gross income by a rate that is equal to the market rate of interest. Thus, an owner can maximize total potential gross income over the economic life of the structure by receiving payment in advance, at the beginning of whatever payment interval is used.

Variability of the payment pattern over time   In the foregoing example the rent payment is assumed to be constant over time. However, changes in the magnitude of the payment over time can affect the total amount of income to be received. If the economic life of the improvement is five years, and over the five-year period the property generates $6,000 in rental payments, the manner in which the full $6,000 is paid to the owner affects total income. For example, assume that the tenant can make payments to the landlord in any of the three patterns shown in Exhibit 6-1.

Utilizing the fundamentals of compound interest theory, the landlord finds that the total potential gross income plus interest return for each of these payment schemes is as follows:

        □ Payment pattern 1 = $8,058
        □ Payment pattern 2 = $8,569
        □ Payment pattern 3 = $7,549

These figures are generated under the assumption that the owner receives the rental payment from the tenant at the beginning of each of the annual periods and that the current interest rate is 10 percent.

If two identical properties return the same total income over identical economic lives, the greatest interest payment is accumulated by the property that has high rent receipts in the first years and lower rent receipts in the latter years of the economic life span. This is evident in the numerical example because payment pattern 2 generates a $6,000 rental payment over the five years of economic life, and in addition generates $2,569 of interest payments during the same five-year period.

Contract rents that differ from market rents Market rent is used as the basis for determining potential gross income for the property that is being appraised. However, after making this calculation, the appraiser might have to consider the impact of a difference between contract rent and market rent. A difference necessitates an adjustment to the potential gross income figure. This adjustment could be positive or negative, depending on whether the contract rent exceeds or is less than the market rent.

If contract rent is less than market rent, the appraiser assumes that when the one-year lease agreement expires, the new contract rent to be established in the future will equal the market rental rate. If contract rent exceeds market rent, the appraiser assumes that when the lease expires at the end of twelve months the owner will be able to rent space only at the rate established by the market, $100 per month.

EXHIBIT 6-1 Three hypothetical payment patterns

	Pattern 1	Pattern 2	Pattern 3
Year 1	$1,200	$2,000	$ 400
Year 2	1,200	1,600	800
Year 3	1,200	1,200	1,200
Year 4	1,200	800	1,600
Year 5	1,200	400	2,000
Total	$6,000	$6,000	$6,000

Factors that Influence the Quality of Potential Gross Income

The factors that influence the qualitative aspect of potential gross income are related to the degree of uncertainty about the actual receipt of the rental payments by the owner. One qualitative factor that the appraiser considers is the financial responsibility of the tenant. The owner of the property anticipates very little uncertainty in collecting the rental payment if the tenant is considered to be financially responsible or has a good credit rating. In other words, the owner of the property faces very little risk that the tenant's financial position will interfere with ability to pay the rent.

A second qualitative factor related to the tenant is the degree of that person's nonfinancial responsibility. Lease agreements contain clauses that require the tenant to perform stipulated actions such as keeping the property in good repair by avoiding undue wear and tear. A tenant who does not act in the prescribed manner may have to be removed by the landlord. If such an action does take place, the rent payment is interrupted until a new tenant is found.

The nature of the rental agreement itself can also affect the level of certainty about the future rent payments. The lease may contain provisions that could nullify the rental agreement. One such provision is known as the *transfer* clause in a residential lease. If the tenant is transferred to a new job that is at least fifty miles away from the apartment building, the tenant can void the lease. Such statements in the lease increase the risk that the owner will not be receiving the market rent over the full term of the lease.

Another qualitative factor that affects potential gross income is the degree of accuracy associated with the projections of future market rent levels. In the process of determining potential gross income, the appraiser must make forecasts about future market rent levels. Therefore, the appraiser must forecast the economic and demographic factors that affect both demand and supply in the market for the space provided by the subject property. All such forecasts are based on uncertainty. Thus, the risk factor associated with forecasting future market rent rates—the risk of forecast error—affects the quality of the potential gross income figure.

Quality of management also can affect potential gross income. The basic assumption made by the appraiser is that the subject property and comparable properties in the market are under "good management." Efficient systems for rent collection can maintain a stable flow of income. In addition, an effective tenant selection process can reduce problems associated with rent collection, vacant apartments, and the turnover rate of tenants. The risk associated with the management function is that the assumption of high-quality management is erroneous or will be incorrect in the future. In either case, the actual level of potential gross income may not be as high as it should be if an inefficient manager does not know the market rent and leases the space at less than market rates.

Income Projections and Their Effect on the Quantity of Potential Gross Income

The preceding discussion on quantitative factors affecting potential gross income (the duration, timing, pattern, and variability of the rental payment) is based on the assumption that the exact magnitude of rent payments is known. However, future market rents and thereby future levels of potential gross income are known with only limited certainty. The appraiser must forecast these future market rent levels by analyzing the market in which the property's services are sold. All the pertinent economic and demographic features affecting both demand and supply must be analyzed. The dynamic changes in these variables must be anticipated.

In essence, the appraiser must consider the economic factors used in both area analysis and neighborhood analysis as well as the full scope of factors used in locational analysis. At a minimum, the appraiser must be able to forecast future levels of real disposable income; the number and composition of the households in the community; the number of properties in competition with the subject property; changes in locational attributes based on shifts in residential, employment, and commercial locations; and changes in neighborhood factors that would make the subject property more or less desirable to the consumer. If the appraiser can forecast an increasing level of demand for the services provided by the subject property, a constant supply of competitive space, a stable neighborhood that maintains its present quality, and little, if any, change in other significant variables, the appraiser can forecast an increase in market rents. However, the exact level of those future market rents is subject to error whether the appraiser uses an educated guess or undertakes some sophisticated mathematical or statistical projection of the future rent level.

Vacancy and Income Loss Considerations

Potential gross income is an estimate of the subject property's maximum income-earning potential given current and future market conditions. However, the appraiser is not interested in what the property could generate in the form of income as an end product. The appraiser is interested in the income level that the property actually should generate from its full potential. In other words, the appraiser calculates potential gross income as the starting point of the income appraisal process but makes an adjustment to potential gross income to obtain an income figure that represents the anticipated revenues of the property. This adjusted income level is known as *effective gross income* and it is defined as "the anticipated income from all operations of the real estate after allowance for vacancy and collection loss."[6]

To estimate vacancy and collection loss, the appraiser considers the following items of information:

1. The vacancy rate by type of residential unit or type of commercial space
2. Rent payment problems such as nonpayment or partial payment of rent
3. Special concessions made to the tenant that have a monetary value
4. Losses due to vandalism or theft

When the earning potential of an income property is considered, the appraiser must realize that some space in that structure may be vacant for some period of time during its economic life. This situation could occur even if the property is fully occupied in the current period. A tenant may have to be evicted because the

THE DECISION TO ESTIMATE MARKET VALUE

rent is not paid or for some other violation of the lease arrangement. Also, demand for such space may decline. In this case, there will be an abundance of available rental space and a shortage of tenants at the current market rent. The owner of the property may have to make concessions such as a rent exemption (a free first month), free parking for the household's second car, or even a contract rent below the current market rent to attract enough tenants to keep the property fully rented. If the owner is not successful with these concessions, space will be vacant in the building. Finally, even if damage by vandals and theft of fixtures have never occurred, such losses can be incurred in the future. Therefore, to establish the effective gross income projections for the property, the appraiser must make a negative adjustment to potential gross income to reflect the four events that can cause vacancy and income loss for the property.

There are three general sources of information about the magnitude of these vacancy and income losses. One source of data is the historical record of the subject property itself. The appraiser can analyze the property's records over the last four or five years to establish a figure for annual losses in the four categories. Then, the appraiser can assume that the magnitude of such losses will be the same in the future if the financial quality of the tenants, the quality of the neighborhood, and the relative market activity of the buyers and sellers remain constant in the future.

The historical records of comparable properties represent the second source of information on these income losses. The appraiser obtains figures for such losses from comparable properties and uses them as a check against the estimates for the subject property.

The third data set consists of surveys that are occasionally made by trade associations. Such surveys usually are made on a national or regional basis for different types of residential and commercial property. They provide the appraiser with an understanding of the vacancy and income losses for similar kinds of property in the nation or at least in the region in which the subject property is located. Since the data are for nonlocal comparable properties, the appraiser views this information as a less important and less definite check against the data gathered about the subject property and local comparable properties.

Potential gross income is the first element of analysis in income property appraisal. From this income figure, the appraiser subtracts vacancy and income losses to obtain a revenue estimate known as effective gross income. Having obtained this figure, the appraiser can examine the next important component of income property appraisal—the current and future operating expense of the property.

ANALYSIS OF OPERATING EXPENSES

The **operating expenses** incurred by the owner of an income-producing property are the annual cash payments that are a necessary cost of generating effective gross income. The important phrase in this definition is "necessary cost of generating effective gross income." To identify the operating expenses of the property, the appraiser must consider only expenditures that are necessary for the operation of the property and that are associated with the property. If an expenditure is associated with the owner's personal needs or the operation of another property, the appraiser must ignore it in the appraisal of the subject property.

Classification of Operating Expenses

Operating expenses traditionally have been grouped into variable expenses, fixed expenses, and reserves for replacement. *Variable expenses* include cash outlays that change with the level of occupancy in the structure. As more residential units or more commercial space is leased to tenants, certain cash outlays increase in magnitude. There are several major expenditure items in this category:

1. *Payroll and personnel* expenses include salaries, social security contributions, payments to unemployment insurance, and all other fringe benefits provided by the property owner to the employees working in the subject property. In some instances, the fringe benefits include a rent concession on the maintenance superintendent's apartment in the subject property.
2. *Management fees* are the expenditures incurred by the owner for rent collection, tenant selection, marketing the property, and other such administrative work. The payment for these management services can be made to an independent property manager, or they may be made to the owner for the time and effort expended in this activity.
3. *Utilities* expense includes all payments made by the owner for electricity, natural gas, heating oil, water, sewer service, and trash collection.
4. *Supplies and materials* expense includes only those items that are used in the normal operation of the property. These supplies and materials are not fixtures of the property; they are the owner's personal property used to make the property habitable and clean. This expense category includes the payments made by the owner for light bulbs, rug cleaning solutions, floor wax, paint, and other general cleaning and repair supplies.
5. *Grounds care* expenses are the maintenance expenditures for improvements made on the property other than to the main building. Maintenance expenditures for parking lots, access roads, and sidewalks would be included in this category, as would expenditures incurred in connection with the lawn, landscaping, the swimming pool, tennis courts, and patios.

The second type of operating expense is known as *fixed expenses*. These cash outlays do not vary with the level of occupancy in the structure. Their magnitude is relatively constant whether the property is fully occupied or whether the property is entirely vacant. Traditionally, the two most important fixed expenditures are as follows:

1. *Property taxes* are the actual tax dollars paid by the owner of the property. Property taxes are considered a fixed operating expense because they are levied by local governments as payment for public services provided to the inhabitants of that property. A well-maintained street net-

work, reliable police protection, and an up-to-date school system, for example, affect both the desirability and satisfaction of the structure to the tenants.

2. *Property insurance,* another fixed expense, requires a cash outlay by the owner to insure the property against such hazards as fire, theft, and vandalism. In addition, the owner must carry liability insurance on those portions of the property for which the courts hold the owner responsible. The property owner should carry liability insurance to cover the common areas against personal injury incurred by tenants and their guests. However, the owner need not carry liability insurance for the space leased by the tenants. The courts hold the tenant responsible for personal injury incurred within the leased space.

The third category of operating expense is *reserves for replacement.* These expenditures are the payments made by the owner for short-lived items such as appliances that are provided with the apartment unit, for heating and cooling equipment in the structure, and for other parts of the building that must be replaced periodically; for example, elevators, escalators, light fixtures, revolving doors, carpeting, and plumbing fixtures. The economic life of these fixtures is much shorter than the economic life of the major improvement or structure. Every five or ten years, they must be replaced. Therefore, the owner must have a reserve of funds from which money can be drawn to replace these items as they wear out.

Expense Items Excluded From the Appraiser's Operating Expense Statement

The operating expense statement used by the appraiser does not include many items that are viewed as expenses by the owner of the property. Conventional profit and loss statements include all expenses incurred by the owner with respect to the property. Some of these expenses are inappropriate for the appraiser's purposes because they are not cash outlays that are a necessary cost of generating the effective gross income from the property. Consequently, the appraiser excludes the following expenses in preparing an operating expense statement for the purpose of income property appraisal.

Income taxes   Personal and corporate income taxes are excluded from the appraiser's operating expense statement because they are expenses of the owner, not of the income-producing property. The exact level of the income tax payment varies with the taxable earnings of the individual or the corporation. Even though these expenditures are important to the owner, and even though they can influence the decision to buy the property, the value estimate must not include them in the total of operating expenditures.

Debt service   Debt service is the annual payment made by the owner of the property to repay the loan. It is the sum of the annual interest charge on the mortgage and the principal repayment made during the year. Even though this payment is an expense incurred by the owner of the property, the expenditure is not necessary to generate effective gross income. The property has the same income-generating potential whether it was purchased with borrowed money or purchased by the owner for cash. If borrowed funds were used, the property has the same income-generating potential whether it was purchased on a thirty-year mortgage or a five-year mortgage. Moreover, the property has the same income-earning potential whether the interest rate on the borrowed fund is 9½ percent per year or 3 percent per year. Consequently, the operating expense statement should not include the mortgage repayment or debt service payment.

The exclusion of debt service from operating expenses can be justified for another reason. The more sophisticated techniques used to generate the rate of capitalization incorporate the debt service consideration into the process of calculating the capitalization rate. In this way, mortgage features are reflected in the appraisal process even though the exact mortgage payment is not considered an expense.

Tax depreciation expenses   Capital recovery or depreciation expenses are an important item and must be considered by the appraiser at some point in the income property appraisal process. The generally accepted manner of treating this expense item is to consider it as a deduction when computing Federal income taxes and not as a separate expense item in the appraiser's operating expense statement.[7]

Capital improvements or capital outlays   These expenditures are made by the owner to improve the property. They are typically payments for remodeling; replacement of functionally obsolescent equipment that still operates but does not suit consumer preferences; and upgrading the level of services by including patios, covered parking, and other amenities. **Capital improvement expenditures** are made only when the owner is certain that the property's income-producing potential will increase sufficiently to cover the cost of the improvement. This increase in the income-producing potential can occur if market rent, and thus the contract rent, can be increased, or if the economic life of the improvement is extended. The appraiser does not treat these expenditures as operating expenses for purposes of income property appraisal.[8] Capital improvement expenditures do not generate current effective gross income as do the products or services provided by operating expenses. Capital improvements increase the level of future effective gross income by raising rent revenues or lengthening the economic life of the property. Thus, the impact of capital improvement expenditures is seen as an increase in the income-generating potential of the property, and this is the way they are reflected in the appraisal process.

Other expenses of the owner   A distinction must be made between certain other expenses that the owner charges against the property and the operating expenses used by the appraiser in the income property appraisal process. True operating expenses are instrumental in generating effective gross income. For this reason, expenditures such as "charitable contributions, traffic or other fines, entertainment expenses, cost of lawsuits, damage awards, and similar extraneous and personal expenditures"[9] must be excluded from the list of operating expenses used by the appraiser. In addition, any payments made by the owner for supervisory or management activities that are neither performed for, nor essential to, the operation of the property must also be excluded.

The Operating Expense Ratio

Knowledge of the subject property's operating expense ratio is useful to the appraiser for two reasons. First, it can provide a check or a benchmark against which the appraiser can judge the reasonableness of the estimation of the subject property's operating expenses. This task is accomplished by examining operating expense and effective gross income data for comparable properties in the local community and in the nation as a whole. Several publications provide this information to the appraiser.[10] Second, the operating expense ratio is useful in judging the property's operating performance.

The typical **operating expense ratio** used by investors and appraisers is found by dividing total operating expenses by effective gross income. An acceptable value for the ratio depends on the nature of the improvement. Apartment buildings that differ in numbers of units, size of the rooms, and elevator systems will have different acceptable operating expense ratios. The ratio for apartments is different from the operating expense ratio for commercial buildings. As a general operational procedure, the appraiser assumes that competent property management acts to keep the level of effective gross income high and the level of total operating expenses low. Therefore, a low operating expense ratio is the ideal.

The appraiser should realize that the level of operating expenses can be lowered by minimizing or reducing expenses. For example, the operating expense ratio can be reduced by lowering the level of repairs and maintenance. However, such a reduction is not always beneficial. If necessary repairs are not made, both the level of operating expenses and the operating expense ratio fall; this should make the property more desirable. But, if the repairs are not made, the physical deterioration can cause increased vacancy levels or reduced contract rents in the future. The net effect may well be a reduction in future levels of effective gross income.

The appraiser and the investor should know the variables used to construct the operating expense ratio. The numerical value of the ratio could be lower if potential gross income, instead of effective gross income, is used as the denominator of the ratio, because vacancy losses are not considered in potential gross income. The operating expense ratio can also be low if some category of operating expenses, such as reserves for replacement, is not included in the numerator of the ratio. Therefore, the appraiser and the investor should ask for a definition of the terms and the values used in generating the operating expense ratio.

THE CONCEPT OF NET OPERATING INCOME (NOI)

After the appraiser has calculated effective gross income and total operating expenses, net operating income can be calculated. It is simply effective gross income minus total operating expenses. The importance of net operating income (NOI) to the appraiser is simple to understand. NOI is the numerator in the valuation formula discussed at the beginning of the chapter. It is the income figure that is divided by a capitalization rate to obtain an estimate of the property's market value.

Current Period NOI and the Need to Forecast Future Levels of NOI

In the preceding discussion of effective gross income and operating expenses, the appraiser calculated these income and expense figures for the current period. Exhibit 6-2 is a numerical representation of the property owner's income statement based on acceptable accounting procedures. Exhibit 6-3 is the appraiser's reconstruction of this income statement into an income property operating statement that is appropriate for the purpose of income property appraisal. Comparison of these two exhibits reveals that the accountant's level of net income is significantly different from the appraiser's estimation of net operating income for appraisal purposes. First, the appraiser has excluded those expense items that are not directly related to the generation of potential gross income. Second, the appraiser has adjusted the rent revenue figure used by the accountant to reflect market rents and not contract rents. Third, the appraiser has incorporated a vacancy and collection loss factor that does not appear in the accountant's statement.

However, an estimate of current period NOI is not the conceptually appropriate income figure to use in the income property appraisal process. The income approach for estimating the current market value of a property is based on the principle of anticipation, which "affirms that value is created by the expectation of benefits to be derived in the future."[11] This definition emphasizes the concept of future benefits. "The primary value of past experience arises from its significance for the estimation of possible future trends and conditions. . . . The assembled data is then analyzed, and appropriate factors are weighed in order to form an opinion

EXHIBIT 6-2 The property owner's income and expense statement

Revenues (24 units)		
Rent receipts: 14 (2-bedroom) units @ $225/mo	$42,840.00	
8 (1-bedroom) units @ $220/mo	21,120.00	
Laundry room collections	1,276.80	
Parking fees ($12/additional space for 2nd car)	1,296.00	
Total revenues		$66,532.80
Expenses		
Management fee (5% of rent receipts)	$ 3,326.64	
Property taxes	6,640.00	
Building custodian (salary—½ time sharing)	6,600.00	
Insurance premium	1,725.00	
Maintenance, repairs, and supplies	3,980.00	
Utilities	7,925.00	
Natural gas $2,871.00		
Water $ 924.00		
Electricity $4,130.00		
Mortgage payments (10%, 20 years)	$22,952.00	
Replacement of appliances	2,400.00	
Depreciation	8,500.00	
Misc. administration costs (legal fees, accountant fees, etc.)	2,400.00	
Total expenses		$66,448.64
Income for the year		$ 84.16

concerning whether the net income stream may be expected (under typical management and business conditions) to continue, to decline, or increase." [12] The current operating statement prepared by the appraiser is the assembled data from the past that can be used as an aid in forecasting future levels of net operating income.

The source of the actual data used in the operating statement is an important issue. Since the appraiser is attempting to place a market value on the subject property, he or she uses income and operating expense data from comparable properties as the main source of information. Then, the specific data from the subject property is used as a check. If the resultant figures are substantially different in any of the income or expense categories, the appraiser checks the estimates to see why the differences occurred. For example, the subject property's operating expenses could be substantially lower than the operating expenses for comparable properties. This situation could result from a greater degree of management efficiency by the owner of the subject property, or it could occur because maintenance and repair expenditures are being deferred. In either case, the actions are not assumed to be typical of the potential buyers in the market. The appraiser will use the estimate of operating expenses generated for comparable properties. However, the appraiser might discover that the subject property uses less energy than its comparable properties that are similar in all other respects except the degree of insulation in the structure. In this case, the appraiser would use this information to lower the operating expense estimate for the appraisal. In summary, the appraiser attempts to discover the market. Consequently, the information from the market, the data on comparables, is the first line of information. The data from the subject property is used as a check and a basis for sound, documentable adjustments to the data from the market.

EXHIBIT 6-3 The reconstructed income and expense statement

Revenues (24 units)		
Potential rent receipts: 14 (2-bedroom) units @ $260/mo		$43,680
10 (1-bedroom) units @ $220/mo		26,400
Less vacancy and collection losses (4%)		−2,800
Parking fees		1,300
Laundry room collections		1,300
Effective gross income		$69,880
Expenses		
Management fee		$ 3,500
Property taxes		6,700
Building custodian		6,600
Insurance premiums		1,750
Maintenance, repairs, and supplies		4,000
Utilities		8,000
Natural gas	2,875	
Water	925	
Electricity	4,200	
Replacement of appliances		2,400
Misc. administration costs		800
Total operating expenses		$33,750
Net operating income		$36,130

Forecasting Future Levels of NOI

Since the income property appraisal process is based on the principle of anticipation, the appraiser must analyze future levels of net operating income. However, the only readily available information is historical data about the operation of the subject property and historical data about the operation of comparable properties. From these data, the appraiser can evaluate short-term and intermediate-term trends in the historical operating expense items. In addition, the appraiser must evaluate the probable impact of dynamic changes in economic and demographic variables on future levels of potential gross income, effective gross income, and net operating income.

To forecast future levels of potential gross income, the appraiser must forecast future trends in the economic and demographic factors that affect that market of which the property is a part. Once these trends are forecast, the appraiser can determine their impact on market rents. For example, assume that the subject property is a small apartment complex in a desirable section of the city. The appraiser can forecast an increase in market rents if the following market trends occur: increases in the number of households in the age groups that desire apartment living; continuation of the neighborhood's desirability and accessibility to employment opportunities; stability in the local zoning pattern that deters construction of competing properties.

If, however, the appraiser forecasts a reduction in the absolute size of the 18- to 25-year-old and the over-55 age groups in the population, if changing neighborhood factors will make the property less desirable, and if comparable properties are being constructed in other more desirable neighborhoods, the appraiser can forecast declining market rent. Many other combinations of market and neighborhood factors could indicate changes in market rent levels. The examples are used to illustrate how market and neighborhood analyses are used in forecasting future market rent.

Having established a probable direction of change in the level of market rents, the appraiser can estimate the change in the level of the property's potential gross income. However, the exact magnitude of the change is still an educated guess.

The appraiser can develop proxy relationships to represent future economic and demographic changes. For example, the appraiser may determine that future increases in the number of households over the next five to ten years will be approximately the same as increases in the population over the past ten years. In addition, the appraiser may determine that construction of new apartments over the next ten years will be approximately equal to construction of new apartments over the past ten years. These two pieces of proxy information provide a basis for forecasting future market rent levels. Similarly, the appraiser can assume that the market rent increase in one- or two-year increments in the future will be equal to the percentage increases by similar increments over the past five years. The appraiser may assume that after the five-year period market rent will remain constant for a decade and then gradually decline as the building reaches the end of its projected economic life of about forty years.

Alternatively, the appraiser may forecast that future levels of the economic and demographic variables will stay approximately as they are today and have been

THE DECISION TO ESTIMATE MARKET VALUE

in the recent past. In addition, historical data for the subject property and comparable properties may reflect that the rent level has been constant over the last five years. In this case, the appraiser can assume that the rent level will stay constant for at least the next five years. After that point, the market rent may decline as the building ages and nears the end of its projected economic life.

The assumption that at some point in time market rents will decline is logical, even if the initial forecast shows an increase in market rent. The structure ages and all economic and demographic factors affecting the property will not remain stable for the remaining economic life of the property. As the building ages, less will be offered for its space because its floor plan and design are less popular (functional obsolescence). Furthermore, as the subject property ages, the adjacent structures in the neighborhood also age. This economic obsolescence of neighborhood features and services reinforces the inevitability of declining market rent in the later years of the property's economic life in its current use. The phrase "in its current use" is important because it indicates that the property is not improved, rehabilitated, or renovated. If capital improvements are made, the building is in a different market after the rehabilitation and enters another period of economic life in the new use.

The appraiser must also forecast future levels of operating expenses. In the majority of cases, the appraiser can rely on published data to obtain a reasonable estimate of what happens to various operating expense items as the building ages. The appraiser can apply this information as a first step in forecasting future levels of expense items starting with the current year's figures as the base. For example, as the building ages, the expenditures for maintenance and repair on a per unit basis increases if the owner is attempting to keep the structure in good condition.

However, the data available from published sources may not be adequate unless past trends can be determined. For example, payments for utilities, property tax, and insurance have increased steadily for several years. Therefore, the appraiser can reasonably assume that utility costs will continue to rise in the near future at a rate that is comparable to their increase in the last three or four years. Insurance rates have been steadily rising as the cost to reconstruct the improvement continues to rise. Thus, a good proxy for changes in the insurance payment would be an extrapolation into the future of changes in building material and construction labor costs over the last three or four years.

A projection of property tax payments is more difficult to make because of the apparent trend to shift the revenue-generating structure of local government away from real property taxes to nonproperty taxes such as income tax or a sales tax. In addition, future levels of property taxes are difficult to predict because of the movements to put a ceiling on local governmental budgets. If such actions are likely or have already been taken in the local community of the subject property, the appraiser can assume that the current property tax bill will not be exceeded in the future, and that the future property tax bill for the subject property may decline. If the local community has established a ceiling for the property tax bill as some percentage of the property's market value, the appraiser can assume that the property tax payment will in some way reflect the path of potential gross income.

Exhibit 6-4 is a net operating income pattern generated for a hypothetical subject property over a ten-year ownership period. The underlying assumptions used to generate the figures in Exhibit 6-4 are as follows:

1. Market conditions are such that market rent will rise over the first years of the economic life of the building and then slowly decline.
2. Vacancy losses will always be at a rate comparable to that of similar properties in the market. Those rates should always reflect existing vacancy rates of those comparable properties.
3. All operating expense items will increase over time with the exception of property taxes, which will decline as the building ages.

The first three years of the remaining economic life are explicitly shown in Exhibit 6-4. The column headings in the table represent the first, second, third, and the fourth through tenth years of the ownership period. To make the calculations and the exhibit less cumbersome, the income and expense items for years 4–10 are represented by a single value. For example, the income figure of $73,010 is given as the yearly effective gross income value for each of the fourth through tenth years. The assumption is that this one income figure stated for each of the years is a good proxy for the actual pattern of income that may exist in this time period. Exhibit 6-4 serves as a basis for the following discussion of the capitalization process.

EXHIBIT 6-4 The reconstructed income and expense statement: Ten-year ownership period.

	Year 1	Year 2	Year 3	Years 4–10
Revenues (24 units)				
Potential rent receipts: 14 (2-bedroom) units	$43,680	$44,520	$45,360	$45,360
10 (1-bedroom) units	26,400	27,000	27,600	27,600
Less vacancy and collection losses (4%)	−2,800	−2,860	−2,950	−2,950
Parking fees	1,300	1,300	1,300	1,500
Laundry room collections	1,300	1,300	1,400	1,500
Effective gross income	$69,880	$71,260	$72,710	$73,010
Expenses				
Management fee (5%)	$ 3,500	$ 3,600	$ 3,650	$ 3,650
Property taxes	6,700	6,900	7,100	7,000
Building custodian	6,600	6,800	7,000	7,500
Insurance premiums	1,750	1,800	1,850	1,950
Maintenance, repairs, and supplies	4,000	4,100	4,200	4,800
Utilities	8,000	8,400	8,800	9,600
Natural gas 2,875				
Water 925				
Electricity 4,200				
Replacement of appliances	2,400	2,400	2,600	2,900
Misc. administration costs	800	800	800	1,000
Total operating expenses	$33,750	$34,800	$36,000	$38,400
Net operating income	$36,130	$36,460	$36,710	$34,610

THE DECISION TO ESTIMATE MARKET VALUE

THE CAPITALIZATION PROCESS

The process of converting net operating income into an estimate of market value is known as the capitalization process. The derivation of the property's net operating income is described in the preceding section. The appraiser's next task is the derivation of the capitalization rate.

Derivation of the Capitalization Rate

The capitalization rate is always composed of two rates of return that serve different purposes. One of these rates is the **basic rate of interest.** It reflects current phenomena in the financial markets where the investor will borrow funds and simultaneously represents a rate of *return on the investment.* The second rate is the **capital recovery rate** for the investment. It represents the accrued depreciation of the improvement over its economic life. It is a *return of the investment.*

A typical investor who purchases income-producing property fully expects to receive a rate of return on the equity that is put into the investment. The reasoning process is similar to that of an investor who puts $40,000 into a savings account with the expectation of receiving a rate of return on that money.

In addition, the typical investor wants a return *of* the investment. Unlike a savings account, the income-producing property can undergo a loss in the value of the equity over time. As the property ages it becomes less valuable. The investor therefore needs some way to recover the equity put into the investment. For example, assume the investor holds the property for ten years and that after ten years the property is worth three-fourths of its current value. Consequently, the investor needs to have that 25 percent reduction in value returned over the period of ownership. In this case, the investor would want 2.5 percent of $10,000 returned in each year. This 2.5 percent is a capital recovery rate that is calculated using a straight-line depreciation technique.

Regardless of whether the basic rate of interest and the capital recovery rate of the investment are stated explicitly as two separate entities, they are both conceptually included in the rate of capitalization.

The overall rate of capitalization   The overall rate of capitalization is derived from the market. The appraiser identifies several comparable properties that have sold in the recent past and obtains both their sales price and level of net operating income. This information can be found in the appraiser's own data files or can be gathered from commercial brokers or even property owners. As an example, assume that a duplicate property to the subject property recently sold for $250,000 and that its NOI is $35,000. In this case, the overall rate of capitalization is obtained by using the following simple equation:

$$\text{NOI/Sales Price} = \$35,000/\$250,000 = 0.14 = 14\%$$

If reliable market data are available for comparable investment properties, the overall rate of capitalization from such market comparisons can be used. However, the necessary data on such comparable properties are frequently not available. Moreover, if the properties are not similar, a significant number of adjustments to the sales price would have to be made, and this technique for obtaining the rate of capitalization would lose its validity and its applicability. The subject property and the comparable properties must have the following elements of similarity if the overall rate of capitalization is to be used:

1. Similar types of property with essentially the same remaining economic lives, physical condition, and relationship of the site to the improvement
2. Similar neighborhood and locational characteristics
3. Similar terms of financing involved in the purchase
4. Similar terms of sale and market conditions prevailing at the time of the sale
5. Similar income streams that represent the same timing, stability, and risk
6. Similar types of buying motivations underlying their purchase
7. Arm's length transactions surrounding the sale.[13] (The term *arms length* is defined as "a transaction freely arrived at in the open market, unaffected by abnormal pressure or by the absence of normal competitive negotiations as might be true in the case of a transaction between related parties.")[14]

If the use of an overall capitalization rate cannot be justified because of the lack of comparable properties, the appraiser must turn to an alternative method of deriving the rate of capitalization. The alternative method requires that the appraiser calculate a basic rate and a capital recovery rate. Some techniques calculate these two entities as separate items. Other techniques calculate a single value that is a composite of a basic rate and a capital recovery rate. This latter process is the more widely used procedure in current appraisal practice.[15] However, in order to explain the underlying concepts involved in the generation of a capitalization rate, the following discussion is very useful.

The basic interest rate The fact that real estate is typically purchased with borrowed money is significant in the process of deriving the basic rate. The typical purchaser of real estate borrows money at a specified interest rate, and the amount of money borrowed is a stated percentage of the value of the property. For example, in the current market, purchasers of real estate may be typically required to pay 10 percent of the sales price as a down payment and allowed to borrow 90 percent of the sales price at an interest rate of 10 percent per year. Given this information, the appraiser can generate the basic interest rate.

The band-of-investment technique The process used to generate the basic rate component of the capitalization rate is known as the **band-of-investment technique.** The following numerical example explains how it is used. Assume the following facts:

THE DECISION TO ESTIMATE MARKET VALUE

L/SP = the ratio of the loan to the sales price typically
given in the mortgage market   = 0.8

i = the interest rate on borrowed funds   = 0.10

E/SP = the ratio of funds that the buyer pays as a down
payment (the equity) to the sales price   = 0.2

i_e = the buyer's expected rate of return on the
investment in the current market   = 0.16

From these facts, the basic interest rate is calculated in the following manner:

$$
\begin{aligned}
(L/SP)\,(i) &= 0.80 \times 0.10 = 0.08 \\
+\ (E/SP)\,(i_e) &= 0.20 \times 0.16 = \underline{0.032} \\
\text{Basic rate} & = 0.112
\end{aligned}
$$

This numerical example, which focuses on the use of one mortgage, yields a basic rate of 11.2 percent. However, one factor in this calculation must still be analyzed. An assumption was made that the typical investor or buyer expects a 16 percent rate of return on an investment made in the subject property. The magnitude of this expected rate of return must be high enough to attract funds to the investment. In the market, the typical investor's opinion about the level of this expected rate of return reflects his or her opinion about risk plus several other factors that affect a real estate investment. This point will be discussed in greater detail later in this section.

The band-of-investment technique can also be used in situations where the buyer anticipates the need for more than one loan to purchase the property. In this instance, one individual holds a first mortgage on the property and a second individual holds a second mortgage (to be discussed in Chapter 18). The individual or financial institution holding a second mortgage is in a less than advantageous position and consequently requires a higher interest payment. The following example illustrates the generation of the basic interest rate when two loans are obtained to purchase the property.

L_1/SP = the ratio of the first loan to the sales price   = 0.70

i_1 = the interest rate on the first loan   = 0.10

L_2/SP = the ratio of the second loan to the sales price   = 0.20

i_2 = the interest rate on the second loan   = 0.12

E/SP = the ratio of the buyer's fund for equity to the
sales price   = 0.10

i_e = the investor's expected rate of return on the
investment   = 0.16

$$
\begin{aligned}
\text{First loan:} \quad & 0.70 \times 0.10 = 0.070 \\
+\ \text{Second loan:} \quad & 0.20 \times 0.12 = 0.024 \\
+\ \text{Equity:} \quad & 0.10 \times 0.16 = \underline{0.016} \\
\text{Basic rate} \quad & 0.11
\end{aligned}
$$

The basic rate calculated from this numerical example is 11 percent. The band-of-investment technique for calculating the basic rate can be used in a similar manner for calculating the basic rate in situations where the investor obtains three or more loans to buy the property. A third loan would be included in the process in the same manner as the second loan. No matter how many loans the buyer obtains, the sum of the loan/sales-price ratios and the equity/sales-price ratio must equal one.

Every investor realizes that there are certain types of investment for which there is very little risk of losing all or even part of the invested funds. Two such investments are government bonds and savings accounts in insured savings and loan associations and commercial banks. The federal government provides the ultimate backing for both of these safe, virtually riskless savings opportunities. Government bonds are considered safe because the federal government's power to tax and, thereby, raise revenues insures that it will not become bankrupt. Deposits in insured savings accounts are backed by two agencies of the federal government, the Federal Deposit Insurance Corporation (FDIC) and the Federal Savings and Loan Insurance Corporation (FSLIC). Each of these safe investments pays a return to the saver in the form of an interest payment. The interest payment on these riskless or safe investments forms the lower limit of the typical investor's expected rate of return. As an example, assume that government bonds are paying a higher rate than savings accounts, and that the rate is 8 percent per year.

A typical investor who places accumulated savings into a real estate investment would expect to receive a rate of return that is at least equal to the interest rate on a safe or riskless investment. However, real estate is not a safe or riskless investment. Therefore, some additional return must be generated to compensate for the risk of loss faced by the investor and future owner of the property. There are no guarantees that in two, three, or five years the property can be sold for an amount of money equal to its current sales price. There are no guarantees that the gross effective income generated by the property will continue at its current level. How much does the typical investor require to compensate for such risk? Evaluation of this risk is highly subjective and may vary greatly from one investor to another. The appraiser, however, must recognize the importance of such risk and must obtain some intuitive understanding of its magnitude for the type of property being appraised. For the numerical example, assume that the appraiser envisions a 3 percent addition to the safe rate of return as sufficient compensation for the risk that the typical investor will face.

The investor who fully considers the real estate market must also evaluate the economic characteristics of the real estate commodity. First, the typical well-informed investor realizes that, unlike the government or the savings account, real estate cannot be converted into cash quickly. In other words, it is not a liquid asset. Real estate is a very illiquid asset. A long period of time usually is required to convert real estate investments into cash without taking a loss in the value of the investment. A government bond can be converted into cash in several business days. A "day-to-day" savings account in a savings and loan association can be converted into cash within a matter of hours. In the case of a long-term savings certificate, the investor may lose an interest payment in order to convert the certificate into cash but does not suffer any loss in the value of the investment. At most, it may take thirty days to turn such a long-term savings account into cash. However, in the case of real estate, it may take several months to convert the property into cash. The typical investor in real estate therefore requires an additional return over and above the safe rate to compensate for the loss of liquidity.

As a numerical example, assume that the typical investor in the market requires an additional 1.0 percent return to compensate for illiquidity. How is this numerical value obtained? The appraiser must have an intuitive feeling and understanding of the typical investor's motivation and concern about this factor. There is no quantitative source that lists an exact level of compensation for illiquidity. At best, the appraiser and the investor know that the illiquidity factor is less in an active market for the property; consequently, the appraiser and the typical investor realize that the illiquidity premium must rise when a dull market is forecast for the near future.

The next factor that the investor recognizes is that a real estate investment requires a certain degree of management that a government bond or savings account does not. Someone must make the disbursements associated with the various categories of operating expenses. Utility bills, tax bills, repair bills, and salaries must be paid. In many cases, an account must be established to hold funds for replacing fixtures and major components of the structure. Someone must maintain the financial records associated with the property. All these activities are time-consuming tasks. They can be performed by the owner or they can be performed by a property manager. In either case, the owner incurs an additional expense. Time must be devoted to this activity, or money must be paid to hire the services of a property manager. The appraiser can estimate the compensation required by the typical investor for the burden of management associated with real estate. Property management companies charge a percentage of the property's gross income. The appraiser can use these management fees as a proxy for the premium that the typical investor would expect as compensation for the extra burden associated with investment in real estate. The management fee depends on the type of property and the volume of services that the property owner requests. As an example, assume that the management fee associated with the type of service and the type of property is 4 percent.

The preceding numerical example indicates how the investor could decide upon an expected rate of return of 16 percent. This numerical value is the sum of the interest payment on the safe riskless investment plus the risk premium, plus the illiquidity premium, plus the percentage of gross income established as the management fee. However, the subjectivity associated with determining the risk of loss and the illiquidity premium make this summation process an unacceptable technique for an appraiser to use to calculate the investor's expected rate of return.[16]

If the appraiser does not use this intuitive summation process to establish directly a numerical value for the expected rate of return, how is a numerical value determined? The answer depends on the appraiser's understanding of the market in which this type of property is sold. From discussions with clients and colleagues, the appraiser can obtain information about the anticipated rates of return and the actual rates of return that typical investors have received from similar investments. Such information might show that most investors in this class of property receive between 15 and 18 percent on their investment. Therefore, the appraiser can deduce that the typical investor would probably receive 17 percent on the equity invested in the property.

Refinements in the band-of-investment technique In the simple band-of-investment technique, the loan/sales-price ratio, the equity/sales-price ratio, the interest rate on the loan, and the investor's expected rate of return on the investment are used in calculating the basic rate. However, the typical investor also considers other factors. First, the investor would be concerned about the maturity date of the mortgage loan. If $50,000 is borrowed at a rate of 10 percent for forty years, the monthly repayment of this loan is less than the monthly payment required to pay back a loan of $50,000 at 10 percent for ten years. Consequently, the length of the mortgage loan is an important consideration for the investor because it affects the size of the monthly mortgage payment. The simple band-of-investment technique ignores the length of the mortgage in its calculations.

Second, the investor would be concerned with the fact that over time the equity/sales-price ratio increases as the mortgage loan is paid off. Assume, for example, that the buyer invests 10 percent of the value of the property on the day of purchase; over time, as the mortgage loan is paid off, the owner's funds account for more than 10 percent of the original sales price. The investor's equity is increased because the principal of the loan is being paid off. In a sense, the investor is investing additional equity funds in the property. The simple band-of-investment technique ignores this phenomena of increasing equity due to mortgage loan payment. Hence, the basic interest rate as calculated by the band-of-investment technique is understated (and the value of the property is overstated).

A related matter of concern to the investor is that this equity increase due to the mortgage repayment is taking place at the mortgage rate of interest and not the investor's expected rate of return. In other words, instead of receiving 16 percent as a return on the increase in equity the investor only receives a 10 percent return. The simple band-of-investment technique ignores this factor.

The third factor that the typical investor considers is the length of time that property will be held. The simple band-of-investment technique does not consider this point. However, it is an important consideration to the investor because the length of ownership of the investment determines the amount of equity increase due to mortgage repayment. If the investor holds the property for ten years instead of five years, the investor's equity increase is greater.

A more sophisticated version of the band-of-investment technique, which takes these additional factors into account, can be used to generate the basic rate. This advanced form of the band-of-investment technique is known as the **Ellwood method** for deriving a rate of capitalization. The Ellwood method mathematically reflects "varying combinations of mortgage and equity ratios over investment or ownership life periods of one to thirty years at preselected mortgage interest and equity yield rates."[17] In other words, the Ellwood technique allows the appraiser to calculate the basic rate by considering the following pieces of information:

□ The mortgage interest rate
□ The loan/sales-price ratio

- ☐ The equity/sales-price ratio
- ☐ The investor's expected rate of return
- ☐ Equity increases due to mortgage repayment
- ☐ The duration of the mortgage loan
- ☐ The investor's anticipated length of the investment

The basic rates that can be derived under different combinations of these factors are presented and published in a series of tables known as the *Ellwood Tables*.[18] In addition, the Ellwood technique allows the appraiser to consider changes in the future resale value of the property.

The basic capitalization rate and specifically the rate component is calculated by using this refined band-of-investment technique. In applying the Ellwood technique, the appraiser must identify the typical investor's ability to obtain mortgage financing and the financial arrangements involved in that mortgage. Because the financial arrangements are considered in the calculation of the basic interest rate, the appraiser does not consider the mortgage payment as an operating expense of the property. Moreover, the risk of ownership and the various costs of ownership are considered in the development of the investor's expected rate of return from the property.

The capital recovery rate The second component of the capitalization rate is the capital recovery rate, which provides for the return of the investment over the property's economic life. Because the property is composed of land plus the structure, and because only the structure is a wasting asset that can lose value as it ages, only the portion of the investment that represents the value of the building needs to be recovered by the investor. The value of the land is not recaptured because the assumption is made that land has an exceptionally long economic life. The capital recovery rate is the percentage of the building's portion of the sale price that needs to be returned to the investor annually over the projected economic life of the building. For example, if a building has a remaining economic life of forty years, then, 2½ percent of the value of the structure must be returned to the investor every year over the forty-year period in order for the investor to obtain 100 percent of the building's initial value. This calculation is made on the assumption that a straight-line recovery of the investment is desired. If the remaining economic life of the property is twenty years, it is easy to calculate that the annual rate of capital recovery must be 5 percent using the straight-line method.

A second method for calculating the capital recovery rate is based on the use of compound interest theory, specifically the **sinking fund factor.** If the property is assumed to have an economic life of forty years, the appraiser and the investor ask a very fundamental question: What percentage of the value would have to be put aside each year in order for the annual accumulation at the end of the economic life span to equal the initial value of the building? The compounding process often assumes that it takes place at the interest rate of a comparable or alternative investment.[19] However, the rate on a safe, riskless investment and even a speculative rate could be used. If the rate is 10 percent per year, and if the economic life of the investment project is forty years, placing 0.226 percent of the sales price into an account every year would provide a fund equal to the sales price at the end of forty years.

If the economic life is only twenty years, at a rate of 10 percent the full sales price can be accumulated by putting aside 1.75 percent of the sales price every year. The capital recovery figures of 0.226 percent for forty years of economic life and 1.75 percent for a twenty-year economic life can be used to generate the capitalization rate. These figures are obtained from compound interest tables, specifically the mathematical function known as "the deposit needed to accumulate" or "the sinking fund factor." Exhibit 6-5 is the compound interest table for 10 percent that shows the sinking fund factor.

The Ellwood technique also determines capital recovery. The Ellwood technique is based on compound interest theory and uses the sinking fund concept for capital recovery. However, it establishes the sinking fund at the investor's expected equity rate of return.[20] In addition, the Ellwood technique uses the sinking fund factor for the length of ownership that the investor anticipates, rather than for the economic life of the property. Then this sinking fund factor is weighted by the original equity position of the investor. The Ellwood technique for establishing a capital recovery rate is a more sophisticated version of the simple sinking fund concept.

In summary, the rate of capitalization is composed of two entities, the basic interest rate and the capital recovery rate. These two components represent the typical investor's concerns about a rate of return *on* the investment and a rate of return *of* the investment. The rate, therefore, of capitalization must consider the basic rate and the capital recovery rate. Once the rate of capitalization is established, the appraiser proceeds to the next phase of the income approach, which is selection and use of a method of capitalization.

The Method of Capitalization

The preceding section explains the components of the capitalization rate *(R)* that is used in the formula $V = NOI/R$. The capitalization rate must consist of a basic rate component and a capital recovery rate component. Current practice among appraisers, however, does not require a separate calculation of these two rates. A recent study of appraisal practices points out that only a small number of appraisals (8 percent) are based on a separate calculation of a capital recovery rate, and that the more sophisticated mortgage-equity techniques, such as the Ellwood technique, and computer simulation models are being used. So, the most frequently used procedures to derive the capitalization rate are sophisticated mortgage-equity models and the establishment of an overall rate from an analysis of the market for comparable properties.[21]

Assuming that the appraiser uses one of these widely accepted methods to obtain the capitalization rate, and that it is determined to be 14 percent, the estimation of the market value of the subject property can proceed. Exhibit 6-4 is a hypothetical example of a forecast of net operating income for a ten-year ownership

EXHIBIT 6-5 Compound interest for 10 percent with the sinking fund factor

Source: Austin J. Jaffe and C. F. Sirmans, *Real Estate Investment Decision Making,*
©1982, p. 518. Reprinted by permission of Prentice-Hall, Inc., Englewood Cliffs, N.J.

10%

Yrs.	Amount of one	Amount of one per period	Sinking fund factor	Present worth of one	Present worth of one per period	Partial payment
1	1.10000	1.00000	1.00000	.90909	.90909	1.10000
2	1.21000	2.10000	.47619	.82645	1.73554	.57619
3	1.33100	3.31000	.30212	.75132	2.48685	.40212
4	1.46410	4.64100	.21547	.68301	3.16986	.31547
5	1.61051	6.10510	.16380	.62092	3.79079	.26380
6	1.77156	7.71561	.12961	.56447	4.35526	.22961
7	1.94872	9.48717	.10541	.51316	4.86842	.20541
8	2.14359	11.43589	.08744	.46651	5.33493	.18744
9	2.35795	13.57948	.07364	.42410	5.75902	.17364
10	2.59374	15.93743	.06275	.38554	6.14457	.16275
11	2.85312	18.53117	.05396	.35049	6.49506	.15396
12	3.13843	21.38428	.04676	.31863	6.81369	.14676
13	3.45227	24.52271	.04078	.28966	7.10336	.14080
14	3.79750	27.97498	.03575	.26333	7.36669	.13575
15	4.17725	31.77248	.03147	.23939	7.60608	.13147
16	4.59497	35.94973	.02782	.21763	7.82371	.12782
17	5.05447	40.54470	.02466	.19785	8.02155	.12466
18	5.55992	45.59917	.02193	.17986	8.20141	.12193
19	6.11591	51.15909	.01955	.16351	8.36492	.11955
20	6.72750	57.27500	.01746	.14864	8.51356	.11746
21	7.40025	64.00250	.01562	.13513	8.64869	.11562
22	8.14028	71.40275	.01401	.12285	8.77154	.11400
23	8.95430	79.54302	.01257	.11168	8.88322	.11257
24	9.84973	88.49733	.01130	.10153	8.98474	.11130
25	10.83471	98.34706	.01017	.09230	9.07704	.11017
26	11.91818	109.18177	.00916	.08391	9.16094	.10916
27	13.10999	121.09994	.00826	.07628	9.23722	.10826
28	14.42099	134.20994	.00745	.06934	9.30657	.10745
29	15.86309	148.63093	.00673	.06304	9.36961	.10673
30	17.44940	164.49402	.00608	.05731	9.42691	.10608
35	28.10244	271.02437	.00369	.03558	0.64416	.10369
40	45.25926	442.59256	.00226	.02210	9.77905	.10226

period, which is discovered to be typical in the current market. The appraiser's analysis of market trends reveals that the property's effective gross income increases but that operating expenses increase at a faster rate over the ownership period.

Given the income and expense figures presented in Exhibit 6-4, the appraiser can estimate current market value. First, the appraiser makes an estimate of an income figure called the stabilized NOI. This is a single value of the NOI that represents the NOI figures in each year for the whole ten-year period. The rationale used to develop the stabilized NOI is based on the establishment of a single number that typifies the stream of future NOI figures. It is not the highest NOI nor is it the lowest. It is not the average NOI value. Conceptually, the stabilized NOI is a single figure whose present value, if it were received in each year, would equal the present value of the actual NOI figures. In the numerical example being used in this chapter, a stabilized NOI of $36,000 is established.

Second, the appraiser divides $36,000 by 14 percent to obtain an estimate of market value that is approximately $257,000. Remember the capitalization rate consists of a return on the initial investment, a return of the investment, and may include an estimate of the change in sales price over the ownership period. If the future sales price is expected to increase, then the capitalization rate decreases causing a rise in the estimated present market value. The most widely used techniques have this value appreciation or depreciation factor included in their determination process.

Even though this final step in the capitalization process seems simple, remember that the capitalization rate is established only after a large number of important factors are analyzed. A list of these factors should serve to remind the reader of the complexity of the underlying thought process. The factors either directly included (Ellwood Technique) or indirectly considered (overall rate from the market) in the calculation of a capitalization are

- The typical mortgage interest rate
- The length of the typical mortgage
- The typical size of the mortgage as a percentage of sales price
- The typical investor's expected rate of return, which in itself considers the rate of return on a safe, riskless investment plus premiums for risk, illiquidity, and management
- The typical investor's equity as a percentage of sales price
- The return on the equity increase as the mortgage balance is paid down
- The typical capital recovery requirements for an investment that may decline in value over the ownership period
- A price appreciation factor for an investment that gains value over the ownership period

The complexity is in the generation of the capitalization rate and the stabilization process for NOI. Once these two magnitudes are known, the simple $V = NOI/R$ provides the market value estimate.

The Estimation of Value and Its Application

In general, the income approach to real property appraisal is applicable if historical records are available for at least the last three to five years of the subject property's actual gross income and operating expenses. In addition, the appraiser would like to see information about income and operating expenses from comparable properties within the local market. If there are no comparable local properties, the appraiser examines comparable properties in nonlocal markets. This nonlocal information could be regional or may even be national. The appraiser also might use local properties that are not closely comparable by making appropriate adjustments. The appraiser uses the income and expense data for comparable properties to estimate the market value of the subject property, and then uses the data from the subject property as a check on the accuracy of the estimate of stabilized NOI.

In the numerical example presented in the preceding section, the subject property's net operating income was assumed to decline slightly over its economic life. This is a realistic assumption because the earning potential of a property typically declines with increasing functional obsolescence and decreasing quality of the property's environment. In addition, as the subject property ages, certain operating expense categories such as maintenance and repair will increase and cause a decline in NOI.

However, circumstances can prevent net operating income from declining over time. Net operating income can remain constant over time if increases in the property's ability to generate effective gross income exactly match the increases in operating expenses as the structure ages. In this case, the future value of the building should equal the present value of the building. Consequently, because the value of the investment is not declining over time, the investor or the owner has nothing to recover and the capital recovery component should equal zero. In other words, the capitalization rate in a situation where net operating income remains constant is equal to the basic interest rate.

Situations can also arise in which net operating income increases in the future as market factors increase the level of effective gross income at a rate faster than operating expenses increase. In this case, the market value of the subject property in the future will be more than the market value of that property today. The appraiser should estimate the increase in market value at some expected date of sale in the future and use this information in determining the capitalization rate.

THE GROSS INCOME MULTIPLIER TECHNIQUE

The **gross income multiplier** technique can be used to estimate current market value of income-earning properties by converting *annual* gross income into an estimate of market value. To apply the gross income multiplier, the appraiser makes the assumption that investors in income-earning properties are rational and well-informed market participants. The appraiser makes a second assumption that the sales price of recently sold comparable properties adequately reflects the investor's judgments about the future NOI of those properties. Inherent in this second assumption is the idea that the sales price paid for these comparable properties adequately reflects future trends in operating expenses and vacancy rates as well as future trends in the market value of the space being provided by those structures.

On the basis of these assumptions, the appraiser divides the sales price of each of the comparable properties by the monthly or annual rent level for its space. At this point, the appraiser must take care to distinguish between contract rent and market rent. Since the gross income multiplier is established by using each comparable property's rent receipts, the gross income multiplier is really based on contract rents. What the appraiser must examine is the relationship between the contract rent and the market rent. If the investor purchases the building knowing that current leases contain contract rents that are below the market rent, but knows the leases expire soon, the current sales price may suggest that the investor paid more for the property than was warranted. In other words, dividing sales price by a contract rent level that is less than the market rent yields a relatively high gross income multiplier.

By establishing gross income multipliers for several comparable properties that have recently sold in the market, the appraiser obtains an order of magnitude for the current multiplier. If the comparable properties were chosen correctly, the several gross income multipliers established for them may deviate from each other by a magnitude of 5 percent or so. This small level of deviation more than likely reflects differences that the market has detected. For example, a 5 percent difference in the multipliers for the comparable properties can reflect differences in age, condition, special features, room size, and/or location of the property. For this reason the appraiser should not adjust gross income multipliers. The appraiser identifies the comparable property that is most like the subject property and uses its gross income multiplier to estimate the market value of the subject. The gross income multipliers of the other comparable properties serve as a check on the accuracy of the market, in other words, on the consistency of the different investors' judgments about the market value of the properties that are very similar.

The appraiser must recognize other limitations when using the gross income multiplier. Since the gross income multiplier relates the appraiser's estimate of market value to a gross income concept, that is, to potential gross income or to effective gross income rather than to net operating income, its use is only valid for certain types of property. The properties used for comparison must exhibit a high degree of uniformity among their operating expense ratios, and this uniformity must be present among the whole set of comparable properties and the subject property itself. Without uniformity in operating expense ratios, the gross income estimate cannot reflect comparability in net operating income among the properties and the subject property. If there is uniformity among operating expense ratios, the assumption of comparability among the net operating incomes of the comparable properties and the subject property is warranted.

A final limitation of the gross income multiplier is the fact that it totally ignores remaining economic life. Use of the gross income multiplier is based on the erroneous assumption that the comparable properties and the subject property have the same economic life span. In reality, comparable properties of the same actual age in the same physical condition may have different levels, and different patterns, of income into the future. If the appraiser is to use the gross income multiplier concept appropriately, this difference in remaining economic life must be incorporated in some way into the selection of comparable properties.

Despite the limitations of the technique, the gross income multiplier is very appealing because of its simplicity. By obtaining estimates of gross income multipliers from the comparable properties, checking to be sure that the divergence among these estimates is not excessively large, and identifying the comparable property most like the subject property, the appraiser can determine a gross income multiplier to use in placing a value on the subject property. This estimate is obtained by establishing the market rent for the subject property on either a monthly or an annual basis and multiplying this figure by the gross monthly income multiplier or the gross annual income multiplier (whichever the appraiser is using). The product of this multiplication is the estimate of market value for the subject property.

In conclusion, "it should be realized that the use of the gross income multiplier cannot and should not be considered as part of the income or capitalization approach to value. To capitalize means to convert the estimated *net* income anticipated over the remaining economic life of the subject property into a sum or present value. The gross income multiplier does not give weight to amounts of operating expense ratios, or to variations in the remaining economic life of properties." [22]

CHAPTER SUMMARY

This chapter explains the procedure used by the appraiser to estimate a current market value for income-earning real estate. To accomplish this task, the appraiser must analyze several crucial factors. The market rent capabilities of the property must be examined both in the current period and in the future. The level of current and future vacancy losses must be estimated. The appraiser must identify the operating expenses of the property and estimate changes in these expenses over time. Then the appraiser obtains an estimate of net operating income for each year in that property's remaining economic life.

After generating these net operating income figures, the appraiser establishes the capitalization rate that will be used to determine the present value of the future stream of net operating income. The capitalization rate is a composite of many factors that reflect typical market situations for several important financial variables. Once the capitalization rate is obtained, it is used to establish the present value of the future stream of net operating income. Due to the principle of anticipation, the current market value of the property is equal to the present value of the stream of future benefits.

Review Questions

1. Distinguish between market rent and contract rent. How is potential gross income determined?
2. Explain the nature and purpose of the appraiser's view of operating expenses. Identify and discuss the several categories of operating expenses.
3. Identify the expense items that are not included on the appraiser's operating expense statement.
4. Identify the components of the capitalization rate and discuss the technique by which each of these components can be calculated.
5. Explain how the appraiser uses revenues, operating expenses, and the capitalization rate to make an estimate of the current market value for an income-earning property.

6. Identify the shortcomings of the simple band-of-investment technique by explaining the factors that more sophisticated techniques consider in the process of deriving the capitalization rate.

Discussion Questions

1. Differentiate between capital improvement expenditures and reserves for replacement.
2. Discuss the impact of rising energy costs on the market value of income earning property. First assume that revenues do not increase while energy costs rise; then assume that rent revenues increase at a rate that is greater than the increase in the energy costs.
3. Analyze and comment on the following statement: It does not matter whether the appraiser is very accurate in making projections of income and operating expenses for the last years of the property's economic life; what matters is that the projections made for the first decade are accurate.

Notes

1. Alfred A. Ring, *The Valuation of Real Estate* (Englewood Cliffs, N.J.: Prentice-Hall, Inc., 1970), p. 208.
2. Byrl N. Boyce (ed.), *Real Estate Appraisal Terminology* (Cambridge, Mass.: Ballinger Publishing Co., 1975), p. 136.
3. Ring, *The Valuation of Real Estate,* pp. 207–8.
4. Halbert C. Smith, *Real Estate Appraisal* (Grid Series in Finance and Real Estate; Columbus, Oh: Grid, Inc., 1976), p. 114.
5. William N. Kinnard, Jr., *Income Property Valuation: Principles and Techniques of Appraising Income-Producing Real Estate* (Lexington, Mass.: D. C. Heath and Co., 1971), p. 202.
6. Textbook Revision Subcommittee, *The Appraisal of Real Estate,* 7th ed. (Chicago, Ill.: American Institute of Real Estate Appraisers, 1978), p. 338.
7. Ring, *The Valuation of Real Estate,* p. 221.
8. Kinnard, *Income Property Valuation,* p. 222.
9. Ring, *The Valuation of Real Estate,* p. 222.
10. For example, *Income/Expense Analysis: Apartments, Condominiums, and Cooperatives,* published annually by the Institute of Real Estate Management, 430 N. Michigan Ave., Chicago, Ill. 60611.
11. *The Appraisal of Real Estate,* p. 32.
12. Ibid., pp. 32–33.
13. Kinnard, *Income Property Valuation,* pp. 190, 194.
14. Boyce, *Real Estate Appraisal Terminology,* p. 15.
15. Kenneth M. Lusht, "The Behavior of Appraisers in Valuing Income Property: A Status Report," *The Real Estate Appraiser and Analyst* (July–August 1979), pp. 49–59.

16. Ring, *The Valuation of Real Estate,* pp. 245–46.

17. Ibid., p. 263.

18. L. W. Ellwood, *Ellwood Tables for Real Estate Appraising and Financing,* 4th ed. (Cambridge, Mass.: Ballinger Publishing Co., 1977).

19. Ring, *The Valuation of Real Estate,* p. 274.

20. Kinnard, *Income Property Valuation,* p. 271.

21. Lusht, in *The Real Estate Appraiser and Analyst,* pp. 50–52.

22. Kinnard, *Income Property Valuation,* p. 145.

Additional Readings

American Institute of Real Estate Appraisers. *Readings in the Income Approach to Real Property Valuation.* Cambridge, Mass.: Ballinger Publishing Co.

BOYCE, BYRL N. and WILLIAM N. KINNARD. *Appraising Real Property.* Lexington, Mass.: Lexington Books, 1984. Chapter 17.

EPLEY, DONALD R. and JAMES H. BOYKIN. *Basic Income Property Appraisal.* Reading, Mass.: Addison-Wesley Publishing Company, 1983. Chapters 7–15.

FRIEDMAN, JACK P. and NICHOLAS ORDWAY. *Income Property Appraisal and Analysis.* Reston, Va.: Reston Publishing Company, Inc., 1981.

KAHN, SANDERS, A., and FREDERICK E. CASE. *Real Estate Appraisal and Investment.* New York: The Ronald Press Co., 1977. Chapters 8–11.

KINNARD, WILLIAM N., JR. *Income Property Valuation: Principles and Techniques of Appraising Income-Producing Real Estate.* Lexington, Mass.: Heath Lexington Books, 1971.

RING, ALFRED A. *The Valuation of Real Estate.* Englewood Cliffs, N. J.: Prentice-Hall, Inc., 1970. Chapters 14–19.

SHENKEL, WILLIAM M. *Modern Real Estate Appraisal.* New York: McGraw-Hill Book Co., 1978. Chapters 10, 11, and 13.

SMITH, HALBERT C. *Real Estate Appraisal.* Columbus, Oh: Grid, Inc., 1976. Chapters 5 and 6.

Textbook Revision Committee. *The Appraisal of Real Estate, 8 ed.* Chicago, Ill.: American Institute of Real Estate Appraisers, 1983. Chapters 14–17.

WENDT, PAUL. *Real Estate Appraisal: Review and Outlook.* Athens, Ga.: University of Georgia Press, 1974. Chapter 6.

7 | Housing Market Analysis

1. What information about housing markets does the consumer need in order to understand future trends in the value of housing?
2. How can information about the characteristics of the real estate market and the economic and demographic factors affecting that market be used by the consumer?

OBJECTIVES

When a student finishes the chapter, he or she should be able to

1. Identify and explain the several characteristics of the real estate market.
2. Identify and explain the demand and supply relationships in these markets.

3. Describe the important economic and demographic factors that affect real estate markets.

4. Use information about the characteristics of the real estate market and the economic and demographic factors to analyze changes that can occur in real estate markets.

IMPORTANT TERMS _____

Absorption Analysis	Net Household Formation
Active Market	New Construction
Buyer's Market	Nominal Income
Demand	Ownership Costs
Disposable Income	Real Income
Dull Market	Seller's Market
Market Disaggregation	Supply
Market Price	Stock of Housing
Market Value	Vacancy Analysis
Most Probable Selling Price	

THE MARKET FOR REAL ESTATE

Characteristics of the Market

Analysis of the real estate market must be based on a thorough understanding of the characteristics of the market. The market for real estate is substantially different from the markets in which other commodities are traded. It is disaggregated, localized, composed of interrelated submarkets, decentralized, and less organized than other markets. Each of these characteristics is explained in the following sections.

Market disaggregation   Real estate is not a standardized commodity. To facilitate analysis, however, real estate can be broken down into distinct categories. The first readily apparent distinction is among the three broad categories of land use—residential, commercial, and industrial. Within the three major categories, additional distinctions can be identified. For residential real estate, the next logical breakdown is between owner-occupied and renter-occupied units. Owner-occupied residences can be classed as single-family detached units and as duplexes and townhouses. The single-family detached housing units can be divided further on the basis of architectural style (ranch, split-level, bi-level), size of the housing unit, size of the lot, the floor plan, number of rooms, number of full baths, basement/attic storage space, fixtures, and so on. The end result of this refinement process is the identification of a relatively standardized commodity that forms a submarket of the real estate market.

The process of distilling a standardized submarket from a more general, less standardized market is called **market disaggregation.** It is the first step in real estate market analysis because it identifies the submarket to be studied.

Localization   Due to the characteristic of immobility, a property is affected by its location and surrounding off-site improvements. Consequently, the market for real estate is local. The same parcel of real estate located at different points in space would have a different perceived value-in-use and value-in-exchange due to these locational attributes. Moreover, if the impact of these attributes is negative, the property owner cannot escape it by moving the commodity to another point in space.

The consequence of localized real estate markets is that a house located in one urban area can be valued differently from an identical house in another urban area solely because of its locational attributes. Moreover, such value differences can also occur in different sections of the same urban area. Therefore, once the market is disaggregated on physical characteristics, the geographic or spatial area must be specified.[1] The area specification or market delineation could be central city versus suburban fringe, northern suburbs versus western suburbs, neighborhod A versus neighborhhood B, and so on:

Existing stock of housing versus the flow of new construction.   Next, newly constructed units must be distinguished from existing units. This distinction is important because newly constructed units are typically viewed as more desirable than used or existing units. New units possess current standards of attractiveness. They tend to be at the fringe of the urban area where open space and larger lots are available. This distinction can be viewed as **market disaggregation** among housing units by the age of the structure. Categories such as newly constructed, one to five years old, six to ten years old, . . . , forty-one years and older can be established.

Interrelationships among submarkets   The housing units within any particular submarket can have many different substitutes. For example, the new single-family detached housing unit of predetermined structural characteristics in the northern suburbs has the following substitutes:

1. Used single-family housing units of the same type in the northern suburbs
2. New and used single-family detached units in the nonnorthern suburbs, which could include some fringe areas of the central city
3. New and used duplexes or townhouses in the northern suburbs
4. New and used apartments in the northern suburbs
5. New and used single-family houses that are slightly bigger or slightly smaller
6. New and used single-family houses of different architectural style
7. New and used duplexes, townhouses, and apartments in the nonnorthern suburbs

Changes in the economic and/or demographic variables in any of these submarkets can affect the new single-family detached housing submarket.

Buyer and seller characteristics   Another characteristic of the real estate market is the fact that at any point in time, or even over a short period of time, there are typically only a few potential buyers and sellers in the real estate market. Typically buyers and sellers are more numerous in the market for single-family detached housing and apartments than in the markets for commercial and industrial property. The number of used single-family homes offered for sale at any point in time is a very small fraction of the total number of such homes. Moreover, the number of newly constructed single-family units offered for sale in a localized market is small in relation to the number of existing units. Similarly, relatively few households are undertaking a search for a different housing unit during a given period of time. Since these potential buyers are spread over many submarkets, few buyers are participating in each submarket at any point in time.

Unlike the participants in other types of markets, buyers and sellers of the real estate are relatively inexperienced. The vast majority of properties offered for sale are owned by people who lack experience in selling the product because they have never sold a parcel of real estate before or are selling only their second or third unit. These people are typically not in tune with current market conditions and may not attempt to overcome this information deficiency. On the demand side, the potential buyers are also inexperienced because they have not participated in the market frequently. These buyers are probably somewhat more informed than the sellers about current market conditions because they have been searching for days, weeks, and maybe even a month or more. However, the information they possess is probably not broad. They may know about the asking price for certain types of houses, but they may not be knowledgeable about the quality of the structure or the impact of off-site improvements on the value of that structure.

Lack of centralized, organized market   Commodity markets for goods such as gold and agricultural products, and financial markets for assets such as stocks and bonds are centralized and organized. However, real estate is bought and sold in very fragmented markets. In other words, real estate is bought and sold in markets that resemble those for automobiles, household appliances, and furniture. These markets for consumer durable goods are less centralized and organized than the markets for financial assets. The search and information costs in such markets are high, and much travel is needed to obtain price information because prices and quality of the product vary. Poor information or not enough good information could lead to the buyer paying more than the market value, or to the seller accepting less than the market value for the parcel of real estate. The conditions required to establish market value are discussed in another section of this chapter.

In a centralized and organized market, the information and search costs are minimized. The market is efficient. The same expenditure of time and effort generates more information in a centralized and organized market than in a decentralized and less-organized market, or the same quantity and quality of information can be gathered with less expenditure of time and effort. Such a market would be helpful to the buyers and sellers of real estate because real estate is not merely a consumer good. It can be an investment in the same sense as a common stock, corporate bond, and government bond are investments. However, the physical feature of immobility and the economic characteristics of location preclude such centralization and organization of the real estate market. Consequently, the purchaser of real estate must realize the need for extra time and effort in gathering information.

Government influence   The real estate market is affected more by governmental activity than any other commodity market. Local government can tax, regulate, condemn through eminent domain, and control real property and its use. Moreover, the federal government affects real estate investment opportunities through the Internal Revenue Code; in the area of finance various governmental and quasi-governmental agencies affect the money markets for mortgages and construction loans; and the government influences the area of housing through legislation and agencies that provide construction and rental supplements for low-income housing. The degree of government involvement is not as high in the market for any other commodity as it is in the real estate market.

The Demand and Supply Relationships

All commodity markets including the real estate market are composed of two distinct groups of participants. First, there is a group of individuals who are able and willing to purchase the commodity—the **demand** side of the market, which represents these consumers. Second, there is a group that is able and willing to produce and make the product available for sale—the **supply** side of the market. These two concepts must be examined for each specific submarket of the real estate market. In the following explanation of demand and supply relationships, the market composed of existing, one- to ten-year-old, moderate-sized, single-family, detached housing units in the northern section of an urban area is used as an example.

The demand curve   The range of possible prices for the commodity can extend from zero dollars to some finite number of dollars. At each of these possible prices, a different number of households will express interest in the property. These price–quantity relationships are shown in Exhibit 7-1. At the price of P_M, households are not interested in obtaining any of these housing units. At a price of zero dollars, the households in the community are able and willing to buy quantity Q_M units of the commodity. The quantity desired at a price of zero is not infinite because of several limiting factors: (1) The total number of households is finite. (2) Some households will not desire this form of housing because it is too small, too cheap, or too far from their jobs. (3) Some households will not be able to incur the other expenses of ownership even if the purchase price were zero.

At each of the possible prices between the end points of the curve, a certain number of households are willing and able to purchase this type of housing unit. For example, quantity Q_A will be purchased at price P_A. As the possible price decreases below P_A, the quantity of housing desired will increase as more households are able and willing to buy this type of residential unit. The demand relationship is easily expressed as an inverse relationship between possible prices and quantities desired. As price declines, quantity desired increases.

The supply curve   The demand curve represents only one side of the market. It expresses only consumer preference and desires for the commodity. The supply curve

THE DECISION TO ESTIMATE MARKET VALUE

expresses the ability and willingness of the owners and builders of residential units to sell their properties. Like demand, the supply must be disaggregated by physical and locational characteristics. However, the supply curve explicitly reflects the distinctions between new and used structures whereas the demand curve treats this distinction as a form of disaggregation. In other words, the demand for new housing units can look like the demand for used or existing units. However, on the supply side, the graph of these curves can take a different shape. Three different supply curves are described in the next sections:

Units offered for sale One supply relationship expresses the ability and willingness of the owners of existing, one- to 10-year-old, moderate-sized, single-family, detached housing units to sell their property. This relationship is shown in Exhibit 7-2. At a price below P_N none of the present owners are willing to sell their housing units, because they know that a price of P_N is necessary to enable them to find equally suitable housing in some other segment of the market. As the possible sales price increases, the number of these residential units offered for sale increases until point R is reached.[2] Here the price is so high that every household unit in this submarket is offered for sale. Because Q_R is the total number of housing units at this time, quantities of such housing units above Q_R do not exist. Therefore, even at possible prices above P_R the quantity of units offered for sale remains at Q_R.

A time element must be kept in mind in analyzing the supply side of the market. In the example, the time span considered is limited to the construction cycle, which can be viewed as 90 days or the length of time during which Q_R (the total stock of existing housing units of the specified type) is constant. As the time period of analysis lengthens beyond 90 days, more houses become one year old, some one- to 10-year-old houses are destroyed by fire, and 10-year-old houses become 11 years old. Thus, for a 180-day period or a 360-day period the existing stock of housing can be equal to, greater than, or less than Q_R, depending upon the relative magnitude of new construction, demolition, and aging of the units.

Existing stock In addition to the supply of existing units that are offered for sale, the supply side of the market for this type of housing could be specified in one other way. The total supply of existing, one- to 10-year-old, moderate-sized, single-family, detached housing units in the northern section of the urban area can be analyzed. This

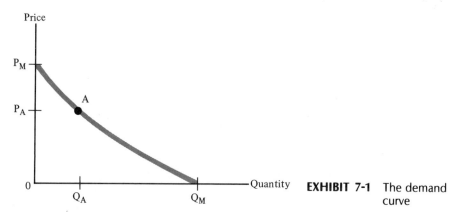

EXHIBIT 7-1   The demand curve

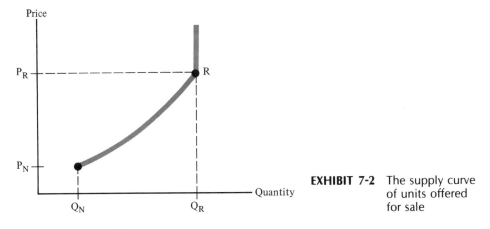

EXHIBIT 7-2 The supply curve of units offered for sale

supply curve is depicted in Exhibit 7-3. It differs from the supply curve in Exhibit 7-2 because this perfectly vertical curve reflects the fact that the total supply of such housing units, whether being offered for sale or not, is perfectly fixed during the time period under analysis. Thus, whether the price of such housing is P_N or P_R, the total number of units in existence is exactly the same, that is, quantity Q_R, at this point in time. However, as the time period changes the existing stock of units can also change for the reasons mentioned in the preceding section.

New construction The third aspect of the supply side to be analyzed is the supply of newly constructed, moderate-sized, single-family, detached housing units in the northern section of the urban area. This supply curve is plotted in Exhibit 7-4. The builders of new housing units require that a minimum price be reached in the market before they undertake any construction activity. This minimum price, depicted as P_K, must be high enough to cover the cost of materials, labor, and land that are used in the production of new residential units. Moreover, the price must be high enough to provide some return to the management or owners of the construction company. If the price is less than P_K, no units will be constructed. If the price is equal to P_K, some positive number of units, such as Q_K, will be erected. As the possible price rises

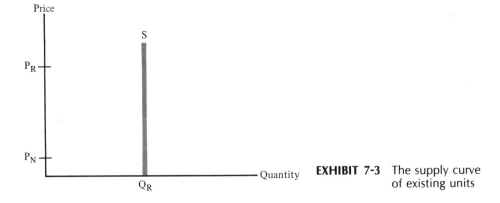

EXHIBIT 7-3 The supply curve of existing units

THE DECISION TO ESTIMATE MARKET VALUE

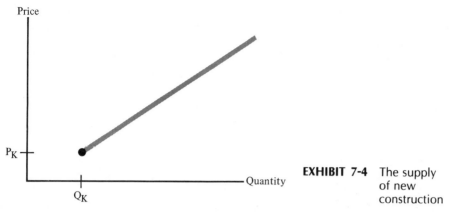

Price

P_K

Q_K

Quantity

EXHIBIT 7-4 The supply of new construction

above P_K, the quantity of units that the builders are able and willing to build will increase.

The Determination of Price in a Market

A market is composed of two distinct groups. One is the group of people who are able and willing to buy the product, the demand side of the market. The other is the group of people who are able and willing to provide the product for sale, the supply side of the market. These two groups interact in the market as depicted in Exhibit 7-5, which represents the market for existing, one- to ten-year-old, moderate-priced, single-family, detached housing units in the northern section of the urban area being offered for sale.

The market allows both groups of people, as groups but not as individuals, to become simultaneously satisfied. There is only a single price–quantity relationship at which this mutual satisfaction occurs—point H in Exhibit 7-5. At price P_H, suppliers are willing to supply Q_H and buyers are willing to buy Q_H housing units. At prices above P_H, the owners of this type housing as a group are willing to sell more units than potential buyers desire. At prices below P_H, the potential buyers as a group are

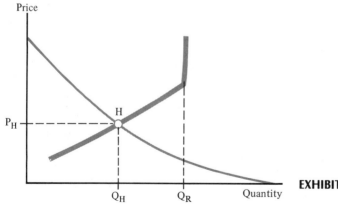

Price

P_H

H

Q_H Q_R Quantity

EXHIBIT 7-5 The market for housing

willing to purchase more units than the owners are willing to sell. If the market is not encumbered in any way, if the potential buyers and potential sellers are allowed to analyze the market and obtain all relevant information, if there is adequate time to negotiate, and if there is no pressure or force exerted on any of the participants, the market for this housing will clear at price P_H and quantity Q_H.

Economic and Demographic Factors that Affect the Market

The economic and demographic environment of a parcel of real estate affects its value. The impact of the environment can be analyzed and the resultant effect can be shown by using demand and supply analysis. Changes in the economic and demographic environment affect the position of the demand and supply curves. In other words, the various economic and demographic factors affect the ability and willingness both of buyers to purchase and of suppliers to provide units of housing at all possible prices in the market. First, the effect on demand is analyzed,[3] then the effect on the supply side is considered.

Demand factors   The economic and demographic factors that affect the level of demand are

- Net household formation
- Age composition of the households
- Household income
- Credit conditions
- Prices of substitutes
- Ownership costs
- Expectations about future prices and mortgage interest rates

Each of these variables is examined below to identify the changes that will cause an increase in demand for a selected type of housing unit. The movement of

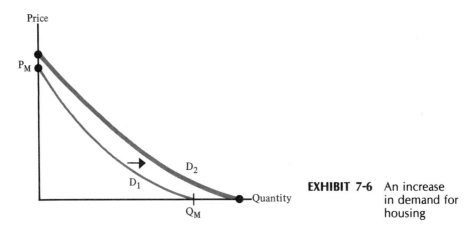

EXHIBIT 7-6   An increase in demand for housing

the demand curve is depicted in Exhibit 7-6 as the shift from D_1 to D_2. This shift represents the fact that potential buyers as a group are willing and able to buy more units of housing at each possible price.

Net household formation As time passes, the number of households in an urban area changes for several reasons. First, children reach the age of maturity (eighteen years old in most states) and choose to reside apart from their parents. When a young adult establishes a physically independent existence, an additional or new household is established. This new household requires living space and causes an increase in demand for some type of housing unit. Second, many households will move into the urban area. These new or additional households require living space and thus cause an increase in demand. These two major types of additions to the number of existing households are the first component of **net household formation.**

At the same time that new household units are being formed through maturation and in-migration, the number of existing household units is being reduced by out-migration from the urban area, death, and the decisions made by adults to share a dwelling unit. The reduction in household units brought about by these circumstances must be subtracted from the new households formed to obtain net household formation. If the resultant figure is positive, the effect will be an increase in the demand for housing.

Age composition of the households Households of different ages tend to prefer different types of housing. The younger households, eighteen to twenty-five years of age, typically choose rental units, and households in the middle years tend to choose owner-occupied housing. Because different urban areas can have different age compositions of households, the markets for various types of housing will be different in each urban area.

As time passes, the age composition of households changes. Single-person households marry to form multiple-person households. Young households become middle-aged households. Such changes over time bring about changes in future housing demand. Moreover, migration of households from one geographic area to another brings about a compositional change in both areas. As a general rule, households headed by young adults and single-person households have a greater propensity to move. Consequently, the market for rental units and smaller houses can increase at the destination and decrease in the area from which these households moved.

The age composition of households also affects the demand for commercial real estate and thus affects the use to which it is put. Different age groups prefer different restaurants, clothing stores, and other retail shops.

In addition to the age composition, the size of the household can affect the type of housing submarket that the household enters. A household whose head is in the middle years can have children or can be childless. This difference in the size of the household can affect a decision about the size of the housing unit desired. The household with two children may require a moderate-sized, three-bedroom, single-family house, whereas the household without children may require a smaller, two-bedroom, single-family house or even a two-bedroom apartment.

Currently, the size of the typical household in this country is decreasing. This compositional change will have an impact on the demand for housing in the future. Demand for smaller housing units will be increasing relative to the demand for larger housing units.

Household income Determining the impact of income changes on the real estate market involves two steps. First, the type of income must be identified. Then the effect of the change on the demand curve can be determined. The majority of households received an income from the sale of labor services. This income can be identified in several ways. It can be the gross income—a measure of the full payment for the work performed—or it can be a net income figure—the dollars remaining after federal and state income taxes and social security taxes are deducted. This net income figure, known as **disposable income,** underlies the household's ability to buy all commodities, including real estate.

Disposable income can be stated in nominal terms or in real terms. The **nominal income** is the household's actual dollars in hand. The **real income** or *purchasing power,* is stated in terms of goods and services that can be bought with those dollars. At two different points in time, the number of dollars a household receives can be the same but the purchasing power can be different. As the price of a consumer good increases, the real income (purchasing power) of each individual dollar decreases and fewer units of goods and services can be purchased. Consequently, *real disposable income* is the demand variable to be examined.

A distinction also must be made between current income and future income. When a household enters into a decision to purchase real estate, it typically commits itself to a stream of future repayments of a loan taken out to purchase the commodity. If the parcel of real estate is a single-family housing unit, the future income stream of the household is an important consideration because it determines the ability to repay the loan. If the property is an income-earning investment, the future income levels from the investment determine the ability to repay the loan. Consequently, for single-family residential property, the level of future real disposable income should be the income variable that determines the level of demand.

In many instances, nominal gross income is used to analyze the demand for real estate. Because this figure is a proxy for the theoretically preferable income figure, the following assumptions are inherent in its use:

1. Future nominal income will be at least as great as current nominal income.
2. Future nominal income will increase at a rate equal to the rate of inflation so that current and future levels of real income will be equal.
3. The tax burden in the future will not be greater than that in the present and thus the levels of future and current nominal disposable income will be the same.

Once the type of income to be examined has been identified, the impact of a change in the income figure can be determined. In traditional economic theory, as the income level increases, the demand for a typical commodity will increase as shown in Exhibit 7-6. An example of this typical situation is the market for T-bone steaks. As the consumer's income increases, the demand for T-bone steaks increases.

In general, the aggregate beef market consists of T-bone steaks, sirloin steaks, round steaks, chuck steaks, hamburger, and beef organ meats. As the income of consumers increases, consumers tend to reorient their purchases from the "low-grade" to the "high-grade" cuts of beef. In other words, as the consumers' income increases, other things remaining constant, they upgrade the quality of beef they buy. Similar upgrading can occur in the housing market. In the case of beef, as income rises some consumers reduce their purchases of beef organs and shift to hamburger; the demand for beef organs falls and the demand for hamburger rises. In addition, the rising income levels enable some consumers of hamburger to shift their expenditure pattern in favor of steaks. Therefore, different impacts occur in different submarkets for beef. As income rises, the lowest grade declines in demand, the middle grades of beef simultaneously increase and decrease in demand, and the highest grade of beef increases in demand. The market for medium-grade beef is difficult to project because the net effect of the demand change must be determined.

In addition to the shift of consumer expenditures to the market for higher grade beef, an increase in demand occurs in each of the submarkets for beef as a result of the increase in income. Consumers who never bought beef can increase their consumption of both hamburger and steak. Demand in a submarket can increase for two reasons—present consumers in the submarket buy more, and more new consumers enter the submarket than leave the submarket.

Demand in housing submarkets increases for the latter reason. As income levels rise, people change from one submarket to the next highest submarket. This shift is detected as an increase in demand for the submarkets that represent the more desired forms of housing, and a reduction in demand for the less desirable forms of housing. In a specific housing submarket, however, there is no increase due to an increase in absolute quantity of housing bought by a single consumer. As income levels rise to twice their former level, the typical consumer does not buy two existing, moderate-sized, single-family, detached housing units in the northern suburbs of the urban area. This consumer might buy a bigger house or a newer house in the same area, or the extra dollars might be turned to the purchase of a second home or a vacation home in another geographical area that is a different submarket.

Credit conditions One of the economic characteristics of the real estate commodity is the fact that its price is a multiple of the buyer's yearly income. The buyer typically must borrow money to purchase the property. The availability of funds for real estate loans and the financial terms associated with the loans therefore are important determinants in the market. On the demand side, as the interest rate on a mortgage loan decreases or as the loan's maturity lengthens, the size of the monthly mortgage payment decreases and more people can enter the market as potential buyers. The consumer's ability to buy has increased. The same result occurs as the down-payment requirement drops. Thus, any of these three changes can cause the increase in demand shown in Exhibit 7-6. (A more complete discussion of mortgage provisions with respect to the interest rate, maturity period, and down-payment requirements is given in Chapter 16.)

Prices of substitute units Each type of real estate has several substitutes. Therefore, each type of housing is affected by changes in the market for its substitutes. As an example, consider a particular type of housing called type X housing. Substitutes for type X housing are the housing alternatives mentioned in the section on interrelationships among submarkets. Call these alternative housing units type Y housing. As the price of any of these residential alternatives increases because of some demand or supply change in their submarket, demand for type X housing increases. This increase in demand for type X housing occurs because the increased price of type Y housing makes that kind of housing unit unavailable to some consumers as a result of income and mortgage loan considerations. Therefore, as the price of type Y housing increases in relation to the price of type X housing, the number of potential buyers of type X housing increases because of a shift of some consumers from type Y to type X units. This increase in demand for type X units is shown in Exhibit 7-6.

Ownership costs An individual who owns real estate incurs a series of expenses related to the operation or utilization of the property. A list of these **ownership costs** follows:

- The property tax bill and any assessments made against the property for improvements to the land
- Property insurance payment
- Maintenance and repair costs
- Utility costs including heating, cooling, water, and sewage disposal
- Mortgage payment, specifically the interest payment component

These expense items must be incurred by the property owner because failure to pay the property tax, the assessment, or the mortgage payment will lead to the exercise of a specific lien against the property. Failure to insure the property could result in a substantial financial loss. Failure to maintain and repair the property could lead to a reduction in the property's value. Failure to pay for utilities causes a reduction in some of the physical and psychic benefits or revenue that the property could generate.

In traditional economic theory, these costs of ownership are incurred to provide goods and services that are complementary goods to housing. Housing cannot be utilized without these complementary expenditures. As the magnitude of these ownership costs decreases, the demand in the market will increase as shown in Exhibit 7-6. A reduction in these costs of ownership allows more potential buyers to enter the market, even if their income level remains constant.

The preceding discussion of demand factors relates them to increases in market demand. An increase in net household formation, income levels, credit availability, and the prices of substitutes will cause an increase in market demand. Conversely, a decrease in the costs of ownership, which include interest payments, causes an increase in market demand. The directional change in these economic and demographic factors can be used to predict a change in market demand for a selected type of housing.

Supply factors   An examination of the supply side of the real estate market must be accomplished by examining new construction separately from the existing stock. This approach is required because these two commodities are viewed to be different by consumers and the supply of each is affected by different economic variables.

New construction The economic variables that affect the supply side of the market for new construction are

  □ The prices of the factors of production used in the construction process
  □ Productivity of the factors of production and technology
  □ The number of builders in the market
  □ Builders' expectations about sales in the near future

An increase in the supply of newly constructed units is shown in Exhibit 7-7 as a shift of the supply curve from position S_1 to Position S_2. This movement can be explained in two ways—the builders are willing and able to construct more units at each of the possible prices, or the builders are willing and able to construct the same number of units but offer them at a lower price. The second situation is shown as a shift of the minimum price from P_{K_1} to P_{K_2}.

The increase in supply depicted in Exhibit 7-7 is brought about by a reduction in the prices of the factors of production used in the construction industry. As the wage rate for construction labor, the price of building materials, the interest rate for construction loans, the price of construction equipment, and the price of raw land decline, the supply of new construction increases. In addition to declining factor prices, improvements in labor productivity and advances in construction technology can cause an increase in supply. Improvements in productivity occur if construction laborers become more experienced and make fewer errors, work faster, and utilize more construction equipment that increases output more than costs. Advances in construction technology could be the use of newer and more sophisticated construction equipment and the adoption of prefabrication techniques that can reduce overall construction costs.

The supply of newly constructed units will also increase as new builders enter the market. Typically, new builders will have approximately the same cost structure as the builders already in the market. If so, supply curve S_2 will not extend below the price of P_{K_1}: The builders who enter the market are willing and able to provide new units on the same terms as the present builders; in other words, the

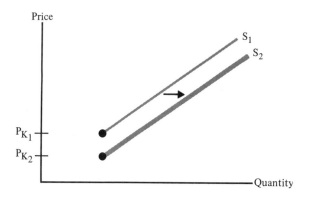

EXHIBIT 7-7 An increase in the supply of new housing

minimum supply price of P_{K_1} will apply to all builders, both the new entrants and the present firms.

Finally, builders have expectations about future sales levels. If they are optimistic about the future, more units will be built this period than were built in the last period because each builder expects that the additional units will sell. This will cause the supply curve of new construction for the current period to increase. On the other hand, if the builders are pessimistic about the future, fewer housing units will be built and the supply curve will decrease.

Existing units The supply of existing units must be examined in terms of the existing units that are offered for sale and the change in the total stock of existing units. The questions to be answered are

□ How many units of existing type X housing will be offered for sale at each possible point?

□ How many units of type X housing exist in the market at this point in time and what factors cause a change in this number of units?

Existing units offered for sale Changes in the supply of units offered for sale during a specified time period reflect the economic and psychological situation of the owners of property in that submarket.[4] The supply of the existing units of type X housing will increase as the owners of this housing attempt to upgrade the quality of their dwelling units. As they demand better housing in submarket Y, they must sell their property in submarket X. This increase in supply in submarket X is depicted in Exhibit 7-8. The supply of these existing units can never increase above quantity Q_R. Below that limit, however, the quantity offered for sale at each possible price can increase. Moreover, as these households attempt to dispose of their type X property, some individual households might be willing to accept an offer of less than price P_N.

The same increase in the supply of these units can occur with the onset of adverse economic conditions affecting owners of type X property. An economic recession with high rates of unemployment or the relocation of industry to another geographic area could create a desire for some households to sell type X housing and seek other less desirable and less expensive forms of housing.

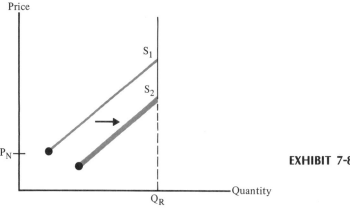

EXHIBIT 7-8 An increase in supply of existing units offered for sale

THE DECISION TO ESTIMATE MARKET VALUE

Change in total stock of existing units There is a direct connection between the market for new construction of type *X* housing and the existing stock of type *X* housing. New construction increases the supply of existing units. It shifts the supply curve shown in Exhibit 7-3 to the right. Other factors also can affect the position of the supply curve for the stock of existing units. Casualty losses due to fire and other forms of destruction, as well as intentional demolition of units, cause the supply to decrease—a leftward movement of the curve. The process of conversion also affects the supply curve. Type *X* housing might be upgraded by means of a room addition or modernization/renovation work into type *Y* housing. Such upgrading causes a reduction in the supply of type *X* housing. Moreover, a lesser form of housing can be upgraded into type *X* housing, causing the supply of type *X* housing units to increase. Consequently, the supply of existing housing in any submarket depends on new construction, casualty loss, demolitions, and conversions to or from that type of housing.[5]

Market Price as a Measure of Value-in-Exchange

In theory, **market price** is determined by the intersection of demand and supply. Is this market-determined selling price the same as the value-in-exchange of the commodity? The answer to this question is yes, but only if the exchange is carried out under certain conditions. These conditions have been defined in real estate appraisal literature in several ways. The following quotation is a list of six points typically identified as constituting the necessary conditions underlying **market value:**

1. Buyer and seller are typically motivated.
2. Both parties are well informed or well advised, and each acting in what he considers his own best interest.
3. A reasonable time is allowed for exposure in the open market.
4. Payment is made in cash or its equivalent.
5. Financing, if any, is on terms generally available in the community at the specified date and typical for the property type in its locale.
6. The price represents a normal consideration for the property sold unaffected by special financing amounts and/or terms, services, fees, costs, or credits incurred in the transaction.[6]

The same points are made in a different way, and several additional considerations are expressed in the following definition:

> There must be several buyers and sellers competing with one another to provide alternatives to other market participants. These buyers and sellers must be informed. They must have reasonable, readily available knowledge about the property being appraised, its probable future income-producing capacity under present use; the alternative uses to which it can be put and the most probable income streams associated with those uses; prevailing market conditions and market standards of investment acceptability; and the character and intensity of their competition. . . . In brief, potential buyers and/or sellers are assumed to possess the typical knowledge about

the property and the market that a prudent market participant can reasonably be expected to have.

Buyers and sellers are further presumed to act "rationally" on the basis of the information they possess. Each party to a transaction is expected to act in his own self-interest to maximize his economic or financial well-being: his profit, the rate of return on investment, and/or the value of his interest in the real estate. Rational behavior consists of behaving logically to achieve the stated investment or market objective with the typical property and market information at hand. . . . A reasonable turnover or marketing period must be allowed for the transaction to take place; there must be no undue time pressure on either buyer or seller. The type of property involved and the existing market conditions determine what a "normal" marketing period is, or should be. . . . It is also assumed that there is no fraud, collusion, or misinformation on the part of either party. . . . Payment must be consistent with the prevailing standards of the market or the type of property interest to be exchanged, and the type of transaction involved. Typical or normal financing and payment arrangements are presumed.[7]

In brief, market value is obtained when these conditions exist in the market. However, because all these conditions rarely exist simultaneously, a less rigorous theoretical concept is used in obtaining value in a real estate market. It is the concept of the **most probable selling price,** which is

The price at which a transaction is most likely to occur under actually existing market conditions and actually prevailing levels of information on the part of buyers and sellers. Most probable selling price is somewhat less rigid and idealistic a concept than market value.

. . . The buyer or user is expected to produce the best return he can under the conditions of existing market information, but not necessarily with the full knowledge stipulated as part of the market value. The estimation of the most probable selling price does not require that the prospective buyer search out every possible alternative type and intensity of use for the property before rationally selecting the best one.[8]

The price determined in the market can be either the market value of the parcel of real estate or the most probable selling price. The distinction depends on the conditions that prevail in the market. In other words, the conceptual issue is related to the characteristics in the real estate market. The most important characteristics as pointed out in the two previous quotations are

□ The knowledge possessed by the market participants

□ Their relative abilities to obtain financing and to structure the exchange

□ The motives and behavior of the participants

□ The time period over which the property is in the market

Participants in the real estate market are not fully knowledgeable because of inexperience and because of the high search costs that must be incurred. Their abilities to obtain financing and to structure the exchange vary greatly. The ability to obtain a loan is based on creditworthiness, which reflects income and past performance in repaying a debt. Some participants have virtually no savings, others have large savings; this factor can affect the size of the loan and the interest rate. Some housing consumers are not rational; they buy a house on impulse or as a result of frustration generated by several months of "house hunting."

Finally, identical houses can be in the market for different lengths of time. One unit may sell in several days and another may not sell for several months. In this situation, the selling prices of the specific units may be different. The house that sold quickly may have been priced at less than its true market value either because the sellers lacked information or because the other house may have been overpriced. Moreover, as time passes the seller of an overpriced unit may reduce the asking price or an uninformed buyer might pay a higher price because of lack of information.

Real estate market analysis produces an estimation of most probable selling price because the characteristics in the typical real estate market are not those required to estimate the true value-in-exchange or market value.

MARKET ANALYSIS

Once the economic and demographic factors that affect market demand and supply have been defined and identified, market analysis can be applied. In this section, the type of activity in the market, vacancy and absorption analysis, dynamic factors, and the relationship of market analysis to community economic base analysis are explored.

Activity in the Market: Active Versus Dull Markets

The level of activity in the real estate market is influenced by changes in the economic and demographic factors that underlie the demand and supply curves. The prediction of such changes is known as market forecasting. "A forecast is an estimate of future happening or condition. It consists of estimating what will most probably happen in the future, based in part on analysis of trends of the recent past, but tempered in the analytical judgment. A forecast is also based on the existence of accrued or stipulated conditions of forces external to the factor(s) being forecast."[9] Market analysis is basically an examination of the economic and demographic variables to predict the impact of their changes on the market.

The Market for Existing Units Offered for Sale

Market analysis can be applied to any specific submarket of real estate. One such submarket could be the existing stock of a selected type of housing that is being offered for sale. The analyst knows a historical fact: this type of housing is currently selling for price P_E and in the current period quantity Q_E units of this type of housing were sold in the market. This fact is shown in Exhibit 7-9. The market analyst undertakes to forecast the price in the next period. Assume the analyst discovers that over the next three months interest rates on mortgages will decline and that there will be a net inflow of households who prefer this type of housing unit. On the basis of the forecast of these economic variables, the analyst recognizes that the demand for this type of housing will increase, causing the price to rise above that given as price P_E. This higher level of demand will intersect the existing supply curve at point F in the next period. The analyst makes this deduction under the condition that the existing supply of such housing remains unchanged.

However, if new construction exceeds demolitions and no conversions occur, the number of units of this housing offered for sale at each possible price might increase in the next period. The new demand and supply curves will intersect in the next period at a point such as G in Exhibit 7-9. In contrast, if demolitions exceed new construction and no conversions take place, the supply of this housing will be less in the next period. The lower level of supply coupled with an increase in demand will lead to a shift from point E to point H.

When the level of demand increases, and this increase is accompanied by a relatively smaller change in supply (either an increase or a decrease), the analyst can forecast an increase in price as well as an increase in the number of units offered for sale. When such price and quantity increases are forecasted, the market is referred to as an active market for this type of housing unit.

An **active market** is a market that exhibits increasing levels of demand accompanied by a relatively smaller change (increase, decrease, or no change) in supply. An active market can be initiated by any change in the economic and demographic factors that cause an increase in demand. For example, an increase in the consumer's real income level, an increase in the price of substitute housing, and a reduction in ownership costs could cause the shift in the demand.

A **dull market** for this type of existing housing unit would be a market in which the price and the quantity traded decline because a reduction in the level of demand is accompanied by a change (increase or decrease) in supply that is of a smaller magnitude. In other words, a dull market is the reverse of an active market. Graphically, an active market is a movement from point E to points such as F, G, and H in Exhibit 7-9, which represent higher prices with higher quantities traded. A

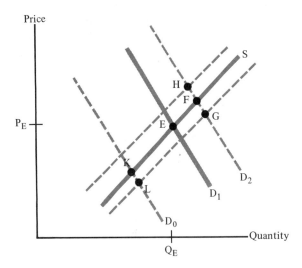

EXHIBIT 7-9 Market for existing units of housing offered for sale

THE DECISION TO ESTIMATE MARKET VALUE

dull market is a movement from point E to points such as K and L, which represent a decline in price accompanied by a decline in the number of units sold.

Active and dull markets are often referred to as a "seller's market" and a "buyer's market," respectively. A **buyer's market** (dull market) has been defined in the following way: "In a buyer's market properties are offered in great numbers but the competition among buyers is not keen. Indeed, few buyers appear at any price."[10] This statement is the same as saying that as the demand declines, the number of units offered for sale increases. For example, in Exhibit 7-9 this phenomenon is depicted by the movement from point E to point K to point L. However, for all practical purposes, a movement from point E to point K can also be viewed as a buyer's market because the price has declined.

A **seller's market** (active market) "would result from the opposite conditions. . . . The supply of real estate decreases . . . sales are more frequent . . . (and there are) increases in demand."[11] Graphically, this situation is depicted in Exhibit 7-9 as a movement from point E to point F to point H. But the movements from point E to point F, and even to point G, can also be considered as a seller's market because the price has risen.

In addition to these active and dull market conditions, two other situations can arise in a housing market. Price and quantity sold move in the same direction in both the active and the dull markets. In the active market, price and quantity sold both increase; in the dull market, the price and quantity sold decrease. However, certain situations in the market can lead to price increases accompanied by a decline in the quantity traded, and to price decreases accompanied by an increase in the quantity traded. These two situations are graphically depicted in Exhibit 7-10. A movement from point E to a point such as R is caused by a decline in the supply of units offered for sale. This situation could occur if demolitions exceed new construction so that stock of this housing unit declines. Or, it could happen if households offer less of these units for sale from the existing stock. The result of these changes is an increased price in the next period accompanied by a reduction in the number of

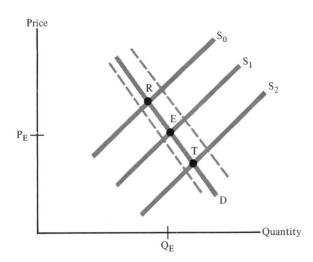

EXHIBIT 7-10 Market for existing units of housing offered for sale

units offered for sale in that period. In contrast, a movement from point E to point T can be caused by an increase in supply as new construction exceeds demolitions causing an increase in the stock, or as households offer more units for sale from the existing stock. The results of this change are a reduction in price and an increase in the number of units traded in the market in the next period.

Such movements are not called buyers' or sellers' markets as previously defined. These changes represent unique market situations that can and do occur in housing markets. By means of the graph in Exhibit 7-11, names can be given to all four types of market changes phenomena. A movement from E as shown in Exhibits 7-9 and 7-10 can take place into any of the four regions shown in Exhibit 7-11. These four regions and the combinations of demand and supply changes that cause the movements into these regions are labeled as Types I–IV market activity. The direction of the market movement and its magnitude depend on the direction and magnitude of the shifts in demand and supply caused by changes in their underlying economic and demographic factors.

A relatively infrequent but possible occurrence is the movement from point E to a point on one of the boundary lines. A move from point E to point Z is such a situation. Is this movement a Type I or Type IV movement? For the sake of simplicity it can be considered a Type I movement. It is an increase in the number of units traded at a constant price in the next period.

The market for new construction   The market for newly constructed housing units can be analyzed in the same way as the market for existing housing units that are offered for sale. Market analysis can lead to forecasts of an active (Type I), dull (Type III), Type II, or Type IV market phenomenon. The distinguishing feature is that the supply of new housing units is affected primarily by construction costs. As the prices of the factors of production (land, labor, equipment, loans, and materials) increase, the supply in the new housing market decreases. On the other hand, the supply in the market for existing units offered for sale is affected primarily by the size of the existing stock and the expectations/aspirations of the owners of real estate and economic/demographic factors that affect the owners' willingness to sell their existing housing units.

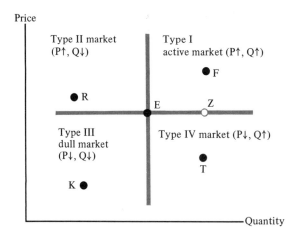

EXHIBIT 7-11   The four types of market activity

THE DECISION TO ESTIMATE MARKET VALUE

Dynamic Factors

Time is an important element in real estate market analysis. The economic and demographic factors underlying a real estate market change as time passes. On the demand side, households move from one geographic location to another. New households start and existing households enter and leave selected real estate submarkets. As the interest rate changes, the ability to buy real estate with a given real income level changes. On the supply side, construction laborers' wage rates, the price of raw land, interest rates on construction loans, and the prices of building materials change. New construction techniques are developed and the number of construction companies in an area fluctuates.

Market analysis must be dynamic to capture the effect of these changes through time. The market analyst must understand current market situations and the impact of the past on the current market. Most importantly, the analyst must forecast the changes that will take place in the future. Thus, market analysis is a study of historical trends, an understanding of current conditions, and a forecast of changes in the economic and demographic factors underlying the demand and supply in the various real estate submarkets. The dynamic interrelationships between current and future markets is examined in the next section on vacancy and absorption analysis.

Vacancy and Absorption Analysis

In the preceding discussion of market analysis, the assumption was made that at the prevailing market price, the number of units desired or demanded of a given housing type was exactly equal to the number of units provided—that is, the market cleared. Such a situation is rare in real estate markets. At any given time, there are existing single-family housing units that are vacant and for sale. There are new single-family housing units that have not been sold while more of these units are being constructed. There are vacant apartments for rent. There are vacant retail stores, offices, and factories. Vacancies occur in the various real estate markets when the prevailing price in the market is greater than the price that would clear the market. In the market for newly constructed housing units shown in Exhibit 7-12, the prevailing price is P_A and the market clearing price is P_E. At the prevailing price, the builders of these new units expect to sell quantity Q_S and therefore are willing and able to construct this output level. However, at this price, potential buyers are only willing and able to buy quantity Q_D units. Consequently, a fraction of the new units actually constructed are unsold and remain vacant. The actual number of new vacancies is the difference between Q_S and Q_D. Typically vacancies are stated as a rate or percentage. Vacancies are zero when P_E equals P_A. At this price, there is a single quantity level Q_S because Q_D is equal to Q_E, which equals Q_S. There is a "normal" or acceptable level of vacancies as perceived by the local builders in each market. These vacant units provide for the smooth operation of the real estate market by allowing for household and business mobility. Deviations from this normal level of vacancies establish the responses that can be seen in the market and are discussed below.

Knowledge of the level of vacancy is important to participants on both sides of the market. On the demand side, the consumer should realize that each vacant unit

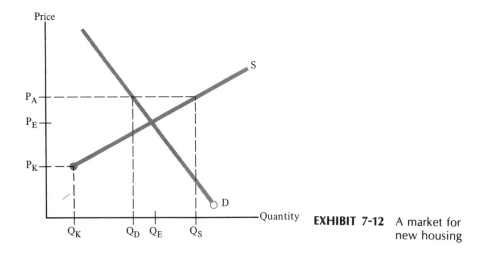

Price

P_A
P_E

P_K

Q_K Q_D Q_E Q_S Quantity

S

D

EXHIBIT 7-12 A market for new housing

costs the builder the periodic interest payment on the loan used to construct that unit. The higher the number of vacancies, the greater the consumer's bargaining strength in the market and thus the greater the consumer's relative ability to obtain a price less than P_A.

On the supply side, low levels of vacancies (below normal vacancies) are to the builder's advantage in the bargaining process. The lower the vacancy rate, the greater the builder's ability to obtain the anticipated price of P_A. More importantly, vacancy analysis provides a signal to the builder about future construction needs in the market. An increase in the number of vacant new units is a clear indication of overconstruction in the submarket. Current vacancies signal the need to produce fewer units in this submarket in the next construction period.

Vacancy analysis is a supply consideration of importance to the builders of real estate projects. Another concept that is important to the same builders is the rate of absorption. However, **absorption analysis** is a demand consideration. It is an analysis of the change in the position of the demand curve in the market. On the basis of Exhibit 7-12, absorption analysis can answer the following types of questions: Given market price P_A, how many units of this housing will consumers demand in the next period? In other words, what will quantity Q_D be in the next period? How long will it take to eliminate or absorb the current number of vacant units?

The answers to these questions are found through market analysis by forecasting changes in the economic and demographic factors underlying demand. For example, if there are vacancies in the market and the analyst can forecast a future decrease in mortgage interest rates coupled with an increase in net household formation, the absorption rate will be positive. Under these conditions, the builders can construct quantity Q_D units of housing and still realize a reduction in vacancies because demand in the next period will be greater than Q_E at a price of P_A. If the analyst can accurately predict the shift in the demand curve, the approximate number of vacant units to be absorbed can be forecast. This information can lead to a conclusion about the number of periods required to sell all the vacant units in that

THE DECISION TO ESTIMATE MARKET VALUE

market if the builders continue to construct units at the current level and other economic and demographic factors remain constant. If the analyst forecasts a declining absorption rate because the changes in economic and demographic factors will lead to declining demand, at current levels of construction the stock of vacant units will increase in the next period. This increase will occur because this period's vacant units may not sell and a significant portion of the units constructed in the next period will not sell at the prevailing price of P_A.

Vacancy analysis and absorption analysis are related concepts that can be helpful to the producers of real estate. These techniques are used to forecast construction activity in future periods on the basis of vacancies, absorption, and future production cost considerations. Vacancy analysis measures the difference between demand and supply at the prevailing market price, the distance Q_D to Q_S at price P_A in Exhibit 7-12. Absorption analysis forecasts the direction and magnitude of the movement in demand. Future production cost considerations forecast the position of the supply curve in the next period.

Relationship of Market Analysis to the Community Economic Base Analysis

A community or urban area contains several real estate submarkets for residential, commercial, and industrial activity within its geographic boundaries. Each of these submarkets is composed of demand and supply elements. In the residential submarkets, demand is almost entirely local. The residents establish the community as the site for their primary residence, whether they are natives or migrants who chose to reside in the community because of jobs or upon retirement. An exception to this locally originated demand is the demand in the second home submarket, which originates primarily from sources external to the local community. In the commercial and industrial sectors, the demand is both local and nonlocal. For example, the demand for retail goods is primarily local but the demand for legal or financial services can be local or nonlocal in origin. The demand for industrial products can also be from local sources or nonlocal sources. Some industrial firms produce for the local market and others produce for the nonlocal market.

An economic model was formulated in the 1950s and 1960s to analyze the growth of a community. This model is known by two names in the real estate industry. It is often referred to as *economic base analysis* but should be more correctly called *export base theory*. A substantial body of literature has been published on the subject. The idea of this model is that a community's commercial and industrial sectors can be divided into two categories on the basis of the sales of their goods and services to local versus nonlocal consumers. Those industrial and commercial firms that sell their products to the nonlocal consumers are known as the *basic component* of the local economy. The firms that sell their goods and services to the local consumers are known as the *nonbasic components* of the local economy. In its original formulation, the theory of economic base held that an expansion in the basic sector of the economy generated the growth and development process of the local economy. As the exportation goods and services grew to accommodate increased demand by external consumers, the local economy grew for two reasons. First, the basic industries needed more employees to meet increased external demand. Second, the firms producing goods for local consumption also had to expand and/or new firms were started to meet the demands of the expanded local labor force in the basic industries.[12]

How does this concept of economic base relate to housing market analysis? As the basic industries and commercial operations expand their output and employment, they foster the expansion of employment in local producers. The effect of this expansion in the local economy is an increased demand in the various housing submarkets and the markets for commercial services. The increase in demand is brought about by an increase in the number of households and a possible increase in their purchasing power. However, the concept of economic base is utilized in another way in the real estate field. It also refers to the inventory of productive resources, the local market potential, and the external market potential of the local community. To produce goods and services, either for export or local consumption, factors of production must be available to produce those items. There must be labor and there must be real estate, or the factor of production known as land. A thorough description of these productive resources is one component of the community's economic base.

The local economy's labor force can be described in two fundamental ways. First, the workers can be identified by the type of industry in which they work. This method would yield information about the number of workers in the construction industry, in the manufacturing industries (heavy and light), in the retail and wholesale industries, and in the food processing industry. Second, the labor force can be identified by its skill level and job orientation. This method would yield information about the number of workers who are classified as professional, administrators, craftspersons, clerical, sales, and production-line workers (laborers).

The local economy's real estate can be described by its components:

1. The number of land units (acres, lots, etc.) and specific uses of this land (residential, commercial, and industrial) can be identified.
2. The area inside existing structures can be stated in square footage available for commercial and industrial users.
3. Current vacant real estate can be enumerated in terms of the number of vacant acres zoned for residential, commercial, or industrial use and the square footage of vacant commercial and industrial buildings.

This information on the labor force and the available real estate can indicate the community's potential to attract new employment opportunities. The new jobs can arise from the expansion of existing firms and the entry of new firms into the area. In addition to these supply factors, other production considerations also affect the community's ability to expand employment opportunities—for example, the availability of local construction financing and the attitude of the local government and the local business community toward the type and quality of firms involved in the expansion. In this sense, the property and income tax structure of the local community, the quantity and quality of public services (roads, utilities, fire protection, school system, etc.), and industrial interrelationships among the present and entering firms are important determinants of the community's ability to develop new employment.

The productive resource known as labor plays a dual role in this development process because each labor unit affects the demand side of the real estate market as well as the supply side. These labor units are related in a definite way to both the number of households and the size of the population. The number of households is an important demand variable in housing markets and the size of the population is an important variable in the demand for commercial space. Thus, the next major component of the community's economic base is a thorough classification of the local population and households. Their size is important, but just as important is their composition by age, income, sex, and marital status. The economic base of the community can be described by breaking the total population and the total number of households down into various age and income categories. The age categories can be stated as five-year groups or as stages of life such as children, adolescents, young adults, middle age, senior citizens. The income categories can be established as less than $3,000, $3,000 to $7,000, 7,000 to $10,000, . . . $50,000 and above. This type of information helps to identify the portion of the total population or household that may enter a specific real estate submarket.

On the supply side of the issue, a percentage of the population makes up the local economy's labor force. The larger the labor force, the greater the economy's productive capability. Moreover, the more skilled the labor force the greater is the productivity and the greater is the economy's productive capacity. One aspect of the economic base of the community consists of an identification of the skill level, by occupational category, of the labor force. Another aspect is an analysis of the adjustment potential of the participation rate of the local population.

In summary, the export base theory is related to real estate markets. As nonlocal consumers desire products produced by local firms, these firms expand. Both a direct increase in the need for residential and industrial space and an indirect increase in the need for commercial space occur as a result. The concept of economic base is also related to real estate markets. The characteristics of the local productive factors determine the local economy's growth potential and also influence demand and supply in various real estate submarkets.

APPLICATION OF MARKET ANALYSIS
FOR REAL ESTATE DECISIONS

Market analysis can be applied to the real estate decision process in three ways. First, it can be used to analyze the market factors for a class or category of real estate in a geographic area. This approach was used in the preceding discussion of market analysis to explore such issues as the market for single-family housing in the northern suburbs, the market for rental units in the central city, and the demand for retail activity of certain types in the urban area or some smaller geographic area.

In these instances, the specific type of residential or commercial land user is analyzing the consumer demand for the product or space and the availability of alternatives in a geographic area. In a sense, this process can be described as a "land use looking for a geographic area in which it can locate." The questions that this form of market analysis can answer are:

☐ What part of the urban area is most desirable for new single-family housing of a certain type?

☐ What part of the city will yield the highest rent level and the lowest vacancy level for a specific type of apartment?

☐ Which section of the urban area will generate the highest sales volume for this type of retail activity?

In addition, this form of market analysis can be used to resolve the following issues:

☐ What is the future level of demand for new selected housing types in the western suburbs of the urban area?

☐ What is the potential sales volume for retail activity in this section of the city?

A second way in which market analysis can be used in real estate decisions can be described as a "land use looking for a site."[13] The type of questions that can be answered by this approach is more specific:

☐ Given that the northern suburbs are the most desirable geographic area for single-family housing, where in that geographic area should the developer build the housing units?

In other words, of the several available building sites in the northern suburbs, which sites should be bought and developed on the basis of the economic and demographic variables that currently prevail in the market, and are forecast to occur, for a certain type of single-family housing?

The third way in which market analysis can be applied is described as "a site looking for a land use."[14] This approach is utilized by a landowner who has vacant land available for development. The question in the owner's mind is the use to which the land should be put. Should the land be developed into a single-family subdivision, an apartment complex, or a condominium project? The task in this case is to analyze the market potential of each of the legally permissible and probable uses to discover the use that yields the highest residual income to the land. In other words, the owner wants to discover the legally permissible highest and best use for the land.

In the following sections, market analysis is applied to real estate decisions in three broad categories—owner-occupied residential units, rental residential units, and nonresidential space.

Owner-Occupied Residential Units

Several actors participate in the various submarkets for owner-occupied residential units—the homebuyer, the developer of new units, and the rehabilitator of existing units. Each of these actors utilize some aspect of market analysis. The homebuyer must weigh two questions: What are my needs? and What are the needs of the next potential buyer of the property? The answer to the second question depends on market analysis. The homebuyer must ask the following questions: When I want to sell this property five or ten years from now, will it fulfill the tastes and preferences of future consumers? Will there be a relatively large number of prospective home-buyers (households) seeking this type of house in this location or neighborhood? In essence, the current homebuyer should attempt to forecast these two demand variables to determine future levels of demand in the submarket that describe the house under consideration. It would be difficult for the homebuyer to forecast income levels, interest rates, or the prices of substitutes. However, an intelligent estimate of tastes and the number of potential consumers is minimally required.

The developer of new single-family housing uses market analysis that is described as "a use looking for a site" or "a site looking for a use." If the developer does not own the land, the type of potential construction is first identified, then the developer looks for the site that gives the highest absorption rate. In this case, market analysis is used to identify a site for the intended use. If the developer owns a parcel of property, several alternative residential uses for the land can be investigated. The developer analyzes the types of housing that will be in greatest demand and estimates the absorption rate and profit potential. The land user or developer in this situation should also analyze the return that can be received from a sale of the property to another person. In this case, market analysis aids the developer in finding a use for the site.

The housing rehabilitator utilizes market analysis that is described as "a use looking for an area." The rehabilitator must forecast demand for the renovated unit in the geographic area where the house is located. The important variables are taste and preference of the consumers toward rehabilitated housing in the neighborhood in which that housing will be found, and the number of potential consumers in the near future (120 or 180 days) when the renovation is completed. In addition, the rehabilitator must know the attitude of the local lenders toward the issuance of mortgage loans in that area of the city. If loans are not available, the preference of the consumers and their numbers are inconsequential.

Rental Property

The same three actors operate in the rental residential markets—the potential buyer who is the investor and the owner of the rental housing, the developer, and the renovator/rehabilitator. The potential buyer of rental residential property utilizes the market analysis described as "a use looking for a site." The investor is concerned with the level of demand for the specific rental units and needs to know the preference pattern and both the current and future number of households in a certain age bracket and income category. The investor also wishes to know the current and future number of competing units. This information is important in determining current and future rent levels and vacancies in the rental units.

The developer of new rental units uses the same form of market analysis as the potential buyer of existing rental units. However, the analysis is applied to a different submarket. New residential units are located in a different geographic area and are functionally different because of new designs for interior and exterior space. Market demand and supply for new units at the fringe of the urban area are different from those in older, more centrally located city neighborhoods.

The renovator of existing rental units requires market analysis in the same sense that the developer does. The renovator needs to know the current number of households willing to buy or to rent the remodeled units. An analysis of the preference patterns of the appropriate age and income brackets is needed to determine the desirability of the renovated units themselves as well as their location. In this case, the renovator is analyzing a special submarket that may have only a few potential customers from a large number of households that have the appropriate demographic and economic characteristics.

Nonresidential Property

For the full range of nonresidential property in general and commercial property in particular, the "use looking for a site" form of market analysis is used when the business neither owns nor leases real estate. However, when the real estate is owned by the business, the form of market analysis utilized is "site looking for a use." For a retailing activity, the entrepreneur identifies several alternative sites that appear to be suitable for the store. Then a study of the trade area or market area surrounding each site is undertaken. The purpose of the analysis is to identify the geographic area from which the store could potentially draw customers. That geographic area is studied to determine the number of potential customers within a reasonable distance of driving time from the potential site. The analysis of potential customers necessitates an understanding of their preferences toward the item or items sold by the store, the number of these potential customers, and their purchasing power. When this has been done for each potential site, the entrepreneur chooses the site that yields the highest profit level. In this case, market analysis provides estimates of potential sales volume. In addition, the costs of operation must be determined to find the site with the greatest profit potential. The future profit level necessitates an analysis of the growth potential of the alternative sites. If several sites yield approximately the same prospective profit level, the choice of the site will be made on the basis of the geographic area that allows the firm to make that profit but simultaneously minimizes the potential for the location of future competitors.

If a site is owned by an individual, the task is to identify the highest and best use for that site. This necessitates an evaluation of the site's use as both a residential and a nonresidential establishment. If the land is zoned only for commercial activity, the owner must analyze the need for a selected commercial activity (i.e., restaurant, shoe store, women's apparel, etc.) and then determine the relative profitability of such activity on the basis of the demographic and economic characteristics of the households in the surrounding geographic area.

CHAPTER SUMMARY

The real estate market has several significant characteristics that set it apart from markets for other commodities and assets. Real estate markets are very disaggregated, localized, interrelated, decentralized, and less organized. In addition, the buyers and sellers in the market are less informed and less experienced than buyers and sellers in other markets. These characteristics influence the demand and supply factors in the real estate market.

The economic and demographic factors on the demand side of the market are net household formation, the age composition of the households, future real disposable income, credit conditions, prices of substitute products, and the ownership costs.

Before the economic and demographic variables affecting the supply side of the market can be identified, the type of supply must be distinguished. The market may consist of newly constructed units, existing units that are being offered for sale, or the total stock of existing units. Each of these three supply types establishes a distinct market. In the market for newly constructed units, the supply of those units is determined by the prices of the resources used to construct them. The variables in the analysis are prices of materials, labor, land, and construction finance costs. In addition, productivity and technology of the construction industry affect the supply of newly constructed units. In the market for existing units that are offered for sale, the supply side is affected primarily by psychological factors and the economic circumstances that may be influencing the potential sellers. Finally, in the market for the existing stock of housing, supply is a function of new construction, demolitions, and conversions.

When the characteristics of the market and the factors affecting demand and supply are understood, the activity in the market can be analyzed. Active markets generally represent rising prices and rising quantities traded; dull markets generally represent declining prices and declining quantities traded. Market situations in which prices are rising and quantities are falling or in which prices are falling and quantities are falling are also considered.

Market analysis, which is the study of the economic activity in real estate markets, begins with an examination of the economic and demographic factors affecting both the demand and the supply sides of the market. Once the important factors have been identified and their impact forecasted, the market analyst can estimate the trend of market price and number of sales that will take place in the future. This information is important for the consumer because it forecasts the possibility of either price appreciation or price declines for single-family housing units. For the investor, market analysis estimates future levels of rent that the owner of residential property can expect.

Review Questions

1. Discuss the characteristics of the market for real estate.
2. Differentiate between demand and supply in the market. Be certain to consider the differences among new construction, existing units offered for sale, and total stock of existing units when explaining the supply side of the market.
3. Identify and explain the important factors on the demand side in a housing market.
4. Identify and explain the important factors on the supply side under each of the three distinct supply conditions.
5. Explain the difference between an active and a dull market. Do these two terms explain all the occurrences that can take place in a real estate market?
6. What is a vacancy? What is vacancy analysis? Assume that there are vacant units in a real estate market. What economic and demographic changes must occur to cause the number of vacant units to decline?
7. What is the absorption rate?

Discussion Questions

1. Assume that you are a market analyst hired by a developer who is constructing single-family detached housing for middle-income and upper-middle-income households. The developer and you both know that the number of vacant units in this market is very small, less than one percent of the existing stock. The developer asks you the following question: Should I build more of these units to be put on the market one year from now; and if so, how many should I construct? As the market analyst, how would you undertake the investigation to solve this problem?
2. Assume that you are a city planner and that you have just learned that a major manufacturing plant is moving into an industrial park in the northern section of the city. The plant is a highly automated production facility that requires skilled blue-collar workers and supervisory personnel. You know, as a fact, that the plant will employ a total of 2,500 production-line workers and 500 supervisory and management personnel. You also know that vacancy in the existing housing stock is less than 0.5 percent for moderately priced apartments, but vacancies in owner-occupied housing are excessively high at 7 percent of the existing stock. What would you expect to happen in the next few months in terms of rezoning requests and submission of plat maps for new development? What housing requirements do you envision for your city given these circumstances and the increase in demand that will occur consequent upon the location of the new plant?
3. You are the owner of a modest ranch house that contains a living room, a kitchen, two bedrooms, and one full bath. You do not want to move,

but you need more space. Your choices are to renovate and enlarge the existing house or to move to a larger house in the same general neighborhood. How do you analyze these two alternatives? What variables do you think should be considered? Under what circumstances would you renovate and enlarge the existing house? Under what circumstances would you sell the existing unit and move to the larger, more suitable house?

Notes

1. The more narrowly a market is disaggregated on the basis of area, location, or neighborhood, the fewer the number of close substitutes for the commodity. In economic terms, market disaggregation in this sense makes the demand curve more price inelastic. Market disaggregation on the basis of physical features also increases the inelasticity of demand.

2. *Reservation demand*—the desire to hold the property. As the possible sales price increases, reservation demand declines, which is the same as saying that the "desire to hold property" declines. See George J. Stigler, *The Theory of Price* (New York: Macmillan Co., 1960), pp. 96–98; and D. Epley, "A Further Note on the Theory of Value," *The Real Estate Appraiser,* Vol. 42, No. 1 (January/February 1976), pp. 13–16.

3. The concept of price elasticity of demand and supply can be introduced into the discussion. However, the authors have chosen to focus the discussion on the variables that cause a shift in the respective curves. Changes in demand and supply are considered but changes in price elasticity are purposely relegated to the notes section. In the latter sense, the authors also decided not to use the terms "income elasticity" and "cross elasticity."

4. The price elasticity of the supply curve can also change. As the desire to hold property weakens at higher prices, the elasticity of the supply curve is increased. If the desire to hold property (reservation demand) weakens at higher prices more than proportionately, the price elasticity will increase—the supply curve will be more elastic at higher sales prices.

5. The concept of economic time enters into the discussion on the supply side. Economic time is measured by the length of time to bring about a change in the stock of housing units. Economic time is the amount of chronological time required to construct or convert housing units. As economic time passes, the existing stock changes; in addition, as economic time passes, the price elasticity of the supply of existing units offered for sale can also change.

6. Byrl N. Boyce (ed.), *Real Estate Appraisal Terminology* (Cambridge, Mass.: Ballinger Publishing Co., 1975), p. 137.

7. William N. Kinnard, Jr., *Income Property Valuation: Principles and Techniques of Appraising Income-Producing Real Estate* (Lexington, Mass.: Lexington Books, D. C. Heath and Company, Copyright 1971, D. C. Heath and Company), pp. 11–12. Reprinted by permission of the publisher.

8. Ibid., p. 13.

9. Ibid., p. 44.

10. Henry E. Hoagland, *Real Estate Principles* (New York: McGraw-Hill Book Co., 1955), p. 202.

11. Ibid.

12. Paul F. Wendt, *Real Estate Appraisal: Review and Outlook* (Athens, Ga.: University of Georgia Press, 1974), Chapter 3. See also Ralph W. Pfouts, ed., *The Techniques of Urban Economic Analysis* (West Trenton, N.J.: Chandler-Davis Publishing Co., 1960).

13. James A. Graaskamp, *A Guide to Feasibility Analysis* (Chicago, Ill.: Society of Real Estate Appraisers, 1970), p. 29.

14. Ibid., pp. 28–29.

Additional Readings

CASE, FRED E. *Real Estate Economics.* Los Angeles, Calif.: California Association of Realtors, 1974. Chapters 4 and 5.

GRAASKAMP, JAMES A. *A Guide to Feasibility Analysis.* Chicago, Ill.: Society of Real Estate Appraisers, 1970. Chapters 1 and 3.

MCKENZIE, DENNIS, and RICHARD M. BETTS. *The Essentials of Real Estate Economics.* New York: John Wiley and Sons, 1976. Chapters 9 and 10.

SHAFER, THOMAS W. *Real Estate and Economics.* Reston, Va.: Reston Publishing Co., 1975 Chapters 7 and 8.

SUMICHRAST, MICHAEL, and MAURY SELDIN. *Housing Markets.* Homewood, Ill.: Dow Jones-Irwin, 1977. Chapters 4–7.

THE DECISION TO ESTIMATE MARKET VALUE

8 | Real Estate Market Analysis and Feasibility Study

QUESTIONS TO BE ANSWERED _____

1. How is a market analysis conducted?
2. What are the major elements of a market analysis?
3. What is a feasibility study?

OBJECTIVES _____

When a student finishes the chapter, he or she should be able to

1. Identify the nature and the major elements of a feasibility study.
2. Describe the nature of the market analysis process.
3. Discuss the concepts of economic base analysis and export base theory.

4. Describe several techniques to update population and household data.

5. Describe the nature and the components of a marketability study.

IMPORTANT TERMS _____

Circular Flow of Income
  Model
Cohort Survival Technique
Construction Cost Study
Consumer Research
Design Study
Economic Base Analysis
Export Base Theory
Feasibility Study
Financial Study
Housing Inventory Method

Location Study
Market Analysis (Study)
Market Disaggregation
Market Segmentation
Marketability Analysis (Study)
Natural Increase and Migra-
  tion Method
Operating Cost Study
Ratio Technique
Survey of the Competition

INTRODUCTION

In general terms, a market analysis examines the economic nature of a market for a specific type of real estate such as single-family housing units or condominium units. More specifically, a market analysis examines the demand and supply factors that affect the market for such a real estate commodity. A feasibility study encompasses a market analysis because a feasibility study is an analysis of all pertinent facts and variables to show whether a proposed project will allow all parties involved to accomplish their investment objectives. A feasibility study requires gathering all relevant economic and financial information and putting these data together in a logical form to reach a conclusion about risk. The word *feasible* means that the risk can be reasonably assumed and the investor's objectives can be reasonably fulfilled.

The feasibility analyst views the property from the standpoint of a client to determine whether the client's objectives can be satisfied. Also, the feasibility study typically includes a recommendation to the client that covers the potential success or failure of the project.

The first step in structuring a feasibility study is to define the focus of the study. The analyst must identify the starting assumptions and the limiting conditions involved in the study. The analyst must ascertain whether the project is

    ☐ A site or a building in search of a user

    ☐ A user in search of a site and certain improvements

    ☐ An investor looking for an involvement in either of the first two situations

By making this distinction, the analyst can establish the logical starting point for the study and thereby eliminate many unnecessary considerations.

A feasibility study can provide the answers to the following five basic questions.

1. What is the anticipated range of return that the investment will generate? Estimates can be derived showing the return on the investment at various levels of income and expenses; various economic circumstances in the local, regional, and national economy; and various individual tax considerations.

2. What is the optimum size and type of structure for the use involved in the property? The analyst examines the issue of building a new structure, remodeling an existing structure, or renting space in an existing structure.

3. What level of amenities and services should be provided in the structure? The analyst evaluates the size and quality of construction, fixtures placed within the structure, parking space requirements, transportation and access requirements, utility requirements, and any other special features that may be appropriate.

4. When should the structure be built, rented, or remodeled? The analyst could recommend that new space is needed immediately, that space should be rented for a period of time to build cash flow, or that remodeling is the best alternative.

5. Where should the building be located? The answer to this question depends on the transportation needs, the location of competitors, the growth of the market area in geographic and economic terms, and any special financial circumstances, either current or anticipated.

TYPES OF FEASIBILITY STUDIES

Typically, a feasibility study contains two major components: **The market study** and **the financial study.** The nature and content of the market study are discussed in this chapter; the nature and content of the financial analysis are presented in Chapter 9. In addition, a feasibility study can contain other specialized components such as a *construction and/or rehabilitation cost study,* an *operating cost study, a location study,* a *design study,* or a *composite of some of these different components.* Any one of these studies can dominate a specific feasibility study, depending on which question or combination of questions the analyst is attempting to answer.

A **market study** is a research effort to determine whether the customers of the product or service provided on the property are sufficient in number to generate an income stream that meets the investor's financial goals. This study is used to measure the demand for the product or service and to delineate a geographic market area. It is used to project market prices or market rent and to determine the quantity, quality, and duration of the income stream for the property and/or its tenants. Quantity is the magnitude of the potential income stream. Quality is related to the nature of the flow—that is, to the financial position of the tenants renting the space and to the capabilities of the management to obtain leases and to keep down operating expenses. The duration of the income flow is the length of time that the necessary level of income is expected to be generated. More specifically, it is a measure of the economic life of the investment.

A very important component of the market study is an estimate of the activity of the competition. How many similar projects are in existence or under construction? Are any competitors ready to initiate a similar project? How does the subject property compare with one that is being placed on the market by the competition? A market study can be used to answer these types of questions.

A **financial study** is used to determine whether the rate of return on a project is large enough to attract capital to that project. The rate of return must be large enough to yield an attractive return on the investment and to cover business and financial risk. The explicit nature of a financial study will be revealed in another part of this text. At that point, there will be a thorough discussion of the types and nature of the risks facing the investor, and the ways that the returns from the investment can be identified and measured.

A **cost study** can be used to obtain an estimate of the construction or rehabilitation costs for a structure designed to satisfy the needs of the user. The analyst examines all of the possibilities among the minimum building requirements, and the types of building materials and specifications that will satisfy those requirements. The cost estimates of each are evaluated against the income and operating expense projections to determine whether investment objectives can be met.

In a second type of cost study, the analyst examines the operating costs of a proposed or existing structure to determine whether operating expenses can be reduced. A questionable, proposed project may be made feasible through such cost reduction even if revenue is stable. Topics of analysis could be the extent to which utilities are provided by the landlord; the use of maintenance and supervisory personnel; the level of maintenance and repair; and special business practices, such as inventory policies and the use of volume discounts to customers. In addition, different financing techniques and practices can affect the debt service payment by reducing the interest and principal repayment expenses.

A **location study** is an attempt to locate all possible sites that will satisfy the needs of the project. The analyst must ascertain the minimum physical on- and off-site requirements of the project—for example, topography, drainage, transport access, open space for parking, transportation facilities for the shipment of materials, and perhaps open space for visibility to enhance market appeal. All possible sites within the geographic area that have these characteristics are identified. Then a market study is done for each of the potential sites. Finally, the financial features of each site are compared with the funds allocated to purchase the land. The investors are attempting to decide the best location in relation to the funds available for land acquisition.

Finally, a **design study** examines the impact on revenues and operating costs of different floor plans, building heights, and density of construction. The end result of the study is a determination of the structural design and building lot layout that will best meet the client's financial objectives.

The construction cost, operating cost, location, and design studies are only mentioned for the reader's information. The main thrust of this chapter is the market study. Then, in other chapters the financial study is presented in detail.

THE MARKET ANALYSIS PROCESS

The market analysis process consists of three major tasks. First, the local economy is analyzed with regard to the nature of its economic activity. This is performed for the current period and forecast into future periods. Second, an analysis is performed for the commodity market in which the subject property is traded. Here market demand and supply factors are analyzed to understand current and future market activity. Third, the specific characteristics of the subject property are analyzed and compared to other properties that can be described as competitive with regard to the services or product that they provide.

These three components of the market analysis process are discussed in the following three major subsections.

Analysis of the Local Economy

An analysis of the local economy consists of three steps. First, the geographic extent of the local economy must be identified. Second, the nature of the economy and its economic activity has to be identified. Third, the level and composition of that economic activity must be forecast into the future.

Defining the local economy   In the most conventional sense, the local economy is defined by political areas. The fundamental building blocks are cities and counties. The city and county are geographic areas enclosed within the political boundaries established by the residents who have chosen to establish the local jurisdiction. The primary differentiating characteristic between the city and the county is the extent of the geographic area. Counties contain more geographic space than cities. Stated in a different way, cities are usually found in counties. Sometimes cities cross county lines. However, for the most part, cities are political jurisdictions located within the boundaries of a county. The relationship among these concepts is shown in Exhibit 8-1. The exhibit also shows the relationship of census tracts to counties, and counties to the metropolitan statistical area (MSA).

The local economy can be a city, it can be a county, and it often is a combination of counties referred to as a Metropolitan Statistical Area (MSA). Depending on the place where the study is being performed, the local economic area can be described by either of these three titles. Therefore, market analysis can be performed for the Atlanta Metropolitan Statistical Area, Champaign County, Illinois, or for the city of Fayetteville, Arkansas.

The important point to remember when defining the local economy is the concept of functional integration. Simply stated, functional integration refers to the

EXHIBIT 8-1 Census divisions in metropolitan areas
Source: U.S. Bureau of the Census, Washington, D.C.

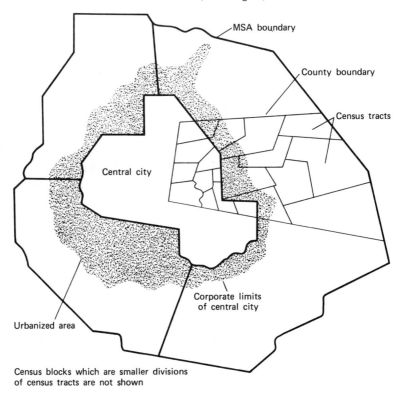

Census blocks which are smaller divisions
of census tracts are not shown

important economic links that exist between the political-geographic areas. Considering the metropolitan statistical area, the counties that constitute the MSA are functionally integrated because there is a significant commuter flow from the peripheral counties to the central county in the MSA.

Describing the nature of economic activity in the local economy   Describing the nature of the economic activity that exists in the local economy can be easily accomplished by means of a simple economic model known as the circular flow of income model. When the relationships in this model are understood, they lead directly to the concepts of **economic base analysis, export base theory,** and **interindustry relationships (the input-output model).**

The internal structure of a local economy is composed of three major sectors: the household sector, the business sector, and the government sector. For the sake of simplicity, the government sector is dropped from consideration so that the focus of attention can be placed on the interrelationships between the household sector and the business sector.

The household sector in the local economy undertakes two activities simultaneously. First, the household sector consists of all individuals and households who

THE DECISION TO ESTIMATE MARKET VALUE

own the factors of production. In other words, the household sector consists of those individuals who reside locally and who

1. Provide labor services to the industries located within the local economy
2. Own land in the local economy
3. Own all the capital goods and capital funds, used locally
4. Provide entrepreneurial talent to local firms

These factors of production are sold to the business sector and in return the household receives wages for its labor services, rent for the use of its land, dividends for the use of its capital goods, interest payment for the use of its capital funds, and profits for the application of its entrepreneurial ability. These relationships are shown in Exhibit 8-2. Exhibit 8-2(a) identifies the real flows—the movement of productive services from the household to the business sector—while Exhibit 8-2(b) shows the money flows—the movement of factor payments in the form of wages, rents, interest, dividends, and profits from the business sector to the household sector.

At the same time that the household sector is providing factors of production to the business sector it is also purchasing consumer goods and services that the business sector produces. This relationship is shown in real terms in Exhibit 8-2(a) as the movement of goods and services from the business sector to the household; it is also shown in money terms in Exhibit 8-2(b) as the flow of money in the form of consumption expenditures from the household to business sector.

The business sector, like the household sector, simultaneously performs two functions in the local economy. First, it uses the productive resources. Second, it produces the consumer goods and services that are purchased by the individuals in the household sector.

The circular flow of income model presented in this form reveals that the local economy is made up of two major sectors and is interrelated by two real flows

Real flows

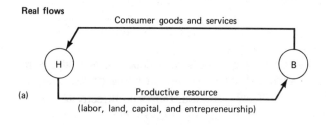

Consumer goods and services

(a)

Productive resource

(labor, land, capital, and entrepreneurship)

Money flows

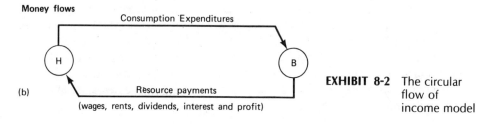

Consumption Expenditures

(b)

Resource payments

(wages, rents, dividends, interest and profit)

EXHIBIT 8-2 The circular flow of income model

and two money flows that reflect those real flows. Understanding the composition of the sectors and the composition of the flows is the first and major conceptual step in understanding the nature of the economic activity in the local economy.

The economic base of the local economy The economic base of the local economy is simply the description of the household and business sectors, and the flows shown in the circular of flow of income model. The household sector can be described by identifying variables such as the following:

1. Size of the population, the number of families, the number of households
2. The age composition of the population, of the heads of families and of the heads of households
3. The income composition of the population, families, and households
4. The size of families and households
5. The occupational composition of the population
6. The sex composition
7. The marital status of the population

This information can be obtained from the *Census of Population* and publications of local planning agencies.

The structure of the business sector can be described by identifying the industrial classifications that exist in the local economy. This can be accomplished by means of the standard industrial classification system (SIC) developed and used by the Bureau of the Census. The SIC classification system identifies industrial activity according to a numerical code of one to four digits that expresses the type of industrial activity that can occur in an economy.

The real flows and the money flows identified in Exhibit 8-2 for consumer goods are closely related. However, it is easier to obtain information on the money flow entitled consumption expenditures than it is to obtain a list of the consumer goods and services themselves. Therefore, information from several sources is used to describe the composition of this flow. The *Census of Retail Trade* is one such publication in which the composition of retail trade for the metropolitan statistical area is broken down by two- and three-digit SIC codes.

The nature and composition of the productive resource flow and the resource payments flow can also be obtained from government publications. First, the workers can be identified by the type of industry in which they work. This method would yield information about the number of workers in the construction industry, in the manufacturing industries (heavy and light), in the retail and wholesale industries, and in the food-processing industry. This is provided by the *Census of Population,* which identifies the number of employees in one-digit SIC Codes for MSAs and counties. Similar information can also be obtained from state offices on a county basis. Second, the labor force can be identified by its skill level and job orientation. This method would yield information about the number of workers who are classified as managerial and professional, technical, clerical, sales, service workers, and production craft and repair workers.

The local economy's real estate can be described by its components. The following kind of information can be provided:

1. The number of land units (acres, lots, etc.) and specific uses of this land (residential, commercial, and industrial) can be identified.
2. The area inside existing structures can be stated in square footage available for commercial and industrial users.
3. Current vacant real estate can be enumerated in terms of the number of vacant acres zoned for residential, commercial, or industrial use and the square footage of vacant commercial and industrial buildings.

Export base theory—The link to the nonlocal area This economic model was formulated in the 1950s and 1960s to analyze the growth of a local economy. This model starts with the idea that the business sector of the local economy contains firms that sell to nonlocal consumers and firms that sell to local consumers, and that the community's commercial and industrial firms can be classified on the basis of the sales of their goods and services to local versus nonlocal consumers. Those industrial and commercial firms that sell their products to the nonlocal consumers are known as the basic component of the local economy. The firms that sell their goods and services to the local consumers are known as the nonbasic components of the local economy. In its original formulation, the theory held that an expansion in the basic sector of the economy generated the growth of the local economy. As the exportation of goods and services grew to accommodate increased demand by external consumers, the local economy grew for two reasons. First, the basic industries needed more employees to meet increased external demand. Second, the firms producing goods for local consumptions also had to expand and/or new firms were started to meet the demands of the expanded local labor force in the basic industries.

As the basic industries expand their output and employment, they foster the expansion of employment in local producers. The effect of this expansion in the local economy is an increased demand in the various housing submarkets and the markets for commercial services. The increase in demand is brought about by an increase in the number of households and a possible increase in their purchasing power.

The significance of the export base theory lies in its signal to the analyst that external factors play a substantial role in the future of the local economy. As discussed in the previous section, economic base analysis describes the internal structure of the local economy. Export base theory alerts the analyst to the need

1. To find the most significant basic industries and firms
2. To identify the important external economic variables that affect the basic industry
3. To trace the impact of changes in the basic sector on the nonbasic sector of the local economy

There is an alternative technique that allows the analyst to combine the concepts of the circular flow of income and export base techniques. This alternative model is the input-output model. In its simplest use, the input-output model is a description device for the internal relationships in the business sector and an alternative to the circular flow of income as a descriptive technique for the economy. However, a discussion of this technique is beyond the scope of this chapter.

Updating and Forecasting the Level of Local Economic Activity

After the real estate market analyst describes the nature of the existing economy using the most recent data from the U.S. Bureau of the Census, the analyst may face two additional tasks. First, if the census data are not current—that is, the analysis is being done in 1985 while the census information reflects the economic relationships of 1980, the analyst must update the key variables such as population, employment, income, and retail sales. Then, once the information is updated, the analyst can use this current information as well as past information to forecast the level of population, employment, income, and retail sales for future periods.

As a point of clarification, there is a difference between a projection and a forecast. A projection is simply the extrapolation of past values for some variable, such as population, through the present period into the future. A forecast, on the other hand, takes data from the past and extrapolates it through the present, but subjects the trend to an analysis given current-day situations. When this analysis is imposed, the trend of the variable into the future may be higher or lower than the value that would arise given a simple projection. The need to make this distinction between a forecast and a projection exists because the real estate market analyst is responsible for forecasting future changes that can affect a parcel of real property or its income stream.

The real estate analyst often makes forecasts based upon the projections of population and employment made by governmental agencies. At times, the real estate analyst must make forecasts concerning the property based upon a projection or a forecast for the national, regional, or local economy. The following sections present information on the traditionally accepted techniques used by the analyst to update and forecast information.

Updating techniques There are several accepted methods for updating population values from the past census, such as 1980, to the current period. Five of these methods will be discussed in the following subsections. They are the housing inventory method, the natural increase and migration method, the cohort survival method, the ratio technique, and graphical/mathematical techniques.

The housing inventory method This updating technique relies on the use of population and household size figures from the previous census. Information from the 1970 and the 1980 Census of Population is used. In addition to the census data, local area data on building permits and demolitions are also used. The method of calculating the current population value starts with 1970 population for the geographic area in question and the appropriate household size for that geographic area. (The geographic area can be the MSA, the county, or a census tract.) Information from the 1980 Census is obtained for household size. Once these data from the past are obtained, the trend in household size is forecast to the current period. The number of current households are estimated by using building permit and demolition data from the local community to get the change in the number of housing units. The analyst produces a population estimate for the current period by multiplying housing units by household size.

The natural increase and migration method This updating technique starts with information from the most recent census of population for age categories and sex composition as they existed in 1980. Then the net change in population is calculated. First, given demographic information about the fertility rate of women in the high child-bearing age category, the number of births per thousand can be established for each year. Then the survival rate, or its counterpart the death rate, by age category is obtained from mortality tables on a year-by-year basis.

The next piece of information required to complete the estimate of 1985 population is an estimate of the net migration of individuals into the geographic area. The best available local source of such information is the "net new electrical hook-ups" for the area in question. This information is available from some utility company for broad geographic areas such as a census tract basis, a zip code, or a county. Net new hookups represent the number of households that have established new service in the local area and did not have existing service in the area, less the number of existing households who have cancelled service in the local area and have not established new serivce at another site in the local area. In other words, it measures the number of households who had electrical service outside the area previously and have now moved to the area and established new electrical service less those households who resided in the area, cancelled their service, and never established a new account because they have left the area.

If net new electrical hookups data are not available, the most recent migration, 1980–current period, must be extrapolated from the previous period, 1975–80. Given the data, this extrapolation can be performed on a year-by-year basis.

The analyst produces the population estimate for the current period by recording 1980 population, adding the estimated births for 1980–current period, subtracting out the deaths for 1980–current period, and then entering the result of migration which could be positive or negative. If the analyst obtains local statistics on actual births and deaths for the 1980–current period, the updated population figure becomes more accurate.

The cohort survival method This population updating technique also utilizes an age breakdown of the population from the most recent census of population. In this case, the breakdown in the age category has to be in five-year intervals because the data are presented in the census in five-year groupings. In other words, the age group that was 21 to 25 in 1980 will be 26 to 30 in 1985.

However, the technique uses the survival rate for these five-year cohorts to obtain the surviving members of each age cohort. A calculation is performed for each of the age groups and the surviving members of each age cohort are placed forward in time. In other words, the age group that was 21 to 25 in 1980 will be 26 to 30 in 1985, but only 99.6% or so will have survived.

The next major component of the cohort survival technique is the calculation of net migration. In the simplest form, the estimate for net migration can be obtained using net new residential hookups. Once it is obtained, this figure is entered in by age group or simply by its total change (plus or minus) to get the 1985 population estimate.

Finally, births during the update period are estimated from data on women in prime child-bearing years and the fertility rate. Births become the estimate for children in the 0 to 5 years of age cohort in 1985.

Ratio technique The ratio technique allows the analyst to estimate the value of an unknown variable from a known value. The analyst may have past and current data for a longer geographic unit, the county, but only has past data for the census tract. The task at hand is to obtain an estimate for the population level in the census tract for the current period. This is accomplished by using the ratio for the known values to estimate the unknown value—present period in the census tract population.

Graphical and mathematical techniques The graphical and mathematical techniques for updating population utilize data from previous periods and project it to the present using either a graph or a mathematical equation that approximates the value of the historical curve. In its simplest form, this technique uses direct observation to project a curve. The analyst looks at a graph of past data and extends the curve. Currently, the most popular technique for approximating the historical values and projecting them is regression analysis. However, a detailed discussion of regression analysis in its mathematical and statistical forms is beyond the scope of this chapter.

Forecasting techniques Each of the updating techniques discussed in the previous section can be used to forecast or project into the future. The procedure involves an additional conceptual step. The updating task brings the data series to the present; the forecasting task extrapolates the present into the future by analyzing the key variables in each method. The forecast can be made under two initiating conditions: the existence of a population projection, or the lack of such a projection.

Forecasting population from an existing projection The ratio technique is the simplest method to use if there is a reputable population forecast or projection in existence. Usually, such data are provided by an agency or department of a state government. It also may be available from a regional planning agency.

First, the analyst displays the actual 1970 and 1980 population data for the county and the census tract. From these data, the historical census tract/county population ratio and the current period values are calculated. Then, the analyst displays the county population projection from the state agency for 1990 and 2000.

The forecast for census tract population involves the following steps:

1. The value of the census tract/county ratio is forecast into the future. This is accomplished by checking the current growth potential in the county and the census tract.
2. The future appropriate value of the ratio is applied to the projected county population.

THE DECISION TO ESTIMATE MARKET VALUE

To obtain the appropriate future value of the census tract to county population ratio, the analyst could check the following supply factors that enable growth in both the county and the census tract:

1. Construction projects under way
2. Available land zoned for residential construction
3. The prospects for rezoning from low-density residential to high-density residential, and from nonresidential to residential uses
4. County plans for road, water, and sewage system extensions into undeveloped areas
5. State and county plans for the provision of public services that might require eminent domain takings of existing residential units

In addition to these supply variables, the analysis also can check the demand for residential space in the respective areas. A more thorough discussion of these demand variables is presented in the chapter entitled "Housing Market Analysis."

Once the level of population in the census tract is forecast, the number of households also can be forecast. This is accomplished by determining the historic trend in household size for the study area, judging its future value, and dividing this estimate into the population forecast.

Forecasting Population without an Existing Projection If an independent population projection is not available from a reputable government or private agency, the ratio method is not applicable. In this case one of the other techniques must be used. For purposes of discussion, the natural increase and migration method will be used.

Since relatively short time periods are of major concern for small area forecasting, the forecast will be made for 1990. The first piece of information needed to make the forecast is the number of females in the primary childbearing years. The exact number of such women will depend on the relative number of women in the 10 to 20 age cohort in 1980 who will move into the 21 to 35 age cohort by 1990, and the number of women in the 25 to 35 age group in 1980 who will move out of the 21 to 35 age cohort by 1990. A first approximation would set the inflow equal to the outflow so that the size of the 21 to 35 age cohort is assumed to be stable at 12,000 women. If this assumption is made, the number of births between 1985 and 1990 can be calculated. Then the deaths between 1985 and 1990 are estimated. So, the net effect of the birth and death component can be established.

The first approximation for net migration could be the simple reinsertion of the 1980 to 1985 net migration value. However, the more conceptually appropriate approach would be an analysis of the historic migration figures compared to the past growth potential of the study area. If the future growth enabling supply factors in the census tract are still favorable, the historic trend can be readily extended into the future. Yet, if the ability to grow is retarded because the supply of land for residential use is limited, the future growth will be much less than the historic trend. In other words, future levels of net migration will be lower, or could even be negative.

In summary, the population can be forecast by combining the natural increase method with the graphical technique to analyze the historic migration trend and compare it to future trends.

Forecasting and Updating Income

Updates and forecasts for levels of income such as median per capita income or household income must be established by the market analyst because updates of income are seldom made, and forecasts are virtually never made by government agencies. The easiest update procedure requires that the analyst obtain consumer price index (CPI) data that adequately represent the area. Since the information to construct the CPI is only gathered in a limited number of geographic areas, the best that can be said is that the CPI seems to be a relatively good proxy, and may reflect the income change with a high degree of accuracy. This statement can be further refined by the following thoughts:

1. When inflation is small in magnitude and stable over time, real income tends to increase.
2. When inflation is large, real income typically declines.
3. Geographic areas with relatively high median incomes tend to capture all of the price change in the form of an income increase.
4. Geographic areas with below-average income levels tend not to capture the full extent of the income change.
5. The change in income tends to lag the change in the price level by about a year.

Given what has been said, an update for income is obtained by multiplying the level of income given in the latest census by the percentage change in the CPI from 1980 to the present and adding this value to the 1980 figure.

Forecasting the level of income requires the judicious use of geographical and ratio techniques. The historic trend in income for the study area is displayed. Then a year-by-year change in income is also displayed; this data stream could be the figures for per capita personal income in the gross national products accounts of the United States. The ratio technique can be used to see how the local area compares to the national figures over time. Once such comparisons are made, the analyst can make a judgment about future levels of local income. The judgment reflects prior knowledge about many factors. Some of the important factors are identified below:

1. The comparison should be made in real terms to eliminate geographic differences in CPI changes.
2. Changes in the participation rate affect the level of household income as well as per capita income.
3. Geographic relocation of industry into and out of the area must be considered.

4. The nature of the local economy in industrial structure with regard to growth versus stagnant industries must be analyzed.

In conclusion, the level of income can be updated and it can be forecast. The analyst can make these forecasts from secondary data, or the analyst can purchase this information from firms that use census data, update it for census tracts, and even project it into the future. Their projections are usually for a 5-year horizon. The authors are familiar with the following companies that make this data available: CACI Inc., Urban Decision Systems, and National Decision Systems.

ANALYSIS OF THE MARKET FOR A SPECIFIC TYPE OF REAL ESTATE

In order to analyze a market for a specific type of real estate, that product must be defined. Real estate is not a standardized commodity; it incorporates residential, retail, office, and industrial property. To facilitate market analysis, one of these broad types of real estate must be initially selected. Then, within this broad category, additional distinctions need to be made. For residential real estate, the next logical breakdown is between owner-occupied and renter-occupied units. If a finer distinction needs to be made, the analyst can distinguish between single-family housing and condominiums as owner-occupied units and rental units in traditional apartments versus rental units in townhouses. The end result of this refinement process is the identification of a relatively standardized commodity that is a distinct submarket under the general heading of residential real estate. The process of identifying such a standardized submarket from a more general, less standardized market is called *market disaggregation.*

Analysis of a Housing Submarket

Once the process of disaggregation identifies the housing unit under analysis, the market analyst obtains information on the economic and demographic factors that affect the submarket. In other words, the analyst seeks information about the demand variables and the supply variables that operate within that market. At this level of the analysis, it is useful to keep in mind that the analyst still has not turned his or her attention to the specific property that forms the basis of the study. Rather, at this stage of the process, the analyst investigates the broad market factors that affect the demand and supply for the category of housing to which the subject property belongs. In other words, if the assignment is an analysis of the market potential for a single-family housing development, at this stage of the analysis the demand and supply variables affecting the market for single-family housing in general are studied.

For the sake of discussion, assume that the assignment is the analysis of a new residential development. The analyst seeks to identify the demand and supply factors that affect the market for newly constructed single-family residential units.

The demand variables   The economic and demographic variables that affect the level of demand for new residential construction are:

☐ Net household formation
☐ The age composition of the households
☐ Household income levels
☐ Credit conditions, especially the mortgage interest rate
☐ The price of substitute housing
☐ Expectations about future price levels for the type of housing being studied

Each of these variables is examined over time to see its direction of change and to get an indication of the demand for new residential construction. If net household formation occurs, household income levels rise, and the prices of substitute housing units increase, the demand for new residential construction of single-family housing units typically will increase. If the mortgage interest rate declines, it also translates into an increase in the demand for new single-family residential units. A more complete discussion of the nature of these variables and their impact on the demand curve is presented in Chapter 7.

The supply variables   The supply of newly constructed single-family housing is determined by the following variables:

☐ The prices of materials, land, labor, and other factors of production used in the construction process
☐ The productivity of labor in the construction process
☐ The number of builders who are operating in the submarket
☐ The expectations that these builders have about future sales levels

The supply of newly constructed units increases as the cost of materials, construction worker wages, land prices, and construction finance costs decline. In addition, supply of newly constructed units also increases as the productivity of labor increases and as additional builders enter the submarket. Finally, holding all of the other variables constant, the supply of new construction can increase if the builders in the market believe that future sales will expand. A more complete discussion of these supply side variables also appears in the chapter entitled "Housing Market Analysis."

Commercial Market Analysis

In the area of commercial property, there are three distinct categories that can form the basis for market analysis. First, there is the market for retail space. If a greater distinction is required, the submarkets under retail space could be regional malls, community shopping centers, neighborhood shopping centers, and free-standing retail establishments. At the next level of disaggregation, the analysis could focus on

THE DECISION TO ESTIMATE MARKET VALUE

the retail space for specific product lines in specific locations—for example, shoe stores in a specific census tract.

The second broad category of commercial property is office space designed for use by activities that serve the local market. This category contains the following services: legal, insurance, medical, dental, tax, accounting, general accounting, real estate brokerage, and other such professional services that are provided for local residents. In this situation, disaggregation can occur by analyzing these activities for a particular location within the local economy.

The third category of commercial property is office space for activities that primarily serve the nonlocal consumer. This category would contain activities such as corporate headquarters (national or regional), stock market brokerage companies who serve clients outside the local economy, insurance company offices, and so on.

Each of these commercial submarkets can be analyzed using demand and supply variables. This discussion follows in the next few paragraphs.

Retail market analysis   The demand variables that are most important in an analysis of retail services are the number of consumers and their income level. Using these data, the level of purchasing power can be calculated. As purchasing power increases, the demand for retail goods and services increases. As a consequence, the demand for retail space also increases. (This cause-and-effect relationship from the demand for the retail good to the demand for retail space is known as the concept of derived demand.)

In addition to purchasing power, the other important demand side variables are the consumer's taste and preference pattern for the products that can be purchased and the spatial distribution pattern of purchasing power. Considering changes in taste and preferences, the consumer rearranges the combination of retail goods purchased from time to time. For example, as new products are offered for sale (videocassette recorders, personal computers, lightweight cassette players with earphones, etc.), they are added into the consumer's market basket and the quantity of other products purchased either decreases or is discontinued. In addition, as the consumer moves through his or her life cycle, different products are bought. For example, the young consumer may spend proportionally more for recreation and entertainment activities, while the older consumer may spend proportionally more for home furnishings, education expenses, and insurance.

The market analyst can obtain information about consumer purchase patterns from two government publications: *Consumer Expenditure Survey,* and *Relative Importance of Components in the Consumer Price Index.* Here, several distinct retail categories are identified and the percentage of before-tax income spent on each retail category is identified. In addition, within each of the broad retail categories, such as men's clothing, different income groups purchase different quality of product lines. For example, the low-income household may buy men's clothing exclusively in discount stores, while the upper-income households may buy men's clothing exclusively in specialty men's shops. The census of retail trade can also provide these percentages.

Office space providing local services   Market analysis for the services and activities provided in this category of commercial property is very similar to the analysis for retail activities. These office services also compare a certain percentage of the consumer's income. Consequently, as the market analyst obtains data for purchasing power, he can apply those percentages to calculate the local residents' demand for medical, legal, dental, and other services.

Office space for nonlocal customers   The demand for office space for this category of services is more difficult to estimate because it requires knowledge about the purchase pattern of nonlocal consumers, the types of industries located in the local economy, the cost of comparable space between the local economy and the nonlocal economy, the relative wage rate between the local economy and the nonlocal economy, and locational amenities that may attract firms to the local economy. These variables affect the demand for local office space by firms that serve the nonlocal consumer.

ANALYSIS OF THE SUBJECT PROPERTY

The analysis of the subject property consists of the following four major tasks:

1. A study of the legal and physical characteristics of the subject property
2. The definition of the competitive trade area
3. A survey and evaluation of the competition
4. Consumer research

Each of these tasks will be discussed in the following subsections. When the analyst focuses on a specific property, the analyst is undertaking a *marketability study*. The *market study* is product or use specific, the *marketability study* is site specific. Yet, even though the focus is different, the two studies are related. The data used in the market study and the information derived from it are inputs to the marketability study.

Analysis of the Legal and Physical Characteristics of the Subject Property

The legal characteristics of the subject property that must be identified and analyzed have been discussed in great detail in earlier chapters. Consequently, at this point these characteristics will only be identified and briefly examined. The first concern of the market analyst is a determination of what activity is legally permissable on the subject property. To obtain information pertinent to this aspect of inquiry, the analyst must examine the following:

1. The zoning ordinance with regard to land-use restrictions, height restrictions, and area regulations
2. Subdivision regulations
3. Construction code requirements
4. Occupancy code requirements

5. Environmental and pollution restrictions

6. Availability of public services

When the analyst examines the various restrictions and requirements imposed by these ordinances and governmental activities, the legally permissable uses that can be placed on the subject site are identified.

Once the legal restrictions are known, the analyst checks the physical restrictions imposed by the subject site. The factors that are analyzed in this section of the study are the following geographic and geological features of the site:

1. Geographic features, which include:
   —size of the land parcel
   —shape of the land parcel
   —frontage
   —width and depth of the land parcel
   —corner influences

2. The geological features of the site, which include:
   —topography
   —surface soil quality and landscaping
   —subsoil and bedrock characteristics
   —drainage and runoff characteristics

3. Physical characteristics of the improvement, which include:
   —the placement of the structure on the site
   —quantitative and qualitative construction details
   —an analysis of the mechanical systems in the improvement
   —an analysis of the physical design and layout of the space within the improvement

These physical features associated with the site and the improvements on the site establish the second set of limiting requirements. Not only must the economic activity be legally permissable, but it also must be physically possible given the physical characteristics of the site and the improvement.

After the legal and physical characteristics of the subject property are analyzed, many uses are eliminated and a few are possible. These legally permissable and physically possible uses for the subject property must now be analyzed in greater detail. In order to carry on a discussion of remaining tasks, assume that either housing or retail activity can be accommodated by the subject property. The following discussion concerning the remaining tasks will be presented by referring to these two forms of economic activity.

Definition of the Competitive Area

The procedures needed to define the competitive trade area for housing and for retail activity contain some common characteristics. First, whether the competitive area is for housing or for retail activity, the most appropriate geographic area to analyze is the area that lies immediately adjacent, or in close proximity to, the subject site.

Sometimes this area is readily identified for the analyst because of natural barriers such as rivers, ridge, lines, mountains or hills, and man-made barriers such as railroad tracks, expressways, and open space in the form of parks. However, for the most part, the geographic extent of the competitive area must be obtained from an analysis of economic variables and consumer behavior.

At its most basic level, consumer behavior is affected by the desire to accomplish simultaneously: (1) minimization of the disutility of travel, and (2) maximization of the amenities that can be obtained on the subject property and from the geographic area in close proximity to the subject property.

The Survey and Evaluation of the Competition

When the survey of the competition is performed, as much information as possible is gathered about the competitors of the activity on the subject property. If the subject property is going to provide housing units, the market researcher must define the competitive, geographic trade area and identify all of the comparable properties as well as all of the strong substitutes for the type of housing units on the subject property. If, on the other hand, the subject property is providing retail activities, the market researcher must identify the retail trade area and all of the direct competitors for the retail establishment located on the subject property.

In general, the structure of the information to be gathered in either the residential or the retail case is quite similar. In either case, the information that should be gathered concerning the competitive and substitute establishments is given by the classification system presented below:

1. Physical and functional characteristics of the structure, which include:
   —architectual style of the building
   —age and condition of the structure
   —special features of the structure such as covered walkways, enclosed entry ways, location of the units within the structure
   —traffic patterns inside the structure, special characteristics of the structure that are viewed as attractive (this could include design features, floor layouts, positioning window opening, lighting, carpeting, size of the individual units in terms of square footage as well as the type of space being provided bedrooms, bathrooms, livingroom, dining room, etc.)
   —special structural features such as balconies, patios, screen porches
2. Amenities, which include:
   —parking features such as number of spaces, location of the parking facilities relative to the entrance of the structure, covered area, etc.
   —security and safety factors
3. Accessibility features, which include:
   —proximity to employment centers, shopping facilities, entertainment, recreational, and cultural activities

—proximity to major streets and public transportation

—proximity to fire and police protection, hospitals

—proximity to schools especially if the subject property contains residential units

4. Financial characteristics, which include:

—sales prices or rent levels for the space

—special financial arrangements associated with the sale or rental of the space (this could include price discounts, rent below the market rate, and the provision of special or supplementary fixtures and appliances)

—special charges that may take place in the future (this category could include special assessments for public improvements, cost of living increases in rent levels, etc.)

The market analyst must obtain this information about the subject property and its competitors to the greatest degree possible given the time and money constraints that may be imposed. The end result of the analysis should be the construction of a table that allows the analyst to compare each establishment with regard to each characteristic identified in the previous discussion. This table is the starting point for the establishment of a market standard and the identification of a competitive differential for the subject property.

Consumer Research

The data gathered in the survey of the competition identify the various characteristics of competitive and substitute properties. However, in an indirect fashion, the data gathered from the survey of the competition also identify consumer tastes and preferences. This information is obtained by checking the absorption rate of the units against the financial, structural, site, and neighborhood/location characteristics. Presumably, the dwelling units in the comparable properties that best satisfy consumer tastes and preferences will have the higher absorption rates, given the relative price of the property. So, the market analyst can start the process of creating a competitive differential by advising the client to design the subject property to include features that are at least as good as those in the properties with the highest historical absorption rates. In this way, the analyst can make the judgment that if consumer tastes and preferences are constant, or are at least highly similar, they will currently select those properties that yield the same amenities as the properties with the high absorption rate.

However, information about consumer tastes, preferences, and attitudes taken from the survey of competition is indirect knowledge. The analyst infers present and future taste and preference patterns from past taste and preference patterns. Situations will occur in which the analyst will require direct knowledge about consumer attitudes, tastes, and preferences. The only way this information can be obtained is through the process of consumer research. The analyst must go to the potential consumer and ask questions that will reveal the pertinent information about desirable characteristics and, in general, about the subject property.

THE RESULTS OF THE MARKET ANALYSIS PROCESS

The data obtained from the process of market and marketability analysis lead the analyst to a determination of the current market rent and vacancy level, as well as a forecast of future levels of market rent and vacancy. This information is used as the "top line" of the financial analysis. In terms of the income property appraisal example presented in Chapter 5, the figures placed into Exhibit 5-4 for potential rent receipts and vacancy losses come from the market analysis process.

In general terms, the data for current market rent come from an analysis of the existing competition by means of their current price quotes and the negotiated price for space. Care must be taken to make sure that the information is not historic, contract rent because market analysis points to the future not to the past. Vacancy data are also obtained from the market analysis process in the same manner as the rent data.

In addition to this current data for rents obtained from the survey of the competition, the analyst can get an idea of what consumers are willing to pay for the space in the subject property by using appropriately designed questions in the consumer survey. These data can even provide information on the differentials that consumers will be willing to pay for certain types of structural amenities such as extra rooms, extra square footage, balconies, fireplaces, and so on.

The survey of the competition and the survey of the consumer also can provide information about the type of product—its qualitative aspects—that is most desired. The survey of the existing competition can show the analyst what product the market provided in the past by identifying its structural features and its location. Moreover, the survey of the competition can show the analyst the absorption rate, or how responsive the market was to that product.

The survey of the consumers can tell the analyst what current consumers want in the way of location, neighborhood, and structural amenities, and what they are willing to pay for the space they desire. Special features can be evaluated for inclusion in the units. The importance of on-site recreational amenities also can be determined.

Armed with these data, investors can determine if the investment meets their financial objectives, mortgage lenders can determine if the property passes their standards for acceptable loans, and developers can determine what to build and where to build it.

CHAPTER SUMMARY

Market analysis is a major component of a feasibility study. Other components are the financial study, the construction cost study, the location study, and the design study. Using these specialized studies, the feasibility study evaluates the property's ability to meet the investor's financial objectives.

The market study addresses several important topics. It identifies the local economy and describes its nature and structure. It analyzes the market(s) in which the subject property will compete. This is first accomplished by studying population and income levels in the past, present, and future. Then, the marketability of the

THE DECISION TO ESTIMATE MARKET VALUE

space or service of the subject property is evaluated by a study of the characteristics of the property; a delineation of the competitive market area; a survey of the competition; and a survey of the tastes, preferences, purchase habits, and so on of the consumers.

This information allows the analyst to forecast the level of revenues and vacancies for the subject property. These forecasts are utilized in the financial analysis that underlies the investment decision.

Review Questions

1. Discuss the nature and content of a feasibility study. Be certain to describe the various component studies that can be included in a feasibility study.
2. Define market analysis and describe the market analysis process.
3. Explain the relationships that are expressed in the circular flow of income model.
4. Define and discuss the economic base model.
5. Define and discuss the export base theory. How does it differ from economic base analysis?
6. Describe the techniques that are used to update and forecast population.
7. Identify the tasks to be accomplished to analyze a specific subject property.
8. What are the legal and physical characteristics that can affect the marketability of the subject property?
9. Describe the nature and content of the survey of the competition.
10. What is consumer research?

Discussion Questions

1. How does the condition of the local economy affect the marketability of a single-family home and the marketability of retail space?
2. How does the condition of the "outside world," the nonlocal economy, affect the marketability of retail space and local housing?
3. Why might the analyst need consumer research to do a complete marketability study for a new apartment project?
4. How does the information from the survey of the competition help the analyst determine rent levels for the subject property?

Additional Readings

APPLEBAUM, WILLIAM. "Methods for Determining Store Trade Areas, Market Penetration and Potential Sales." *Journal of Marketing Research* 3 (May 1966): 127–141.

BAILEY, JOHN B., PETER F. SPIES, and MARILYN KRAMER WEITZMAN. "Market Study + Financial Analysis = Feasibility Report." *Appraisal Journal* 45 (October 1977): 550–77.

BARRETT, G. VINCENT. "Appraisal Should Be Market Study: Techniques of Analysis." *Appraisal Journal* 47 (October 1979): 538–55.

BARRETT, G. VINCENT, and JOHN P. BLAIR. *How to Conduct and Analyze Real Estate Market and Feasibility Studies.* New York: Van Nostrand Reinhold Co., 1982.

DASSO, J. "Economic Base Analysis for the Appraiser," *Appraisal Journal* (July 1969).

DETOY, CHARLES J., and SOL L. RABIN. "Office Space: Calculating the Demand," *Urban Land* 31 (June 1972): 4–13.

ELDRED, GARY W., and ROBERT H. ZERBST. "Consumer Research and the Real Estate Appraiser." *Appraisal Journal* 44 (October 1976): 443–52.

GRAASKAMP, JAMES A. *A Guide to Feasibility Analysis.* Chicago: Society of Real Estate Appraisers, 1970.

HUFF, D. "A Probabilistic Analysis for Shopping Center Trade Areas." *Land Economics* (February 1963): 81–90.

KELLY, H. "Forecasting Office Space Demand in Urban Areas." *Real Estate Review* (Fall 1983): 87–95.

MESSNER, STEPHEN D., BYRL N. BOYCE, HAROLD G. TRIMBLE, and ROBERT L. WARD. *Analyzing Real Estate Opportunities: Market and Feasibility Studies.* Chicago, Ill. Realtors National Marketing Institute, National Association of Realtors, 1977.

RABIANSKI, J. "An Alternative to Economic Base Analysis." *The Real Estate Appraisal* (September–October, 1977): 49–54.

SUMICHRAST, M. "Housing Market Analysis." *The Real Estate Handbook,* ed. by M. Seldin. Homewood, Ill.: Dow Jones-Irwin, 1980: 314–337.

VERNOR, JAMES D. *Readings in Market Research for Real Estate.* Chicago, Ill.: American Institute of Real Estate Appraisers, 1985.

9 | Real Estate Equity Investment

QUESTIONS TO BE ANSWERED

1. What factors must an individual investor consider in deciding whether to purchase income-earning property?
2. What techniques should the individual investor understand and use as part of the decision-making process?

OBJECTIVES

When the student finishes the chapter, he or she should be able to

1. Explain the nature of an equity investment in real estate.
2. Understand the various objectives that typical investors wish to achieve.
3. Identify and discuss the risks and obstacles associated with real estate equity investment.

4. Explain the generation of before-tax cash flow.

5. Describe the nature and uses of financial and profitability ratios.

6. Describe the nature and uses of present value and internal rate of return calculations.

7. Explain feasibility analysis.

IMPORTANT TERMS _____

Before-Tax Cash Flow	Internal Rate of Return
Breakeven, or Default, Ratio	Investment
Business or Income Risk	Leverage (Positive)
Cost of Capital	Liquidity
Debt Service Coverage Ratio	Operating Expense Ratio
Equity	Periodic Cash Flow
Equity Dividend Rate	Present-Value Technique
Equity Yield Rate	Price Appreciation
Estate Building	Principal Risk
Feasibility Analysis	Purchasing Power Risk
Financial Risk	Pyramiding
Gross Rate of Return	Real Estate Equity Investment
Holding-Period Analysis	Sensitivity Analysis
Interest or Money Market Risk	Tax Shelter

INVESTMENT CONSIDERATIONS

Every potential investor in real estate must have pertinent information about the investment opportunity and the various economic and financial factors that can affect it. In addition, the investor should establish personal goals or expectations about the financial returns to be derived from the investment. Neither real estate investments nor any other investment can fulfill everyone's financial objectives. The investor should evaluate the strengths and weaknesses of the real estate investment in comparison with those of other investment opportunities.

The Nature of Equity Investment in Real Estate

When private individuals or corporations accumulate savings, they investigate various uses to which this unspent money can be applied. In other words, private individuals and corporations look for investment opportunities. The term **investment** is used in this sense throughout this textbook. Investment is the use of accumulated savings to purchase an asset that has potential income-earning ability.

Types of investment opportunities   The individual can choose from a large number of investment alternatives for accumulated savings. A person can enter some investments directly by assuming ownership of a document that is an income-earning asset—for example, savings accounts, corporate bonds, government bonds, and common and preferred stocks. The expected return for the savings accounts and bonds is greater than zero and is fixed in magnitude. The interest payment is stated in advance when the asset is purchased. In contrast, common and preferred stocks are investments for which the rate of return is variable. The dividends paid by the corporation depend on the company's earnings level and profits.

In addition to financial assets, an individual can invest in many types of nonfinancial assets such as commodities, business ventures, precious metals, gems, art objects, and antiques. The rate of return on each of these investments varies because the yield depends on such factors as the investor's bargaining ability, the establishment and operation of a business concern, and knowledge about future levels of demand and consumer tastes.

Real estate provides opportunities for investment in both financial and non-financial assets. An investor who purchases part or all of a parcel of real property—a nonfinancial asset—makes an *equity investment.* An investor who purchases a financial asset called a mortgage makes a *mortgage investment.* Both types of real estate investment are examined in detail in the following section.

Real estate equity investment versus mortgage investment   The real estate equity investor owns real property. The investor typically pays part of the sales price from savings and borrows the remainder. The extent to which borrowed funds are used does not affect the level of the investor's ownership rights. Whether the investor pays 10 percent, 50 percent, or 100 percent of the sales price from savings, the rights to use and dispose of the property do not change. At the time of purchase, the term **equity** specifically denotes the buyer's funds or assets that are used to acquire the property. If a 20 percent down payment is made from the investor's savings, the equity in the property is equal to 20 percent of the sales price.

The income-earning capability of an equity investment in real estate depends on a multitude of factors that can affect potential gross income, effective gross income, and operating expenses, and thereby affect the level of net operating income. The individual investor's income tax considerations also affect the level of earnings that can be derived from a specific parcel of real estate.

Mortgage investment is very rarely chosen by an individual. Financial institutions such as savings and loan associations, commercial banks, and life insurance companies generally utilize this type of investment. Mortgage investment is not ownership. The financial institution lends money to a person to buy real estate. In return, the financial institution receives an asset or legal document called the mortgage. The rate of return that the financial institution receives is known as the mortgage interest payment. In the past, it has typically been a fixed rate of return to the financial institution if the mortgage is held to maturity. The return is determined by the interest payment that is calculated at the time the mortgage instrument is signed by the borrower and the lender. Some forms of mortgage, however, have a rate of return that is not fixed or constant (the variable rate mortgage is described in Chapter 16). In this situation, the interest payment made by the borrower changes over time to reflect fluctuations in the level of interest rates in the economy.

The purpose of this chapter is to examine the equity investment in real estate because it is the type of investment chosen most often by people who wish to invest in real estate. In later chapters, we will explore the mortgage investment and the viewpoint of the mortgage investor, because the equity investor needs to understand the considerations and objectives of the financial institutions that loan money for the purchase of real estate.

INVESTOR OBJECTIVES

The rational investor analyzes all available opportunities for the use of savings. This analysis takes place in the framework established by the investor's individual financial goals and objectives. Some investors will assume more risk if there is a strong possibility of a high rate of return. Other investors will give up a periodic income flow for the prospect of an increase in the value of the asset over time. These investors are willing to take the risk that the investment will increase in value if the right economic or market circumstances occur.

The rational investor considers not only the income flow, the rate of return, and the growth of the investment's value, but also the possibility of converting the asset into cash without a loss during the transaction—the **liquidity** of the asset. As a general rule, an asset that is traded in an organized, active market tends to be more liquid than an asset that must be traded in a disorganized or fragmented market. Consequently, common stocks, preferred stocks, corporate bonds, and government bonds tend to be more liquid than real estate.

Once the investor decides what traits are desirable in a specific investment, a choice can be made from the many alternatives. The purpose of this section is not to compare real estate and non-real estate investments but to identify the various objectives that typically pertain to the real estate investment. Some of these objectives are appropriate to an investment decision in financial securities, such as stocks and bonds, and other objectives are applicable only to real estate investments.

Periodic Cash Flow

One investor objective is a return of dollars from the investment on some definite periodic basis, known as **periodic cash flow.** In the case of a common stock, this periodic return (or cash flow) is the quarterly or semiannual dividend check that may be issued by the company. For the investor in corporate or government bonds, the periodic cash flow is the interest payment received quarterly or annually. For the equity investor in real estate, the periodic cash flow is that portion of actual gross income that remains after operating expenses and other expenses associated with the property are paid. (A complete discussion of cash flow from a real estate investment is presented later in this chapter.)

Liquidity

A second investor objective is the ability to convert the asset into cash without a loss of value in the transaction. Common and preferred stocks that are listed with a major stock exchange can be converted into cash at the prevailing market rate within several business days. The investor receives the market value as of the time the asset was sold. From these funds, the investor pays the selling costs associated with the transaction. Corporate and government bonds can also be sold in organized markets for the current market value established in those markets. No organized national market is available for equity investments in real estate. Real estate markets are local; they are differentiated on the basis of the physical characteristics of the property. Moreover, at any given point in time, the number of potential buyers may be small. In some instances, there may not be even one buyer for the property. The process of converting the real estate asset to cash will probably take a relatively long time—60 to 180 days for residential property, several months for commercial property, and perhaps a year or more for industrial property. Consequently, real estate is probably the most illiquid investment alternative.

Price Appreciation

Some investors may not be concerned about a periodic income flow or even the liquidity of the asset because the primary objective is to hold the property while its market value increases. The term **price appreciation** refers to this situation. The investor expects the sales price of the property to increase over the next five or ten years by an amount that is greater than the earnings that might be received from alternate investments. The underlying assumption made by the investor in this case is that the real estate investment is part of an active market both currently and during the entire time the property is held. An investor whose main objective is price appreciation also might seek a periodic cash flow as a secondary objective.

Increase in Equity Through Mortgage Reduction

This investment objective is related to the need for cash flow from the property. What the investor hopes to achieve is an actual gross income level from the property that is great enough to cover all operating expenses as well as the mortgage payment. If the investment is paying for itself, the investor need not divert any income from other sources to pay off the mortgage on the property. The investor's equity, or percentage of ownership, increases as the borrowed funds are repaid over time. If the property is held for ten years, and if at the end of that time the investor must sell the property for its original purchase price, the investor still has a financial gain because the equity is a greater percentage of that price at the end of the ten-year period than it was on the day of purchase.

As an objective, this form of equity increase makes sense only in a market where the price of the commodity is increasing or at least staying constant. If the price of the property declines over the ownership period, the investor is really getting a larger percentage of a smaller number of dollars. If prices are declining, equity increase through mortgage reduction as an objective may be futile because the decline in the property's price may be greater than the increase in equity over the period of time that the property is held by the investor.

Tax Shelter

The tax laws of the federal and state governments have created another investment objective—obtaining a **tax shelter.** Since an income-producing structure is viewed as a wasting asset, the Internal Revenue Code allows the property owner to subtract a percentage of the value of that structure from the property's income stream. The tax codes allow several different methods for the calculation of this depreciation rate (the allowable forms of depreciation are described in Chapter 10). A tax shelter is achieved when the income subject to taxation that is generated by the property is negative (taxable income is negative). When the taxable income from the property is negative, the investor is able to shelter or protect income that is received from other sources, even salary, from federal and state income taxation. Furthermore, to the extent that depreciation charges taken as an income tax deduction are not measures of actual accrued depreciation (physical deterioration, functional obsolescence, and economic obsolescence), the investor is able to shelter part of the net operating income generated by the property from taxation.

High Rate of Return on Equity

Many people choose real estate as an investment to obtain high rates of return on equity. Typically, a good, financially sound real estate investment generates a positive periodic cash flow that can create a higher rate of return than an investment in stocks or bonds. However, the investor should realize that this higher rate of return is a compensation for factors that negatively affect real estate investment. Real estate investments are riskier than the typical investment in a financial asset such as stocks or bonds because real estate investments involve a greater degree of uncertainty about the income stream. A portion of the higher rate of return is designed to compensate the investor for this risk. In addition, real estate investments are less liquid and require more personal attention on the part of the investor than investments in financial securities.

There are two important rates of return that are used in a discussion of real estate equity investments. The first is the **equity dividend rate.** This rate is formed by dividing the periodic cash flow by the investor's equity. A more technically precise definition will be offered later in this chapter. However, conceptually, this definition is applicable. The other rate of return is the **equity yield rate.** In simple terms, this is the rate of return to the investor's equity obtained from periodic cash flow, price appreciation, and reduction in the unpaid balance of the mortgage. A more precise definition of this rate of return will also be offered later in this chapter.

Leverage

Leverage refers to a technique that can allow the investor to achieve objectives of high periodic cash flow, price appreciation, tax shelter, and so on, by using borrowed funds. A frequently used measure of leverage is the relationship between the rate of return generated by the property and the rate the investor must pay on the money borrowed to purchase that property. Another way to explain this concept of leverage is to say that the NOI from the investment property exceeds the mortgage payment by enough to produce a return on the equity greater than the mortgage rate of interest. In this situation, the investor is utilizing funds obtained from a lender to generate an income flow that is large enough to pay all operating expenses plus the cost of borrowed funds and still provide a positive cash payment. This cash flow is divided by the number of dollars of equity invested in the property to determine the equity dividend rate from the investment. If this rate exceeds the mortgage rate on borrowcd money, the investor is benefiting financially by using other people's funds to purchase investment property. Consequently, the investor wishes to find a property that provides positive leverage—a rate of return on the investment that is greater than the mortgage interest rate. Another form of leverage is the amount of funds the investor can borrow as a percent of the property's value. The higher the loan-to-value ratio, the greater the leverage.

Estate Building or Pyramiding

Estate building is another technique that can be used to achieve certain investment objectives. It is based on the premise that the investor currently owns a property that generates a gross income large enough to cover all operating expenses and the mortgage payment and still returns a positive cash flow. The investor can use such property in a trade for another piece of property that is larger or more profitable and thus more valuable. This process of estate building is encouraged by a tax code provision that allows the investor to defer capital gains taxation into the future (the tax-deferred exchange provision is described in greater detail in Chapter 10).

Pyramiding is also dependent on prior ownership of a good investment. However, the investor does not exchange one property for another. Instead, the equity increase in the initial investment is used as collateral to acquire additional property. When equity has increased, the original property can be refinanced to free cash that can be used to buy a second property, or the increased equity in the first property can be used as collateral for a loan to buy the second property.

Hedge Against Inflation

The investor also wishes to protect the purchasing power of the equity investment. This objective can be accomplished by a combination of price-appreciation and rate-of-return considerations. The investor would like to earn a return from the periodic cash flow and price appreciation that is great enough to offset alternative opportunities, illiquidity, management expenses, and risk. In addition, the investor would like the same return to be large enough to cover increases in the price level, as measured by the consumer price index, as well as provide a reasonable rate of return. So, if the investor desires a 16 percent return when inflation is 2 percent per year, the same investor wants a 24 percent return when inflation is 10 percent per year. This investment objective is typically achieved in an active real estate market when demand is increasing.

Psychological Factors

Some investors may derive nonmonetary benefits from the prestige associated with ownership of real property. Friends and relatives tend to be more impressed by ownership of an apartment building than with the possession of an account at the local savings and loan association, even if the equity position in the apartment complex is the same as the dollar value deposited in the savings account.

Conversely, certain psychological considerations can deter an investor from owning real property. This deterrent is "simply the awesome prospect of acquiring a piece of commercial or residential property, and finding ourselves in the position of being somebody's landlord. It is one thing to recognize and seize upon a good buy in the real estate market. It is quite another thing, however, to take on a role of absentee landlord for a piece of property inhabited by living and breathing people who are, at best, demanding, and, at worst, out to take you for everything they can get."[1] The prestige of ownership can be an incentive for real estate investment for some individuals, but the fear of ownership responsibilities of a physical asset that affects the lives of individuals can deter other potential investors.

RISKS AND OBSTACLES AFFECTING THE EQUITY INVESTMENT

Most types of investments involve risks and obstacles. The risks faced by the real estate investor tend to be greater than those faced by investors in financial securities. However, a parcel of real estate in a good location that has very little competition from other properties and is traded in an active market is likely to be a safer investment than many common stocks. Moreover, such a real estate investment is possibly safer than a bond issued by a corporation that has a small portfolio of assets and whose expenses have exceeded income for the past several years.

Risks

In general, risk is the possibility of financial loss in an investment opportunity arising from uncertainty about the future. The basic sources of risk are unfavorable changes in the economic environment affecting an investment with a fixed location, and a poor information flow coupled with high information search costs. The risks described in this section affect all investment alternatives, but they are examined with specific references to the real estate investment.

Business or income risk   Future levels of actual gross income may not be as large as forecast. In addition, the pattern or timing of future actual gross income flows may not be as forecast.[2] Such risk arises from both internal and external sources. The external sources are unanticipated changes in economic and demographic market factors that cause the level of market rent to fall below the investor's expectations. The internal source of business risk is the assumption of competent management. If this assumption does not hold true in the future, the vacancy loss will be higher if the inefficient manager is unable to find suitable tenants and accepts tenants with poor credit ratings.

Financial risk   Future levels of net operating income may not be sufficient to allow the owner to pay the mortgage from the revenues generated by the property. This problem can arise as a repercussion of business risk when the level of effective gross income in future periods is less than the amount forecast. Financial risk also can arise because the levels of future operating expenses were underestimated in the forecast. Operating expenses are affected by internal and external factors. Internally, the assumption of competent management may be erroneous and operating expenses for the property may increase at a greater rate than operating expenses for comparable properties that have competent management. Externally, operating expenses can be underestimated because the investor was unable to project rapid or sharp increases in such expense items as utilities, maintenance, property taxes, insurance, and the price of replacements for appliances and structural components.

Principal risk   The future sales price of the property may be less than anticipated.[3] This risk can arise because the investor anticipates an active future market for the sale of the property in which the property's value is expected to increase, when, in fact, the market value of that property declines. Also, principal risk can arise if the investor unrealistically forecasts a rate of price appreciation greater than the rate that actually occurs. In the first of these situations, the future sales price may be less than the current sales price. In the second case, the actual future sales price may be higher than the current price but still significantly less than the sales price forecast.

Interest or money market risk   The future value of the investment may be less because the basic rate component of a capitalization rate may be higher in the future than it was at the time of the initial appraisal and investment decision.[4] In terms of the band-of-investment technique, this risk can arise if mortgage interest rates rise in the future, if the expectations about typical rates of return increase, or if the typical loan in the future is made with a lower equity/value ratio. All of these changes are difficult to calculate for the future. If future capitalization rates are higher than current capitalization rates, and this increase is not expected, the actual value of the property in the future may be much less than the future value forecast.

Purchasing power risk   The dollars the investor will receive in the future may have less purchasing power than anticipated. The cause of this risk is inflation. Such risk arises when the investor underestimates the rate of inflation in the future.

Obstacles

Many obstacles can affect the investor's ability to analyze a real estate investment opportunity thoroughly. In general, these obstacles are the problems the investor faces in gathering adequate information to make an accurate forecast of future income and expenses. Certain difficulties inherent in the real estate sales transaction do not occur in the purchase of a financial security. The following list of obstacles is representative of the problems of the real estate investor:

1. Objective information sources about the subject property are difficult to find.
2. The amount of usable data on comparable properties is limited.
3. Reliable price quotations are not available on a frequent basis.
4. There are typically only a few buyers and sellers.
5. Real estate transactions are typically cumbersome, time consuming, and very often inefficient.
6. Each transaction is usually undertaken after a search of ownership records because of the possibility of title errors.
7. The exchange typically requires much negotiating and bargaining, which can be difficult and time consuming.
8. Specialized legal factors and tax considerations increase the complexity and costs of the transaction.[5]

Generally, these obstacles do not affect investment alternatives in the stock and bond markets or in savings accounts. The information and data problems associated with real estate investment increase business and financial risks above the levels faced by investors in stocks and bonds. The extra time and dollar costs associated with the real estate transaction either serve as a disincentive to enter into the real estate investment or necessitate a higher rate of return to compensate for the increased time and money expenditure involved.

RELATIONSHIP BETWEEN THE INCOME APPROACH TO VALUE AND INVESTMENT ANALYSIS

The income approach to determining current market value is very similar to the approach used to determine investment value. In this section, the similarities and differences between the two approaches are explored. First, the nature and purpose of investment analysis are compared with the nature and purpose of estimating current market value of an income-earning real estate asset. Then, the income and expense items included in each technique are examined.

Nature and Purpose of Investment Analysis

The income approach for estimating the current market value of a specific parcel of real estate focuses on market forces and their effect on the subject property. The appraiser attempts to analyze the typical investor whose expectations are reflected in the demand side of the market for this class of property. Within this frame of reference, the appraiser primarily examines market phenomena that affect all aspects of this type of property. Market rents are analyzed. The mortgage rate and loan-to-value ratio available to the typical investor are used in the construction of the capitalization rate. The typical investor's expected rate of return is also used in determining the capitalization rate. In this process, the appraiser does not consider the income and expense items of the specific investor. In investment analysis, the investor is concerned not only with market phenomena but also with personalized income and expense factors that are specific to the property under analysis. In other words, the income property appraisal technique informs the investor of the price the market will pay for the property whereas investment analysis leads the investor to a conclusion about the specific price that he or she should offer for the property.

Another way to consider the relationship between market value and investment value is to assume that there are many possible investors for a specific property. Each investor is competent and rational but each has a different set of objectives. If each investor receives sufficient information, each one can make an evaluation of the value of the property to him or her—the investment value. Now, if these investment values were plotted along a line, a normal (bell-shaped) curve should result. Many investors will calculate approximately the same investment value. A few calculations will yield very high or very low investment values. In this sense, market value (or most probable selling price) can be explained as the mean or median of the distribution of possible investment values.

Income Items in Investment Analysis

In general, investment analysis involves the same revenue considerations that are used in income property appraisal. However, the focus is slightly different. First, contract rents are of primary importance in the initial years that the property is owned. To the appraiser, contract rents are viewed as an adjustment that is necessary to make potential gross income a more reasonable representation of the property's income-earning capability. In investment analysis, the contract rents are the source of revenue for the initial years. The investment analyst takes the contract rents as given and uses them to calculate the level of income for the length of the contract period. After these rental agreements terminate, the investment analyst, like the income property appraiser, searches to identify market rent levels and utilizes these figures to forecast revenues.

Generally, the other sources of revenue that are not affected by contractual agreement and are not related to the provision of space within the structure are treated the same way in investment analysis as they are in income property appraisal. These other income sources are forecast on the basis of the investor's understanding of their future market trends. Thus, as the cost of appliances increases, so does the charge for doing a load of wash in the apartment complex's laundry facility.

Vacancy and collection losses in investment analysis also are viewed in relation to the rental agreements that are in force for the first years of ownership. An investor can identify specific tenants and examine the leases they signed. If the tenants are individuals or corporations with good credit ratings, the investor can assume collection losses over the rental agreement period will be zero. If the leases do not contain escape provisions for the tenant, the investor can assume the vacancy rate for that space will also be zero for the length of time the rental agreement is in force. Upon termination of the rental agreements, the investment analyst, just like the income property appraiser, must turn to the market to forecast future levels of vacancy and collection losses.

Expense Items in Investment Analysis

The purpose of investment analysis is to obtain an estimate of the value of the property to the specific investor. An evaluation of the expense items in investment analysis starts with the owner's income statement from the subject property, as shown in Exhibit 9-1. The investor must use the same expenses that the income property appraiser uses. In addition, the investor must consider those expense items that are excluded from the appraiser's reconstructed income statement for the subject property. In other words, the investor does consider income taxes, depreciation allowances, capital improvement expenditures, and the exact level of the interest payment on the mortgage. All four of these excluded items are considered to obtain the investor's "before-tax" and "after-tax" cash flow.

The next section of the chapter examines the before-tax cash flow concept. First, the process of generating before-tax cash flow is explained and then it is used to judge the performance of the real estate investment in the initial period as well as in the future. The next chapter, which covers the income tax aspects of the investment decision, includes an explanation of the income tax considerations that allow the investor to obtain after-tax cash flow from before-tax cash flow.

EXHIBIT 9-1 Property owner's income and expense statement: Expected six-year ownership period

	Year 1	Year 2	Year 3	Year 4	Year 5	Year 6
Revenues (24 units)						
Potential rent receipts:						
14 (2-bedroom) units	$43,680	$44,520	$45,360	$45,360	$45,360	$45,360
10 (1-bedroom) units	26,400	27,000	27,600	27,600	27,600	27,600
Less vacancy and collection losses (4%)	0	−2,860	−2,950	−2,950	−2,950	−2,950
Parking fees	1,300	1,300	1,300	1,400	1,400	1,500
Laundry room collections	1,300	1,300	1,400	1,500	1,500	1,500
Effective gross income	$72,680	$71,260	$72,710	$72,910	$72,910	$73,010
Expenses						
Management fee	$3,500	$3,600	$3,650	$3,650	$3,650	$3,650
Property taxes	6,700	6,900	7,100	7,200	7,100	7,100
Building custodian	6,600	6,800	7,000	7,200	7,300	7,400
Insurance premiums	1,750	1,800	1,850	1,900	1,900	1,950
Maintenance, repairs, and supplies	4,000	4,100	4,200	4,200	4,300	4,400
Utilities	8,000	8,400	8,800	9,000	9,000	9,200
Natural gas 2,875						
Water 925						
Electricity 4,200						
Replacement of appliances	2,400	2,400	2,600	2,700	2,800	2,900
Misc. administration costs	800	800	800	900	900	1,000
Total operating expenses	$33,750	$34,800	$36,000	$36,750	$36,950	$37,600
Net operating income	$38,930	$36,460	$36,710	$36,160	$35,960	$35,410

GENERATION OF BEFORE-TAX CASH FLOW

An investor obtains a numerical value for before-tax cash flow by calculating NOI and subtracting the annual mortgage payment or debt service from that figure. The underlying reason for calculating before-tax cash flow is the investor's desire to obtain an estimate of the revenue generated by the property after all operating expenses and mortgage expenses are subtracted from revenue. In other words, before-tax cash flow represents the dollars that the investor would receive after the revenue from the property has been used to cover the major outlays the investor incurs.

The reader should remember that different steps may be used by different professional organizations to derive before-tax cash flow in this chapter and after-tax cash flow in the next chapter. The steps differ because an organization may want to emphasize particular types of cash flows that are important to its members. These estimates of after-tax cash flow are identical among all the procedures.

Derivation of Net Operating Income for Investment Analysis

The income and expense items analyzed by the investor to obtain net operating income are the same as those the appraiser uses in establishing net operating income for income property appraisal. The investor must establish a level of gross income for the property in the current year and estimate levels of gross income for future years. These income figures are established by referring to contract rents while the contracts or leases are in force. Then the investor relies on market analysis to establish market rent levels in those future periods for which no leases are in effect. Vacancy and collection losses also must be determined just as the appraiser determines such losses. Other sources of revenue must be identified and the magnitude of these funds must be estimated for future periods. Then the investor must establish the level of operating expense for the current period and prepare a forecast of the level of operating expenses by category. Once this is done, the investor has an income statement similar to that shown in Exhibit 9-1. For simplicity, the assumption is made that the investor will hold the property for the next six years. Moreover, the following assumptions about income and expense items also are reflected in Exhibit 9-1. (This numerical example is consistent with the example presented in Chapter 6 on income property appraisal.)

1. All fourteen of the two-bedroom apartment units are currently rented for $260/month. None of these leases is in force for the second year.

2. All ten of the one-bedroom apartments are currently rented for $220 each. None of these leases extends beyond the first year.

3. Market analysis shows that the level of demand for this type of property in this part of town will grow moderately into the future. This information translates into the fact that in the second year the market rent will

rise to $265/month and $225/month on the two-bedroom and one-bedroom apartments, respectively.

4. In the third year, market rent levels will increase by $5 per unit per month—for each type of apartment to $270 and $230, respectively. These rent levels are assumed to remain in force for the following years.

5. The vacancy rate for comparable properties in the local market is 4 percent. This rate is deemed to be applicable for the second through sixth years because of forecasted market conditions in the future. However, in the current year all apartments are leased.

6. Historic data on expenses reveal that for the last four years expense items have been growing at a constant rate. Operating expenses are assumed to increase at approximately the same rate for the next five years.

On the basis of these income and expense items, net operating income can be generated for the current year and each of the five future years.

Debt Service

Once net operating income is calculated, the next step in generating before-tax cash flow is the deduction of debt service (or the mortgage payment) from net operating income. This process is shown in Exhibit 9-2. Debt service has two components, the interest payment made on the loan and the principal repayment. (Mortgage payment schemes and provisions are examined in detail in Chapters 16 and 17.) Assume that the mortgage repayment scheme for the first mortgage is the constant level installment plan, whereby the total monthly mortgage payment stays constant over time. However, as the loan matures, part of the principal is paid back and thus the interest

EXHIBIT 9-2 Property owner's income and expense statement: Continuation of Exhibit 9-1

	Year 1	Year 2	Year 3	Year 4	Year 5	Year 6
Net operating income	$38,930	$36,460	$36,710	$36,160	$35,960	$35,410
Debt service: First mortgage*						
Interest payment	19,289	19,094	18,704	18,314	17,729	17,339
Principal repayment	3,315	3,510	3,900	4,290	4,875	5,265
Total mortgage payment	22,604	22,604	22,604	22,604	22,604	22,604
Debt service: Second mortgage†						
Interest payment	3,000	2,400	1,800	1,200	600	
Principal repayment	5,000	5,000	5,000	5,000	5,000	
Total mortgage payment	8,000	7,400	6,800	6,200	5,600	
Before-tax cash flow	$8,326	$6,456	$7,306	$7,356	$7,756	$12,806

* First mortgage = $195,000; 0.75 loan/sales price ratio
† Second mortgage = $25,000 @ 12% for 5 years; principal repayment = $5,000/year with interest on unpaid balance
Total equity = $40,000

rate applies to a smaller unpaid balance in each of the successive years. Consequently, in each successive year, the interest payment declines. Because the total payment on a monthly basis is constant, the principal repayment increases over time.

Then assume that the mortgage repayment scheme on the second mortgage is a straight principal reduction method whereby the principal is repaid in equal yearly installments and the interest is charged on the unpaid balance. (The nature of these repayment schemes and the difference between a first and a second mortgage will be discussed in Chapters 16 and 17.)

Exhibit 9-2 presents data on debt service for both mortgages over the ownership period. The total mortgage payment made on the subject property in the first year of ownership will be $30,604. This payment is divided into a total mortgage interest payment of $22,289 and a principal reduction of $8,315 that is an equity increase brought about by the reduction in the mortgage balance.

When the total debt service payment is subtracted from NOI the resultant figure is before-tax cash flow. In the first year of the ownership period, before-tax cash flow is $8,326.

INITIAL PERIOD RATES OF PERFORMANCE

When before-tax cash flow is calculated for the current year, several financial and profitability ratios can be derived. These ratios are determined from the various income and expense items used in the calculation of the before-tax cash flow. At the most rudimentary level, the investment decision can be based on an analysis of initial period financial and profitability ratios that are calculated from the first year's income and expense items. Although a strict adherence to these initial period ratios is viewed as conceptually inadequate, an understanding of the facts displayed by these ratios is important for the investor.

Financial Ratios

The investor needs to understand three financial ratios: the operating expense ratio; the debt service coverage ratio; and the breakeven, or default, ratio. Each provides information about the financial capability of the investment opportunity. The common focus of these financial ratios is the ability of the investment's income stream to support the different expenses that the investor incurs for the property.

Operating expense ratio   The **operating expense ratio** was first explained in connection with income property appraisal (Chapter 6). It is the level of operating expenses divided by gross income, either potential gross income or effective gross income. The numerical value of the operating expense ratio generated by effective gross income is always larger than the value of the ratio generated by potential gross income. This difference is obvious because vacancy and collection losses are usually positive, making effective gross income a smaller number than potential gross income when these losses are subtracted out. In appraisal analysis, the operating expense ratio is important as a check on the efficiency of operation of the subject property. The underlying assumption is that the subject property should have an operating expense ratio similar to that of the comparable properties in the local market.

For the typical investor, the operating expense ratio indicates the property's capability of generating income large enough to cover the full operating expenses. Ideally, the investor should seek a property with the smallest possible operating expense ratio. At the extreme, the investor would want the operating expenses to be as close to zero as possible without jeopardizing the physical maintenance of the building and the desirability of the units within that building. Generally, the operating ratio is considered to be acceptable within a certain range. The typical operating expense ratio for residential income-producing properties should be within a range of 35 to 40 percent of gross potential income.[6] However, the acceptable operating expense ratio depends on the type of property. Obviously, high-rise apartments with elevators have a higher operating expense ratio than low-rise apartments without elevators because elevators run on electric power and they require repair and maintainance. For certain types of investments, the ratio can be as large as 50 percent. An operating expense ratio that exceeds this percentage should warn the typical investor that the property may not be capable of generating enough effective gross income to provide a net operating income large enough to meet the mortgage payment, or that the property is being managed inefficiently.

On the other hand, the operating expense ratio could be very low. Even though this would appear to be favorable, the investor should seek information about the reasons for the low rate. The seller could be operating a sound, high-quality building that requires few repairs and is energy efficient. But, the low operating expense ratio could occur if the seller is deferring maintainance, cutting back on utilities, and reducing reserves for replacing short-lived items like appliances and mechanical systems. In this latter situation, the investor would be buying high future operating expenses. As a safety measure, the investor should obtain information about the operating expense ratio for comparable properties to use as a check on the subject property.

The initial period operating expense ratio for the numerical example in Exhibit 9-1 is 46.4 percent. This ratio is calculated by dividing $33,750 by $72,680. In this example, potential gross income in year 1 is equal to effective gross income in year 1 because the vacancy and collection losses are zero.

Debt service coverage ratio   The **debt service coverage ratio** is the level of net operating income divided by the annual mortgage payment. This financial ratio indicates whether the property is able to generate a level of net operating income large enough to cover the full mortgage payment. If the numerical value of this ratio is less than one, the mortgage payment is greater than the amount of effective gross income remaining after operating expenses have been paid. If the ratio exceeds one, the property is capable of meeting all of its operating expenses and the mortgage payment and still providing the investor with a positive level of before-tax cash flow. Conceptually, the minimum acceptable debt service coverage ratio for the investor should be equal to one plus enough cash to provide for that investor's expected rate of return before taxes. However, a common rule of thumb is that a debt service coverage ratio of one and a quarter or more on residential income property is acceptable[7] but, as financial and market factors change, lenders may require a higher debt service coverage ratio. Finally, the magnitude of the ratio changes with different classes of investments.

The initial period debt service coverage ratio is calculated by dividing NOI by the annual mortgage payment. The relevant mortgage data required to calculate the debt service coverage ratio are given in Exhibit 9-2. Using this debt service information and the value of NOI calculated in Exhibit 9-1, the ratio is the NOI of $38,930 divided by the sum of the two mortgage payments, $30,604. The value of the debt service coverage ratio is 1.27 and is considered an acceptable level.

Breakeven, or default, ratio   The numerator of this financial ratio is the sum of operating expenses and the mortgage payment. In other words, the numerator of the ratio identifies all expense items plus the mortgage payment that must be made from the income generated by the property. The denominator of the ratio is either potential or effective gross income. If the value of this ratio is greater than 1, the investor knows that the property is not generating a level of gross income adequate to pay the expenses incurred in the operation and the purchase of the property. If the ratio is less than 1, the property is generating an income stream large enough to cover all operating expenses and the debt service, as well as to maintain some level of vacancy within the property.

The initial period breakeven ratio for the numerical example in Exhibits 9-1 and 9-2 is 88.5 percent. It is calculated by dividing the sum of operating expenses ($33,750) and debt service on the two mortgages ($22,604 + $8,000) by the effective gross income of $72,680.

After the breakeven ratio is calculated, it can be subtracted from 100 percent to find the vacancy and collection loss percentage that the property can withstand before a zero return is generated for the investor. In the numerical example, the breakeven ratio is 88.5 percent. It indicates that the property being analyzed can withstand a vacancy rate of 11.5 percent before the sum total of operating expenses and mortgage payments is greater than effective gross income.

Obviously, the investor desires the lowest possible breakeven, or default, ratio. The typically acceptable breakeven ratio on a residential income-producing property is in the range of 80 to 85 percent of potential gross income.[8] This level of the ratio would allow enough remaining cash to cover an unexpected increase in the vacancy rate and to provide a positive cash flow to the investor before income tax impacts are calculated.

Profitability Ratios

The financial ratios described in the preceding section indicate the property's ability to generate an income flow large enough to cover operating expenses and mortgage payments. The profitability ratios discussed in this section show the relationship of income and expense items to the investor's equity in the property. In other words, the profitability ratios can be viewed as measures of the rate of return on the investment.

Equity dividend rate   The equity dividend ratio is the before-tax rate of return on equity in the investment. It is before-tax cash flow divided by the dollars of equity invested in the property. The before-tax equity dividend rate for the first year as shown in Exhibits 9-1 and 9-2 is 20.8 percent ($8,326/$40,000). Once it is calculated, this rate of return can be compared with the investor's expectations about a rate of return that should be obtained from the investment. The actual return should be large enough to provide for the interest payment available from a safe, riskless investment plus premiums for illiquidity, risk, and management of the property. If the initial period equity dividend ratio exceeds the investor's expected rate of return, the income-earning property is viewed as a good investment opportunity. If, however, the equity dividend ratio is less than the expected rate of return, the investor realizes that some burden, such as risk or illiquidity, is being borne without compensation.

The reciprocal of the equity dividend ratio is known as the payback period. For example, the before-tax equity dividend ratio for the property in Exhibits 9-1 and 9-2 is 20.8 percent. The reciprocal of this figure is one divided by 0.208, which yields 4.8 years. The payback period is an estimate of the number of years that the property must be held before the total cash flow equals the equity position of the investor. It is not considered a return of the investment because at the end of 4.8 years the investment still has a positive value.

Gross rate of return on equity   The equity dividend ratio pertains only to before-tax cash flow. However, another payment accrues to the investor each year that the property generates funds to pay the mortgage. Each mortgage payment is composed of an interest payment and principal repayment. Consequently, the equity increases each year as the principal repayment is added to the original equity of the investor. The **gross rate of return** on equity represents the relationship between the total yearly return and the original equity position. The gross return on equity is the ratio of before-tax cash flow plus mortgage principal repayment (the equity increase through mortgage reduction) divided by the investor's equity. In the numerical example in Exhibits 9-1 and 9-2, the before-tax gross return on equity in the first year is the sum of $8,326 + $3,315 + $5,000 divided by $40,000, or 41.1 percent.

As long as the principal repayment is greater than zero, the gross rate of return on equity exceeds the equity dividend rate. The importance of the gross rate of return is simply that it shows an additional element of the property's earning potential.

Disadvantages of Initial Period Rates of Performance

Many shortcomings are associated with the use of initial period ratio analysis to evaluate the attractiveness of a property as an investment opportunity. First, there may be a difference between the level of income and expense items in the initial period and their level in future time periods. Many factors can change between the first and second year. For example, if contract rents in the first year exceed market rents, when the contracts terminate at the end of the first year future income will decline. The level of potential gross income in year 2 will be less than it is in year 1. In this case, all other things being equal, the level of before-tax cash flow is less in the second year. This decline will cause the equity dividend ratio and the gross rate of return on equity to be lower in the second year. Alternatively, potential gross income in the second and successive years may increase while expense items in those years increase even more. In this situation, before-tax cash flow will fall, causing a reduction in the value of the equity dividend ratio and the gross rate of return in the second year.

The second problem with initial period ratio analysis is that the value of the property at the time of the sale is not considered. The initial period ratios pertain only to items inherent to cash flow analysis and the equity position of the investor. They totally ignore changes in the value of the property between its date of purchase and its date of sale. Market analysis indicates that the sale price of property can increase or decrease depending on the changes in the economic and demographic factors affecting the market. Therefore, a more thorough investment analysis would have to include consideration of the value of the asset upon sale. This added dimension of the analysis is consistent with one of the investment objectives mentioned earlier in this chapter—investors would like to benefit from price appreciation of the asset. In the event that the asset does not increase in value, they would like to know how the value decline affects the rate of return they will obtain from the property.

The third disadvantage of initial period ratio analysis is that the investor needs to know what the future levels of cash flow and the future sales price of the property are worth in dollar terms at the time the investment is being made. In other words, the investor needs to know the present value of payments that will be made at different times in the future. Only when the present values of these future payments are known can the investor evaluate the financial desirability of the investment.

The underlying concept for establishing the present value of future income flows can be seen in the following example. If you know that the current interest rate is 5 percent on a savings account at a local savings and loan association, you are in a position to make the following decision. A friend of yours offers to give you either $100 today or $104 a year from now. Which option do you take? At the 5 percent rate of interest, you are $1 ahead if you take the $100 today and place it in the savings account at 5 percent. This action would yield $105 at the end of the year instead of the $104 offered. Now turn this example around. Your friend offers you $95.24 payable today or $100 at the end of a one-year period of time. Which offer do you accept? The answer is simple. It does not matter because the present value of both these payments is the same. If you take the $95.24 and place it in the bank at 5 percent interest per year, the value at the end of the year will be $100. Thus, $95.24 is the present value of $100 to be received one year from now if the interest rate is 5 percent.

Due to the three disadvantages of initial period ratio analysis, the investor must seek measures of performance that reflect future circumstances of the investment. The two methods for determining the investment's performance in the future are present value analysis and internal rate of return analysis.

AN ESTIMATE OF THE INVESTMENT'S FUTURE PERFORMANCE

The process of evaluating future performance involves an analysis of the present and future benefits to be derived from the property over a period of ownership that is called the *anticipated holding period* (income projection period). The investor, like the appraiser, projects potential gross income, vacancy rates, and operating expenses for the property. This information allows the investor to analyze the property's likelihood of meeting the objectives of periodic cash flow, equity increase through mortgage balance reduction, and equity increase through price appreciation. Using revenue and expense data from the subject property, the investor can project future levels of net operating income. Then, using the annual debt service, **before-tax cash flow** for each year of expected ownership can be calculated. These calculations are shown in Exhibit 9-1.

After projecting the levels of before-tax cash flow for the six-year holding period, the investor must estimate the sales price of the property at the end of the holding period. In Exhibit 9-1, an assumption is made that there will be no significant change in the future sales price; that is, the investor is assuming no price appreciation will take place in the market for this property. Remember that price appreciation should not be expected as a matter-of-fact occurence. It only occurs if the market circumstances warrant such an increase. Having made the assumption of zero price appreciation, the investor can analyze the investment potential of the property as it is affected by future changes in revenues and costs.

To start the analysis, the investor must identify a discounting interest rate. Conceptually, the investor follows the same process as that undertaken by the income property appraiser. The appraiser defines a capitalization rate to convert NOI into a value estimate of current market value; the investor defines a discount rate to convert before-tax cash flow into an estimate of value. The important point is the choice of the discounting interest rate. One way of establishing the discounting rate is to use the investor's expected rate of return on the investment, **the equity yield rate.** In this way, the analysis would reflect the investor's knowledge about safe rates and expected needs for risk, illiquidity, and management coverage.

Another concept for defining the discounting interest rate is the **cost of capital** concept. An entity such as a corporation can borrow in a variety of ways; it can issue bonds, common stock, or preferred stock, or it can borrow directly from a bank. The cost of capital is the rate of return that the corporation must pay for such funds. Depending on the method chosen, different components are used to calculate the cost of capital. For the real estate equity investor, the cost of capital is the cost of borrowed funds; that is, the interest rate on the mortgage, plus an adjustment for the opportunity cost of using equity funds in real estate investment instead of some other investment opportunity.

The numerical example used in this chapter assumes that the investor in question is a typical investor in the market. Therefore, his or her expected return from the investment will be 16 percent (as identified in Chapter 6). If the investor is a risk averter, a high value will be assigned to the risk and illiquidity premiums causing an expected return greater than 16 percent. If the investor is a risk-taker, a low value will be assigned to risk and illiquidity and the expected equity yield rate might be less than 16 percent. In conclusion, assume that the individual making the investment decision in the numerical example is a typical investor and is seeking a 16 percent return.

Present-Value Calculation

An analysis of the initial period financial and profitability ratios for the example in Exhibits 9-1 and 9-2 reveals the following facts: the operating expense ratio, based on effective gross income is 46.4 percent; the debt service coverage ratio is 1.27 percent; and the breakeven ratio is 88.5 percent. Each of these financial ratios is within the reasonable range for a good investment.

The two profitability ratios also indicate that the investment can be considered good on the basis of initial period analysis. The equity dividend rate is 20.8 percent and the gross rate of return on equity is 41.1 percent. Both of these profitability ratios exceed the investor's expected rate of return of 16 percent.

However, the question that the investor must still ask is whether or not the purchase price is acceptable. In Chapter 6 (on income property appraisal), a most probable selling price of $257,000 was estimated for the property. The seller, however, established a firm, minimum price of $260,000 from which he or she is unwilling to deviate. The buyer used this potential purchase price to calculate mortgage and equity values. Should an offer of $260,000 be extended by the buyer? The initial period ratios suggest that such an offer could be made. However, this decision should not be made until the future is analyzed in addition to the present and the past, both of which are reflected in the current year figures. The final answer to this question can be determined by utilizing a method known as **present-value** that considers the present value of before-tax cash flows for the holding period, plus the present values of the expected change in the sales price that will be received in the sixth year (equity increase due to price appreciation), plus the equity increase due to the decrease in the unpaid mortgage balance. The second column of Exhibit 9-3 shows the actual figures for cash flow and the components of equity increase or change. The present value of these concepts is determined by utilizing the concept of "present worth of one dollar."

EXHIBIT 9-3 Present value of before-tax cash flow and equity increase at 16 percent

Year	Before-tax cash flow	Factor @ 16%	Present value
1	$ 8,326	0.862	$ 7,177
2	6,456	0.743	4,797
3	7,306	0.640	4,676
4	7,356	0.552	4,061
5	7,756	0.476	3,692
6	$12,806	0.410	5,250
			$29,653
Equity increase through mortgage balance reduction	$50,155	0.410	$20,564
Equity change due to sales price change	0	0.410	0
			$50,217

In simple terms the "present worth of one" tells us what a one-dollar payment in the future is worth in the present at a given interest rate. Since the investor is considered to be a risk-averter seeking an equity yield of 16 percent when the market is only stipulating a 14 percent rate, the present-value calculation is based on the individual investor's expected equity yield requirement. Exhibit 9-4 shows the calculation of the "present worth of one" factors for the first six years at 16 percent. The numerical value 1/1.16 is equal to 0.862 in year 1. Exhibit 9-5 presents the "present worth of one" factors at 16 percent for the first forty years (see column 5 of Exhibit 9-5). Utilizing the factors generated in Exhibit 9-4, the before-tax cash flow figures in Exhibit 9-3 provide the present-value calculations at the investor's 16 percent expected equity yield rate. In year 1, the before-tax cash flow of $8,326 is multiplied by 0.862 to obtain the present value of $7,177

A similar calculation is made for years 2 through 6. If the property is sold in year 6, the present value of the equity increase through mortgage reduction is calculated by multiplying $50,155 by 0.41, the discounting factor in the sixth year.

In the analysis of the figures in Exhibit 9-3, remember that an assumption was made about price appreciation. The assumption was that sales price would not increase over the six-year holding period. The investor should not always assume that price appreciation will occur just because it has occurred in the past. The investor should know enough to analyze the market to see if sales prices will rise. To emphasize this point, the present value of the change in sales price in this case is assumed to be zero. The present value of the investment opportunity based on before-tax considerations is the sum of the present values of each of the six before-tax cash flows, equity increase through reduction of the mortgage balance, and the change in the sales price. On the basis of the calculations, the present value of the investment's before-tax cash flow and equity increase is equal to $50,217, approximately one and a fourth times the initial equity of $40,000.

The initial period financial and profitability ratios indicate that the investment is a good opportunity, and the present-value calculations of before-tax cash flows, equity increase from mortgage balance reduction, and future sales price (which is assumed to be equal to the purchase price) also indicate that the investment is a good opportunity. The investor could purchase the property and feel reasonably assured that the total return to be derived warrants the use of the initial $40,000 in equity. The present-value calculation of $50,217 at a 16 percent rate shows the investor that the future stream of benefits to be derived from the property over the next six years is adequate to cover the investor's desire for a safe rate of return plus premiums for risk, illiquidity, and management expenses.

EXHIBIT 9-4 Present worth of one at a discounting interest rate of 16 percent

Year	Calculation of discount rate	Factor
1	$1/1.16$	0.862
2	$1/(1.16)^2$	0.743
3	$1/(1.16)^3$	0.641
4	$1/(1.16)^4$	0.552
5	$1/(1.16)^5$	0.476
6	$1/(1.16)^6$	0.410

THE DECISION TO INVEST

EXHIBIT 9-5   Annual Compound Interest Rate (16%)

Source: Austin J. Jaffe and C. F. Sirmans, *Real Estate Investment Decision Making*, ©
1982, p. 524. Reprinted by permission of Prentice-Hall, Inc., Englewood Cliffs, N.J.

n	Amount of one	Amount of one per period	Sinking fund factor	Present worth of one	Present worth of one per period	Partial payment
1	1.16000	1.00000	1.00000	.86207	.86207	1.16000
2	1.34560	2.16000	.46296	.74316	1.60523	.62296
3	1.56090	3.50560	.28526	.64066	2.24589	.44526
4	1.81064	5.06650	.19738	.55229	2.79818	.35738
5	2.10034	6.87714	.14541	.47611	3.27429	.30541
6	2.43640	8.97748	.11139	.41044	3.68473	.27139
7	2.82622	11.41387	.08761	.35383	4.03856	.24761
8	3.27842	14.24009	.07022	.30503	4.34359	.23022
9	3.80296	17.51851	.05708	.26295	4.60654	.21708
10	4.41144	21.32147	.04690	.22668	4.83323	.20690
11	5.11727	25.73290	.03886	.19542	5.02864	.19886
12	5.93603	30.85017	.03242	.16846	5.19711	.19241
13	6.88579	36.78620	.02718	.14523	5.34233	.18718
14	7.98752	43.67199	.02290	.12520	5.46753	.18290
15	9.26552	51.65951	.01936	.10793	5.57546	.17936
16	10.74801	60.92503	.01641	.09304	5.66850	.17641
17	12.46769	71.67303	.01395	.08021	5.74870	.17395
18	14.46252	84.14072	.01189	.06914	5.81785	.17189
19	16.77652	98.60323	.01014	.05961	5.87745	.17014
20	19.46076	115.37975	.00867	.05139	5.92884	.16867
21	22.57448	134.84051	.00742	.04430	5.97314	.16742
22	26.18640	157.41499	.00635	.03819	6.01132	.16635
23	30.37622	183.60139	.00545	.03292	6.04424	.16545
24	35.23642	213.97761	.00467	.02838	6.07262	.16467
25	40.87425	249.21402	.00401	.02447	6.09709	.16401
26	47.41412	290.08827	.00345	.02109	6.11818	.16345
27	55.00038	337.50239	.00296	.01818	6.13636	.16296
28	63.80045	392.50277	.00255	.01567	6.15204	.16255
29	74.00852	456.30322	.00219	.01351	6.16555	.16219
30	85.84988	530.31173	.00189	.01165	6.17720	.16189
35	180.31407	1120.71296	.00089	.00555	6.21534	.16089
40	378.72116	2360.75724	.00042	.00264	6.23350	.16042

One remaining fact that needs to be considered before the investor knows
the full scope of possible returns is the impact of the Internal Revenue Code. This
issue is examined in Chapter 10. The actual investment decisions can be made only
after calculation of after-tax cash flow.

A problem that arises with the use of the discount rate in investment analysis is based on the understanding that the rational and prudent investor will analyze
several different investment opportunities. Some of them may be real estate investment opportunities, and others undoubtedly would be opportunities in financial securities such as stocks and bonds. In the preceding example, a high discount rate was
used to find the present value of the investment opportunity in this particular income-producing property. Before the investor commits $40,000 to this project, alter-

native opportunities should also be analyzed. One such opportunity could be a safe, riskless investment such as a six-year savings certificate that pays 8 percent per year. What is the present value of the returns to be obtained from this investment opportunity? A numerical example of the calculations to answer this question is provided in Exhibit 9-6. A discounting interest rate of 9 percent is chosen because it represents a safe, riskless investment opportunity (8 percent) plus a premium for illiquidity (1 percent).

If the $40,000 were placed in the savings certificate, it would pay $3,200 at the end of the first year. However, the present value of $3,200 to be received a year from now is $2,934. In the second year, the principal plus accumulated interest is $43,200. At the end of the second year, the investor will receive an interest payment of $3,456. However, the present value of $3,456 paid two years from today is only $2,910. At the end of the sixth year, the present value of the total return on the $40,000 initial savings is $17,211.

From this comparison, the most desirable alternative seems clear. The present value of the financial gain to be received from the real estate equity investment is $50,217 at a discount rate of 16 percent. On the other hand, the present value of the gain to be received from the savings certificate is $17,211 at a discount rate of 9 percent. The investment in the income-earning real estate asset provides approximately three times the return even after the additional risk and management expenses are reflected in the higher discount rate.

What should the investor do if the real property investment generated a present value of only $17,211 while the savings certificate still offered the same return of $17,211? Does the higher discount rate adequately reflect all of the added risk making the investor indifferent between the two opportunities? The answer is no to the second question and choose the savings certificate to the first question. These answers are based on the following statements. First, the cash flows, equity increase through mortgage balance reduction, and price appreciation to be received from a real estate investment are treated *as if they are certain to be received* just as the payment from the savings certificate is certain to be received. However, this certainty does not apply to the cash flows and price appreciation generated by real estate. Therefore, if these two alternatives offer the same present value of returns, even at

EXHIBIT 9-6   Present value of the return on 6-year savings certificate paying 8 percent per year

Year	Principal	Interest payment	Discount factor @ 9%	Present Value
1	$40,000	$3,200	.917	$2,934
2	43,200	3,456	.842	2,910
3	46,656	3,732	.772	2,881
4	50,388	4,031	.708	2,854
5	54,419	4,353	.650	2,830
6	58,773	4,702	.596	2,802
				$17,211

different discount rates, the investor should examine the certainty and variability of those returns. "The discounting process makes no specific allowance for risk. Even the use of relatively higher discount rates, while having the effect of producing lower present values, does not actually take into account the element of risk associated with the specific property. When comparisons are made among the present values and/or rates of return among investment alternatives, the alternatives should represent cash flows of similar risk and duration.[9]

An alternative approach that can be used to make the investment decision is the calculation of the return instead of the present value of the investment. This process, known as the internal rate of return technique, also utilizes a discounting factor.

Internal Rate of Return (IRR)

To apply the **internal rate of return** (IRR) technique, the investor must have an estimate of cash flow, equity increase through mortgage balance reduction, and the expected sales price of the investment. However, the investor does not need to state a discounting interest rate (as is the case in the present-value technique). The discounting rate is the unknown to be estimated in this procedure.

The calculation of the internal rate of return is not simple because our numerical example involves the solution of an equation that contains the discounting rate raised to the sixth power. Currently, the sophisticated investor uses computer technology to solve this problem. If the investor is not trained in computer modeling, or does not have such facilities at hand, the problem can be solved by a process of elimination. First, a discount factor is chosen; then it is incorporated into the formula; and finally it is utilized to calculate the present value of future returns to be received. If the present value of future benefits is less than the initial equity, the discount factor that was chosen is too large. If the present value of the benefits is greater than the initial equity, the discount factor that was chosen is too small. By a process of elimination, a discount factor can be identified that brings about an equality between the future returns and initial costs of the investment.

Exhibit 9-3 contains information about present values of cash flow, equity increase through mortgage reduction, and change in sales price. When a discount rate of 16 percent is used, the present value of the total returns exceeds the initial equity outlay. Therefore, the actual internal rate of return is more than 16 percent. The process of elimination would show the internal rate of return to be approximately equal to 22 percent. This rate is the equity yield rate that the investor would receive from the property that was analyzed.

The investor now compares the 22 percent internal rate of return calculated for this specific investment opportunity with the expected rate of return needed to compensate for risk, illiquidity, and management of the real estate asset, in addition to a safe rate on a riskless investment. The internal rate of return of this real estate investment opportunity exceeds the typical investor's expected 16 percent rate of return. The investor can conclude that a purchase price of $260,000 and a $40,000 initial equity are reasonable if the estimates of future revenues and operating expenses hold true.[10]

Other Analyses

Both the present value of the investment and the internal rate of return are affected by the factors used in the generation of before-tax cash flow as well as by the market factors that affect the future sales price of the property. Because of possible changes in these factors, the investor must undertake two related studies. First, the impact of changes in these factors on the investment decision should be understood. The investor must study the sensitivity of the present-value calculation or the internal rate-of-return calculation to changes in revenue, operating expenses, and the future sales price. The investor should also examine the expected length of time that the property may be owned. These two studies are known as sensitivity analysis and holding-period analysis. They are being discussed as separate entities even though they are intellectually intertwined.

Sensitivity analysis   The investor does not know with certainty the future level of any income or operating expense item; nor does the investor know with certainty the future resale price of the property. However, a most probable range of these income, expense, and resale figures can be determined. The investor must identify the most volatile income and expense items and establish the most pessimistic and the most optimistic future levels for those items. Then, holding all of the other income and expense items constant, the investor can insert the most pessimistic estimates and the most optimistic estimates to recalculate the level of present value or the internal rate of return under these opposite conditions. Thus, the investor establishes a range for either the present value or the internal rate of return within which the actual present value or internal rate of return should fall.

From the present-value calculation, the investor can make several kinds of decisions. If, under the most pessimistic conditions, the present value of the investment exceeds the initial equity, the investor can feel very confident that the investment opportunity is good on the basis of both initial period estimates and analysis of future performance. On the contrary, if the present value of the investment calculated under the most optimistic circumstances is below the initial equity, the investor knows that even under the best of circumstances the investment is undesirable.

Holding-period analysis   Every investor must make a decision about the length of time the real estate equity investment will be owned. Various economic and financial factors affect the decision about the planned holding period for any particular real estate investment. Several alternative strategies for establishing the holding period are presented in the following statement:

> While ten years is recommended as a planning horizon for general use in analyzing projects that are looked to for future cash flows, an alternate approach would be to make the planning horizon equal to the number of years in which *positive* cash flows

are expected to be received. . . . Another possible choice would be the number of years during which tax-shelter benefits are expected to be received. . . .[11]

These strategies can be appropriate for investors who view periodic cash flow as the primary investor objective.

If the investor's objective is price appreciation, the property is usually acquired for one of three reasons:

1. The investor sees the opportunity to buy a property that is currently being sold for less than its market value.
2. The investor purchases property with a strong expectation of a significant change in its economic use in the near future. Such a change in use can occur because of market factors that create a higher investment use, or because a zoning ordinance change can allow a change in the use of the land.
3. The investor sees that the rate of return is well above the current rate of inflation and believes it will increase as the rate of inflation increases. This situation can arise when the rental payment for commercial property is tied directly to changes in the consumer price index, or when the market for the residential property is strong and there is a possibility of increasing rents and net operating income by at least as much as the consumer price index increases.

If the investor's objective is price appreciation, the planned holding period depends on the underlying reason for the purchase. In the situation of a purchase for quick resale, the holding period is equal to the time required for the sale to occur. If a hedge against inflation is the reason for the purchase, the holding period is the length of time over which either the equity dividend ratio or some other rate of return exceeds the rate of inflation. This time horizon could be one year or two decades.[12]

In the numerical example in Exhibits 9-1 and 9-2, the holding period is established on the basis of price appreciation and periodic cash flow. Expectations are that the market value of the property will remain constant or slightly increase over the six-year period and that simultaneously the before-tax cash flow will be positive. During this period of time, the market rental rate will first increase and then remain constant before declining slightly in the seventh or eighth years. If the holding period were extended to include the tenth, eleventh, and maybe the twelfth year, the assumption about a stable market value for the property might not be sound. As the market rent level in those years declines and expenses rise, an investor who might purchase the property in the twelfth year would probably see that the discounted stream of future benefits is not large enough in year twelve to warrant a sales price that is equal to the present-day sales price. In this case the sales price would decline and the yearly levels of before-tax cash flow would also decline.

The holding period should be identified and established on the basis of the investor's objectives. However, the sophisticated investor will recalculate the holding period, quite possibly on a yearly basis, to see what impact the changing economic environment has on the levels of cash flow and future sales price.

Refinancing and Other Considerations

Over the six-year holding period, a change in the mortgage money market might cause the investor to seek refinancing of the original mortgage. In other words, because of economic circumstances in the mortgage market, the mortgage interest rate in the third year or so could be substantially less than the 10 percent rate that the investor initially obtained to purchase the property. Assume that in the third year the mortgage rate in the market falls to 7 percent. In this case, the investor could go to a second lender, obtain a mortgage on the property, and use the funds received to pay the mortgage that was undertaken in the first year. The investor's benefit from this financial change is a reduction in the total debt service requirement. As the level of the mortgage payment declines, the level of before-tax cash flow increases if all other expenses and income items stay the same.

Refinancing the loan at a lower interest rate is obviously beneficial to the investor. However, the investor may also benefit from refinancing the loan at the same interest rate because of certain tax-code provisions (discussed in Chapter 10). When the loan is refinanced, the interest deduction allowed by the federal government is larger and the after-tax cash flow is affected.

The owner controls very few of the income and expense items shown in Exhibit 9-1. The market controls potential rent receipts and vacancy losses. The market also controls parking fees and, to a lesser extent, laundry room revenues. The owner can negotiate the management fee, but only within limits. The property tax bill is beyond the investor's control even with the right to argue for a reduction in the assessment value of the property. The insurance premiums are quoted and the only choice is to underinsure the property; but even this choice is limited by the demands of the lender to keep the property insured to the value of the unpaid loan.

The items most directly controlled by the investor are the dollars paid for maintenance and repairs, the expenditures for utilities (in this case, utility expenditures to heat and light the common areas, not the apartments themselves), and replacement of appliances. If the investor minimizes maintenance and repair expenditures, the value of before-tax cash flow in each year can increase. Similarly, measures to reduce utility costs—such as eliminating lights in the parking area between the hours of twelve and six in the morning, and lowering the thermostat on the heating unit serving the common areas of the property—can increase the level of before-tax cash flow. Finally, as appliances wear out over the holding period, leases can be renegotiated so that the landlord does not provide kitchen appliances. In this way, the investor eliminates the need to accumulate funds to replace worn-out refrigerators, ranges, and dishwashers and hence increases before-tax cash flow.

The investor can influence the level of before-tax cash flow substantially by manipulating the few items on the income and expense statement that are under his or her control. However, the investor should realize that minimizing these expense items will have future repercussions on the profitability and marketability of the property. As maintenance and repair expenditures are reduced, the degree of physical deterioration increases and reduces future resale value. As fully equipped kitchens are eliminated from the units, the rent potential in future years may decline or at least not rise at a rate comparable to that of units providing fully equipped kitchens. In a sense, the investor is trading the savings on expense items for future losses in rent receipts or resale value.

THE FEASIBILITY STUDY

The feasibility study was introduced in the first section of the previous chapter. At that point, two important components of a feasibility study were identified—the market study and the financial analysis. This section serves to bring that same point to the reader's attention now that before-tax investment analysis is completed. The market study yields information about current revenues and vacancies as well as forecasts of future levels of rents and vacancies. Financial analysis takes data from the market study, combines it with expense data, and calculates performance and profitability ratios. The two studies work hand in hand to help the investor make a rational decision about involvement in an investment project.

FORMS OF OWNERSHIP IN A REAL ESTATE EQUITY INVESTMENT

In the preceding discussion of equity investment, the owner and investor are viewed as a single individual. However, in many situations a single individual cannot raise enough money to be the only person involved in an equity investment. For example, the purchase of a large apartment complex or a small shopping center would require an investor to raise several million dollars. Some of this money would be used as a down payment and the remainder would be in the form of a mortgage. In this situation, if the best mortgage term available is an 80 percent loan-to-value ratio and the sales price of the property is $3 million, the initial down payment would be $600,000. A single individual may not be able to raise $600,000 to enter this specific investment opportunity. Consequently, other ownership forms are utilized in real estate equity investments. Three of these forms are the partnership, the corporation, and the equity investment trust. They are described in Chapter 17.

CHAPTER SUMMARY

An individual can choose from among many kinds of investment opportunities— savings accounts, common stocks, corporate bonds, government bonds, and real estate equity investments. To make a rational choice, each investor must define his or her investment objectives, which may be price appreciation, periodic cash flow, equity increases through mortgage reduction, tax shelter, leverage, estate building, or a combination of these objectives. In addition, the investor must understand the risks inherent in the various investments.

Having chosen real estate equity as the desired type of investment, an individual must examine the financial aspect of the potential investment property. The first step in this process is the estimation of revenues, total operating expenses, and the debt service to obtain a value for before-tax cash flow. Then intial period rates of performance are used to calculate the operating expense ratio, the debt service coverage ratio, and the breakeven ratio to determine whether the income generated by the property is great enough to cover various categories and combinations of the property's expenses. Next, the investor can calculate the profitability ratios, such as the equity dividend ratio, as a measure of the return on the investment.

However, the initial period performance ratios do not provide projections of future levels of income and expenses, the time value of money, price appreciation, and income tax factors such as capital gains and depreciation recapture that only come into effect upon sale of the property. Consequently, more sophisticated tools are used in the investment decision—present-value or internal rate-of-return techniques.

Finally, the investor should realize that a feasibility study may be needed. By using financial analysis, market analysis, and locational analysis the investor can develop a full understanding of the investment opportunity and its desirability as a method of achieving his or her objectives.

Review Questions

1. Discuss the difference between financial and nonfinancial assets. How does this distinction relate to real estate investment opportunities?
2. What is a real estate equity investment?
3. Identify and explain the various objectives that a real estate equity investor may have.
4. Identify and explain the various risks that a real estate equity investor may face.
5. Explain the process by which before-tax cash flow is obtained.
6. Identify and describe the initial period rates of performance.
7. Explain the disadvantages or shortcomings of initial period rates of performance.
8. Describe the present-value and internal rate-of-return techniques. How do these techniques overcome some of the disadvantages of initial period ratio analysis?
9. What is sensitivity analysis and how might an investor use it?
10. What is holding-period analysis and how is it related to investor objectives?
11. When might it be reasonable for the investor to refinance the property?
12. Define feasibility analysis and describe its component parts.

Discussion Questions

1. Refer to the numerical example presented in the chapter. Analyze the investment on the assumption that total operating expenses in the sec-

ond through the sixth year are 10 percent more than those forecast in Exhibit 9-1, and that because of price appreciation the expected sales price in the sixth year is $280,000.

2. Analyze the investment decision portrayed in Exhibits 9-1, 9-2, and 9-3 on the assumption that the investor did not obtain a second mortgage and the investor's equity is $65,000.

Notes

1. Don G. Campbell, *The Handbook of Real Estate Investment* (New York: Bonanza Books, 1968), p. 13.

2. William N. Kinnard, Jr., *Income Property Valuation: Principles and Techniques of Appraising Income-Producing Real Estate* (Lexington, Mass.: D.C. Heath and Co., 1971), p. 116.

3. Ibid., p. 117.

4. Ibid.

5. Stephen E. Roulac, *Modern Real Estate Investment* (San Francisco, Calif.: Property Press, 1976), pp. 49–50.

6. Henry E. Hoagland; Leo D. Stone; and William B. Bruggeman, *Real Estate Finance,* 6th ed. (Homewood, Ill.: Richard D. Irwin, Inc., 1977), p. 265.

7. Ibid.

8. Ibid., p. 267.

9. Stephen D. Messner; Irving Schreiber; and Victor L. Lyon, *Marketing Investment Real Estate: Finance Taxation Techniques* (Chicago, Ill.: REALTORS National Marketing Institute of the National Association of REALTORS, 1975), p. 44.

10. There are several conceptual problems associated with the use of the IRR technique that are beyond the scope of a principles text. There is also a modification to the *IRR* calculation process known as the Financial Management Rate of Return *(FMRR)* technique. For further information concerning these points, see the investment analysis texts listed in the section on additional readings.

11. Robert J. Wiley, *Real Estate Investment: Analysis and Strategy* (New York: The Ronald Press Co., 1977), p. 196.

12. Ibid., pp. 190–197.

Additional Readings

EPLEY, DONALD R., and JAMES A. MILLAR. *Basic Real Estate Finance and Investments.* New York: John Wiley & Sons, 1980. Chapters 14, 15, and 19.

GRAASKAMP, JAMES A. *A Guide to Feasibility Analysis.* Chicago, Ill.: Society of Real Estate Appraisers, 1970.

GREER, GAYLON. *The Real Estate Investment Decision.* Lexington, Mass.: Lexington Books, 1979. Chapters 1, 3, 5, 7, and 9.

JAFFEE, AUSTIN J., and C. F. SIRMANS. *Real Estate Investment Decision Making.* Englewood Cliffs, N.J.: Prentice-Hall Inc., 1982.

KAHN, SANDERS, and FREDERICK E. CASE. *Real Estate Appraisal and Investment.* New York: The Ronald Press Co., 1977. Chapter 23.

KINNARD, WILLIAM N., JR. *Income Property Valuation Principles and Techniques of Appraising Income-Producing Real Estate.* Lexington, Mass.: D.C. Heath and Company, 1971. Chapter 11.

MAISEL, SHERMAN J., and STEPHEN E. ROULAC. *Real Estate Investment and Finance.* New York: McGraw-Hill Book Co., 1976. Chapters 20 and 22.

MESSNER, STEPHEN D.; IRVING SCHREIBER; and VICTOR L. LYON. *Marketing Investment Real Estate.* Chicago, Ill.: REALTORS' National Marketing Institute, 1975. Chapters 1–4.

PYHRR, STEPHEN A., and JAMES R. COOPER. *Real Estate Investment.* New York: John Wiley & Sons, 1982.

ROULAC, STEPHEN E. *Modern Real Estate Investment.* San Francisco, Calif.: Property Press, 1976. Chapters 1 and 20.

WENDT, PAUL, and ALAN R. CERF. *Real Estate Investment Analysis and Taxation.* New York: McGraw-Hill Book Co., 1979. Chapters 1 and 2.

WILEY, ROBERT J. *Real Estate Investment: Analysis and Strategy* . New York: The Ronald Press Co., 1977. Chapters 3-8, and 10.

10 | Taxation of the Real Estate Investment

2. Explain the nature and purpose of depreciation techniques permitted in the Internal Revenue Code.

3. Define taxable income and show how it is used in the investment decision.

4. Explain the concepts of capital gain and depreciation recapture and show how they are used in calculating the tax obligation of the property owner upon sale of the property.

5. Describe capital gain tax deferral techniques permitted in the Internal Revenue Code.

IMPORTANT TERMS

Accelerated Cost Recovery
System (ACRS)
Accelerated Depreciation
Additional Depreciation (Excess)
Adjusted Basis
After-Tax Cash Flow
Capital Gain
Declining Balance Depreciation Methods

Depreciation Recapture
Income Tax Depreciation
Techniques
Salvage Value
Straight-Line Depreciation
Sum-of-the-Years' Digits
Tax Deferral Techniques
Taxable Income
Useful Life

EFFECTS OF INCOME TAX CODE ON OWNER-OCCUPIED REAL ESTATE

Owners of a single-family house who occupy that house for their own purposes are significantly affected by income tax provisions of both the federal and state governments. The purpose of this section is to describe the typical tax effects on such individuals during ownership and at the time the property is sold. The information in this section is drawn mainly from two publications issued by the Department of the Treasury's Internal Revenue Service, *Tax Information for Home Owners* (Publication #530) and *Tax Information on Selling or Purchasing Your Home* (Publication #523). The homeowner should review these free publications frequently to discover any changes in the federal income tax code that affect owner-occupied units.

Tax Savings During Ownership

Annual itemized deductions   The federal income tax code allows a homeowner to take certain annual deductions during the ownership period. Deductions are itemized expenditures associated with homeownership that are made by the homeowner; they can be subtracted on the income tax form from the owner's earnings for the year. The IRS allows the following expenditures as deductions:

1. The mortgage interest that is paid on either the money borrowed to purchase the home or the interest paid on the money borrowed to make repairs, improvements, or additions to the house

2. The real property tax that is actually paid to the local government or local taxing jurisdiction during the year

3. Mortgage prepayment penalties, which are costs that can be incurred by the homeowner if the mortgage loan is repaid before its maturity date

4. Other types of payments, such as state and local sales taxes on utilities, and the interest paid when the homeowner makes a late payment for either utilities or real property taxes

5. The portion of fire and other casualty loss to the home that exceeds $100 after any insurance reimbursement. Casualty or theft loss on personal property in the home is deductible to the extent that the loss exceeds $100 for each casualty or theft. When real property has been damaged, the loss is calculated as (1) the loss in value that is the difference between the value of the property before the damage and the value of the property after the damage; or (2) the adjusted basis of the property at the time of the loss. The deduction is the lesser of these amounts. This value is then reduced by the amount of the insurance compensation received. If the remaining figure is positive it is reduced further by a $100 statutory minimum, and also reduced by 10 percent of the taxpayer's adjusted gross income. The remaining figure is an itemized deduction

6. Casualty losses for furniture and fixtures not entirely destroyed. In this case, the deductible amount is computed for each item, as it was in #5 above. The amount of the deduction is the decrease in value, less any insurance compensation and less $100 and 10 percent of AGI for each casualty loss

7. Other itemized expenditures not related to the cost of homeownership. These deductions can be taken by tenants as well as landlords. For example, the tax code allows deductions for taxes paid on personal property, medical and dental expenses, educational expenses, union or employee organization dues, charitable contributions, and interest on consumer loans

Certain expenditures made by the homeowner cannot be deducted on the annual income tax form unless the property is rental property that either earns an income for the owner or is being used for business purposes. The following expenditures are in this category:

1. Expenses for maintenance and repairs to the house

2. Insurance premiums paid for homeowners' insurance polices and for mortgage insurance

3. Depreciation charges

4. Utility bills

The federal tax code makes a distinction between repairs and improvements. It defines a repair as an expenditure made to maintain the house in an ordinarily efficient operating condition. A repair expenditure does not add to the value of the property or increase its physical life. Examples of repairs are painting, fixing gutters, repairing the roof, plastering walls, and replacing broken windows. In contrast, an improvement expenditure materially increases the value of the property, lengthens its economic life, or adapts it to a new use. Examples of improvement expenditures are the construction of a room addition or new wing, modernizing a bathroom or kitchen, finishing the basement, putting up a fence, installing new plumbing or electrical wiring, replacing an old roof, and paving the driveway. If ordinary repairs are done as part of an improvement project, the tax code allows the entire expenditure to be treated as an improvement. Improvement expenditures are a major consideration when the property is sold, but repair expenditures are not.

Costs incurred during purchase   In addition to the annual itemized deductions, certain expenses incurred by the homeowner when the property is purchased are deductible in the year of the purchase. One of these items is any real property tax proration paid by the buyer on the day the property is received. This payment from the buyer to the seller arises because the seller usually pays the property taxes on an annual basis. If the property is sold six months into the tax period, the seller will require a payment of half of these taxes from the buyer. This expenditure is tax deductible because it is a property tax payment made by the buyer.

A second tax-deductible expenditure associated with the purchase of a house is any additional interest charge, typically known as "points" on the loan. The lender makes such charges when the mortgage interest rate is at the legally allowable ceiling established by state usury laws, or is less than the return the lender could receive on alternative nonmortgage investments. These charges allow the lender to receive an effective interest rate that exceeds the interest rate stated on the mortgage. Therefore, depending on the type of mortgage (conventional or VA), the buyer and/or seller may have to pay one to two percent of the value of the loan at the time the property is purchased and the loan is made. (Points are examined in greater detail in Chapter 19.)

If the points are paid on the value of the loan that was obtained to purchase the taxpayer's principal residence, this expenditure is deductible. However, the deductibility applies only if the charging of points is an established business practice in the geographic area where the loan was made, and as long as the number of points claimed by the taxpayer does not exceed the number generally charged in the area.

The tax savings generated by the annual deductions and other deductible expenses can be significant. The homeowner should keep records on both the annual deductions and the year-of-purchase deductions to extract the maximum benefit from the tax code. Depending on the property owner's effective tax rate, these deductions could amount to a deduction of $4,000 or $8,000, a tax savings of $1,000 to $3,000 per year for the typical homeowner.

Tax credits   The homeowner may claim tax credits for certain expenditures that conserve the use of energy for heating and cooling the home. The types of qualifying expenditures include:

THE DECISION TO INVEST

☐ Insulation of floors, walls, ceilings and attics

☐ Installation of doors and windows

☐ Caulking and weatherstripping of doors and windows

☐ Installation of multiglazed or heat-absorbing windows and doors

☐ Automatic energy-saving thermostats

☐ Replacement furnace burners that reduce fuel consumption

☐ Electric or mechanical ignition systems that replace a gas pilot devise

☐ Other energy savings expenditures

The allowable tax credit for these items is set at a maximum of $300 (15 percent of expenditures up to $2000). The home must have been substantially completed before April 20, 1977, and the equipment must be installed prior to December 31, 1985.

Expenditure for alternative energy equipment such as solar, wind, and geothermal devices for the principal residence is also a tax credit item. The tax credit is a maximum of $4,000 (40 percent of the first $10,000 spent) for new equipment with at least a five-year recovery period.

Tax Liability at Termination of Ownership

The homeowner should know about three important concepts when the property is sold—the adjusted basis of the property, the capital gains, and techniques for the deferral of capital gains.

Adjusted basis calculation   In the Internal Revenue Code, the basis of the property is the value of that property for tax purposes. The first and probably most important component of basis is the cost of the property. If the home was purchased on the open market, the first element of basis is the price paid for the property. If the home was constructed new, the basis consists of the price of the land plus the construction costs of the improvements on the land. In addition to the sales price or construction costs, expenditures made for improvements and additions to the property increase the **adjusted basis** of the property.

The homeowner should keep accurate records of the adjusted basis of the property as well as the value of the furnishings and fixtures. These figures are important in making calculations of casualty losses or damage to property. In addition, these figures serve as the starting point for calculating capital gains on the property.

In certain circumstances depreciation affects the adjusted basis. Depreciation is not allowed as a deduction from the adjusted basis for an owner-occupied unit, but if the property owner rents the property or uses some portion of the property for business purposes, a depreciation deduction is allowed. In the case of rental property, the full structure can be depreciated. If part of the property is used for business purposes, only that part can be depreciated.

Capital gains and losses   The homeowner realizes a capital gain when the property purchased before June 22, 1984, is sold after one year of ownership, or, if the property was purchased after June 22, 1984, it is held for six months and sold for more than the adjusted basis of the property. In other words, a **capital gain** is generated when the sales price exceeds the original purchase price of the property plus the dollar value of improvements that have been made to it. The calculation of a gain requires the homeowner to identify the exact sales price received at the time of the sale and to make adjustments to this price to include costs incurred in fixing up the house for sale and selling it.

Selling expenditures consist of the brokerage commission paid to the real estate broker or the expenditures made by the owner in the process of selling the property without a broker. These selling expenses include newspaper advertisements, increased telephone usage, and other such expenditures required to find a buyer, as well as any legal fees incurred by the seller in conjunction with the sale and any points the seller is required to pay.

"Fix-up" expenditures are incurred to make the house more saleable. They may include such expenses as painting the interior and exterior surfaces of the house, wallpapering, installing new carpets, and installing new appliances or fixtures.

The following established rules regulate which fix-up expenses can be used in the adjustment process:

1. The work must be performed during the ninety days preceding the day upon which the sales contract is signed by both parties.
2. The expenditures cannot be made later than thirty days after the date of sale as it appears on the contract.
3. The expenditures cannot be considered as improvement expenditures.
4. The expenditures cannot be deducted by the individual as operating expenses when calculating taxable income in the year of sale. They are deducted in the process of establishing the capital gain (loss).

To calculate the capital gain, the seller first subtracts the selling expenses and the fix-up expenses from the sales price of the property. This step yields a value for the adjusted sales price. Then the seller subtracts the adjusted basis from the adjusted sales price. The remainder is a capital gain if the amount is positive or it is a capital loss if the amount is negative.

If the property is sold during the first six months of ownership, any gain is not considered a long-term capital gain; it is viewed as a short-term capital gain. In this case, the short-term gain is considered as ordinary income and is taxed at its full value.

Capital gain deferral and exclusion   If a capital gain is realized from the sale of the property, the seller has a substantial period of time in which to utilize that capital gain for the purchase of a replacment residence before reporting it to the Internal Revenue Service as a taxable capital gain.

If the seller chooses to purchase a replacement home within 24 months of the sale of the original home, and this replacement is of equal or greater value than the residence that was sold, the capital gains tax can be deferred into the future. The capital gains will continue to be deferred until the principal residence is sold and an equally valuable substitute is not purchased.

If an individual sells his or her principal residence and buys a residence of lower value, the difference between the adjusted basis is subject to taxation in the current year; part of the capital gain is deferred and part of the capital gain is subject to taxation in the current year. The entire capital gain can be deferred if the home-owner undertakes improvement to the replacement residence, such as adding a room or remodeling the basement into a den or extra bedroom.

If the seller decides to rent a residence and not purchase, after 24 months the seller must report 40 percent of the capital gain as part of his or her taxable income. Typically, this is done by filing an amended tax form (1040X) for the year in which the property was sold. However, a seller fifty-five years old or older before the date of the sale who decides not to purchase a replacement home is accorded special treatment. If the property was used as the individual's main residence for three of the last five years preceding the sale, the taxpayer receives a once-in-a-lifetime tax exclusion of up to $125,000 ($62,500 for married people filing separately) from the sale of that personal residence. The important phrases are "up to $125,000 ($62,500 for married people filing separately)" and "once-in-a-lifetime"—if this exclusion is elected at age 56 to shelter a capital gain of $60,000, it cannot be elected a second time at age 68 if a second home is sold and another capital gain is generated.

EFFECTS OF INCOME TAX CODE ON INCOME-PRODUCING PROPERTIES

The tax impact on income-earning property is related to three key concepts within the tax law—useful life, adjusted basis, and depreciation. The information in this section of the chapter is based on two publications of the Department of the Treasury, Internal Revenue Service, *Tax Information on Depreciation* (Publication #534) and *Sale and Other Disposition of Assets* (Publication #544).

Concept of Useful Life

The **useful life** of the asset is the IRS's term for the time period over which the asset will provide benefits to the owner that exceed the costs incurred by the owner in utilizing that asset to earn income. The tax code states that the useful life can be the period of time over which the asset may be useful to the investor in the operation of a business or the production of income, or it can be the same as the physical life of the structure. In the past, prior to 1981 the tax code allowed the investor to choose the shorter of these two time periods.[1] The tax code also stated that no average useful life was applicable for all parcels of real estate. Consequently, the investor was able to determine the useful life of the real property on the basis of its particular operating conditions and the investor's experience. The useful life of a real estate asset can depend on many factors; for example, the degree and intensity of its use, its age when it was acquired, the owner's maintenance and repair routine, the investor's policy toward improvements, and the climate in which the real estate asset is located. Moreover, the tax code also recognized the fact that useful life can change over time as a result of changing economic conditions that affect the property.

Due to these factors, the investor could enter into a written agreement with the Internal Revenue Service to reach a mutually acceptable estimate of useful life. The investor was responsible for initiating this discussion by filing an application in advance or attaching a statement to the tax return for the year in which the property was purchased. The following points had to be discussed in the document:

☐ The character and location of the property
☐ The original cost, other basis items, and the date the property was acquired
☐ Any proper adjustments to the basis
☐ The estimate of useful life and salvage value
☐ The method and rate of depreciation
☐ Any other facts or circumstances that are pertinent in the decision-making process to obtain a reasonable estimate of useful life and salvage value

As part of this process, the IRS wanted an estimate of **salvage value** of the real estate investment. In the Internal Revenue Code, the salvage value was defined as the amount the investor estimates will be realized upon either sale or some other form of disposition of that asset when it is no longer useful to the investor as a source of income. Salvage value was estimated at the time the property was obtained.

After December 31, 1980, when the Economic Recovery Tax Act (ERTA) became effective, these concerns about useful life were removed. ERTA mandated statutory recovery periods that are unrelated to the concept of useful life as a measure of economic life, and shorter than the previous useful life guidelines published by the IRS. The new system also disregards salvage value.

THE ACCELERATED COST RECOVERY SYSTEM (ACRS)

The accelerated cost recovery system (ACRS) starts with an identification of the classes of "recovery property," which means tangible property that depreciates when it is used in a trade or business, or as an investment held for the production of income. The following example shows the classes of recovery property and the type of property in each class of recovery property:

Classes of recovery property	Type of property included in each category
15 years and 18 years 3 years	Personal property used in the investment, primarily cars and light trucks
5 years	Personal property used in the investment, single-purpose agricultural or horticultural structures, and storage facilities used for petroleum distribution
10 years	Residential manufactured homes
15 years and 18 years	Most real property

In this example, personal property can include assets such as appliances, furniture, carpeting, cleaning equipment, and maintenance equipment used in the process of generating income. If these items are not fixtures, they can be depreciated over three to five years instead of fifteen or eighteen years as real property.

Adjusted and Unadjusted Basis

The unadjusted basis of income-earning property is simply the acquisition cost of the real estate, either the purchase price or the price for land and construction. The adjusted basis is obtained by adding any improvement expenditures and subtracting depreciation that was claimed. (If the owner does not claim any depreciation, the IRS requires the adjusted basis be reduced by the amount calculated using the straight-line depreciation technique.)

The adjusted basis also can be reduced for any casualty loss to the property. However, in the calculation of both the annual depreciation and the casualty loss, the investor must realize that real estate is composed of a depreciable and a nondepreciable component. Real estate consists of the improvement, which is depreciable, and the land, which is not depreciable. The investor, therefore, must apportion the original basis or acquisition price of the property into two components—the acquisition price of the land and the acquisition price of the improvement(s). The investor is not allowed to depreciate more than the value of the improvement nor is the investor allowed to claim a casualty loss that exceeds the value of the adjusted basis of the improvement at the time the loss occurs.

The unadjusted basis is used to calculate the annual depreciation charge. The adjusted basis is used for the calculation of capital gains. The distinction is very important to keep in mind.

As a point of clarification, if the investor makes a substantial improvement to a structure, the IRS treats the improvement as a separate building rather than considering it a component of the original structure. This allows the investor to use the regular ACRS recovery period for the improvement. The definition of a "substantial improvement" requires that the improvement increase the worth of the entire structure by at least 25 percent and that the improvement is made three years or more after the building was placed into service.

Depreciation Methods

Two depreciation methods are allowed under the Internal Revenue Code—straight-line depreciation and accelerated depreciation which is the ACRS. To a limited extent, investors can choose the type of depreciation method that best meets their investment objectives. Therefore, an understanding of each technique and the manner in which the annual depreciation charge is determined is important for real estate investors. Before the legally allowable and appropriate depreciation technique can be chosen, the investment's useful life must be established.

Straight-line depreciation   Assume that the recovery period of a real estate equity investment is eighteen years. The investor learns from the appraisal report that the estimated market value of $260,000 is divided into its two components in such a way that the value of the land is $35,000 and the value of the improvements is $225,000.

The annual depreciation percentage under the **straight-line depreciation** method is very simple to calculate. Over the eighteen years the investor would like to receive *a return of the investment*. In other words, over this eighteen-year period, the owner would like to write off the value of the structure. The straight-line depreciation method is based on the fact that in each of the eighteen years an equal percentage of the improvement's value is charged against the income that the property generates. An annual charge of 0.055556 for eighteen years will recover 100 percent of this value. This establishes a depreciation charge of $12,500 per year for each of the eighteen years. The annual allowable depreciation charges under the straight-line method and other depreciation methods are compared in Exhibit 10-1.

If the straight-line method is elected as the depreciation method, the following options are available:

Classes of recovery property	Permissible recovery periods under ARC
3 years	3, 5, or 12 years
5 years	5, 12, or 15 years
10 years	10, 25, or 35 years
15 years and 18 years	15, 35, or 45 years

If the investor decides to choose the straight-line method for depreciation, the investor must then specify the recovery period. As a rule of thumb, the shorter periods are usually selected.

Accelerated Depreciation Methods

In contrast to the straight-line method, several depreciation methods generate an annual depreciation charge in the first years of ownership that exceeds the annual depreciation charge in the last years of ownership. The two methods that provide this feature of **accelerated depreciation** are the declining balance depreciation method and the sum-of-the-years' digits depreciation method.

Three types of **declining balance methods** are allowed by the Internal Revenue Code—the double-declining or 200 percent declining balance method, the 175 percent declining balance method, and the 150 percent declining balance method. The 200 percent and 175 percent methods apply to real property. The 150 percent method only applies to personal property. The investor who uses the 200 percent or double-declining method can apply 200 percent of the annual depreciation rate allowed under the straight-line method over the useful life of the property. Under the straight-line depreciation method, the annual rate in the numerical example is 0.055556 per year over an eighteen-year useful life period. Under the 200 percent declining balance method, the annual depreciation is 0.11111 for the same time period. However, the 0.11111 is not applied to the figure $225,000 in each taxable

EXHIBIT 10-1 Comparison of the annual depreciation charge generated under alternative depreciation methods

Year	Straight line	Accelerated forms	
		200%	175%
1	12,500	25,000	21,875
2	12,500	22,222	19,748
3	12,500	19,753	17,828
4	12,500	17,558	16,095
5	12,500	15,607	14,530
6	12,500	13,873	13,118
7	12,500	12,332	11,842
8	12,500	10,962	10,691
9	12,500	9,744	9,652
10	12,500	8,661	8,713
11	12,500	7,699	7,866
12	12,500	6,843	7,101
13	12,500	6,083	6,411
14	12,500	5,407	5,788
15	12,500	4,806	5,225
16	12,500	4,272	4,717
17	12,500	3,798	4,258
18	12,500	3,376	3,844
	225,000		

year. It is applied to the undepreciated value of the structure in each of those years. A numerical calculation of the 175 percent declining balance method is shown in Exhibit 10-2.

In the first year of ownership, the undepreciated balance is $225,000. Applying the 0.11111 depreciation rate gives a depreciation charge for the first year of $25,000. After the investor writes off this amount in the first year, the undepreciated balance in the second year is $200,000. Applying the annual rate of 0.11111 to this amount yields a depreciation charge in the second year of $22,222. This procedure continues for each year to establish the annual depreciation charge from the first through the eighteenth year of the recovery period.

Comparing columns 1 and 2 in Exhibit 10-1 clarifies the concept of accelerated depreciation. For the first five years of the recovery period, the 200 percent declining balance method allows an annual depreciation charge that exceeds the straight-line depreciation charge in each of these five years. In the sixth year the annual depreciation charge under the 200 percent declining balance method is less than the annual depreciation charge under the straight-line method. The adjective *accelerated* implies that under the declining balance method, the investor can depreciate the project more rapidly than under the straight-line method. In a sense, the investor accelerates the maximum allowable depreciation charge over the useful life by taking large write-offs in the first year and small write-offs in the last years.

The 175 percent and the 150 percent declining balance methods can be applied in a manner similar to that used to apply the 200 percent declining balance method. The only difference among these methods is the rate of depreciation. In the

EXHIBIT 10-2 The 175 percent declining balance method

Year	Undepreciated balance	175% rate	Annual depreciation $	Annual depreciation %
1	225000	0.097222	21875	9.722
2	203125	0.097222	19748	8.777
3	183377	0.097222	17828	7.924
4	165549	0.097222	16095	7.153
5	149454	0.097222	14530	6.458
6	134924	0.097222	13118	5.830
7	121806	0.097222	11842	5.263
8	109964	0.097222	10691	4.752
9	99273	0.097222	9652	4.290
10	89621	0.097222	8713	3.872
11	80908	0.097222	7866	3.496
12	73042	0.097222	7101	3.156
13	65941	0.097222	6411	2.849
14	59530	0.097222	5788	2.572
15	53742	0.097222	5225	2.322
16	48517	0.097222	4717	2.096
17	43800	0.097222	4258	1.892
18	39542	0.097222	3844	1.708
–	35698	0.097222	–	–
				84%

example, for the 150 percent declining balance method the rate is 150 percent of the 0.055556 depreciation rate allowed under the straight-line method, which is 0.083333. For the 175 percent declining balance method the annual depreciation rate is 0.097222. The fourth column in Exhibit 10-1 lists the annual depreciation charges for the 175 percent method. The student can check for understanding of the calculation procedure by calculating the depreciation charges for the 150 percent declining balance method. However, the IRS does not allow a calculation of these declining balance methods. Instead, the IRS provides tables such as the ones shown in Exhibit 10-3 for the taxpayer to use. These tables appear in publication #534 entitled *Depreciation.*

Focusing attention on the annual depreciation percentage column for the 175 percent declining balance method reveals the allowable percentage charges against the original depreciable base. For example, $21,875 divided by $225,000 for the first year equals 9.722 percent; $19,748 divided by $225,000 equals 8.777 percent for the second year; and $3,844 divided by $225,000 equals 1.708 percent for the eighteenth year.

The IRS-approved tables of depreciation percentages for eighteen-year property are given as Exhibit 10-3. Comparing information from Exhibit 10-2 with the approved eighteen-year percentages shows that the IRS rates are approximately the same as those for the 175 percent calculations in Exhibit 10-2 for years one through seven. But the IRS rates are higher for years eight to eighteen. This occurs because the IRS rates add to 100 percent, while the depreciation rates for the 175

EXHIBIT 10-3 The accelerated cost recovery system

Source: Department of Treasury, IRS, Publication 534 "Depreciation" (for 1984 returns)

18-year Real Property
(placed in service after June 22, 1984)

	Month placed in service											
Year	1	2	3	4	5	6	7	8	9	10	11	12
1st	9%	9%	8%	7%	6%	5%	4%	4%	3%	2%	1%	0.4%
2nd	9%	9%	9%	9%	9%	9%	9%	9%	9%	10%	10%	10%
3rd	8%	8%	8%	8%	8%	8%	8%	8%	9%	9%	9%	9%
4th	7%	7%	7%	7%	7%	8%	8%	8%	8%	8%	8%	8%
5th	7%	7%	7%	7%	7%	7%	7%	7%	7%	7%	7%	7%
6th	6%	6%	6%	6%	6%	6%	6%	6%	6%	6%	6%	6%
7th	5%	5%	5%	5%	6%	6%	6%	6%	6%	6%	6%	6%
8–12th	5%	5%	5%	5%	5%	5%	5%	5%	5%	5%	5%	5%
13th	4%	4%	4%	5%	4%	4%	5%	4%	4%	4%	5%	5%
14–17th	4%	4%	4%	4%	4%	4%	4%	4%	4%	4%	4%	4%
18th	4%	3%	4%	4%	4%	4%	4%	4%	4%	4%	4%	4%
19th	–	1%	1%	1%	2%	2%	2%	3%	3%	3%	3%	3.6%

15-year Real Property (other than low-income housing)
(placed in service after 12/31/80 and before 3/16/84)

	Month placed in service											
Year	1	2	3	4	5	6	7	8	9	10	11	12
1st	12%	11%	10%	9%	8%	7%	6%	5%	4%	3%	2%	1%
2d	10%	10%	11%	11%	11%	11%	11%	11%	11%	11%	11%	12%
3d	9%	9%	9%	9%	10%	10%	10%	10%	10%	10%	10%	10%
4th	8%	8%	8%	8%	8%	8%	9%	9%	9%	9%	9%	9%
5th	7%	7%	7%	7%	7%	7%	8%	8%	8%	8%	8%	8%
6th	6%	6%	6%	6%	7%	7%	7%	7%	7%	7%	7%	7%
7th	6%	6%	6%	6%	6%	6%	6%	6%	6%	6%	6%	6%
8th	6%	6%	6%	6%	6%	6%	5%	6%	6%	6%	6%	6%
9th	6%	6%	6%	6%	5%	6%	5%	5%	5%	6%	6%	6%
10th	5%	6%	5%	6%	5%	5%	5%	5%	5%	5%	6%	5%
11th	5%	5%	5%	5%	5%	5%	5%	5%	5%	5%	5%	5%
12th	5%	5%	5%	5%	5%	5%	5%	5%	5%	5%	5%	5%
13th	5%	5%	5%	5%	5%	5%	5%	5%	5%	5%	5%	5%
14th	5%	5%	5%	5%	5%	5%	5%	5%	5%	5%	5%	5%
15th	5%	5%	5%	5%	5%	5%	5%	5%	5%	5%	5%	5%
16th	–	–	1%	1%	2%	2%	3%	3%	4%	4%	4%	5%

percent method in Exhibit 10-2 add to 84 percent. Also notice that the IRS rates are applied to the original depreciable base.

The component method of depreciation The component method for calculating the annual depreciation charge was permitted prior to 1981. The Economic Recovery and Tax Act of 1981 eliminated it as one of the investor's options. So, currently, only the composite methods such as the straight-line and the declining balance methods exist. However, the component method can still be used for property placed in service prior to 1981. As a brief explanation, the component method of depreciation yields results similar to those obtained under the accelerated depreciation methods. The component method allowed a greater proportion of the total depreciation to be written off in the early years of the investor's ownership period.

However, there was an important difference between the component method and the composite method of depreciation. Using the component method the investor divided the value of the improvement into separate values for the various components of the structure. In a physical sense, an income-earning residential investment was divided into major components, such as the roof; the structure; the heating, ventilating, and air-conditioning system (HVAC); the plumbing system; the electrical system; the doors, stairs, and windows; and other short-lived fixtures such as carpeting, wall coverings, and appliances. Each of these components was given a useful life and depreciated over its recovery period. So, the structure may have been depreciated over a twenty-five-year period, while the roof and HVAC system depreciated over a ten-year period. The results of this technique were high initial depreciation charges and low charges in the last years.

Internal Revenue Code Guidelines on Depreciation

Prior to 1981, the IRS made distinctions among investment property with regard to

1. Its use—residential versus nonresidential
2. Its age—new or used
3. Its remaining useful life—twenty years or less versus twenty-one years or more

Based on these distinctions, different depreciation techniques were permitted. Since January 1, 1981, the procedure is greatly simplified. Today, none of these distinctions exist.

The current IRS guidelines on depreciation for property placed into service after December 31, 1980, follow. The phrase "placed into service" means that the property is in a state of readiness and is available for a specifically assigned function such as personal residential activity, or the generation of income in a trade or business, or as an investment.

A. Real Property
 1. Residential and nonresidential investments. The investor in residential units can choose the straight-line or the ACRS method for the appropriate recovery period, which is typically eighteen years. If the straight-line depreciation is chosen, the investor can elect an eighteen, thirty-five, or forty-five-year recovery period. If the ACRS method is elected, the investor is allowed to switch to the straight-line method. No distinction is made between new or used property or its physical age.
 2. Low-income housing. The investor in residential units for low-income house-

holds can choose the straight-line method, or the ACRS method with a switch to straight-line at the appropriate time.

B. Personal Property

Personal property included in the investment for depreciation purposes includes appliances, furniture, carpeting, drapery, and air conditioners. These items cannot be fixtures. In addition, coin-operated washers and dryers, maintenance and repair equipment, and other personal property used in the production of income from the investment are also included. For such personal property, the ACRS recovery period is either three or five years and the IRS provides the applicable depreciation percentages in Publication 534 entitled *Depreciation*. For example, 5-year recovery property can be depreciated on the following basis regardless of the month it is placed in service:

1st Year	15%
2nd Year	22%
3rd through 5th Year	21%

Since the guidelines allow the investor to switch from the ACRS to the straight-line method, a time for such a switch needs to be determined. A comparison of the annual depreciation charges in Exhibit 10-1 reveals the time period when an investor may choose to elect a change from an accelerated depreciation method to the straight-line method. An investor who originally chose the 175 percent declining balance method could elect to switch to the straight-line method in the seventh year if the property is held that long. In the seventh year, the annual depreciation charge allowed under the 175 percent declining balance method is less than the annual charge allowed under the straight-line method. The straight-line depreciation charge would be used until the improvement is fully depreciated over the eighteen-year recovery period. The total amount to be depreciated is $225,000, which is the acquisition price of the improvement but not the land. If the owner used the 175 percent method over the first six years, a total of $103,194 will have been claimed over that period of time. The remaining $121,806 of the building's value will be depreciated in the seventh through the eighteenth year.

However, if the switch is made in the seventh year, the undepreciated balance of $121,806 yields an annual depreciation charge of $10,150 over the twelve remaining years. Using the 175 percent method for the seventh and eighth year yields annual depreciation charges of $11,842 and $10,691, which exceed $10,150. So the switch from the 175 percent to the straight-line method should not be made until the ninth year. Recalculating the undepreciated balance after eight years yields the following figures:

$225,000	Depreciable base
−$125,727	Depreciation taken in years 1–8
$99,273	Undepreciated balance for years 9–18
$9,927	Annual depreciation for years 9–18

The straight-line annual depreciation charge of $9,927 exceeds $9,652 allowed under the 175 percent method for year nine and all subsequent years. So, the switch should occur in the ninth year.

TAX ASPECTS OF THE INVESTMENT DECISION

The Internal Revenue Code has a major impact on the real estate equity investment decision. The potential investor must examine the effects of the tax code during the period of ownership and at the time the property is sold. Moreover, these effects must be evaluated in relation to the investor's own effective tax rate.

Tax Liability During Ownership

During the ownership period, the investor is primarily interested in how the tax code treats the expense and debt service items that are considered in establishing the level of before-tax cash flow, and what benefits may be received in the form of a tax shelter. The investor first calculates the taxable income that will be received from the property, then calculates the value of after-tax cash flow, which is considered to be the "bottom line" of the income and expense statement.

Calculating taxable income   Calculating **taxable income** for the real estate investment starts with the amount of net operating income. From that figure, the investor subtracts the mortgage interest payment, the annual depreciation charge, and several other property-oriented tax deductions. The numerical calculation of taxable income for the six-year holding period is presented in Exhibit 10-4.

The first deduction from net operating income is the mortgage interest payment. The full value of the mortgage payment is not deducted. The tax code does not allow the investor to deduct the principal repayment component of debt service

EXHIBIT 10-4 Calculation of taxable income and after-tax cash flow

Item	Year 1	Year 2	Year 3	Year 4	Year 5	Year 6
Net operating income	$38,930	$36,460	$36,710	$36,160	$35,960	$35,410
Less:						
Interest on first mortgage	19,289	19,094	18,704	18,314	17,729	17,339
Interest on second mortgage	3,000	2,400	1,800	1,200	600	0
Depreciation (175%)*	20,250	20,250	18,000	15,750	15,750	13,500
Other deductions	0	0	0	0	0	0
Taxable income	−3,609	−5,284	−1,794	+896	+1,881	+4,571
Net tax savings (tax shelter)**	+1,624	+2,378	+807	−403	−846	−2,057
After-tax cash flow (before-tax cash flow + net tax savings)	9,950	8,834	8,113	6,953	6,910	10,749
Equity increase from mortgage loan reduction						
Yearly	8,315	8,510	8,900	9,290	9,875	5,265
Cumulative	8,315	16,825	25,725	35,015	44,890	50,155

* Using the percentages from Exhibit 10-3 for an improvement valued at $225,000 and put in service in January of year one.
** Effective tax rate = 45%

because the IRS does not view the principal repayment as an expense incurred by the owner of income-earning property. The IRS considers it a repayment of the individual's obligation to the lender. The mortgage interest payment, in contrast, is considered to be an expense of ownership and, consequently, is a tax-deductible item.

The second deduction from net operating income is the annual depreciation charge. Depreciation is not a true expense of ownership because it does not represent funds that the owner actually pays out in each accounting period. It is a tax concept used to recognize the fact that a real estate investment will undergo physical deterioration, functional obsolescence, and economic obsolescence over its useful life. The IRS code recognizes that the investor both desires and deserves a return of the investment over the useful life of the property.

The Internal Revenue Code allows several other deductions in the calculation of taxable income. Certain expenses incurred in the year of purchase can be deducted but not at their full dollar value in that year. The Internal Revenue Code requires these expenses to be prorated over some period of time. This category of expenses includes the points paid by the investor to obtain the mortgage loan and the prepaid interest payment that the borrower might make in the first year. These two expenses must be prorated over the length of the mortgage loan.[2] The interest payments the owner incurs on the construction loan obtained to build the investment and the property taxes that were paid over the construction period are prorated over a ten-year period.[3] In Exhibit 10-4 the amortized initial period expenses are assumed to be zero for the subject property.

Once the mortgage interest payment, depreciation, and other deductions have been calculated over the holding period, the useful life of the property, or the maturity of the mortgage loan—whichever is applicable—they can be used to determine taxable income over the investor's planned holding period. Exhibit 10-4 shows the calculation of the taxable income level for the six-year holding period. In the first four years, the taxable income is a negative number. This situation provides a tax shelter.

Tax shelter   The IRS provisions allow the owner of the property to subtract the negative taxable income figure from the adjusted gross income figure on the federal income tax form in each of the first three years of ownership. In other words, the negative taxable income generated by the investment reduces the investor's tax liability from other income sources in those years. In the first year, for example, the investment property is sheltering the individual's other earnings to the extent of $3,709.

After the taxable income is calculated, the next step in the investment decision is to calculate the value of the *net tax savings*. This calculation yields a dollar figure to represent either the tax benefits provided by a negative taxable income or the tax obligation created by a positive taxable income. To make this calculation, the investor must know the *effective tax rate* that he or she will pay in each year over the holding period.

The investor's effective tax rate is not the investor's marginal tax rate. The effective tax rate is the portion of the investor's adjusted gross income that is paid as income taxes. Since the investor probably has deductions that are not associated with the real estate investment, the effective tax rate is less than the marginal tax rate. For example, the investor who is a homeowner can deduct the mortgage interest payments on the home as well as the real property taxes on the home. In addition, the investor can have a large deduction for medical expenses, charitable contributions, educational expenses, personal property casualty losses, union or professional association dues, etc. Consequently, "the effective rate is the critical one in analyzing tax deductions. Specifically, many investors as well as promoters and salespeople incorrectly use their top marginal tax bracket to calculate the value of a potential tax saving."[4]

However, in common practice the marginal tax rate is used much more frequently than the effective tax rate. When the marginal tax rate is used the investor should realize that all of the cash flow from the property may not be subject to the same marginal tax rate. This rate increases as gross income increases. So, if the cash flow is small, it will all probably be taxed at the same marginal rate. But, if the cash flow is large, part of it could be taxed at a lower rate and the other part of it at a higher rate as the investor moves into a higher income bracket.

In the numerical example given in Exhibit 10-4 the investor's effective tax rate is assumed to be 45 percent. The net tax savings attributable to the investment is calculated by treating 45 percent of the taxable income as an addition to before-tax cash flow if taxable income is negative, or as a reduction in cash flow if the taxable income is positive. The net tax savings in each of the six years calculated at a rate of 45 percent is presented in Exhibit 10-4.

After-tax cash flow   After the net tax savings is calculated, its numerical value can be added to before-tax cash flow. The resultant figure is **after-tax cash flow.** It represents the numerical value of the cash flow that the investor can expect in each of the years of the holding period after the income tax impact has been determined. The after-tax cash flow figures are also presented in Exhibit 10-4.

EXHIBIT 10-5   Present value of the investment based on after-tax cash flow, sale price change (appreciation), and equity increase

Year	After-tax cash flow	Factor at 16%	Present value
1	$9,950	0.862	8,577
2	8,834	0.743	6,564
3	8,113	0.640	5,192
4	6,953	0.552	3,838
5	6,910	0.476	3,289
6	10,749	0.410	4,407
PV of After-Tax Cash Flow			31,867
Equity change due to change in sales price	0	0.410	0
Equity increase through mortgage balance reduction	$50,155	0.410	$20,564
		Present Value—Total Return	$52,431

After-tax investment decision   The investor can use the after-tax cash flow figures in Exhibit 10-5 to evaluate the desirability of the investment. Initial period profitability ratios can be examined. For example, the after-tax equity dividend rate is equal to the initial period after-tax cash flow divided by equity. In the calculations, $9,995 divided by $40,000 equals 24.99 percent. A second initial period profitability ratio is the after-tax gross yield on equity. It is a measure of the after-tax cash flow plus mortgage principal repayment or equity buildup divided by the equity position. In the example, $9,995 plus $8,315 divided by $40,000 yields a rate of 45.78 percent. These two initial period profitability ratios suggest that the investment is a financially sound opportunity because they both exceed the investor's 16 percent expected rate of return on equity.

The rational investor should also examine the present value of the benefits to be derived from the property. An example of this calculation is given in Exhibit 10-5. The present value of the after-tax cash flow is $31,906. The present value of the equity increase arising from a reduction in the mortgage is $20,564. The equity increase is viewed as a single payment received by the investor in the sixth year because it is not received until the property is sold. In this sense, it is different from the after-tax cash flow because this periodic payment is received by the owner at the end of each accounting period. Finally, the sales price of the property in the sixth year is assumed to be the same as the purchase price.

The investor now can begin to make a rational judgment. The initial period profitability ratios indicate that the investment is a good opportunity, and the present value of the benefits, $52,470, exceeds the initial equity of $40,000. However, the analysis is still not complete. The tax impact at the time of sale of the property must be analyzed. Thus, all of the following factors must be considered in the process of analyzing an investment opportunity.

1. The amount, the timing, and the pattern of the before-tax cash flows that arise from the property over its entire holding period.
2. All tax effects, both tax shelter and tax liability, that arise during the holding period.
3. The cash proceeds (or obligations, as the case may be) from sale after analyzing all tax factors, including capital gains tax and the ordinary income tax liability on the recapture of the excess of accelerated depreciation over straight-line depreciation.
4. Recognition of the time value of money. A dollar received today has more value than a dollar received tomorrow. Money has a time value because when its payment is deferred, the ultimate recipient must sacrifice the regular "savings rate of interest" that could be earned at the bank and must forego special opportunities that may be available.[5]

The present-value calculation gives information on more of these factors than the initial period rates of performance. The present-value example used in this chapter enables the investor to consider cash flows from operations over the holding period, tax shelter effects over the holding period, and the time value of money. The after-tax equity dividend rate gives no information on cash flows after the initial period or on the time value of money.

Investment and other tax credits   The following types of tax credits can be claimed by the taxpayer. These credits reduce the tax liability on the property and should therefore enter the calculation of after-tax cash flow:

□ Taxpayers who buy personal property for business use may claim a credit of 10 percent of that investment if the recovery period is five years or more, or 6 percent of the investment if the recovery period is three years
□ Taxpayers who rehabilitate qualified buildings may claim a credit for
—15 percent of expenditures if the commercial and industrial building is thirty to thirty-nine years old
—20 percent of expenditures if the commercial or industrial building is forty or more years old
—25 percent of expenditures for certified historic residential and nonresidential structures

To get the credit, the taxpayer must use a straight-line method with an eighteen-year recovery period, and the expenditure must be greater than $5,000 or the adjusted basis of the property. The credit also applies to only the portion of the property's value that is at risk for the investor.

In the next section, the tax factors that come into effect upon termination of ownership are examined.

Tax Liability at Termination of Ownership

Five major tax factors can affect the investor when the property is sold—adjusted basis, capital gains taxation, depreciation recapture, tax preference, and tax deferral techniques.

Adjusted basis   The basis of income-earning property that is acquired by purchase is simply the purchase price of that property, regardless of the type of financial arrangements used in the acquisition. If the purchase price of the property is $250,000, the basis is $250,000 whether the buyer buys the property for cash or only pays 10 percent of the purchase price in cash and assumes a mortgage for the remaining 90 percent. If the property is inherited or received as a gift, the basis for the property is its market value on the date it is received. If an improvement is constructed, the basis is the purchase price of the land plus the construction costs.

Once the basis is known, adjustments to the basis can be made over the ownership period. These adjustments can be either additions to or subtractions from the initial unadjusted basis. The additions to basis are the costs of improvements made to the property. Improvements are either an addition to the property that prolongs the useful life of the property, or an addition to the property that has a useful life of more than a year. (Repairs, in contrast, merely replace some worn-out or damaged item and do not increase the useful life of the property; repair costs are treated as an operating expense deduction in the year incurred rather than as an addition to the basis.)

The major subtraction from the original unadjusted basis is depreciation that is allowed during the period of time the property is owned. The investor *must* deduct depreciation from the basis. If no depreciation claim is made by the owner, the Internal Revenue Code implies that a depreciation charge calculated by means of the straight-line technique will be subtracted from the basis.[6] If the investor deducts more than the straight-line depreciation charge, either intentionally or unintentionally, the basis is reduced by the actual amount of depreciation that is deducted.

The adjusted basis of income-earning property is the original purchase price plus the value of improvements to the structure less either the annual straight-line depreciation charge or the actual depreciation charge taken by the owner (if it is greater than the straight-line depreciation charge).

If the structure is rehabilitated, and if investment tax credits are claimed, 100 percent of the tax credits must be subtracted from the basis to obtain the adjusted basis. If the structure is a certified historic structure, only 50 percent of the tax credit is subtracted from the basis.

Capital gains taxation   If the property were acquired prior to June 23, 1984, and sold after more than one year of ownership, or, if the property were acquired after June 22, 1984, and sold after six months, the investor pays capital gains on the long-term gain received over the period of ownership. The magnitude of the capital gain is determined by finding the difference between the adjusted sales price and the adjusted basis. The adjusted sales price is the actual sales price received by the investor less selling expenses and fix-up expenses incurred during the sales period (described in the first section of this chapter).

The 1978 revision of the tax code specifies that 40 percent of the capital gain is subject to taxation as ordinary income in the year of the sale. Consequently, the investor must add 40 percent of the capital gain to his or her gross income for that year. The calculation of the expected capital gain is shown in Exhibit 10-6. The sales price is estimated to be $260,000 in the sixth year. The investor anticipates selling costs to be 5 percent of the sales price and fix-up costs to be $2,000 for painting the exterior. No capital improvements are planned. Total depreciation charges claimed over the six-year holding period will be $103,500. The capital gain is the adjusted sales price less the adjusted basis, which calculates to be $88,500. The capital gains tax is 40 percent, so $35,400 must be added to the investor's ordinary income as stated on his or her income tax return.

Depreciation recapture   When an investor sells income-earning residential property on which accelerated depreciation was used, the Internal Revenue Code requires the investor to calculate a figure known as additional depreciation; this same concept was known as excess depreciation in earlier years. Additional depreciation is the difference between the annual depreciation charge used under an accelerated method and the annual depreciation charge that would have resulted from use of straight-line depreciation. In Exhibit 10-6, the investor claims $103,500 in annual depreciation charges over the six years of ownership. Under the straight-line depreciation method,

EXHIBIT 10-6   Calculation of the expected capital gain

Sales price in 6th year	$260,000
Broker's commission (5%)	−13,000
Fix-up expenses (exterior painting)	−2,000
Adjusted sales price	$245,000
Original basis	$260,000
Capital improvements	0
Total depreciation charges − Years 1 to 6 (from Exhibit 10-4)	−103,500
Adjusted basis	$156,500
Capital gains (adjusted sales price less adjusted basis)	88,500
Capital gains subject to tax (40% of gain) ($103,500 × .40)	35,400
Capital gains impact on investor ($35,400 × .45)*	15,930

* .45 is the effective tax rate

the total depreciation charge would be $75,000. The difference between these figures, the additional depreciation, amounts to $28,500.

The Internal Revenue Code requires that upon sale of the residential income-earning property, the additional depreciation must be treated as part of the investor's ordinary income to the extent of the capital gain in the year the property is sold. This process is called depreciation recapture. (This requirement applies if the property was purchased after the 1969 Revenue Act.) The only exceptions to this rule are low-income housing projects, whether or not they are government subsidized. For this class of property, the additional depreciation that is recaptured as ordinary income is 100 percent of the excess less 1 percent for each month that the property is held in excess of 100 months. In other words, if a low-income housing project is held by the owner for less than 100 months (8⅓ years), all of the additional depreciation will be recaptured. If the investment is held for 200 months (16⅔ years), no depreciation recapture will occur. If the property is held for 150 months the investor must add 50 percent of the additional depreciation to that year's income from all sources.

The investor can avoid depreciation recapture entirely if the straight-line depreciation technique is elected. Only a capital gain is recognized, no depreciation recapture occurs. This complexity reveals the need for good investment and tax planning at the time the acquisition decision is being made.

Minimum tax on tax preference items   Excess depreciation and long-term capital gains are known as tax preference items. The federal government desires to impose the maximum tax liability upon the investor. To do this, the Internal Revenue Code as stated in the 1981 Revenue Act instructs the taxpayer to figure a minimum tax on the long-term gain from the sale of the property. In addition, the Internal Revenue Code instructs the taxpayer to figure a minimum tax on excess depreciation. When both of these figures are calculated, the individual is required to pay the *higher* of the following two tax calculations: (1) the minimum tax or (2) the regular tax payment that the individual investor would have to pay in that year based on the proceeds from the sale of the investment as well as all other sources of the investor's income.

The purpose of the minimum tax is to eliminate the possibility that the investor could escape payment of any taxes because of financial situations arising from the sale of the property.

The minimum tax liability is calculated in the following way. First, the investor must add together the excess depreciation that is subject to recapture and the *untaxed* long-term capital gains. In the example, the excess depreciation is $25,650, and the untaxed capital gain is $61,200. The sum of these two figures is $86,850. The investor has a specific exemption of $30,000 ($40,000 if a joint return) which is subtracted from $88,200. Then the remainder is taxed at 20 percent. After these calculations are made, the minimum tax imposed on the investor is $11,640 ($9,640 if a joint return). Consequently, no matter what favorable tax advantages could have arisen, the investor is responsible for paying the minimum tax.[7]

A complete calculation of the minimum tax liability requires the consideration of other tax preference items such as additional depreciation on leased personal property, the stock dividend exclusion, interest on all-savers certificates, and other more highly specialized items.

Tax deferral techniques The Internal Revenue Code allows the investor to defer payment of capital gains tax and depreciation recapture until the time the capital gain is actually received.[8] The deferral of these two items is a very important consideration to the investor because the funds that are not paid to the government at the time of sale can be considered as equity funds in the purchase of the other investment property. In a sense, the capital gains tax and the depreciation recapture are invested in the new property.

In the numerical example in Exhibit 10-6, the capital gain of $88,500, and more specifically the tax on the gain of $35,400, may not affect the calculation of the investor's total income in the sixth year. The investor might choose to undertake the process of estate building. The Internal Revenue Code encourages such activity through its provisions for capital gains taxation. The capital gains tax may not have to be paid if the investor exchanges for another parcel of real estate that is of equal or higher value.

The first requirement for a tax-deferred exchange is that the income-earning properties being traded are of "like kind." The term *like kind* refers to the nature or character of the income-producing property. The tax code does not require consideration of the quality of the property in terms of its construction or its condition, nor does the tax code require consideration of the size of the properties that are being exchanged. What the tax code does require is that real estate be exchanged for real estate. This ruling would allow a trade of investment property for investment property (commercial space for an apartment building), investment property for business property (an apartment building for a retail store that the investor will now operate), and improved property for land. However, it would not allow an exchange of investment real estate for a residence. Moreover, real estate cannot be exchanged for personal property because these assets are not viewed as being of "like kind."[9]

The second requirement for a tax-deferred exchange is that the property must be held for a reasonable period of time before the owner resells it. Therefore, the tax-deferred exchange does not apply to property that is resold in a short period of time after it is acquired.

When an exchange is made between two investors, typically one investor receives a property that is worth more than the property currently owned and the other investor receives property that is worth less than the property currently owned. In this situation, the financial arrangement must contain a cash payment or an exchange of personal property as well as real property. This cash payment or personal property is offered as part of the trade (the "boot") by the individual who currently owns the lower-valued property. The cash is received by the individual who trades the higher-valued property for the property of less value. In this exchange, the cash payment or the value of the personal property received by the investor who is trading to a lower-valued property is subject to taxation only if a capital gain is realized. The other investor defers all capital gains taxation.

In a tax-deferred exchange, both investors must calculate the basis of the properties that they own after the exchange. They retain the adjusted basis that they originally had before the exchange and they use the cash payment or the value of the personal property as an adjustment to the basis after the exchange. The investor who receives the cash payment or personal property subtracts its value from the adjusted basis. Through this process each investor really takes on the tax basis held by the other investor. Each investor's basis in the new property is the basis in the old property less the boot received plus the gain recognized. The important point is that both of the investors who entered into the tax-free exchange are able to defer capital gains tax and depreciation recapture. One investor defers all capital gains tax and depreciation recapture and the other investor is required to pay on the cash or personal property received on the day of the trade if a capital gain occurred.

The Internal Revenue Code also contains a second procedure by which capital gains can be deferred—the *installment sale method*. The deferral of capital gains taxes arises in this case because the full capital gain earned through the sale is not received in total in the year of the sale. The capital gain is spread over the years of the installment plan that is created at the time of the sale. Therefore, the investor pays capital gains taxes over a multi-year period instead of having to pay the full capital gains tax in the year of the sale.

To calculate the taxable portion for each year, the seller must first calculate *gross profit*. It is the selling price less the adjusted basis, selling expenses, and recapturable additional depreciation. (If the property were your home, the capital gain that could be postponed or excluded is also subtracted.) The selling price includes all financial benefits the seller receives from the buyer. These benefits include cash, the fair market value of securities, the unpaid balance of a mortgage that the buyer assumes, and the value of the installment note that the buyer signs as part of the deal. Once the gross profit is calculated, the *contract price* is determined by subtracting the mortgage balance that the buyer assumed from the selling price. Then, gross profit is divided by contract price to obtain the *gross profit percentage*.

The gross profit percentage is applied to the payments received in all years to obtain the capital gain in that year. This capital gain is treated in the usual manner—i.e., 40 percent of it is added to ordinary income and taxed at the seller's effective tax rate in that year.

The last major point in the installment sale is the interest rate stated for the installment loan. If the interest rate in the contract is at least 9 percent simple rate per year for any such note on a sale that took place after July 1, 1981, then the issue of *unstated interest* does not arise. However, if the installment note contains an interest rate that is less than 9 percent, then additional calculations must be made. If the deal does not pass the "test for unstated interest," you must apply an interest rate of 10 percent per year compounded semiannually. More information can be obtained on the installment sale provisions from IRS Publication #537, entitled *Installment Sales.*

Analysis of After-Tax Investment Returns

Having analyzed the tax impacts that arise during the period of ownership and at the time of the sale, the investor can undertake a thorough analysis of the investment opportunity. From the calculations shown in Exhibits 10-4 and 10-5, the investor knows the present value or the after-tax cash flow, the equity increase arising from the mortgage repayment, and the change in the sales price over time. In addition to these figures, the investor must consider the effects of capital gains tax, depreciation recapture, and the minimum tax.

The capital gains calculation is shown in Exhibit 10-6. The gain is $88,500. The portion of this gain that must be added to the investor's gross income in the year of sale is $35,400. The impact of the capital gain on the investor is $15,930 in additional federal taxes if the individual maintains an effective tax rate of 45 percent. The addition of $35,400 to the investor's income probably can cause the investor to be in a higher marginal tax bracket and thus will increase the effective tax rate. Therefore, a tax impact of $15,930 may be an understatement of the effect that the capital gain may have on the investor's tax liability to the federal government.

The tax impact of depreciation recapture is calculated and shown in Exhibit 10-7. Since the investor chose the 175 percent declining balance method instead of the straight-line depreciation technique, there is additional (excess) depreciation to recapture. This additional depreciation must be added to the investor's income in the year of the sale when the capital gain is reported.

The minimum tax calculation indicates an expected minimum tax payment in the year of the sale of $10,320. If the investor sells the property in the sixth year, the tax impact of the capital gain together with the tax impact of depreciation recapture will exceed $10,320. The minimum tax can be put aside because the investor's total tax liability from all sources in that year exceeds $10,320. However, the investor would not be able to avoid the minimum tax even if capital losses were increased on other investments.

The investor must now calculate the present value of the after-tax cash flow, equity increase through mortgage reduction, and the tax impacts that arise from the capital gain and depreciation recapture. The present-value calculation at a discounting interest rate of 16 percent is shown in Exhibit 10-7. The present value of the return on the investment is $40,681. Should the investor purchase this property? The answer is yes.

The present value of the investment, taking into consideration all of the factors shown in Exhibit 10-7 is greater than the initial equity of $40,000. If, however,

EXHIBIT 10-7 The after-tax investment decision

Present-value calculations at 16%

After-tax cash flow for years 1-6 (taken from Exhibit 10-5)	+31,867
Equity increase due to mortgage reduction ($50,155 × .410)*	+20,564
Capital gains tax impact ($15,930 × .410)*	−6,531
Depreciation recapture impact ($28,500 × .41 × .45)**	−5,258
Present value of the investment	$40,642

* .41 = PV factor in year 6 at 16%
** .45 = Individual effective tax rate

the present value of the investment were less than the $40,000 figure, the investment would still be a good opportunity for several reasons. First, the analysis to this point has not fully considered the role that the initial equity plays in the calculation. To complete the analysis, the investor must calculate the present value of the initial equity, which will be returned at the end of the holding period. In our example, the investor locks the initial equity into the property for six years. This $40,000 that returns six years in the future has a present value of $16,400 ($40,000 × 0.41). So, the full value of the investment in the current period is $16,400 greater than calculated in Exhibit 10-7. Stated in a different manner, the investment would be a good investment opportunity as long as the present value *as calculated in Exhibit 10-7* equals or exceeds $40,000 minus $16,400, which is $23,600.

Second, if any of these figures change, the investment decision may also change. As a case in point, assume that the investor decides to undertake a tax-deferred exchange or use the property to collateralize a second property. In this situation, both the capital gains and the depreciation recapture will be deferred. The present value of the investment at the end of the sixth year will be $52,470. The deferral of capital gains into the distant future makes them less significant in the present value calculation. Also, as the depreciation period runs its course, recapture diminishes as the excess depreciation of the early years is balanced by lower depreciation charges in later years.

Third, negative recommendation could also change if significant price appreciation was expected over the six-year holding period. Sixty percent of the gain is not taxed so the present value of the total return would increase. To show this point, assume that there was a 10 percent appreciation in the price of the property over the holding period. Calculate the after-tax present value of the investment's future returns under the assumption that the property would be sold at the end of the sixth year. In the calculation, assume that fix-up expenses, adjusted basis, and total depreciation as shown in Exhibit 10-6 stay the same.

PENDING LEGISLATIVE CHANGES

At the time that this text was entering the publication process, the U.S. Congress was considering several measures that could affect the content of this chapter. Several key concerns or legislative initiatives are briefly discussed below. If these changes do occur, see how they change and how they can be included into the discussion that is presented in this chapter.

1. The ACRS may be changed to include a nineteen year recovery period for property that was eighteen year property but purchased after a predetermined date.
2. Investment tax credits may be repealed.
3. The capital gain tax rate may be changed.
4. The deductibility of mortgage interest payments and state and local property taxes may be revised.
5. The marginal tax brackets may be revised.
6. The ACRS may be changed to reflect the impact of inflation on the value of an income earning asset.

CHAPTER SUMMARY

Both the homeowner and the equity investor are affected by the Internal Revenue Code. The Internal Revenue Code affects each of these individuals during the time the property is owned, as well as at the time the property is sold. The homeowner is allowed to make annual deductions for mortgage interest payments and real property taxes. When the single-family residence is sold and a capital gain is made, the homeowner must pay tax on the capital gain unless that tax liability is deferred by the purchase of a replacement residence of equal or greater value.

For the real estate equity investor, the tax effects are more complicated. During the ownership period, the investor must establish the useful life, salvage value, and a depreciation technique for the property. The depreciation charge is an additional annual deduction allowed by the Internal Revenue Code. Upon the sale of the property, the equity investor must calculate the capital gain, the excess depreciation to be recaptured, and the minimum tax that must be paid. If a capital gain is made, and if excess depreciation was claimed, a tax liability must be paid unless the investor makes use of tax-deferral techniques known as the tax-free exchange or the installment sales plan.

Review Questions

1. What expenditures associated with homeownership does the Internal Revenue Code allow as annual deductions? Which expenditures are not allowed?
2. Define adjusted basis and discuss the components of adjusted basis for both the single-family homeowner and the real estate equity investor.
3. Define long-term capital gain and explain how it is calculated for both the single-family homeowner and the real estate equity investor.

4. Discuss the methods by which long-term capital gain can be deferred by the single-family homeowner and the real estate equity investor.

5. Explain how the equity investor calculates a 200 percent declining balance.

6. Explain the nature and the purpose of the ACRS.

7. What are the Internal Revenue Code guidelines for the use of depreciation techniques for various categories of real estate?

8. Explain the process by which taxable income is calculated and how it is used by the equity investor to calculate the tax impact and consequently the level of after-tax cash flow.

9. How is additional (excess) depreciation calculated? What is depreciation recapture?

Discussion Questions

1. Explain how the decision to purchase a home might be affected if the federal government eliminated the homeowner's right to deduct annual expenditures that directly pertain to the physical asset.

2. Calculate the annual depreciation charges shown in Exhibit 10-1 on the assumption that real estate becomes twenty-year property in the ACRS in the future.

3. For the investment decision portrayed in Exhibits 10-4 through 10-7, analyze the impact on the investment of each of the following changes that take place independently of each other.

    (a) No second mortgage is used, so equity increases to $65,000.

    (b) The investor chose a straight-line depreciation charge instead of the 175 percent declining balance.

    (c) The investor's effective tax rate is 60 percent.

    (d) Capital gains are taxed at 60 percent instead of 40 percent.

    (e) The future sales price of the property is $280,000.

Notes

1. Jerome Y. Halperin et al., *Tax Planning for Real Estate Transactions,* prepared for Farm and Land Institute of the National Association of REALTORS (no place of publication given: Cooper and Lybrand, 1979), p. 319.

2. Ibid., pp. 90–92.

3. Ibid., p. 97.

4. Sherman J. Maisel and Stephen E. Roulac, *Real Estate Investment and Finance* (New York: McGraw-Hill Book Co., 1976), pp. 357–58.

5. Stephen E. Roulac, *Modern Real Estate Investment* (San Francisco, Calif.: Property Press, 1976), pp. 360–61.

6. Halperin et al., *Tax Planning for Real Estate Transactions,* p. 105.

7. *Supplement to Tax Planning for Real Estate Transactions.*

8. Halperin et al., *Tax Planning for Real Estate Transactions,* pp. 144, 166.

9. Ibid., p. 166.

Additional Readings

GREER, GAYLON. *The Real Estate Investment Decision.* Lexington, Mass.: Lexington Books, 1979. Chapter 6.

GREER, GAYLON. *The Real Estate Investor and the Federal Income Tax.* New York: John Wiley & Sons, 1978.

HALPERIN, JEROME Y.; FRANCIS J. GREY; CARL M. MOSER; and HERBERT A. HUENE. *Tax Planning for Real Estate Transactions.* Chicago, Ill.: Farm and Land Institute of the National Association of REALTORS, 1978. Chapters 4–5, 7–8, and 11.

KAHN, SANDERS, and FREDERICK E. CASE. *Real Estate Appraisal and Investment,* New York: The Ronald Press Co., 1977. Chapter 23.

MAISEL, SHERMAN J., and STEPHEN E. ROULAC. *Real Estate Investment and Finance.* New York: McGraw-Hill Book Co., 1976. Chapter 21.

MESSNER, STEPHEN D.; IRVING SCHREIBER; and VICTOR L. LYON. *Marketing Investment Real Estate.* Chicago, Ill.; REALTORS' National Marketing Institute, 1975. Chapters 7–12.

PYHRR, STEPHEN A., and JAMES R. COOPER. *Real Estate Investment.* New York: John Wiley & Sons, Inc. 1982.

ROULAC, STEPHEN E. *Modern Real Estate Investment.* San Francisco, Calif.: Property Press, 1976. Chapter 13.

WENDT, PAUL, and ALAN R. CERF. *Real Estate Investment Analysis and Taxation.* New York: McGraw-Hill Book Co., 1979. Chapters 4 and 5.

WILEY, ROBERT J. *Real Estate Investment: Analysis and Strategy.* New York: The Ronald Press Co., 1977. Chapters 4–6, 10–11.

11 | The Listing Motive and Contract

QUESTIONS TO BE ANSWERED

1. How important are listings to a broker?
2. What are acceptable listing techniques?
3. What are the advantages and disadvantages of the types of listings?

OBJECTIVES

When a student finishes the chapter, he or she should be able to

1. Explain the need and importance of identifying the characteristics of the local real estate market and, in particular, the market in which the agent wants to concentrate.
2. Identify several of the statistics an agent can gather from local sources to examine market trends.

3. Describe the relationship between the client and the agent.
4. Discuss the various types of listing contracts and state the advantages and disadvantages of each.
5. Explain the components of an exclusive right-to-sell listing contract.
6. Explain why listing is important to the agent.
7. Describe the National Association of REALTORS Code of Ethics and the state licensing rules and regulations pertaining to listings and the listing contract.

IMPORTANT TERMS

Affirmative Marketing Agreement
Breach
Commission Split
Dual Agency
Exclusive Agency Listing Contract
Exclusive Right-to-Sell Listing Contract
Farm
Fiduciary Relationship

Listing
Listing Agent
Multiple Listing Service (MLS)
Net Listing
Open Listing Contract
Principal
Procuring Cause
Real Estate Agent
Selling Agent
Special Agency with the Buyer
Special Agency with the Seller

Most real estate transactions involve the services of a real estate agent. Therefore, the consumer, whether a buyer or a seller of real estate, should understand the agent-principal relationship, the importance of listings to agents, the agent's techniques in obtaining listings and selling property, the various types of listings, and the legal and ethical aspects of listings. The consumer with this knowledge is able to make an informed decision about whether to list property with an agent, which agent to employ, and what type of listing contract to use.

AGENT AND CLIENT RELATIONSHIP

A Listing

The term **listing** is used to describe the contractual relationship between the agent and the owner of property. The owner typically instructs the agent to find a buyer who is ready, willing, and able to purchase the property. The agent expects to be compensated for accomplishing this task by being paid a commission, usually calculated as a percentage of the selling price.

Agent-principal relationship   In a typical listing between the owner of property and an agent, the firm is viewed as the **agent** and the owner as the **principal.** The agency relationship must be created for the firm by the principal broker in the firm. Although a firm could have several brokers, only one could have the authority to contract. Thus, this relationship can be described as being between the authorized listing broker representing the firm and the principal (the owner of the property). The listing is a contract of employment between the principal and the agent.

Agency   The listing contract typically used between the agent and the principal establishes a **special agency.** The agent is authorized to carry out only the instructions given by the owner. For example, the owner normally tells the agent to locate a buyer who is "ready, willing, and able to purchase the property" through whatever means of advertising and contact with potential buyers the agent considers to be legal, ethical, and most effective. The agent is given authority to pursue a wide range of actions and to seek a number of potential buyers.

A **special agency** can also be created if the principal authorizes the agent to perform a limited task. For example, the principal may be a buyer who wants a real estate agent to find a ten-acre tract of land with running water, not more than ten miles from the city limits, for less than $50,000. The agent is given specific instructions to perform a specific task and does not have authority to pursue a number of alternatives.

Satisfaction of principal's instructions   The principal always retains the right to determine whether the agent has satisfactorily carried out the instructions and whether the commission should be paid. For example, the owner indicates approval of the agent's actions to find a buyer who is ready, willing, and able to purchase the property by accepting the buyer's offer in the sales contract.

Payment of the commission   A question often arises about the distinction between when the commission is earned and when it is actually paid. The broker has legally earned a commission when the seller accepts the offer in the sales contract. The seller, by accepting, has indicated approval of the buyer. As a matter of caution, however, the state REALTORS Association may recommend—for the benefit of all parties—that the commission not be paid until the closing. At that time, all parties are certain the buyer can acquire the needed funds and will proceed with the transaction. Also, the buyer has either reviewed the abstract or has obtained a title insurance policy from the seller to confirm that the seller can convey all rights of ownership for the property. If the commission is paid when the sales contract is accepted by the seller, legal problems can arise if the buyer defaults before the closing, such as recovering the commission from the agent.

Dual agency   The state real estate license law may allow a concurrent **dual agency** between one agent and both a buyer and a seller. For example, an agent holding an agency contract with a buyer may sell that person a property on which the agent has an agency listing. The agent represents both principals and collects two commissions in such a transaction. States may allow this dual agency and dual commission transaction provided that both parties are informed in writing in advance of the transaction.

THE DECISION TO BUY OR SELL

Two agents and two principals   A relatively new trend is for the *buyer* to contract with an agent to locate or purchase a property. If the property in question is represented by a listing agent, the two agents may be *advisaries* in negotiating the price. Thus, this transaction has two principals, two agents, and one parcel.

Fiduciary relationship   The listing contract places the agent in a **fiduciary relationship** to the principal. In other words, the listing contract creates and requires trust, confidence, and loyalty from the agent.

Loyalty to the principal   To be loyal to the principal, the agent must follow all instructions, transmit all pertinent facts influencing the agency or the transaction, promote the interests of the principal, uncover all reasonable facts, eliminate any conflicts of interest, account for all monies pertaining to the transaction, and exercise reasonable skill, but the agent cannot exceed his or her authority, profit from the sale above the agreed amount, or represent his or her own interest in the property to the client without full disclosure of the interest in advance.

Breach of the Listing

A breach of the listing contract can occur in several ways, and it can affect the seller and the buyer as well as the agent.

Breach by the buyer   Consider a situation in which the agent has found a buyer who is ready, willing, and able to purchase the property, and the seller has accepted the buyer by signing the sales contract. The buyer suddenly changes his or her mind and will not appear at the closing although the seller has satisfied the terms of the listing and sales contract. The agent has fulfilled the terms of the listing contract, but the property is not sold. In this case the buyer *forfeits* the earnest money (see Chapter 13) that was paid when the sales contract was signed. It is divided between the agent and the principal according to the terms in the listing contract. Typically, the agent is reimbursed for expenses first, and any remainder is divided evenly between the agent and the principal. The agent may not receive more than the amount he or she would have received if the transaction had been completed.

Breach by the seller   The seller can breach a listing contract in two ways. One is simply by telling the agent that he or she wants to break the listing. Typically, the listing contract requires a specific number of days notice be given with a payment of funds to the agent to compensate for the time and expenses invested in the property. Second, the seller can breach the contract by refusing to accept an offer for the **asking price** by a buyer who is ready, willing, and able to purchase the property. In this case, the agent may have legitimate grounds to claim a commission because the instructions given by the seller were satisfied successfully.

Cancellation of the listing   The listing contract typically is considered to be cancelled when the principal dies, the agent or the principal files for bankruptcy, the property is destroyed, or the agent fails to retain a valid real estate license.

IMPORTANCE OF LISTINGS TO THE AGENT

The Need for Listings

A real estate firm has an incentive to establish as many agency relationships with as many principals as possible for two reasons. First, the firm's salespeople need an inventory to show prospective buyers. If the firm does not have an inventory of properties of various price ranges and types, the salespeople cannot satisfy the needs and desires of a prospective buyer. If the inventory is insufficient, the firm must rely on the listings of competitors and consequently the commissions must be shared. A shared commission is not the maximum commission. Second, the firm will always receive a part of the commission from its own listings regardless of who sells the property. For these two reasons, listing is sometimes described as the "bread and butter" of a brokerage office.

A properly listed property   A cliché used in the real estate business is that "A properly listed property is a sold property." A proper listing typically has the following characteristics:

1. *The list price is close to the market value.* The seller should list the property for a price that is comparable to the prices of recently sold similar properties. A price that is too high will discourage prospective buyers.
2. *The agent has explained the meaning of the listing contract to the seller.* The agent should always spend whatever time is necessary in explaining to the seller the clauses and terms of the employment relationship. The seller should be told that the agent is working for the seller, the terms of that employment contained within the contract, and that a commission is to be paid when the agent's duty is accomplished.
3. *The agent has made reasonable effort to uncover all pertinent facts about the property.* The agent needs to inquire about the condition of the property to determine whether it has any unfavorable features, such as sewer or septic tank problems, termite infestation, or water drainage problems.

Other characteristics of a listing depend on individual preferences. For example, a proper listing might also include the following features:

4. *A request by the agent to the seller to remove all personal property that does not remain with the real property.* If a buyer does not actually view these items, no confusion will arise later about whether they are included in the purchase price.
5. *A request by the agent to the seller to provide a survey of the property boundaries.* The buyer who is informed in advance of the precise boundary of the property knows exactly what is being purchased.
6. *A request by the agent to the seller to provide an up-to-date abstract.* By accepting this provision when the property is listed, the seller agrees to

provide the abstract and pay the expense. If the buyer later requests title insurance, the abstract can be used as the basis for the insurance policy.

7. *A request by the agent to the seller to give the buyer possession of the property on the day of closing.* A buyer who completes the closing but does not take possession has little control over damages to the property or a later failure by the seller to vacate the premises.

In a normal market, the proper listing of a property should eliminate many of the potential problems involved in its sale.

Listing agent   The **listing agent** is concerned mainly with the needs and desires of the seller. The seller must be convinced that the agent's firm employs salespersons who are professional and competent, and that the property will be represented to the maximum number of potential buyers. In addition, the agent can counsel the seller on the firm's ability to help transfer to another property after the sale.

Selling agent   The **selling agent** counsels the buyer, shows the available inventory, helps arrange financing, helps to prepare the offer, and in some circumstances presents the contract to the seller. The selling agent attempts to sell the buyer a property from the firm's own inventory. If the firm is both the listing agent *and* the selling agent, it retains all of the commission.

Control of the listing.   The listing agent has control of the property that is listed. No other agent can "jump the listing" by talking directly to the principal without the consent of the listing agent. Exhibit 11-1 shows a typical agency-principal relationship between the ABC Realty Company and James and Mary Dunn. ABC Realty holds an exclusive right-to-sell listing contract (explained later in this chapter). No other agency can show the Dunns' property without the approval of the ABC Realty. This listing is part of ABC's inventory, and the property is shown to that firm's prospective buyers. If ABC Realty is also the selling agent, that firm retains the whole commission.

Exhibit 11-2 depicts a situation in which another firm enters as the selling agent. The potential buyer contacts XYZ Realty to view the Dunns' property. The broker for XYZ calls the broker for ABC to gain permission and access to the property. XYZ can help the buyer write a contract, but the document must be presented to ABC, the listing agent. The broker for XYZ cannot present the contract directly to the Dunns without permission of ABC Realty. To do so would be "jumping the listing."

Commission splits   All salespersons must remember that a commission can be paid only by the firm where the individual is employed. In Exhibit 11-2, a salesperson for XYZ Realty cannot accept a commission directly from ABC Realty. It must be paid to XYZ first, and XYZ pays its salesperson.

Techniques for Obtaining Listings

The first step in forming a plan for obtaining listings is to set a goal for the number of new listings desired within a given time period. The number is determined by the

EXHIBIT 11-1 Typical agency-principal listing relationship

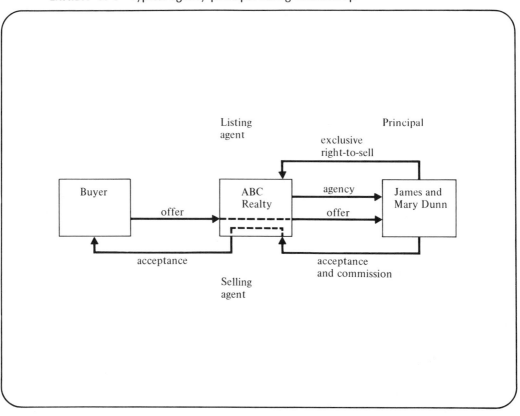

policies of the brokerage firm and the income desired by the individual. In addition, some firms pay an advance against future commissions on every listing produced, and a salesperson can use this information to plan income. One national franchise organization recommends that every salesperson concentrate on the "2 and 1" goal of two new listings and one sale per month.

The farm   All real estate agents should have their own **farm.** The **farm** represents a group of potential clients that one agent serves. It can be defined as a neighborhood, a price range, or a group of individuals clustered around an employment center. For example, an agent could define his or her farm as all properties between Center Street on the south, River Boulevard on the east, Sky Drive on the north, and the public zoo on the west. The farm could be defined as all properties priced above $75,000 in the community. Also, it could be defined as all individuals who are employed at the Northwest Shopping Mall, the First National Bank, or the Speedy Electronics plant. The agent attempts to meet everyone enclosed in the farm, identify him/herself as a real estate agent, and serve their needs. The agent should maintain thorough records for each property or individual contacted within the farm in order to stay aware of current needs of potential clients.

THE DECISION TO BUY OR SELL

EXHIBIT 11-2 Typical listing relationship with a listing agent, a sales agent, and a principal

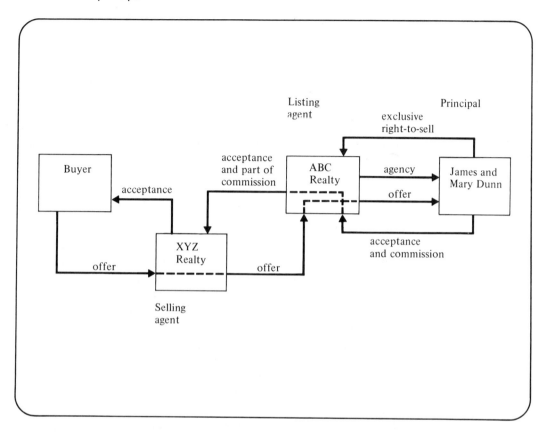

Use of the business card   The personal business card is the cheapest form of advertising. An agent should be innovative in distributing the card: for example, leaving it with the tip in a restaurant, inserting it with payments on all bills, and giving it to friends. Every agent within a firm should have a card with current, correct information and no cross outs, write overs, dog-earred edges, or discolorations.

Telephone technique   Since one of the agent's main tools is the telephone, the techniques of giving and soliciting information by telephone must be refined. An agent should practice answering incoming calls regarding ads in the newspaper, requests about signs in the yard, requests for showings, and requests for appointments by owners who are prospective clients. A good telephone technique can be practiced by role-playing between the salesperson and the broker, who can offer constructive criticisms.

Efficient use of time   One of the best methods of acquiring listings is to develop a daily schedule to make the most efficient use of time. Such a schedule might include the following items:[1]

Step 1. *Develop a good attitude.* A salesperson must have a positive attitude. One method of developing this attitude is to allot time each morning to concentrate on a statement such as "This is going to be a great day, and I will make it that way." Concentrating on a positive statement and evaluating it helps to generate a positive attitude.

Step 2. *Arrive at the office at an early hour.* Every salesperson should arrive at the office at an early hour, say 7:30 A.M. The cliché "Once you lose an hour in the morning, you spend the rest of the day looking for it" is true in the real estate sales job.

Step 3. *Send all new correspondence.* The first hour should be spent answering all new correspondence and communicating with new potential clients.

Step 4. *Visit the farm.* Approximately two or three hours a day should be spent visiting the farm to maintain a close, current contact.

Step 5. *Visit and study the inventory.* To show a property effectively, the agent must be familiar with its features.

Step 6. *Seek referrals.* About one or two hours a day should be spent soliciting referrals. Anyone in the farm who might be able to identify clients should be visited to obtain potential new listings. One of the best methods of acquiring a referral is to ask for it.

Step 7. *Solve daily problems.* All daily problems should be resolved by contacting the office or returning to it by 5 P.M.

Step 8. *Make listing appointments.* Prospective owners who might list with the firm should be visited at dinner time or early evening when they are most likely to be at home.

Step 9. *Maintain this schedule.* An agent should maintain this schedule for a predetermined number of days each month, say fifteen to eighteen, to acquire listings. Additional time of five or six days can be spent showing property to potential buyers and presenting contracts, arranging financing, ordering an abstract, and any other business associated with a sale. By maintaining the schedule, the agent can concentrate on listing property and still have several days for contacting buyers and showing the property. Additional emphasis can be placed on the latter two activities in any particular month if the agent has been successful in listing.

Understanding the Agent's Motive

An understanding of the real estate agent's motivation to obtain listings enables the potential seller to evaluate which agent can best represent the property. For example, the seller could ask the agent to describe his or her farm to determine the agent's area of specialty. The seller could ask the agent about the available inventory that the firm has under contract and to describe similar properties currently for sale in the community. Answers to these questions can help the seller decide whether the firm is active in the right market and can give the property a favorable competitive position in relation to other properties on the market in the community.

A prospective seller should know that the agent may be more motivated to list the property than to sell it. Consequently, the seller should always seek information from the prospective agent about steps that will be taken by the firm to find a buyer. Advertising campaigns, newspaper ads, letters, yard signs, and all promotional efforts should be discussed in advance of listing the property.

A prospective buyer should be aware that an agent may not show all the suitable properties on the market because the firm is motivated to show only properties that are in its own inventory of listings. Another firm's listings will be shown only if the buyer's desires cannot be satisfied.

DETERMINING THE MARKET

Both the consumer and the agent can benefit from examining the local real estate market and becoming familiar with its characteristics.[2] The agent wants to list the types of properties that have the highest volume of sales and therefore needs to determine the price range and location of such properties. The buyer or seller needs answers to several questions: "What is the best time of year to list a property worth $80,000?" "What is the average waiting period for the average sale?" "What is the amount of the average sale?" "How many homes in general are selling?" "Is the market strong with numerous sales and is adequate financing available?" Several useful statistics on past sales, which reflect local market characteristics, can provide the information needed by the agent and the consumer.

Statistics on Past Sales

Several sets of statistics accumulated on one midwestern city provide an example of how such figures can be used. A competent real estate firm in any locale can gather similar data as a basis for understanding the local market and its trends.

One set of data classified by value for one neighborhood is shown in Exhibit 11-3. Clearly, 55 percent of the sales were valued from $30,000 to $49,999. Adding the first two classes together reveals that almost 81 percent of all sales were less than $69,999. Thus, homes valued at $89,999 and less account for almost 92 percent of the sales.

EXHIBIT 11-3 Frequency of sales

Price range	Number of sales	Frequency	Cumulative frequency
$30,000–$49,999	545	55.0%	55.0%
$50,000–$69,999	256	25.8	80.8
$70,000–$89,999	106	10.7	91.5
$90,000–$109,999	52	5.2	96.7
$110,000–$129,999	29	2.9	99.6
$130,000–$149,999	2	.2	99.8
Over $150,000	2	.2	100.0
	992	100.0%	

Exhibit 11-4 is a simple tally of the number of rooms compared with the average selling price for the property in the same neighborhood. Comparing the data used in Exhibit 11-3 with the data used in Exhibit 11-4 reveals that approximately 81 percent of the homes sold had six or fewer rooms. Another interesting observation is the amount of increase in the average prices from adding a room. For example, increasing the house from three to four rooms raised the average price from $30,000 to $35,500, an increase of $5500. Enlarging the house from six to seven rooms increased the average price by $27,100. The data do not give the reasons for the increase.

EXHIBIT 11-4 Number of rooms and value for homes

Rooms	Average price
3	$ 30,000
4	35,500
5	38,700
6	55,500
7	82,600
8	90,200
9	106,800

Exhibit 11-5 lists the square feet of living area purchased on the market in the same neighborhood. Fifty percent of the homes have 1,814 square feet or less area and 75.2 percent have 2,091 square feet or less. The average area purchased during the time period was 1,610 square feet, and the most frequent area (mode) was 1,950 square feet.

EXHIBIT 11-5 Square feet of living area for homes purchased

Square feet of living area	Frequency (%)	Cumulative frequency (%)
1261–1537	25.1	25.1
1538–1814	24.9	50.0
1815–2091	25.2	75.2
2092–2368	14.8	90.0
Over 2369	10.0	100.0
Average = 1610 sq. ft.		
Mode = 1950 sq. ft.		

Exhibit 11-6 shows the lot values that were purchased during the time period. Clearly, 50.1 percent of the lots sold during this time period were valued at $19,999 and less. The value $29,999 and less accounted for 90.5 percent of all lots.

EXHIBIT 11-6 Lot values

Lot Value	Frequency (%)	Cumulative Frequency (%)
$10,000–$14,999	25.6	25.6
$15,000–$19,999	24.5	50.1
$20,000–$24,999	27.0	77.1
$25,000–$29,999	13.4	90.5
$30,000–$34,999	9.5	100.0

THE DECISION TO BUY OR SELL

Exhibit 11-7 shows the sales by value per month for the same neighborhood. The figures can be used to ascertain a selling cycle to answer the question "In which month of the year should a property of a given price be placed on the market?" For example, a property priced in the $90,000 to $100,000 range during this time period had the best chance of selling during July when almost six sales (57 × 0.105) in that price range occurred. September was also the best month for homes valued at $110,000 to $129,999, almost four sales (68 × 0.058) were in that month.

EXHIBIT 11-7 Frequency of sales by selling price each month

	Jan	Feb	Mar	Apr	May	June	July	Aug	Sep	Oct	Nov	Dec
$30,000–$49,999	34.8%	59.1%	66.7%	4.7%	43.8%	66.2%	61.4%	48.8%	49.3%	55.6%	40.0%	0%
$50,000–$69,999	30.4	22.7	12.1	32.4	29.2	18.5	10.5	35.0	31.9	33.3	45.0	0
$70,000–$89,999	8.7	9.1	12.1	14.7	14.6	7.7	14.0	8.8	10.1	5.6	10.0	0
$90,000–$109,999	18.0	4.5	6.1	2.9	4.2	4.6	10.5	5.0	2.9	5.5	5.0	0
$110,000–$129,999	8.1	4.5	3.0	2.9	4.2	1.5	3.5	2.5	5.8	0	0	0
$130,000–$149,999	0	0	0	0	2.1	1.5	0	0	0	0	0	0
Over $150,000	0	0	0	0	2.1	0	0	0	0	0	0	0
Total number of sales	23	22	33	34	48	65	57	80	68	36	20	0

The foregoing statistics are easily obtainable and provide a basis for several conclusions:

☐ The single highest frequency of sales is in the $30,000–49,999 range. Increasing the upper limit to $69,999 covers more than 80 percent of all sales.

☐ An average-priced house at $38,700 will contain five rooms, a house priced at $55,500 will contain six rooms, and a house priced at $82,600 will contain seven rooms.

☐ Fifty percent of all houses sold have 1,814 square feet or less of living area, and 75.2 percent of all houses sold have 2,091 square feet or less.

☐ Fifty percent of all homes sold are on lots valued at $19,999 or less, and 77.1 percent of all homes are on lots valued at $24,999 or less.

☐ Homes within specific price ranges sold more frequently during certain months of the year.

Listing Strategy

The agent can use the statistics on past sales to maximize the listings obtained for the amount of time invested. Typically the agent would attempt to list and specialize in properties in the highest volume market. For example, the agent's basic objective might be to "list all homes priced under $50,000." The locations of sales at those prices could be pinpointed on a map to develop a farm or a listing area. An agent most likely would not specialize in the higher-priced homes because the frequency of their sales is low in relation to the market. The lower-priced homes, say those under $50,000, show a higher frequency of sales.

INTERVIEWING THE SELLER

Prior to accepting a listing, an agent needs to discuss several points with the prospective client to ensure that no misunderstanding will arise and that the sale will progress smoothly.[3]

Seller's Reasons for Listing the Property

The agent must discover the prospective client's exact reasons for wanting to sell the property. A person who is being transferred may need the equity from the property urgently. A family that is either looking for a larger house or planning to build may be in less hurry to sell. Understanding the seller's motives enables the agent to serve the seller most effectively.

Seller's Knowledge of Selling and Purchasing Property

The agent needs to determine how much the seller knows about contracts, financing, and other components of a sale and purchase. With this information the agent is able to judge the amount of time needed to educate the seller about the sales process.

Appropriate Sales Price

The property must be listed at a competitive price to sell. The seller cannot expect the agent to obtain an offer to purchase the property at an unreasonable price. An agent should be wary of a seller who demands that the property be advertised at a price higher than its actual value. Taking a listing under such terms can create ill will.

The Agent's Plan for the Sale

All prospective sellers should be presented with a plan for the sale of their property. This plan should inform the seller of the type of advertising to be used, any plans for contacting prospective out-of-town buyers, times for showing the property, and any other unique features. The seller who knows the sales plan is not likely to become apprehensive if the agent does not show the house within a few days.

Property Condition and Time of Showing

The client and the agent should agree on the optimal time for showing the property if it is occupied. The seller must be aware of the need to keep the house in good condition and spotlessly clean for a good showing. Also, the agent may want to ask

THE DECISION TO BUY OR SELL

PROPERTY DESCRIPTION

Owner James D. and Mary R. Dunn	Date Listed December 1, 1986 **(CITY PROPERTY)**
Owner's Address 2232 Smokey Hills, Anywhere USA	Bus. Phone 575-4505 Res. Phone 521-2234
1st Mtg. $ 29,475 + @ 9 % Monthly Payment of $ 241.39	Includes Taxes, Insurance, (Interest and Principal)
Date of Mortgage $30,000 on Feb. 1, 78 Held by First Federal Savings and Loan, Anywhere, USA	
2nd Mtg. $ none Payable	Held By
Insurance Rate $720. annual on Dec. 1 Taxes $ 630.	Special Improvement $ 225.
Lot 12 Blk. 3 Addition Smokey Hills	Survey Jan. 78
Size of Lot: F 120. R 120 S 150 S 150 Lot Faces west Water yes Gas yes Sewer yes Septic Tank no	
Alley es Sidewalk yes Curb yes St. Paved yes Blks. to B. L. not applicable to School 10 blocks	

Stories	Material	No. Bd. Rms. 4	Patio rear	Floor Furnace no Attic Fan no Insulated yes
1 No. Rooms	brick veneer	Slp. Pchs. No	Den yes	Min. Cash Payt. negotiable
	Roof asphalt	No. Baths 2	Porch rear	Carport no-garage
	Heat central-gas	Dw. Str. Lav. 1	Attic no	Air Cond. yes
		Utility yes		

Occ. By owners	Rntd. for $ Mo. Lease Exp.	Poss.
Keys at MLS Box on front door Listed by Janet Watson	Option Exp.

REMARKS:
A two bedroom rental unit above the garage goes with the property. It rents for $175. per month. The lease expires on December 1, 1987

District	Location of Property	Type of Prop.	Price
	northeast section off highway 45	ranch	52,500

the owner to leave the house before a showing to enable the prospective buyer to discuss the property candidly.

Listing Agreement and Property Description

Typically, the agent must explain the terms of the listing contract to inform the client of his or her responsibilities and obligations to pay the commission. In addition, the property must be described accurately on the listing. The legal address and the current financing arrangements must be verified and explained carefully in the property description (see Exhibit 11-8) to enable other agents to identify precisely the property that is being sold for the price advertised. Also, all fixtures that are excluded under the listing price must be identified and explained.

TYPES OF LISTING CONTRACTS

Exclusive Right-to-Sell Listing Contract

The distinguishing characteristic of an **exclusive right-to-sell listing** is that the listing broker is entitled to a commission regardless of who sells the property. The primary advantage to the broker is that the money and effort expended on advertising and showing the property will be to his or her benefit. The advantage to the owner is that a broker who holds an exclusive right-to-sell listing will usually put the most effort into selling the property. Even if the owner sells the property during the listing period, the broker is entitled to a commission. Moreover, a real estate firm may have prearranged agreements to show and sell property listed by other firms; a predetermined commission split is paid if the property is sold. Brokers prefer exclusive right-to-sell listings because of the protection of commission feature. (See Exhibit 11-9)

Exhibit 11-9 shows the terms of a typical exclusive right-to-sell listing contract. The provisions of the contract are described hereafter.

Agency   The first section of the contract establishes the agent-client relationship and sets forth several points of agreement between the broker and the client.

Time period The listing runs for a specific time period with a definite beginning and ending date. The state real estate license law may prohibit an automatic extension period. The broker is given the exclusive right-to-sell agency within this period.

Multiple listing service The seller has the option of requesting that the property be placed in a **multiple listing service** (MLS). Typically, the seller requests this service because it gives the property maximum exposure with other participating brokers. The broker must pay the advertising expenses and agrees to cooperate with other brokers.

The broker may attempt to discourage the seller from placing the property in MLS if the property is a "good listing"—that is, if it is well maintained, located in an area of strong demand, and priced competitively. The broker knows that such a property could sell rapidly and does not want to share the commission. One alternative to this situation is for the seller to give the broker a specified period of time, say ninety days, to sell the property before it *must* be placed in MLS.

Right to cancel The terms of breaking the contract with the agent are identified. A specific number of days notice must be given and a penalty must be paid.

Referrals The owner agrees to refer to the broker all requests for information about the sale.

Price   The next section of the listing contract contains provisions related to the price of the property.

List price The broker and the seller agree on the list price. Once this price is stated on the contract, the agent cannot advertise the property for sale at any price higher or lower.

The list price is the asking price. Common practice is to ask the appraised value plus 5 to 10 percent. A property appraised for $50,000 would be listed at $50,000 plus, say, the maximum of 10 percent or $5,000, for a total of $55,000. This price enables the seller to negotiate in response to conditions offered by a buyer. In addition, prospective buyers typically offer less than the list price. Thus, the *list price* is equal to the *asking price,* which may or may not equal the *sales price* negotiated between the buyer and the seller.

EXHIBIT 11-9 Exclusive right-to-sell listing contract

EXCLUSIVE RIGHT-TO-SELL LISTING

December 1   19 86

AGENCY

Time Period. For the services of the following named
real estate broker, I list with this broker, from
___December 1___ 19 _86_ to ___March 1___ 19 _87_, inclusive, the property described below. I give this broker
the exclusive right to sell this property within the
time period.

MLS. I /xx/ authorize   / / do not
authorize this broker to list the property with any
multiple listing service in which he is a member, at
the broker's expense, and to accept the cooperation and
assistance of other brokers.

Right to Cancel. I may cancel this contract within the
listing period by giving __15__ days notice and paying
a fee to the broker of _$2,000.00_.

Referrals. I agree to refer to this broker all parties
expressing an interest in purchasing this property.

PRICE

List Price. The broker will advertise this property at
a price of _$52,500_. The broker agrees to present all
offers to purchase at a lower price to me for my consideration.

Deposits. The broker may accept deposits on offers to
purchase and retain them until closing or my rejection
of the offer.

Fixtures and Personal Property Included. The above
list price includes all household fixtures normally
considered to be included in a comparable property.
Exceptions include the following: The pool table does
not remain, the master bath drapes should be removed,
the storage shed in the backyard does not remain.

Encumbrances. I authorize the holder of any note
secured by this property to disclose to the broker the
precise terms of the note.

COMMISSION

Amount. I agree to pay the broker _7_ % of the selling
price for (a) the sale or exchange of the property
within the listing period by any person, OR (b) the
sale or exchange of the property within 120 days after
the lising expiration to any potential buyer shown the
property by the broker during the listing period. I
UNDERSTAND THAT THIS COMMISSION IS NEGOTIABLE.

Capable Buyer. The buyer must be ready, willing, and
able to purchase the property as evidenced by the successful completion of the closing.

Default. If I default on an accepted contract of sale,
I agree to pay the broker the commission.

EXHIBIT 11-9 (continued)

TITLE

Evidence of Good Title. In the event of sale or exchange, I agree to furnish at my option, an abstract of title or a commitment for title insurance in an amount equal to the purchase price. I will pay either expense.

Title. In the event of sale or exchange, I agree to furnish a _general_ warranty deed conveying a marketable title in which my wife or husband will join, free and clear of all taxes and liens.

POSSESSION

Delivery of Keys. I agree to deliver posssession and the keys no later than the closing.

APPORTIONMENTS

Real Property Taxes and Special Assessments. Delinquent property taxes shall be paid before closing. Current taxes and special assessment taxes shall be prorated through the day of closing.

Rents, Interest, Premiums. Prepaid rents, water rents, sewer rents, and mortgage interest shall be prorated through the day of closing.

MAINTENANCE AND DAMAGES

The broker shall not be responsible for maintenance of the premises nor damages unless such damage is caused by the broker's negligence.

DISCRIMINATION

The broker or owner shall not discriminate against any potential buyer because of race, creed, or national origin.

ABC Realty
Agent

James D. Dunn
James D. Dunn   Owner

Arthur Son
by: Broker

Mary R. Dunn
Mary R. Dunn   Owner

Deposits The broker agrees to accept and hold all deposits attached to offers on the property. This money is held in a trust account that is separate from all personal funds.

Fixtures included The list price includes all fixtures that are normally considered to be attached. Any exceptions, such as draperies, shelving, curtain rods, refrigerator, or a pool table, should be identified.

Encumbrances The owner authorizes the holder of any note on the property to disclose the terms.

Commission   Several stipulations pertaining to the agent's commission are agreed upon in the listing contract.

Amount The agent's commission is stated as a percentage of the sales price. It is paid for a successful sale during the listing period or during the 120 days after the listing period if the agent's efforts were the procuring cause or primary cause of the buyer's purchase of the property. The latter provision protects the agent if a potential buyer who is shown the property by the agent during the listing period does not decide to buy until after the listing has expired.

A competent real estate firm maintains records of its showings. Any attempt by the seller and the buyer to withhold a commission and sell at a lower price after the listing has expired will be met by a demand from the firm for the commission if the transaction occurs within 120 days of the listing contract's expiration date.

The commission between the agent and the seller must be negotiable. Charging a "going rate" or "recommended rate" may be an antitrust violation, such as price fixing or collusion.

Capable buyer The seller agrees to pay the commission when the agent presents a buyer who is ready, willing, and able to purchase the property as evidenced by a successful closing.

Default The condition for default by the seller on an accepted sales contract does not require that notice be given to the agent, but the seller must pay the stipulated commission.

Title   The seller agrees to furnish *evidence of good title* in the form of an abstract or title insurance. The seller agrees to pay the required expense of such evidence. The seller has the option of indicating the *type of deed* that will be provided. Writing in the type of deed serves to remind the agent to verify the warranty on the deed.

Possession   The seller will not remain in possession of the property after the closing, as evidenced by the *delivery of the keys* at the closing. The seller can negotiate possession after closing if the buyer is willing. The seller should be asked to pay the buyer a competitive level of rent and post a deposit against physical damage to the property.

Apportionments   The allocation of certain expenses between the buyer and seller is stipulated.

Real taxes and special assessments The seller must pay delinquent property taxes before the closing. Real taxes and special assessments are prorated between the buyer and seller through the day of closing (prorations are explained in detail in Chapter 21, "Preparing for the Closing").

Rents, interest, premiums Prepaid rents, water rents, sewer rents, and mortgage interest are to be prorated between the buyer and seller through the day of closing.

Maintenance and damages The broker is not responsible for maintenance of the premises or for damages unless they are caused by the broker's negligence.

Discrimination The owner and broker agree not to discriminate against any potential buyer on the basis of race, religion, ethnic origin, and/or sex.

Signatures The listing contract should be signed by all of the owners of the property. The presence of all signatures indicates a willingness of all owners to sign the deed later. The signature of a wife indicates her desire to release her dower and homestead rights (not all states have dower and homestead). In addition, the contract should be accepted by the principal broker of the firm because the firm is the agent.

Multiple Listing Contract

A multiple listing contract is an exclusive right-to-sell listing contract with one exception. The principal asks the agent to place the property in the multiple listing service so that it can be offered by other cooperating brokers. Thus, others may sell this property, and the agent agrees to a **commission split.**

The multiple listing contract is available only in areas where the local board of REALTORS has formed a multiple listing service (MLS). The service is composed of cooperating real estate firms that agree to share their listings to give the principal's property the maximum exposure. The commission split between the listing agent and the selling firm is governed by the MLS bylaws. Typically, the listing firm receives more than 50 percent of the total commission.

The owner benefits by placing the property in MLS because it provides the maximum amount of advertising among local firms. In addition, the principal still has an exclusive agent to represent his or her needs.

Exclusive Agency Listing Contract

The **exclusive agency listing contract** is identical to the exclusive right-to-sell listing contract with one exception. The owner may sell the property and pays no commission unless the agent can prove that the firm was the procuring cause of the sale. The firm, however, is guaranteed that it is the only agent representing the owner.

For an owner, this arrangement may appear to be the best—to have one agent attempting to sell the property and still maintain the right to sell without paying a commission if the opportunity arises. However, the agent may not invest much time or money in selling the property because he or she might not collect a commission to cover expenses and time. Consequently, an unethical agent may write the listing contract to prevent the property from being listed by a competing firm but may not do much to find a suitable buyer.

Open Listing Contract

Open listings carry no exclusive rights. An owner can give an open listing to any number of brokers at the same time and can still find a buyer without paying a commission. This arrangement gives the owner the greatest freedom of any listing form, but an agent has little incentive to expend time and money showing the property because someone else may be compensated if the property is sold. A firm's only protection is that it is entitled to a commission if it does find a buyer at the listing price and terms. Due to the agent's reluctance to develop a sales effort, few if any offers will be received and the result may be no sale or a sale below market price. If a broker does find a buyer, however, the commission charged will be the same as with an exclusive right-to-sell.

A broker who has an open listing or an exclusive agency listing is entitled to a commission if he or she can prove that the property's sale was due primarily to his or her efforts. Suppose a broker shows an open listing property to a client and, during the listing period or during an extension, the client goes directly to the owner and concludes a deal. Even though the owner negotiates the transaction and prepares the sales contract, the broker is entitled to a full commission for finding the buyer. The same would be true if the owner and the buyer used a third person to purchase the property to avoid paying a commission. State laws protect the broker who in good faith has found a buyer at the request of an owner.

When an open listing is given to two or more brokers, the one who first produces a buyer is entitled to the commission. For example, broker 1 shows the property to client C, but no sale is made. Later C goes to broker 2 and makes an offer, which is accepted by the owner. Although two brokers have attempted to sell the property, only one has succeeded and he or she is the one entitled to a commission. The fact that broker 1 receives nothing, even after expending considerable effort, illustrates why brokers dislike open listings.

Net Listing Contract

A **net listing** contract is created when an owner states the price wanted for the property and then agrees to pay a commission equal to any amount the broker obtains over that price. It can be written in the form of an exclusive right-to-sell, exclusive agency, or open listing. If a homeowner asks for a "net $40,000" and the broker sells the home for $50,000, the commission is $10,000. Many owners believe that by using the net listing, they are forcing the broker to obtain the commission from the buyer by marking up the price of the property. Due to public misunderstanding about net listings and because they provide grounds for questionable commission practices, some states prohibit them outright, and most brokers avoid them even though requested by property owners.

In a net listing contract, the compensation is not definitely specified. The broker retains as compensation all monies received in excess of the selling price set by the seller. The broker, however, is required to reveal the exact selling price to the buyer and seller.

Negotiation of the Commission and Antitrust

The amount of commission that the owner will pay the broker for services is a matter of negotiation between the seller and broker.[4] The usual arrangement is to express the amount on the listing contract as a percentage of the sale or exchange price, although a stated dollar amount could be used if the owner and broker agreed. The broker recognizes that if the fee is too low, the firm will not spend time and effort finding a buyer. Typically, a commission or fee ranges from 5 to 8 percent of the selling price for houses, condominiums, and small apartment buildings, and from 6 to 10 percent for farms, ranches, and vacant land. On multimillion dollar improved properties, commissions may drop to the 2 to 4 percent range.

The commission must be negotiable. Over the last seventy years, the courts have heard numerous price-fixing cases in which real estate boards and real estate groups have been accused of fixing the commission. Consequently, the commission must be negotiable to avoid antitrust violation. The commission must be reasonable. The owner cannot expect to take advantage of this point to negotiate a commission that is not a reasonable compensation for the agent's services. No agent will accept the listing contract and expect to invest time and money if the expected compensation is unreasonably low.

Other Points of Law

Several other points of law affect the listing contract and the agent's collection of a commission. The agent is entitled to collect a commission under the following conditions:

1. The agent must hold a valid real estate license at the time of the sale. This point is contained in many state license laws.
2. A valid listing contract must be in effect at the time of the sale. An agent cannot expect to collect a commission unless the property is listed. Thus, an agent should verify the validity of the listing contract before presenting a sales contract to the seller for acceptance.
3. The agent must be able to prove that he or she was the procuring cause of the sale. This requirement typically is met by the broker who is the first to present to the principal an offer that is accepted.

NATIONAL ASSOCIATION OF REALTORS CODE OF ETHICS AND LICENSE LAW REGULATIONS

The National Association of REALTORS has a 23-point Code of Ethics that covers in general all steps of a real estate transaction. These points, paraphrased below, require that a REALTOR

1. Be informed on real estate matters
2. Be informed on laws, legislation, government regulations, and market condition
3. Protect the public and eliminate damaging practices

4. Avoid controversy with fellow REALTORS
5. Share with other REALTORS and be loyal to the Board of REALTORS
6. Urge exclusive right-to-sell listings
7. Protect the client's interest, and treat all fairly
8. Not accept a commission from more than one party in the same transaction unless all parties involved know the facts
9. Attempt to discover all adverse factors that a diligent investigator would uncover
10. Provide equal service to all
11. Provide competent service
12. Have no undisclosed interest in property for which a professional service may be rendered
13. Have no undisclosed interest in offers to purchase property listed by the firm
14. Arbitrate disputes
15. Provide all pertinent facts to the proper tribunal
16. Inform the principal of all profit and expenditures
17. Recommend legal counsel and do not engage in the unauthorized practice of law
18. Not commingle funds
19. Present a true picture
20. Provide each party with all agreements in writing
21. Respect the agency of another
22. Cooperate with other brokers, and negotiate with listing broker
23. Not criticize competitors

Although these points apply to all phases of the transaction, several apply in particular to a listing.

Point 6 calls for REALTORS to urge exclusive right-to-sell listings. For reasons given earlier, the exclusive right-to-sell contract is the most advantageous for the agent and the principal. Point 7, requiring the agent to protect the client's interest and treat all fairly, reflects the agent's fiduciary relationship with the client.

Under point 8, the REALTOR can accept a commission from more than one party to a transaction only if all parties are informed of the circumstances. Similarly, points 12 and 13 require that the agent have no undisclosed interest in either property for which the firm may provide a professional service or in an offer to purchase. A dual agency may be allowed if the agent informs all parties involved. Conflicts of interest should be avoided.

Point 19 means that the agent should always represent the property clearly and accurately.

Point 20 states that each party should be given a copy of all agreements in writing. The principal should always be given a copy of the listing contract.

Points 21 and 22 pertain to the relationship with other brokers. A REALTOR must respect other agencies and cooperate with other brokers. One agent should not "jump the listing" by talking directly to the seller without the permission of the listing agent. Each firm should recognize and respect the agency relationships established by competitors.

State Regulation of Listings

The state real estate commission (or commissioner) typically enforces regulations covering the procurement of listings and the use of advertising and signs. Typically, state regulations stipulate that the listing agent

1. Must accept the responsibility of ascertaining all of the pertinent facts about adverse factors influencing the value
2. Cannot collect a commission unless a valid listing contract is in effect
3. Can offer to purchase the property for personal reasons only if the interest of the firm is disclosed in advance to the principal
4. Can collect a commission from the buyer *and* the seller on the same property *only* if both are informed in advance
5. Can place a sign on the property with the owner's permission (the sign must be removed promptly when the transaction is complete)
6. Must provide the principal with a copy of the listing contract
7. Must include the name of the firm and/or the name of the broker in all advertising
8. Must include a definite expiration date on all listing contracts. An automatic extension date typically is not allowed

Affirmative Marketing Agreement[5]

An **affirmative marketing agreement** is a document signed by the Department of Housing and Urban Development and members of the local real estate board who agree to cooperate to support equal opportunity in housing. Among other commitments, certain *advertising requirements* are imposed on real estate firms that sign the agreement:

1. Within sixty days after the agreement is signed, and quarterly thereafter, a notice that advertises the agreement must be placed in the local newspaper.
2. The local newspaper shall print a "publisher's notice" on each page containing real estate advertising. One alternative is to print the Fair Hous-

ing and Equal Opportunity sign in every ad larger than six column inches.

3. The Fair Housing and Equal Opportunity sign must be displayed in a prominent location by each board member who signs the agreement.

Misrepresentation

All agents must represent the facts about the property in a clear and accurate manner. Misrepresentation of facts can be intentional or accidental.

Intentional misrepresentation   Intentional misrepresentation is fraud if the affected party can *show intent,* prove that the *information was used as the basis for making a decision,* and *provide data that he or she was damaged from the transaction.* Several remedies may be available. First, the affected party may file a complaint with the state real estate commission. After an investigation and hearing, the commission may revoke or suspend the agent's license. Second, if the state has a recovery fund, the damaged party can ask the real estate commission to award actual damages. Third, the damaged party can sue the agent in civil court for additional damages or for the total amount.

Unintentional misrepresentation   In most cases, misrepresentation is unintentional. For example, the potential buyer may ask the agent, "Does this farm have a good water supply?" The agent might reply that it does without bothering to check. This response could be viewed as misrepresentation to the buyer if the farm does not have a good supply of water. An agent *should not provide unverified facts to the potential buyer.* An alternative is to refer the buyer's questions to the owner. The agent could have responded, "I don't know," or "Let's ask the owner."

To protect real estate firms against unintentional misrepresentation, some states have established a recovery fund that can be used to pay damaged consumers. In addition, the agent could still lose his or her license for grossly flagrant disregard of pertinent facts. Many firms carry "errors and omission insurance" to cover damages caused by their erroneous information or omission of information.

SALE BY OWNER VERSUS USE OF A REAL ESTATE AGENT

A question frequently asked by potential sellers is, "Why can't I sell the property myself and avoid paying a commission?" The answer is that a homeowner always has the option of selling his or her own property. The decision to sell the property oneself or to list it with an agent depends on the seller's *knowledge* and *time.* Does the seller have the knowledge for advertising, finding potential buyers, showing the property, negotiating a sales contract, helping the buyer with the financing, ordering the abstract, employing an attorney, purchasing title insurance if necessary, ordering a new deed, and employing a neutral party to conduct the closing? Furthermore, a seller who has the knowledge may not have time to devote to selling the property. A businessperson, executive, or professional may know something about real estate transactions, contracts, and financing but simply may not be able to take enough time to sell the property. In fact, the time expended in selling the property may be valued at more than the amount of the commission, especially if the transaction involves special arrangements in the contracts or the financing. A competent real estate agent provides or arranges for all the services that the property owner may not know about and may not have the time to carry out.

In some regions of the country, fee agents and discount agents have become active in the real estate business. These firms advertise a range of services that they can provide. The seller may select one or several and pays a predetermined fee for those services only. Such agents, who are in competition with firms that charge a commission as a percentage of the selling price, hope to generate a large cash flow through the volume of transactions.

All potential sellers must carefully evaluate their knowledge and time. If the seller knows little about the real estate transaction, or does not have time to take care of all the details involved in selling the property, a good real estate agent can provide a service that is worth the commission. The possibility of using a fee agent or a discount real estate agent should be evaluated with respect to the seller's knowledge and time. In any case, a real estate agent should be selected on the basis of a successful record of professionalism and competence.

CHAPTER SUMMARY

An owner of property may elect to "list" property with a real estate agent to promote its sale. A listing typically is a written contract containing instructions for the agent to locate a potential buyer who is "ready, willing, and able to purchase the property." Also, the contract contains other important provisions such as the price to be advertised, the amount of the commission, the time period for the contract to remain in effect, and a description of the property and the fixtures that are included in the price.

Real estate agents seek to acquire as many listings as possible because once a property is listed, the listing agent will eventually receive a portion of the commission regardless of who sells the property during the contract period. All real estate agents should have definite goals for the number of properties to be listed and sold and for their income level during a particular period of time. These goals can be translated into a daily work schedule to provide a basis for an organized daily routine and the maximum use of time.

In any community, statistics are available on market trends in property prices and sizes as well as number and frequency of sales. A potential seller can use such data to determine the best time of year to sell property of a certain price, the level of competition in the market, and the length of time that may elapse before the property is sold. The agent can use such data to determine the most profitable types of properties to list and their location.

Listing contracts range from the exclusive right-to-sell, whereby the agent receives a commission regardless of who sells the property, to an open listing, whereby the owner can establish an agency relationship with any number of firms. The best contract for both the agent and the owner is the exclusive right-to-sell, which enables the agent to invest adequate time and money in the sale of the property with the assurance of collecting a commission when the transaction is completed.

Many aspects of the listing contract are covered in the National Association of REALTORS Code of Ethics and in the state real estate license law rules and regulations. These points relate to the ethical conduct of agents among themselves and with the public.

Review Questions

1. What is a listing? What type of relationship between the agent and client is created by the listing contract?
2. What is a special agency in a listing?
3. Is there a difference between when a commission is earned and when the commission is paid? Explain.
4. What is a dual agency? When can a broker be a dual agent without violating a code of ethics or state license law regulations?
5. Outline the agent's requirements to be loyal to the client.
6. Is the agent motivated by different goals in obtaining listings and in selling? Describe them.
7. When is a property properly listed?
8. What is the difference between a listing agent and a selling agent?
9. Outline techniques that an agent could use to obtain listings.
10. Why should an agent attempt to determine market trends? Describe several sets of statistics that could be used in delineating market trends.
11. Why should the agent interview the prospective seller? Outline points that need to be covered during the interview.
12. Contrast the following types of listing contracts:
   exclusive right-to-sell   net
   exclusive agency   multiple-listing
   open
   What are the advantages and disadvantages of each?
13. Outline the typical components of an exclusive right-to-sell contract.
14. What components of the NAR Code of Ethics and the state rules and regulations cover listings and the listing contract?

Discussion Questions

1. Can a real estate agent successfully combine listing *and* selling? What set of circumstances would cause an agent to do both?

2. Does the potential *buyer* have any representation in a real estate transaction when the agent is showing property listed under a special agency?

3. Can you think of any situations in which an agent might have a conflict of interest in being loyal to the seller and still answer questions from the buyer about the property?

4. Are the techniques for obtaining listings any different from those used in selling any other product?

5. Does the listing agent always have an incentive to show the firm's listings first? Why?

6. Are there any circumstances in which the agent and the principal would use a listing contract other than the exclusive right-to-sell?

Notes

1. Harry Ladd, "Tracking Time," *Real Estate Today,* Vol. 13 (June 1980), pp. 25–29; Hugh Robertson, "Making Time Mean Money," *Real Estate Today,* Vol. 13 (March 1980), pp. 49–52.

2. William C. Weaver, "Measuring the Market," *Real Estate Today,* Vol. 9 (July 1976), pp. 7–9.

3. Art Godi, "Put Yourself in the Seller's Shoes," *Real Estate Today,* Vol. 9 (July 1976), pp. 38–40; Len Church, "Discover the Seller's Motivation," *Real Estate Today,* Vol. 9 (July 1976), pp. 41–45; "Manual Dexterity," *Real Estate Today,* Vol. 12 (December 1979), pp. 50–57.

4. Donald R. Epley and Cameron Parsons, "Real Estate Transactions and the Sherman Act: How to Approach an Antitrust Suit," *Real Estate Law Journal,* Vol. 5 (Summer 1976), pp. 3–14.

5. Much of the information in this section comes from the National Association of REALTORS, *Affirmative Marketing Handbook* (January 1977), and NAR, *REALTORS Guide to Practice Equal Opportunity in Housing* (September 1976). An interested reader may order a copy of the Federal Fair Housing Law by writing to the Department of Housing and Urban Development, Assistant Secretary for Equal Opportunity, Washington, D.C. 20410. See also "The Affirmative Marketing Agreement: Good for the Country and Good for Business," *Real Estate Today,* Vol. 13 (September 1980), pp. 55–56; Armin Guggenheim, "Do You Offer Equal Service to All Prospects?" *Real Estate Today,* Vol. 13 (April 1980), pp. 19–21.

Additional Readings

BLOZAN, DARLENE. "The Keys to a Successful Career." *Real Estate Today* (July/August, 1983): 54–55.

CLODGO, PHILLIP. "Raise a Crop of Listings with the Farm Listings." *Real Estate Today* 9 (September 1976): 22–23.

"Effective Telephone Techniques." *Real Estate Today* 8 (October 1975): 11–15.

HEAVENER, MAC. "Knock on Doors for Knock-out Sales." *Real Estate Today* 9 (August 1976): 44–45.

HENSZEY, BENJAMIN. "Broker's Liability: Cause for Concern." *Real Estate Review* 8 (Fall 1978): 57–60.

IACOBUCCI, H. PAUL. "Put That Business Card to Work." *Real Estate Today* 9 (April 1976): 46–48.

MILLER, NORMAN G. "The Changing Structure of Residential Brokerage." *Real Estate Review* 8 (Fall 1978): 46–51.

NICOLOFF, DOROTHY. "The Soft Sell Works." *Real Estate Today* 9 (March 1976): 34–37.

NORMAN, THOM. "Handling Ad Calls." *Real Estate Today* 8 (October 1975): 16–18.

"Objections Overruled." *Real Estate Today* 9 (August 1976): 32–37.

SOKOL, LORETTA. "War on Open Listings." *Real Estate Today* 9 (February 1976): 52–53.

STARRETT, EILEEN. "Follow-Up After the Sale." *Real Estate Today* 6 (July 1973): 34–39.

WARSTLER, GARY. "Classified Ads: Give 'em What They Want." *Real Estate Today* 8 (January 1975): 14–17.

YOUNG, SAM. "Turning Ad Calls into Appointments." *Real Estate Today* 9 (March 1976): 50–51.

12 Methods of Marketing and Persuasion

What are good marketing and persuasion techniques to use for generating business, obtaining an offer, and presenting the offer to the owner?

OBJECTIVES ─────────────────────────────────

When a student finishes the chapter, he or she should be able to

1. Explain the role of marketing and persuasion techniques in a typical real estate transaction.
2. Contrast an employee with an independent contractor and explain the advantages of each.
3. Describe the characteristics of a good salesperson.

4. Explain the techniques for finding potential buyers for property.

5. Identify the reasons for counseling the buyer and outline the topics typically discussed by the agent.

6. Describe the techniques that can be used in showing property.

7. Describe steps that an agent should follow in presenting an offer to a seller.

8. Demonstrate methods of persuasion that can be used in a real estate transaction.

9. Discuss the parts of the National Association of REALTORS Code of Ethics and the state license laws and regulations that apply to marketing techniques.

IMPORTANT TERMS

Affirmative Marketing Agreement
Blockbusting
Civil Rights Act of 1968
Close on the Buyer
Code for Equal Opportunity in Housing
Direct Prospecting
Division of Twos
Employee
Farm

Independent Contractor
Indirect Prospecting
Management by Objectives
Panic Peddling
Qualifying the Buyer
Racial Steering
Reflexive Statement
Role Playing
That's Right—That Leaves . . .
Tie-down
Yes-response Question

INTRODUCTION

This chapter explains common techniques and tactics practiced by real estate agents as methods of persuasion. The objective of the chapter is twofold: (1) to give the potential real estate agent knowledge about common methods of persuasion and (2) to inform the consumer about these matters, which can be used as a basis for making sound decisions in situations involving a real estate purchase or sale.

In this chapter, the agent is assumed to be fair and honest and practices good sales techniques. Knowing the techniques described should enable all participants in the market to undertake a real estate transaction rationally and intelligently.

APPROACHES TO THE REAL ESTATE SALES JOB

To be successful in selling real estate or any other commodity, a person must know and use effective approaches to the sales job. Any salesperson sells only knowledge and time and must be able to give knowledge that satisfies the needs of the clients in a minimum amount of time. Using an effective approach to the sales job gives the agent a competitive edge in the market.

Establishing Motivation and Attitude[1]

Any aspect of selling must be approached with a positive attitude and a high level of motivation. Selling should be viewed as a vocation that is composed of *challenges and opportunities rather than problems.* One method of developing a positive attitude and generating motivation is to establish a routine that allows fifteen minutes every day before going to the office when only positive statements are repeated, examined, and repeated. For example, the statement "It's going to be a great day, I am a professional, and I want to prove it to you" repeated several times, examined, and repeated again can greatly improve a salesperson's daily work.

Avoiding negativism   The positive attitude and approach to selling should not be influenced by the selling negativism of colleagues. Once the positive attitude has been developed, the agent should not listen or be sympathetic to the negative remarks, problems, or defeatist attitudes expressed by others who are not doing as well professionally. For example, an agent with a positive attitude must be very careful about spending too much time on a coffee break with other agents who have not been successful in meeting their goals. Their tendency will be to blame their failures on such factors as the economy, a poor broker, stiff competition, insomnia and lack of energy, and high costs of construction. Dwelling on these points is an inefficient use of time that can drain emotions away from the challenges.

Fear of failure   One of the very first steps in developing a positive attitude toward selling is to *overcome any fear of failure.* Hearing the word "no" is one of the most frightening experiences to a new salesperson because it is usually interpreted as failure and rejection. One way of viewing a "no" is to realize that it earns money! For example, assume that a new agent learns from the broker that, on the average, the sale of this firm's listing is worth $875 in commission. Also, company data reveal that approximately twenty people have been contacted on each listing prior to each sale. Consequently, each "no" for whatever reason is worth $43.75 to the agent ($875/20). A new agent should think of each "no" response as earning $43.75 commission.

This conclusion is a simplified version of the law of large numbers, which says that if enough potential buyers are contacted, a percentage of them will buy. It is a good basis for building a positive attitude.

Management by Objectives

All agents should develop a plan for achieving their goals. The objectives are the goals toward which an individual directs his or her efforts. The planning process is used to devise the day-to-day schedule to accomplish the goals.

Objectives are important because they can be interpreted into day-to-day operations. They give direction, provide a basis for making decisions, and an individual can use them to evaluate successes and failures.

For example, Bill Smith has established an objective of earning $29,000 in gross commissions the first year. If Bill's firm is giving salespeople an average of $875 for each of the firm's listing that is sold, Bill estimates that he must raise about $24,000 from listings sold because his specialty is showing and closing on residential homes. Bill must find 28 buyers ($24,000/$875 = 27.4). If the firm's data show that an average of 20 potential prospects are contacted prior to each sale, Bill must contact an average of 560 (28 × 20) potential buyers. Bill estimates 264 working days per year and therefore must contact two or three potential buyers on the average per day.

Bill plans to raise the additional $5,000 by showing commercial listings. Because the commission on such property depends on the price and the property, no general data can be used. However, Bill plans to contact at least two potential buyers per week or 104 for the year. Bill figures that one sale from the 104 will net the remaining $5,000.

Bill's objectives can be interpreted into a day-to-day work schedule that will allow contacts with at least two or three potential buyers per day and two commercial prospects per week. For example:

7:00 A.M.	Rise.
7:30	Adjust attitude to positive thoughts by repeating positive statements.
8:00	Arrive at the office and handle office matters.
9:00	Leave office and visit the properties for sale to know the inventory.
10:00	Contact potential buyers from office at home or from a private public phone; never return to office during the day as I may become involved in the negative attitudes of my colleagues.
Noon	Lunch with a commercial prospect.
1:00 P.M.	Contact additional buyers and show property.
3:00	Call or visit satisfied customers to ask for referrals.
4:00	Return to office to answer phone messages and write follow-up correspondence to potential buyers who have just been contacted.
5:00	Present contracts of sale to sellers; write listing contracts.
7:00	Contact potential clients who could not be reached earlier in the day; return home when finished.

Evaluation   Any plan must be examined periodically to evaluate successes and failures. One of the best methods of evaluating performance is to maintain good data and files on a daily basis. Also, the agent may need these data to provide evidence that he or she has not discriminated in showing.

One method of evaluation is to examine performance every weekend to determine the amount of time and effort to be expended in the following week. In addition, a cumulative total of all figures for the year-to-date should be maintained so that each week can be compared with the total performance, and each can be compared with the previous week.

Knowledge

No agent can hope to serve the public, be a professional, and make a reasonable living from commissions unless he or she has the basic knowledge and skills required to accomplish the objectives. A good approach to follow is first to acquire the basic skills required for the profession, and then to spend at least one week each year in continuing education classes that sharpen and update those skills.

Perhaps the best source of information on market persuasion techniques is the courses sponsored by the National Association of REALTORS and the State REALTORS Association. A state association may sponsor periodically a Graduate REALTORS Institute, which includes sessions on topics such as prospecting, listing, and closing. Graduates are awarded the GRI designation. Technical information on appraising, finance, law, contracts, construction, or similar topics can be acquired from the Institute, college courses, and special seminars sponsored by national real estate groups such as the NAR, the Institute of Real Estate Management, the American Institute of Real Estate Appraisers, and the Society of Real Estate Appraisers.

Role Playing[2]

Occasional role playing is important because (1) it is one of the most effective teaching techniques and (2) it enables the participant to receive criticism on knowledge and techniques from an outside source. Such evaluation and criticism is constructive because the participant learns how others perceive his or her actions.

The objective of **role playing** is to simulate an actual situation, let the participant apply his or her knowledge in handling it, and provide constructive criticism. Any situation can be simulated, from telephone techniques to answering questions from a potential buyer. Several roles can be played by the learning participant.

One-on-one:	In this simulation, a broker provides direct evaluation to the participant. It is most effective for teaching or evaluating telephone procedures.
All against one:	All agents in an office can periodically assume the role of a seller (buyer) and ask questions that simulate actual problems. The agent is collectively criticized on his or her responses.
Hat trick:	Written questions or problems are collected from agents in the firm and placed in a hat. Each person in the group must evaluate the questions or problems and provide an answer to the others by simulating the situations.
Make up your own:	Real-life situations can be simulated periodically to cover all possible problems that may arise. An agent

THE DECISION TO BUY OR SELL

who is prepared in advance for potential pitfalls is well trained and should have confidence.

Personality Traits of a Successful Salesperson

Traits of a successful salesperson can be learned from attending a sales meeting or knowing successful independent contractors. In either case, techniques or procedures for success can be shared and evaluated. In addition, a checklist of desirable traits can be generated and reviewed periodically. Such traits include

Decisiveness:	Ability to make decisions.
Can take the initiative:	Can assume leadership and stay in control of a transaction.
Knowledgeable:	Knows all phases of the business.
Perceptive:	Listens to other people carefully.
Flexible:	Open-minded and willing to adjust to the desires of the client.
People-oriented:	Enjoys meeting people.
Self-aware:	Self-disciplined, self-motivated, and a self-starter.
Hard worker:	Willing to work long hours to accomplish individual goals.

By comparing his or her own traits with those listed, the salesperson can identify the ones that need improvement and can make a conscious effort to strengthen them.

THE AGENT-FIRM RELATIONSHIP

A real estate agent may be employed by a firm as an employee or may sell services to a purchaser (firm) as an independent contractor. An agent is an **employee** if someone in the firm has the right to control his or her actions. This supervisor must have the *right to control,* and the fact that the right has never been exercised is not important. In an employer-employee relationship, the employee does not have to be called an "employee."

An **independent contractor** uses his or her own methods and materials, neither expects nor receives training from the firm, determines his or her work schedule, receives pay by the job or straight commission, pays all expenses and taxes, and furnishes all tools and materials of the trade. Materials and tools furnished by the firm should be itemized in a contract that requires these items as a basis of providing services or should be repaid by the independent contractor.

For both employees and independent contractors, the amount of compensation paid to the agent is negotiated between the firm and the agent.

Guidelines

The Tax Equity and Fiscal Responsibility Act of 1982 established three "safe harbor" requirements that must be met to ensure that salespeople will not be treated as employees for federal tax purposes:

1. Salesperson must be a licensed real estate agent.
2. Substantially all of the salesperson's compensation must be directly related to sales or other output as opposed to the number of hours worked.
3. A written agreement must exist between the salesperson and the person for whom he or she works. This agreement must state that the person for whom he or she works will not treat the agent as an employee for tax purposes.

Employer Requirements

An employer must pay FICA taxes on the employee's wages, state and federal unemployment taxes, worker's compensation, and other necessary expenses for maintaining payroll records.

Conflict Between the IRS and the License Law

The state license law may require a broker to assume the responsibility for sales personnel working for the firm, which implies a right to control. In contrast, the independent contractor as seen by the IRS functions without the broker's right to control his or her actions. This apparent conflict is a national issue rather than a state problem.

FINDING BUYERS

Once a property is listed with the firm, the agent must attempt to find a suitable buyer. An agent *prospects* for a buyer just as the agent prospects for a listing. The seller benefits from the agent's ability to find a buyer and needs to understand the prospecting process. In addition, knowledge of the agent's techniques can assist the seller in evaluating the agent's performance.

Positive Attitude

In any business that involves selling, a positive attitude is a key to success. The agent should view every potential real estate buyer as an interesting challenge.

Data on Buyers

Typically, data describing the typical buyers within a region are difficult to obtain. No central source maintains files of aggregate statistics on buyers. Furthermore, sources such as lenders who might have some data in unaggregate form regard these facts as confidential. Consequently, no profile of past buyer characteristics is available. Potential buyer demand can be estimated from census information describing the employment and income levels of the area. These data are somewhat limited because they show only potential and do not indicate migration from outside the area or among neighborhoods.

Direct Prospecting

Direct prospecting is the effort of the agent to find an interested buyer among specific individuals or groups. Many sources of names can be investigated.

Farm of listings[3]   The first place to look for an interested buyer is the current file of listings in the office. A seller who has already listed property with the agent's firm has expressed a willingness to sell, a willingness to work with the firm exclusively, and a *need for another property after the sale.* If the agent has a property that satisfies the needs of a seller already in the file, a match may be readily available.

In addition, individuals in the agent's **farm** may have expressed a willingness to move if the "right" property can be found. By matching needs and wants of such persons, the agent has the opportunity not only to sell a property to an interested party in the farm but also to list the buyer's present property.

Multilist   The second group of sellers to check are those whose property is listed with other firms. Once a sale is completed on one of these properties, the seller will need other property. The contact with the seller of property listed with another firm must be accomplished according to the regulations of the State REALTORS Association.

Neighbors   Residents within two square blocks of the property will be reasonably familiar with the property and its general condition. They will know the wants and needs of their friends and neighbors in the area and the region. Also, they will prefer that new neighbors be friends with whom they can associate. Therefore, they may be willing to give names of possible buyers.

Satisfied customers   Satisfied customers with whom the agent has worked in the past may be a good source of potential buyers, including themselves. A satisfied customer might be ready to move on or to move up to a more expensive neighborhood.

Immigrants to the area   Individuals who are being transferred to the area or are retiring to the area can be contacted by phone or sent a copy of the listing. Names of transferees can sometimes be obtained from the chamber of commerce and the personnel departments of local firms. Retirees from outside the area are difficult to identify in advance.

Referrals   A good commercial agent sells almost all of his or her commercial listings by referral only. The property is not advertised in the newspaper or placed in a multiple listing service. For good commercial property, qualified buyers are not difficult to find. The property is "placed" with the proper buyer to satisfy his or her particular needs. Consequently, the agent has no need to advertise and typically has more buyers than properties.

Expired listings   Expired listings of sellers identify potential buyers who may have recently sold their property. These parties should be contacted according to the rules of practice recommended by the State REALTORS Association.

Names in the newspaper   A clipping service in the office can identify parties who are moving into the area from information presented in public relations announcements.

Legal transaction section   In some communities, a newspaper or newsletter publishes a summary of the legal documents filed in the county courthouse. A deed that is recorded showing a transaction from *A* to *B* means to the agent that *A* is now in need of new property.

Indirect Prospecting

Indirect prospecting is not aimed specifically at certain individuals or groups. The motive of the agent is to advertise the property and wait for a buyer to express an interest.

Yard sign   With the seller's permission, a sign is always placed in the yard of a property for sale to inform parties living nearby and driving past that the property is available.

Newspaper ad   The agent will invest his or her own funds to advertise the property in the local newspaper.

Use of multiple listing   The property will receive maximum exposure to all interested parties if the seller agrees to advertise the property in the multiple listing service, if one is available.

COUNSELING THE BUYER

One of the most important steps in matching a buyer with the right property is to counsel the buyer early in the transaction. The purpose of the counseling is to determine the buyer's desires and financial capability and to obtain the buyer's confidence and loyalty. The agent can select the most suitable property to show the buyer by determining the buyer's needs, motivation to buy, and financial capability. The process of obtaining this information is called **qualifying the buyer.**[4]

Warming the Buyer

To begin the counseling process with the buyer, the agent should imagine that the buyer is very cold and probably somewhat apprehensive about finding the right property and spending a large sum of money. Thus, the agent should offer coffee or soft drinks and establish a friendly atmosphere in which communication and confidence can be created. All agents should spend whatever time is necessary at the very beginning to develop rapport with the buyer.

Determining the Buyer's Knowledge of the Market

The agent can determine the buyer's knowledge of the local market by asking several direct questions such as Are you familiar with local market trends? and Have you ever visited ____(city)____ before? and Do you have any friends or relatives living in ____(city)____ ? A "no" response to each of these questions will inform the agent that the buyer should be given facts about local trends before visiting prospective properties. The buyer will thus have a more realistic concept of prices when he or she views properties.

Determining the Buyer's Needs

The agent needs to know the buyer's needs: What amount of square footage is necessary? How many baths and bedrooms are needed? Is a garage or carport desired? Should the house have brick veneer or cedar siding? What school district is desired? How far from work should the property be? Is a flat lot or a sloping lot preferred? Should there be trees? Should the property be new or old? What style is desired in the construction? Answers to these questions and others that the agent might add give a profile of the buyer's needs that can be compared with features of properties for sale.

Determining the Buyer's Motivation

Is the buyer actually committed to buying, or just a looker? Does the buyer need to purchase a property immediately to replace one that was sold, or is the buyer simply expressing his or her desires in case a suitable property comes on the market in the future? Answers to these questions determine the buyer's urgency for purchasing property. In addition, the agent should discover whether the buyer wants to locate in a specific neighborhood because of the "snob appeal" of associating with a certain social class. Buying in a neighborhood for its social status may involve paying a higher price for a house with fewer of the desired features. Further, a family might sacrifice to purchase a higher priced property within a choice school district. The agent also should find out whether some member of the family has a strong preference for a special feature such as colonial architecture, a sunken bath, a large backyard, a recreation room in the basement, or a short commuting distance from work. Need and motivation should be evaluated simultaneously. In the end, *motivation* will typically become the dominating factor in a buying decision.

Determining the Buyer's Financial Capability

The agent must learn the buyer's financial capability of raising the down payment necessary for the mortgage and of meeting the lender's requirements on size of income. The agent must know whether the buyer's needs and motivation are consistent with the buyer's financial capabilities of actually purchasing the property. If the buyer does not volunteer information on assets and income, the agent can acquire the facts indirectly by asking, for example, "The required down payment on the property we are viewing is $10,000—can you raise that much cash, and can you afford the $375.60 monthly payment?" No agent wants to waste time showing property priced beyond the buyer's ability to purchase it.

Making Decisions for the Buyer

Knowing the buyer's needs, motivations, and financial ability to purchase property enables the agent to decide which properties to show. By selecting a maximum of three, the agent makes a decision for the buyer as to which of all available properties are most suitable. Using this approach, the agent can utilize time efficiently rather than conduct a "guided tour" of all properties in the area.

Obtaining the Buyer's Confidence and Loyalty

Very few prospective buyers approach an agent's office with all the details and information needed for the purchase of property. In addition, very few buyers have taken the time to evaluate the agent's professional reputation. Consequently, the agent needs to discuss such matters as local property trends, types of loans available, costs, and school districts with the buyer *prior* to viewing any property. The agent demonstrates professionalism by providing pertinent information that is needed to make decisions to save the buyer time.

Explaining Services Offered

The agent should demonstrate the ability to satisfy the buyer's needs by telling the buyer how many listings the office has available in various school districts and choice locations within the city. In addition, the agent should explain that the office is a member of the Multiple List Service (if applicable) and cooperates with other offices to show other listings.

Commitment to the Buyer

The agent should make a firm commitment to helping the buyer satisfy his or her needs by using simple direct statements such as "I want to be your agent because I understand your desires, and I think that I can satisfy them. I will work with you for whatever time is needed to find the property that is satisfactory." In addition, the agent should ask for the buyer's loyalty in not working with other agents. This approach ensures coordination, avoids duplication of effort, and prevents later misunderstanding about the payment of a commission.

SHOWING THE PROPERTY[5]

The procedure for showing property can be described as a technique for *obtaining the offer*. The buyer must decide that he or she wants the property and must make an offer to the seller. The agent should evaluate each step of the showing to enhance the likelihood of the buyer's decision to make an offer.

The phrases *showing the property, obtaining an offer,* and *closing the buyer* are used interchangeably. The agent shows the property for the intention of obtaining an offer from the buyer to purchase it. Obtaining an offer from the buyer is the same as closing the buyer. The following steps can be used by the agent to show property at its best and to create a mood conducive to the buyer's decision to buy.

Inspecting the Premises in Advance

Since the objective is to present the property at its best, the agent should always inspect the premises before the showing. In essence, *the property must be ready to be shown.* If the property is vacant, damage such as broken pipes, leaking faucets, buckled flooring, or vandalism may have occurred since it was last seen. If the property is occupied by the current owner or renter, the occupants must be given adequate warning of a pending showing.

In addition, property can be shown most effectively when the occupant or the owner is not present. The seller may reveal apprehensions that detract from the property's good points. Inadvertent remarks such as, The basement once had a water leak from a spring but it was fixed, may cause the buyer to look elsewhere.

Learning All the Property's Features

An agent cannot sell a property without knowing its characteristics. The general rule to follow is *know the inventory.* What is the school district?, How many square feet does it have?, Is it on sewer or septic tank?, When were the last capital improvements made and what were they? are examples of questions that should be answered immediately.

An agent needs to understand which pertinent facts about the property must be revealed. For example, is it the agent's responsibility to verify that the house does/does not have termites and to communicate that fact to the buyer? Must the agent reveal to the buyer that the basement of the house once had a water problem that has been corrected? Must the agent reveal a change in school district boundaries that might cause the property value to decrease? Must the agent reveal all pertinent information that might influence the buyer's decisions, or should the agent be responsible only for answering questions that the buyer raises to acquire the facts?

As a general rule, *the agent should disclose any pertinent facts about the property that might influence the property value and should devote a reasonable effort to uncovering such information.* Depending on the circumstances, the agent should simply tell the seller to correct any problems so that the buyer can be informed that there are no problems.

Another interesting matter is the amount of information the seller is expected to relay to the agent about the property. For example, does the seller have to tell the agent about problems with the drainage from the septic tank? Must the seller inform the agent that the basement had a water leak that has been corrected? Must the seller inform the agent of evidence of termite infestation?

If information pertinent to the market value or the sale is not disclosed prior to the sale, the agent and/or the seller may be accused by the buyer of misrepresentation. The buyer may contend that (1) either the agent or the seller acted in an unprofessional and unethical manner by failing to disclose information that could be uncovered with reasonable effort, (2) the buyer relied on the available information that did not include those facts to make a decision, and (3) the buyer was damaged by a loss in value after the transaction. To avoid this difficulty, *the agent should attempt to uncover this information and disclose the relevant facts prior to the sale.*

Showing a Maximum of Three Properties

If the agent has counseled the buyer properly and has ascertained the buyer's needs and motives for buying, a maximum of three properties can be shown. The buyer should find one of those properties satisfactory and should be willing to make an offer for it. If the buyer is not willing to purchase after viewing the third property, the agent has not succeeded in discovering the factors that the buyer uses in making a decision.

By selecting three properties from the total inventory, the agent is making a decision for the buyer. For example, a buyer may state that he or she wants to buy in the best school district, needs 1,500 square feet, wants a two-car garage, needs two baths and three bedrooms, wants a large back lot, needs to be within five miles from work, and has only $10,000 in cash. The agent picks the three properties that best satisfy those needs and desires and restricts the showing to those three properties.

Showing a maximum of three properties separates the professional agent who has spent time uncovering the buyer's needs from the "tour guide" who shows the potential buyer every property on the market. If the agent does select the tour-guide option, the buyer most likely will conclude his or her tour by examining more closely and expressing interest in those two or three properties that the professional agent could have selected initially by adequate communication with the buyer.

Showing the Special Features of the Neighborhood

By selecting the best route to the property, the agent can show that the neighborhood has adequate shopping nearby and schools at a reasonable distance. The agent should emphasize the attractive features of the neighborhood such as the income class and professional status of the residents, type of lots, seclusion, and the architectural style. The agent's car should always be parked across the street and not in the driveway. The buyer should be able to view the whole property from the front at once. A car parked in the driveway restricts the property's total effect. In addition, driving too close may be psychologically overwhelming to the buyer, who may want to maintain a distance from the transaction.

Discovering the Premises

The agent should unlock the front door and let the buyer discover the premises. The agent does not initially point to the major features, because the buyer will find features that he or she considers important. Also, the agent's opinions may differ

THE DECISION TO BUY OR SELL

from the buyer's. For example, the agent may view the large picture window as a bonus because of the scenery, but the buyer may see the window as a cause of energy loss. The agent follows rather than leads the buyer through the property, because the agent's presence in a room may make it seem smaller and may obstruct the buyer in discovering the premises. At all times, the agent should be aware of conversation or remarks that reveal how the prospect actually feels about the property, real needs rather than the ones expressed, and the prospect's seriousness in purchasing the property.

Summarizing and Emphasizing Characteristics that Satisfy the Needs and Motives of the Buyer

At the conclusion of each showing, the agent should attempt to motivate the buyer by enthusiastically emphasizing those features that satisfy the needs and motives expressed by the buyer.

Countering the objection   All agents need to develop, master, and practice techniques for countering objections.[6] The agent should expect the objection as the buyer's effort to slow the decision process. By stating an objection, the buyer is asking for time to think because of fear of the unknown. The objection usually is expressed as a negative remark or question such as, The master bedroom is too small, The backyard is too big, or It costs too much money. The procedure to follow in responding to the objection includes several steps:

1. Make an immediate decision as to whether the objection is legitimate or just the buyer "thinking out loud."
2. If the statement is not legitimate, ignore it.
3. If the statement is legitimate, respond first with a **reflexive statement** to lower the buyer's resistance. A reflexive statement repeats the same information in the form of a question. For example, if the buyer says, "I think that the backyard is too small," the agent can say, "You really don't think the backyard is very large, do you?" This response does not give any new information but solicits additional information from the buyer. The agent rewords the objection in the form of a question and then answers the question. For example, the agent might say, "I certainly am glad you asked that question about the backyard. Let's answer it. The yard appears to be large enough to hold your swing set and barbeque and doesn't have much grass to mow. Didn't you say that you don't want property with a lot of maintenance?"

All objections should be answered if they are legitimate.

Evaluation of Failure

If the buyer is not ready to purchase after the third property is shown, the agent should find out why the buyer is not satisfied. The agent asks the buyer for feedback about problems and starts anew.

The agent may decide to release a prospect who is not serious and thus gives up a claim to a commission. A release by an agent or buyer is determined by the intent and actions of the two parties involved. If the agent feels that he or she can do nothing else for the buyer and decides not to invest more time and effort, or if the buyer expresses a desire to work with another agent, the first agent loses a claim to the commission.

CIVIL RIGHTS ACT OF 1968 AND THE CODE FOR EQUAL OPPORTUNITY

Civil Rights Act of 1968[7]

In April 1968, Congress passed the **Civil Rights Act** supporting the concept of equal housing opportunity for all people. Sometimes called the Federal Fair Housing Law, this act makes discrimination illegal against any person because of race, color, religion, sex, or national origin. This covers the sale or rental of housing or residential lots, advertising the sale or rental of housing, financing of housing, and the provision of real estate brokerage activities. Equal Housing Opportunity is advertised by the symbol, ⌂.

Code for Equal Opportunity

In 1972, the NAR approved a **Code for Equal Opportunity in Housing** and urged member boards to adopt it. This code can be summarized as follows:

- ☐ In the sale, purchase, exchange, rental, or lease of property, all members will offer equal services to all.
- ☐ Members have no right to volunteer information on the racial, creedal, or ethnic composition of the neighborhood.
- ☐ Members shall not promote panic peddling (defined later in this chapter).
- ☐ Members shall not print, display, or circulate material that indicates a racial preference.
- ☐ Members who violate this code in spirit or action are subject to disciplinary action.

Affirmative Marketing Agreement

In 1975, the NAR concluded negotiations with HUD and recommended to its member boards the adoption of the **Affirmative Marketing Agreement.** This recommendation follows the concept that voluntary action to provide and promote equal opportunity in housing is preferable to forced government action. Confirmation of this agreement by the local board and its members will reduce the risk of other agents being accused of a violation of the Civil Rights Act by the actions of one member firm. The agreement becomes a local vehicle of demonstrating and illustrating compliance and support of civil rights. The Affirmative Marketing Agreement is a voluntary action by the board, and the signatures of individual firms is voluntary also.

Specific Provisions

The act prohibits discrimination on the basis of race, color, sex, religion, and national origin with respect to the sale or rental of dwellings and vacant land that may have residential use. Commercial and industrial transactions are excluded. Real estate agents, in an office that is being investigated because of a discrimination complaint, are automatically guilty of discrimination if the equal housing opportunity sign, ⌂, and logo are not on display.

The act covers: single-family housing when an agent is employed by a listing; multifamily units with five or more units; multifamily units with four or fewer units, provided that the owner does not reside in one unit; single-family housing owned by a development corporation; and single-family housing owed by a private individual who owns more than three houses and sells more than one in a two year period in which he or she has not been the most recent resident.

The act excludes: single-family housing owned by a private owner when an agent is not employed by a listing and no discriminatory advertising is used; owner occupied dwellings of four or less units; non-commercial property owned by a religious group and sold to people of the same religion, provided that membership in the religion is not discriminatory; and non-commercial lodgings of a private club for use by its members.

Common Questions[8]

Several common questions asked by agents and consumers follow with the answers:

Q: What is **panic peddling?**
A: Panic peddling occurs when the agent makes statements such as "The neighborhood is declining because of the number of (race)," even though the statement is factually accurate. *Panic peddling refers to statements between the salesperson and the prospective seller that are made to induce a sale.*

Q: What is **racial steering?**
A: Racial steering occurs when the prospective buyer is offered choices that attempt to influence the housing location because of race. Racial steering is an *external* concept that originates in the choices offered. If the buyer chooses a particular location, the decision is internal and not included in this definition.

The law does not prohibit encouragement of integration. Legal racial comments can be made between the broker and the potential buyer. Thus, the action of a white family moving into an all-black neighborhood could be legal under the law providing that steering and panic peddling have not occurred. **Blockbusting** exists when a neighborhood was integrated by the use of panic peddling to gain the listings.

Q: What two theories can be used to determine if a salesperson has violated the civil rights law?

A: The first involves the accusation that a salesperson did not make housing available on the basis of race, sex, country of national origin, or creed. This complaint usually takes the form of "less favorable treatment" and covers actions such as delaying submission of a valid offer, failing to service the potential buyer, inducing the seller to reject the offer, and offering the property on less favorable terms. The second theory includes those cases where the salesperson used the location of minorities as an inducement for nonminorities to sell their property. This covers blockbusting and panic peddling.

    Knowledge of the law is not regarded as sufficient. A prudent salesperson must be able to demonstrate compliance in day-to-day activities.

Complaints[9]

Alleged violations of the Federal Fair Housing Act may be sent directly to HUD for investigation or filed in federal court. If the local board has adopted the Affirmative Marketing Agreement, complaints may be investigated by its Professional Standards Committee.

ADVERTISING AND TRUTH-IN-LENDING

Real estate agents are subject to the terms of the Truth-in-Lending Act (Regulation Z). Full disclosure of the financing terms are *not* required if an ad contains (a) no specifics about credit or (b) the annual percentage rate and the amount of the loan. Typically, any other credit terms require full disclosure, and the ad must contain the deferred credit price, the finance charge expressed as an annual percentage rate, amount of the downpayment, and the cash price. Section 8 of Chapter 21 gives examples of the statements that require full disclosure and of those that do not.

PRESENTING THE SALES CONTRACT TO THE SELLER

Presenting the sales contract is not just a matter of giving the seller the contract and waiting to see whether it's accepted.[10] The buyer or the agent (if one is involved) should give considerable forethought to the process of "presenting an offer" to ensure that the seller will view the transaction as favorable.

    An understanding of contract presentation is useful to the consumer as well as to the agent. The consumer who is a prospective buyer needs to understand what the sales agent is doing with the offer and how the seller is being approached. The consumer who is a seller needs to know what factors to consider when an agent arrives with an offer.

Preparing the Buyer for a Counteroffer

Once the buyer has signed the contract of sale, he or she should expect a counteroffer from the seller if the terms are not identical to those in the listing. Time spent by the agent at this stage to prepare the buyer mentally for a rejection and a counteroffer facilitates additional negotiations. For example, assume that the listing price is $75,000 and the buyer has offered $69,000. The agent's explanation might be, "You realize that you are offering $6,000 less than the seller wanted. I will do everything I can to encourage acceptance of this offer, but you should realize that it could be rejected. If the seller does reject this offer, I will ask for a counteroffer naming the terms including the price that will be accepted. I just want you to know that I will do everything possible to have your price accepted, but because it is less than the listing price I may be back with a counteroffer." The process of offer–counteroffer/offer–counteroffer may continue for several days until the two parties have found a set of terms acceptable to both of them.

The agent may be required by state law to present a contract once it is written by an interested party. For example, in Arkansas an agent must present a contract of sale within one business day after its receipt regardless of the terms.

A common question is whether a prospective buyer should offer a purchase price that is equal to the list price or that is lower. Normally, the seller will list property at a price slightly higher than he or she expects to receive, especially if there is no hurry to sell. The listing price will *typically* not be more than 10 percent higher than the property's appraised value. Thus, the buyer may have nothing to lose by offering a price that is 10 percent lower than the list price. However, in a housing market where the buyers outnumber the available properties for sale, the buyer may want to offer the list price to ensure an acceptance because of a relative shortage of housing units.

Preparing to Present the Offer

The offer should be presented to the seller the same day it is signed by the buyer, if possible. The buyer has a legal right to cancel the offer with no penalty within the time period allowed on the contract, generally several days. An agent should take just enough time to prepare for the presentation before visiting the seller, regardless of the time of day. This preparation involves several steps that enable the agent to present the offer most favorably:

1. All of the owners should be visited in their homes or places of business. The offer price should not be disclosed over the telephone. The agent can call the seller and arrange an appointment, saying, for example, "Mr. Seller, I have an offer on your property that I'd like to discuss with you. I'm going to be in your neighborhood this evening—would it be more convenient to stop by at 6:00 or 6:30?" The first question the seller will ask is, "How much is the offer?" The agent should not disclose this price, especially if it is not the list price. The agent's response to this question is, "I really feel that this decision is too important to discuss on the telephone and that you would prefer to examine the total offer. I'll be happy to explain the details to you this evening."

2. The agent should determine the net proceeds the seller will receive from the list price and the offer price. The difference between these two sums is the accurate figure to use in discussing price differences and, especially, in examining differences in down payments and financing arrangements. A lower price can result in higher net proceeds. If so, a difference of $1,000 or $2,000 in the selling price may involve only a $600 to $800 difference in net proceeds.

3. The agent should determine how much interest has been shown in the property recently. Is this offer the first in the last month or perhaps the fourth or fifth? What price was offered before? How long has the property been for sale? Such information indicates how much persuasion the agent should exert toward the seller. For example, if the current offer is $2,500 less than the list price on the tenth day, the seller is more likely to reject the offer than if it is the third offer for $2,500 less than the list price on the 115th day.

4. The agent should make a list of the reasons why the seller should accept the offer. What benefits would the seller receive? How does this offer compare with previous ones? What is the likelihood of additional offers? Are the net proceeds the maximum amount that the seller can realistically expect to receive? How does this net amount influence the seller's future plans? How does this offer influence the seller's future moving plans? Advance preparation on these questions gives the agent the information needed to answer questions the owner is likely to raise. In addition, having this information can build the agent's confidence.

5. The agent should anticipate any reasons the seller may give for rejecting the offer and should prepare an explanation. The seller may feel the property has not been on the market for a sufficient length of time. He or she may believe that a better price will be offered. The seller may dislike some of the terms, such as the date for vacating the premises. The agent must think of responses to such objections.

6. If a broker is presenting an offer on property that was listed by a salesperson, the latter should be contacted before the presentation as a matter of courtesy and to discover any additional pertinent information about the seller's needs and motivations. If a broker has obtained an offer to purchase a property listed by another firm, the custom in the area and the state license law determine whether the selling broker ignores the listing broker, or both brokers go to the seller, or the former gives the offer to the latter to present to the seller. In Arkansas, for example, the selling agent must give the offer to the listing broker who presents it to the seller.

7. No offer should be presented to a seller unless the agent has checked his or her own records or those of another listing firm to ensure that the listing contract is still valid. The agent may conclude the transaction successfully and then discover that the listing has expired. If a listing agreement is not in force, the agent may have difficulty collecting a commission from the seller.

8. The broker should know the favorable attributes of the prospective buyer. A seller generally wants to know that his or her property will be left with a responsible party. The seller should be told the good features of the buyer's background as assurance that the property will remain in approximately the same condition after the sale.

9. The agent works for the seller under a typical listing contract. An agent who thinks the price is unreasonable should counsel the seller to make a counteroffer at a price the seller believes is fair.

10. By explaining to the seller the amount of time, advertising, and expense that has been invested in obtaining the offer, the agent can encourage the seller to consider the offer seriously.

11. The agent should establish a timetable with the seller for bringing the transaction to a successful closing. This process establishes in the seller's mind the possibility of additional negotiations and simultaneously sets the limits on what the agent will be able to do with another offer from the buyer, should it be written.

12. The agent should evaluate his or her skills after every transaction, being careful to note weak and strong points. If the transaction was a failure, why did it end that way? What could have been done to avoid the result?

Visiting the Seller

The visitation with the seller can be conducted in a logical sequence of steps.

First, small talk from the agent is necessary to relax the atmosphere. Once a cordial environment has been created, the agent describes the buyer's family, place of employment, reasons for liking the property, and reasons for thinking the offer is fair. The seller who feels that the buyer is reputable and will take care of the property will be preinclined to accept the offer. The description of the buyer should require only a short time, say three minutes.

Second, the agent explains any of the "subject to" conditions or contingencies in the offer, such as items to be included in the sale price (for example, the carpeting, draperies, curtain rods, shelving, dishwasher, and refrigerator), the closing date, date of moving, and type of deed. By obtaining the seller's agreement on these points, the agent improves the chance of closing on the transaction. In considering these points, the seller mentally lets go of the property piece by piece and begins to think of the property as being sold. Discussion of these terms should require as much time as needed to cover the important issues.

Third, the agent explains the negotiations that have passed with the buyer and describes the other property the buyer has seen. The seller is more likely to accept the offer if he or she is aware that the agent has spent considerable time in counseling the buyer and viewing other properties. At this point, the agent gives the seller the offering price.

Fourth, if the agent believes the offer is satisfactory, he or she should give the reasons why the seller ought to accept it. The amount of net proceeds and the seller's benefits from the transaction can be explained. Answers to the seller's possible objections can be given in advance. The agent should know the seller's objectives in selling the property and therefore should be able to explain how the offer satisfies those objectives. If the agent does not believe that the offer is reasonable, he or she should tell the seller and help prepare a counteroffer.

Once these four steps have been completed, the agent shows the agreement and asks the seller to sign it. The agent's attitude should be that the seller will sign.

Overcoming Seller's Reluctance to Accept

If the seller shows reluctance in accepting the offer, several persuasive points could be mentioned:

1. *Risk in not signing.* The buyer has the legal right to cancel the offer at any time within the period identified in the offer. If the housing market has more houses for sale than potential buyers, the seller does have some risk that the buyer will cancel before the seller accepts the offer.

2. *Enjoyment of the premises.* If the seller is not receiving the full list price, the loss could be compared with the loss taken on a personal automobile. The seller may think nothing of incurring a $600–$800 loss in value per year on a car, but may not be willing to accept that loss on real estate. Perhaps the differences between the list price and offer price could be viewed as the cost of enjoyment, as in the case of the automobile.

3. *Amount of appreciation.* Perhaps the seller has misestimated the amount of appreciation of the property, assuming a rate of 8 percent each year, for example, when in reality the rate was 6 percent. The seller should judge that rate in comparison with rates of appreciation in competing types of investments.

4. *The seller as a new buyer.* The seller who wants to move should not think of him/herself as a seller but rather as a buyer. Upon accepting an offer, the seller will become the buyer of another property. Consequently, the seller's choice is to retain the property or to become a buyer. The seller can take what is a sure price or take a chance of receiving more in a short period of time. The agent can calculate the additional net proceeds that could be obtained by waiting and ask the seller if the difference is worth the chance of failure.

5. *Peace of mind.* The agent could ask the seller how much peace of mind is worth. By accepting the offer, the seller eliminates worry about selling the property before reentering the market as a buyer. There is no longer a need to negotiate. The seller has the satisfaction of selling the property and can concentrate on moving. This point is very persuasive to anxious sellers.

6. *Difference in net proceeds.* The difference in net proceeds between the list price and the offer price should be reexamined. This is the important figure to consider in weighing the other points.

7. *Conditions of the local market.* The agent should reexamine the conditions of the local market with the seller to emphasize trends that may influence

the possibility of receiving a higher offer in the future. A market characterized by more houses than buyers does not indicate much future activity for the property.

METHODS OF PERSUASION

In explaining property characteristics to a buyer or answering questions or objections, an agent can give information in a manner that helps the other party make a decision. These techniques, called *methods of persuasion,* help the agent or seller to obtain an offer and help the agent or buyer to obtain an acceptance.[11] A potential buyer or seller should recognize these techniques to avoid making a quick, uninformed decision without careful consideration of the consequences. In addition, the techniques apply to everyday situations in which information is given to obtain a decision.

The Tie-Down

The **tie-down** is a reflexive statement that ends with a question. The purpose of the tie-down is to provide a response to a statement, solicit more information, and ask for a response. The agent gives no new information and waits for the buyer (seller) to respond.

For example, a buyer who is being shown a property may say, "This room is certainly small." The agent's response is, "This room isn't very large, is it?" This statement is reflexive in that it is simply a response to the buyer's statement without giving any additional information. The question at the end—"isn't it?"—demands a reply from the buyer. Numerous examples of tie-down can be given, such as:

- ☐ It is colorful, isn't it?
- ☐ Your furniture would fit in this room very nicely, wouldn't it?
- ☐ Both cars could be parked in that space, couldn't they?
- ☐ That room would make a good reception area, wouldn't it?

The use of a question requiring a positive response creates a good rapport.

Division of Twos

The **division of twos** is a method of asking the buyer to make a choice between two alternatives presented by the agent. Either choice is acceptable to the agent and the buyer. For example, the agent has shown the buyer three houses and concludes that the third is unacceptable. At the end of the showing, the agent asks the buyer, "Would you prefer to make an offer on house number one or house number two?" This question conveys a positive attitude that the buyer *will make an offer* and that one of the first two properties is acceptable. This technique helps the buyer make a decision.

That's Right—That Leaves . . .

A response by the agent of **"That's right"** or **"That leaves . . ."** is another version of division of twos. The buyer is given a set of two choices. After the buyer selects one alternative, the agent remarks "That's right" for a desired response or "That leaves . . ." for an incorrect response. In either case, the client is led toward a decision acceptable to both parties.

Numerous examples can be found in all types of decisions. As an illustration, consider a salesperson who asks a prospective purchaser after viewing several properties, "Would you rather submit a loan application at First Federal or First National?" (The salesperson really prefers the service given by First Federal.) If the buyer responds that First Federal is acceptable, the salesperson's response is one that means "That's right," which could be "That was a great choice—let's go there." If the buyer's response should be First National, the salesperson says, "Good—that leaves First Federal. That was a great choice. Let's go to First Federal." This process can be repeated for several steps until the desired conclusion is reached.

The Yes-Response Question

A yes-response question or comment requires a positive attitude and elicits a yes from the client. A good example is the tie-down. The question at the end solicits a yes response from the person to whom it is directed. For example, the agent can point out major features of the property that the buyer has not noticed. While pointing to these features, the agent can make statements ending with a question:

- ☐ The storage space is large, isn't it?
- ☐ The bathrooms are decorated well, aren't they?
- ☐ The kitchen has been well kept, hasn't it?

A slight variation of these statements places the question at the beginning:

- ☐ Don't the appliances appear to have had good care?
- ☐ Hasn't the property been well-maintained?

These remarks differ from the tie-down, because the buyer does not make the initial statement. By using these remarks at the end of the showing, the agent can create a positive frame of mind and put the buyer in the habit of saying yes. Both effects are conducive to making an offer.

Ask for the Offer

Depending on the personalities involved, the agent may be able to ask directly for the offer. A strong-willed buyer who can make decisions readily may be approached directly by the agent with a question such as, Shall we write an offer on property 2 before someone else buys it? No agent should be afraid of asking for an offer.

Ask for a Referral

All of the methods of persuasion described are techniques of generating business by obtaining an offer on property. An agent should also pursue a regular plan of visiting satisfied clients to ask for referrals for additional business. Satisfied clients should readily give names of friends who need the services of a professional real estate agent.

Close on the Buyer

The phrase **close on the buyer** means that the agent tries to obtain an offer from the buyer. A successful close on the buyer is a signed offer with an earnest money check. All of the techniques described are methods of persuasion that can be used to close on the buyer.

One approach sometimes recommended to agents for progressing smoothly to the close is to fill in a blank sales contract during each showing. For example, an agent may be showing residential property to a couple. The wife exclaims that the draperies are beautiful, and the agent writes on the contract that the draperies will remain. The husband asks if the refrigerator goes with the property, and the agent asks, "Does it fit into your plans for it to stay?" The husband responds, "No," and the agent writes that the refrigerator does not stay. The husband asks when the property will be vacant, and the agent asks, "What date would best fit into your plans?" The couple discusses various dates and responds that forty-five days is the most convenient. The agent writes on the contract that the premises must be vacated by the forty-sixth day after acceptance. By the end of the showing, a completed contract is ready for the property. All that is needed is the buyer's signature and an earnest money check. This technique should minimize the buyer's resistance to signing.

NATIONAL ASSOCIATION OF REALTORS CODE OF ETHICS AND STATE LICENSE LAW AND REGULATIONS

Code of Ethics

Every real estate agent who agrees to abide by a code of ethics and pays the required fee may receive the designation *REALTOR* or *REALTOR-ASSOCIATE* and may use the symbol "R" in advertising. The twenty-four articles of the code are listed in Chapter 11. Many articles can be interpreted as methods of marketing and persuasion. For example:

Article 1. Be informed on real estate matters.

Article 2. Be informed on laws, legislation, government regulations, and market condition.

Article 3. Protect the public, and eliminate damaging practices.

Article 4. Avoid controversy with fellow REALTORS.

Article 5.	Protect client's interest, and treat all fairly.
Article 6.	All parties to the transaction must know all facts.
Article 7.	Provide equal service to all.
Article 8.	Provide competent service.
Article 9.	Present a true picture.
Article 10.	Provide each party with agreements in writing.
Article 11.	Respect the agency of another.
Article 12.	Cooperate with other brokers, and negotiate with listing broker.
Article 13.	Do not criticize competitors.

State License Law and Regulations

The state real estate license law often contains provisions covering the unethical conduct or unprofessionalism of the agent. In addition, many rules and regulations enacted by the state regulatory authority pertain to listing, contacting the seller after the property has been listed with another firm, presenting offers, and advertising. These requirements typically prohibit an agent from[12]

1. Making any substantial misrepresentations
2. Making any false promise likely to influence, persuade, or induce
3. Pursuing a continued and flagrant course of misrepresentation or making false promises through agents, salespersons, advertising, or otherwise
4. Accepting a commission or valuable consideration as a real estate salesperson for the performance of any of the services specified . . . from any person, except the licensed broker by whom he or she is employed
5. Failing, within a reasonable time, to account for or remit any monies coming into his or her possession that belong to others
6. Being unworthy or incompetent to act as a real estate broker or salesperson in such a manner as to safeguard the public interests
7. Paying a commission or valuable consideration to any person for ads or services performed in violation of this act
8. Any other conduct, whether of the same or a different character from that specified above, that constitutes improper, fraudulent, or dishonest dealing.

Infractions are punishable by loss of the agent's license, suspension of the license, or a reprimand.

CHAPTER SUMMARY

Methods of marketing and persuasion should be understood both by real estate agents and by consumers. Knowing these techniques enables all participants in a real estate transaction to make rational decisions.

Every agent should define carefully his or her objectives and form a day-to-day plan of accomplishing those goals. This plan can be used to evaluate successes and failures and provides a basis for the efficient budgeting of time. An agent should periodically update his or her skills and knowledge and should strive to develop the characteristics of a successful salesperson.

An agent may work for a firm as an employee or may be an independent contractor. An employee is controlled by the firm but an independent contractor is not. The latter is employed for the knowledge that he or she already possesses and is self-directing.

Techniques for finding potential buyers include direct prospecting, whereby a specific individual is contacted or indirect prospecting, whereby the property is advertised and the agent waits for an interested party to come forward. The techniques range from using the firm's farm of listings to advertising the property in a multiple-listing service.

Counseling the buyer is a crucial first step in the selling process. An agent must discover the buyer's needs and motivation to match the right buyer with the right property.

Before showing property to a prospective buyer, the agent must know the terms of the listing contract and the characteristics of the property. Moreover, the agent must be able to apply effective methods of showing property and responding to the buyer's objections.

Before presenting an offer to a seller, the agent must follow a series of preparatory steps as a basis for answering questions, responding to objections, and writing a counteroffer. The agent's task of answering questions and countering objections is easier if he or she knows and has practiced methods of persuasion, such as the division of twos, the yes-response question, the tie-down, and "That's right—That leaves. . . ."

Typically, state license law and the rules and regulations of the state regulatory authority control unethical and unprofessional conduct, including methods of marketing and persuasion. Violation of these laws or rules and regulations can cause the agent to lose his or her license.

Review Questions

1. What is the proper motivation and attitude for a career in selling? Why is this important?
2. What does the phrase *management by objectives* mean to a real estate agent?
3. How is an employee distinguished from an independent contractor?
4. What approach can an agent use periodically to evaluate successes and failures?
5. How does direct prospecting compare with indirect prospecting? Give examples of each.
6. Why is counseling the buyer important to the agent? What information is the agent attempting to discover?

7. What steps should an agent follow in showing property to a prospective buyer?

8. What steps should an agent follow in presenting an offer to the seller?

9. How should an objection be countered?

10. What is the purpose of a counteroffer? Who gives it?

11. How do the NAR Code of Ethics and the state license law and rules and regulations cover the agent's conduct in using methods of marketing and persuasion?

Discussion Questions

1. Can an agent rely on a strong personality instead of practicing all of the approaches identified in the chapter and still be a success?

2. Are the marketing and persuasion techniques described in the chapter really just a "hard sell"?

3. If an agent uses these methods of persuasion, will a potential buyer feel that he or she was forced into a sale and become angry?

4. Why doesn't the agent show a potential buyer everything on the market and just let the buyer choose rather than spending valuable hours applying marketing procedures?

5. Can you think of other good recommendations for showing property or presenting an offer to the seller?

6. If these marketing and persuasion techniques can be used in everyday life, why don't more people use them? Is there a negative reaction toward selling?

7. Is there a typical selling personality? Can an agent who lacks such characteristics still be a success in real estate sales?

Notes

1. David W. Gillis, "Developing Attributes for Success," *Real Estate Today,* Vol. 13 (February 1980), pp. 26–28; Aaron Hemsley, "Overcoming Behavior Obstacles," *Real Estate Today,* Vol. 13 (April 1980), pp. 12–18; Harry Ladd, "Tracking Time," *Real Estate Today,* Vol. 13 (June 1980), pp. 25–29; Hugh Robertson, "Making Time Mean Money," *Real Estate Today,* Vol. 13 (March 1980), pp. 49–52.

2. James J. Onder and Barbara Tuma, "The Role-Play Technique—Its Use in Real Estate Training," *Real Estate Today,* Vol. 13 (June 1980), pp. 30–36.

3. Rick Brown, "Successful Farming," *Real Estate Today,* Vol. 13 (June 1980), pp. 45–48.

4. Donald Hull, "A Complete Guide to Qualifying," *Real Estate Today,* Vol. 13 (February 1980), pp. 40–44.

5. Jack Donnell, "The Art of Showing," *Real Estate Today,* Vol. 12 (December 1979), pp. 33–36.

6. "Objections Overruled," *Real Estate Today,* 9 (August 1976), pp. 32–37.

7. Much of the information in this section comes from the National Association of REAL-TORS, *Affirmative Marketing Handbook* (January 1977), and NAR, *REALTORS Guide to Practice Equal Opportunity in Housing* (September 1976).

8. Ibid.

9. Ibid.

10. Drummond Gaines, "How to Close," *Real Estate Today,* Vol. 13 (June 1980), pp. 5, 50–52.

11. A number of sources were useful in this section. See "Solving the Most Common Problems in Selling," *Real Estate Today,* Vol. 5 (November 1972), pp. R1–R24; Bud Andrus, "Put Yourself in the Client's Shoes," *Real Estate Today,* Vol. 4 (April 1971), pp. 6–8; "The New Psychology of Selling," *Real Estate Today,* Vol. 8 (August 1975), pp. 9–24; and Tom Hopkins, "Questions to Close By," *Real Estate Today,* Vol. 8 (November–December, 1975), pp. 16–20.

12. These requirements are similar to those in Donald Epley, *Arkansas Supplement for Modern Real Estate Practice* (Chicago, Ill.: Real Estate Education Co., 1984), pp. 1–2.

Additional Readings

HEAVENER, MAC. "Knock on Doors for Knock-out Sales." *Real Estate Today* 9 (August 1976): 44–45.

KOLE, ROBERT A., "Teaching the Basics: Telephone Techniques," *Real Estate Today* 8 (October 1975): 11–15.

NICOLOFF, DOROTHY. "The Soft Sell Works." *Real Estate Today* 9 (March 1976): 34–37.

NORMAN, THOM. "Handling Ad Calls." *Real Estate Today* 8 (October 1975): 16–18.

"Objections Overruled." *Real Estate Today* 9 (August 1976): 32–37.

STARRETT, EILEEN. "Follow-Up After the Sale." *Real Estate Today* 6 (July 1973): 39–41.

YOUNG, SAM. "Turning Ad Calls into Appointments." *Real Estate Today* 9 (March 1976): 50–51.

13 | The Real Estate Sales Contract

QUESTIONS TO BE ANSWERED

1. What are the essential features of a valid contract?
2. What are the usual contents of the real estate sales contract?

OBJECTIVES

When the student finishes the chapter, he or she should be able to

1. Identify and explain the legal classifications used to describe contracts.
2. Identify and describe the essential features of a valid contract.
3. Analyze the real estate sales contract on a clause-by-clause basis.
4. State the various methods by which the parties to the contract can discharge their obligations.

5. Identify and explain the legal excuses for not discharging contractual obligations.

6. Identify and explain the legal remedies available to the aggrieved party when a breach of contract occurs.

IMPORTANT TERMS _____

Acceptance	Mistake of Fact
Bilateral Contract	Mistake of Law
Breach of Contract	Nominal Damages
Consideration	Offer
Discharge of Contract	Specific Performance
Duress	Undue Influence
Express Contract	Unenforceable Contract
Fraud	Unilateral Contract
Liquidated Damages	Valid Contract
Material Fact	Void Agreement
Misrepresentation	Voidable Contract

CLASSIFICATION OF CONTRACTS

Contracts can be classified according to their legal characteristics. Contracts can be categorized as valid, voidable, void, and unenforceable, as bilateral or unilateral, and as express or implied. The ability to distinguish among these contract categories and the underlying legal characteristics is important in real estate decision making. The purpose of this chapter is to describe the general characteristics of all contracts, as well as the terms and provisions of the real estate sales contract and its provisions.

Valid, Voidable, Void, and Unenforceable Contracts

A **valid contract** fulfills all the legal requirements imposed by the body of law known as contract law and can therefore be enforced by the courts of law. A **voidable contract** is a valid contract, but one party to the contract can exercise the right to avoid or to set aside the contractual obligations incurred. The best-known example of a voidable contract is one between an adult and a minor. Under the law, the minor has the right to avoid or rescind a valid contract at the minor's discretion. Consequently, this contract is classified as "voidable" because the minor has the right of avoidance.

A **void agreement** is not a valid contract. It is an attempt to enter into a contract that does not fulfill the requirements imposed by contract law and therefore has no legal effect and is not recognized by the courts.

An **unenforceable contract** is a valid contract, but it is not recognized by the courts if any legal action is brought before the court to enforce it. Many types of contracts, including the real estate sales contract, must be in writing in order for the courts to hear cases involving their enforcement. If such a contract were made orally, and if one of the parties failed to meet the obligations imposed in the contract, this oral contract could not be brought to the courts. The contract is valid, but the courts will not enforce it. The distinction between the unenforceable contract and the void agreement is that the unenforceable contract is a valid contract and the void agreement is not a valid contract.[1]

Bilateral and Unilateral Contracts

A **bilateral contract** is an agreement reached between two or more people. One person makes an offer or a promise to the other; if the second person accepts the offer, a bilateral contract is formed. As part of this process, each of the two parties to the contract makes a promise or performs an act and simultaneously receives a promise from the other party. A **unilateral contract** contains a promise or offer by only one of the parties to the contract. In other words, one person makes a promise or extends an offer and the other person receives the benefit of the promise or offer contingent upon the performance of some act. An example of a unilateral contract is the reward that one person offers for the return of a lost object or pet. If the lost object is returned, the finder will receive a financial reward. The owner of the object or pet promises to pay cash if an unknown party performs an act—that is, finds and returns the missing entity.[2] A listing agreement (discussed in Chapter 11) is a unilateral contract that is used in the real estate business.

The real estate sales contract is a bilateral contract. When two individuals enter into an agreement to exchange property, one individual offers cash and/or other financial assets in order to receive the property. The second individual gives up the property in order to receive the cash. Each of the two parties gives up an asset and receives another asset in return.

Express and Implied Contracts

An **express contract** is an explicit agreement. It can be either oral or written. The fundamental requirement is that the individuals discuss and then agree to the terms and conditions. A contract can also result from inferences about facts and circumstances. Such a contract is referred to as a contract "implied in fact." The agreement between the parties is derived from the presumed intent of the individuals as indicated by their conduct and their acts. "A contract may be implied in fact whenever one person knowingly accepts a benefit from another person and the circumstances make it clear that the benefit was not intended as a gift. The person who accepts the benefit impliedly promises to pay the fair value of the benefit that he receives."[3]

The real estate sales contract can be characterized as a valid, bilateral, express contract. It contains all of the legally essential features of a valid contract. It is made by two individuals after due deliberation and full agreement about the terms of the sale. In the next section the legal requirements for valid contracts are examined in greater detail.

THE DECISION TO BUY OR SELL

ESSENTIAL FEATURES OF A VALID
AND ENFORCEABLE CONTRACT

A valid contract is defined simply as "a legally binding agreement—one that is enforceable by law. This agreement results from an exchange of acts, or of promises to do or not to do certain things."[4] A full understanding of a contract, however, requires more than just an understanding of the simple definition. A contract must have the following essential legal features in order to be valid and enforceable in a court of law:

- [ ] An agreement
- [ ] A consideration
- [ ] Competent parties
- [ ] Reality of consent
- [ ] Legality of purpose
- [ ] Necessity of writing in certain instances

A real estate sales contract must contain each of these features (see Exhibit 13-1).

An Agreement

Two acts constitute an agreement—the offer and the acceptance. The offer is the initial step undertaken in the formation of a contract between two individuals. In a real estate transaction, the offer is made by the potential buyer or an agent who is working for the buyer. An **offer** is a conditional promise made by the potential buyer to the seller of the property. The promise is viewed as being conditional because the potential buyer is not bound by the promises unless the seller responds to the offer in an appropriate and proper fashion.[5] The seller's appropriate and proper response is the acceptance of the offer. An **acceptance** is thus an indication by the seller of a

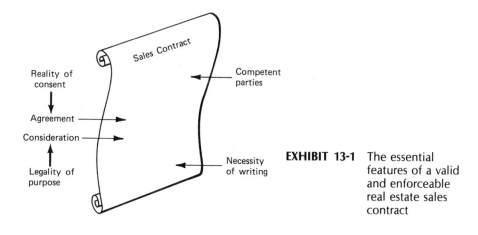

EXHIBIT 13-1 The essential features of a valid and enforceable real estate sales contract

willingness to be bound by the terms of the offer. These two actions—the offer and the acceptance—constitute the agreement that is essential to a valid contract.

Offer   An offer must be:

- ☐ definite and certain
- ☐ complete
- ☐ communicated to the seller
- ☐ intended to create a legal obligation between the two parties

To be definite and certain, the offer must be clearly intelligible to a reasonable person and "must be made under such circumstances that the person receiving it has reason to believe that the other party (offeror) is willing to deal on the terms indicated."[6] Definiteness and certainty are required because the courts may have to determine whether or not the parties to the contract performed in compliance with the specified terms. If the terms of the transaction are vague, left out, or impossible to measure, there is no contract. The price to be paid by the buyer, the condition of the property, and the time of delivery are important terms of the sale that should be specified and not left vague. If for some reason these terms are not clearly specified, the contract is still enforceable if the court is convinced from the existing evidence that both the buyer and seller intended to be bound by the terms specified within the contract. If a time of performance is not stated or if a price is not specified, the court will imply a "reasonable time" for performance and a "reasonable price" for the commodity.[7]

The offer must also be complete if the contract is to be enforceable in a court of law. "All the terms of the contract must be settled, and none must be left to be determined by future negotiation."[8] The offer cannot contain a statement that calls for future discussion of a term or condition of sale. A statement such as "price to be negotiated at the time of the exchange" is not sufficient. The courts have ruled that they cannot complete an unfinished contract, and thus the incomplete contract would be unenforceable, even though it could still be valid.

An offer must be communicated and delivered by the buyer to the seller in order for the contract to be effective. The communication can be made directly by the buyer or by an agent of the buyer. The offer can be made directly to the seller or to an agent of the seller, the real estate broker or salesperson, if the seller has given the agent the power to accept an offer. Communication and delivery of the offer are necessary because the seller cannot act upon the offer until it has been communicated and delivered.

An offer can be effective even though a delay occurs in reaching the seller. When an offer is made, a delay is normally viewed as resulting from the negligence of the buyer or trouble with the means of communication chosen by the buyer. For example, the buyer may choose to communicate and deliver the offer by means of a telegraph company or the U.S. Postal Service. If either of these agents of the buyer causes a delay, the court feels that the seller should not bear the loss resulting from that delay. Therefore, the seller can take a reasonable amount of time to respond even if the effective time of the offer has expired. If the delay is apparent to the seller, however, the seller's acceptance of the offer must be communicated to the prospective buyer "within a reasonable time after the offer would normally have been received. If he knows that there has been a delay in communicating the offer, he cannot take advantage of the delay."[9]

The last characteristic of the offer, and of a contract in general, is the intention by both the prospective buyer and the seller to create a legal obligation. The two parties to the contract must agree about the specified terms. Consequently, a distinction must be made between a serious offer and a statement that is made either in jest or anger. The courts will not hold a person legally responsible for a statement made in jest or anger. A person is not considered to be making an offer when exasperation over a disabled automobile results in a statement such as "I'd sell this piece of junk for a nickel!"

In addition, a distinction is made between a serious offer and what the courts consider "invitations to bid." Individuals can make oral statements about general terms they might consider in a transaction. These statements may be made to open a discussion about specific terms of the sale. The courts generally understand that the \detailed terms of the sale will be discussed, communicated, reduced to writing, and signed before any agreement between buyer and seller is held to be legally binding. A statement such as "Make me a serious offer for the car and I'll sell it" is considered an invitation to bid that can start a discussion that may or may not end in a contractual agreement.

Acceptance   The other half of the agreement is the acceptance. "An acceptance occurs when the party to whom the offer has been made agrees to the proposal or does what is proposed. If the acceptance is to result in an enforceable agreement, it too must meet certain requirements."[10] An acceptance must be:

- ☐ Made only by the person or persons to whom the offer was made
- ☐ Unconditional and identical to the terms of the offer
- ☐ Communicated to the offeror (prospective buyer)

The first of these points needs very little explanation. For a contract to be valid, the person accepting the offer must be the person to whom the offer was made. If the seller has given the authority to a lawyer or broker to accept an offer, the buyer can deliver the offer to the seller's agent.

The acceptance must occur without any conditions added to the offer and without any exceptions deleted from the offer. In other words, the seller must either accept or reject the offer as it is stated without changing the offer in any way. Any change in the terms required by either the seller or the buyer is made through a process of negotiation. During this negotiation process, the buyer and seller can enter into a series of offers and counteroffers. The original offer is made by the buyer. If the seller does not like all the terms, the seller can express a counteroffer in which some of the original offer appears unchanged and some portion is deleted, added, or changed. The buyer can accept, reject, or amend the counteroffer. If the buyer accepts the counteroffer, the contract is created. Notice that the buyer and seller have changed roles—the buyer is the acceptor (offeree) and the seller is the offeror.

By amending the counteroffer, the buyer can establish a second counteroffer. The seller can accept, reject, or amend this amended counteroffer. If the seller accepts this version of the original offer, the contract is created. At this stage the buyer is once again the offeror and the seller is the acceptor. This negotiation process can continue until a final offer is extended and accepted by the appropriate party. This final offer is the legal offer that must be accepted unconditionally.

Finally, the acceptance must be communicated and delivered to the buyer. As part of the acceptance process, the prospective buyer may require the acceptance to be delivered in a certain way. For example, the buyer may stipulate that an acceptance will not be effective until the offer is actually or physically received. If the acceptance is transmitted by mail or by telegraph, custom and tradition indicate when the acceptance is received. "Acceptances sent by mail generally take effect when properly posted, with correct address and sufficient postage. A telegram takes effect as an acceptance when handed to the clerk at the telegraph office or telephoned to the telegraph office."[11]

An agreement is legally enforceable only when actions occur on the part of the buyer and the seller. A person is not legally responsible to reply to an offer that is made by another individual. In other words, an offer cannot be stated in such a way that silence is considered as an acceptance. Suppose an agreement in a contract contains statements made by the buyer to the effect that the offer is considered as accepted if a reply to the contrary is not forthcoming.[12] This would not result in a contract coming into existence because of the silence of the offeree (except for certain unusual situations not necessary to this discussion).

Termination of the offer   The offer stays in effect until one of four actions occurs:

☐ The seller rejects it
☐ The seller makes a counteroffer
☐ The buyer revokes the offer
☐ Unforeseen circumstances invalidate the offer

The first two actions should be clear from the previous discussion. The other two actions require elaboration. The buyer can revoke the offer by direct action or by terms stated in the offer. The buyer can call upon the seller by telephone or by personal visit and withdraw the offer prior to its acceptance; this is the direct action. The buyer can state a definite period of time in the contract for which the offer lasts. He can say "This offer will be in effect until 6:00 P.M. on the 9th of March 198X," or the buyer can say "This offer will be in effect for three days." Typically, offers for residential property last for three to five days. A longer period of time is stipulated for commercial and income-producing residential property.

If the time period for the offer passes, the offer has lapsed or expired. If a definite time period for the offer is not stated in the contract, the offer is assumed to be in effect for a "reasonable period of time." It is best to avoid any such interpretation, so always state an expiration date for the offer.

EXHIBIT 13-2 The offer and the acceptance

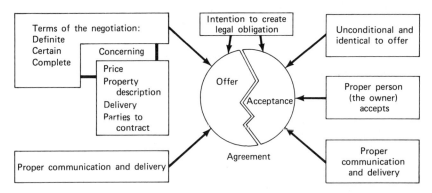

Unforeseen circumstances also can invalidate the offer. The buyer can die while the offer is in effect. If this occurs before the acceptance, the offer is terminated. If the buyer dies after the offer is accepted, the contract can be in effect if a binder-on-heirs clause is in the contract, or if state law interprets a signed contract as binding on the deceased person's estate and heirs. Destruction of the property prior to the acceptance also terminates the offer. However, if destruction occurs after the acceptance—i.e., the contract is signed, legal problems can arise. See the discussion about "the risk of loss" clause in the contract in a later section of this chapter.

Consideration

In addition to the agreement, a valid contract requires that each party to the bargain actually give something to the other. In a sales contract for real estate, the **consideration** is the exchange of valuable assets. Typically, the buyer gives a financial asset and receives the parcel of real estate, and the seller receives cash or some other valuable asset and gives the real property.

Historically, the courts and the laws governing contracts did not make judgments about the economic worth of the assets exchanged as the consideration. The courts were primarily interested in the fact that the consideration took place. It was sufficient in the law if the parties to the contract received something of legal value. The law was not concerned with the question of whether the bargain struck by the parties was an equitable or inequitable economic exchange. Today, however, legal philosophy has changed substantially. Contracts that are too one-sided or grossly inequitable are considered economically unreasonable and unenforceable under current legal standards.[13]

If the consideration is an exchange of assets other than cash, the value of those assets should be approximately equal in order for the contract to be valid. However, "if the consideration on each side of an agreement involves money, the consideration must be equal."[14] Another aspect of consideration is the time period during which the consideration occurs. "Past consideration is insufficient to support a present promise. The consideration must consist of some present surrender of a legal right. Some act that has taken place in the past will not suffice."[15] Certain minor exceptions to this rule can be interpreted by a lawyer specializing in real property law. However, the rule for consideration generally requires the exchange to be an exchange of current assets.

Consideration is the mutual exchange that takes place subsequent to the offer and acceptance components of the agreement. "As a general rule, mutual promises furnish a sufficient consideration to support a valid enforceable contract. However, each of these mutual promises must be valuable, certain, and not impossible of performance or they will not suffice as consideration. As a general proposition, if one party is not bound by his promise, neither is bound."[16] A contract for the exchange of real property must involve an exchange of assets that are of approximately equal value. The exact nature of the consideration and its component parts are explained later in this chapter.

Competent Parties

The individuals who enter into a contract must each have the legal capacity to make a contract. In other words, both individuals must have the ability to make legally binding agreements. Such people are known as **competent parties.** People who do not have the legal capacity to contract are those who are under the legal age, those who are considered insane, and those who are seriously intoxicated by liquor or drugs. Moreover, in certain states, convicts and enemy aliens from countries at war with the U.S. are also considered "incompetent" to enter into a contract.[17]

The concept of legal competence is based on the courts' interpretation of the individual's ability to understand the nature of the transaction involved in the contract. In the law, a contract cannot be enforced against an individual who does not have the ability to understand the agreement and the consequences of the agreement. For example, the law assumes that young people are not experienced in business and therefore should be protected against their own immaturity and the possibility that older people may take advantage of them. Minors, consequently, are given the right to disaffirm or avoid most of the contracts they might enter. However, minors are being held responsible for contractual agreements for necessities such as food, shelter, and clothing. Consequently, a person entering into a contract with a minor may require that a guardian sign the agreement in addition to the minor. In this case, the adult can be held liable for any damages if the minor chooses to disaffirm or avoid the contract.[18]

Because of the basic tenet that the parties to a contract must understand the nature of the transaction and its consequences, individuals who signed a contract under the influence of alcohol or drugs are assumed to be incompetent. These individuals have a reasonable time after they attain sobriety to reconsider. Finally, because of the need to understand, contracts are not enforceable against insane people who are legally defined as "mentally deranged."

Reality of Consent

For a contract to be recognized as valid, it must be free of mistakes, misrepresentations, fraud, undue influence, and duress. The consent of each individual party to the contract must be real and intentional. Without this consent the contract is either void or voidable.

Mistakes   Two types of mistakes are recognized in the law. One type is a **mistake of fact.** This mistake occurs when certain pieces of information or conditions in the contract are not true; for example, when the identity of a party to the contract is mistaken, or when the identity of the subject property is mistaken, or when the true nature of the agreement is mistaken. These mistakes generally do not void a contract but could make it voidable. The second type of mistake is a **mistake of law.** It occurs when a person who has full knowledge of the facts makes an erroneous conclusion about the legal effect of those facts. Currently, this mistake cannot be the grounds for avoiding a contract.[19]

The important aspect of a mistake of fact is related to the people who make the mistake. If both parties to the contract made a mistake of fact (a mutual, belated mistake of fact), the contract is either voidable or nonexistent, depending on the circumstances.[20] If only one party to the contract made a mistake of fact, the courts do not view the situation as grounds for automatically rescinding the contract. The courts usually consider that "the majority of such mistakes result from carelessness or lack of diligence on the part of the mistaken party and should not, therefore, affect the rights of the other party."[21] In other words, the contract is not automatically voidable but it could be. Therefore, both parties to a contract should work to eliminate any mistakes.

Misrepresentation and fraud   A mistake must be distinguished from a misrepresentation. A mistake is a misunderstanding or misconception that a person has about a fact. In contrast, a **misrepresentation** is an incorrect or improper statement about a fact that is made by an individual. A misrepresentation makes a contract voidable by the party to whom the misrepresentation was made. However, the contract is voidable only if the misrepresentation refers to a material fact. In the law, a **material fact** is defined as information or evidence that a reasonable person would consider important when determining a course of action or reaching a decision.[22]

A contract is voidable if a misrepresentation of a material fact was part of the basis for reaching the agreement. The misrepresentation can be intentional or unintentional. If it's intentional, the misrepresentation is classified as **fraud.** In either case, "the victim of the misrepresentation may rescind the contract because the loss is the same whether the false statements were made innocently or intentionally. In the case of fraudulent misrepresentation, the victim is given a choice of the additional remedy of a suit for dollar damages."[23]

In addition, the law recognizes the possibility of concealment of a material fact or nondisclosure of that fact. In this situation, the courts presume that the concealment or nondisclosure was intentional. However, such conduct must be proved by statements or acts of the person charged with concealment or nondisclosure; circumstantial evidence does not constitute such proof. If the intent to conceal is proven, the contract is voidable by the aggrieved party.[24]

If the courts are to judge whether a misrepresentation or a fraud occurred, a distinction must be made between a statement of fact and an opinion. The ultimate decision as to whether a statement is fact or opinion is a matter for the jury in a court trial. However, as a general guideline, a *fact is that which actually exists or actually occurred.* It is reality. In the case of a proven false statement of fact, the contract is voidable. In contrast, *opinion is a belief, a view, or judgment.* A belief is stronger than an impression but is not positive or absolute knowledge. As a general rule, erroneous or uninformed opinions are not viewed as a basis for voiding a contract. However, if an individual states an opinion as one thing but in fact it is just the reverse, the individual has misstated a fact. The fact is the true nature of the opinion. In this situation, if the intentional misrepresentation can be proven, the contract is voidable on the basis of the fraudulent action that occurred. In addition, ". . . false opinions regarding the quality of the product or its value may . . . be considered misrepresentations of fact where the parties do not have equal knowledge of the facts or equal access to them." (See Exhibit 13-3.)[25]

The buyer should be aware that the value of the property is an opinion, except if such statement is made by an expert. At best, it is the opinion of the appraiser arising from the appraisal process. If the buyer does not seek a professional opinion but accepts the seller's statement, the buyer should be aware that "Representations as to the value of the property, though greatly exaggerated, do not ordinarily justify a cancellation of the contract when the other party had an opportunity to learn the truth or falsity of the representations. If the buyer has an opportunity to examine the land, it is his or her duty to make use of this opportunity."[26] In addition, very general and "unwarranted praise that does not include concrete misrepresentation of specific facts does not entitle the buyer to back out of the deal."[27] The buyer should be wary of such general statements as You can't go wrong, You won't regret this deal, or It's the best buy you'll ever see.

Duty to speak   Historically, the laws governing the formation of contracts have followed the concept of caveat emptor (let the buyer beware), especially in relation to real estate transactions. "The parties to a contract are required to exercise ordinary business sense in their dealings. As a result, the general rule is that silence in the

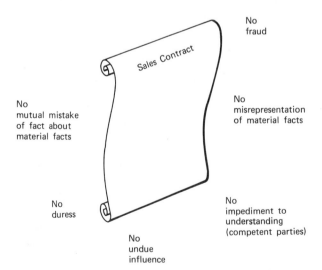

EXHIBIT 13-3   The reality of consent

THE DECISION TO BUY OR SELL

absence of a duty to speak does not constitute fraud. Where there is a duty to speak, concealment of a material fact is equivalent to a fraudulent misrepresentation."[28]

However, the law recognizes three situations in which a person has a duty to speak the truth. In these situations, failure to make true statements about a material fact constitutes fraudulent action. One situation pertains to the relationship between the seller of the property and real estate broker. In this fiduciary relationship, both parties have the duty to speak the truth and to make a full disclosure of all the facts.

The second situation in which a person has a duty to speak reflects the courts' interpretation of justice, equity, and fair play. If an important material fact is known by one person but not by the other, the courts could rule that the contract is voidable. This situation can arise in a real estate transaction if the property being traded has a hidden defect. The defect can be a physical defect in the improvement that is not visible upon inspection of the property, or the defect can be legal, such as a tax lien or a mechanic's lien against the property or even an easement that has not been filed. In these situations, it is the seller's duty to inform the purchaser of the defect. If the seller fails to inform the purchaser of a hidden defect that is known to exist, the courts will probably view this action as fraud.[29]

The third situation arises when a person misstates or unintentionally misrepresents an important material fact. Upon discovering this misrepresentation, the person is obligated to correct the mistake immediately or when negotiations are renewed. If the aggrieved party in this case can prove that the person making the unintentional misrepresentation subsequently learned of the error and did not correct it, a case can be made in the courts to avoid the contract.

These situations in which a person has a duty to speak have one aspect in common—the fact "that one of the parties has the erroneous impression that certain things are true, whereas the other party is aware that they are not true and also knows of the misunderstanding. It therefore becomes his duty to disclose the truth. And unless he does so, most courts would hold that fraud exists. This does not mean that the potential seller or buyer has to disclose all of the facts about the value of the property he is selling or buying. It is only when he knows that the other party to the agreement is harboring a misunderstanding on some vital matter that the duty to speak arises."[30]

Duress and undue influence **Undue influence** is the unfair advantage that one person has over another because of a relationship between the parties. If undue influence is proven, the contract is voidable by the individual who was unfairly or unduly influenced. **Duress** is the use of force or the threat of personal injury to make a contract against the free will of the individual. Contracts entered under duress are voidable by the party who was forced into the agreement.[31]

Legality of Purpose

Contracts must involve legal promises, actions, and objects. If illegal acts or objects form the basis of a contract, the law considers the contract to be illegal and consequently unenforceable in courts of law. An interpretation of unlawful or illegal purposes is based on activities or objects that are specifically prohibited by law, contrary to the rules established under common law, or contrary to stated public policy. Any contract that violates a statute or an ordinance is illegal and consequently is considered to be a void agreement.[32]

Necessity of Writing

In general, contracts can be initiated by means of an oral or a written agreement. Oral agreements, however, are subject to failure of memory, misrepresentation, and possibly even fraud. To overcome these problems, the English Parliament passed the Statute of Frauds in 1677. This statute requires that certain contractual agreements be evidenced by some written form of agreement. A contract to buy and sell real property or any partial interest in real property is governed by the Statute of Frauds and consequently must be evidenced in a writing.[33]

The Statute of Frauds does not require that all terms in the contract be reduced to writing. What is required is that some signed, written piece of evidence exist that gives the court a reason to believe that an agreement was made. The written evidence can be the contract itself or a memorandum, a written document that outlines the nature of the agreement and gives a judge reason to believe the two parties wanted to enter into a legally binding contractual agreement. "To satisfy the Statute of Frauds the memorandum of the contract must contain the names of seller and buyer, a sufficient description of the land, the contract price, the terms of sale, if other than cash, and . . . the signature of the party against whom suit is brought on the contract. A few states require both parties to sign the contract, and there appears to be a trend in this direction."[34]

To comply with the various state statutes of frauds, the parties to the contract must be identified, the offer and acceptance must be stated, and the consideration must be identified. However, details about the time and the performance of the contract need not be stated in writing.

Contracts that do not comply with the necessity of writing as stipulated by the Statute of Frauds are not necessarily fraudulent or illegal. However, the necessity-of-writing provision attempts to prevent fraud that can easily arise when oral contracts are used. Oral contracts are sufficient if there is no need to go to court to settle some difference between the buyer and the seller. However, failure to satisfy the writing requirement of the Statute of Frauds "simply means that the contract cannot be enforced in a court of law."[35]

AN ANALYSIS OF THE REAL ESTATE SALES CONTRACT

The purpose of the real estate sales contract is to bind two individuals to the sale and the purchase of a property under certain specified, mutually agreeable terms and provisions. The real estate sales contract is the required written evidence of the offer and the acceptance of the consideration between two competent parties to the contract. This legal instrument does not convey any ownership rights to the property. It does not pass the rights of ownership from one individual to the other. It is merely written evidence of a mutual agreement to undertake the transfer of ownership rights to the physical commodity known as real estate.

No standard real estate contract is in use throughout the country. However, certain basic features are found in most real estate sales contracts. The features are explained in reference to the sample contract in Exhibit 13-4. It is one of many printed forms that can be used as a real estate sales contract.

The Agreement and the Consideration

The first part of a real estate sales contract pertains to the agreement reached by the parties and the consideration that will be exchanged by those individuals. An examination of the sales contract in Exhibit 13-4 reveals that the buyer "offers to buy" the property under the terms established in the document. Clause 1 of the contract is the offer. The seller's acceptance appears at the bottom of the page in a clause, which precedes the seller's signature and contains the phrase "the above offer is accepted." These two clauses, and the inferences therein, form the agreement required for a contract. The buyer offers to purchase under the conditions stated in the contract, and the seller accepts that offer as stated in the contract.

The consideration is identified in Clauses 2, 3, 4, and 5 of the contract. In Clause 2, the property is identified. The description of the property can take two forms. The full legal description of the property can be given in the clause or it can be attached to the document if the attachment is identified in Clause 2. Alternatively, as in this document, the mailing address can be specified with the understanding that the buyer and seller both realize that the mailing address is not the legal description and that the legal description will be provided on the document that actually passes ownership rights. In some states, when land containing an improvement (ordinarily a house or commercial structure) is traded, the mailing address can be used. However, when land without an improvement is sold, the legal description must appear on the sales contract.[36] The legal implication of Clause 2 is that the seller will give the buyer the property contingent upon a simultaneous action in which the buyer gives the seller an asset of equivalent value.

The second part of the consideration is specified in Clauses 3, 4, and 5. These three clauses are the financial section of the real estate sales contract. In Clause 3, the buyer identifies the price he or she is willing to pay for the property when the exchange is made. At this point, both the buyer and the seller have promised to give something and simultaneously receive something.

The financial transaction, however, can be accomplished in a number of ways. Notice that Clauses 3 and 5 provide several options. The buyer can make a down payment and attempt to obtain a mortgage loan. These two components make up the financial asset that the buyer will give to the seller. When the buyer receives the funds from the lender, those funds will be used to pay off the seller's obligation under his or her mortgage.

In addition, Clause 5 mentions "earnest money"—the funds that the buyer places on deposit with the real estate broker to serve as both an indication of intent

EXHIBIT 13-4 Contract forms provided by the Arkansas REALTORS® Association.

REAL ESTATE CONTRACT
For Residential Resale Property
(Offer and Acceptance)

TIME _____ AM/PM DATE _____ , 19 _____

1. **BUYER:** _____ , offers to buy, subject
to the terms set forth herein, the following property.

2. **PROPERTY DESCRIPTION AND ADDRESS:** _____

_____

_____

_____

_____

3. **PURCHASE PRICE:** The Buyer will pay $_____ for the property at Buyer's closing. The down payment shall be $_____ with the balance
subject to the following conditions:

A. ☐ **NEW LOAN:** ☐ Conv. ☐ FHA ☐ VA _____ Fixed Rate _____ Varying Rate

The Buyer's ability to obtain a loan to be secured by the property in an amount not less than $_____ , payable over a period of not less

than _____ years, with interest not to exceed _____ % per annum.
Unless otherwise specified, all loan costs and prepaid items shall be paid by Buyer. If said loan is not available or is not closed, Buyer agrees to pay for loan
costs incurred, including appraisal and credit report, unless failure to close is caused by Seller.

B. ☐ **LOAN ASSUMPTION:** The Buyer's ability to assume existing loan payable to _____

in the approximate amount of $_____ , currently payable at approximately $_____ per month, including ☐ principal,
☐ interest, ☐ existing taxes, and ☐ existing insurance. Payments on existing loan to be current at Buyer's closing.

_____ Fixed Rate _____ Varying Rate. Note interest not to exceed _____ % at Buyer's closing.

C. ☐ **OTHER:** _____

_____

4. **APPLICATION FOR FINANCING:** If applicable, Buyer agrees to make application for a new loan or loan assumption within _____ days from date of this
contract.

5. **EARNEST MONEY:** Buyer herewith tenders a check for $_____ to be deposited upon acceptance as earnest money, which shall apply on
purchase price or closing costs. If title requirements are not fulfilled, it shall be promptly refunded to Buyer. If Buyer fails to fulfill his obligations, the earnest money
shall become liquidated damages, WHICH FACT SHALL NOT PRECLUDE SELLER OR AGENT FROM ASSERTING OTHER LEGAL OR EQUITABLE RIGHTS
WHICH THEY MAY HAVE BECAUSE OF SUCH BREACH.

6. **CONVEYANCE:** Conveyance shall be made to Buyer, or as directed by Buyer, by general warranty deed, except it shall be subject to recorded restrictions and
easements, if any, which do not materially affect the value of the property. Unless expressly reserved herein, such conveyance shall include mineral rights owned
by Seller.

7. **ABSTRACT OR TITLE INSURANCE:** The owner(s) of the above property, hereinafter called Seller, shall furnish, at Seller's cost, a complete abstract reflecting
merchantable title satisfactory to Buyer's attorney; however, Seller shall have an option to furnish Buyer, in place of abstract, a policy of title insurance in the
amount of the purchase price, and submission of an abstract shall not constitute a waiver of this option. If objections are made to title, Seller shall have a reasonable
time to meet the objections or to furnish title insurance.

8. **PRORATIONS:** Taxes and special assessments due on or before Buyer's closing shall be paid by Seller. Any deposits on rental property are to be transferred to
Buyer at Buyer's closing. Insurance, current general taxes and special assessments, rental payments, and any interest on assumed loans shall be prorated as of
Buyer's closing unless otherwise specified herein.

9. **CLOSING:** The closing date, which will be designated by Agent, is estimated to be on or about _____ .
However, any unforeseen delays such as arranging financing or clearing title specifically do not void this contract.

10. **POSSESSION:** Possession shall be delivered to Buyer:
A. ☐ Upon Buyer's closing date.
B. ☐ After Buyer's closing date, but no later than _____ days after Buyer's closing. In this event, Seller agrees to pay at Buyer's closing $_____ per day
from Buyer's closing to date possession is delivered and to leave this sum with Agent to be disbursed to the parties entitled thereto on the date possession is
delivered.

11. **FIXTURES AND ATTACHED EQUIPMENT:** Unless specifically excluded herein all fixtures and attached equipment, if any, are included in the purchase price.
Such fixtures and attached equipment shall include, but not be limited to, the following: window air conditioners, carpeting, indoor and outdoor light fixtures,
window and door coverings, gas or electric grills, awnings, mail boxes, garage door openers and remote units, water softeners, propane and butane tanks, antennas
and any other items bolted, nailed, screwed, buried or otherwise attached to the real property in a permanent manner.

12. **TERMITE CONTROL REQUIREMENTS:**
A. ☐ None.
B. ☐ Purchase price to include a current termite control policy issued by licensed operator.
C. ☐ Purchase price to include termite control policy and inspection report, as required by HUD, VA, or lender.

13. **INSPECTIONS AND REPAIRS:** Buyer certifies that Buyer has inspected the property and is not relying upon any warranties, representations or statements of
Agent or Seller as to age or condition of improvements, other than those specified herein. 13A and 13B do not apply to new previously unoccupied dwellings.

A. ☐ Buyer accepts the property in its present condition, subject only to the following: _____

_____

B. ☐ The following items, if any, shall be in normal working order at Buyer's closing: dishwashers, disposals, trash compactors, ranges, exhaust fans, electrical
systems, heating and air conditioning systems, plumbing system, and _____
Buyer shall have the right, at Buyer's expense, to inspect the above items prior to Buyer's closing. If any of the above items are found not to be in normal working
order, Buyer may notify Seller in writing prior to Buyer's closing. After such notice as provided herein, Seller agrees to pay the cost of repair of such items in-

cluding FHA, VA or other lender requirements, up to but not exceeding $_____ . If cost of such repairs will exceed the above amount, and Seller refuses
to pay the additional cost, Buyer may accept the property in its condition at Buyer's closing with credit on the purchase price in the above amount, or Buyer may
declare this contract null and void. If Buyer does not give notice of defects in writing prior to Buyer's closing, all subsequent repairs shall be at Buyer's expense.

14. **RISK OF LOSS:** The risk of loss or damage to the property by fire or other casualty occurring up to the time of Buyer's closing is assumed by the Seller.

15. **EXPIRATION OF OFFER:** This offer shall expire unless written acceptance is received by listing agent before _____ AM/PM on _____ 19 _____

16. **OTHER CONDITIONS:** _____

_____

_____

THIS IS A LEGALLY BINDING CONTRACT WHEN SIGNED BY BOTH BUYER AND SELLER. IF NOT UNDERSTOOD, SEEK LEGAL ADVICE.

_____   _____   _____
Selling Agency   Supervising Broker Signature   Buyer

_____   _____
Selling Associate Signature   Buyer

The above offer is accepted _____ 19 _____ at _____ AM/PM I/WE agree to pay the below named agent a fee of

_____ for professional services rendered in securing said offer. If for any reason the earnest money provided for herein is forfeited by Buyer
under the provisions hereof, same shall be divided equally between Seller and Agent after payment of incurred expenses.

_____   _____   _____
Listing Agent Firm & Principal Broker   Supervising Broker   Seller

_____   _____
Listing Associate   Seller

Arkansas Realtors Association #61-R-83

362

to honor the contract and a guarantee that the broker and the seller will receive compensation if the buyer does not honor the contract. These funds are not an additional cash payment, because the earnest money is applied to the downpayment at the time the property is traded. The seller wants an earnest money deposit that is large enough to cover any expenses that might have been incurred plus compensation for the contract not being fulfilled. The seller may have to pay part or all of the broker's commission if the buyer backs out and therefore wants the earnest money to at least cover that expense. Generally, however, earnest money is not sufficient to cover the full commission.

The buyer does not want to place the deposit in the hands of the seller. The buyer would prefer that the funds be placed in an escrow account in the hands of a third party such as a bank. The funds would be released at the closing. Often the seller wants the money deposited with the broker. If the buyer agrees to this provision, the seller should be made legally responsible for these funds; that is, if the funds are lost or stolen the seller must replace them. This provision should encourage the seller to allow the earnest money to be deposited in an escrow account.[37] Many states legally require that earnest money deposits be placed in escrow accounts under the control of the broker.

In addition to earnest money, the downpayment, and the possibility of obtaining a new loan, other options can be stipulated in the financial section of the real estate sales contract. The potential buyer could assume the seller's loan. In this situation, most typically with the lending institution's approval, the buyer accepts the seller's responsibility to pay off a mortgage. If this option is taken, the buyer would pay the difference between the value of the unpaid mortgage and the sales price to the seller at the closing.

Another option that could be exercised in the financial section is the issuance of a loan by the seller to the buyer. In this situation, a mortgage instrument of some form is drafted and signed by the buyer and seller. The buyer promises to pay the seller a certain mutually agreeable interest rate and also agrees to a predetermined repayment scheme. (Such loans are discussed in Chapters 16 and 17.)

The financial section of the real estate sales contract describes the financial asset that the buyer will give the seller in exchange for the property. The three components in the financial section are:

1. The earnest money deposit
2. The cash that will be paid by the buyer at the time the property is traded
3. The mortgage provision, which can take three possible forms:
   (a) The buyer can obtain a new loan.
   (b) The buyer can assume the loan that was originally issued to the seller.
   (c) The buyer can obtain a loan directly from the seller (purchase money mortgage).

Various combinations of these financial arrangements can be used. For example, the property identified in Exhibit 13-4 could have sold under the following alternative conditions:

	CASE I	CASE II
Earnest money deposit	$ 1,000	$ 2,500
Cash at closing	3,000	2,500
Mortgage assumption	38,000	45,000
Loan from the seller to the buyer	8,000	0
	$50,000	$50,000

These four components amount to a $50,000 financial asset that the buyer will give the seller in exchange for the property.

The Contingency Provisions

The buyer may choose to incorporate several contingency clauses into the real estate sales contract. The sections of Clause 3 relating to a new loan and a loan assumption start with the phrases "The buyer's ability to obtain a loan" and "The buyer's ability to assume an existing loan." These statements provide a contingency by which the buyer can escape or avoid the contract. However, the contingency arises only if the buyer is unable to obtain a new mortgage or to assume the existing mortgage. As protection for his or her own interests, the seller should make sure that the mortgage terms the buyer is seeking are reasonable given the current market. If current interest rates are 11 percent per year and loan maturity is twenty-five years, the seller would be foolish to sign a contract in which the buyer is asking for a 5 percent mortgage for fifty years.

A second contingency clause commonly used in a sales contract provides that the offer is contingent upon the buyer's ability to sell the residential unit that is currently owned. In this situation, the buyer makes an offer on a replacement residence before an offer is received on the residence that he or she currently owns. Because the buyer would need the equity from the current home to purchase the new home, the contract could not be fulfilled if the current residence were not sold. If the buyer insists upon a contingency clause, the seller should insert a contingency statement that gives the buyer three to five business days to honor the contractual obligations if the seller receives a second offer on the property.

The third contingency clause that the buyer can add to the sales contract provides that the offer will be contingent upon inspection of the property on the day of the closing. The buyer may insist on this clause to ensure that the seller will not be negligent in repairs and ordinary maintenance between the date the contract is signed and the date on which the property changes ownership, which may be two or three months later. The clause implies that the buyer reserves the right to void the contract if the property is not in the same condition as it was on the day the contract was signed. This contingency clause is used in addition to (and should not be confused with) Clause 13, which is entitled Inspections and Repairs. This clause is a statement made by the buyer that the property was inspected and found to be satisfactory with regard to its age and the condition of improvements at the time the contract was signed.

THE DECISION TO BUY OR SELL

In Section B of Clause 13, the status of appliances and mechanical systems is disclosed in the phrase "The following items, if any, shall be in normal working order at closing. . . ." The contingency clause for these items is expressly stated as "buyer shall have the right, at buyer's expense, to inspect the above items prior to closing." If these items are not in working order, the seller can pledge a sum of money to pay for necessary repairs.

The contingency clauses are placed in the contract by the buyer as protection against certain possible occurrences. The first contingency clause protects the buyer from a financial obligation that could not be discharged if a loan were not available. The second contingency clause protects the buyer from a financial obligation that could not be discharged unless the current dwelling in which the household lives is sold. Finally, the third contingency clause protects the buyer from taking possession of property that is not in the same physical condition as the property that was the basis for the contract.

Miscellaneous Provisions

The miscellaneous provisions are stated in Clauses 6 through 17 of the real estate sales contract in Exhibit 13-4. Clause 6, the conveyance clause, is a statement describing the type and form of the deed that the seller will give to the buyer as indication of ownership. The deed is a legal instrument that passes ownership of the property. The conveyance clause specifically names a "general warranty deed" as the instrument that the buyer and seller agree to exchange as evidence of ownership. A more detailed discussion of the deed appears in Chapter 21.

Clause 7, the abstract or title insurance clause, is related to the conveyance clause. Even though the buyer and seller have agreed to exchange a general warranty deed as evidence of title, the buyer wants proof that the seller does have the full rights of ownership that he or she is selling to the buyer. The buyer, therefore, requires that the seller furnish an abstract of title that is satisfactory to the buyer's attorney. The abstract of title is a legal document showing the property's history of ownership. By checking through the chain of ownership, the buyer's attorney can determine whether the current seller is in possession of the full rights of ownership that the buyer is expecting to receive.

The abstract or title insurance clause, Clause 7, also gives the seller the option of providing a paid title insurance policy in the amount of the purchase price instead of a title abstract. Title insurance offers the owner protection against loss of the property due to some defect in the title or ownership rights that the seller passes to the buyer. The seller could offer title insurance only if the title were good, as shown by an abstract and title search that was done when the seller purchased the property. If a title insurance policy is cheaper than the cost to obtain a new abstract, use of the title insurance option would be to the seller's financial benefit. Title search, examination, abstract, and opinions, as well as title insurance, are examined in Chapter 19.

Clause 8 is entitled "Prorations." It contains an agreement that the buyer will compensate the seller for any payments that the seller made for property taxes, water bills, and insurance payments applicable to the period of time after the property changes ownership. Assume that property taxes and property insurance payments are due at the first of the year and that these bills must be paid semiannually. On January 1, the seller of the property would have paid amounts such as $400 for property taxes and $125 for property insurance as the semiannual payments for these two items. The property changes ownership on February 10, as stated in Clause 9. Thus, the seller paid property taxes and property insurance for 180 days but held the property for only 40 days. On the day the property changes owners, the seller has paid for 140 days' worth of property taxes and insurance on behalf of the buyer. The rational seller would like to be reimbursed for this expenditure. The prorations clause will require that at closing the buyer compensate the seller for (140/180) ($400) + (140/180) ($125), which is a grand total of $408.33. (A more complete discussion of proration is given in Chapters 21 and 22.)

Clause 9 is the closing clause that establishes a date and a time at which the buyer and seller and interested third parties, such as the buyer's attorney and the broker, will meet to consummate the transaction. This is the day and time when the property changes ownership. (A complete description of the closing process is given in Chapter 22.)

Clause 10 accompanies Clause 9 because it is a statement of possession. The buyer owns the property immediately after the closing procedure is completed. However, the buyer and seller must agree on when the buyer takes possession of the property. It is in the buyer's best interest to take possession upon closing; however, circumstances may cause the seller to insist on retaining possession of the property for a short period of time after the transaction takes place. In this event, the seller must agree to pay rent for the premises until the day possession of the property is delivered to the new owner.

Clause 11 is the fixtures and attached equipment clause. The purpose of this clause in the sales contract is to identify the items of personal property that are considered part of the real estate. The clause makes specific reference to items such as window air conditioners, carpeting, garage door openers and their remote units, and antennae that are to be viewed by both parties as transferring with the real estate. The clause defines a fixture on the basis of attachment. Those items that are "bolted, nailed, screwed, buried, or otherwise attached to the real property in a permanent manner" are fixtures.

However, the clause allows the parties to the contract to define some fixtures as personal property. The phrase "unless specifically excluded" means that the seller should make a list of specific items that are not to be traded with the property. The buyer also may include a list of personal property items that he or she would like to have traded with the property. This clause and the additions to the clause made by both the buyer and seller should identify any and all disputable items and whether or not those items will be considered part of the transaction. Many disputes arise as a result of the failure to specify these items.

Clause 12 specifies the termite and pest control requirements typically stipulated by the buyer. As shown in Exhibit 13-4, the buyer requires that the seller provide a letter of clearance stating that there is no termite damage and that termites were not found on the property. The need for this letter of clearance generally arises

THE DECISION TO BUY OR SELL

in the Southern and Western states. The exact nature of the guarantee stated in the letter varies among the states. In most states, the letter guarantees that no infestation is present on the day of the inspection. In some states, the letter either guarantees no termite damage or identifies its extent if it has occurred. In some states, the letter guarantees that chemicals were applied to ward off insects. Regardless of the requirements, this letter should be issued by a company that specializes in pest control and insect extermination.

Clause 13 is the inspections and repair clause. It identifies the buyer's right to inspect the property and the seller's responsibility to keep the property in good repair until the closing. An important part of the clause is the statement that the buyer expects all appliances and mechanical equipment to be in normal working order at the time of the closing. If they are not, an agreement is made between the buyer and the seller about the extent of the repair expenditure that the seller wishes to incur.

The second part of Clause 13 is the inspection clause. The buyer should arrange for some formal inspection before the contract is signed. The inspection should be no sooner than the day of the closing, or it could be the day after the property is vacated by the seller if the seller vacates before the closing. At the inspection, the buyer makes certain that all fixtures to remain with the property are in place and that all appliances and mechanical systems are in working order.

Clause 14, the risk of loss clause, identifies the responsibility for any casualty loss caused by fire, flood, windstorm, vandalism, etc., that might occur between the time the sales contract is signed and the time of closing. States differ in the manner in which liability is assigned in this case. Some states hold the purchaser liable for loss during this time period and other states hold the seller liable.[38] The clause in Exhibit 13-4 specifically states that any loss or damage that may occur up to the time of the closing is assumed by the seller. If this clause is not included in the contract, a legal disagreement can occur. The seller could claim that the responsibility for the loss is borne by the buyer after the contract is signed. The buyer could claim that the responsibility is the seller's until after closing. To avoid court procedures, the parties to the contract should insist on the inclusion of a clause obligating one of the parties to carry property insurance of sufficient magnitude to completely replace the improvements.

Clause 15 identifies the expiration date of the offer. The buyer should state an exact number of days during which the offer is outstanding. However, the buyer should realize that he or she must deliver the offer and communicate it to the seller without unreasonable delay. For example, in this contract the buyer gives the seller five days to accept the offer. If the offer is signed on January 3 but is not delivered to the seller until January 7, the buyer is not fulfilling the legal responsibilities of delivery and communication. In this event, the courts probably would award the seller a reasonable amount of time after January 8 to sign the contract.

Clause 16 provides space to specify matters not discussed in preceding clauses or to raise issues not covered in the preprinted clauses. This clause can be used to clarify the issue of fixtures and attached equipment. The clause can also state that the buyer will assume the seller's property insurance.

Other aspects of the transaction can be addressed in this clause. For example, an installment assessment clause is an agreement between the buyer and the seller about the treatment of any outstanding assessments against the property. Such assessments might have arisen because of the construction of sewer lines, storm drainage systems, or roadways. The public improvements have an impact on the value of the property (as explained in Chapter 2); they either increase the value of the property in an absolute sense or keep the value from declining in relation to that of other properties that are served by such improvements. The local government makes these assessments against the property and the property owner is responsible for paying them. The assessment can be paid in one installment, but most local governments allow the assessment to be paid in several installments over a number of years. If the owner does not pay these assessments, the local government has a tax lien against the property. Consequently, the buyer should be aware of any such assessments against the property and their financial and legal ramifications.

A financial problem arises about the payment of the installments that are due in the future. Should the buyer pay them after the property is purchased or should the seller pay them before or at the closing? The answer depends on the relationship between the sales price of the subject property and its comparable properties. If the sales price of the subject property is on a par with that of comparable properties that have these public improvements, the seller should be instructed to pay these assessments at the closing or just before. The buyer should insist on this procedure to avoid double payment for the improvement through the sales price and the outstanding assessment payments. If the seller cannot pay the assessment by the closing or chooses not to pay it, the buyer should negotiate a reduction in the sales price equal to the value of the outstanding assessment that is owed to the local government.

If the sales price of the subject property is equivalent to that of comparable properties *without* the off-site improvement, the buyer should pay the installments. In this instance the buyer is receiving the benefit of the improvements as potential price appreciation. The same situation can arise if the sales price of the subject property is less than the sales price of comparable properties *with* the improvement and the difference is equal in value to the unpaid assessment.

In Clause 16, the installment assessment provision can be written to obligate the seller to pay the full assessment before closing, or to pay only those installments falling due before the closing.[39]

The execution section of the contract follows Clause 16. The important signatures are the buyer's and the seller's because these signatures give evidence of the offer and acceptance. Furthermore, any interested parties, such as the brokers, should sign the contract so that they will also be bound by its terms and conditions. In Exhibit 13-4, the selling broker and the listing broker signed the contract, as did the buyer and the seller. The very last section appearing on the sample contract is an agreement between the seller and the brokers about the brokers' commissions.

A question may arise about the need for the signatures of witnesses, the need for an acknowledgment, and the necessity of recording the document. Generally, witnesses are not essential to the validity of a sales contract. A witnessing of the document is not necessary unless the parties wish to have the document recorded and state law requires that the contract be witnessed. Moreover, sales contracts are generally not acknowledged (witnessed by a public official such as a notary public), and because they are short-term contracts they are generally not recorded.[40] However, state statutes should be checked to determine the exact requirements in the state where the property is located. This is one reason for employing a lawyer who is trained in real property law.

The last of the miscellaneous clauses is typically included in a sales contract for a new house. The contract displayed in Exhibit 13-4 is identified as a resale contract. But it can also be used for the transaction surrounding a newly constructed house. If it is used in this capacity an additional clause should be added to cover the installation of insulation. A 1980 ruling by the Federal Trade Commission requires the builder to specify the amount of insulation that will be installed in the house. A preprinted version of such a clause appears in Exhibit 13-5. Notice that the clause only specifies what amount of insulation will be installed. The buyer may have to check on the adequacy of the R-values of the insulation installed. In many areas the electric utility company and/or the natural gas utility company will provide consumer information about the R-values recommended in the locality. If the utility companies do not provide such information a reputable insulation contractor will.

EXHIBIT 13-5 Reprinted with the permission of the Arkansas Realtors Association.
1980 FTC RULING INSULATION: Insulation (is/will be) installed as follows:

	TYPE	THICKNESS	R-VALUE
EXTERIOR WALLS	_____	_____	_____
INTERIOR WALLS	_____	_____	_____
CEILINGS (in all areas)	_____	_____	_____
WALLS for which above information varies, (such as special insulation in bedroom)	_____	_____	_____

The above information has been furnished by the insulation manufacturer or home builder and is relied on by Seller and Agent.

THE OPTION

An option is a written contract that gives a potential buyer a right to buy the property prior to a specified date. The potential buyer pays the seller an agreed-upon sum of money to hold the property off the market until either the option is exercised or expires. Both the option payment and the holding period are part of the negotiation process.

The option also must contain a valid agreement and consideration. The purchase price and the property description need to be specified. The greatest number of complications regarding the option arise when it is made part of a lease. For this discussion, see the section on "special-purpose clauses" in Chapter 15.

DISCHARGE, NONPERFORMANCE, AND BREACH
OF CONTRACT

After the real estate sales contract is negotiated and signed by the buyer and seller, the rights and duties created by that contract remain in force until one of three things occurs: (1) the contract is discharged, which means that the rights and duties created by that contract are fulfilled in some manner; (2) one of the individuals who entered into the contract receives legal permission for nonperformance of the duties incurred in the contract; or (3) one individual party to the contract fails to perform according to the terms and provisions established in the contract.

The legal ramifications of contract law are important to all parties involved in a real estate transaction. These individuals need to understand the rights and responsibilities incurred in the contract, the legally permissible reasons for not fulfilling the terms of the contract, and the repercussions that may arise if an individual fails to fulfill the commitments specified within the real estate sales contract.

Discharge or Performance of the Contract

The legal system fully intends that the usual method of discharge for a contract is the *complete performance* by both parties of the obligations that each incurred under the contractual agreement. Each party to the contract must perform the actions or fulfill the promises that were made, and each party expects the other individual to do the same.

In the majority of contracts, the obligation of one individual in the contract is to pay for a commodity or for a service that is rendered. In the real estate sales contract, the commodity is the parcel of real property. Two questions related to payment are "What constitutes payment?" and "What is good evidence that payment has been made and that the obligation has been discharged?"[41]

Clearly, the transfer of money that is legal tender constitutes payment. However, the payment is less clear when it is made by means of a negotiable instrument such as a check or a promissory note. In this case, absolute discharge of the obligation does not occur until the debt specified by the check or promissory note is discharged. In other words, the contract is not discharged until the seller deposits the check in the bank and the account is credited with the appropriate sum of money. In the case of a promissory note, the contract is not discharged until the promissory note is paid off. The delivery of the check or the promissory note does not constitute a discharge of the contract. The contractual agreement is completed when the full consideration as specified in the contract has been completely discharged.[42]

If a negotiable instrument such as a check or promissory note is to be used as an absolute discharge of the financial responsibility, the parties to the contract must so agree. The purchase-money mortgage must be agreed to as an absolute discharge of the contract, or else the contract is not discharged until the buyer pays off the loan received under the purchase-money mortgage. Moreover, if the financial section of the contract calls for a cash payment at closing, and that cash payment is made by check, the contract is not discharged until the seller has the face value of the check deposited in his or her bank account.

THE DECISION TO BUY OR SELL

The usually accepted form of evidence for full-payment discharge of the contract is a receipt for payment that clearly states the amount paid and the transaction to which the payment related. A cancelled check can be viewed as evidence that payment was made. However, for the evidence to be conclusive, the cancelled check should stipulate the purpose for which payment was given. The buyer can specify on the face of the check that the endorsement and the cashing of that check acknowledges full satisfaction of the obligation.[43] To avoid legal complications, the only acceptable checks should be cashier's checks or certified checks.

In addition to complete performance of the obligations stipulated in the contract, other means can be used to discharge a contract legally. One of the individuals involved in the contract can find a substitute. In other words, a party to the contract who becomes unwilling to meet the terms of the contract may find another person who is willing to assume those duties and obligations. This new party must agree to assume all of the responsibilities and duties of the original party who is seeking to be freed from the obligations of the contract. Moreover, both parties to the original contract must agree to the substitution. This process of finding an acceptable, willing substitute for one of the original parties is called *novation*.[44] It is a way of fully and legally discharging the obligations of a contract.

Another type of novation is the mutually agreeable substitution of a different obligation for one of the original obligations specified in the contract.[45] For example, the real estate contract may have been signed by both the buyer and seller with the stipulation that the kitchen appliances remain with the property. The seller now realizes that the appliances match the decor of the new house that was purchased and seeks the buyer's approval to substitute $700 for the appliances. If the buyer agrees, the original obligation to leave the appliances is superseded by the new obligation to pay $700 and the contract can be discharged.

The obligations incurred in the contract also can be legally discharged by the process of *accord and satisfaction*. An *accord* is a reformation of the agreement made between the two parties to the contract. One of the individuals undertakes to give an asset or to perform an action that is different from the one specified in the contract. Simultaneously, the other party to the contract must accept this asset or action. The term *satisfaction* denotes that the substitution was made with the agreement of all parties to the contract. The legal doctrine of accord and satisfaction requires that there be a dispute or uncertainty about the consideration specified in the contract. A compromise agreement is reached between the parties to the contract, their differences are reconciled (this is the accord), and the mutual obligations are satisfactorily discharged (this is the satisfaction). There is a clear understanding that the parties have entered into a new and substitute contract and that in so doing they have surrendered the legal right to take the dispute or the settlement agreement into court.[46]

The difference between novation and the doctrine of accord and satisfaction is the difference between substitution inside the original contract and the formation of a new contract to replace the original agreement. In a novation, a party to the contract is substituted or a specification in the agreement is substituted, but there is no dispute or misunderstanding about the terms of the contract. Under the doctrine of accord and satisfaction, a new contract is struck that replaces the original contract. The new contract arises because of a disagreement or misunderstanding about the original contract. Bear in mind, however, that if the satisfaction does not follow the accord, then the original obligation may still be enforced.

Legal Excuses for Nonperformance

Even though the contract binds two individuals to a certain agreement, one of the individuals can be relieved of the responsibilities of performing a contract by a legal excuse for nonperformance. Since competent parties are required for a valid contract, a legal incompetent, such as a minor, can be excused from having to perform the obligations specified in a contract. Also, if reality of consent is lacking, the party who did not give his or her true consent can be legally excused from the contract. Other legal excuses for nonperformance are:

- ☐ Failure to perform a condition precedent
- ☐ An intention not to hold the other party to the terms of the contract, a waiver
- ☐ Prevention
- ☐ Frustration
- ☐ Impossibility

Many contracts are drawn with the specification that one of the parties must perform an act or fulfill a promise before the other party's obligation is incurred. In other words, the performance of one of the parties depends on a prior or preceding action by the other party to the contract. This situation is known as a *condition precedent.* If the initial action or promise is not undertaken and fulfilled, the obligation of the other party is not incurred. Consequently, failure to perform the condition precedent is a legal excuse for the other party to be relieved of contractual obligations.

An example of a condition precedent in a real estate sales contract is a requirement made by the buyer that the seller perform some repair and maintenance work prior to the closing. Let's assume the ceilings in the living and dining rooms are warped and discolored because of leaks in the roof. The buyer may require that prior to closing the seller patch the roof to stop the leaks and paint both the living and dining rooms. If the seller agrees to these repairs but does not perform the tasks, a condition precedent established in the contract is not completed and the buyer has a legal excuse for nonperformance of his or her obligation in that contract. As a general rule in such cases, the courts' interpretation has been that if the condition precedent is relatively insignificant, its performance is not required to make the contract legally binding. In such cases, the party who was expecting the condition precedent to be performed merely deducts the financial damages caused by the other person's nonperformance from the sales price of the property.

If the condition precedent in the example required merely patching a few leaks in the roof and repainting the rooms, failure to perform the condition precedent may not be a reason to void the contract. In this situation, the buyer would reduce the cash payment made to the seller by the expenses incurred to patch the roof and repaint the living and dining rooms. If stopping the leaks necessitated putting a new roof on the building, however, and if this was fully understood by the two parties, the seller's failure to perform the condition precedent would be a legal excuse for the buyer to escape the obligations incurred by the contract.

If the work is performed, a different set of legal questions can arise if the buyer is not fully and completely satisfied with the quality of the work. For example, assume that the leak is repaired but only half of the roof was reshingled. The front of the house has old shingles and the back of the house has new shingles. However, the leak is stopped, and the living and dining rooms have been painted. The buyer is not satisfied because only half the roof is new and, in addition, the stains show through the two coats of new paint. Does the buyer have an excuse for nonperformance? The answer to this question depends on the issue of substantial performance—the work must be performed in such a way that it meets acceptable community standards in order for the courts to interpret that the obligation was discharged. The leak was stopped by replacing only half of the roof shingles. The walls were painted with two coats of paint as is customary, but the discoloration was so severe that a third and maybe fourth coat of paint would be needed to cover it. The courts could rule in this case that the seller did meet the condition precedent and that the buyer must fulfill the contractual obligations incurred.

In matters such as these, the contractual obligations must be closely scrutinized. If the contract states that the leaks must be stopped, the seller bears the obligation only to stop the leaks. This could be accomplished by tarring a section of the roof or by partial reshingling. If the buyer had wanted the entire roof replaced, an explicit statement to that effect should have been entered into the contract. The seller may have signed a contract that stated Stop the leaks, or Patch the roof, but may not have signed a contract that stated Replace the roof.

The second legal excuse for nonperformance is the waiver. The waiver is an action or statement by one party to the contract that indicates an intention not to enforce the provisions of the contractual agreement that the other party is obligated to perform.[47] The person granting the waiver therefore gives up the opportunity to enforce a legal right and thereby loses that right. A waiver of one peson's right to force the other person's performance of the contract provides a legal excuse for nonperformance by the other person.

The third legal excuse for nonperformance is prevention. The law stipulates that if a person prevents the performance of a contract or in some way makes the performance impossible by direct action, that person "will not be permitted to take advantage of the nonperformance. If one party by his conduct makes it impossible for the other to perform, the one failing to perform has no liability. It is an implied condition of every contract that neither party will prevent performance by the other or the carrying out of a contract in the normal course of events."[48]

The fourth legal excuse for nonperformance is impossibility of performance. Four specific situations can be used to show the rationale underlying the concept of impossibility:[49]

1. The performance of the contract becomes illegal after a law is enacted that makes either the act or the object illegal.

2. One of the parties to the contract dies or contracts an incapacitating illness.

3. Destruction of an object or other material that is essential to the completion of the contract will relieve the obligations established in the agreement.

4. An element essential to the contract is missing. "This situation has never been satisfactorily defined, but apparently, when some element or property that the parties assumed existed or would exist is in fact lacking, the agreement may be rescinded. . . . It must be definitely proved that performance is substantially impossible because of the missing element. For example, a contract to build an office building at a certain location. Because of the nature of the soil, it is utterly impossible to build the type of building provided for in the agreement; the agreement must therefore be terminated. The missing element is the proper condition of the soil."[50]

Impossibility must be differentiated from hardship. "As a general rule, . . . circumstances that impose additional hardship on one party do not constitute an excuse for breach of contract. The fact that the promised performance of a contractual obligation may be more difficult than expected at the time the promise was made does not discharge the promisor from his duty to perform."[51]

The fourth legal excuse for nonperformance of a contract is frustration. An event can take place that does not create actual impossibility but does prevent the fulfillment of the obligations incurred in the contract. "Frustration has the effect of excusing nonperformance and arises whenever there is an intervening event or change of circumstances that is so fundamental as to be entirely beyond that which was contemplated by the parties. Frustration is not impossibility, but it is more than mere hardship . . . It includes impracticability caused by extreme or unreasonable difficulty or expense when the cause is not foreseeable. If the event was reasonably foreseeable, frustration is not an excuse for nonperformance. If the parties could have reasonably anticipated the event, they are obliged to make provisions in their contract protecting themselves against it."[52]

Breach of Contract

A **breach of contract** is failure to perform the acts or promises stipulated as the terms of the contract. Breach of contract is nonperformance of a contract, but without a legally acceptable excuse. If one party to the contract does not perform according to the terms and agreements of that contract, the other party may be financially injured as a result of nonperformance. The injured party has legal recourse in this event. The courts may require that the contract be fulfilled or they may provide that the injured party receive compensation for the injury or damages incurred because of the breach of contract.

The legal actions that the injured party can undertake are known as *remedies*. The law provides for three general classes of remedies:

☐ Rescission or cancellation
☐ A lawsuit to obtain financial compensation for the damages suffered
☐ A lawsuit to obtain specific performance of the contract

When one party to the contract fails to perform according to the agreement, the other individual has the right to return to the same legal and financial position that was maintained prior to the formation of the contract. In other words, the party to the contract who did not breach the agreement should be restored to the position he or she was in before signing the contract. This remedy is known as *rescission*. In this situation, both parties return any consideration they may have received, and the entire contract is rescinded. The rescission process can be accomplished voluntarily by agreement between the parties or it can be instituted by court order at the request of the injured party. Cancellation is the same as recission with the exception that the injured party retains the right to sue for damages.[53]

The second remedy available to the injured party in a breach of contract is a lawsuit to recover a financial loss that will be incurred subsequent to the breach of contract. "In awarding damages for breach of contract, the court tries to place the injured party in approximately the same position that party would have been in had the breach not occurred."[54] The damages awarded to fulfill this legal tenet are known as compensatory damages. Their magnitude is usually determined by the extent of the financial injury.

In certain situations, the parties to the contract may foresee the possibility that a breach of contract may occur. Consequently, they may agree on an amount of money that would be paid to the injured party in case the default does take place. In this situation, the predetermined sum of money is known as **liquidated damages**. "This arrangement is common when actual damages would be difficult to prove and is enforceable if the amount is reasonable. If damages are not reasonable, the court will deem them to be a penalty and will not enforce the agreement."[55] The earnest money deposit can be viewed as liquidated damages in case of a breach of the sales contract yet the aggrieved party usually receives the right to sue for additional damages. (The distribution of the earnest money deposit among the aggrieved parties—the seller and the broker—is usually specified in the listing agreement, which was discussed in Chapter 12.)

The courts also award damages on the basis that a breach of contract is an illegal action. If no fraud is intended, the courts may award **nominal damages** to the injured party. These nominal damages are granted in recognition that the rights of one of the parties, the injured party, have been violated. Typically, nominal damages are in the neighborhood of one dollar. They are awarded only when no financial loss is suffered by the aggrieved party to the contract.

The third remedy for breach of contract is **specific performance.** Often money damages are not an adequate remedy. In this event, the courts may grant the injured party a court order requiring that the defaulting party perform the contract according to the specific terms included in the agreement. The court order requires the specific performance of the contractual obligation. This remedy typically is used when the assets involved in the contract are considered to be unique and different from even similar types of assets. Works of art and real estate are considered to be such unique assets. "The law today still considers each parcel of real estate to be absolutely unique and different from any other parcel of real estate no matter where it is located."[56] Consequently, the injured party can request the specific performance of the contract instead of money damages.

EXHIBIT 13-6   The contract process

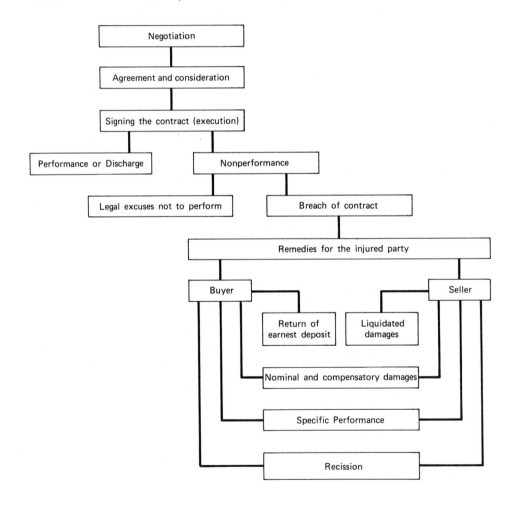

MISREPRESENTATION RELATED TO CONTRACT
PERFORMANCE

Misrepresentations can occur and pass unnoticed even if the material facts are available in sources of information that are readily and equally available to both parties to a contract. In these situations, the "misrepresentation of a material fact would not always entitle the other party to cancel the contract. For example, some courts say that a buyer has no right to rely on a misrepresentation when the sources of information are equally available to both parties."[57]

One such situation involves the zoning ordinance. The seller could misrepresent the nature of the land-use restriction that affects the property. In this situation, "an unintentional misrepresentation of existing state or local law affords no basis for rescission, since the law is presumably a matter of common knowledge, open and available to all who desire to explore its mysteries."[58] The important phrase in this statement is "no basis for rescission."

Misrepresentation can be related to matters that would be disclosed by the buyer's inspection of the property. The buyer is not entitled to rely on the seller's representation about matters that would be disclosed by the buyer's inspection of the property. The buyer cannot rely on the seller's statements about the condition of the building when the buyer has actually made a careful inspection of that property. In such cases, the buyer is relying on observations and not on the seller's representation. The buyer may be able to sue for damages but may not be able to rescind the contract even if the seller has made a misrepresentation.[59] However, if the parties are not dealing on equal terms—that is, the buyer is not able to recognize a structural flaw—the buyer might be allowed to void the contract. "For example, when a buyer inspects the land but makes no attempt to check the seller's representations as to the area, the buyer may rescind the contract if there is a misrepresentation in this respect . . . but a buyer who learns of a defect, such as decay or crumbling of the foundation, has no right to make a merely casual inspection. He must make a careful inspection."[60] Many legal authorities view this last case where the buyer is forbidden to rely on certain representations made by the seller as a bad legal rule. "In effect, it legalizes fraud in many situations. Many courts have discarded this barbarous rule, and no doubt it will disappear in time. No rogue should enjoy his ill-gotten plunder for the simple reason that his victim is by chance a fool."[61]

The parties to the contract should make use of all readily available public information and take every opportunity to inspect the property. In certain situations, a misrepresentation will not be grounds to void a contract even though the misrepresentation can be the basis for filing a suit to obtain damages. The body of law relating to misrepresentation in contracts is slowly changing to eliminate any possibility that a person could profit from another person's gullibility or ignorance. However, the change is slow and the buyer should not assume that his or her interests are totally protected in the law.

The telling of "half-truths" is another problem. The courts tend to view the revealing of only part of the truth as being the same as telling a lie. If a seller states a fact that in and of itself is true, the seller must also state all of the other facts that either qualify or modify the correct information that was previously stated. If these qualifying facts are not stated, the seller can face court action. Many such actions have resulted in the seller's liability to pay damage to the buyer.[62]

Finally, a misrepresentation, either intentional or unintentional, may not be discovered until the contract has actually been performed. After the closing date when the agreement has been fulfilled and the consideration exchanged, the buyer may discover that a misrepresentation was made. It is important to remember "that the buyer is seldom in a position to discover the seller's misrepresentations until he has taken possession of the property."[63] Some of the more common grounds for misrepresentation in such cases are:

- ☐ The magnitude and sources of the property's income, profits, and volume of business
- ☐ The location of the property's boundary lines
- ☐ The exact frontage of the property or the age of the improvements on the property
- ☐ The soil's drainage capacity and characteristics
- ☐ The existence or nonexistence of encumbrances such as easements and liens[64]

Both buyer and seller should be careful about their statements and understanding of these factors pertaining to the property being exchanged.

CHAPTER SUMMARY

The real estate sales contract is a valid, bilateral, express contract. As a valid contract, it contains all of the essential features required by the body of law known as contract law. It is a stated agreement negotiated between the two parties through the offer and acceptance process about an exchange of assets that are approximately equal; this exchange is the consideration that is satisfactory to the two parties to the contract. The contract is initiated and executed with the full and real consent of all parties to that contract. In addition, the object or action involved in the contract is legal. Finally, the real estate sales contract is expressed in written form.

The real estate sales contract contains many clauses and provisions. The two most important are the agreement and the consideration. The potential buyer and the seller reach a mutually acceptable decision about the exchange of assets that will take place. The buyer offers a certain financial package that consists of an earnest money deposit, cash at closing, and debt financing in exchange for the parcel of real estate. The seller accepts this financial package in exchange for the real property asset. After this financial agreement is reached, the buyer and the seller focus their attention on a series of other issues. Depending on the situation, these other issues can be of primary or secondary importance.

The body of contract law presupposes that all contracts will be honored by the parties involved. In this sense, the expectation is that all contracts will be discharged according to the conditions and terms specified within the document. However, in certain situations contracts are not discharged. There may be a legal excuse for this nonperformance, or one of the parties may breach the contract. Both the buyer and the seller should be fully aware of the legal excuses for nonperformance, as well as the legal remedies available to them in the event of a breach of contract by the other party.

Review Questions

1. Explain the differences among valid, void, voidable, and unenforceable contracts.
2. Identify and explain the essential features of the offer and the acceptance.
3. In a real estate sales contract, what is the consideration?
4. Who are competent parties?
5. Distinguish between mistakes in fact and mistakes in law.
6. Distinguish between a material fact and an immaterial fact.
7. Define misrepresentation. When does it become fraud?
8. Under what circumstances do parties to a real estate sales contract have the duty to speak?
9. What four items can be discussed in the financial section of the real estate sales contract?
10. What are the three most common contingency provisions in a real estate sales contract?
11. Briefly discuss as many provisions of the sales contract as you can.
12. There are three ways of discharging a contract. One is to have both parties to the contract comply with all of the terms and obligations incurred in that contract. The other two ways are novation and accord and satisfaction. Explain the concepts of novation and accord and satisfaction.
13. What are the legal excuses for nonperformance of a contract?
14. Describe the remedies available to the injured party when a breach of contract occurs.

Discussion Questions

1. Besides the legal requirement stipulated under the regulations of the Statute of Frauds, discuss the conceptual reasons why a real estate contract should be in written form.
2. Choose a friend or another student in the class and assign the role of buyer to one of you and the role of seller to the other. Then draft a real estate sales contract for an imaginary piece of property using simple, declarative statements such as The buyer will. . . . Compare the agreement and provisions of your contract with those in the contract shown in Exhibit 13-4.

3. The term *substantial performance* is introduced in Chapter 1. Compare and contrast it with *specific performance.*

Notes

1. Robert N. Corley and William J. Robert, *Principles of Business Law* (Englewood Cliffs, N.J.: Prentice-Hall, Inc., 1979), p. 96.

2. McKee Fisk and Norbert J. Mietus, *Applied Business Law,* 11th ed. (Cincinnati, Ohio: South-Western Publishing Co., 1977), p. 143.

3. Corley and Robert, *Principles of Business Law,* p. 97.

4. Fisk and Mietus, *Applied Business Law,* p. 135.

5. Corley and Robert, *Principles of Business Law,* p. 115.

6. Ibid., p. 117.

7. Ibid.

8. Robert Kratovil and Raymond J. Werner, *Real Estate Law* (Englewood Cliffs, N.J.: Prentice-Hall, Inc., 1979), p. 106.

9. Corley and Robert, *Principles of Business Law,* p. 118

10. Fisk and Mietus, *Applied Business Law,* p. 141.

11. Ibid., p. 143.

12. Ibid.

13. Corley and Robert, *Principles of Business Law,* pp. 141–42.

14. Ibid., p. 145.

15. Ibid., p. 147.

16. Ibid., p. 148.

17. Fisk and Mietus, *Applied Business Law,* p. 136.

18. Ibid., p. 165.

19. Jack C. Estes and John Kokus, *Real Estate License Preparation Course for the Uniform Examinations for Salespersons and Brokers* (New York: McGraw-Hill Book Co., 1976), p. 49.

20. Corley and Robert, *Principles of Business Law,* p. 167.

21. Ibid., p. 168

22. Ibid., p. 163.

23. Ibid., p. 161.

24. Ibid., p. 162.

25. Ibid., p. 163.

26. Kratovil and Werner, *Real Estate Law,* p. 138.

27. Ibid.

28. Corley and Robert, *Principles of Business Law,* p. 64

29. Ibid.

30. Ibid., p. 165.

31. Estes and Kokus, *Real Estate License Preparation Course,* p. 49.

32. Corley and Robert, *Principles of Business Law,* p. 180.

33. Fisk and Mietus, *Applies Business Law,* p. 153.

34. Kratovil and Werner, *Real Estate Law,* p. 98.

35. Fisk and Mietus, *Applied Business Law,* p. 283.

36. H. Glenn Mercer and Homer C. Davey, *National Guide to Real Estate* (Prentice-Hall Series in Real Estate; Englewood Cliffs, N.J.: Prentice-Hall, Inc., 1972), pp. 79-80.

37. Kratovil and Werner, *Real Estate Law,* p. 116.

38. Milton R. Friedman, *Contracts and Conveyances of Real Property* (New York: Practicing Law Institute, 1975), pp. 365-86.

39. Ibid., pp. 28-30.

40. Harold F. Lusk and William B. French, *Law of the Real Estate Business* (Homewood, Ill.: Richard D. Irwin, Inc., 1975), p. 321.

41. Corley and Robert, *Principles of Business Law,* p. 258.

42. Ibid.

43. Ibid., pp. 258-59.

44. Ibid., p. 260.

45. Ibid.

46. Ibid., p. 259.

47. Ibid., p. 242.

48. Ibid., p.243.

49. Ibid., p. 244-45.

50. Ibid., p. 245.

51. Ibid., p. 243.

52. Ibid., p. 246.

53. Fisk and Mietus, *Applied Business Law,* pp. 214-15.

54. Ibid., p. 216.

55. Ibid., p. 217.

56. William B. French, Stephen J. Martin, and Thomas E. Battle Ill, *Guide to Real Estate Licensing Examinations for Salespersons and Brokers* (Boston, Mass.: Warren, Gorham, and Lamont, 1978), p. 163.

57. Kratovil and Werner, *Real Estate Law,* p. 139.

58. Corley and Robert, *Principles of Business Law,* p. 164.

59. Kratovil and Werner, *Real Estate Law,* p. 138-39.

60. Ibid., pp. 139-40.

61. Ibid., p. 140.

62. Ibid., p. 143.

63. Ibid., p. 137.

64. Ibid.

Additional Readings

CORLEY, ROBERT N., and WILLIAM J. ROBERT. *Principles of Business Law.* Englewood Cliffs, N.J.: Prentice-Hall Inc., 1979. Chapters 7–12, 14, and 15.

FARMER, ROBERT A. *What You Should Know About Contracts.* New York: Cornerstone Library, 1979.

FRIEDMAN, MILTON R. *Contracts and Conveyances of Real Property.* New York: Practicing Law Institute, 1975.

KRATOVIL, ROBERT, and RAYMOND J. WERNER. *Real Estate Law.* Englewood Cliffs, N.J.: Prentice-Hall Inc., 1983. Chapter 11.

LUSK, HAROLD F., and WILLIAM B. FRENCH. *Law of the Real Estate Business.* Homewood, Ill.: Richard D. Irwin, Inc. 1984. Chapter 12.

14 Property Management and the Residential Lease

QUESTIONS TO BE ANSWERED

1. What must I know about property-management services in order to make a decision about managing the property?
2. What must I know about a residential lease if I enter into the agreement as either a tenant or a landlord?

OBJECTIVES

When the student finishes the chapter, he or she should be able to

1. Discuss the scope of services offered by a property manager.
2. Explain the nature of the residential lease agreement.
3. State the rights and responsibilities of both the landlord and the tenant in a lease.

4. Describe the various clauses that appear in a residential lease.

5. Discuss the consumer-oriented issues involved in the landlord-tenant relationship.

6. State the ways a lease can be terminated.

7. Discuss the consequences that arise when the lease agreement is breached.

IMPORTANT TERMS

Assignment	Dispossession Proceedings
Eviction	Security Deposit
Constructive Eviction	Subletting

INTRODUCTION

When the investor decides to purchase the property, a collateral decision must also be made. Should the investor/property owner manage and operate the property or find a competent property manager to perform the task? In order to answer this question, the investor must know the full scope of administrative responsibilities that an investment property might require. Then, the investor has to decide which of these services a property manager will be contracted to perform. Consequently, an understanding of the property-management function is important. To achieve this understanding, the nature of the various management services that a property manager can provide must be identified, and a general discussion of the duties and responsibilities of a professional property manager must be undertaken.

THE PROPERTY-MANAGEMENT FUNCTION

In general, property management is a professional activity that assists property owners in achieving their investment objectives. Depending on the individual and on the market circumstances, these investment objectives can vary. However, for the most part, the investor will probably seek to maximize the total return on the investment over the holding period. Obtaining this objective would require a combination of maximizing after-tax cash flow and maximizing equity increase through mortgage reduction and price appreciation. The property manager can provide many different services to help the investor achieve this goal. These property-management services are discussed in the following subsections.

Management of the Physical Asset

The professional property manager should be able to establish an adequate and well-defined maintenance program for the property. In order to perform this service, the property manager must understand the nature of physical deterioration. He or she must be able to make a physical inspection of the property and determine which items require immediate repair and which items can have maintenance and repair deferred. In addition, the property manager must be able to estimate both the amount of funds that should be budgeted for repairs and maintenance in any given year and the amount of funds necessary to be set aside as a replacement reserve.

Moreover, the property manager should be able to identify the difference between corrective maintenance, which is the repair and replacement of physically deteriorated items in the building, and preventive maintenance, which is the replacement of items prior to breakdown. This ability to distinguish between corrective and preventive maintenance is important, because a well-established, well-executed, preventive-maintenance program can minimize total maintenance and repair expenditures. Well-executed preventive maintenance may be less costly than corrective maintenance.

In addition to the knowledge about the physical aspects of the property, the property manager must understand the nature of maintenance service contracts and be able to analyze the nature of competitive bids that are issued to perform both corrective and preventive maintenance. Finally, as part of the responsibility to the physical asset, the property manager should be able to supervise personnel who are responsible for maintenance activity, whether these individuals are paid by the property owner directly or reimbursed for services performed on a contract basis.

Knowledge of the physical asset also extends to knowledge of the concept of functional obsolescence. The property manager should realize what features of the building are functionally obsolescent, especially those features that are curable. In this capacity, the property manager can advise the property owner about the economic feasibility of improvement expenditures to overcome functional obsolescence. For instance, lighting fixtures might be replaced, window space could be enlarged, air conditioning might be installed, kitchens and bathrooms could be modernized, and so on. These improvements become feasible if the property manager can show that the extra revenue generated by these features exceeds their cost. The property manager should also realize that features with incurable functional obsolescence, such as inefficient floor plans and small rooms by current standards, also affect the rent-generating capabilities of the property. Both functional and economic obsolescence will be considered again in later subsections.

Management of Financial Records

The property manager should be able to perform the necessary financial accounting functions that are required for the property. This includes the generation of an owner's income and operating expense statement on both a monthly and an annual basis. An example of such a statement on an annual basis is provided in Chapter 6. The property owner may choose to buy this service separately from the management of the physical asset or even from the rent-collection service (to be discussed later). In essence, the property owner would be buying the property manager's skills as an accountant.

Management of the Tenant-Acquisition
and Tenant-Selection Processes

In the very simplest terms, the property manager should be able to merchandise the rental space in his or her control. In order to fulfill this function, the property manager should understand the various aspects of merchandising that will attract potential tenants. The property manager should know the effectiveness of newspaper advertising, of mailing of individualized brochures, and of the placement of "for rent" signs on the property itself. The property manager should know which of these techniques is currently most successful in the community.

However, the process of tenant selection may well be the most important aspect of the property manager's task in this category of management services. In this sense, the property manager may be required to play both an active and passive role. In an active sense, the property manager may wish to identify the characteristics of the tenants who would be most susceptible to advertising and who would be most desirable for the property owner. Knowing these facts, the property manager would go out and establish advertising programs to attract these tenants. On the passive side, the property manager must have some basis for selecting the tenants to whom space will be delivered. (Tenant-selection criteria will be discussed in the next major section of this chapter.)

Management of the Rent-Collection
and Lease-Negotiation Processes

The property manager can also provide rent-collection and lease-negotiation services. In this sense, the property management firm would be the depository for rent payments that are made by the tenants. The property manager would also provide a procedure by which delinquent rents could be collected. For example, if the rent is due on the first of the month, but no later than the fifth of the month, the property manager could send out a late notice on the sixth of the month reminding the tenant of the late payment. Then, if the payment is not received by the tenth or the fifteenth of the month, the property manager can send out a second notification informing the tenant of both the lateness of the payment and legal action that will be undertaken if the payment is not made by the fifteenth of the month. In this way, the property manager removes one of the more distasteful aspects of rental property from the shoulders of the property owner.

The property manager can be given the responsibility to initiate and negotiate leases on behalf of the property owner. If this service is purchased from the property manager, it frees the property owner from the necessity of thoroughly understanding a body of crucial knowledge. The property owner should realize that there are certain legal obligations and responsibilities that are imposed both on the tenant and on the owner. The nature of these legal obligations and responsibilities are embodied in lease laws that change over time from state to state. Information about lease provisions will be presented as a major portion of this chapter under the heading of "The Residential Lease."

Management of the Financial Asset

In addition to the responsibilities of managing the physical asset and maintaining the financial records, the property manager can also provide the following investment counseling services:

1. Analyze the variables that enter into the property owner's decision to purchase the income-earning property. For this reason it is important for the property manager to understand the basics of investment analysis.
2. Determine the level of market rent for the property and use this estimate to establish contract rents when the lease is signed.
3. Advise the owner on the nature and magnitude of operating expenses.
4. Advise the owner on the tax aspects of the investment decision by analyzing the quantity and quality of maintenance and repair expenditures versus improvement expenditures, and establishing a useful life and salvage value for the property, which can be used in the permissible depreciation scheme.
5. Advise the owner on alternative ways to maximize equity increase through price appreciation by identifying several improvement alternatives and specifying the possible impact on rent receipts.
6. Advise on refinancing and the use of those funds to achieve specified investor objectives such as tax shelter or pyramiding.
7. Advise on the lease provisions, including the rent agreement that will help to fulfill the property owner's investment objectives.

In summary, the property manager can serve as an investment analyst if the property manager has these skills and if the property owner is certain that the manager is capable and competent to give such advice.

Depending on the property owner's personal and investment objectives, a predetermined combination of these property-management services should be identified in a management agreement between the property manager and the property owner. The final package of services depends on the property owner's wishes and the property manager's capabilities. Typically, the investor/property owner makes a decision that he or she does not want to maintain direct responsibility for the various aspects of managing the physical asset, maintaining financial records, marketing the property, selecting tenants, collecting rents, and negotiating leases. A smaller number of property owners turn to the manager for investment consultation. However, in either case, the investor expects that the property manager minimizes the owner's responsibility toward managing and operating the property by providing qualified, competent, efficient, and effective management services.

General Aspects of the Property-Management Function

The full scope of the property manager's responsibility often extends beyond the day-to-day operations of the property and the economic performance of the property. In addition to the services discussed in the previous section, the property manager is also responsible for the supervision and evaluation of personnel who work in and on the subject property. If the property manager is an efficient and effective employee supervisor, operating expenditures can be reduced because of increased labor productivity.

Moreover, the property manager is often considered to possess social responsibilities to the community and neighborhood. The property-management function affects people who work or live in the property, people who live in the immediate area, and the community in which that property is located: (1) The subject property and the property management firm itself are both sources of employment. (2) The subject property provides space for residential, commercial, or industrial activity, which in turn provides both employment opportunities for members of the community and consumer goods and services to the community. (3) The physical condition of the property affects the value of surrounding property.[1] Therefore, the management firm has an ethical and professional responsibility to its clients, the property owners; to the tenants in the space that is being leased; to the neighborhood that is affected by the property's condition; and to the public at large, who may work or conduct business on the property.

SELECTING A PROPERTY MANAGER

The investor/property owner should realize that there are individual differences among people who identify themselves as property managers. An understanding of the differences that can arise among individuals is important in the selection process of a property manager. "Most practitioners in the field of real estate management are property supervisors."[2] The difference between a property supervisor and a property manager lies in the manner in which they view their job, the way in which they operate to discharge their responsibilities, the manner in which they make decisions, and the criteria by which they measure their success. The exact title that these individuals use is less important than the way that they relate to the scope of the assigned responsibilities that are given them by the property owner in the management agreement. In order to reach an understanding of the difference between a property manager and a property supervisor, the property owner must determine whether the individuals are (1) effective as well as efficient in discharging their responsibilities, and (2) whether they are given the authority as well as the responsibility to carry out their assigned tasks.[3]

A basic difference between the property manager and the property supervisor is whether their approach to solving problems concerning the operation of the physical asset ends with an efficient solution or an effective solution. A property supervisor is efficient because he or she seeks solutions to problems. "Given an apartment complex to manage, the property supervisor maintains the structure, collects rents and enforces lease agreements, buys efficiently and approves contracts, hires and supervises the resident manager, and takes care of tenant grievances. He does all this efficiently having learned given solutions to given problems."[4] A property manager, on the other hand, is effective because he or she not only seeks solutions (as does the property supervisor) but also attempts to understand the problems that arise. The property manager wants to know why something happened and then, after reaching an understanding of the causes of the problem, pursues an immediate solution to the problem as well as a technique or process that can be used to handle the problem in the future if it arises. More importantly, the property manager then establishes a procedure that will eliminate the creation of the similar problem. In this sense, the investor/property owner is looking for an individual who not only can solve problems but can establish procedures to minimize their creation. The property manager is an active agent while the property supervisor is a reactive agent. The property supervisor responds to problems as they arise and utilizes a storehouse of knowledge gathered over years of experience or from colleagues to solve given problems, while the property manager attempts to create new or innovative processes to forestall problems.

Another difference between a property manager and a property supervisor lies in the degree of responsibility with which each is charged, and more importantly, whether the necessary level of authority accompanies that responsibility. The property manager's responsibility is stated in the property-management agreement that was signed by the property owner and by the property-management company. However, these responsibilities must be accompanied by the necessary authority to meet the objectives stated by the property owner. The property manager should possess the authority to hire and fire personnel, to issue various maintenance contracts, establish appropriate merchandising procedures and tenant-selection procedures, decide on the role of preventive versus corrective maintenance, establish rent-collection procedures, and negotiate leases. If the property manager does not have this authority, he or she may be frustrated attempting to meet the property owner's stated objectives. For example, if the primary objective is to minimize operating expenditures, the property manager should be given the authority to discharge inefficient workers and to hire workers that can perform the job. Moreover, the property manager should be given the authority to decide on the distribution of funds between preventive and corrective maintenance. If this authority is not granted, repairs can occur only after an item or piece of equipment has broken down; this situation might be the costlier of the two options.

In summary, the investor/property owner is looking for a property manager who can resolve a crisis but does not manage by crisis. The property owner is looking for an individual who anticipates problems, plans ahead, and resolves these potential problems before they occur.

Realizing that these are the personal qualifications that the property owner is seeking in a property manager, the individual chosen must in some way be able to show that he or she is professionally qualified. First of all, a property manager should be a licensed broker and professionally certified through the Institute of Real Estate Management (IREM) or the Building Owners and Managers Institute. The Certified Property Manager (CPM) designation is offered through the Institute of Real Estate Management while the Real Property Administrator (RPA) designation is offered through the Building Owners and Managers Institute International, Inc. When the property owner determines that the individual property manager or the owners of the property-management firm are qualified in this manner, a greater degree of assurance about the provision of competent, effective, and efficient property-management services will exist. However, the property owner should periodically check the quality of services that he or she is receiving in order to determine whether high-quality work is being performed.

If the decision is made to hire a property manager, a principal/agent relationship is formed between the property owner and the property manager. The responsibilities of the manager are offered to the property owner in exchange for a management fee stipulated in the management agreement. This agreement is a written contract that is structured to meet the needs of the property owner, the specific property, and the capabilities of the property manager. There are a number of items that should be covered in this management contract. All the owners of the property and the agent as well as any authorized representatives should be named and should execute the agreement. The commencement date and the term of the contract should be explicitly stated, and there should be a clause that gives the property manager the authority to enter into leasing agreements, maintenance contracts, and employment contracts in the name of the owners.

Focusing on more specific activities, the management contract should contain a clause that outlines the property manager's authority to undertake repairs and maintenance on the structure, to collect rents, to make disbursements for operating expenses, to select tenants, to undertake advertising and merchandising campaigns, etc. In addition, the property manager should insist on a clause that specifies the rate of remuneration for the services performed, and on a clause that identifies the manner and form by which the agreement can be terminated. Also, the property manager should insist on a statement that holds the agent harmless for any liability that arises out of the management of the property. As a rule of thumb, the property manager will need at least a two- or three-year contract in order to fulfill the objectives stated for the property-management function.[5]

SELECTION CRITERIA FOR RESIDENTIAL TENANTS

It is not possible for the property manager to make a complete analysis of every member of a family or household who applies for residential space in the subject property. However, the property manager should obtain information about certain characteristics of the tenant. The purpose of the discussion in this section is to identify a number of criteria that can be used as a basis for tenant selection.[6] Some of these criteria can be supported by available objective data, while other criteria cannot be supported by such data. In this latter event, the property manager must operate subjectively and realize that there is a degree of uncertainty about any conclusions.

Occupancy Period

The property manager should attempt to find tenants whose tenancy will be long term or medium term, but definitely not short term, in nature. Frequent turnover in occupancy generally creates greater than normal expenditures for advertising and "turn-key" operations (fix-up expenses that are routinely performed to the apartment between tenancies). In addition, frequent turnover can lead to a revenue loss because of vacancy periods between tenancies. Therefore, if it is possible, a record of prior occupancies of prospective tenants should be carefully scrutinized by the property manager. This kind of information is generally requested on the tenant application form. However, in many cases the form requests information about only the prior residence, not a history of residence over the past two, three, or five years.

A tenant with a history of short occupancies would, on the surface, appear to be a relatively undesirable tenant. However, there are some mitigating circumstances that the property manager should attempt to discover. The underlying reason for the frequency of moves should be established. The property manager can then judge whether the moves are justified. One general point that the property manager should keep in mind is that the typical household is currently more mobile than in the past. Young adults change jobs frequently, or change geographic locations frequently by transferring within the same company. In these instances, the household does not lose employment but merely uses the job change as a stepping stone to a better or higher paying position. In this event, the property manager would be getting a "good" tenant and would be gambling on the length of occupancy. On the other hand, other tenants may have a history of short occupancies that were welcomed and probably initiated by their previous property managers. In this case, the tenant could have been destructive or noisy. The effective property manager prefers the first group of tenants and avoids the second group of tenants.

Housekeeping Ability

A large portion of building maintenance is a matter of housekeeping. Cleanliness of the tenants' quarters and of the public or common space has a significant impact on the desirability of property to prospective tenants. Consequently, tenants who are good housekeepers are preferred to tenants who are untidy. Moreover, the maintenance expenditures are less in a building with good, clean tenants than it would be under other circumstances. However, the level of a prospective tenant's housekeeping ability is difficult to discern. A rough approximation could be the person's general appearance, but this would not be an accurate or exact measure of the household's attitude toward cleanliness.

Compatibility

The property manager should realize that to a degree the personal happiness of each tenant is dependent upon the compatibility of all tenants in the building. In residential property, the tenants could have some important common characteristics such as income, age, and social background. Three other issues—living habits, household size (which implies the existence of children), and credit—are discussed in the following subsections.

Discrimination and social responsibility   The search for tenant compatibility in residential units should not lead the property manager to make unwarranted assumptions about the need for any form of discrimination. Racial, ethnic, religious, and sexual discrimination in housing is forbidden by law. The property manager is not paid to operate by illegal means. Additionally, discrimination against some specific group may be an inappropriate management tactic and an undesirable social activity. From a management perspective, discrimination against a certain group could increase vacancies if this group is the dominant market segment for the property. In a social context, most advanced societies are committed to providing decent housing in a suitable living environment to its members. (The definition of decent housing is a highly debated issue that is beyond the scope of this text.)

The property manager is charged with managing the subject property in order to meet certain investment objectives. In order to accomplish the end of maximizing rental revenues, the property manager must strive to achieve a high degree of tenant satisfaction, but discrimination on the basis of race, ethnic origin, creed, and sex should not be part of the management plan.

The question of children   "Even the person most sympathetically disposed toward children recognizes the fact that unless controlled, children can be a major source of destruction."[7] Some property owners and property managers have attempted to solve this problem by simply refusing to rent to families with children. This issue relates to the social impact aspect of property management mentioned in the previous subsection. The property manager may be caught between the desires of the owner and the needs of society. In this situation a decision must be made. There are some guidelines that can be used to reach that decision. First of all, certain characteristics of the building can warrant a prohibition against households with young children. For example, the building may contain structural or design characteristics that would be hazardous to a young child, but not to an adolescent or an adult. In this situation, it would seem reasonable to ban households with young children from the property.

As a general tendency, but not necessarily a universal truth, families with children tend to be more stable and permanent than households without children. If the parents are responsible and can control the child so that unnecessary destruction does not occur, the property manager may be able to reduce vacancy losses by renting to families with children.

The existence of children can affect the relationship between the families with children and the other tenants. Families with children may be an irritant to childless couples because of the noise level that is directly related to the existence of children. Yet, possibly, families with children may lead a more orderly and socially conforming life that would not be an irritant to the other tenants. Typically, a family with small children does not play its stereo or television in a loud manner after ten o'clock at night, nor do they have loud, late night parties on weekends.

Finally, the question of market acceptance becomes extremely important for the property manager. The owner of the subject property may wish to impose a ban on households with children in a part of the city, or in a neighborhood where childless couples do not choose to live. In this case, the ban on children, which is the property owner's personal preference, does not make economic sense as a management objective and the property manager should inform the owner of this inconsistency.

Needless to say, the question of renting to households with children is a difficult issue because it involves the rights of the property owner to use his or her property within the limits of the law and it involves the household's right to find adequate, decent housing for itself. These rights are not mutually exclusive.

Living habits   While property managers should certainly believe in the right of the tenant to live life as he or she chooses, the property manager should be concerned when the life style of one tenant jeopardizes the right of privacy for other tenants in the property. Laws tend to protect the sanctity of the home and thereby make it difficult to recover possession of a house or apartment that has been rented to a tenant who subsequently becomes a nuisance to his neighbors. Tenants who do not pay their rent are comparatively easy to evict. On the other hand, legal remedies for deficiencies in deportment and conduct are extremely vague.[8] Consequently, greater emphasis should be placed on obtaining information that could identify the quality of tenants and their life style or living habits.

Credit Rating

The ability to pay rent remains as one of the more important, if not most important, tenant selection criteria. The property manager knows this fact and utilizes his or her judgment regarding necessary credit information about prospective tenants. In the analysis of the prospective tenant's credit rating, the property manager should ascertain the tenant's ability to pay the stipulated rent, and the tenant's stability of employment. A credit check provides information with a greater degree of accuracy about rent-paying ability than about stability of employment. The property manager can make a direct comparison between the tenant's income less outstanding debts, and the ability to pay rent. However, there is no such direct relationship between the name of the tenant's employer, the position the tenant holds in the company, and the stability of the tenant's job. In this case, the property manager must rely on experience and general knowledge of the firm in the area. If the firm is experiencing sales growth, employment in that firm tends to be stable. However, if the firm's sales are cyclical, a reasonable assumption is that the newer employees will be the first to be laid off. This information can prepare the property manager to evaluate the prospects of renting units to new employees in a firm with a highly volatile employment pattern.

THE RESIDENTIAL LEASE

Knowledge of the use and structure of the real estate lease is important in real estate decision making, because many situations require an individual to enter into a lease. The individual may be subject to a lease as a tenant in an apartment or as a tenant in commercial space. As a commercial tenant, the individual may require retail space in a shopping center or office space in an office building. The individual who decides to purchase income-producing real estate will be subject to a lease as the owner or landlord of either residential units or commercial space. Consequently, an individual should be informed of all legal and financial aspects of the lease.

In simple terms, a lease is a legal document that specifies the extent of the rights of ownership that the landlord transfers to the tenant and the responsibilities that each party to the lease incurs. In Chapter 1, the rights of ownership are identified as the rights to use, to possess, to exclude, and to dispose of the property. The rights of the tenant are broadly defined as those aspects of the right to use, to possess, to exclude, and to dispose that are transferred from the property owner to the tenant. The discussion of less-than-freehold estates (also called leasehold estates) explains that the tenant is not given the right to dispose of the property. However, the extent of the transferred rights to use, possess, and exclude is not described in detail. Therefore, the purpose of this section is to expand the discussion of the nature and the extent of the rights of ownership that are transferred from the owner to the tenant when a leasehold estate is established.

As a background for the material presented in this section, the reader should review the description of less-than-freehold estates in Chapter 1. More specifically, the reader should examine the differences among tenancy for years, tenancy from period to period, tenancy at will, and tenancy at sufferance.

The residential lease is a legal document containing the terms and conditions that bind the landlord (the lessor) and the tenant (the lessee) when certain rights of ownership are transferred from the landlord to the tenant. In its conceptual form, the lease contains three major components:

1. The agreement between the landlord and the tenant and the consideration that is exchanged
2. The rights and responsibilities of both the landlord and the tenant as stated in the document or as implied in the body of law pertaining to landlord-tenant relationships
3. Provisions related to other issues that are important to either the landlord, the tenant, or both of them

The Agreement and the Consideration

In the chapter on the sales contract, the terms *agreement* and *consideration* are defined and discussed in relation to the offer and acceptance process in the sales contract. In the execution of a lease for residential space, the offer and acceptance components of the agreement usually take place at a single point in time. The landlord and the prospective tenant reach an agreement within a few minutes. The landlord usually indicates an asking price for the property; the potential tenant makes an offer to the landlord that is equal to the asking price, and the landlord accepts the offer. However, the tenant's offer need not be equal to the landlord's asking price. In this situation the landlord and the prospective tenant enter into a series of counteroffers until an agreement is reached.

The offer made by the tenant must be definite and clear and the acceptance by the landlord must be unconditional. In the negotiation of a residential lease, the delivery and communication process is simplified because both parties are usually in the same room when the negotiation is under way. The execution of a residential lease very seldom involves the services of a third party such as a broker. However, the landlord may hire a property manager to serve as an agent responsible for tenant acquisition and the general management activities associated with the property.

The consideration exchanged between the landlord and tenant is the use of space for a financial payment known as rent. Since the lease is viewed as a contract, the consideration must be clearly stated. The space must be identified in such a way that there is no confusion about its extent. The rent payment must be clearly understood by both parties. The magnitude of the payment and the medium of exchange must be identified. For example, if the amount specified is $250, both magnitude of the rent payment and the medium of exchange (U.S. dollars) are clearly defined. In some situations, the landlord will exchange the use of space for services that the tenant can provide. For example, the tenant might be an accountant or a plumber. The landlord might exchange the use of the apartment for twenty-five hours of the tenant's time per month. In this case, the magnitude of the rent is twenty-five hours and the medium of exchange is professional services.

The lease also includes a statement about when, where, and how the rent payment will be made. In most residential leases, the landlord requires the rent to be paid in advance at the first of the month. If a statement indicating this aspect of the rental payment is not included in the lease, the rent payment is not due until the end of the time period. If the lease is a month-to-month lease, the rent is due at the end of the month. If the lease is a yearly lease, the rent payment is not due until the end of the year. Consequently, the landlord must be certain that the lease specifies when the rent is to be paid. The usual statement requires that the payment be made in advance on the shortest reasonable time period that can be used.[9]

The "where and how" aspects of the rental payment can be stated in a variety of ways. The lease may specify that the rent is due on the first day of each month and must be delivered to the landlord no later than the fifth day of the month. Such a statement gives the tenant the freedom to pay the rent to the landlord or agent in person or to send it by mail. How the rent is paid is usually associated with the medium of exchange. The rent payment is defined in terms of U.S. dollars, but custom dictates that the payment can be in cash or by check. In some instances, the landlord may wish to state that the $250 rental payment is to be delivered in cash, not by check, on the first day of every month in person.

Another aspect of the rent payment that can be covered in a lease is rent concessions. The landlord may wish to give some form of free rent to the tenant. An example is the exchange of an apartment for the tenant's personal services. The landlord may give an apartment free of charge to the building superintendent as partial payment for the superintendent's services. If vacancy rates in the area are high, the landlord may decide not to lower the monthly rent payment, but to provide free rent for a month to individuals who lease space in the building. Any rent concessions to be given by the landlord should be clearly stated in the lease. The magnitude of the concession should be stated, the length of time over which the concession lasts should be identified, and the services to be provided by the tenant should be specified.

The other side of the consideration is the space for which the tenant pays rent. The magnitude and the extent of that space must be identified in the lease. In a lease that pertains to an apartment in a multiunit apartment building, the address of the building and the apartment number might be sufficient as a legal description. However, if any other space besides the apartment is to be provided, this additional space must be specified in the lease. Such space may be basement or attic storage facilities or parking in either reserved or covered spaces.[10]

If the rent payment is made for a single-family detached house, the mailing address is not a sufficient description of the premises.[11] A lease written for a house that is identified by street number generally includes a yard as part of the leasing agreement. However, unless the full extent of the property is defined, confusion can occur about the extent of the yard that is included in the lease. To avoid such confusion, a lease for a single-family detached house should contain the property's legal description. If a legal description is not feasible, the lease should describe the property as clearly as possible. The mailing address of the house and a clear statement about the extent of the surrounding land should be given. If the property is enclosed by a fence, the extent of the land could be stated by using the phrase "the land area enclosed within the wire mesh fence." If the land is not enclosed by a fence, a statement such as "the house and the immediately adjacent half acre" can be used. The latter phrase is still subject to confusion, but it does define the land near the house as part of the rental agreement.

Rights and Responsibilities of Landlord and Tenant

The body of law pertaining to landlord–tenant relationships identifies certain rights and responsibilities of the two parties to the lease. If possible, the exact nature and extent of these rights and responsibilities should be defined and specified within the lease. However, if they are not specified in the lease, the body of law governing landlord–tenant relationships has established precedents that can be used to arbitrate any disagreement between the landlord and the tenant. Seven of these major rights and responsibilities are described hereafter.

Delivery of possession   The first responsibility of the landlord is to deliver possession of the space to the tenant. Each lease must state the period of time during which the landlord promises possession of the space to the tenant. The provision may be stated as "January 1, 1985, through and including December 31, 1985." With such a statement, the landlord promises possession to the tenant beginning with the first day of January. The laws of the states are not in unanimous agreement about the nature of the landlord's promise. In some states the landlord is held responsible for giving the tenant *actual possession* of the premises, whereas in other states the landlord is only responsible for giving the tenant the *right of possession.* The difference between actual possession and the right of possession is important. In states where the tenant is granted actual possession, the landlord is responsible for taking whatever action is necessary to put the tenant into the property on the first of January. If a holdover tenant is still in the property, the landlord must initiate action to remove that tenant. In states where the landlord gives only the right of possession, the tenant is responsible for taking whatever action is necessary to obtain actual possession. To avoid any legal problems, "the tenant, for his own protection, should insist that the lease provide that the landlord would put the tenant in actual possession of the leased premises at the beginning of the term."[12]

If the phrase "actual possession" appears in the lease or if it is part of the legal provisions of the state, the landlord will be in jeopardy if the property is not delivered to the tenant on the first day of the stated term of the lease. To protect against a suit for damages that may arise if actual possession cannot be delivered on time, the landlord would like to insert a clause that postpones the beginning of the term of the lease until the premises have become available. Such a clause eliminates the landlord's risk of being sued for damages but simultaneously ties up the tenant for an indefinite period of time. In this situation, the tenant would have to wait until the property becomes available to execute the agreement that was made. As protection against this indefinite wait, the tenant should insist that the obligation to pay rent does not start until the day of actual possession and should insist on a cutoff date.[13] If actual possession is to be delivered on January 1, the tenant could specify that the lease agreement is voided if the property is not delivered on or before January 15.

Use of the property   Unless the lease restricts the tenant's use of the property, the tenant can use the property for any legal purpose. However, the landlord can place a clause in the lease that restricts the tenant's right to use. "A landlord may, for example, restrict the premises to residential use only, to occupancy by no more than a certain number of persons, to the provision or selling of certain services or goods only, or to any other lawful purpose."[14] Such a restriction will be strictly interpreted by a court. If the restriction is in any way ambiguous, it will be interpreted in favor of the tenant and against the landlord. Consequently, any restrictions on the use of the property should be drafted with great care.[15]

Tenant's right to exclude versus landlord's right of entry   The lease transfers the rights to possess and to use the property from the landlord to the tenant. In general, the tenant's right to use and to possess the property gives the tenant complete control of that property. Anyone who enters the property, including the landlord, without the tenant's consent is considered to be trespassing.[16] This rule, however, is subject to two important exceptions:

1. The law recognizes the landlord's right to enter onto the property in order to collect rent.
2. The landlord can enter the property in order to prevent waste—i.e., anything that is, or could cause, damage to the property, and to stop any nuisance.[17]

If a landlord has sufficient evidence that a water pipe had ruptured or plumbing was leaking in the tenant's property, the landlord could enter the property to repair the pipe or the leak in order to prevent damage to the property. However, in many states, if waste is not being committed, the landlord does not have the right to enter the property without the consent of the tenant, even for repairs. In these states, the landlord's right of entry for general repairs is typically granted through a clause inserted in the lease by the landlord. (The full extent of the landlord's right to repair is described in the next section.) A landlord who wrongly enters the tenant's property can be sued. The suit can take one of three forms: (1) The tenant can sue for nominal damages because, in civil law, the landlord committed a wrongful act. (2) The tenant can obtain an injunction against the trespass if the landlord enters the property on a continuing basis. (3) Because the lease is viewed as a contract, the tenant can sue under contract law, because the landlord has violated one of the provisions of the contract.[18]

Repairs and maintenance   In general, the landlord has not been responsible under common law to maintain and repair the property that was leased to the tenant. This basic rule is expressed by the phrase *caveat lessee,* which translates "let the tenant beware." "In essence, the landlord had no duty to maintain or repair the leased premises either before or after its occupancy. The same general principle was applicable to the tenant. The tenant's only responsibility was to preserve what he or she originally received—that is, to prevent deterioration of the leasehold subject to ordinary wear and tear."[19] However, this basic rule is currently under question in the body of legal knowledge known as landlord–tenant relationships. When the basic rule of "let the tenant beware" was originally devised, the leases were for a uniquely identified and specified piece of property, generally a parcel of agricultural land to be used and occupied by a single tenant. The major component of the leasehold was the land; the improvement or dwelling was incidental. Moreover, the landlord was absent and the tenant, who was in possession, had the tools and skills to maintain and repair whatever structure was on the property. This agrarian situation is drastically different from the current situation involving leased residential property. Today, apartment buildings are inhabited by many tenants who typically have neither the tools nor the skills to even attempt repair and maintenance work. Consequently, "whatever a written lease may provide, neither landlord nor tenant of current urban housing expects a tenant to repair."[20] This legal view, as expressed in many legal cases and the statutes of most states, now imposes an expressed or implied obligation on the landlord to maintain and repair the property that is leased to the tenant.[21] In other words, the current legal view is that the landlord makes an implied warranty of habitability in a lease.[22]

The question of habitability of property is very subjective. At best, the condition of habitability or fitness for living would force the landlord to comply with the housing codes of the locality. However, the specificity of housing codes varies greatly. Depending on the municipality, the codes may contain statements such as the following: "Each dwelling unit must be serviced by hot and cold running water and must contain private toilet and bath facilities." The housing code might specify a prohibition against exposed electrical wiring and unprotected heights such as stairways and balconies. Some codes require heat during cold weather but do not state the minimum temperature that must be provided for each dwelling unit. Finally, some codes specify that the property must be maintained in a clean and sanitary manner, which implies the landlord's responsibility for trash and rubbish removal.

To avoid confusion, the lease should specify the obligations of both the tenant and the landlord to maintain and repair the property. In the case of a single-family detached house, the courts tend to view the tenant as being responsible for repair and maintenance of the property under his or her control if the lease does not specify the landlord's responsibility for making repairs.

In the case of an apartment building, if a lease provision specifying the responsibilities to repair and maintain is lacking, recent court rulings obligate the landlord to make repairs. In addition, the landlord is usually held responsible for the repair and maintenance of the common areas of the apartment building such as its entrances, stairways, and hallways, as well as any structural components of the building such as floors, ceilings, walls, foundation, and roof.

The tenant should be aware of the fact that in some states the common law provisions may still dominate and the recent rulings about implied warranties of habitability may play a secondary role. In such states, the absence of a clause specifying the landlord's responsibilities to maintain and repair leaves the burden of repair upon the tenant. The tenant has the obligation to maintain the property in the same condition as it was at the time possession was taken. This obligation is limited, however, to maintenance and repair that is required as a result of normal wear and tear of the property. Moreover, common law does not require the tenant to perform any structural work that involves improvement of the property or structural replacement of any of its components.[23]

Even in states where the implied warranty of habitability is of primary concern to the courts, the landlord does not have an obligation to improve the property to a condition better than the condition when the tenant took possession. In this case, the landlord is required only to maintain the premises in the condition they were in at the time the lease was signed.[24]

If the lease has a clause stating that the landlord will be responsible for the repairs and maintenance of the property, a landlord's breach of this promise entitles the tenant to make the repairs and to charge the expense of these repairs to the landlord. However, the tenant has this right only after issuing proper notification of the need for repair to the landlord, and after the landlord refuses to make such repairs. The tenant cannot repair the property on the landlord's behalf until the landlord has been given a reasonable opportunity to make the repairs.[25]

If the landlord fails to fulfill the promise to repair, and the tenant undertakes to have the repairs made by a third party, the third party is treated as an agent of the landlord. If the tenant gives the landlord adequate notice of the intention to have the work done by the third party and the landlord agrees, and the work is performed in an appropriate manner, nonpayment for the work in most states could presumably result in a mechanic's lien against the landlord's property.[26] In some other states, the statutes limit the repair expenditures to an amount that does not exceed one month's rent. The tenant may pay for the repair and deduct it from the rent payment.[27]

If a tenant plans to exercise the right to repair at the landlord's expense, the tenant should anticipate objections from the landlord and the possibility of a dispute about the facts of the case. The landlord may deny that there was any need for the repair; the landlord may claim that the need for repair was due to the tenant's negligence; or the landlord may argue that the repairs went beyond the scope of necessary work—that is, the property was improved above and beyond what was required to cure the defect. Therefore, the tenant should make a complete and clear record showing the conditions before the repair work started. Photographs could be used for documentation. In addition, the tenant may require justification from the workers about the level of expenditures and the needed work to forestall the landlord's complaint that the expense was excessive because unnecessary work was performed.[28]

In addition to the right to make the repair and deduct the expense from the rent, or to pass the bill to the landlord, the tenant has other options. If the landlord is obligated to make repairs and does not, the tenant can select one of the following remedies:

1. Vacate the property if it is uninhabitable.
2. Occupy the property without repair and reduce the rent payment proportionately. (This may result in litigation if the tenant reduces the rent in an amount in excess of the actual reduction in value of the leased premises.)
3. Pay the full rent and sue the landlord for decrease in rent value caused by the defects that the landlord has failed to repair.[29]

The tenant should either examine the statutes governing landlord-tenant relationships or seek legal advice on these matters before proceeding with a course of action. The tenant's rights and the landlord's responsibilities differ from state to state.

Liability to third parties   When a third party is injured on the property, the law can hold either the tenant or the landlord liable for the injury depending on the circumstances created by the lease. There are three categories of third parties—invitees, licensees, and trespassers. An invitee is an individual who enters upon the property with either the express or implied consent of the tenant. The invitee enters the property to conduct business with the tenant. In the case of residential property, deliverypersons, mail carriers, and meter readers would be considered invitees. The tenant has a responsibility to keep the property in a reasonably safe condition, and to warn the individual of any condition that might be considered harmful. A licensee also is a person who enters the property with either the expressed or implied consent of the tenant. In the case of residential property, a licensee would be a guest of the tenant. A licensee must be warned of dangerous conditions, and the tenant must refrain from any conduct that might injure the visitor. Finally, the trespasser is an individual who enters the property without the consent of the tenant. A trespasser takes the property as it is. However, the tenant cannot act to create a harmful situation for a trespasser. If the tenant knows that a trespasser enters the property, the tenant must take reasonable care not to cause the trespasser any injury.[30]

The responsibilities of either the landlord or the tenant to invitees and licensees depend on the lease arrangement. If the tenant has leased the entire property, as is the case when a single-family detached house is rented, the tenant bears full responsibility under the law. To guard against a personal-injury suit, the tenant should maintain personal-liability insurance. In this situation, the landlord is responsible only for warning the tenant of any known but hidden dangerous conditions on the property. If the landlord does not warn the tenant of these conditions, and the tenant is injured as a result of the landlord's failure, the landlord is liable for the tenant's injury.[31] The landlord's liability to third persons depends on the relationship between the landlord and such third parties, as well as on the circumstances of the particular case:

> The courts have generally held the landlord liable to third persons where injured as the result of the dangerous or defective condition of real estate leased to a tenant, if the leased real estate is to be used for public purposes. Such real estate as entertainment halls, amusement parks, athletic arenas, wharves, and so forth, would fall into this class. However, the landlord's liability does not extend to all real estate leased for purposes that require that the premises be open to the public. Such real estate as retail stores, restaurants, offices, and so on would be included in this last class.[32]

As a rule, if the tenant leases the entire property, the residential tenant should maintain liability insurance because the property is going to be used for his or her private purposes. The commercial tenant should also maintain liability insurance because the nature of the public use may not free the tenant from liability to an injured party.

If the property is leased to several tenants and the landlord retains possession of the common areas of the structure that are used by the tenants, the courts are in uniform agreement about the landlord's liability. In this case, if the common areas become unsafe because of the landlord's negligence, "the landlord will be liable to persons who are injured as a result of his negligence. The landlord is liable not only to such injured tenants, but also to third parties such as guests of tenants or persons making business calls on the tenants if such persons are injured while lawfully using the passageways, elevators, or other commonly used portions of the premises."[33] In this same situation, the tenant retains responsibility for injuries that occur in the leased apartment or commercial space. Consequently, the tenant should carry liability insurance against personal injury that may occur within the leased area.

Right to assign and sublet   Unless a clause in the lease limits this right, the tenant can assign or sublet his or her rights in the property without the landlord's permission.[34] An **assignment** is a process by which the original tenant transfers his or her *entire* unexpired rights in the leased property to a new tenant. The new tenant steps into the role of the original tenant. In other words, the new tenant who receives the property through an assignment becomes responsible to the landlord for all of the provisions and obligations specified in the lease that were issued to the original tenant. Under the provisions of the lease, the landlord can require the new tenant to pay the rent, to use the property as specified in the lease, and to conform to all other stipulations in the lease. However, if the new tenant does not make the rent payment, the landlord can legally compel the original tenant to make it. In the law, an assignment of leased property does not free the original tenant from the contractual duties imposed in the lease.[35]

Subletting is the process by which the original tenant enters into a separate and distinct lease arrangement with a new tenant. This arrangement between the original tenant and the new tenant does not involve the landlord. Subletting is a transfer of a *portion,* but not all, of the original tenant's rights in the leased property. In other words, a sublet presupposes that the original tenant maintains some portion of the property. This portion can either be physical or temporal. The original tenant subleases some part of the space that was originally leased, or the original tenant subleases some portion of the time remaining in the original lease. For example, the original tenant could sublet one of the bedrooms in a two-bedroom apartment to a friend while retaining possession of the other bedroom, or the original tenant could sublet the entire apartment to a friend for the last three months of a lease. Thus, the process of subletting involves a transfer of only a portion of the original tenant's leased property and does not contain a provision by which the new tenant is directly liable to the landlord.

The distinction between an assignment and a sublet is important for the landlord to understand. It affects the contractual obligations and the landlord's right to sue in case the rent-payment obligation is breached. If the property is assigned, the landlord must first attempt to obtain payment from the new tenant. Only after failing with the new tenant can the landlord sue the original tenant for payment. If the property is sublet, the original tenant is liable for the rent payment without any interruption in the legal process. If the new tenant, the sublessee, fails to make a rent payment, the landlord can sue the original tenant directly. In either event, the ultimate responsibility for the payment of rent and other relevant contractual arrangements is with the original tenant. Subletting, however, is preferred by most landlords because it can minimize the potential legal problems.[36]

Even though the landlord has legal recourse against the original tenant under both the assignment and the sublet, the landlord would like to limit the tenant's right to sublet or assign. To limit this right, the landlord must place a clause in the lease indicating the limitation. Typically the clause states that the original tenant cannot assign or sublet without the landlord's written permission and thus gives the landlord the opportunity to check the new tenant's creditworthiness. The tenant, however, should stipulate within that clause that the landlord cannot withhold consent unless there is a valid reason for doing so.[37] Only the courts can decide what is or is not a valid reason, but a reasonable person would accept the following factors as valid excuses to deny an assignment or a sublet: a history of rent delinquency, present status of unemployment, a history of destructive or disrupting behavior, and any other factors that indicate an inability or a lack of desire to fulfill contractual obligations in the lease.

Clauses Relating Common Points of Concern Between Landlord and Tenant

In addition to the major rights and responsibilities of the landlord and the tenant, the residential lease addresses other matters of concern to the parties to the lease. This section describes the clauses that typically appear in a residential lease to resolve matters of common concern.

Fixtures   As defined in Chapter 1, fixtures are items of personal property attached to the structure so as to become part of the realty. When property is leased, the tenant may choose to attach his/her personal property to the improvement owned by the landlord. Once these items are attached, they are known by the generic name of *tenant's fixtures* or, more specifically, the *tenant's domestic fixtures.* The disposition of these fixtures must be identified in the lease. Specifically, the tenant wants a clause in the lease that allows the removal of these domestic fixtures at the expiration of the lease. If such a clause is included, the landlord should seek protection by requiring that the property be restored to its original form or that the removal shall not damage the property. For example, the tenant who installs bookshelves or installs special lighting fixtures views these items as personal property and wants to remove them at the expiration of the lease term.

The purpose of the fixtures clause is to obtain an understanding with the landlord at the beginning of the lease that items of personal property belonging to the tenant will not be considered as the landlord's fixtures at the expiration of the lease. If the lease expires and the tenant moves out without removing these domestic fixtures at that time, they become the property of the landlord.[38]

Landlord's right to enter to show the property   The landlord does not have the right to enter the property unless it is specified in the lease, or unless the landlord is entering to collect the rent or to stop waste against the property. Due to this prohibition on their right to enter, landlords typically insert a clause into the lease that gives them some rights to show the property to a new tenant before the original lease expires. This clause generally comes into effect only after the original tenant has indicated that the lease will not be renewed.

Typically, the clause contains wording to the following effect:

> The landlord will have the right to show the property to a new or prospective tenant during reasonable hours and upon reasonable notification to the original tenant.

If this clause appears in the lease and the tenant signs the lease, the landlord has a right to enter the property to show the property to a new tenant. A question can arise about reasonable time of day and reasonable notification. Many people shop for residential property after dinner and on weekends. Consequently, the landlord may insist that early evening hours and weekends are reasonable times to show the property. The tenant may contend that these are the most inconvenient times to show the property. Moreover, the landlord may wish to notify the tenant fifteen to thirty minutes before bringing a prospective tenant to view the property. The tenant may rightly claim that reasonable notification is measured in terms of days and not fractions of hours. To prevent hostility and arguments, the landlord and the tenant should define what is meant by reasonable times and reasonable notice in the lease.

Disputes about showing property tend to arise in apartment buildings that have no vacancies. If apartments are vacant, the landlord can show the unoccupied units to prospective tenants and not disturb the current tenants.

Hazard insurance   The owner or landlord must have adequate insurance coverage against hazards such as fire and windstorms. The landlord who rents an entire structure to a single tenant can insert a lease clause requiring the tenant to carry such insurance and to provide adequate proof of the coverage. In the case of an apartment building, the landlord should always carry hazard insurance to cover the entire property.

The tenant who rents space in an apartment building should carry hazard insurance to cover damage to personal property within the leased space. If a fire occurs due to the negligence of another tenant, or the negligence of a visitor to the property, the landlord is typically not viewed as responsible. Consequently, the landlord will not have to compensate the tenant for losses of personal property.

Security deposits   Although most states have enacted the landlord's lien or the landlord's attachment on the tenant's personal property as a security measure to guarantee payment of the rent as specified in the lease, both of these processes are subject to inconvenience, delay, and the cost of enforcing the legal action. Due to the inconvenience and the cost, the practice arose of requiring the tenant to deposit money with the landlord to secure the payment of rent. The **security deposit** is intended to protect the landlord against default in rent payment as well as losses due to the tenant's negligent behavior in relation to the landlord's property. Security deposits are not intended for the landlord's use to repair damages to the property that result from normal wear and tear.[39]

Typically, the security deposit is viewed as a fund established by the tenant to secure the faithful performance of the obligations incurred under the lease. This interpretation entitles the tenant to a return of the security deposit at the termination of the lease. If no damages were caused by negligence on the part of the tenant, the tenant should receive the entire deposit. Disagreement often arises, however, about what is and is not negligent behavior and about what is and is not normal wear and tear. To avoid confusion, a clause can be included in the lease that describes normal wear and tear and negligent behavior. Fraying of carpeting may be considered normal wear and tear, whereas rips and discoloration from spills may be viewed as caused by the tenant's negligent behavior. Knife marks on kitchen counters and damage to the exterior of appliances, such as chips or cracks in the porcelain, could be considered the result of negligent behavior. Discoloration and pitting of new surfaces should be considered normal wear and tear. Holes in the walls are seldom considered normal wear and tear.

Another aspect of the security deposit is the arrangement under which it is held. State laws generally determine the relationship between the landlord and the tenant pertaining to the security deposit. This relationship between the two parties to the lease can take one of three forms:

1. *Debtor-creditor.* In this instance, the security deposit belongs to the landlord, who can use these funds as he or she sees fit. The security deposit does not have to be separated or segregated from the landlord's other assets. This situation provides the least possible protection for the tenant, because the repayment of the security deposit depends on the landlord's personal resources.

2. *Trustee-beneficiary.* In this situation, the landlord receives the funds for the security deposit and has those funds in her or his possession. However, a fiduciary responsibility is created that requires the landlord to maintain these funds for the benefit of the tenant and to account for any

misuse of the funds. In this relationship, the landlord is required to act in the tenant's best interest with regard to the security deposit.

3. *Pledgor-pledgee.* In this case, the security deposit is given to the landlord, remains in the landlord's possession, but legally belongs to the tenant. The landlord must keep these funds separate from his or her personal assets and may not use them for private purposes. This is a more suitable arrangement for the tenant because the security deposit will always be available, regardless of the landlord's financial position.[40]

In states where the security deposit is considered a pledge or a trust, the landlord must exercise prudence and due care in protecting the security deposit. However, the landlord is not liable for its loss or any reduction in the value of the funds as long as prudence and due care are exercised.[41] Typically, in these states, the landlord discharges this obligation by establishing a separate bank account for the funds. The bank account is probably an interest-bearing account, but the majority of states do not require that the landlord pass these interest payments on to the tenant. In those few states that do require the landlord to pay interest to the tenant for the security deposit, the interest payment is some nominal amount such as 3 percent, substantially below the rate paid on interest-bearing savings accounts.

Utility payments   Responsibility for utility payments must be settled in the lease. In some instances, the landlord pays all utilities such as electricity, natural gas, water, and trash collection. In other situations, the landlord provides trash collection and water, but requires the tenant to pay for electricity and heating of the apartment. The arrangement should be specified clearly in the lease.

Notification of renewal   A lease provision commonly included by the landlord requires the tenant to provide written notice of the intention to renew the lease. The clause typically states that the tenant must inform the landlord sixty or thirty days before the expiration of the current lease of an intention to renew the lease. In addition, the clause could state that the landlord has the right to change the conditions of the new lease. This provision enables the landlord to either increase rent or change the utility payment plans or some other aspect of the lease when the lease is renewed.

Transfer clause   The tenant is responsible for fulfilling the provisions of the lease even if the tenant is transferred to a new job in a new locality. To avoid this jeopardy, the tenant should insist on a clause providing a release of the lease obligations if a relocation takes place. The transfer clause usually stipulates that the tenant's responsibilities terminate if a new job is taken that is fifty, seventy-five, or some other reasonable number of miles away from the residential unit for which the lease is written.

Miscellaneous rules and regulations   In addition to the preceding specific clauses, the typical lease contains a section stating various rules and regulations that the landlord wishes to impose. For example, this section of the lease might contain the following statements:

1. No pets allowed on the premises.
2. Children are not allowed to congregate in the common hallways and passageways of the building.
3. Tenants will refrain from playing stereos, radios, or TV's in a loud manner after 10:00 P.M.
4. The laundry room must be used for doing laundry, but only during the hours from 9:00 A.M. to 9:00 P.M.
5. Each tenant must park in the assigned parking space for the apartment.

These rules and regulations specify the landlord's preferences about the behavior pattern of the individual tenants in an apartment building. The landlord's concern is to establish a code of behavior that maximizes the benefits to be received by all individuals living in the building. Consequently, each individual may have to be restrained from performing actions of pure self-interest that he or she finds beneficial or enjoyable. For example, one tenant may prefer to do the laundry at 2:00 A.M. but in so doing would disturb other tenants. The rule for use of the laundry room facilities is designed to benefit the community and not the individual.

Consumer Issues in the Landlord-Tenant Relationship

The residential lease agreement is affected by many consumer-oriented matters. One is the issue of implied habitability. As explained in the section on rights and responsibilities of landlord and tenant, the courts currently hold that the landlord makes an implied warranty that the residential property will conform to minimum acceptable standards of livability. This section examines other consumer-oriented issues that affect the landlord-tenant relationship.

Limits imposed on the landlord's right to select tenants   Under common law, the landlord had the right to rent property to whomever he or she pleased. This rule implied the right to refuse to rent to specific individuals and to refuse lease renewals to specific tenants. Currently, court decisions and statutes are beginning to impose limits on these rights. The federal and state fair housing acts expressly forbid the landlord to use race, ethnic origin, creed, or sex as a basis for a decision to issue a lease or renew a lease on property. However, the landlord still retains the right to make decisions based on creditworthiness, which can reflect employment history, promptness of discharging financial responsibilities, and adequacy of the prospective tenant's income level to meet the rent obligation. In some instances, the landlord is required to show cause for nonrenewal of leases and even to show cause of the need for a rent increase. The latter cases typically involve housing constructed with federal subsidies or financing.[42]

Landlord's duty to protect the tenant from criminal acts   Traditionally, the landlord did not have a responsibility or duty to protect the tenant from criminal acts committed by third parties. However, under the notion that a lease is a contract for the use and possession of space, the courts are beginning to place this responsibility on the landlord. This new rule is especially applicable if the landlord advertises that security protection is being offered in the building. In other instances, the courts have held the landlord liable for security protection when the condition of the property was such that it facilitated the criminal act. For example, a landlord was held liable for losses due to burglary because adequate locks were not furnished for the apartments. A landlord was held liable for losses due to robbery in a common area of a building because the tenant, who was the victim, showed that the landlord had failed to provide adequate lighting.[43]

Tenant's right to withhold rent   Traditionally, the landlord had the right to evict the tenant for nonpayment of rent. However, the courts are recognizing that a lease contains an implied warranty of habitability. In general, this means that the property is free from building and housing code violations. Some states allow the tenant to withhold all or part of the rent on the premise that the building or apartment is not habitable. Another remedy is the rent escrow whereby the tenant makes the rent payment to a third party, such as the court or a trustee. The third party holds the rent until the violations are corrected and the building is once again habitable. In some instances, the third party is given the right to use the rental proceeds to make the repairs needed to fulfill the landlord's obligation to provide adequate living space.[44]

Tenant's promise to comply with legal requirements affecting the property   A lease typically requires that the tenant comply with all statutes, ordinances, and rules that are applicable to the property. In addition, the lease holds the tenant responsible for the correction and elimination of any nuisances and hazards that might be created by direct or indirect actions of the tenant. The legal interpretation of this requirement does not relate directly to the physical structure. The law does not hold the tenant responsible for structural changes to comply with statutes and ordinances; such compliance is viewed as the landlord's responsibility.[45] Rather, the tenant must comply with statutes and ordinances that affect the use of the property, for example, the zoning ordinance and the safety and health aspects of the housing code.

A lease can be written in which the tenant does assume responsibility for making the physical property conform to legal requirements. In this situation, the lease would provide that the tenant incur the financial obligation to make the structure comply with all legal requirements affecting the property. However, such arrangements are uncommon in residential property leases; they are more prevalent in long-term leases on other types of property.

Tenant unions   The single tenant in a multiunit apartment building has very little bargaining power with the landlord. To establish countervailing power, tenants have organized into unions for the purpose of bargaining with landlords. Tenant unions typically bargain with the landlord on such key issues as:

1. The negotiation of a new lease to be used between all of the individual tenants and the landlord. In this case, the negotiation can cover the level of rent, the quality of services, and any and all other clauses within the lease.

2. The development of a procedure to handle tenant complaints and to arbitrate disputes between the landlord and the tenants.
3. Formulation of a mutually satisfactory way to bring the building into compliance with housing codes, and to establish measures to provide adequate security for both the persons and the property in the dwelling units and the common areas.[46]

Evaluating the Residential Lease

Both the tenant and the landlord must approach a lease seriously and with full knowledge of the consequence of each of the clauses. Moreover, the body of law affecting leases obligates the parties to a lease to certain types of activity and responsibilities, even if those matters are not specified in the document.

The legal document known as a residential lease is not standardized. Even though printed forms of the lease are available in every community, two different landlords who own adjacent properties can use different printed forms. Consequently, the consumer should not assume that all printed forms used in the community contain the same stipulations. Each lease should be read and understood. Both parties to the lease should fully understand the rights they wish to retain, the responsibilities they are willing to incur, and the obligations they would like to impose on the other party to the contract. Exhibit 14-1 is one printed form of a residential lease. The reader can evaluate this sample lease by indicating in the margin which clauses are included and which clauses are not included in the form.

The discussion of the residential lease presented in this section of the chapter covers the major aspects of this legal document that most commonly affect the typical landlord and tenant. In addition, certain highly specialized or special-purpose clauses can be used in a residential lease.

TERMINATION OF LEASES

Leases can be terminated in a multitude of ways. Both the tenant and the landlord should understand the types of lease terminations and their effects.

Expiration of the Term of the Lease

The most usual way for a lease to terminate is by the expiration of the mutually agreed period of tenancy. At that point in time, the tenant surrenders possession and use of the property to the landlord, and the landlord regains the leasehold estate and consequently has all the rights of ownership in the property.

Mutual Agreement to Terminate

The lease may terminate before its expiration date if the landlord and tenant agree to its termination. For example, the tenant may hold a lease on the property for a definite period of time (a tenancy for years) and may find during the term of the lease

EXHIBIT 14-1   Courtesy of Miller's Book and Office Supply Company.

APARTMENT LEASE

GEORGIA,
County

THIS AGREEMENT, made and entered into this_____day of_____

Nineteen Hundred and_____between_____

_____of the first part,

hereinafter called Lessor, and_____

of the other part, hereinafter called Lessee,

WITNESSETH: That the said lessor does this day lease unto said lessee, Apartment

No._____of the building of the lessor situated at_____

Known as_____, in the City of   , to be used and occupied by

the lessee as residence, and for no other use or purpose whatsoever, for the term of_____

beginning on the_____day of_____and ending on the_____day

of_____, at and for the agreed monthly rental of_____

_____Dollars, payable on the first day of each and every

month during the term, in advance, to_____

_____, or at any such other place and to such other person as the lessor may

from time to time designate in writing.

The following express conditions are a part of this lease, and are assented to by the lessee:

FIRST. The lessee shall not assign this lease, nor sublet the premises, nor any part thereof, nor use the same, or any part thereof, or permit the same, or any part thereof, to be used for any other purpose than as above stipulated, nor make any alterations therein, or additions thereto, without the written consent of the lessor; and all additions, fixtures, or improvements which may be made by lessee, except movable household furniture, shall become the property of the lessor, and remain upon the premises as a part thereof, and be surrendered with the premises at the termination of this lease.

SECOND. All personal property placed in the premises above described shall be at the risk of the lessee or owner, and lessor shall not be liable for any damages to said personal property, or to the lessee, arising from the bursting or leaking of water or steam pipes, or from any act of negligence of any co-tenant or occupants of the building, or of any other person whomsoever.

THIRD. Lessor will furnish the premises hereby leased without charge to lessee during the proper seasons and during reasonable hours, with steam heat for heating said premises, and lessor will also furnish during reasonable hours, hot and cold water free of charge; the reasonable hours to be determined by the lessor. But in the event the heating apparatus shall need repairs, or if from other causes beyond the control of the lessor, including federal or municipal control, shortage of quantity or inferior quality, it should be necessary to cut off, reduce or stop the same, the lessor shall not be liable for any damage of any sort whatsoever arising out of its failure to furnish such heating or water service, as lessor may determine. Should any of the electrical equipment, belonging to the premises, become unserviceable, the lessor shall have a reasonable time, after notification, to determine the responsibility, and have same repaired, without any liability to the lessee for damage or inconvenience.

FOURTH. In the event the leased premises are destroyed or rendered untenantable by fire, storm, earthquake or other casualty not caused by the negligence of the Lessee, this lease shall be at an end from such time except for the purpose of enforcing rights which may have then accrued hereunder. The rental shall then be accounted for between the Lessor and the Lessee up to the time of such injury or destruction of said premises, the Lessee paying up to said date and the Lessor refunding the rents collected beyond such date.

Should any part of said premises be rendered untenantable by any of said agencies, the rental shall abate in the proportion which the injured part bears to the whole leased premises, and such part so injured shall be restored by the Lessor, at his option, as speedily as practicable, when the full rent shall recommence and the lease continue according to its terms.

FIFTH. The prompt payment of the rent for said premises upon the dates above named, and the faithful observance of the rules and regulations printed upon this lease, and which are hereby made a part of this covenant, and of such other and further rules and regulations as may be hereafter made by the lessor, are the conditions upon which the lease is made and accepted; and any failure upon the part

EXHIBIT 14-1 (continued)

of the lessee to comply with the terms of said lease, or of any of said rules and regulations now in existence, or which may be hereafter prescribed by the lessor, shall, at its option, work a forfeit of this contract and of all of the rights of the lease thereunder; and thereupon the lessor, its agents or attorneys, shall have the right to re-enter said premises and remove all persons therefrom forcibly or otherwise; and the lessee hereby expressly waives any and all notice required by law to terminate tenancy and also waives any and all legal proceedings to recover possession of said premises; and expressly agrees that a violation of any of the terms of this lease, or of said rules and regulations now in existence, or which may hereafter be made, said lessor, its agents, or attorneys may immediately re-enter said premises and dispossess lessee without legal notice or the institution of any legal proceedings whatsoever.

SIXTH. The lessor or any of his agents shall have the right to enter said premises during all reasonable hours, to examine the same, or to make such repairs, additions or alterations as may be deemed necessary for the safety, comfort or preservation thereof, or of said building, or to exhibit the said premises, and put and keep upon the doors or windows thereof a notice "FOR RENT" at any time within thirty (30) days before the expiration of this lease. The right of entry shall likewise exist for the purpose of removing placards, signs, fixtures, alterations or additions, which do not conform to this agreement, or to the rules and regulations of the building.

SEVENTH. Lessee agrees to maintain said premises in the same condition, order and repair as they are at the commencement of said term, excepting only reasonable wear and tear arising from the use thereof under this agreement, and to make good to said lessor, immediately upon demand, any damage to the heating or water apparatus, or electric lights or wires, or any fixtures, appliances or appurtenances of said premises, or of the building, caused by act or neglect of lessee, or any person or persons in the employ or under the control of the lessee.

EIGHTH. Lessee hereby waives and renounces for self and family any and all homestead and exemption rights they may have now, or hereafter, under or by virtue of the Constitution and laws of the State of Georgia, or of any other State, or of the United States, as against the payment of said rental, or any portion thereof, and should the rental herein specified be collected by law or an attorney at law the lessee herein agrees to pay all court costs and 20% attorney's fees.

NINTH. If said Lessee shall abandon or vacate said premises before the termination of this lease or any renewal thereof, the same or any part thereof may be re-let by said Lessor for such rent and upon such terms as said Lessor may see fit, and if full rental hereinbefore named shall not thus be realized, the said Lessee hereby agrees to pay all deficiency, including any expense incurred by such re-letting.

TENTH. The parties hereto agree that the said Agent, its successors, representatives or assigns, in consideration of services rendered in procuring this contract and of services to be rendered under the same shall, if the monthly rental rate exceeds $20.00, have one-fourth (¼) of the first month's rent collected in cash, and for the remaining months five per centum (5%) of the gross rentals to arise hereunder, or any renewals thereof; should the monthly rental rate be $20.00 or less, the commission shall be ten per centum (10%) of the gross rentals to arise hereunder. The commission is now by the lessor, with the assent of the lessee, assigned to said Agent, its successors, representatives or assigns. Any person who may acquire an interest in said premises shall take notice hereof and be bound hereby.

ELEVENTH. This lease is for the term hereinbefore stated and is to be considered re-newed from term to term thereafter unless a written notice to the contrary is given by either party to the other at least sixty (60) days prior to the expiration of the term of any existing re-newal thereof.

IN WITNESS WHEREOF, The parties have hereunto affixed their hands in duplicate, the day and year first above written.

Signed, sealed and delivered in the presence of

EXHIBIT 14-1 (continued)

RULES AND REGULATIONS

Which are Referred to in the within Lease and made a part thereof

1. The sidewalks, entry passages, halls, public corridors and stairways shall not be obstructed by tenants, or used by them for any purpose other than those of ingress or egress.

2. The floors, skylights and windows that reflect or admit light into any place in said building shall not be covered or obstructed by tenants. The water closets, and other water apparatus, shall not be used for any other purpose than those for which they were constructed, and no sweepings, rubbish, rags, ashes, or other substances shall be thrown therein. Any damage resulting to them, or to steam heating apparatus from misuse, shall be borne by the tenant who, or whose servants, shall cause it.

3. No tenant shall do, or permit anything to be done, in said premises, or bring or keep anything therein, which shall in any way increase the rate of fire insurance on said building or on property kept therein, or obstruct or interfere with the rights of other tenants, or in any way injure or annoy them, or conflict with the laws relating to fires, or with the regulations of the Fire Department, or with any insurance policy upon said building or any part thereof, or conflict with any of the rules and ordinances of the Board of Health.

4. Tenants, or servants shall maintain order in the building, shall not make or permit any improper noises in the building, smoke tobacco in the corridors or interfere in any way with other tenants, or those having business with them.

5. Nothing shall be thrown by the tenants, or servants, out of the windows or doors, or down the passages or skylights of the building.

6. All tenants and occupants must observe strict care not to leave their windows open when it rains; and for any default or carelessness in these respects, or any of them, shall make good any injury sustained by other tenants, and to the lessor for damage to paint, plastering, or other parts of the building, resulting from such default or carelessness.

7. No painting shall be done, nor shall any alterations be made, to any part of the building by putting up or changing any partition or partitions, door or doors, window or windows, nor shall there be any nailing, boring or screwing into the woodwork or plastering, without the consent of the lessor or his agents.

8. All glass, locks and trimmings in or upon the doors and windows, respectively, belonging to the building, shall be kept whole, and whenever any part thereof shall be broken, the same shall be immediately replaced or repaired, and put in order under the direction and to the satisfaction of the lessor, or his agents, and shall be left whole and in good repair, together with the same number and kind, or kinds, of keys, as may be received by such tenant on entering upon possession of any part of said building or during the tenancy.

9. No additional locks to be put upon any door without the consent of the lessor, and any and all locks placed on any door to remain for the benefit of the lessor.

10. Tenants, at the termination of their lease of the premises, to return all keys of doors and water closets.

11. If lessee desires awnings outside or shades inside the windows, to be erected at lessee's expense, they must be of such shape, color, material and make as may be prescribed by the lessor.

12. Servants will be permitted to have ingress and egress through servants' entrances only except nurses when with children

13. No marketman will be allowed to pass through the main hall, and market supplies, etc., must be delivered through the servants' entry only.

14. Heating apparatus and light fixtures in halls and stairways and porch are under the exclusive control of the janitor.

15. All garbage or refuse must be sent down to the basement from apartments at such times as required by janitor of the building. Tenants to provide garbage cans satisfactory to the lessor.

16. When practical, tenants will be required to have their household goods brought into and taken out of the building through the rear entrance.

17. The front porches are not common property for all tenants. Each tenant must confine his or her use of said porches to that portion directly in front of their respective apartments.

18. All reports of repairs or any irregularities must be made in writing to our office.

19. The lessor reserves the right to make such other and reasonable rules as in his judgment may from time to time be needed for the safety, care and cleanliness of the premises, and for the preservation of good order therein.

20. No animals, birds, bicycles or other vehicles shall be allowed in the corridors, hall, elevators or elsewhere in the building and the agent reserves the right to remove any and all objections and nuisances, and the failure on the part of the agent to remove same promptly does not constitute a waiver in this regard.

21. All victrolas, pianos, radio horns, and other musical devices must discontinue at eleven o'clock p. m. No saxophones or band instruments shall be practiced on at any time nor will the giving of music lessons, vocal or instrumental, be permitted in the building.

22. The management cheerfully concedes the tenants' right to have parties, or a large number of guests, but in so doing shall insist that perfect order prevail, and that boisterous conduct be avoided. A continued violation of this regulation will, at the option of the lessor, void this lease.

23. Dogs and cats are strictly prohibited in this building.

24. If any of the above agreements or covenants are broken, said lease may be cancelled immediately as though tenant were holding over for non-payment of rent, at the option of the lessor, or his agents.

25. As many keys for outside doors or mail-boxes will be furnished as lessee desires. A deposit of fifty cents (50c) per key is required. Said deposit to be refunded when keys are returned to lessor or his agents.

26. The lessor reserves the right to make such other and reasonable rules and regulations as in his judgment may from time to time be needed for the safety, care and cleanliness of the premises, and for the preservation of good order therein.

27. Special stipulations.

that it would be beneficial if the full lease term were not enforced. In this event, the tenant approaches the landlord and asks to be relieved of the responsibilities and obligations specified in the lease. The landlord may choose to allow the tenant to vacate the property and thus regains possession of the leasehold. In this case, the lease has terminated because both the landlord and the tenant have agreed that it should. A more obvious example of a lease termination by mutual agreement is a lease based on the concept of tenancy at will.

The process of mutual agreement is also known as the process of *surrender and acceptance.* The tenant offers to surrender the property to the landlord, and the landlord accepts the property. The process of surrender is different from abandonment. A lease does not automatically terminate when the tenant walks away or abandons the leasehold estate; in this case, the tenant is still legally liable for the unpaid portion of the rent through the expiration date of the lease.

Merger of the Freehold and Leasehold Estates

A lease can terminate if the tenant purchases the property. In this case, the owner of the leasehold estate becomes the owner of the freehold estate, thereby canceling the lease.

Breach of Covenants

A breach of the conditions of the lease by either party can bring about its termination. When a tenant breaches the conditions of the lease, the landlord has many alternatives. First, if the breach is nonpayment of the rent, the landlord can sue for the rent that is in default. In addition, the landlord may have to institute legal action to regain possession of the property. Some states include these two legal actions in one suit and other states require separate legal actions for rent recovery and for recovery of possession.[47] This type of termination enables the owner to regain possession of the property, but does not end the tenant's obligation. When the landlord takes possession—or more accurately, regains possession—he or she should take possession as an agent of the tenant. This legal distincton allows the landlord to hold the original tenant liable for the rent while searching for a new tenant to place in the property.[48]

If the breach of contract involves nonpayment of rent or retaining possession of the property at the end of the term (tenancy at sufferance), the landlord is allowed in most states to undertake an action known as a *summary proceedings* or a **dispossession proceedings.** The landlord petitions the court in the local jurisdiction to regain possession of the property. The landlord files a statement that describes the tenancy and sets forth the breach of contract that occurred. The court evaluates the petition, gives the tenant an opportunity to respond, and then evaluates the case. If the tenant fails to respond or if the court rules against the tenant, a court order is issued to the tenant to vacate the property. In some states, this court order is known as a summons and in others it is a warrant or a notice. If the tenant does not peaceably leave the property after the court order has been issued, a local public official or a marshall may forcibly remove the tenant.

State laws governing the type of breach that establishes a dispossession summary proceedings vary greatly. In some states, the actions causing a breach are specified. In these states, the breach usually involves a major condition or agreement in the lease, such as holding over and nonpayment of rent. In some states, a breach of the lease can be caused by an unapproved use of the property. This violation of the use agreement can also be grounds for a summary proceedings. In some states, a breach of the tenant's financial obligations to pay real estate taxes, hazard insurance, repairs/maintenance, or other such financial items can serve as the basis for a summary proceedings. In other states, a breach of any clause in the lease can serve as the grounds for summary proceedings.[49]

If summary proceedings cannot be instituted against the tenant, the landlord must enter into a longer and more expensive legal action to remove the tenant. To avoid such action, the landlord can attempt to draw the lease agreement in such a way that all breaches are brought into the class for which summary or dispossession proceedings can be obtained. In states that identify only a breach of the rent obligation as grounds for a summary proceedings, the landlord could include a clause in the lease stating that any payment the tenant must make for utilities, repairs/maintenance, insurance premiums, or real estate taxes can be made by the landlord in the event that the tenant does not pay those bills, and thus such payment would be considered "additional rent." Failure by the tenant to pay these financial obligations would enable the landlord to petition the court for a summary proceedings instead of a more lengthy and costly legal action for ejection.

A landlord may breach the contract by depriving the tenant of use or possession of the entire leased property or a substantial portion of that property by either a positive act or a default. This action or default, which must be intentional and permanent, is known as a **constructive eviction** by the landlord. It occurs when the tenant's use of the property is restricted or disturbed, either by the landlord's direct action or by his or her failure to act when there is a duty to act. Examples of acts that can be viewed as constructive eviction are demolition of a stairway or access point to the property that is leased, failure to repair an elevator that serves the leased property, failure to repair and maintain the property in conformity with housing codes and the warranty of implied habitability, failure to provide heat on cold days, permitting the property to be infested with vermin, and not repairing clogged sewage pipes that cause noxious odors and can be a health hazard.[50]

A breach of the lease by either the tenant or the landlord can lead to an eviction. If the tenant fails to meet the contractual obligations, the landlord undertakes **eviction** or ejection action known as dispossession proceedings. If the landlord breaches an express covenant or an implied covenant, his or her action or default can lead to a reduction in the tenant's ability to use or inhabit the property—that is, to a constructive eviction.

SPECIAL-PURPOSE CLAUSES IN A RESIDENTIAL LEASE

Neither the landlord nor the tenant expects an apartment building to be damaged, destroyed, or condemned under eminent domain proceedings. The typical assumption is that if such events occur the tenant will meet the obligations of the lease and neither default nor abandon the leased property. However, clauses can be placed in the lease to identify the tenant's responsibilities in such cases. Other clauses can be used to cover situations in which a landlord intends to use the property as collateral for a loan, or intends to sell the property.

Damage or Destruction of the Structure

The residential lease can make provisions for the possibility that the structure can be damaged or destroyed. In common law, when land and a building were leased by the landlord to the tenant, the tenant was not freed of the responsibility to pay rent if the improvement was destroyed. However, a large number of states have abolished this unrealistic rule. In such states, if the building is destroyed or is damaged to such an extent that it is not usable by the tenant, the tenant is relieved of liability to pay the rent.[51]

To avoid any confusion, the lease should clearly state the tenant's and the landlord's responsibilities in the event that the property is destroyed or damaged. The provisions in the lease should specify

☐ Rent payment adjustments
☐ The right of the tenant to terminate the lease in case of substantial damage
☐ The time period allowed for the landlord to make repairs
☐ The tenant's right to terminate if the repairs are not made in a timely manner
☐ The degree or nature of the repairs

A provision for reduced rent while repairs are being made would enable the tenant to remain in the property after it is damaged. A clause requiring repairs to be completed within a specified time period would allow the tenant to be excused from the lease if the repairs were not done promptly. The landlord could stipulate that the property will be repaired only to the same quality level as before the damage.

The clause covering damage and destruction is very difficult to write. It must encompass many factors and anticipate numerous situations. The lease can easily provide for fire damage to an apartment or for water damage from firefighting efforts in another apartment, but what happens when fire destroys an elevator system in a high-rise apartment building? The penthouse apartment is not damaged by the fire, but the tenant no longer has the same degree of accessibility as before the fire. What rights does this tenant have to adjust the rent, terminate the lease, or expect timely completion of repairs?

Such contingencies can be considered in the lease, but the agreement will be difficult to reach. The tenant will want to stipulate a rent reduction to compensate for reduced accessibility, even though the apartment is not damaged by the fire. Moreover, the tenant would want the repairs performed immediately. The landlord, however, would not want to reduce rents because this financial loss is generally not insurable, or, if it is, the premium would increase. The landlord would also like a reasonable amount of time to perform the repairs so that the work can be handled as normal business by the contractor and not as a special rush job requiring overtime on premium pay scales for the workers.

Condemnation Procedures Against the Property

The landlord could include a clause in the residential lease that would automatically terminate the lease on the day the property is taken by eminent domain proceedings. If this termination clause does not appear in the lease, the tenant may have a legal claim to some portion of the proceeds that the landlord obtains from the condemnation. The lease passes the rights of use, possession, and exclusion from the landlord to the tenant. The process of condemnation takes these rights from the tenant and, consequently, the tenant can claim compensation for the loss of these rights of ownership. To avoid any such legal problems with a short-term residential lease, the landlord wants the tenant's rights of use, possession, and exclusion to terminate on the day of condemnation. For long- and medium-term commercial leases, the problems created by condemnation are more significant.

Landlord's Right to Mortgage the Property

When a lease is signed, the tenant's rights in the property are subordinated to any mortgages or other liens currently recorded against the property. However, once the lease is executed, a new mortgage with the property as collateral would be subordinate to the lease. To avoid this situation, the landlord could put a clause in the lease that would make the tenant's rights subordinate to a new mortgage. Such a clause stipulates that the tenant allows the landlord to increase the value of the existing mortgage, to refinance the current mortgage, or to take out another mortgage against the property, and that any of these liens is superior to the lease.

Abandonment of the Property by the Tenant

Residential leases can provide for the contingency of abandonment of the premises by the tenant before the expiration date of the lease. The lease can state that the tenant continues to be liable for the rent until expiration of the lease. In this situation, if the landlord is able to find a new tenant, the original tenant is relieved of responsibility when the new lease is signed. However, if the new tenant is obtained at a rent level that is less than the contract rent stipulated on the original lease, the original tenant is still liable for the difference. In some states, the original tenant who abandons the property is automatically released from liability when the landlord finds a new tenant and a new lease is signed. In other states, the original tenant is not relieved of liability unless the landlord gives notice of intention to relieve the original tenant of the responsibility to pay the rent.[52] Sometimes the landlord is allowed to charge the expenses of advertising and redecorating the property against the original tenant.[53]

The responsibilities of the landlord in the case of abandonment are also not clear. Some states put the landlord under an obligation to seek a suitable tenant to replace the original tenant. Other states do not require that the landlord actively pursue a new tenant. In this situation, however, the courts compel the landlord to accept a suitable tenant to replace the one who abandoned the property.[54] This is not a harsh rule because in the ordinary course of events the landlord would prefer to rent the property to a suitable replacement than to leave the property vacant. "Rent collections from an existing tenant are money in the landlord's hands, whereas the liability of the previous tenant is a doubtful asset."[55]

Default by the Tenant

If a tenant fails to pay the mutually agreed upon rent, the tenant is in default of the lease provisions. In this case, the landlord has several remedies against the tenant. Depending on the legal jurisdiction in which the property is located, any or all of these remedies may apply. First, the statutes may create a lien on the tenant's personal property and financial assets. If the statutes do not create the lien, it can be created by inserting a clause into the lease.[56]

Second, a provision in common law known as *distraint* or *distress* allows the landlord to seize the tenant's property as security for the payment of rent. The landlord's right of distraint applies only when the tenant is in default, and it can be exercised only against the tenant's personal property that is on the leased property. However, if the tenant removes personal property after the default occurs, the landlord has the right under this common-law concept of distraint to seize the tenant's personal property no matter where it is found.[57]

Exercise of the right of distraint can lead to physical injury and bodily harm for either the tenant or the landlord. To eliminate this possibility, many jurisdictions have enacted legal proceedings to substitute a fair, judicial process for what often have been inequitable and oppressive methods used by the landlord in the process of distraint. This third remedy is typically known as the *landlord's attachment.* It enables the landlord legally to obtain the tenant's property as security against the eventual repayment of the rent while the courts are evaluating the merits of the landlord's claim.[58]

Sale of the Property

If the landlord sells or gives away the property, the new owner accepts that property subject to the rights of the tenant. The new landlord remains responsible for fulfilling all the landlord's obligations as stipulated in the lease, unless the lease specifically includes a clause relieving the new landlord of such liability.[59] This requirement is legally binding in the majority of states; however, the tenant should either insist on a clause to this effect in the lease or obtain legal opinion as to whether or not this stipulation is enforceable in the state in which the property is located.

If a new owner's rights are subordinate to the leasehold in the local jurisdiction, many landlords will place a clause in the lease that cancels the lease in the event that the property is sold. This clause obviously works to the benefit of the landlord.

Without such a clause, the buyer would have to purchase the property subject to or subordinate to the existing lease. The new owner's ability to control the property and the tenant-selection process would be reduced. This situation is not a major problem in short-term residential leases, but could be detrimental in longer-term commercial leases.

CHAPTER SUMMARY

Knowledge of the scope of services that can be provided by the property manager is important information for the investor/property owner. It provides the basis for making a decision about the management of the subject property after it is purchased. The full scope of property-management services consists of managing the physical asset, the financial records, the tenant-selection process, the lease negotiation process, and the financial asset as an investment.

Knowledge of the real estate lease is important in real estate decision making, both to the tenant in residential space and to the equity investor in income-producing property. Each party to a lease has certain rights and responsibilities relating to the delivery of possession, the use of the leased property, responsibility for maintenance and repair, liability for personal injury, the right to enter the property, and the right to assign or sublet the lease. Both parties to the lease must be concerned and informed about their legal responsibilities and their rights in these matters.

In addition to these rights and responsibilities, the residential lease contains numerous clauses pertaining to matters of mutual concern to the landlord and the tenant. In a residential lease the two parties must reach an agreement about the tenant's fixtures, the landlord's right to show the property, the necessity to maintain hazard and liability insurance, the disposition of security deposits, notification of renewal, payment of utilities, and termination of the lease due to the tenant's transfer from the area. In a commercial lease, the parties must agree on provisions for commercial fixtures, improvements made by the tenant, the landlord's right to relocate the tenant after the lease is signed, and breakdowns of mechanical equipment.

Leases are terminated in a variety of ways. Typically, leases for residential property terminate on the expiration date for the estate for years. A lease can be terminated by mutual agreement between the landlord and tenant. Also, the tenant may purchase the property and thereby eliminate the need for the lease agreement. The tenant or the landlord may fail to meet the legal obligations incurred in the document. In this case, either one of the parties may be in breach of the lease agreement and thus in breach of contract.

Review Questions

1. What services can a property manager provide to the client?
2. What criteria are used in the tenant-selection process?
3. What is the consideration that is exchanged between the landlord and the tenant in a residential lease?

4. In general terms, describe the rights and responsibilities of both the landlord and the tenant in the following matters:

(a) delivery of the leased property
(b) the landlord's rights to enter
(c) the tenant's right to assign and sublet the property
(d) the tenant's use of the property
(e) liability for personal injury to third parties

5. Explain the need for a fixtures clause in the residential lease.

6. Why are security deposits needed? What was the landlord's original or common law security against default? What is the current practice? What relationships can be established between the landlord and the tenant with regard to the security deposits?

7. What consumer issues are involved in landlord-tenant relationships?

8. State the various ways in which a lease can be terminated. In a breach of the contract, what is the difference between dispossession proceedings and constructive eviction?

Discussion Questions

1. Compose a list of questions you might ask a property manager to identify what services you might wish to purchase.

2. Find another person in your class, identify yourselves as the two parties to a residential lease, and draft a two-page lease in everyday language. Then ask a third member of the class to critique it for content.

3. Draft an agreement and consideration clause for a residential lease based on a tenancy-at-will agreement instead of a tenancy-for-years agreement.

Notes

1. William Walters, Jr., *The Practice of Real Estate Management* (Chicago, Ill.: Institute of Real Estate Management, 1979), p. 45.

2. Ibid., p. 37.

3. Ibid., pp. 24–28.

4. Ibid., p. 25.

5. W. Donald Calomiris, "Property Management," *Real Estate Handbook,* ed. by Maury Seldin (Homewood, Ill.: Dow-Jones Irwin, 1980), p. 528.

6. James C. Downs, *Principles of Real Estate Management* (Chicago, Ill.: Institute of Real Estate Management, 1975), pp. 323–39.

7. Ibid., p. 327.

8. Ibid., p. 328.

9. Robert Kratovil and Raymond J. Werner, *Real Estate Law* (Englewood Cliffs, N.J.: Prentice-Hall, Inc., 1979), pp. 460–61.

10. Milton R. Friedman, *Friedman on Leases* (New York: Practicing Law Institute, 1974), pp. 17–18.

11. Harold F. Lusk and William B. French, *Law of the Real Estate Business* (Homewood, Ill.: Richard D. Irwin, Inc., 1975), p. 396.

12. Ibid., p. 398.

13. Friedman, *Friedman on Leases,* pp. 56–57.

14. Benjamin H. Henszey and Ronald M. Friedman, *Real Estate Law* (Boston, Mass.: Warren, Gorham, and Lamont, 1979), p. 269.

15. Lusk and French, *Law of the Real Estate Business,* pp. 405–6.

16. Ibid., p. 405.

17. Henszey and Friedman, *Real Estate Law,* p. 261.

18. Ibid.

19. Ibid., p. 262.

20. Friedman, *Friedman on Leases,* p. 394.

21. Henszey and Friedman, *Real Estate Law,* p. 262.

22. Jerome G. Rose, *Landlords and Tenants* (New Brunswick, N.J.: Transaction Books, 1973), pp. 38–40.

23. Ibid., p. 40.

24. Ibid., p. 41.

25. Friedman, *Friedman on Leases,* p. 438–39.

26. Ibid., p. 400.

27. Kratovil and Werner, *Real Estate Law,* p. 468.

28. Friedman, *Friedman on Leases,* p. 441.

29. Kratovil and Werner, *Real Estate Law,* p. 467.

30. Lusk and French, *Law of the Real Estate Business,* p. 412.

31. Ibid.

32. Ibid., p. 413.

33. Ibid.

34. Henszey and Friedman, *Real Estate Law,* pp. 264–65.

35. Ibid., p. 265.

36. Kratovil and Werner, *Real Estate Law,* pp. 471–72; Henszey and Friedman, *Real Estate Law,* p. 265.

37. Lusk and French, *Law of the Real Estate Business,* p. 419.

38. Kratovil and Werner, *Real Estate Law,* p. 14.

39. Rose, *Landlords and Tenants,* pp. 77–78.

40. Ibid., p. 79.

41. Ibid., p. 80.

42. Kratovil and Werner, *Real Estate Law,* pp. 479–80.

43. Ibid., p. 480.

44. Ibid., p. 477.

45. Friedman, *Friedman on Leases,* pp. 471–73.

46. Kratovil and Werner, *Real Estate Law,* p. 481.

47. Rose, *Landlords and Tenants,* p. 71.

48. Lusk and French, *Law of the Real Estate Business,* p. 420.

49. Rose, *Landlords and Tenants,* p. 88.

50. Ibid., p. 38.

51. Kratovil and Werner, *Real Estate Law,* p. 470.

52. Ibid., p. 474.

53. Ibid., p. 473.

54. Ibid., p. 474.

55. Ibid.

56. Rose, *Landlords and Tenants,* p. 73.

57. Ibid., p. 74.

58. Ibid., p. 76.

59. Kratovil and Werner, *Real Estate Law,* p. 472.

Additional Readings

DOWNS, JAMES C. *Principles of Real Estate Management.* Chicago, Ill.: Institute for Real Estate Management, 1975.

FRIEDMAN, MILTON R. *Contracts and Conveyances of Real Property.* New York: Practicing Law Institute, 1975.

———. *Friedman on Leases.* New York: Practicing Law Institute, 1974.

HENSZEY, BENJAMIN H., and RONALD M. FRIEDMAN. *Real Estate Law.* Boston, Mass.: Warren, Gorham, and Lamont, 1979. Chapter 11.

KRATOVIL, ROBERT, and RAYMOND J. WERNER. *Real Estate Law.* Englewood Cliffs, N.J.: Prentice-Hall, Inc., 1983. Chapter 37.

LUSK, HAROLD F., and WILLIAM B. FRENCH. *Law of the Real Estate Business.* Homewood, Ill.: Richard D. Irwin, Inc., 1984. Chapter 19.

ROSE, JEROME G. *Landlords and Tenants.* New Brunswick, N.J.: Transaction Books, 1973.

SHENKEL, WILLIAM M. *Modern Real Estate Management.* New York: McGraw-Hill Book Co., 1980.

WALTERS, WILLIAM, JR. *The Practice of Real Estate Management.* Chicago, Ill.: Institute for Real Estate Management, 1979.

15 | The Commercial and Industrial Lease

QUESTIONS TO BE ANSWERED

1. What must I know about the selection of commercial tenants if I am an owner of commercial property?
2. What must I know about a commercial lease if I enter into the agreement as either a landlord or a tenant?
3. How does a lease for vacant land differ from the typical commercial lease?

OBJECTIVES

When the student finishes the chapter, he or she should be able to

1. Explain the nature of the commercial lease agreement.
2. State the rights and responsibilities of the landlord and the tenant in a lease.

3. Describe the various clauses that appear in a commercial lease.

4. Explain the nature and purpose of the ground lease.

5. Describe the nature and purpose of the sale and leaseback agreement.

IMPORTANT TERMS

Escalated Lease
Graduated Payment Lease
Gross Lease
Ground Lease
Indexed Lease

Net Lease
Percentage Lease
Sale and Leaseback Agreement

TENANT-SELECTION CRITERIA FOR COMMERCIAL PROPERTIES

The selection of tenants for commercial property focuses on criteria that are comparable to those discussed in relationship to residential tenants and on criteria that are unique to a commercial tenant. A discussion of these criteria is presented in the following subsections.

Credit and Financial Rating (Profitability)

The commercial tenant should be able to fulfill the financial obligations stipulated in the lease. In other words, the tenant should be able to pay the rent. If the prospective tenant is an established business, the property owner or property manager could check the tenant's credit rating and ask to see the audited financial records of the business or its published annual report. In this way, the financial capacity to pay rent can be determined.

If the prospective tenant is a new enterprise, the property owner/manager has less concrete evidence upon which to base a decision. Initially, the property owner/manager could check the credit rating of the owner of the business. Then, the property owner/manager could analyze the nature of the business by comparing the product or service it is offering with the potential market for that product or service. In order to reach an understanding of the nature of the market, the property owner/ manager can (1) ask to see the tenant's market study that was performed, (2) ask if a financial institution provided a business loan to establish an inventory and/or to purchase equipment and fixtures used in the business, (3) rely on his or her own market experience to judge the prospective tenant's potential for success. The property owner/manager's eventual decision will be based upon some combination of this information.

Tenant Reputation

The value of commercial space is related to the prestige or reputation of the tenants who are located in the structure. The property owner/manager should recognize that the reputation of existing commercial tenants affects the desirability of the property to prospective tenants. If the property provides space to a group of prestigious tenants, the close physical proximity of these tenants will be desirable to prospective tenants and will allow the property owner/manager to command a higher rent level. Consequently, the property owner/manager should do everything in his or her power to obtain highly regarded tenants.

Unique Space Requirements

A commercial tenant may be perfectly acceptable from the point of view of reputation, credit, and profitability and yet be unsatisfactory because of unique requirements regarding space. Several examples of this should prove beneficial. For instance, the location of a late-night restaurant on the top floor of a high-rise office building might be inappropriate if there is no way to provide security to the portions of the building not being used by the patrons of the restaurant. Most structures solve this problem by having direct access, by elevator, from the lobby to the restaurant while all other portions of the structure are secured from intrusion by the restaurant's patrons. Another example might be the location of a bicycle repair shop or a roller skate rental store in the middle of a shopping mall. In this situation, a problem could arise between the needs of the shoppers in the mall and the patrons of the bicycle shop or roller skate store. The mode of travel and the travel pattern of bike riders and roller skaters can interfere with pedestrian traffic to the stores in the mall. Consequently, even though the prospective tenant is desirable in all respects, the space requested in the center of the mall would be inappropriate. The property owner/manager must analyze the prospective tenant's space needs with regard to the existing tenants in the structure.

In a more specific sense, the tenant's space requirements should also be compared to the existing capability of the space and its potential for renovation (its functional efficiency). The prospective tenant might have special space needs that cannot be met by the property. The prospective tenant might need high ceilings for storage or display purposes but the ceiling height cannot be changed. The prospective tenant might need soundproofing, which cannot be provided due to construction features of the building. The prospective tenant might need special access to and from the store, which cannot be provided. For any of these reasons or a variety of others, the prospective tenant might not be suitable for the space in the subject property.

Expansion Requirements

In the process of selecting tenants, the manager must be aware of the likelihood that in the future the tenant may require an increase of space. Such expansion problems can be troublesome because if the building is not able to fulfill this need for increased space, the tenant's occupancy will be temporary. Consequently, the property manager should analyze the growth potential of prospective clients. If expansion needs are going to develop quickly, and if the building cannot meet the tenant's future needs, it may be better in the long run not to rent to this tenant.

Compatibility and Affinity

One aspect of tenant compatibility was discussed in the previous section on unique space requirements. Commercial tenants should be compatible in the sense that the activities of one tenant do not deter or interfere with the flow of customers to the other tenants. The customers of a bicycle repair shop located in the middle of a shopping mall could cause such interference if they entered through the regular pedestrian area of the mall. However, the aspect of tenant compatibility that is being discussed in this section is the concept of locational affinity among retail stores.

The successful property owner/manager selects commercial tenants based on consumer perceptions about the close interrelationships among certain types of commercial enterprises. For example, the existence of major department stores and specialty clothing shops in a shopping mall or a commercial district increases the degree of comparative shopping that the consumer can undertake. Consequently, shopping malls generate a large volume of pedestrian traffic, which affects the sales volume of each store. If a good combination of commercial tenants is established, the mix is mutually beneficial to all of the tenants.

Several studies show that consumers perceive compatible relationships between major department stores and specialty clothing shops, between clothing stores and shoe stores, between women's clothing shops and jewelry shops, between men's clothing stores and women's clothing stores, and between women's clothing shops and family clothing shops. Research also has shown that if the consumer perceives a difference between the products offered by two or more similar stores, there is a locational compatibility among these businesses. This explains the close, spatial proximity of competing clothing shops, shoe stores, and even automobile dealerships.

The successful property owner/manager chooses the mix of commercial tenants in a shopping center to maximize the benefits that the tenants will receive from being in close proximity to stores with which they share a locational compatibility. He or she avoids situations that will place incompatible tenants in close proximity because such a spatial relationship will deter customers from at least one of the businesses.

THE COMMERCIAL LEASE

The commercial lease is a legal document that describes the agreement reached between a landlord who owns property that can be rented as commercial space and a tenant who is a private businessperson. Commercial leases are written for tenants such as retail stores, restaurants, movie theaters, and drug stores. In addition, commercial leases are written for office space that is needed by doctors, dentists, optometrists, attorneys, appraisers, real estate brokers, and other professional individuals. The commercial lease is generally similar to the residential lease, but is different in certain respects. The following discussion of the commercial lease explains the significant points of difference.

The Agreement and the Consideration

In a commercial lease, the landlord and the tenant must reach an agreement about the rent to be paid and the space to be provided. Unlike the residential lease, in which the rent payment is usually stated as a flat fee, the commercial lease can stipulate any of a variety of payment schemes. Moreover, the commercial lease includes special provisions about the space.

Rent payment schemes   The commercial lease takes a special name that reflects the rent payment scheme agreed to by the landlord and the tenant. Hence, commercial leases are referred to by the following names:

- ☐ Gross lease
- ☐ Net lease
- ☐ Percentage lease
- ☐ Escalated or indexed lease
- ☐ Graduated-payment lease

Each of these rent-payment arrangements is described hereafter.

Gross lease The **gross lease** is a commercial counterpart of the flat or fixed rent payment lease for residential property. Under a gross-lease arrangement, the tenant pays a predetermined, fixed amount for the space on a periodic basis. This fixed amount of rent covers all of the financial responsibilities that the tenant incurs for possessing and using the space. The payment can be stated as $475 per month or as $12 per square foot of space per year.

Net lease The **net lease** breaks the rent payment into components; one component is fixed and the other one can change over time. In this arrangement, the tenant promises to pay the landlord a fixed sum on a periodic basis and in addition promises to pay some of the expenses that the landlord incurs against the property. The most typical expenses paid by the tenant under a net-lease arrangement are the real property taxes and/or insurance premiums. A net lease can be written in which the tenant promises to pay a flat fee plus the real property taxes, a flat fee plus the hazard insurance premiums, or a flat fee plus the real estate taxes and the hazard insurance premiums. If the tenant pays two expense items, the leasing arrangement is often called a *net-net lease.* In this instance, the tenant might be paying a flat fee plus property taxes and insurance.

Other charges also may enter into a net-lease arrangement. The lease can require the tenant to bear the financial responsibility for maintaining and repairing the structure. If the tenant is required to pay the real estate taxes, the insurance premium, and the maintenance/repair costs, the lease is often referred to as a net-net-net, or triple-net, lease. Many people in the real estate industry use the triple-net lease phrase to imply that the tenant is in essense paying all of the landlord's normal operating expenses.

Percentage lease In a **percentage lease,** the landlord and the tenant agree that the rent payment will reflect the gross sales or gross revenues of the tenant's commercial establishment. The landlord must specify or define the concept of gross sales revenue. To do this, the landlord must understand the nature of the tenant's business. For example, a retail store may sell merchandise directly over the counter to customers on the premises and in addition sell merchandise by mail. In this case, the landlord and tenant must agree to the definition of gross sales as being equal to only the over-the-counter sales or to the over-the-counter sales plus mail order sales. The definition of gross sales is important because it directly affects the tenant's rent payment and thereby affects the landlord's actual gross income from the property.

In another situation, the tenant may have a policy of selling merchandise to employees at cost and/or providing employees with subsidized cafeteria or vending machine service. The tenant would like to have these sales excluded from the calculation of gross sales because no profits are being made. The agreement to exclude these sales should be stated in the lease.

Since the gross sales of the commercial establishment may be related to the hours and the days on which the store is open, the tenant and the landlord should agree to a schedule of dates and times during which business will be conducted. The landlord may rent space to a tenant whose business is seasonal. The tenant's year may start in the early spring and continue through the late fall or the Christmas season. This situation is common in vacation communities, shopping complexes along interstate highways that primarily serve the tourist, and concession areas along beaches. The landlord and the tenant must agree to the rent-payment provisions that will apply while the business is closed. The landlord would need a small fixed sum to defray expenses that are incurred even when the property is not in operation because the property is still in use by the tenant.

The landlord's income under a percentage lease is affected by the success of the commercial establishment. The landlord can share in both the success and the failure of the tenant's business. Consequently, an astute landlord would like the following two provisions incorporated into a percentage lease:

1. *A fixed minimum rent payment.* The landlord should insist that the lease contain a statement establishing the rent payment as a fixed minimum amount to which the percentage is added; or the lease should require the tenant to pay whichever is the higher sum—the minimum payment decided by agreement between the two parties or the percentage of the gross sales.

2. *A recapture clause.* This clause enables the landlord to regain the property if the tenant's business is not successful over a predetermined time. For example, the landlord may want the lease to terminate if the tenant has

paid only the minimum rent for twelve consecutive months. In this way, the landlord regains possession of the property and is able to search for another tenant whose business may be more successful.

The final point of negotiation is the exact percentage to be applied to the tenant's gross sales. Obviously, the tenant desires the lowest possible rate and the landlord wants the highest rate. The compromise is easily reached because each type of business in operation in each market is paying a certain approximate rate. This information can be obtained from a commercial property broker, a property manager, or even the owner of a comparable business operation.

Escalated or indexed lease When the escalated or indexed lease arrangement is used, the landlord and the tenant agree that the first year's rent will be a flat or fixed amount, but that this amount will change on a periodic basis, usually yearly, when some index changes. This agreement necessitates a second agreement on the index that will be used to adjust the gross rent. The index can be the consumer price index, the wholesale price index, or any other index related to commodity prices. However, "the use of any such index has been criticized on the ground that an index . . . based on variations in commodity prices, does not accurately reflect costs of building operation, which are most closely related to real estate taxes, wages, and the cost of building materials. The cost of living, as an escalation factor, has been used less frequently than taxes and operating expenses."[1]

An index directly related to the property is more realistic and reasonable to both the landlord and the tenant. The information contained in such an index pertains to their day-to-day activity and reflects changes they can comprehend that affect them personally.

If the index is established as the change in the level of real estate taxes, or as the change in the level of total operating expenses, the lease agreement should stipulate that the landlord is responsible for providing each of the tenants with an audited statement of operating expenses incurred by the property. However, the landlord should be aware that a tenant may object to a rent increase based on an increase in operating expenses that does not benefit the tenant directly. For example, the energy costs for operating the elevator and/or escalators may increase total operating costs and thereby force an increase in the rent of tenants on the first floor of the building. The landlord should be prepared for arguments or, more likely, counterproposals by these tenants. Furthermore, the landlord may not wish to use total operating expenses as the index because the operating statement of the property is the landlord's own personal affair and he or she may not want to share such information with the tenants.

Changes in real estate taxes could be a substitute for the total operating expenses, but they may not be an adequate measure of increasing costs in the future. If municipal governments shift from the real estate tax to the sales tax or an income tax to generate revenues, the landlord may find that real estate taxes stay constant while other categories of operating expenses increase. The landlord could choose utility rate changes as the index. The knowledgeable tenant, however, would realize that utility rates have been rising at a substantially greater rate than most other operating expense components and therefore would object to an index based on utility rate changes.

The choice of the index is a serious matter for both the tenant and the landlord. Each party must understand operating expenses and should have a general understanding of their relative increases in order to have equal bargaining power in establishing the index.

Finally, each tenant's share of the total increase in the index may have to be established. If a single tenant leases the entire property, the calculation is simple; the tenant pays the entire increase. However, if several tenants are renting spaces of different sizes, the problem is complicated. In the latter case, the landlord must show each tenant his or her percentage of the total space and must relate that percentage to the total increase in the index. Thus, the tenants who rent large units of space pay a proportionately greater share of the increased rent than tenants who rent smaller units of space.

Graduated payment lease Under the graduated payment scheme, the landlord and the tenant mutually agree on a rent-payment pattern that will continue into the future. The agreement may stipulate that the tenant will pay $350 per month for use of the commercial space in the first year of operation, $450 per month in the second and third years of the lease, and $600 per month in the remaining years of the lease. This agreement is established at the outset of the leasing period and remains in force for the remainder of the lease. The graduated payment can take any one of a multitude of forms. For example, an alternative could be a rent payment of $350 per month for the first year, $450 per month in the second and third years, and a minimum of $500 per month plus 1 percent of the gross sales per month for the remainder of the lease. In this case, the lease is a hybrid of the graduated payment and the percentage leases.

These repayment schemes greatly complicate the agreement process underlying a commercial lease. Both parties to the lease may have biases for or against a certain lease arrangement. Consequently, owners of commercial space and tenants who desire such space must be willing to negotiate and must understand the ramifications of their actions. In the real estate industry, individuals who facilitate commercial lease negotiations are typically known as commercial brokers. Their services can be very valuable in the negotiating process.

Agreement on competitive space   In addition to the negotiations about the rent-payment scheme, the landlord and the tenant may need to reach an agreement about space usage. Such agreements are common in leases for space in shopping centers. If the shopping center is small in total rentable floor space, or if the shopping center does not attract many customers, certain tenants may want a clause in the lease that eliminates the landlord's right to rent space to a competitor. For example, an individual or corporation that desires to put a drugstore into a low-revenue shopping center may not want the landlord to put a second drugstore into the complex. The Federal Trade Commission now provides that such a clause is anticompetitive and is therefore an antitrust violation. However, the landlord should critically evaluate the tenant's need for such an arrangement. Certain establishments may not be able to face competition if the sales volume of the shopping center is small but could face competition in a shopping center with a larger sales volume. For example, large shopping centers can support, and in most cases do support, two drugstores. Moreover, certain types of stores can become profitable only in a large shopping center.

Consequently, the landlord must know something about the size of the market required to make stores profitable. A landlord who is leasing space in a large shopping center might not want to allow one tenant to limit the number of direct competitors. A large shopping center could reasonably accommodate more than one women's apparel store, shoe store, fast-food restaurant, and men's apparel shop. In essence, the landlord must know the difference between retail stores that benefit from proximity to stores selling similar products and those that suffer from close competition. As a first approximation, the landlord can use observation, visiting a successful shopping center and seeing that there are two or three department stores, four or five women's apparel shops, three or four men's apparel shops, two or three fast-food restaurants, etc. However, the decision is important and the landlord may wish to seek the advice of a real estate market analyst.

Term of the lease   Commercial leases are generally regarded as medium-term leases whose expiration date is set between three and ten years in the future. The term of the lease is negotiated between the landlord and the tenant. Usually the term of the lease is considered in relation to the rental payment scheme and the future state of the economy. For example, if inflation is expected to continue into the future, the tenant would like a gross lease at the lowest possible rate for the longest term that can be negotiated. In the same situation, the landlord would prefer either an indexed lease or a percentage lease and might be satisfied with giving a long-term lease. The tenant might agree to a percentage lease with a relatively short term, for example, three years or so. This arrangement would give the tenant the opportunity to renegotiate the lease or the freedom to seek a more profitable or less expensive site in the future.

The longest leases for an improvement generally are those for industrial property. Very seldom do such leases remain in force for less than fifteen or twenty years. Possibly the longest-term lease is the ground lease, which is described in another section of the chapter. Some states have established a minimum of fifty years for this type of lease.

Legal description   The description of the premises that the tenant leases must be clearly stated. If the tenant leases an entire property, the mailing address may be sufficient description for the tenant's purposes, but only if the tenant has no use for the external surroundings. Because a future need may arise for that space, the tenant may want the lease to define some portion of the surrounding land as being in the tenant's possession.

If the tenant leases only a portion of a property, a thorough description of the leased property is very important. In this situation, the lease should contain a description of the geographic location of the tenant's space within the owner's building. A verbal description may suffice, but a floor plan would be more appropriate. A copy of such a diagram should be attached to the lease to identify the leased space clearly and unambiguously.

Landlord and Tenant Rights and Responsibilities

The rights and responsibilities of the two parties to a residential lease also apply to the parties to a commercial lease. Regardless of the type of lease, residential or commercial, the parties involved are concerned about delivery of possession, use, personal liability, rights to assign and sublet, rights of entry, and obligations to repair and maintain. These issues were discussed in detail in the chapter on the residential lease.

Clauses Relating Common Points of Concern
Between Landlord and Tenant

Many of the clauses discussed in relation to residential leases are also important clauses in commercial leases. The purpose of this section is to explain the relevance of those clauses to commercial property and to introduce other clauses that are significant only in commercial leases.

Fixtures clause   The tenant's fixtures include a subcategory known as *trade fixtures*. These items are personal property that the tenant in commercial space installs on the property and that he or she fully intends to detach and remove when the lease expires. These trade fixtures should be clearly identified and specified in the lease to prevent confusion later. The tenant does not have the right to claim trade fixtures that were installed by the landlord. If trade fixtures are in place, these items of real property belonging to the landlord must be distinguished from the tenant's trade fixtures, which are his or her personal property.

Improvements by the tenant   The probability of the tenant making improvements to the property is higher for commercial than for residential property. The lease should contain a clause that eliminates any and all confusion about the ownership of such improvements. Typically, any such improvements to the property become the property of the landlord. Agreement must be reached, however, about the person who is responsible for the expense involved in making the improvement. The landlord may agree to pay for the improvements as part of the lease negotiation, or the landlord may give permission to the tenant to put in the improvements. The latter arrangement can create financial problems for the landlord. If the tenant contracts for the improvements but does not pay, the contractor can seek a mechanic's lien against the property. Usually, if the tenant is permitted to construct the improvements, the expenses are added to the tenant's rent-payment provision in the lease agreement if they are not directly paid by the tenant. In this way, the landlord can pay for the improvements with the tenant's funds and avoid the possibility of a mechanic's lien.

Landlord's right to relocate the tenant   When attempting to lease space in a commercial property, the landlord should realize that all the space will not be leased simultaneously. The leasing process takes time and problems can arise as the landlord attempts to achieve a 100 percent occupancy level. Consider an example in which the commercial property is an office building. One of the first tenants to sign a lease could be a small business operation that requires a small area within the property.

The landlord and this tenant reach an agreement about a portion of the property's ground floor, and the lease is signed by both parties. Then another desirable prospect approaches the landlord for commercial space. This prospective tenant is much larger than the original tenant and therefore requires an entire floor in the four-story building. This tenant wishes to have the ground floor, part of which is already leased to the small tenant. The prospective tenant will not accept space on two floors and is adamant about these requirements. Consequently, the prospective tenant probably will not rent.

The landlord should have foreseen the possibility of this situation arising and could have prevented it by including a clause known as "landlord's right to relocate the tenant" into the first tenant's lease. This clause would allow the landlord to move the first tenant into alternative space. That alternative space must be comparable space in terms of the tenant's needs and should be no smaller than the space originally specified in the lease. If these conditions are not met, the landlord and the tenant would have to agree to a rent reduction. Moreover, if the landlord exercises the right to relocate, the tenant's position cannot be worsened in any way. Any expenses associated with the relocation would be borne by the landlord. If the tenant had installed trade fixtures, they would have to be dismantled and moved or replaced at the landlord's expense in the new space. The landlord's right to relocate a tenant has been challenged in court and held to be legal. The courts have ruled that the landlord's right to relocate the tenant does not destroy the tenant's right of possession and use of the property.[2]

Breakdown clause   In many commercial operations, the landlord supplies the tenant with services and facilities other than the space that is being rented directly. The landlord may promise to provide cleaning services, elevator/escalator service, and air conditioning and therefore needs protection against liability if these services are interrupted. In the case of mechanical equipment, such as the elevator, the escalator, and the air conditioner, the lease could include a clause that frees the landlord from liability if these services are discontinued for repair, inspection, or other reasons beyond the landlord's control. In case of the labor services or cleaning services, the clause may read that the landlord is not liable for interruption of services due to labor disputes, such as strikes or walkouts.

The breakdown clause also provides that the tenant's responsibility to pay rent will not be suspended during the period of service interruptions. The interruption of these services may last for more than a few days, however, and may render the property unusable. Therefore, the tenant would want a contingency clause that allows for a rent abatement until the premises are once again usable. The tenant should realize, however, that any stipulation about rent abatement, even in the situation described, would not be welcomed by the landlord or by a lender who holds the mortgage on the property.[3]

Hours-of-business and merchandise-inventory clauses   Shopping center leases typically contain a clause that defines the hours of business during which the stores are to stay open. In general, the hours of the anchor tenants—the major department stores—are imposed as the standard hours that all tenants are to maintain. This stipulation benefits the landlord because it keeps the shopping center in operation for the maximum number of reasonable hours. During this time all stores are open so the customer does not see a patchwork of open and closed stores as he or she walks through the mall. Under these circumstances the total sales of the shopping center should be increased and the landlords' revenues from a percentage lease should also be greater.

However, the small tenants could be disadvantaged financially by these stipulated hours of business. The cost of staying open during marginal hours, such as the hours late in the evening or on Sunday afternoon, may exceed the additional sales made during these times. Consequently, the smaller tenants' interest will be served by attempting to negotiate the "stay open" or hours-of-business clause out of the lease. However, the landlord usually has the upper hand in the negotiation of this clause. To counter this unequal bargaining position, several lawsuits have been filed recently by small tenants to have this clause voided in their leases.

Commercial leases should also identify the inventory of merchandise that the tenant keeps on the premises and offers for sale. This clause is usually stated in general terms, such as the tenant will stock merchandise on the premises that is consistent with operations at other locations. This statement is suitable for a branch store. But, for a single store operation, the clause could state that the stock of merchandise be consistent with the inventory holdings of competing stores.

This clause protects the landlord from a tenant who is attempting to minimize sales in order to take advantage of the recapture clause that appears in a percentage lease. If sales are too low, the lordlord will cancel the lease and the tenant can move without penalty.

Utilities The payment of utilities should be identified in the lease to the greatest extent possible. Typically, the landlord pays for the common areas and the tenants pay for their leased space. However, there are utility payments that cannot be divided neatly. For example, the owner of a shopping center with an enclosed mall and open store fronts will have to pay for some portion of heat and air conditioning because the total utility bill cannot be subdivided easily among the tenants. In this case the owner should put a "stop clause" into the lease. This clause defines the extent to which the owner will pay for utilities. When the utility bill exceeds the predetermined maximum, the extra expense is divided among the tenants in a predetermined manner. The basis could be square footage under lease. The purpose of the clause is to limit the landlord's utility payment during the lease term.

Signs The commercial lease should also contain a clause that describes the nature and placement of the tenant's identifying name and advertising. The landlord does not want a hodgepodge of different-sized signs, in dramatically gaudy and contrasting colors, in inconvenient places. Nor does the landlord want the store windows and mall areas covered with advertising and placards. Therefore, the nature and use of signs by the tenant and the display of advertising should be specified in the lease.

Evaluating the Commercial Lease

An individual who either owns or requires the use of commercial space should understand the many provisions that can be included within a commercial lease. Furthermore, the individual should realize that the commercial lease, just like the residential lease, is not a standardized document. Printed forms of the commercial lease are available, but they cover only the most typical situations. Every commercial lease is unique in some important way. Therefore, neither the landlord nor the tenant should assume that a printed commercial lease addresses all of the matters of concern because the interests of these two parties do not coincide on most issues.

This section of the chapter describes the most common and generally important clauses of the commercial lease. However, certain special-purpose clauses also may be needed in the document because of unique technical considerations that arise between the two parties to the lease.

Exhibit 15-1 is an example of a commercial lease. The reader can evaluate this lease by examining each clause and considering its effect for both the landlord and the tenant.

THE GROUND LEASE

The **ground lease** is an agreement between a landlord and a tenant for the lease of vacant land. An important provision of the lease is the tenant's promise to erect a building on the vacant land. This promise necessitates a thorough discussion between the two parties about the length or term of the lease and the disposition of the improvement when the lease expires. Generally the ground lease is a long-term lease. Few such leases are written for less than twenty years and in some states fifty years is stipulated as the minimum term of a ground lease.[4]

When the tenant fulfills the promise to build the structure, the structure legally becomes the property of the landlord. Consequently, the tenant should discuss the financial settlement that will occur when the lease terminates. The tenant may insist on compensation for the value of the structure at the expiration of the lease. The landlord and the tenant may agree that an appraiser will be consulted to estimate the replacement value of the structure at that future date. If the term of the lease is long enough, the replacement cost of the structure may be insignificant. For example, a fifty-year-old industrial plant may be so functionally obsolete and physically deteriorated that its replacement cost less depreciation is zero. Whatever the situation at the end of the lease, the landlord and the tenant should reach some agreement at the beginning of the lease about the value of the improvement and whether the landlord will compensate the tenant for the improvement.

In the majority of cases, the ground lease is written as a triple-net lease agreement. The tenant typically incurs the obligation to pay a flat rate to the landlord plus all property taxes and assessments against the property, construction costs of the building, insurance on the improvement, and all expenses for maintenance and repair. In addition, the tenant assumes all responsibility for personal injury to third parties. Consequently, the landlord is relieved of all expenses associated with the property. The landlord receives a fixed periodic payment of rent; more importantly, all value increases to the land accrue to the landlord. The tenant receives the use of the land and the long-term use of the building specifically designed to meet his or her needs.

EXHIBIT 15-1

Courtesy of Miller's Book and Office Supply Company.

STANDARD COMMERCIAL LEASE CONTRACT
FORM 48

MILLER'S BOOK & OFFICE SUPPLY CO   ATLANTA

THIS LEASE, made this _____ day of _____ , 19___ , by and

between _____ , first party, (hereinafter called "Landlord");

and _____ , second party, (hereinafter called "Tenant");

and _____ , third party, (hereinafter called "Agent");

WITNESSETH:

Premises

1. The Landlord, for and in consideration of the rents, covenants, agreements, and stipulations hereinafter mentioned, reserved, and contained, to be paid, kept and performed by the Tenant, has leased and rented, and by these presents does lease and rent, unto the said Tenant, and said Tenant hereby agrees to lease and take upon the terms and conditions which hereinafter appear, the following described property (hereinafter called premises), to wit:

and being known as _____

No easement for light or air is included in the premises.

Term

2. To have and to hold the same for a term of _____ beginning on the _____ day of _____ , 19___ and ending on the _____ day of _____ 19___ , at midnight, unless sooner terminated as hereinafter provided.

Rental

3. Tenant agrees to pay Landlord, by payments to Agent of Landlord, who negotiated this lease, at office of Agent in _____ Georgia, promptly on the first day of each month in advance, during the term of this lease, a monthly rental of _____

Agent's Commission

4. The commission to be paid in connection with this transaction has been negotiated between Landlord and Agent, and Landlord agrees to pay Agent, as compensation for services rendered in procuring this lease, _____ and Landlord, with consent of Tenant, hereby assigns to Agent aforesaid commission. If the term of this lease is extended, or if new lease is entered into between Landlord and Tenant covering leased premises, or any part thereof, or covering any other premises as an expansion of, or substitute for, the premises herein leased, then in either of said events, Landlord, in consideration of Agent's having procured Tenant hereunder, agrees to pay Agent_____ under such extension, amendment, or new lease. Agent agrees that, in the event Landlord sells leased premises, and upon Landlord's furnishing Agent with an agreement signed by Purchaser assuming Landlord's obligations to Agent under this lease, Agent will release original Landlord from any further obligations to Agent hereunder. Tenant agrees that if this lease is validly assigned by him he will secure from asignee an agreement in writing by assignee recognizing assignment held by Agent and agreeing to pay rental to Agent herein named during the term of this lease. Agent is a party to this contract solely for the purpose of enforcing his rights under this paragraph, and it is understood by all parties hereto that Agent is acting solely in the capacity of agent for Landlord, to whom Tenant must look as regards all covenants, agreements and warranties herein contained, and that Agent shall never be liable to Tenant in regard to any matter which may arise by virtue of this lease. Voluntary cancellation of this lease shall not nullify Agent's right to collect the commission due for the remaining term of this lease. In the event that the premises are condemned, or sold under threat of and in lieu of condemnation, Agent shall, on the date of receipt by Landlord of the condemnation award or sale proceeds, be paid Agent's commission, reduced to its present cash value at the then existing legal rate of interest, which would otherwise be due to end the term contracted for under paragraph 2 above.

Purchase of Property by Tenant

5. In the event that tenant acquires title to the leased premises at any time during the term of this lease, any renewals thereof, or within six months after the expiration of the term hereof or the extended term hereof, then Landlord shall pay Agent a commission on the sale of the property of the Landlord in lieu of any additional rental commissions. Such sales commission, as negotiated between parties, is to be _____

Utility Bills

6. Tenant shall pay all utility bills, including, but not limited to water, sewer, gas, electricity, fuel, light, and heat bills, for the leased premises and Tenant shall pay all charges for garbage collection services or other sanitary services rendered to the leased premises or used by Tenant in connection therewith. If Tenant fails to pay any of said utility bills or charges for garbage collection or other sanitary services, Landlord may pay the same and such payment may be added to the rental of the premises next due as additional rental.

Use of Premises

7. Premises shall be used for _____ purposes and no other. Premises shall not be used for any illegal purposes; nor in any manner to create any nuisance or trespass; nor in any manner to vitiate the insurance or increase the rate of insurance on premises.

Abandonment of Leased Premises

8. Tenant agrees not to abandon or vacate leased premises during the period of this lease, and agrees to use said premises for purpose herein leased until the expiration hereof.

Repairs by Landlord

9. Landlord agrees to keep in good repair the roof, foundations, and exterior walls of the premises (exclusive of all glass and exclusive of all exterior doors), and underground utility and sewer pipes outside the exterior walls of the Building, except repairs rendered necessary by the negligence of Tenant, its agents, employees, or invitees. Landlord gives to Tenant exclusive control of premises and shall be under no obligation to inspect said premises. Tenant shall promptly report in writing to Landlord any defective condition known to it which Landlord is required to repair, and failure to so report such defects shall make Tenant responsible to Landlord for any liability incurred by Landlord by reason of such defects.

EXHIBIT 15-1 (continued)

Repairs by Tenant

10. Tenant accepts the leased premises in their present condition and as suited for the uses intended by Tenant. Tenant shall, throughout the initial term of this lease and all renewals thereof, at its expense, maintain in good order and repair the leased premises, including the building and other improvements located thereon, except those repairs expressly required to be made by Landlord. Tenant further agrees to care for the grounds around the building, including the mowing of grass, paving, care of shrubs and general landscaping. Tenant agrees to return said premises to Landlord at the expiration, or prior to termination, of this lease in as good condition and repair as when first received, natural wear and tear, damage by storm, fire, lightning, earthquake or other casualty alone excepted.

Elevators, (if any), are accepted by Tenant as in satisfactory operating condition on this date, and Tenant, at his own expense, shall maintain said elevators in good operating condition during the term of this lease, or any extension thereof.

Tax Escalation

11. Tenant shall pay upon demand, as additional rental during the term of this lease and any extension or renewal thereof, the amount by which all taxes (including, but not limited to, ad valorem taxes, special assessments and any other governmental charges) on the premises for each tax year exceeds all taxes on the premises for the tax year_____. In the event the premises are less than the entire property assessed for such taxes for any such tax year, then the tax for any such year applicable to the premises shall be determined by proration on the basis that the rentable floor area of the premises bears to the rentable floor area of the entire property assessed. If the final year of the lease term fails to coincide with the tax year, then any excess for the tax year during which the term ends shall be reduced by the pro rata part of such tax year beyond the lease term. If such taxes for the year in which the lease terminates are not ascertainable before payment of the last month's rental, then the amount of such taxes assessed against the property for the previous tax year shall be used as a basis of determining the pro rata share, if any, to be paid by Tenant for that portion of the last lease year. Tenant's pro rata portion of increased taxes, as provided herein, shall be payable within fifteen days after receipt of notice from Landlord or Agent as to the amount due. The Agent's commission shall not apply to any such additional rental resulting from the provisions of this paragraph unless billing and collection thereof is handled by Agent at the request of the Landlord.

Destruction of, or Damage to Premises

12. If premises are totally destroyed by storm, fire, lightning, earthquake or other casualty, this lease shall terminate as of the date of such destruction, and rental shall be accounted for as between Landlord and Tenant as of that date. If premises are damaged but not wholly destroyed by any such casualties, rental shall abate in such proportion as use of premises has been destroyed, and Landlord shall restore premises to substantially the same condition as before damage as speedily as practicable, whereupon full rental shall recommence.

Indemnity

13. Tenant agrees to indemnify and save harmless the Landlord against all claims for damages to persons or property by reason of the use or occupancy of the leased premises, and all expenses incurred by Landlord because thereof, including attorneys' fees and court costs.

Governmental Orders

14. Tenant agrees, at his own expense, to promptly comply with all requirements of any legally constituted public authority made necessary by reason of Tenant's occupancy of said premises. Landlord agrees to promptly comply with any such requirements if not made necessary by reason of Tenant's occupancy. It is mutually agreed, however, between Landlord and Tenant, that if in order to comply with such requirements, the cost to Landlord or Tenant, as the case may be, shall exceed a sum equal to one year's rent, then Landlord or Tenant who is obligated to comply with such requirements is privileged to terminate this lease by giving written notice of termination to the other party, by registered mail, which termination shall become effective sixty (60) days after receipt of such notice, and which notice shall eliminate necessity of compliance with such requirement by party giving such notice unless party receiving such notice of termination shall, before termination becomes effective, pay to party giving notice said sum of compliance in excess of one year's rent, or secure payment of said sum in manner satisfactory to party giving notice.

Condemnation

15. If the whole of the leased premises, or such portion thereof as will make premises unusable for the purposes herein leased, be condemned by any legally constituted authority for any public use or purpose, then in either of said events the term hereby granted shall cease from the date when possession thereof is taken by public authorities, and rental shall be accounted for as between Landlord and Tenant as of said date. Such termination, however, shall be without prejudice to the rights of either Landlord or Tenant to recover compensation and damage caused by condemnation from the condemnor. It is further understood and agreed that neither the Tenant nor Landlord shall have any rights in any award made to the other by any condemnation authority notwithstanding the termination of the lease as herein provided. Landlord agrees to pay to Agent, from the award made to Landlord under condemnation, the balance of lease commissions, reduced to then present cash value, as provided in paragraph 4 hereof, and agent may become a party to the condemnation proceeding for the purpose of enforcing its rights under this paragraph.

Assignment and Subletting

16. Tenant may sublease portions of the leased premises to others provided such sublessee's operation is a part of the general operation of Tenant and under the supervision and control of Tenant, and provided such operation is within the purposes for which said premises shall be used. Except as provided in preceding sentence, Tenant shall not, without the prior written consent of Landlord endorsed hereon, assign this lease or any interest hereunder, or sublet premises or any part thereof, or permit the use of premises by any party other than Tenant. Consent to any assignment or sublease shall not destroy this provision, and all later assignments or subleases shall be made likewise only on the prior written consent of Landlord. Assignee of Tenant, at option of Landlord, shall become directly liable to Landlord for all obligations of Tenant hereunder, but no sublease or assignment by Tenant shall relieve Tenant of any liability hereunder.

Removal of Fixtures

17. Tenant may (if not in default hereunder) prior to the expiration of this lease, or any extension thereof, remove all fixtures and equipment which he has placed in premises, provided Tenant repairs all damage to premises caused by such removal.

Cancellation of Lease by Landlord

18. It is mutually agreed that in the event the Tenant shall default in the payment of rent, including additional rent, herein reserved, when due, and fails to cure said default within five (5) days after written notice thereof from Landlord; or if Tenant shall be in default in performing any of the terms or provisions of this lease other than the provision requiring the payment of rent, and fails to cure such default within thirty (30) days after the date of receipt of written notice of default from Landlord; or if Tenant is adjudicated bankrupt; or if a permanent receiver is appointed for Tenant's property and such receiver is not removed within sixty days after written notice from Landlord to Tenant to obtain such removal; or if, whether voluntarily or involuntarily, Tenant takes advantage of any debtor relief proceedings under any present or future law, whereby the rent or any part thereof is, or is proposed to be, reduced or payment thereof deferred; or if Tenant makes an assignment for benefit of creditors; or if Tenant's effects should be levied upon or attached under process against Tenant, not satisfied or dissolved within thirty (30) days after written notice from Landlord to Tenant to obtain satisfaction thereof; then, and in any of said events, Landlord at his option may at once, or within six (6) months thereafter (but only during continuance of such default or condition), terminate this lease by written notice to Tenant; whereupon this lease shall end. After an authorized assignment or subletting of the entire premises covered by this lease, the occurring of any of the foregoing defaults or events shall affect this lease only if caused by, or happening to, the assignee or sublessee. Any notice provided in this paragraph may be given by Landlord, or his attorney, or Agent herein named. Upon such termination by Landlord, Tenant will at once surrender possession of the premises to Landlord and remove all of Tenant's effects therefrom; and Landlord may forthwith re-enter the premises and repossess himself thereof, and remove all persons and effects therefrom, using such force as may be necessary without being guilty of trespass, forcible entry or detainer or other tort.

EXHIBIT 15-1   (continued)

Reletting by Landlord	19. Landlord as Tenant's agent, without terminating this lease, upon Tenant's breaching this contract, may at Landlord's option enter upon and rent premises at the best price obtainable by reasonable effort, without advertisements and by private negotiations and for any term Landlord deems proper. Tenant shall be liable to Landlord for the deficiency, if any, between Tenant's rent hereunder and the price obtained by Landlord on reletting.
Exterior Signs	20. Tenant shall place no signs upon the outside walls or roof of the leased premises except with the written consent of the Landlord. Any and all signs placed on the within leased premises by Tenant shall be maintained in compliance with rules and regulations governing such signs and the Tenant shall be responsible to Landlord for any damage caused by installation, use, or maintenance of said signs, and Tenant agrees upon removal of said signs to repair all damage incident to such removal.
Entry for Carding, etc.	21. Landlord may card premises "For Rent" or "For Sale" thirty (30) days before the termination of this lease. Landlord may enter the premises at reasonable hours to exhibit same to prospective purchasers or tenants and to make repairs required of Landlord under the terms hereof, or to make repairs to Landlord's adjoining property, if any.
Effect of Termination of Lease	22. No termination of this lease prior to the normal ending thereof, by lapse of time or otherwise, shall affect Landlord's right to collect rent for the period prior to termination thereof.
Mortgagee's Rights	23. Tenant's rights shall be subject to any bona fide mortgage or deed to secure debt which is now, or may hereafter be, placed upon the premises by Landlord.
No Estate in Land	24. This contract shall create the relationship of Landlord and Tenant between the parties hereto; no estate shall pass out of Landlord. Tenant has only a usufruct, not subject to levy and sale, and not assignable by Tenant except by Landlord's consent.
Holding Over	25. If Tenant remains in possession of premises after expiration of the term hereof, with Landlord's acquiescence and without any express agreement of parties, Tenant shall be a tenant at will at rental rate in effect at end of lease; and there shall be no renewal of this lease by operation of law.
Attorney's Fees and Homestead	26. If any rent owing under this lease is collected by or through an attorney at law, Tenant agrees to pay ten percent (10%) thereof as attorneys' fees. Tenant waives all homestead rights and exemptions which he may have under any law as against any obligation owing under this lease. Tenant hereby assigns to Landlord his homestead and exemption.
Rights Cumulative	27. All rights, powers and privileges conferred hereunder upon parties hereto shall be cumulative but not restrictive to those given by law.
Service of Notice	28. Tenant hereby appoints as his agent to receive service of all dispossessory or distraint proceedings and notices hereunder, and all notices required under this lease, the person in charge of leased premises at the time, or occupying said premises; and if no person is in charge of, or occupying said premises, then such service or notice may be made by attaching the same on the main entrance to said premises. A copy of all notices under this lease shall also be sent to Tenant's last known address, if different from said premises.
Waiver of Rights	29. No failure of Landlord to exercise any power given Landlord hereunder, or to insist upon strict compliance by Tenant with his obligation hereunder, and no custom or practice of the parties at variance with the terms hereof shall constitute a waiver of Landlord's right to demand exact compliance with the terms hereof.
Time of Essence	30. Time is of the essence of this agreement.
Definitions	31. "Landlord" as used in this lease shall include first party, his heirs, representatives, assigns and successors in title to premises. "Tenant" shall include second party, his heirs and representatives, and if this lease shall be validly assigned or sublet, shall include also Tenant assignees or sublessees, as to premises covered by such assignment or sublease. "Agent" shall include third party, his successors, assigns, heirs, and representatives. "Landlord", "Tenant", and "Agent", include male and female, singular and plural, corporation, partnership or individual, as may fit the particular parties.
Special Stipulations	In so far as the following stipulations conflict with any of the foregoing provisions, the following shall control:

This lease contains the entire agreement of the parties hereto, and no representations, inducements, promises or agreements, oral or otherwise, between the parties, not embodied herein, shall be of any force or effect.

IN WITNESS WHEREOF, the parties hereto have hereunto set their hands and seals, in triplicate, the day and year first above written.

Signed, sealed and delivered as
to Landlord, in the presence of:

_____   _____(SEAL)
                                                    (Landlord)

_____   _____(SEAL)
Notary Public   (Landlord)

Signed, sealed and delivered as
to Tenant, in the presence of:

_____   _____(SEAL)
                                                    (Tenant)

_____   _____(SEAL)
Notary Public   (Tenant)

Signed, sealed and delivered as
to Agent, in the presence of:

_____   _____

                                                    By:_____(SEAL)
                                                        Agent

Most provisions in a ground lease are very similar to those in a commercial lease. The topics discussed between the landlord and the tenant in a commercial lease form the basis of the agreement between the landlord and the tenant in the ground lease. However, there are some major differences.

First, in a commercial lease if the tenant defaults, the landlord's typical remedy is the legal right of attachment against the tenant's personal property and a suit for breach of contract. In the ground lease, the tenant has erected a valuable building on the landlord's property, and this building serves as the landlord's security against the default of rent payments.

Second, the tenant typically borrows money to construct the building. The lender will want collateral for the loan. Since the building usually becomes the real property of the landlord, the only collateral the tenant can offer is the ground lease and its inherent rights of use and possession of the property. Thus, a lease provision is needed that gives the tenant the full right to mortgage the leasehold. Moreover, the tenant should realize that the lender wants protection against the landlord if the tenant defaults on the mortgage and the lender must take over the lease. In this event, the lender will want the right to assign the lease to a new tenant without the landlord's interference. In other words, the tenant in a ground lease should insist that the lease contain provisions allowing for unimpaired rights to mortgage the leasehold and to assign or sublet the property.[5]

Third, the landlord and the tenant must understand their respective rights and responsibilities if the property is sold. The landlord retains the right to sell the property, but the tenant is implicitly assured that the property is sold to a new owner who fully recognizes and honors the unexpired term of the lease and all other provisions stipulated in the original lease. In this way, the tenant is protected against the loss of the rights of possession and use in the event that the property is sold. In other words, the buyer takes possession of the property subject to the existence of the lease.

Finally, if the leasehold is to be mortgaged by the tenant, the lender would want the lease to require formal notification from the landlord of any default by the tenant. In addition, the lender would like the right to step in and clear away any default to prevent a forfeiture of the lease, which serves as the collateral for the leasehold mortgage.

The ground lease is beneficial to both parties. The landlord receives a periodic rent payment, is freed of major expenses associated with owning vacant land, and receives any increase in the value of the land. The tenant receives the use and possession of the land, use and possession of the building, which in most cases is specifically designed for his or her needs, and may receive compensation for the value of the structure at the expiration of the lease. The tenant can also receive income tax benefits derived from deductibility of depreciation allowances, interest payments on the leasehold mortgage, and ground rent as a business expense.

THE SALE AND LEASEBACK AGREEMENT

The **sale and leaseback provision** is an arrangement whereby the current owner and user of commercial or industrial property decides to offer the property for sale, but only on the condition that the prospective buyer simultaneously enters into a lease in which the current owner retains the rights to use and possess the property. The current owner initially must make an own-or-rent decision. The owner must analyze the company's financial position to see whether the ownership of the real estate asset is or is not more beneficial than leasing the rights to use and possess that same property. Each of these options has advantages and disadvantages.[6] The owner must consider the following items:

1. *The equity in the property.* The owner of commercial or industrial real estate has an equity position in the property. The question to be resolved is whether that equity is needed in the operation of the business. If the property were mortgaged, or if a second mortgage were taken out against the equity, the owner would only receive a portion of the equity—i.e., the loan-to-value ratio might be only 80 percent. However, the owner might be able to use the equity to make the business more productive. New capital equipment could be purchased or the inventory of the business could be expanded. The owner must weigh the relative benefits of keeping the equity in real property or converting it to personal property such as machines and inventory.

2. *Income tax consideration.* Generally, the owner of income-producing property is able to deduct the interest payments on the mortgage, real property taxes, and depreciation allowances from income earned in the current year. If the same property is leased, the entire rental payment becomes an expense of the business and thereby a deduction against the income of the business. This deduction could become an important tax consideration in later years as the yearly depreciation allowance becomes smaller and smaller.

3. *Fixed asset holdings.* The fixed asset can be converted to a cash asset. The liquidity position of the business is improved, and thus the capacity to borrow funds is increased.

4. *Change in role from landlord to tenant.* When the property is sold and leased back, the owner of the business is no longer the owner of the property. The landlord becomes a tenant. Consequently, that businessperson is obligated to the provisions of the lease with its stipulated rent payment and other terms. The tenant may have to relocate at the expiration of the lease or renegotiate the lease agreement. The original owner can protect his or her future interests by negotiating an option to repurchase the property in the original lease. An option to renew might also be included in the original lease.

The preceding list is not an exhaustive list of the factors that must be analyzed. The owner of the property must make a thorough analysis of the before- and after-sale impacts of the sell/leaseback decision. Only then can the sale and leaseback arrangement be identified as either a good tactic to be used or a poor tactic to be avoided.

The other party to the sale and leaseback arrangement is the prospective buyer or the future owner of the property. This individual's decision is based on the factors discussed in the real estate equity investment chapter. The investor in a sale and leaseback arrangement should analyze the rate of return to be obtained from the investment and compare it to the rates of return available from alternative investments. In this context, the investor is analyzing the periodic cash flow, equity increase through mortgage reduction, the price appreciation, and all the other factors and considerations involved in the real estate equity investment decision.

The sale and leaseback agreement is a lease agreement in the sense that a lease is part of the consideration that the two parties exchange. The original owner, who becomes the tenant, is concerned with use and possession of the property and may insist on certain arrangements in the lease that clearly define the use and possession requirements. There is no standard form for the lease drawn up in a sale and leaseback agreement. Both parties negotiate and compromise to obtain the best financial terms possible.

SPECIAL-PURPOSE CLAUSES IN A COMMERCIAL LEASE

The commercial lease can be affected by several special situations. In medium- and long-term leases, the tenant and the landlord both have rights of ownership that can be used as collateral for a loan. The landlord owns the freehold estate and the tenant owns a leasehold estate. The two parties must agree to the manner and method by which each will be treated if the other uses the ownership rights he or she controls as security for a loan. If condemnation proceedings take place against the property, the fact that the tenant owns a leasehold may establish the tenant's right to make a claim against the compensation paid by the local government to the property owner. The extent and nature of the tenant's claim under condemnation must be analyzed and understood by the two parties in the lease. Finally, the tenant may wish to purchase the freehold estate at some point in the future. The tenant could have this right stated in the lease in the form of an option-to-purchase clause.

Landlord's Right to Mortgage the Property

When a lease is written and signed, it is automatically subordinate to all current mortgages that are recorded or that the tenant knows exist. The lease is superior, however, to a future mortgage that may be created unless the lease contains a provision expressly stating a subordinate relationship. Obviously, a landlord desires this type of subordination clause in the lease, and printed lease forms generally include such a clause. Few landlords would be willing to waive this subordination clause.

The effect of the subordination clause on the tenant is profound. If a new mortgage is made, the subordination clause allows the lender to terminate the lease and evict the tenant if the landlord defaults on the mortgage. In some states, the lender has the option of confirming the lease and leaving the tenant in possession of the property with no change other than a new landlord.[7] However, in these states, this process is the lender's option and not the tenant's right. In other states, the lender has no choice because foreclosure automatically terminates the lease. In states where termination is automatic, the lender may voluntarily agree to subordinate the mortgage to the lease if the lease is held by a very desirable tenant. The lender accomplishes this by placing an appropriate clause in the mortgage. Thus, foreclosure proceedings will not terminate that desirable tenant's lease and the new landlord (the lender) takes over the property with the desirable tenant in possession of the premises.[8]

If the tenant is evicted because of the landlord's default on a mortgage that was executed after the lease came into force, the tenant may or may not have a right to sue the landlord for damages. The grounds for the suit would be the landlord's breach of contract, specifically, breach of the landlord's promise of "quiet enjoyment." However, the tenant's rights in this situation depend on the language of the lease and the wording of the quiet-enjoyment clause.[9] The quiet enjoyment clause can be interpreted as the landlord's guarantee that the tenant will not be disturbed in his or her possession of the property because of circumstances at the time the lease is signed. In a sense, it is the landlord's guarantee that at the time the lease is executed, the landlord has full and complete rights of ownership in that property and possesses a good or marketable title. The problem arises because the quiet-enjoyment clause may not be construed as applying to the loss of title due to future liens against the property.

The tenant should seek to limit his or her risk in the event that the landlord defaults on a mortgage that is issued subsequent to the lease. Several methods can be used to limit the tenant's risk of eviction. First, the tenant can attempt to insert a clause limiting the future mortgage to a specific sum. Alternatively, the tenant may agree to subordinate the lease only to a mortgage that is made by a financial institution. "Lending institutions are limited by law to the amount they may loan, generally to a conservative fraction of the value of the property. Furthermore, lending institutions are apt to be less likely than a private mortgagee to rush into a foreclosure. All of this presupposes that if the mortgage is conservative in amount, it is less likely to go into default than a mortgage that is excessive in amount."[10]

Second, the tenant who is in possession of the entire property can seek to limit the mortgage in such a way that the mortgage payment or the debt service does not exceed the rent paid on a monthly or yearly basis when added to the property's operating expenses.[11] In this way, the tenant attempts to establish a situation in which the landlord's default is unlikely because the property is generating enough net operating income to cover the debt service. The tenant, however, should realize that this approach does not guarantee an elimination of the landlord's risk of default and the tenant's associated risk of eviction. If the landlord is paying most of the operating expenses and those expenses increase in the future, the net operating income that the landlord derives from the property can fall below the level of debt service.

Neither the landlord nor the tenant can subordinate a future mortgage to the existing lease by their actions. Such a subordination can occur only if the lender is willing to agree to waive the right of eviction.[12] The tenant may find it easier to obtain "a nondisturbance instrument" from the future lender. At the time the future mortgage is executed, the tenant asks the lender to sign a document stating that the lender will not terminate the lease in the event of a foreclosure. The lease is still subordinate to the future mortgage, as the landlord and future lender desire, but the tenant has a guarantee that his or her possession of the property will not be disturbed if the landlord defaults. The lender, however, will give a nondisturbance agreement only to a very desirable tenant.[13]

The tenant may be able to insert a nondisturbance clause into the original lease. This clause would state that the lease shall be subject to and subordinated to any future mortgage but that the lender must agree not to terminate the lease in the event of a foreclosure proceeding. Such a clause clearly states that the lease is subordinate to the future mortgage. It therefore should be agreeable to the landlord and the future lender, but it also accords the tenant some degree of assurance that possession of the property will not be disturbed in the event of the landlord's default on the mortgage. Before agreeing to such a clause, the lender will examine the entire lease for terms that may have a disadvantageous effect after default and foreclosure. For example, the lease may require advance payment of rent in the early years of the lease. This provision would leave the lender with a tenant who had already paid rent to the landlord and consequently may owe no rent for the period of the lease still in effect. In other words, the lender would have a tenant and no rent revenues. Other such arrangements in the lease would prevent a future lender from issuing a loan even if the nondisturbance clause were used.[14]

The tenant who is unsuccessful in obtaining a nondisturbance clause in the lease, and consequently must sign a lease that subordinates his or her interests to future mortgages, can minimize the risk of eviction by inserting a clause that gives the tenant the right to pay the mortgage if the landlord defaults.[15] This clause should also contain an agreement giving the tenant some way of shifting the burden back to the landlord, for example, by subtracting the mortgage payments from the tenant's rent responsibilities. Alternatively, the landlord can agree that these payments made by the tenant are in reality a loan to be paid back within a certain time period and carrying a certain rate of interest. The tenant would prefer the first of these remedies because the landlord who defaults on the mortgage will probably not be in a financial position to repay the loan issued by the tenant. Therefore, the tenant would insist on the right to deduct the mortgage payments from the rent. If the mortgage payment exceeds the rent, the tenant should request possession of the property until the total value of the rent abatement is equal to the total mortgage payment made. In other words, in the event of the landlord's default, the term of the lease can be lengthened to a period of time that exceeds the length of the mortgage.

This clause designed to minimize the risk of eviction is simple to implement if a single tenant controls the entire property. If there are several tenants, they must all have this clause in their individual leases and must agree on their share of the mortgage payment to be covered. If the other leases on a multiunit structure do not contain this clause, the latest tenant can insist on a companion clause that allows him or her to be a receiver of rental payments from the other tenants in the event that the landlord defaults. Furthermore, this clause should stipulate that the tenant has the right to use the rent obtained as a receiver to pay the mortgage payments that are in default.

Tenant's Right to Mortgage the Leasehold

Just as in the cases of assignment and sublet, the tenant has the right to mortgage the leasehold unless a specific prohibition is stated in the lease.[16] The tenant may find it desirable to maintain the right to mortgage the leasehold. If the property is in a good location, the use and possession of the property is a valuable asset. For example, if a tenant holds a long-term lease on a building at the corner of the busiest commercial intersection in town, and if the business is successful because of the ideal location, the space is valuable not only to the current tenant but also to a new tenant who could establish the same retail operation. Consequently, a lender might issue a loan for which the collateral is only the right to use and possess that property.

The landlord should have no objection to a mortgage on the leasehold if he or she has the right of approval. If the tenant defaults on the mortgage, the lender on the leasehold takes over the use and possession of the property and also all the obligations imposed in the lease. Consequently, the landlord will not lose any revenue if the lender is a reputable person with a good credit standing or an established financial institution.

Option to Purchase

The purchase option can be viewed as a series of clauses in a commercial lease giving the tenant the possibility of buying the leased property. Probably the most important element of the purchase-option clause is the determination of the purchase price. The landlord and the tenant can agree on a definite, future sales price at the time the property is leased and simultaneously can identify the manner in which payment will be made. Alternatively, the landlord and tenant may agree to stipulate the sales price as being equal to the market value of the property on the day of sale at some time in the future. In this case, the landlord and the tenant should also agree on the manner in which the future market value of the property will be determined. Other issues to be settled are the manner in which the appraiser is chosen and whether either party has the right to withdraw if the estimated market value is too high for the tenant or too low for the landlord.

The two parties can reach a mutual agreement about a single appraiser and accept that appraiser's estimate of market value, or they can agree to hire their own appraisers and establish the average of the two market values as the sales price, or they can reach any other agreement that is mutually acceptable.

The landlord and the tenant may both wish to establish an escape provision for the option-to-purchase agreement. If the purchase price is established at the time the lease is signed and if the lease is long-term, the sales price may not adequately reflect price appreciation. Consequently, the sales price stated in the purchase option would be substantially less than the market value of the property. In this event the landlord would like the right to refuse the purchase option. Conversely, if the purchase price is defined as the market value of the property at the time of the sale, the tenant may find the price to be prohibitively high compared with his or her resources and ability to obtain financing. In this event the tenant would like the right to withdraw. An alternative to the tenant's right of withdrawal could be a contingency clause making the purchase option contingent upon the tenant's ability to obtain mortgage financing at the market rate of interest at the time of the sale.

When the purchase option is exercised, it creates an irrevocable sales contract for the property.[17] The parties to the lease become the parties to the sales contract also. They should take care, therefore, to draft the purchase option in such a way that it reflects all the information required in a sales contract. The purchase option should specifically and thoroughly cover the sales price, the terms of payment, contingency clauses, closing arrangements, the nature of the deed passing ownership, and any other contractual arrangements pertaining to the sales contract. A simple way of drafting the purchase option is to prepare a sales contract in which the sales agreement is determined, attach the sales contract to the lease, and refer to it in the purchase-option clause in the lease.[18]

The purchase option can be written in such a way that it remains in force for the entire period of time covered by the lease, or for a clearly stated period of time that is shorter than the lease. In the latter case, the option can be stated to be in effect for "the first three years of the lease" or "until midnight of December 31, 19XX."

The purchase option should also specify the manner in which the tenant exercises the option. To avoid any future confusion or unnecessary legal complications, the parties should agree that the option is exercised in writing. The tenant drafts a note to the landlord in which he or she clearly states the intention of accepting the purchase option as specified in the lease. Many purchase-option clauses require that the tenant give advance notice of intent to exercise the option. The nature of the advance notice should be clearly described within the purchase option, and the tenant's written statement concerning the exercise of the option should be dated and delivered to the landlord within the specified time period.

When the purchase option is included in the lease, both the tenant and the landlord must give serious consideration to their respective legal rights in the property. The landlord and the tenant must agree about the landlord's right to encumber the property with future mortgages, leases, and easements. The two parties must also agree both to the tenant's right of assignment and to whether the purchase option is assigned when the lease is assigned.

The tenant's purchase option may make it impossible for the landlord to obtain a mortgage on the property unless the purchase option is subordinated to any future mortgage. The tenant should not allow future mortgages to supersede the purchase option for the same reason that he or she would not want a future lender's right to supersede the lease provisions. In addition, the tenant may not wish the landlord to use the property as collateral for a loan after the purchase-option clause is stated because the purchase option, viewed as a sales contract, does not anticipate the manner in which the mortgage would be handled. If the purchase option is exercised, will the landlord pay off the mortgage? Or will the tenant assume the mortgage? These issues should be resolved at the time the lease is signed and the purchase option is specified. In most instances, neither party is in a position, in the current period, to define the specific details of a nonexistent future mortgage.

If a purchase option is included in a lease, the right to exercise the option is transferable if the lease itself is transferable.[19] Conversely, if the lease contains a prohibition against the tenant's right to assign and sublet, that prohibition also applies to the purchase option. "But a covenant against assignment of the lease will not prevent an assignment of the option after its exercise, or invalidate the agreement by the tenant, made prior to the exercise of the option, to convey the property to a third party."[20] Once the purchase option is exercised (that is, the tenant makes the purchase offer and the landlord accepts it), the sales contract that is thereby established frees the tenant from any restrictions against assignment specified in the lease.

The landlord may choose not to give the tenant the unconditional purchase option described in the preceding paragraphs. The landlord may choose to give the tenant a limited right to buy the property. Among the many terms used to describe this arrangement are "first option," "first privilege to buy," or "a first right of refusal." In general, these clauses do not create a purchase option as discussed in this section; they merely give the tenant the right to buy the property if the landlord receives an acceptable offer from a third party. If this provision is included in the lease, both the landlord and the tenant should be well aware of the rules covering these limited, right-to-buy provisions. In a few states, they are viewed as establishing an unconditional right for the tenant to buy the property. In a few other states, these clauses are considered unenforceable under the Statute of Frauds because they do not define the nature of the agreement or the nature of the consideration—essential elements for a valid, enforceable contract. In those jurisdictions where first-right-of-refusal clauses are considered unenforceable, the courts can rule that the arrangement is enforceable if the clause simply states that the tenant will buy the property on the same terms as were offered by the third party. The use of these first-right-of-refusal clauses should be thoroughly investigated by both the landlord and the tenant. They should consult an attorney who knows the legal aspects of commercial leases and the laws governing real estate transactions within the state in which the property is located.[21]

Condemnation

Condemnation proceedings, or the taking of property under eminent domain, terminates a lease because both the landlord and the tenant are deprived of their ownership rights. The landlord loses the right to dispose of the property and the tenant loses the rights of use and possession. Consequently, condemnation frees the landlord of any responsibility to provide possession and simultaneously frees the tenant from liability to pay rent to the landlord.

Every lease should contain some provision for condemnation. In short-term residential leases, the clause merely states that the landlord's responsibility to provide space under the lease agreement terminates upon the seizure of the property under eminent domain. In longer-term commercial leases, the two parties should reach an agreement about the exact nature of the clause. In a commercial lease, the landlord and tenant may have agreed that the rent is paid in advance. The clause should contain some statement that if condemnation occurs, advance rent payments should be prorated over the time period during which the tenant held possession. The landlord may have to refund some of the advance rent to the tenant when the property is condemned.

Condemnation proceedings take both the freehold and the leasehold estates for a public purpose with the provision that fair compensation be paid. Obviously, the landlord should be compensated because he or she is losing property; but the tenant is also losing the right to use and possess the space. For example, a tenant who has a lease on a commercial property may be losing the right to use and possess that property for the five unexpired years of the lease. Consequently, a tenant can have a claim against the monetary award made to the landlord.[22] The tenant can claim a value for the unexpired portion of the lease, as well as a value for the fixtures and improvements added to the structure.

The simplest way to handle the possibility of condemnation is to have the tenant waive all rights to an award if condemnation occurs. If the tenant does not choose to waive all claims in the event of a condemnation, however, specific agreements must be reached defining the tenant's compensation. The landlord and tenant may agree that upon condemnation, the landlord will compensate the tenant on some prorated, mutually agreed basis for the tenant's expenditures for fixtures and improvements. The tenant is justified in asking for this compensation because the fixtures and improvements installed by the tenant increase the appraised value of the structure. The tenant can rightfully claim the increase in value received by the landlord because of the existence of these fixtures.

Calculation of the value of the unexpired lease is a special topic in appraisal theory. The value of the unexpired portion of the lease exists only when the contract rent is less than the market rent.[23] In essence, the tenant is receiving the right to use and possess the space at a dollar value below the amount charged for comparable properties. To estimate the value of the unexpired term, the appraiser calculates the present worth of the difference between the contract rent and the current market rent. This amount would set the upper limit for the tenant's claim. In the reverse situation, if the true market rent is less than the contract rent, the unexpired portion of the lease has no compensable value because the tenant should be willing to be free from the lease in order to rent comparable space at a lower rate in the current market.

Right of Redemption

In many states, although a tenant may have defaulted on the obligation to pay rent when more than five years remain on the unexpired lease, the tenant has the right to pay the unpaid rent and thereby obtain possession of the property. Since the landlord does not consider such a tenant to be a good tenant, the landlord would want to eliminate this tenant's right to regain the property. Therefore, the landlord insists on a clause in the lease that waives the tenant's right of redemption. If a waiver of the right of redemption does not appear in a long-term lease, the landlord faces the danger that a dispossessed tenant will claim the right to regain possession and use of the property, even after initially defaulting on the rent.

CHAPTER SUMMARY

There are several criteria that a property owner or a property manager must examine when selecting a commercial tenant. The business's financial rating, profitability, reputation, space requirements, expansion potential, and compatibility should be analyzed before a commercial lease is executed with any tenant.

In a commercial lease, each party, the landlord and the tenant, has certain rights and responsibilities related to the delivery of possession, the use of the leased property, the responsibility for maintenance and repair, the liability for personal injury, the right to enter the property, and the right to assign or sublet the lease. Both parties to the lease must be concerned and informed about their legal responsibilities and their rights in these matters.

In addition to these rights and responsibilities, the commercial lease contains numerous clauses pertaining to matters of mutual concern to the landlord and the tenant. In a commercial lease, the parties must agree on provisions for commercial fixtures, improvements made by the tenant, the landlord's right to relocate the tenant after the lease is signed, and breakdowns of mechanical equipment.

Commercial leases are typically written for space in a structure. A ground lease is a special lease agreement to establish a leasehold for vacant land. It generally lasts for a longer period of time than the average commercial lease, and it contains clauses pertaining to the tenant's right to any structures or improvements erected on the landlord's property. Another special arrangement is the sale and leaseback agreement whereby the owner of the property sells it to a prospective buyer while maintaining a claim on the leasehold.

Review Questions

1. Discuss the several tenant selection criteria that should be analyzed by the property owner or the property manager before a commercial lease is executed.
2. Identify and describe the various rent-payment schemes that can be established within a commercial lease.
3. Discuss the issues that surround the commercial tenant's fixtures (trade fixtures) and any improvements that are made by the tenant.
4. What is a ground lease? What benefits does the landlord receive from a ground lease? What specific matters should concern the tenant when negotiating the ground lease?
5. Describe the sale and leaseback agreement. What benefits may the original owner-tenant receive? What benefits may the new owner receive?

Discussion Questions

1. Should the tenant's profit level be used as the basis for establishing a percentage lease agreement? Discuss the advantages and disadvantages of this issue in detail.

2. In a percentage lease the landlord may insist on a recapture clause. What is a recapture clause? Should the tenant attempt to eliminate this clause from the lease at the time the provisions of the lease are being negotiated?

3. Assume that inflation, as measured by either the Consumer Price Index or the Wholesale Price Index, will continue at high levels (10% to 12%) for the next decade. You are a prospective tenant seeking space in a shopping center to operate a clothing store. After evaluating the various rent-payment schemes and the term of the lease, what arrangements would you like to have incorporated into the lease agreement?

4. Under the conditions stipulated in question 3, you are now the landlord. What provisions would you want to include in the lease? Is there a difference between the landlord's position and the tenant's position? If so, can you design a compromise that might be suitable to the two parties?

5. One fact of business is that many new commercial enterprises fail. Some of these businesses have a graduated payment lease. Can the graduated payment lease be a factor that causes the failure of some of these businesses?

6. Can a ground lease be written for air rights?

7. Refer to the exhibits in Chapters 9 and 10 that are used to analyze the profitability of an investment opportunity. Relate the lease and the various agreements reached within that document to the cash flow analysis presented in those exhibits. What revenue or cost items are affected? How do the ratios of performance change? What happens to the present value?

Notes

1. Milton R. Friedman, *Friedman on Leases* (New York: Practicing Law Institute, 1974), p. 92.

2. Ibid., pp. 46–47.

3. Ibid., p. 484.

4. Robert Kratovil and Raymond J. Werner, *Real Estate Law* (Englewood Cliffs, N.J.: Prentice-Hall, Inc., 1979), p. 463.

5. Ibid.

6. Irving Korb, *Real Estate Sale-Leaseback* (Washington, D.C.: Society of Industrial Realtors, 1974), pp. 5–10; Henry Hoagland, Leo D. Stone, and William B. Brueggeman, *Real Estate Finance* (Homewood, Ill.: Richard D. Irwin, Inc., 1979), pp. 342–48.

7. Milton R. Friedman, *Friedman on Leases* (New York: Practicing Law Institute, 1974), p. 290.

8. Ibid.

9. Ibid., p. 291.

10. Ibid., p. 292.

11. Ibid.

12. Ibid., pp. 292–93.

13. Ibid., p. 293.

14. Ibid., pp. 293–94.

15. Ibid., p. 296.

16. Harold F. Lusk and William B. French, *Law of the Real Estate Business* (Homewood, Ill.: Richard D. Irwin, Inc., 1975), p. 396.

17. Friedman, *Friedman on Leases,* p. 635.

18. Lusk and French, *Law of the Real Estate Business,* p. 425.

19. Friedman, *Friedman on Leases,* p. 621.

20. Ibid., pp. 621–22.

21. Ibid., p. 622.

22. Lusk and French, *Law of the Real Estate Business,* p. 417.

23. *The Appraisal of Real Estate* (Chicago, Ill.: American Institute of Real Estate Appraisers, 1983), p. 545.

Additional Readings

FRIEDMAN, MILTON R. *Contracts and Conveyances of Real Property.* New York: Practicing Law Institute, 1975.

_____. *Friedman on Leases.* New York: Practicing Law Institute, 1974.

HENSZEY, BENJAMIN H., and RONALD M. FRIEDMAN. *Real Estate Law.* Boston, Mass.: Warren, Gorham, and Lamont, 1979. Chapter 11.

KRATOVIL, ROBERT, and RAYMOND J. WERNER. *Real Estate Law.* Englewood Cliffs, N.J.: Prentice-Hall, Inc., 1983. Chapter 37.

KORB, IRVING. *Real Estate Sale-Leaseback.* Washington, D.C.: Society of Industrial Realtors, 1974.

LUSK, HAROLD F., and WILLIAM B. FRENCH. *Law of the Real Estate Business.* Homewood, Ill.: Richard D. Irwin, Inc., 1984. Chapter 19.

ZOLL, CLIFFORD A. *Guide to Commercial Property Leasing.* Chicago, Ill.: REALTORS National Marketing Institute, 1979.

16 | The Residential Mortgage and the Application Process

QUESTIONS TO BE ANSWERED

1. How can a person raise cash for a downpayment?
2. What is the mortgage application process?
3. What types of mortgages are available?

OBJECTIVES

When a student finishes the chapter, he or she should be able to

1. Explain the differences between and the role of equity and debt funds in a real estate transaction.
2. Identify and discuss additional sources of equity funds.
3. Explain the differences among refinancing, financing, and buying equity.

4. Discuss the covenants within a residential mortgage that are uniform among all 50 states.

5. Identify and discuss covenants that may be unique to a particular state.

6. Contrast a mortgage to a deed of trust.

7. Explain the purpose of the promissory note and identify the clauses within it.

8. Contrast the steps an applicant must follow in applying for a conventional loan with the steps in applying for a loan carrying default insurance or a guarantee from the FHA, VA, or FmHA.

9. Compare the requirements upon the lender covered within the Real Estate Settlement Procedures Act, Equal Credit Opportunity Act, Regulation Z, and the Depository Institutions Deregulation and Monetary Control Act.

10. Explain the criteria that a local lender would typically use to evaluate a residential loan application.

11. Contrast the various default insurance or guarantee programs available and the agencies that grant them.

12. Explain the characteristics and purpose of a conventional fixed-rate mortgage, a variable-rate mortgage, a renegotiable-rate mortgage, a graduated-payment mortgage, and an alternative-rate mortgage.

13. Identify and explain additional mortgages and contracts that could be used in a residential real estate transaction.

IMPORTANT TERMS

Acceleration
Alienation Clause
Alternative Mortgage Loan (AML)
Alternative Rate Mortgage (ARM)
Amortization
Annual Percentage Rate (APR)
Assignment
Assumption (Equity Buy)
Assumption Contract
Blanket Mortgage
Buydown
Certificate of Eligibility
Certificate of Reasonable Value (CRV)

Conventional Loan
Debiting Factor
Debt Funds
Debt Service
Deed of Trust
Depository Institutions Deregulation and Monetary Control Act (DIDMCA)
Due on Sale Clause
Equal Credit Opportunity Act
Equity Funds
Estoppel Certificate
Farmers Home Administration (FmHA)
Federal Housing Administration (FHA)

Garn-St. Germain Act of 1982
Good Faith Estimate of Clos-
ing Costs
Graduated Payment Mortgage
(GPM)
Housing and Urban Recovery
Act of 1983
Intermediate Theory
Lien Theory
Origination Fee
Point(s)
Real Estate Settlement Proce-
dures Act (RESPA)

Renegotiable Rate Mortgage
(RRM)
Seller Financing
Shared Appreciation Mortgage
(SAM)
Title Theory
Truth-in-Lending
(Regulation Z)
VA Guaranteed Loan
Variable Rate Mortgage (VRM)
Verification of Deposit
Verification of Employment
Veterans Administration (VA)

INTRODUCTION

Most residential real estate transactions would not be possible without a mortgage.
Both buyers and sellers therefore need to be familiar with the mortgage application
process and the characteristics of mortgages. Real estate agents also must be knowledgeable of these matters, because they often counsel buyers about local mortgage
terms and availability as well as possible sources of cash for a downpayment.

THE NEED TO BORROW FUNDS TO PURCHASE
PROPERTY

The price of houses generally necessitates the use of debt funds by real estate purchasers. Rarely does an individual have enough funds to pay the total price in cash.
Residential construction costs have increased over the past several years at an enor-
mously high rate and the prospects for the future do not indicate a decline. In
addition, the market forces of supply and demand have caused significant increases
in the selling price in some regions. The high price of houses and the high interest
rate, in combination with the high cost of living in today's society, have forced the
majority of prospective real estate purchasers to borrow funds for the purchase of a
house.

Debt Funds

Assets belonging to other parties that are used to buy property are called **debt funds.**
The prospective borrower approaches a financial lender and borrows a sum of money
that is added to his or her own funds to equal the total purchase price. The lending
institution loans the funds only if the borrower satisfies the loan qualifications by
having a good credit history, showing employment stability, and revealing good
prospects for income. The amount of the loan is based on the amount requested by
the borrower, the appraisal of the real estate in question, the lender's policies cover-

ing the amount loaned on any one property, and regulations governing the lender. The real estate is used as collateral for the loan, and the instrument created is called a *mortgage*. The borrower is called the *mortgagor* because he or she creates the debt and promises to repay it. The lending institution is called the *mortgagee* because it receives and accepts the offer to create and repay a financial obligation.

The amount of the loan is typically equal to a predetermined percentage of the selling price or to the appraised value, whichever is lower. For example, a lending institution might tell a potential customer that it will loan 90 percent of the selling price or the appraised value, whichever is less. The remaining 10 percent is called the *down payment* and must be raised from the borrower's own assets. The amount that the lender will loan can be divided by the lower of the selling price or the appraised value to form a ratio called the *loan-to-value (L/V) ratio*. The difference between the selling price and the amount loaned by the lender is the *down payment* to be paid by the borrower. The **debt service** is the total principal and interest payment on the loan.

Refinancing and Financing

The term *refinancing* means taking out a new first mortgage at prevailing market conditions to replace a current first mortgage loan. When a *buyer* refinances a current mortgage, the intent is generally to obtain better terms or conditions than those in the current mortgage on the desired property. When an *owner* refinances the current mortgage on the property owned, the purpose is generally to raise cash. For example, consider a house valued at $50,000 with a current loan balance of $30,000 and an 8.5 percent interest rate. The owner could probably refinance the house by taking a $40,000 loan at 13 percent interest for twenty-five years, provided that the neighborhood shows prospects for future growth and the owner's income is good. The owner uses the $40,000 to repay the balance of $30,000 on the first loan and retains $10,000. The owner has "taken out part of the equity."

The term *financing* is often used for the transaction whereby a new first loan is obtained on unmortgaged property. Examples include new property, parcels for which cash was paid, or property on which a loan had been previously paid in full.

Equity Funds

Equity funds are personal assets used for the purchase of property. The amount of equity in any property can be found by using either of two methods, which give the same answer. The first, called the *final-value approach*, consists of subtracting the amount of any debt owed on the property from the selling price. The second method, called the *value-added approach*, consists of summing the down payment, the principal payments on the mortgage balance, and the appreciation or depreciation.

For example, James and Judy Smith have owned their home for two years. They paid $40,000 for it, borrowed $36,000 on a mortgage, and currently owe $34,500. They estimate that the home has increased 12 percent in value. The equity can be computed either way:

THE DECISION TO FINANCE THE TRANSACTION

Final Value

Estimated selling price ($40,000 $\times$ 0.12 = $4,800)	$44,800
Minus the current mortgage balance	34,500
Equity	$10,300

Value Added

Down payment	$ 4,000
Payments to the mortgage	1,500
Principal appreciation ($40,000 $\times$ 0.12 = $4,800)	4,800
Equity	$10,300

Most lenders do not grant loans equal to 100 percent of the value of the property. They set an L/V ratio and require the customer to pay the balance in cash as the down payment. Thus, immediate equity is created in a property as soon as it is purchased. Default by the buyer and possible foreclosure are minimized by the lender when the loan is less than 100 percent and the buyer has invested personal assets in the property.

SOURCES OF CASH FOR A DOWN PAYMENT

Methods of Raising Additional Cash

A potential borrower may have a good credit history, good employment stability, and good prospects for income, but not enough cash to make the down payment on the property desired. Assume that in the foregoing example James and Judy Smith only had $2,000 when they first looked at their present home. Since they needed $4,000 in cash as the down payment, they faced an immediate need to raise additional equity funds.

Unsecured loan   One alternative is to obtain a short-term, unsecured personal loan from a commercial bank. An unsecured loan does not have any collateral pledged to cover the loan in case of default, is typically for a small amount ($2,500 or less) and has a short term of maturity. In addition, a commercial bank will not be willing to extend credit unless the applicant has an account with the bank and, in some cases, has a credit history already established with the bank.

Secured loan   Another alternative is to obtain a secured loan from a bank. The borrower must pledge collateral to cover the risk of default. Proof of ownership of the collateral is left in the possession of the bank until the loan is paid in full. Typically, the loan is larger in amount than an unsecured loan, and the term to maturity is longer.

Seller financing   Another method of raising cash for the required down payment is to ask the seller to extend credit for the difference (or for part of the difference) between the selling price of the property and the amount loaned by the financial institution. The seller can do this by instruments such as a second mortgage, an installment note, or a purchase money mortgage. A second mortgage is explained in Chapters 17 and 18. An *installment note* is a promise to repay under certain terms such as monthly payments, 12 percent interest, and maturity of ten years. Payments are made regularly to the owner just as they are made to the lender of the first mortgage. The difference between a second mortgage and the installment note is basically that the second mortgage has the property as security and the installment note does not. The *purchase money mortgage* is defined as a mortgage whereby the seller extends credit as part of the buyer's offering price. The original mortgage and the credit extended by the seller can be placed under one mortgage document. Further examples and characteristics of an installment note and a purchase money mortgage are discussed in Chapter 18, "Creative Financing."

Other possible sources of equity funds   A borrower may be able to raise additional funds by seeking an advance on future wages, using cash value in a life insurance policy, borrowing cash from relatives, or selling other assets. In addition, the amount of equity needed may be reduced in some cases if the borrower provides some of the work on the transaction or does work on the property rather than employing others to do it (sweat equity).

TYPICAL RESIDENTIAL MORTGAGE CHARACTERISTICS

The term *mortgage* is used to define a type of long-term real estate loan wherein the property that is purchased is used as collateral. It is a *conditional ownership of property* that is contingent upon the new buyer satisfying the terms of the mortgage, which include a promise to make the payments when due. If this condition is not satisfied, the mortgagee can reclaim ownership by following predetermined steps of *foreclosure.*

Title Theory Versus Lien Theory

A state legislature can enact a set of laws interpreting the mortgage by either of two concepts. One is called **title theory** and refers to the older common-law thinking that the mortgagee (the lender) retains the deed and actually owns the property. The mortgagor (the buyer) is given possession and the right to collect income from the property as long as the monthly payments are made when due. Once the final payment is rendered, the deed is transferred. In this case the mortgage is an instrument to identify the terms of the arrangement when a debt is made. According to the other concept, **lien theory,** the deed is actually passed to the new mortgagor (the buyer) and the mortgagee (the lender) retains a lien right that can be exercised upon default. To the borrower the differences between the two concepts are technical and have no effect. The differences are important to the lender, however, because they involve claims to the rights of possession and the collection of rents in the case of default.

The third concept is followed in some states where the state statute interprets the mortgage under title theory and the courts interpret it under a lien theory. These states are called **intermediate theory** states.

A Residential Mortgage

The typical residential mortgage used by lenders in the United States since the 1930s has several characteristics: (1) The mortgage interest rate remains constant throughout the term of the mortgage provided that the mortgage debt is not taken over by a new mortgagor prior to maturity. (2) The maturity date is fixed once it is determined. (3) The periodic payments to the debt service for mortgage reduction and interest remain constant. (4) The **amortization** is *full*—that is, the mortgage debt is reduced to zero by the last payment. The newer contemporary mortgages such as the alternative rate mortgage and the graduated payment mortgage involve alterations to a combination of these four points and are discussed in another section of the chapter.

Exhibit 16-1 shows a typical conventional mortgage that is recommended by the Mortgage Corporation and the Federal National Mortgage Association. The first seventeen Uniform Covenants apply to all states. Any covenants that pertain to individual state laws are added. This document illustrates the five basic characteristics of a legal contract: the parties are able to contract by being of legal age and sane, the document is in writing, consideration or something of value is given, the object of the contract is legal, the consent is real, and the makers have affixed their signatures.

Another term for "covenant" is "promise." The lender asks the borrower to make certain promises to protect the collateral value of the asset and to eliminate the possibility that a tax lien will be imposed on the property. A general description of each of these promises follows.

1. *Payment of principal and interest.* The borrower agrees to pay the principal and interest when due.
2. *Funds for taxes and insurance.* Unless the lender approves otherwise, the borrower shall pay 1/12 of the annual property tax payment and 1/12 of the annual insurance premium into an account that shall be used to make these annual payments when due.
3. *Application of payments.* Payments under numbers (1) and (2) are credited first to taxes and insurance, then to interest, then to the principal, then to future advances.
4. *Charges, liens.* The borrower shall give notice to the lender of all claims to the property and agrees to pay them.
5. *Hazard insurance.* The borrower shall maintain an insurance policy covering the premises.
6. *Preservation and maintenance of the premises.* The borrower shall keep the property in good repair.
7. *Protection of lender's security.* If the borrower breaks any of the covenants, the lender shall take whatever action is necessary to protect its interests.

EXHIBIT 16-1 Uniform covenants

MORTGAGE

THIS MORTGAGE is made this. . .First. . . . . .day of. . February, 1986. . . . .,
. . . . . between the Mortgagor, Michael and Nita Ann Watson . . . .
. . . . (herein "Borrower"), and the Mortgagee, Fourth . . . .
Federal Savings and Loan . . . ., a corporation organized and existing
under the laws of. Arkansas . . . ., whose address is. 1205 North . . . .
. 15th Street, Little Rock, AR . . . . (herein "Lender").

WHEREAS, Borrower is indebted to Lender in the principal sum of. . sixty eight thousand . . . .
. ($68,000) . . . . .Dollars, which indebtedness is evidenced by Borrower's note
dated. February 1, 1986 . . . . . . (herein "Note"), providing for monthly installments of principal and interest,
with the balance of the indebtedness, if not sooner paid, due and payable on. February 1, 2011 . . . .
. . . .;

To SECURE to Lender (a) the repayment of the indebtedness evidenced by the Note, with interest thereon, the
payment of all other sums, with interest thereon, advanced in accordance herewith to protect the security of this
Mortgage, and the performance of the covenants and agreements of Borrower herein contained, and (b) the repayment
of any future advances, with interest thereon, made to Borrower by Lender pursuant to paragraph 21 hereof (herein
"Future Advances"), Borrower does hereby mortgage, grant and convey to Lender the following described property
located in the County of. . . .Pulaski . . . ., State of Arkansas:

Lot 16, Block 3, of the Hidden Valley Subdivision as shown on the plat
recorder in the Circuit Clerk's Office on page 72 of Deed Book 106 in
Pulaski County.

which has the address of. . . . .#16. Hidden. Valley, Little. Rock, AR. 72201 . . . .,
                             [Street]   [City]
. . . . (herein "Property Address");
         [State and Zip Code]

TOGETHER with all the improvements now or hereafter erected on the property, and all easements, rights,
appurtenances, rents, royalties, mineral, oil and gas rights and profits, water, water rights, and water stock, and all
fixtures now or hereafter attached to the property, all of which, including replacements and additions thereto, shall be
deemed to be and remain a part of the property covered by this Mortgage; and all of the foregoing, together with said
property (or the leasehold estate if this Mortgage is on a leasehold) are herein referred to as the "Property".

Borrower covenants that Borrower is lawfully seised of the estate hereby conveyed and has the right to mortgage,
grant and convey the Property, that the Property is unencumbered, and that Borrower will warrant and defend
generally the title to the Property against all claims and demands, subject to any declarations, easements or restrictions
listed in a schedule of exceptions to coverage in any title insurance policy insuring Lender's interest in the Property.

EXHIBIT 16-1 (continued)

UNIFORM COVENANTS. Borrower and Lender covenant and agree as follows:

1. Payment of Principal and Interest. Borrower shall promptly pay when due the principal of and interest on the indebtedness evidenced by the Note, prepayment and late charges as provided in the Note, and the principal of and interest on any Future Advances secured by this Mortgage.

2. Funds for Taxes and Insurance. Subject to applicable law or to a written waiver by Lender, Borrower shall pay to Lender on the day monthly installments of principal and interest are payable under the Note, until the Note is paid in full, a sum (herein "Funds") equal to one-twelfth of the yearly taxes and assessments which may attain priority over this Mortgage, and ground rents on the Property, if any, plus one-twelfth of yearly premium installments for hazard insurance, plus one-twelfth of yearly premium installments for mortgage insurance, if any, all as reasonably estimated initially and from time to time by Lender on the basis of assessments and bills and reasonable estimates thereof.

The Funds shall be held in an institution the deposits or accounts of which are insured or guaranteed by a Federal or state agency (including Lender if Lender is such an institution). Lender shall apply the Funds to pay said taxes, assessments, insurance premiums and ground rents. Lender may not charge for so holding and applying the Funds, analyzing said account, or verifying and compiling said assessments and bills, unless Lender pays Borrower interest on the Funds and applicable law permits Lender to make such a charge. Borrower and Lender may agree in writing at the time of execution of this Mortgage that interest on the Funds shall be paid to Borrower, and unless such agreement is made or applicable law requires such interest to be paid, Lender shall not be required to pay Borrower any interest or earnings on the Funds. Lender shall give to Borrower, without charge, an annual accounting of the Funds showing credits and debits to the Funds and the purpose for which each debit to the Funds was made. The Funds are pledged as additional security for the sums secured by this Mortgage.

If the amount of the Funds held by Lender, together with the future monthly installments of Funds payable prior to the due dates of taxes, assessments, insurance premiums and ground rents, shall exceed the amount required to pay said taxes, assessments, insurance premiums and ground rents as they fall due, such excess shall be, at Borrower's option, either promptly repaid to Borrower or credited to Borrower on monthly installments of Funds. If the amount of the Funds held by Lender shall not be sufficient to pay taxes, assessments, insurance premiums and ground rents as they fall due, Borrower shall pay to Lender any amount necessary to make up the deficiency within 30 days from the date notice is mailed by Lender to Borrower requesting payment thereof.

Upon payment in full of all sums secured by this Mortgage, Lender shall promptly refund to Borrower any Funds held by Lender. If under paragraph 18 hereof the Property is sold or the Property is otherwise acquired by Lender, Lender shall apply, no later than immediately prior to the sale of the Property or its acquisition by Lender, any Funds held by Lender at the time of application as a credit against the sums secured by this Mortgage.

3. Application of Payments. Unless applicable law provides otherwise, all payments received by Lender under the Note and paragraphs 1 and 2 hereof shall be applied by Lender first in payment of amounts payable to Lender by Borrower under paragraph 2 hereof, then to interest payable on the Note, then to the principal of the Note, and then to interest and principal on any Future Advances.

4. Charges; Liens. Borrower shall pay all taxes, assessments and other charges, fines and impositions attributable to the Property which may attain a priority over this Mortgage, and leasehold payments or ground rents, if any, in the manner provided under paragraph 2 hereof or, if not paid in such manner, by Borrower making payment, when due, directly to the payee thereof. Borrower shall promptly furnish to Lender all notices of amounts due under this paragraph, and in the event Borrower shall make payment directly, Borrower shall promptly furnish to Lender receipts evidencing such payments. Borrower shall promptly discharge any lien which has priority over this Mortgage; provided, that Borrower shall not be required to discharge any such lien so long as Borrower shall agree in writing to the payment of the obligation secured by such lien in a manner acceptable to Lender, or shall in good faith contest such lien by, or defend enforcement of such lien in, legal proceedings which operate to prevent the enforcement of the lien or forfeiture of the Property or any part thereof.

5. Hazard Insurance. Borrower shall keep the improvements now existing or hereafter erected on the Property insured against loss by fire, hazards included within the term "extended coverage", and such other hazards as Lender may require and in such amounts and for such periods as Lender may require; provided, that Lender shall not require that the amount of such coverage exceed that amount of coverage required to pay the sums secured by this Mortgage.

The insurance carrier providing the insurance shall be chosen by Borrower subject to approval by Lender; provided, that such approval shall not be unreasonably withheld. All premiums on insurance policies shall be paid in the manner provided under paragraph 2 hereof or, if not paid in such manner, by Borrower making payment, when due, directly to the insurance carrier.

All insurance policies and renewals thereof shall be in form acceptable to Lender and shall include a standard mortgage clause in favor of and in form acceptable to Lender. Lender shall have the right to hold the policies and renewals thereof, and Borrower shall promptly furnish to Lender all renewal notices and all receipts of paid premiums. In the event of loss, Borrower shall give prompt notice to the insurance carrier and Lender. Lender may make proof of loss if not made promptly by Borrower.

Unless Lender and Borrower otherwise agree in writing, insurance proceeds shall be applied to restoration or repair of the Property damaged, provided such restoration or repair is economically feasible and the security of this Mortgage is not thereby impaired. If such restoration or repair is not economically feasible or if the security of this Mortgage would be impaired, the insurance proceeds shall be applied to the sums secured by this Mortgage, with the excess, if any, paid to Borrower. If the Property is abandoned by Borrower, or if Borrower fails to respond to Lender within 30 days from the date notice is mailed by Lender to Borrower that the insurance carrier offers to settle a claim for insurance benefits, Lender is authorized to collect and apply the insurance proceeds at Lender's option either to restoration or repair of the Property or to the sums secured by this Mortgage.

Unless Lender and Borrower otherwise agree in writing, any such application of proceeds to principal shall not extend or postpone the due date of the monthly installments referred to in paragraphs 1 and 2 hereof or change the amount of such installments. If under paragraph 18 hereof the Property is acquired by Lender, all right, title and interest of Borrower in and to any insurance policies and in and to the proceeds thereof resulting from damage to the Property prior to the sale or acquisition shall pass to Lender to the extent of the sums secured by this Mortgage immediately prior to such sale or acquisition.

6. Preservation and Maintenance of Property; Leaseholds; Condominiums; Planned Unit Developments. Borrower shall keep the Property in good repair and shall not commit waste or permit impairment or deterioration of the Property and shall comply with the provisions of any lease if this Mortgage is on a leasehold. If this Mortgage is on a unit in a condominium or a planned unit development, Borrower shall perform all of Borrower's obligations under the declaration or covenants creating or governing the condominium or planned unit development, the by-laws and regulations of the condominium or planned unit development, and constituent documents. If a condominium or planned unit development rider is executed by Borrower and recorded together with this Mortgage, the covenants and agreements of such rider shall be incorporated into and shall amend and supplement the covenants and agreements of this Mortgage as if the rider were a part hereof.

7. Protection of Lender's Security. If Borrower fails to perform the covenants and agreements contained in this Mortgage, or if any action or proceeding is commenced which materially affects Lender's interest in the Property, including, but not limited to, eminent domain, insolvency, code enforcement, or arrangements or proceedings involving a bankrupt or decedent, then Lender at Lender's option, upon notice to Borrower, may make such appearances, disburse such sums and take such action as is necessary to protect Lender's interest, including, but not limited to, disbursement of reasonable attorney's fees and entry upon the Property to make repairs. If Lender required mortgage insurance as a condition of making the loan secured by this Mortgage, Borrower shall pay the premiums required to maintain such insurance in effect until such time as the requirement for such insurance terminates in accordance with Borrower's and

EXHIBIT 16-1 (continued)

Lender's written agreement or applicable law. Borrower shall pay the amount of all mortgage insurance premiums in the manner provided under paragraph 2 hereof.

Any amounts disbursed by Lender pursuant to this paragraph 7, with interest thereon, shall become additional indebtedness of Borrower secured by this Mortgage. Unless Borrower and Lender agree to other terms of payment, such amounts shall be payable upon notice from Lender to Borrower requesting payment thereof, and shall bear interest from the date of disbursement at the rate payable from time to time on outstanding principal under the Note unless payment of interest at such rate would be contrary to applicable law, in which event such amounts shall bear interest at the highest rate permissible under applicable law. Nothing contained in this paragraph 7 shall require Lender to incur any expense or take any action hereunder.

8. Inspection. Lender may make or cause to be made reasonable entries upon and inspections of the Property, provided that Lender shall give Borrower notice prior to any such inspection specifying reasonable cause therefor related to Lender's interest in the Property.

9. Condemnation. The proceeds of any award or claim for damages, direct or consequential, in connection with any condemnation or other taking of the Property, or part thereof, or for conveyance in lieu of condemnation, are hereby assigned and shall be paid to Lender.

In the event of a total taking of the Property, the proceeds shall be applied to the sums secured by this Mortgage, with the excess, if any, paid to Borrower. In the event of a partial taking of the Property, unless Borrower and Lender otherwise agree in writing, there shall be applied to the sums secured by this Mortgage such proportion of the proceeds as is equal to that proportion which the amount of the sums secured by this Mortgage immediately prior to the date of taking bears to the fair market value of the Property immediately prior to the date of taking, with the balance of the proceeds paid to Borrower.

If the Property is abandoned by Borrower, or if, after notice by Lender to Borrower that the condemnor offers to make an award or settle a claim for damages, Borrower fails to respond to Lender within 30 days after the date such notice is mailed, Lender is authorized to collect and apply the proceeds, at Lender's option, either to restoration or repair of the Property or to the sums secured by this Mortgage.

Unless Lender and Borrower otherwise agree in writing, any such application of proceeds to principal shall not extend or postpone the due date of the monthly installments referred to in paragraphs 1 and 2 hereof or change the amount of such installments.

10. Borrower Not Released. Extension of the time for payment or modification of amortization of the sums secured by this Mortgage granted by Lender to any successor in interest of Borrower shall not operate to release, in any manner, the liability of the original Borrower and Borrower's successors in interest. Lender shall not be required to commence proceedings against such successor or refuse to extend time for payment or otherwise modify amortization of the sums secured by this Mortgage by reason of any demand made by the original Borrower and Borrower's successors in interest.

11. Forbearance by Lender Not a Waiver. Any forbearance by Lender in exercising any right or remedy hereunder, or otherwise afforded by applicable law, shall not be a waiver of or preclude the exercise of any such right or remedy. The procurement of insurance or the payment of taxes or other liens or charges by Lender shall not be a waiver of Lender's right to accelerate the maturity of the indebtedness secured by this Mortgage.

12. Remedies Cumulative. All remedies provided in this Mortgage are distinct and cumulative to any other right or remedy under this Mortgage or afforded by law or equity, and may be exercised concurrently, independently or successively.

13. Successors and Assigns Bound; Joint and Several Liability; Captions. The covenants and agreements herein contained shall bind, and the rights hereunder shall inure to, the respective successors and assigns of Lender and Borrower, subject to the provisions of paragraph 17 hereof. All covenants and agreements of Borrower shall be joint and several. The captions and headings of the paragraphs of this Mortgage are for convenience only and are not to be used to interpret or define the provisions hereof.

14. Notice. Except for any notice required under applicable law to be given in another manner, (a) any notice to Borrower provided for in this Mortgage shall be given by mailing such notice by certified mail addressed to Borrower at the Property Address or at such other address as Borrower may designate by notice to Lender as provided herein, and (b) any notice to Lender shall be given by certified mail, return receipt requested, to Lender's address stated herein or to such other address as Lender may designate by notice to Borrower as provided herein. Any notice provided for in this Mortgage shall be deemed to have been given to Borrower or Lender when given in the manner designated herein.

15. Uniform Mortgage; Governing Law; Severability. This form of mortgage combines uniform covenants for national use and non-uniform covenants with limited variations by jurisdiction to constitute a uniform security instrument covering real property. This Mortgage shall be governed by the law of the jurisdiction in which the Property is located. In the event that any provision or clause of this Mortgage or the Note conflicts with applicable law, such conflict shall not affect other provisions of this Mortgage or the Note which can be given effect without the conflicting provision, and to this end the provisions of the Mortgage and the Note are declared to be severable.

16. Borrower's Copy. Borrower shall be furnished a conformed copy of the Note and of this Mortgage at the time of execution or after recordation hereof.

17. Transfer of the Property; Assumption. If all or any part of the Property or an interest therein is sold or transferred by Borrower without Lender's prior written consent, excluding (a) the creation of a lien or encumbrance subordinate to this Mortgage, (b) the creation of a purchase money security interest for household appliances, (c) a transfer by devise, descent or by operation of law upon the death of a joint tenant or (d) the grant of any leasehold interest of three years or less not containing an option to purchase, Lender may, at Lender's option, declare all the sums secured by this Mortgage to be immediately due and payable. Lender shall have waived such option to accelerate if, prior to the sale or transfer, Lender and the person to whom the Property is to be sold or transferred reach agreement in writing that the credit of such person is satisfactory to Lender and that the interest payable on the sums secured by this Mortgage shall be at such rate as Lender shall request. If Lender has waived the option to accelerate provided in this paragraph 17, and if Borrower's successor in interest has executed a written assumption agreement accepted in writing by Lender, Lender shall release Borrower from all obligations under this Mortgage and the Note.

If Lender exercises such option to accelerate, Lender shall mail Borrower notice of acceleration in accordance with paragraph 14 hereof. Such notice shall provide a period of not less than 30 days from the date the notice is mailed within which Borrower may pay the sums declared due. If Borrower fails to pay such sums prior to the expiration of such period, Lender may, without further notice or demand on Borrower, invoke any remedies permitted by paragraph 18 hereof.

NON-UNIFORM COVENANTS. Borrower and Lender further covenant and agree as follows:

18. Acceleration; Remedies. Except as provided in paragraph 17 hereof, upon Borrower's breach of any covenant or agreement of Borrower in this Mortgage, including the covenants to pay when due any sums secured by this Mortgage, Lender prior to acceleration shall mail notice to Borrower as provided in paragraph 14 hereof specifying: (1) the breach; (2) the action required to cure such breach; (3) a date, not less than 30 days from the date the notice is mailed to Borrower, by which such breach must be cured; and (4) that failure to cure such breach on or before the date specified in the notice may result in acceleration of the sums secured by this Mortgage, foreclosure by judicial proceeding and sale of the Property. The notice shall further inform Borrower of the right to reinstate after acceleration and the right to assert in the foreclosure proceeding the non-existence of a default or any other defense of Borrower to acceleration and foreclosure. If the breach is not cured on or before the date specified in the notice, Lender at Lender's option may declare all of the sums secured by this Mortgage to be immediately due and payable without further demand and may foreclose this Mortgage by judicial proceeding. Lender shall be entitled to collect in such proceeding all expenses of foreclosure, including, but not limited to, reasonable attorney's fees, and costs of documentary evidence, abstracts and title reports.

19. Borrower's Right to Reinstate. Notwithstanding Lender's acceleration of the sums secured by this Mortgage, Borrower shall have the right to have any proceedings begun by Lender to enforce this Mortgage discontinued at any time

EXHIBIT 16-1   (continued)

prior to entry of a judgment enforcing this Mortgage if: (a) Borrower pays Lender all sums which would be then due under this Mortgage, the Note and notes securing Future Advances, if any, had no acceleration occurred; (b) Borrower cures all breaches of any other covenants or agreements of Borrower contained in this Mortgage; (c) Borrower pays all reasonable expenses incurred by Lender in enforcing the covenants and agreements of Borrower contained in this Mortgage and in enforcing Lender's remedies as provided in paragraph 18 hereof including, but not limited to, reasonable attorney's fees; and (d) Borrower takes such action as Lender may reasonably require to assure that the lien of this Mortgage. Lender's interest in the Property and Borrower's obligation to pay the sums secured by this Mortgage shall continue unimpaired. Upon such payment and cure by Borrower, this Mortgage and the obligations secured hereby shall remain in full force and effect as if no acceleration had occurred.

20. Assignment of Rents; Appointment of Receiver; Lender in Possession. As additional security hereunder, Borrower hereby assigns to Lender the rents of the Property, provided that Borrower shall, prior to acceleration under paragraph 18 hereof or abandonment of the Property, have the right to collect and retain such rents as they become due and payable.

Upon acceleration under paragraph 18 hereof or abandonment of the Property, Lender, in person, by agent or by judicially appointed receiver, shall be entitled to enter upon, take possession of and manage the Property and to collect the rents of the Property including those past due. All rents collected by Lender or the receiver shall be applied first to payment of the costs of management of the Property and collection of rents, including, but not limited to, receiver's fees, premiums on receiver's bonds and reasonable attorney's fees, and then to the sums secured by this Mortgage. Lender and the receiver shall be liable to account only for those rents actually received.

21. Future Advances. Upon request of Borrower, Lender, at Lender's option prior to release of this Mortgage, may make Future Advances to Borrower. Such Future Advances, with interest thereon, shall be secured by this Mortgage when evidenced by promissory notes stating that said notes are secured hereby.

22. Release. Upon payment of all sums secured by this Mortgage, Lender shall release this Mortgage without charge to Borrower. Borrower shall pay all costs of recordation, if any.

23. Waiver of Homestead, Dower, Redemption, and Appraisement. Borrower hereby waives all rights of homestead exemption in, and statutory redemption of, the Property and all right of appraisement of the Property and relinquishes all right of dower in the Property.

IN WITNESS WHEREOF, Borrower has executed this Mortgage.

Michael Watson .... —Borrower
Michael Watson

Nita Ann Watson .... —Borrower
Nita Ann Watson

STATE OF ARKANSAS, ... Pulaski .... County ss:

On this First ...... day of ... February, 19.86 , before me, the undersigned officer, personally appeared ..Michael and Nita Ann Watson.. known to me (or satisfactorily proven) to be the person(s) whose name(s) .they........ subscribed to the within instrument and acknowledged that t.he.y executed the same for the consideration and purposes therein contained. And on the same day also voluntarily appeared before me, the undersigned officer, Nita Ann .Watson .... , wife of the said.. Michael .Watson ...., known to me (or satisfactorily proven) to be the person whose name is subscribed to the within instrument, and in the absence of her husband declared that she had, of her own free will, executed the foregoing Mortgage and signed and sealed the relinquishment of dower and of homestead therein for the consideration and purpose therein set forth, without compulsion or undue influence of her said husband.

IN TESTIMONY WHEREOF, I hereunto set my hand and official seal.

...... *Jon Brown* ....
Jon Brown

....
Title of Officer
Real Estate Loan Officer

8. *Inspection.* The lender may enter the property with reasonable notice.

9. *Condemnation.* Condemnation damages are paid to the lender up to the sum secured; any excess goes to the borrower.

10. *Borrower not released.* Any extension of time for the mortgage or change in the amortization schedule does not release the borrower from the repayment commitment.

11. *Forbearance by lender not a waiver.* Any lack of action by the lender shall not be interpreted as a relinquishment of that right.

12. *Remedies cumulative.* All remedies in this mortgage that are available to the lender can be exercised concurrently or successively.

13. *Successors and assigns bound.* These covenants bind the successors of the lender and other parties receiving assigned benefits from the borrower.

14. *Notice.* Notice to the borrower shall be given by certified mail to the address on the mortgage. Notice by the borrower to the lender is given by certified mail also.

15. *Uniform mortgage.* Should any part of this mortgage conflict with local law, the remainder of the mortgage shall still remain valid.

16. *Borrower's copy.* The borrower shall be given a copy of this mortgage.

17. *Transfer of property; assumption.* The lender has the right to foreclose or raise the interest rate if the debt is assumed by a new buyer without the lender's approval. This section of the mortgage is often called the **due on sale** clause, which is one type of "alienation" clause. Any time the security is transferred to another party without the lender's approval, the lender is alienated from the transaction and reacts by either calling the debt due and payable or increasing the interest rate.

Nonuniform covenants   Nonuniform covenants are added to comply with state laws. Since state statutes vary significantly, the student should obtain a standard FNMA/FHLMC form used by lenders to determine the typical state covenants in his or her state. The following are examples of possible clauses:

18. *Acceleration remedies.* The lender may move the maturity date to the current date if the borrower breaches any of the covenants.

19. *Borrower's right to reinstate.* The borrower can stop any of the foreclosure proceedings prior to the judgment by rectifying the breach and paying the lender any monies owed.

20. *Assignment of rents.* As additional security, the borrower assigns the rents in the property to the lender.

21. *Future advances.* Before the expiration of this mortgage, the lender may make additional advances to the borrower that are still secured by this document.

22. *Release.* The lender will extinguish all commitments made by this mortgage upon payment of the debt.

23. *Waiver of dower, homestead, redemption, and appraisement.* The borrower extinguishes all of these rights including statutory redemption. *Dower* is the right of a widow to claim a portion of her husband's estate. *Homestead* is the right of the head of a household to claim an exemption for a portion of the family home from the claims of certain creditors. *Redemption* is the right of *statutory redemption,* which gives the mortgagor in some states the option of paying the mortgage debt within a specific time period after a foreclosure sale and reclaiming ownership. *Appraisement* refers to the right of the mortgagor to insist upon an appraisal of value at the time of foreclosure to estimate the property value to be solicited during the foreclosure sale.

The nonpayment of the monthly obligation in covenant number (1) is the most common cause of default on a mortgage. The borrower should remember that number (7) says that the lender may take whatever action is necessary if the borrower breaks *any* of the promises.

Promissory Note

A promissory note is defined as the borrower's personal obligation to repay the debt and is viewed as evidence of the debt. One promissory note signed by the borrower always accompanies the mortgage. A typical note to accompany the mortgage (Exhibit 16-1) is shown in Exhibit 16-2. A general description of its components follows:

1. *Date.* The date of the note is identified.
2. *Mortgagor and mortgagee.* The mortgagee is identified and the location where payments are to be made is stated.
3. *Interest rate, monthly payment, and maturity date.* The annual mortgage interest rate, monthly payment, and maturity date are specified.
4. *Acceleration clause.* The lender has the option of moving the maturity date to the current date as a first step in foreclosure if any payments are missed or if any of the covenants are breached.
5. *Interest escalation clause and grace period.* The lender has the right to charge an increased interest rate on delinquent payments. Payments are defined as delinquent after a predetermined period.
6. *Prepayment penalty.* The lender may assess the borrower additional interest if any payments are made in advance.
7. *Notice.* Any notice of breach by the borrower shall be mailed to the lender by certified mail.

Deed of Trust

In some states, a **deed of trust** (trust deed) is used in lieu of a mortgage. The new owner (trustor) transfers legal title to a neutral third party (trustee) as security for

EXHIBIT 16-2

NOTE

US $ .68,000 . . . . Little Rock . . . ., Arkansas

City

. . .February .1, ..., 19 .86 .

FOR VALUE RECEIVED, the undersigned ("Borrower") promise(s) to pay . Fourth . Federal . . . .
. Savings .and .Loan . . . ., or order, the principal sum of
. . .Sixty-Eight .Thousand .($68,000) . . . . .Dollars, with
interest on the unpaid principal balance from the date of this Note, until paid, at the rate of . .12.50 . . . .
. . . . .percent per annum. Principal and interest shall be payable at . Fourth . Federal . . . . . .
. Savings .and .Loan . . . ., or such other place as the Note holder may
designate, in consecutive monthly installments of . . Seven . hundred . forty . one . dollars . and . . . .
. . . . .44/100 . . . . .Dollars (US $ .741.44 . . . .), on the . First . . . .
. . . . .day of each month beginning . . . . .March . . . . .1 . . . . ., 19 .86 . . Such monthly installments
shall continue until the entire indebtedness evidenced by this Note is fully paid, except that any remaining indebtedness, if not sooner paid, shall be due and payable on . .February .1, .2011 . . . .

If any monthly installment under this Note is not paid when due and remains unpaid after a date specified by a notice to Borrower, the entire principal amount outstanding and accrued interest thereon shall at once become due and payable at the option of the Note holder. The date specified shall not be less than thirty days from the date such notice is mailed. The Note holder may exercise this option to accelerate during any default by Borrower regardless of any prior forbearance. If suit is brought to collect this Note, the Note holder shall be entitled to collect all reasonable costs and expenses of suit, including, but not limited to, reasonable attorney's fees.

Borrower shall pay to the Note holder a late charge of . .12.50 . . . . .percent of any monthly installment not received by the Note holder within . . . .21 .days after the installment is due.

Borrower may prepay the principal amount outstanding in whole or in part. The Note holder may require that any partial prepayments (i) be made on the date monthly installments are due and (ii) be in the amount of that part of one or more monthly installments which would be applicable to principal. Any partial prepayment shall be applied against the principal amount outstanding and shall not postpone the due date of any subsequent monthly installments or change the amount of such installments, unless the Note holder shall otherwise agree in writing.

Presentment, notice of dishonor, and protest are hereby waived by all makers, sureties, guarantors and endorsers hereof. This Note shall be the joint and several obligation of all makers, sureties, guarantors and endorsers, and shall be binding upon them and their successors and assigns.

Any notice to Borrower provided for in this Note shall be given by mailing such notice by certified mail addressed to Borrower at the Property Address stated below, or to such other address as Borrower may designate by notice to the Note holder. Any notice to the Note holder shall be given by mailing such notice by certified mail, return receipt requested, to the Note holder at the address stated in the first paragraph of this Note, or at such other address as may have been designated by notice to Borrower.

The indebtedness evidenced by this Note is secured by a Mortgage, dated . February .1, .1986 . . . .
. . . ., and reference is made to the Mortgage for rights as to acceleration of the indebtedness evidenced by this Note.

Michael Watson
Michael Watson

. . . . #16 Hidden Valley, Little Rock . . . . *Nita Ann Watson*
Nita Ann Watson

. . . . Arkansas, 72201 . . . .
Property Address *(Execute Original Only)*

ARKANSAS —1 to 4 Family—8/79—FNMA/FHLMC UNIFORM INSTRUMENT periodic payments made to the lender (beneficiary). The trust deed simply serves as an alternative to the mortgage. In a deed of trust transaction, the trustor gives (a) a promissory note to the beneficiary and (b) a trust deed to the trustee. In contrast, in a mortgage, a nonpossessionary security interest is given to the lender, who holds it until the debt is repaid. Upon payment of the debt in a deed of trust, the property interest that was in the trust is released from the trust.[1] In other words, under a deed of trust, the buyer receives the deed when the debt is paid.

Since no mortgage exists that gives the beneficiary a security interest, a time-consuming foreclosure process can be avoided in the case of default. In addition, the holder of the promissory note can easily transfer the commitment without an assignment, as required under a mortgage.

With a deed of trust, the borrower may not enjoy a statutory right of redemption in some states. In addition, the proof of repayment of the debt to release the property interest from the trust is the responsibility of the trustor (new owner). This process requires accurate record-keeping.[2]

The trustee must be an independent third party selected with the consent of all parties. The trustee has a fiduciary relationship with the trustor and the beneficiary and must accept liability for the terms of the trust.

A deed of trust contains a provision that gives the trustee the power to sell the property in the event of a default in the payments. In many states, mortgages can be foreclosed by exercise of a *power of sale clause* and without any court proceedings. If the instrument is a regular mortgage, the power of sale may be conferred on the mortgagee in some states. In Colorado, the power of sale must be exercised by an official known as the public trustee; in Minnesota, the sale is made by the sheriff or a deputy; and in Georgia, the deed to secure debt that is used in lieu of a mortgage is foreclosed by the grantee (the lender) by exercise of his or her power of sale.

Foreclosure by exercise of the power of sale clause is not permitted by law in a number of states. In other states, laws do not forbid use of this method, but it is not the customary method of foreclosure. In states where it is employed, the mortgage or trust deed outlines the events of default that will give the trustee or mortgagee power to sell the premises. Also, it specifies the notice of sale that must be given and the other formalities that must be followed in making the sale.

The fact that a deed of trust contains a power of sale clause does not prevent a foreclosure suit. If the judicial foreclosure procedure is followed by the beneficiary and the selling price is less than the unpaid balance of the debt, the beneficiary (the lender), in those cases where *deficiency judgments* are not prohibited by state law, can go back to court and sue to obtain a deficiency decree.

When the note is repaid in full the lender sends the trustee a *request for reconveyance*. The trustee cancels the note and issues a *reconveyance deed* to the trustor (new owner).

Exhibit 16-3 is a typical deed of trust for the State of Colorado. A general description of its unique features follows. The promissory note to accompany the deed of trust is the same as the one in Exhibit 16-2.

1. *Deed of trust document.* A deed of trust is being used rather than a mortgage.

EXHIBIT 16-3

DEED OF TRUST

THIS DEED OF TRUST is made this. First . . . . day of . February, 1986 . . . .
19 80 ., among the Grantor, . . . Michael and Nita Ann Watson . . . .
. . . . (herein "Borrower"), the Public Trustee of
. . . . Pueblo . . . . County (herein "Trustee"), and the Beneficiary, . Fourth . . . . .
. . . . Federal Savings and Loan . . . . , a corporation organized and
existing under the laws of . Colorado . . . . , whose address is . 1819 . . . .
. . . . West. 16th, . Pueblo, . Colorado . . . . (herein "Lender").

BORROWER, in consideration of the indebtedness herein recited and the trust herein created, irrevocably grants
and conveys to Trustee, in trust, with power of sale, the following described property located in the County of
. . . . Pueblo . . . . , State of Colorado:

Lot 16, Block 2, Hidden Valley Subdivision, as shown on the plat filed in the
Recorder's Office on page 89 of Deed Book 109 in Pueblo County.

which has the address of . . . . #16 .Hidden. Valley,. Pueblo,. Colorado . . . . ,
                                              [Street]   [City]
. . . . (herein "Property Address");
          [State and Zip Code]

TOGETHER with all the improvements now or hereafter erected on the property, and all easements, rights,
appurtenances, rents (subject however to the rights and authorities given herein to Lender to collect and apply such
rents), royalties, mineral, oil and gas rights and profits, water, water rights, and water stock, and all fixtures now or
hereafter attached to the property, all of which, including replacements and additions thereto, shall be deemed to be
and remain a part of the property covered by this Deed of Trust; and all of the foregoing, together with said property
(or the leasehold estate if this Deed of Trust is on a leasehold) are herein referred to as the "Property";

To SECURE to Lender (a) the repayment of the indebtedness evidenced by Borrower's note dated . February.
. .1, 1986 . . . . (herein "Note"), in the principal sum of . . Sixty-eight thousand . . . .
. . ($68,000) . . . . Dollars, with interest thereon, providing for monthly
installments of principal and interest, with the balance of the indebtedness, if not sooner paid, due and payable on
. February 1, 2011 . . . . ; the payment of all other sums, with interest thereon, advanced
in accordance herewith to protect the security of this Deed of Trust; and the performance of the covenants and
agreements of Borrower herein contained; and (b) the repayment of any future advances, with interest thereon, made
to Borrower by Lender pursuant to paragraph 21 hereof (herein "Future Advances").

Borrower covenants that Borrower is lawfully seised of the estate hereby conveyed and has the right to grant and
convey the Property, that the Property is unencumbered, and that Borrower will warrant and defend generally the title
to the Property against all claims and demands, subject to any declarations, easements or restrictions listed in a
schedule of exceptions to coverage in any title insurance policy insuring Lender's interest in the Property.

COLORADO—1 to 4 Family—6/75—FNMA/FHLMC UNIFORM INSTRUMENT

EXHIBIT 16-3 (continued)

UNIFORM COVENANTS. Borrower and Lender covenant and agree as follows:

1. Payment of Principal and Interest. Borrower shall promptly pay when due the principal of and interest on the indebtedness evidenced by the Note, prepayment and late charges as provided in the Note, and the principal of and interest on any Future Advances secured by this Deed of Trust.

2. Funds for Taxes and Insurance. Subject to applicable law or to a written waiver by Lender, Borrower shall pay to Lender on the day monthly installments of principal and interest are payable under the Note, until the Note is paid in full, a sum (herein "Funds") equal to one-twelfth of the yearly taxes and assessments which may attain priority over this Deed of Trust, and ground rents on the Property, if any, plus one-twelfth of yearly premium installments for hazard insurance, plus one-twelfth of yearly premium installments for mortgage insurance, if any, all as reasonably estimated initially and from time to time by Lender on the basis of assessments and bills and reasonable estimates thereof.

The Funds shall be held in an institution the deposits or accounts of which are insured or guaranteed by a Federal or state agency (including Lender if Lender is such an institution). Lender shall apply the Funds to pay said taxes, assessments, insurance premiums and ground rents. Lender may not charge for so holding and applying the Funds, analyzing said account or verifying and compiling said assessments and bills, unless Lender pays Borrower interest on the Funds and applicable law permits Lender to make such a charge. Borrower and Lender may agree in writing at the time of execution of this Deed of Trust that interest on the Funds shall be paid to Borrower, and unless such agreement is made or applicable law requires such interest to be paid, Lender shall not be required to pay Borrower any interest or earnings on the Funds. Lender shall give to Borrower, without charge, an annual accounting of the Funds showing credits and debits to the Funds and the purpose for which each debit to the Funds was made. The Funds are pledged as additional security for the sums secured by this Deed of Trust.

If the amount of the Funds held by Lender, together with the future monthly installments of Funds payable prior to the due dates of taxes, assessments, insurance premiums and ground rents, shall exceed the amount required to pay said taxes, assessments, insurance premiums and ground rents as they fall due, such excess shall be, at Borrower's option, either promptly repaid to Borrower or credited to Borrower on monthly installments of Funds. If the amount of the Funds held by Lender shall not be sufficient to pay taxes, assessments, insurance premiums and ground rents as they fall due, Borrower shall pay to Lender any amount necessary to make up the deficiency within 30 days from the date notice is mailed by Lender to Borrower requesting payment thereof.

Upon payment in full of all sums secured by this Deed of Trust, Lender shall promptly refund to Borrower any Funds held by Lender. If under paragraph 18 hereof the Property is sold or the Property is otherwise acquired by Lender, Lender shall apply, no later than immediately prior to the sale of the Property or its acquisition by Lender, any Funds held by Lender at the time of application as a credit against the sums secured by this Deed of Trust.

3. Application of Payments. Unless applicable law provides otherwise, all payments received by Lender under the Note and paragraphs 1 and 2 hereof shall be applied by Lender first in payment of amounts payable to Lender by Borrower under paragraph 2 hereof, then to interest payable on the Note, then to the principal of the Note, and then to interest and principal on any Future Advances.

4. Charges; Liens. Borrower shall pay all taxes, assessments and other charges, fines and impositions attributable to the Property which may attain a priority over this Deed of Trust, and leasehold payments or ground rents, if any, in the manner provided under paragraph 2 hereof or, if not paid in such manner, by Borrower making payment, when due, directly to the payee thereof. Borrower shall promptly furnish to Lender all notices of amounts due under this paragraph, and in the event Borrower shall make payment directly, Borrower shall promptly furnish to Lender receipts evidencing such payments. Borrower shall promptly discharge any lien which has priority over this Deed of Trust; provided, that Borrower shall not be required to discharge any such lien so long as Borrower shall agree in writing to the payment of the obligation secured by such lien in a manner acceptable to Lender, or shall in good faith contest such lien by, or defend enforcement of such lien in, legal proceedings which operate to prevent the enforcement of the lien or forfeiture of the Property or any part thereof.

5. Hazard Insurance. Borrower shall keep the improvements now existing or hereafter erected on the Property insured against loss by fire, hazards included within the term "extended coverage", and such other hazards as Lender may require and in such amounts and for such periods as Lender may require; provided, that Lender shall not require that the amount of such coverage exceed that amount of coverage required to pay the sums secured by this Deed of Trust.

The insurance carrier providing the insurance shall be chosen by Borrower subject to approval by Lender; provided, that such approval shall not be unreasonably withheld. All premiums on insurance policies shall be paid in the manner provided under paragraph 2 hereof or, if not paid in such manner, by Borrower making payment, when due, directly to the insurance carrier.

All insurance policies and renewals thereof shall be in form acceptable to Lender and shall include a standard mortgage clause in favor of and in form acceptable to Lender. Lender shall have the right to hold the policies and renewals thereof, and Borrower shall promptly furnish to Lender all renewal notices and all receipts of paid premiums. In the event of loss, Borrower shall give prompt notice to the insurance carrier and Lender. Lender may make proof of loss if not made promptly by Borrower.

Unless Lender and Borrower otherwise agree in writing, insurance proceeds shall be applied to restoration or repair of the Property damaged, provided such restoration or repair is economically feasible and the security of this Deed of Trust is not thereby impaired. If such restoration or repair is not economically feasible or if the security of this Deed of Trust would be impaired, the insurance proceeds shall be applied to the sums secured by this Deed of Trust, with the excess, if any, paid to Borrower. If the Property is abandoned by Borrower, or if Borrower fails to respond to Lender within 30 days from the date notice is mailed by Lender to Borrower that the insurance carrier offers to settle a claim for insurance benefits, Lender is authorized to collect and apply the insurance proceeds at Lender's option either to restoration or repair of the Property or to the sums secured by this Deed of Trust.

Unless Lender and Borrower otherwise agree in writing, any such application of proceeds to principal shall not extend or postpone the due date of the monthly installments referred to in paragraphs 1 and 2 hereof or change the amount of such installments. If under paragraph 18 hereof the Property is acquired by Lender, all right, title and interest of Borrower in and to any insurance policies and in and to the proceeds thereof resulting from damage to the Property prior to the sale or acquisition shall pass to Lender to the extent of the sums secured by this Deed of Trust immediately prior to such sale or acquisition.

6. Preservation and Maintenance of Property; Leaseholds; Condominiums; Planned Unit Developments. Borrower shall keep the Property in good repair and shall not commit waste or permit impairment or deterioration of the Property and shall comply with the provisions of any lease if this Deed of Trust is on a leasehold. If this Deed of Trust is on a unit in a condominium or a planned unit development, Borrower shall perform all of Borrower's obligations under the declaration or covenants creating or governing the condominium or planned unit development, the by-laws and regulations of the condominium or planned unit development, and constituent documents. If a condominium or planned unit development rider is executed by Borrower and recorded together with this Deed of Trust, the covenants and agreements of such rider shall be incorporated into and shall amend and supplement the covenants and agreements of this Deed of Trust as if the rider were a part hereof.

7. Protection of Lender's Security. If Borrower fails to perform the covenants and agreements contained in this Deed of Trust, or if any action or proceeding is commenced which materially affects Lender's interest in the Property, including, but not limited to, eminent domain, insolvency, code enforcement, or arrangements or proceedings involving a bankrupt or decedent, then Lender at Lender's option, upon notice to Borrower, may make such appearances, disburse such sums and take such action as is necessary to protect Lender's interest, including, but not limited to, disbursement of reasonable attorney's fees and entry upon the Property to make repairs. If Lender required mortgage insurance as a condition of making the loan secured by this Deed of Trust, Borrower shall pay the premiums required to maintain such insurance in effect until such time as the requirement for such insurance terminates in accordance with Borrower's and Lender's written agreement or applicable law. Borrower shall pay the amount of all mortgage insurance premiums in the manner provided under paragraph 2 hereof.

Any amounts disbursed by Lender pursuant to this paragraph 7, with interest thereon, shall become additional indebtedness of Borrower secured by this Deed of Trust. Unless Borrower and Lender agree to other terms of payment, such amounts shall be payable upon notice from Lender to Borrower requesting payment thereof, and shall bear interest from the date of disbursement at the rate payable from time to time on outstanding principal under the Note unless payment of interest at such rate would be contrary to applicable law, in which event such amounts shall bear interest at the highest rate permissible under applicable law. Nothing contained in this paragraph 7 shall require Lender to incur any expense or take any action hereunder.

8. Inspection. Lender may make or cause to be made reasonable entries upon and inspections of the Property, provided that Lender shall give Borrower notice prior to any such inspection specifying reasonable cause therefor related to Lender's interest in the Property.

EXHIBIT 16-3   (continued)

9. Condemnation. The proceeds of any award or claim for damages, direct or consequential, in connection with any condemnation or other taking of the Property, or part thereof, or for conveyance in lieu of condemnation, are hereby assigned and shall be paid to Lender.

In the event of a total taking of the Property, the proceeds shall be applied to the sums secured by this Deed of Trust, with the excess, if any, paid to Borrower. In the event of a partial taking of the Property, unless Borrower and Lender otherwise agree in writing, there shall be applied to the sums secured by this Deed of Trust such proportion of the proceeds as is equal to that proportion which the amount of the sums secured by this Deed of Trust immediately prior to the date of taking bears to the fair market value of the Property immediately prior to the date of taking, with the balance of the proceeds paid to Borrower.

If the Property is abandoned by Borrower, or if, after notice by Lender to Borrower that the condemnor offers to make an award or settle a claim for damages, Borrower fails to respond to Lender within 30 days after the date such notice is mailed, Lender is authorized to collect and apply the proceeds, at Lender's option, either to restoration or repair of the Property or to the sums secured by this Deed of Trust.

Unless Lender and Borrower otherwise agree in writing, any such application of proceeds to principal shall not extend or postpone the due date of the monthly installments referred to in paragraphs 1 and 2 hereof or change the amount of such installments.

10. Borrower Not Released. Extension of the time for payment or modification of amortization of the sums secured by this Deed of Trust granted by Lender to any successor in interest of Borrower shall not operate to release, in any manner, the liability of the original Borrower and Borrower's successors in interest. Lender shall not be required to commence proceedings against such successor or refuse to extend time for payment or otherwise modify amortization of the sums secured by this Deed of Trust by reason of any demand made by the original Borrower and Borrower's successors in interest.

11. Forbearance by Lender Not a Waiver. Any forbearance by Lender in exercising any right or remedy hereunder, or otherwise afforded by applicable law, shall not be a waiver of or preclude the exercise of any such right or remedy. The procurement of insurance or the payment of taxes or other liens or charges by Lender shall not be a waiver of Lender's right to accelerate the maturity of the indebtedness secured by this Deed of Trust.

12. Remedies Cumulative. All remedies provided in this Deed of Trust are distinct and cumulative to any other right or remedy under this Deed of Trust or afforded by law or equity, and may be exercised concurrently, independently or successively.

13. Successors and Assigns Bound; Joint and Several Liability; Captions. The covenants and agreements herein contained shall bind, and the rights hereunder shall inure to, the respective successors and assigns of Lender and Borrower, subject to the provisions of paragraph 17 hereof. All covenants and agreements of Borrower shall be joint and several. The captions and headings of the paragraphs of this Deed of Trust are for convenience only and are not to be used to interpret or define the provisions hereof.

14. Notice. Except for any notice required under applicable law to be given in another manner, (a) any notice to Borrower provided for in this Deed of Trust shall be given by mailing such notice by certified mail addressed to Borrower at the Property Address or at such other address as Borrower may designate by notice to Lender as provided herein, and (b) any notice to Lender shall be given by certified mail, return receipt requested, to Lender's address stated herein or to such other address as Lender may designate by notice to Borrower as provided herein. Any notice provided for in this Deed of Trust shall be deemed to have been given to Borrower or Lender when given in the manner designated herein.

15. Uniform Deed of Trust; Governing Law; Severability. This form of deed of trust combines uniform covenants for national use and non-uniform covenants with limited variations by jurisdiction to constitute a uniform security instrument covering real property. This Deed of Trust shall be governed by the law of the jurisdiction in which the Property is located. In the event that any provision or clause of this Deed of Trust or the Note conflicts with applicable law, such conflict shall not affect other provisions of this Deed of Trust or the Note which can be given effect without the conflicting provision, and to this end the provisions of the Deed of Trust and the Note are declared to be severable.

16. Borrower's Copy. Borrower shall be furnished a conformed copy of the Note and of this Deed of Trust at the time of execution or after recordation hereof.

17. Transfer of the Property; Assumption. If all or any part of the Property or an interest therein is sold or transferred by Borrower without Lender's prior written consent, excluding (a) the creation of a lien or encumbrance subordinate to this Deed of Trust, (b) the creation of a purchase money security interest for household appliances, (c) a transfer by devise, descent or by operation of law upon the death of a joint tenant or (d) the grant of any leasehold interest of three years or less not containing an option to purchase, Lender may, at Lender's option, declare all the sums secured by this Deed of Trust to be immediately due and payable. Lender shall have waived such option to accelerate if, prior to the sale or transfer, Lender and the person to whom the Property is to be sold or transferred reach agreement in writing that the credit of such person is satisfactory to Lender and that the interest payable on the sums secured by this Deed of Trust shall be at such rate as Lender shall request. If Lender has waived the option to accelerate provided in this paragraph 17, and if Borrower's successor in interest has executed a written assumption agreement accepted in writing by Lender, Lender shall release Borrower from all obligations under this Deed of Trust and the Note.

If Lender exercises such option to accelerate, Lender shall mail Borrower notice of acceleration in accordance with paragraph 14 hereof. Such notice shall provide a period of not less than 30 days from the date the notice is mailed within which Borrower may pay the sums declared due. If Borrower fails to pay such sums prior to the expiration of such period, Lender may, without further notice or demand on Borrower, invoke any remedies permitted by paragraph 18 hereof.

NON-UNIFORM COVENANTS. Borrower and Lender further covenant and agree as follows:

18. Acceleration; Remedies. Except as provided in paragraph 17 hereof, upon Borrower's breach of any covenant or agreement of Borrower in this Deed of Trust, including the covenants to pay when due any sums secured by this Deed of Trust, Lender prior to acceleration shall mail notice to Borrower as provided in paragraph 14 hereof specifying: (1) the breach; (2) the action required to cure such breach; (3) a date, not less than 30 days from the date the notice is mailed to Borrower, by which such breach must be cured; and (4) that failure to cure such breach on or before the date specified in the notice may result in acceleration of the sums secured by this Deed of Trust and sale of the Property. The notice shall further inform Borrower of the right to reinstate after acceleration and the right to assert in the foreclosure proceeding the non-existence of a default or any other defense of Borrower to acceleration and sale. If the breach is not cured on or before the date specified in the notice, Lender at Lender's option may declare all of the sums secured by this Deed of Trust to be immediately due and payable without further demand and may invoke the power of sale and any other remedies permitted by applicable law. Lender shall be entitled to collect all reasonable costs and expenses incurred in pursuing the remedies provided in this paragraph 18, including, but not limited to, reasonable attorney's fees.

If Lender invokes the power of sale, Lender shall give written notice to Trustee of the occurrence of an event of default and of Lender's election to cause the Property to be sold. Lender shall mail a copy of such notice to Borrower as provided in paragraph 14 hereof. Trustee shall record a copy of such notice in the county in which the Property is located. Trustee shall publish a notice of sale for the time and in the manner provided by applicable law and shall mail copies of such notice of sale in the manner prescribed by applicable law to Borrower and to the other persons prescribed by applicable law. After the lapse of such time as may be required by applicable law, Trustee, without demand on Borrower, shall sell the Property at public auction to the highest bidder for cash at the time and place and under the terms designated in the notice of sale in one or more parcels and in such order as Trustee may determine. Trustee may postpone sale of all or any parcel of the Property by public announcement at the time and place of any previously scheduled sale. Lender or Lender's designee may purchase the Property at any sale.

Trustee shall deliver to the purchaser Trustee's certificate describing the Property and the time when the purchaser will be entitled to Trustee's deed thereto. The recitals in Trustee's deed shall be prima facie evidence of the truth of the statements made therein. Trustee shall apply the proceeds of the sale in the following order: (a) to all reasonable costs and expenses of the sale, including, but not limited to, reasonable Trustee's and attorney's fees and costs of title evidence; (b) to all sums secured by this Deed of Trust; and (c) the excess, if any, to the person or persons legally entitled thereto.

19. Borrower's Right to Reinstate. Notwithstanding Lender's acceleration of the sums secured by this Deed of Trust, Borrower shall have the right to have any proceedings begun by Lender to enforce this Deed of Trust discontinued at any time prior to the earlier to occur of (i) the fifth day before sale of the Property pursuant to the power of sale contained in this Deed of Trust or (ii) entry of a judgment enforcing this Deed of Trust if: (a) Borrower pays Lender all sums which would be then due under this Deed of Trust, the Note and notes securing Future Advances, if any, had no acceleration occurred; (b) Borrower cures all breaches of any other covenants or agreements of Borrower contained in this Deed of Trust; (c) Borrower pays all reasonable expenses incurred by Lender and Trustee in enforcing the covenants and agreements of Borrower contained in this Deed of Trust and in enforcing Lender's and Trustee's remedies as provided in paragraph 18 hereof, including, but not limited to, reasonable attorney's fees and Trustee's expenses and withdrawal fee; and (d) Borrower takes such action as

EXHIBIT 16-3 (continued)

Lender may reasonably require to assure that the lien of this Deed of Trust, Lender's interest in the Property and Borrower's obligation to pay the sums secured by this Deed of Trust shall continue unimpaired. Upon such payment and cure by Borrower, this Deed of Trust and the obligations secured hereby shall remain in full force and effect as if no acceleration had occurred.

20. Assignment of Rents; Appointment of Receiver; Lender in Possession. As additional security hereunder, Borrower hereby assigns to Lender the rents of the Property, provided that Borrower shall, prior to acceleration under paragraph 18 hereof or abandonment of the Property, have the right to collect and retain such rents as they become due and payable.

Upon acceleration under paragraph 18 hereof or abandonment of the Property, Lender, in person, by agent or by judicially appointed receiver, shall be entitled to enter upon, take possession of and manage the Property and to collect the rents of the Property including those past due. All rents collected by Lender or the receiver shall be applied first to payment of the costs of management of the Property and collection of rents, including, but not limited to, receiver's fees, premiums on receiver's bonds and reasonable attorney's fees, and then to the sums secured by this Deed of Trust. Lender and the receiver shall be liable to account only for those rents actually received.

21. Future Advances. Upon request of Borrower, Lender, at Lender's option prior to release of this Deed of Trust, may make Future Advances to Borrower. Such Future Advances, with interest thereon, shall be secured by this Deed of Trust when evidenced by promissory notes stating that said notes are secured hereby.

22. Release. Upon payment of all sums secured by this Deed of Trust, Lender shall request Trustee to release this Deed of Trust and shall produce for Trustee duly cancelled all notes evidencing indebtedness secured by this Deed of Trust. Trustee shall release this Deed of Trust without further inquiry or liability. Borrower shall pay all costs of recordation, if any, and shall pay the statutory Trustee's fees.

23. Waiver of Homestead. Borrower hereby waives all right of homestead exemption in the Property.

IN WITNESS WHEREOF, Borrower has executed this Deed of Trust.

.... *Michael Watson* ....
Michael Watson —Borrower

.... *Nita Ann Watson* ....
Nita Ann Watson —Borrower

STATE OF COLORADO, ... Pueblo .... County ss:

The foregoing instrument was acknowledged before me this First .... day of February, ..., 19. 86, by .James. D. .Snooker ....

Witness my hand and official seal.

My commission expires:

.... James. D. .Snooker .... *James D Snooker* ....
Notary Public

(Space Below This Line Reserved For Lender and Recorder)

467

2. *Three parties to the contract.* The trustor, trustee, and the beneficiary are identified.
3. *Power of sale clause.* The trustee has the right of power of sale in case of default.
4. *Release.* Upon payment of all sums under this mortgage, the lender will extinguish any commitments by the borrower.

Equity Buy and Assumption Contract

A buyer can purchase property by *buying the equity* and *assuming* the remaining debt. This type of transaction is typically called an **assumption** because the lender usually requires an **assumption contract** that commits the buyer to future debt payments. The buyer pays in equity a sum equal to the difference between the selling price and the current mortgage balance.

In the acceleration clause, number 18 in Exhibit 16-1, the lender retains the option of foreclosing on the mortgage if the owner transfers the property by selling the equity without telling the lender in advance. The lender wants the option of approving the new owner's credit prior to the transaction, and of possibly raising the interest rate.

Exhibit 16-4 is an assumption contract for a transaction in Alabama. Its components are described in general:

1. *Identification of grantors.* The sellers are identified.
2. *Original mortgage amount.* The original mortgage amount is stated.
3. *Property sale.* The property has been sold.
4. *Lender agreement.* The lender agrees to the transaction.
5. *New interest rate.* The lender and the new buyer agree to this interest rate on the remaining debt.
6. *Remaining debt assumed.* The remaining debt owed is stated.
7. *Monthly payments identified.* The monthly debt service on the remaining debt is identified.
8. *Borrower's liability.* The original borrowers still maintain liability for the debt.

Buying, Subject to the Mortgage

A purchaser may buy property by agreeing with the seller to take over the existing payments and paying the owner his or her equity in the property. Typically, the purchaser does not sign a promissory note. In the event of foreclosure, the seller will be liable to the lender for the amount of a possible deficiency judgment. Thus, the buyer has purchased the property *subject to* the existing loan as opposed to assuming any liability for it.

EXHIBIT 16-4   Assumption agreement

ASSUMPTION AGREEMENT

STATE OF ALABAMA   )
COUNTY OF TUSCALOOSA)

WHEREAS, Fourth Federal Savings and Loan loaned Michael and

Nita Ann Watson, husband and wife, the sum of Sixty-Eight Thousand

($68,000) Dollars evidenced by Note and Mortgage dated February 1,

1986 recorded in Mortgage Book 78 Page 567 Probate Office of Tuscaloosa

County. WHEREAS, said Borrowers have sold the said property to the

undersigned Purchasers and said Purchasers desire to assume and agree to

pay said indebtedness and to perform all the obligations under said

Loan Contract, and said Association is willing to consent to said

transfer of title and assumption of said indebtedness at an interest

rate of 12.5 percent per annum, but is not willing to release said

Borrowers from their present liability on said Note and Mortgage;

THEREFORE, in consideration of the mutual covenants and agreements

herein contained, IT IS HEREBY AGREED AS FOLLOWS:

1. The Association does consent to the sale and conveyance
   of said premises by the aforesaid Borrowers to said
   Purchasers.

2. The Purchasers do hereby assume and agree to pay said
   mortgage indebtedness, evidenced by said Note and Mortgage,
   and to perform all of the obligations provided therein,
   it being agreed and understood that as of this date the
   indebtedness is Sixty-Seven Thousand, One Hundred Two
   Dollars and 57/100 ($67,102.57) and that the interest
   rate shall be twelve and one-half (12.5) per cent per
   annum and that monthly payments shall be made beginning
   on the 1st day of February, 1986 in the sum of Seven
   Hundred Forty-One Dollars and 44/100 per month, to be
   applied first to interest and the balance to principal
   until said indebtedness is paid in full.

3. The Borrowers agree that their present liability under said
   mortgage loan shall not be impaired, prejudiced or affected
   in any way whatsoever by this agreement, or by sale or conveyance of said premises, or by the change in the terms,
   time, manner or method of payment of said indebtedness, or
   any part thereof, contracted by the Association and the
   Purchasers or by the Transferees of the Purchasers, whether
   or not such changes or such transfers have been consented
   by the Borrowers. This assumption by said Purchasers is
   joint and several and shall bind them, their heirs, personal
   representatives, successors and assigns.

IN WITNESS WHEREOF, the parties have hereunto executed this

instrument on this _1st_ day of ~~February~~ , 198_6_ .

BORROWERS: PURCHASERS:

Michael Watson   _Ben Buyer_

Nita Ann Watson   _Sue Buyer_

                                              FOURTH FEDERAL SAVINGS AND LOAN

APPLYING FOR A MORTGAGE

Shopping for a Lender

One of the best recommendations that can be given to a prospective property owner is to allocate sufficient time to shop among financial lenders and compare terms to find one that offers a real estate mortgage containing terms that fit the individual's needs. A real estate loan is likely to be the single largest debt that a person will create in a lifetime, and the terms of that debt should suit the borrower. The following typical loan terms can vary among lenders:

- *Size of the down payment.* The size of the required cash down payment typically ranges from 5 to 20 percent of the selling price or the appraised value, whichever is lower.
- *Mortgage interest rate.* The exact mortgage interest rate can vary by 1 to 2 percentage points with the size of the down payment. The greater the amount of the down payment, the lower the interest rate until it reaches a minimum.
- *Amount of default insurance.* The amount of default insurance that the lender requires the borrower to purchase depends on the size of the down payment. Normally loans for less than 75 to 80 percent of the property value will not require default insurance.
- *Length of the grace period.* A grace period defines the period of time in which the borrower can make the mortgage payment and still have it counted as paid on time. Grace periods range from a week to thirty days.
- *Prepayment penalty.* A prepayment penalty may be charged the borrower for making payments to the mortgage balance ahead of schedule. This penalty is typically stated as interest on the mortgage amount paid in advance. Penalties can range from none to several months' interest.
- *Interest rate escalation clause.* This clause within the promissory note identifies the penalty that is assessed the borrower if the mortgage payments are not made within the grace period. This penalty is usually figured by escalating the mortgage interest rate to a higher figure on the unpaid payment only.
- *Federal Housing Administration insurance, Veterans Administration guarantee, and the Farmers Home Administration guaranteed loans.* Not all lenders are approved to grant local loans covered by default insurance or a default guarantee issued by these agencies. A borrower can simply ask whether the lender has been approved.

The first step for a prospective borrower is to accumulate all the cash that can be made available for a down payment. The second step is to find a lender that will grant the amount of loan needed by the buyer to purchase the property desired. This involves shopping among lenders and comparing terms of mortgages. Normally,

THE DECISION TO FINANCE THE TRANSACTION

a borrower wants the longest maturity possible, the longest grace period possible, no prepayment penalty, no due-on-sale clause, and the lowest interest rate escalation possible. Whether default insurance is required depends on the size of the down payment.

Necessary Information for a Mortgage Application

Mortgage loans are typically classified as *conventional* or *nonconventional.* A **conventional loan** has neither default insurance nor a guarantee from the Federal Housing Administration, Farmers Home Administration, or the Veterans Administration. A *nonconventional loan* has default insurance or a guarantee from one of these agencies. The application procedures differ somewhat, depending on the type of loan and the default insurance or guarantee being sought.

Conventional loan   Anyone can apply for a conventional loan. The application procedure usually includes the following steps:

1. The applicant submits a residential loan application form like the one shown in Exhibit 16-5.
2. The lender completes the Good Faith Estimate of Closing Costs.
3. Applicant is given the HUD booklet containing an explanation of RESPA.
4. The lender requests a credit report from the credit bureau on the applicant's credit history.
5. The lender requests a form, Verification of Employment, to ensure that the applicant has steady and permanent employment.
6. The lender may ask the applicant to complete a form, Verification of Deposit, to ensure that the down payment exists and can be readily transferred to the lender.
7. The lender collects a fee for the appraisal and the charge for the credit report.
8. The lender either makes the appraisal or contracts with an appraiser to do it.
9. The whole file on the applicant is sent to the loan committee, which consists of selected officials from the lender's staff and directors who evaluate the file and render a decision.

Veterans Administration guaranteed loan   A local lender can loan its own funds to an eligible veteran and ask the VA to guarantee up to $27,500 (1985 figures) or 60 percent of the loan amount, whichever is less, against default. The application procedure usually consists of the following steps:

1. The applicant submits the residential loan application.
2. A VA application is completed by the lender.
3. A **certificate of reasonable value (CRV)** is requested from VA. This certificate contains the selling price or the appraised value, whichever is

EXHIBIT 16-5

RESIDENTIAL LOAN APPLICATION

MORTGAGE APPLIED FOR ☛	☐ Conventional ☐ VA	☐ FHA ☐	Amount $ ___	Interest Rate ___ %	No. of Months ___	Monthly Payment Principal & Interest $ ___	Escrow/Impounds (to be collected monthly) ☐ Taxes ☐ Hazard Ins. ☐ Mtg. Ins. ☐ ___

Prepayment Option

SUBJECT PROPERTY

Property Street Address	City	County	State	Zip	No. Units

Legal Description (Attach description if necessary)	Year Built

Purpose of Loan: ☐ Purchase ☐ Construction-Permanent ☐ Construction ☐ Refinance ☐ Other (Explain)

Complete this line if Construction-Permanent or Construction Loan ☛	Lot Value Data	Original Cost	Present Value (a)	Cost of Imps. (b)	Total (a + b)	ENTER TOTAL AS PURCHASE PRICE IN DETAILS OF ☜ PURCHASE.
	Year Acquired $ ___	$ ___	$ ___	$ ___		

Complete this line if a Refinance Loan	Purpose of Refinance		Describe Improvements	☐ made	☐ to be made	
Year Acquired	Original Cost	Amt. Existing Liens			Cost: $ ___	
	$ ___	$ ___				

Title Will Be Held In What Name(s)	Manner In Which Title Will Be Held

Source of Down Payment and Settlement Charges

This application is designed to be completed by the borrower(s) with the lender's assistance. The Co-Borrower Section and all other Co-Borrower questions must be completed and the appropriate box(es) checked if ☐ another person will be jointly obligated with the Borrower on the loan, or ☐ the Borrower is relying on income from alimony, child support or separate maintenance or on the income or assets of another person as a basis for repayment of the loan, or ☐ the Borrower is married and resides, or the property is located, in a community property state.

BORROWER				CO-BORROWER			
Name		Age	School Yrs ___	Name		Age	School Yrs ___
Present Address	No. Years ___ ☐ Own ☐ Rent			Present Address	No. Years ___ ☐ Own ☐ Rent		
Street				Street			
City/State/Zip				City/State/Zip			
Former address if less than 2 years at present address				Former address if less than 2 years at present address			
Street				Street			
City/State/Zip				City/State/Zip			
Years at former address	☐ Own ☐ Rent			Years at former address	☐ Own ☐ Rent		

Marital Status	☐ Married ☐ Separated ☐ Unmarried (incl. single, divorced, widowed)	DEPENDENTS OTHER THAN LISTED BY CO-BORROWER NO ___ AGES ___	Marital Status	☐ Married ☐ Separated ☐ Unmarried (incl. single, divorced, widowed)	DEPENDENTS OTHER THAN LISTED BY BORROWER NO ___ AGES ___

Name and Address of Employer	Years employed in this line of work or profession? ___ years	Name and Address of Employer	Years employed in this line of work or profession? ___ years
	Years on this job ___ ☐ Self Employed*		Years on this job ___ ☐ Self Employed*
Position/Title	Type of Business	Position/Title	Type of Business
Social Security Number***	Home Phone	Business Phone	Social Security Number***	Home Phone	Business Phone

GROSS MONTHLY INCOME				MONTHLY HOUSING EXPENSE**			DETAILS OF PURCHASE	
Item	Borrower	Co-Borrower	Total		PRESENT	PROPOSED	Do Not Complete If Refinance	
Base Empl. Income	$	$	$	Rent	$		a. Purchase Price	$
Overtime				First Mortgage (P&I)		$	b. Total Closing Costs (Est.)	
Bonuses				Other Financing (P&I)			c. Prepaid Escrows (Est.)	
Commissions				Hazard Insurance			d. Total (a + b + c)	$
Dividends/Interest				Real Estate Taxes			e. Amount This Mortgage	( )
Net Rental Income				Mortgage Insurance			f. Other Financing	( )
Other† (Before completing, see notice under Describe Other Income below.)				Homeowner Assn. Dues			g. Other Equity	( )
				Other:			h. Amount of Cash Deposit	( )
				Total Monthly Pmt.	$	$	i. Closing Costs Paid by Seller	( )
				Utilities			j. Cash Reqd. For Closing (Est.)	$
Total	$	$	$	Total	$	$		

DESCRIBE OTHER INCOME

☐ B—Borrower C—Co-Borrower	NOTICE: † Alimony, child support, or separate maintenance income need not be revealed if the Borrower or Co-Borrower does not choose to have it considered as a basis for repaying this loan.	Monthly Amount
		$

IF EMPLOYED IN CURRENT POSITION FOR LESS THAN TWO YEARS COMPLETE THE FOLLOWING

B/C	Previous Employer/School	City/State	Type of Business	Position/Title	Dates From/To	Monthly Income
						$

THESE QUESTIONS APPLY TO BOTH BORROWER AND CO-BORROWER

If a "yes" answer is given to a question in this column, explain on an attached sheet.	Borrower Yes or No	Co-Borrower Yes or No	If applicable, explain Other Financing or Other Equity (provide addendum if more space is needed).
Have you any outstanding judgments? In the last 7 years, have you been declared bankrupt?			
Have you had property foreclosed upon or given title or deed in lieu thereof?			
Are you a co-maker or endorser on a note?			
Are you a party to a law suit?			
Are you obligated to pay alimony, child support, or separate maintenance?			
Is any part of the down payment borrowed?			

*FHLMC/FNMA require business credit report, signed Federal Income Tax returns for last two years, and, if available, audited Profit and Loss Statements plus balance sheet for same period.
**All Present Monthly Housing Expenses of Borrower and Co-Borrower should be listed on a combined basis.
***Neither FHLMC nor FNMA requires this information.

FHLMC 65 Rev. 8/78   FNMA 1003 Rev. 8/78

EXHIBIT 16-5 (continued)

This Statement and any applicable supporting schedules may be completed jointly by both married and unmarried co-borrowers if their assets and liabilities are sufficiently joined so that the Statement can be meaningfully and fairly presented on a combined basis; otherwise separate Statements and Schedules are required (FHLMC 65A/FNMA 1003A). If the co-borrower section was completed about a spouse, this statement and supporting schedules must be completed about that spouse also. ☐ Completed Jointly ☐ Not Completed Jointly

ASSETS		LIABILITIES AND PLEDGED ASSETS			

Indicate by (*) those liabilities or pledged assets which will be satisfied upon sale of real estate owned or upon refinancing of subject property

Description	Cash or Market Value	Creditors' Name, Address and Account Number	Acct. Name if Not Borrower's	Mo. Pmt. and Mos. left to pay	Unpaid Balance
Cash Deposit Toward Purchase Held By	$	Installment Debts (include "revolving" charge accts)		$ Pmt./Mos.	$
Checking and Savings Accounts (Show Names of Institutions/Acct. Nos.)					
Stocks and Bonds (No./Description)					
Life Insurance Net Cash Value Face Amount ($)		Other Debts Including Stock Pledges			
SUBTOTAL LIQUID ASSETS	$				
Real Estate Owned (Enter Market Value from Schedule of Real Estate Owned)		Real Estate Loans			
Vested Interest in Retirement Fund					
Net Worth of Business Owned (ATTACH FINANCIAL STATEMENT)					
Automobiles (Make and Year)		Automobile Loans			
Furniture and Personal Property Other Assets (Itemize)		Alimony, Child Support and Separate Maintenance Payments Owed To			
		TOTAL MONTHLY PAYMENTS		$	
TOTAL ASSETS	A $	NET WORTH (A minus B) $		TOTAL LIABILITIES	B $

SCHEDULE OF REAL ESTATE OWNED (If Additional Properties Owned Attach Separate Schedule)

Address of Property (Indicate S if Sold, PS if Pending Sale or R if Rental being held for income)	Type of Property	Present Market Value	Amount of Mortgages & Liens	Gross Rental Income	Mortgage Payments	Taxes, Ins. Maintenance and Misc.	Net Rental Income
		$	$	$	$	$	$
TOTALS →		$	$	$	$	$	$

LIST PREVIOUS CREDIT REFERENCES

B–Borrower C–Co-Borrower	Creditor's Name and Address	Account Number	Purpose	Highest Balance	Date Paid
				$	

List any additional names under which credit has previously been received _____

AGREEMENT: The undersigned applies for the loan indicated in this application to be secured by a first mortgage or deed of trust on the property described herein, and represents that the property will not be used for any illegal or restricted purpose, and that all statements made in this application are true and are made for the purpose of obtaining the loan. Verification may be obtained from any source named in this application. The original or a copy of this application will be retained by the lender, even if the loan is not granted. The undersigned ☐ intend or ☐ do not intend to occupy the property as their primary residence.

I/we fully understand that it is a federal crime punishable by fine or imprisonment, or both, to knowingly make any false statements concerning any of the above facts as applicable under the provisions of Title 18, United States Code, Section 1014.

_____ Date _____ _____ Date _____
Borrower's Signature   Co-Borrower's Signature

INFORMATION FOR GOVERNMENT MONITORING PURPOSES

Instructions: Lenders must insert in this space, or on an attached addendum, a provision for furnishing the monitoring information required or requested under present Federal and/or present state law or regulation. For most lenders, the inserts provided in FHLMC Form 65-B/FNMA Form 1003-B can be used.

FOR LENDER'S USE ONLY

(FNMA REQUIREMENT ONLY) This application was taken by ☐ face to face interview ☐ by mail ☐ by telephone

_____ _____
(Interviewer)   Name of Employer of Interviewer

FHLMC 65 Rev. 8/78   REVERSE   FNMA 1003 Rev. 8/78

473

lower. A VA appraiser completes this document and gives it to the lender.

4. The **certificate of eligibility** is obtained from the applicant. The VA must issue a new certificate with each loan application to inform the lender of the size of guarantee that can be applied to the loan.

5. The lender asks the applicant to complete the forms for Verification of Employment and Verification of Deposit.

6. The applicant signs a statement of liability and nondiscrimination. The borrower must be released from the liability on a past mortgage before he or she can commit the $27,500 guarantee to this loan. An unused portion of the $27,500 can be applied to the purchase.

7. The buyer and the seller sign an interest rate agreement, which states that there are no hidden charges.

8. If the veteran lacks cash for a down payment, an escape clause can be requested for the mortgage application in case the appraised value is lower than anticipated.

9. The lender obtains a credit report on the veteran.

10. The applicant receives a Good Faith Estimate of Closing Costs and a copy of the HUD booklet explaining the features of RESPA.

Federal Housing Administration loan   A local lender can loan its own funds and ask the FHA to issue default insurance to protect the lender against nonpayment by the borrower. Anyone can apply for this type of loan from an FHA-approved lender. The procedure for applying usually includes the following steps:

1. The applicant submits a residential loan application.

2. The lender requests a certificate of reasonable value on the property. The FHA appraiser reports the selling price *and* the appraised value to the lender.

3. The lender obtains a Verification of Employment form and a Verification of Deposit form from the applicant.

4. The lender requests a credit report on the applicant.

5. The buyer and seller sign an interest rate agreement, which states that the transaction has no hidden charges or kickbacks.

6. The buyer, seller, and the agent sign an affidavit of truth.

7. The applicant receives a Good Faith Estimate of Closing Costs and a copy of the HUD special booklet explaining the RESPA.

The maximum amount that the FHA would insure in 1985 was 97 percent of the first $25,000 and 95 percent of the remaining mortgage up to a maximum of $67,500. Thus, for a $50,000 mortgage, FHA would insure $48,000 ($24,250 + $23,750). The remaining $2,000 would be paid by the borrower as a down payment.

Direct endorsement   Recently started, direct endorsement is a program that allows all of the previous steps to be conducted by the local lender *prior* to submitting the loan forms to the FHA office. Essentially, the application is submitted to FHA after the closing, and the mortgage can be closed as fast as the lender can process the forms. This new program is a move by the FHA to place the loan decision authority into the lender's office rather than a regional FHA office.

New authority   The Housing and Urban Recovery Act (HURRA) of 1983 gave the FHA authority to initiate several new programs including the following:

- *Indexed mortgages.* Permits adjustment of the monthly payments and outstanding balances according to changes or percentages of changes in a selected price index.
- *Adjustable rate mortgages.* Permits adjustments in the monthly payment amount according to changes in a specified national interest rate index. Any single rate increase cannot exceed one percent, and the maximum increase cannot be over 5 percent above the initial contract rate.
- *Shared appreciation mortgages.* Permits the mortgagee to share in a predetermined percent of the property's appreciated value.
- *Lower down payment for lower-priced homes.* For properties appraised at $50,000 or less, the down payment will only be 3 percent of the appraised value plus closing costs.

Comparison of conventional, FHA, and VA terms   A brief comparison of selected terms (1985) is important information to the potential borrower.

	Conventional	FHA	VA
Due on sale clause	May exist	Does *not* exist	Does *not* exist
Interest rate	Fixed or variable; set by local lender	Fixed or variable; set by local lender	Fixed only
Points	Anyone may pay them	Anyone may pay them	Anyone but the buyer (veteran) pays the points
Prepayment penalty	May exist	If a 30-day notice is given, no penalty is charged	No penalty is charged
Protection of *lender* in the case of *borrower default*	May require large down payment or private mortgage insurance	Provides insurance for a large amount of the total loan	Provides a guarantee that the lender won't lose over $27,500
Source of funds	From the local lender	From the local lender	From the local lender

The interest rate under a conventional loan may be fixed for the life of the loan, or it may vary depending upon the mortgage type. Beginning in November 1983, the interest rate under the FHA mortgage is set by the local lender as opposed to past rates, which have been set in Washington, D.C. The interest rate used by the VA is set by the Washington office, and does not change over the life of the loan.

Farmers Home Administration loan   The Farmers Home Administration (FmHA) is part of the U.S. Department of Agriculture. The agency attempts to provide credit for rural areas. Home ownership loans can be used to buy, build, improve, repair, or rehabilitate rural homes and related facilities. Loans also are available for financing farm operations. The procedure for applying usually includes the following steps:

1. The applicant completes a loan application form.
2. The applicant agrees to a credit check by the lender.
3. The borrower provides an employment verification form as evidence of a steady job with income.

Two sources of loans are available to a potential borrower under this program. The first is a loan from a local lender that is guaranteed by the FmHA. The second is a direct loan from the FmHA in special circumstances.

Federal Land Bank loan   The Federal Land Bank (FLB) is part of the Farm Credit System, which was established by Congress to help extend credit to the rural areas. This agency may accept applications and approve loans from its own funds for residential housing. The procedure for applying includes the following steps:

1. The applicant completes a loan application form.
2. The applicant agrees to a credit check.
3. The borrower provides a legal description of the property and agrees to an appraisal of the property.

No local lender is involved in the loan since the borrower acquires the funds directly from the FLB. The prospective mortgagor should remember that the FLB gives only a variable rate mortgage (VRM). This mortgage allows the lender to periodically change the interest rate and the monthly payments. (VRMs are discussed more in detail later in this chapter.)

EQUAL CREDIT OPPORTUNITY ACT

The intent of the Equal Credit Opportunity Act of 1974 (later amended) was to prevent lenders from underemphasizing and denying credit on the basis of sex, marital status, age, national origin, race, color, or religion.[3] For example, a lender must maintain the credit history of each account in the name of both husband and wife if the account demonstrates both parties' ability to pay. Each denial of credit must be given justification for the action. A female applicant does not have to have a credit application endorsed unless males have that requirement also. Questions on pregnancy and birth control cannot be asked nor can national statistics on birth or birth control be used to deny credit. Questions and information on sex cannot be used as part of the credit evaluation. Each applicant must be given a copy of the act, and all documents pertaining to the transaction must be kept for fifteen months.

The borrower's income from sources such as alimony or welfare cannot be automatically eliminated. It must be examined and counted as qualifying for the loan if the pattern of receipt illustrates sufficient longevity and quantity, and the source of the income is sufficiently reliable.

REAL ESTATE SETTLEMENT PROCEDURES ACT

The Real Estate Settlement Procedures Act (RESPA) has two purposes: (1) It informs the potential consumer about the costs of this loan so that credit terms may be compared among institutions. (2) The consumer is given the right to select the individuals or firms providing services required on the loan such as an attorney, appraiser, and title company. The potential borrower does not have to use the firms or individuals that the lender prefers.

Three parts of this act are important to the applicant: (1) The applicant must be given a copy of the act; (2) The potential borrower must be given a copy of the Good Faith Estimate of Settlement Costs, which includes either the exact costs or an estimate of the costs of acquiring this loan and which identifies the party, buyer or seller, who is expected to pay each cost; (3) The borrower must be given HUD Form 1, which is a final statement of the settlement costs, within a reasonable time following the closing, or within one business day preceding the closing if the borrower requests it.

TRUTH-IN-LENDING ACT (REGULATION Z)

The intent of the **Truth-in-Lending Act,** effective July 1969 and amended in March 1977, is to inform borrowers about the true cost of credit, knowledge they can use to compare costs.[4] Customers are encouraged under the act to shop around for appropriate credit terms. Additional points of the act cover the issuance of credit cards, maximum liability for nonauthorized use of credit cards, and information that must be given to the lessee of personal property about the cost of leasing. The act is administered by the Federal Reserve Board as Regulation Z.

Lenders Covered

The Truth-in-Lending Act applies to credit card issuers and to lenders who charge for granting loans that are repaid in at least four installments.[5] All real estate transactions for personal, household, family, and agricultural uses are covered regardless of the amount. A lease for personal property, which covers personal, household, and family use, is covered if the lessee is obligated for less than $25,000 and the duration is more than four months.

The act covers "arrangers of credit" who have arranged credit more than twenty-five times in the preceding year or more than five times for a transaction secured by a dwelling. This requirement typically excludes an owner/occupant of a single-family home who attempts to sell the property. Also, a real estate agent is not included under an arranger of credit unless special conditions exist, such as the agent taking a second mortgage for a commission or selling property from the agent's own inventory.

Finance Charge and the Annual Percentage Rate

The *total* finance charge and the **annual percentage rate (APR)** must be disclosed to the borrower. The finance charge for real estate loans includes interest, finder's fee, loan fee, discount, time price differential, points, carrying charge, and the credit life premium if it is required.[6]

It does *not* include charges that would be paid, regardless of whether credit, such as legal fees, survey cost, recording fee, title insurance premium, and credit report costs, is extended.

The annual percentage rate can be calculated by a number of methods depending on the manner in which finance charges are determined. One method is to divide the finance charge for one billing period by the median balance for that period and then multiply the result by the number of periods in one year.

Advertising[7]

Regulation Z covers advertising containing the terms of the purchase (sale). Full disclosure of the terms is not required if the advertisement contains (a) no specifics about credit *or* (b) the annual percentage rate and the amount of the loan. Typically, any description of other credit terms requires full disclosure. Examples requiring full disclosure would be the following:

$75 down	No payment until June
No extra financing charge	Only $78 per week

The following examples would not require full disclosure:

- ☐ Easy credit
- ☐ Low down payment
- ☐ Financing arranged while you wait

Once full disclosure is required, the following items must be described within the advertisement:

1. Annual percentage rate, which reflects the finance charge
2. The deferred payment price

3. Cash price of the item or the amount of the loan
4. Amount of the down payment

Rescission

The lender must notify the customer that he or she has the right to cancel the credit arrangement within three days. In real estate, this requirement applies to a first mortgage for a purpose other than the customer's dwelling and to a second mortgage. The right of rescission is intended to protect the homeowner from liens filed by unethical sellers of appliances, home improvements, or furniture.

EVALUATION OF CREDIT

Loan Credit Committee

Once the credit information about the buyer has been obtained by the lender, it is given to the financial institution's loan credit committee for approval or disapproval. The credit information obtained by the lender includes (1) applicant's past history of debt repayment, (2) applicant's previous credit experience, (3) past bankruptcies, (4) pending lawsuits, (5) monthly income of applicant, (6) applicant's assets and liabilities, and (7) the purpose of the loan. The loan credit committee considers all these items to determine the borrower's overall creditworthiness which is the basis for their approval or disapproval of the loan.

Borrower Creditworthiness

The lender is especially concerned that the loan be used for property that the owner will occupy or closely supervise. Owner-occupants usually have pride of ownership in maintaining their property and typically continue to make the monthly payments during all economic conditions.

The lender assesses the borrower's attitude toward the proposed loan. The lender is looking for applicants who show a mature attitude and understanding of the loan obligations and exhibit a strong desire for ownership. At one time, age, sex, and marital status were important factors in the lender's decision to lend or not to lend. Often the young and the old had trouble getting loans as did women and single, divorced, or widowed individuals. Today, the Equal Credit Opportunity Act prohibits discrimination in extending credit. Lenders are no longer permitted to discount income earned by women even if it is from a part-time job or it is earned by a woman of child-bearing age. Also, the money received by a divorced person for alimony or child support must be counted. Young adults and single persons cannot be turned down because the lender feels they are not established. Senior citizens cannot be turned down if life expectancy exceeds the early risk period of the loan and collateral is adequate. The emphasis now in borrower analysis is on *job stability, income adequacy, net worth,* and the *credit rating.*

The lender asks questions about how long the applicant has held his or her present job and the stability of that job. An applicant who has marketable job skills and has been regularly employed with a stable employer is considered the least risk. Borrowers whose income can rise and fall erratically, such as commissioned salespersons, present greater risks. Persons whose lack of skills or lack of job seniority results in frequent unemployment are more likely to have difficulty repaying a loan. The lender also inquires about the number of dependents the applicant must support with his or her income. This information indicates the amount that will be left for monthly payments.

The prospective borrower's income should be sufficient to meet the mortgage debt service payment and the other monthly debts. Two criteria have been used to judge the level of debt: (1) The monthly payment of mortgage amortization and interest typically has not exceeded 25 percent of the household income. (2) Additional debts exceeding ten months in duration should not consume more than 10 percent of the household income. Thus, the household's long-term debt commitments should not be greater than 35 percent of its monthly income.

Recent trends seem to indicate that buyers may be willing to pay and lenders willing to accept a higher percent of the household income to purchase housing. In some regions, these percentages are as high as 40 to 50 percent of household income. These trends have been reflected in the two following criteria used by FHA in 1986 to determine loan eligibility:

1. First-year-only ratio: (total housing expense including principal, interest, taxes, insurance, maintenance, and utilities) divided by (gross family income minus federal income taxes). $\leq 38\%$

2. Fixed-payments ratio: (total housing expense plus fixed expenses including Social Security, state income tax, child care, child support, alimony, all revolving accounts, loans with over twelve payments left, etc.) divided by (gross family income minus federal income taxes). $\leq 53\%$

The lender will examine the applicant's record of debt repayment. A credit report that shows no unfavorable information is most desirable. Applicants with no previous credit experience will have difficulty proving that they intend to pay, and those with a history of collections or judgments will have a poor chance of receiving a loan. Other factors the lender considers are past bankruptcies on the part of the applicant and any pending lawsuits that might result in judgments against the applicant. Additionally, an applicant who has guaranteed the repayment of someone else's debt by acting as a co-maker or endorser may be considered a poor risk. Finally, the lender may take into consideration whether the applicant has adequate insurance protection in the event of major medical expenses or a disability that prevents returning to work.

TYPES OF DEFAULT INSURANCE

A lender can be protected against the borrower's default by means of private mortgage insurance (PMI), Federal Housing Administration insurance, a partial guarantee by the Veterans Administration, or Farmers Home Administration insurance.

Conventional Loan With Private Mortgage Insurance

Default insurance issued by the FHA or the FmHA covers all of the loan. The guarantee given by the Veterans Administration covers up to a maximum of $27,500 of the loan. However, the prospective buyer may not be a veteran, may not want insurance on the whole loan, or may have chosen to buy a house that lacks some feature required by the FHA, VA, or FmHA. Consequently, the buyer can ask the lender for a conventional loan. If the buyer's down payment is not sufficient to minimize the risk of default in the early years of the loan, the lender may require that the buyer purchase mortgage insurance from a private insurer.

All fifty states have an insurance regulation covering the amount of private mortgage insurance that the lender can require the buyer to purchase. Typically, the regulation covers the loan amount during the early years when the risk of borrower default is the greatest. In almost all cases, the borrower can avoid the purchase of the PMI if the down payment amounts to 20 to 25 percent of the property value. Down payments of a smaller magnitude necessitate buying insurance.

PMI has several advantages. With PMI, the buyer can purchase a property that will not pass an FHA, VA, or FmHA appraisal. The lender can grant loans up to 95 percent of the value and insure the risky part for the first years. Moreover, PMI can be combined with the VA $27,500 guarantee to allow a veteran to purchase a more expensive home—the first $27,500 is covered by the VA and the remainder by PMI.

Private mortgage insurers   In 1957, the Mortgage Guaranty Insurance Corporation (MGIC) was formed in Milwaukee, Wisconsin, as a privately owned business venture to compete with the FHA in insuring home mortgage loans. Growth was slow but steady for the first ten years. In the late 1960s, MGIC underwent a sudden burst of growth because the increase in red tape at the FHA was causing a six- to eight-week delay in its processing of applications. In contrast, MGIC offered a three-day service. Also, FHA terms were not suited to changing conditions. Moderately priced homes required larger down payments with FHA insurance than with private insurance, and the FHA-imposed interest rate ceiling hindered rather than helped many borrowers. In addition, private mortgage insurance was priced at one half the FHA fee. In 1971, the Federal Home Loan Bank Board approved the use of private mortgage insurers. The result was that by 1972 private insurers were insuring more new mortgages than the FHA.

Currently about a dozen firms offer private mortgage insurance. Like FHA insurance, PMI insures lenders against losses due to nonpayment of low-down payment mortgage loans. Unlike the FHA, PMI insures only the top 20 to 25 percent of a loan, not the whole loan. This allows a lender to make 90 and 95 percent L/V loans with a reduced possibility of foreclosure losses. For example, on 90 percent L/V loans, the borrower by placing 10 percent cash down assumes the top 10 percent of risk exposure to falling real estate prices. PMI covers 10-15 percent of the next 90 percent.

The borrower can purchase a home with a cash down payment of either 5 or 10 percent. Under the 10 percent down-payment program, the borrower pays a mortgage insurance fee of ½ of one percent the first year and ¼ of one percent thereafter. When a loan is partially repaid to a certain amount, the premiums and coverage can be terminated at the lender's option.

Private mortgage insurers try to keep their losses to a minimum by first approving the lenders with whom they will do business. Particular emphasis is placed on the lender's operating policy, appraisal procedure, and degree of government regulation. Once approved, a lender simply sends the borrower's loan application, credit report, and property appraisal to the insurer. On the basis of these documents, the insurer either agrees or refuses to issue a policy. Although the insurer relies on the appraisal prepared by the lender, the insurer may send its own appraiser to verify the quality of the information being submitted. If an insured loan goes into default, the insurer has the option of either buying the property from the lender for the balance due or letting the lender foreclose and then paying the lender's losses up to the amount of the insurance. As a rule, insurers take the first option because it is the more popular with the lenders. It leaves the lender with immediate cash to reloan, and the insurer with the task of foreclosing.

In summary, any request by the borrower for a conventional mortgage with an L/V ratio of 80 to 95 percent will almost always necessitate the purchase of PMI. The amount of the coverage depends on the amount loaned. A request for a mortgage with an L/V ratio of 80 to 75 percent or less will probably not involve PMI.

Conventional Mortgage Without PMI

A conventional loan without private mortgage insurance is generally obtainable from any financial institution that makes loans on residential property. A conventional loan without PMI almost always has a lower loan-to-value ratio than a loan with PMI. On a high L/V loan, the lender may lose part of the money loaned if the buyer defaults. If the lender has to foreclose, the property may not bring what it is worth. Therefore, if the lender has made a 95 percent loan without PMI and the property sells for less than the mortgage amount of foreclosure, the lender has lost cash and may file a deficiency judgment against the borrower. As a result, lenders generally will not make more than an 80 percent loan-to-value conventional loan without PMI. Such loans require a large down payment.

Federal Housing Administration

The Federal Housing Administration (FHA) was created under the National Housing Act of 1934. Among other things, it provides insurance on loans that can be amortized over a period of years. FHA does not lend money. It merely insures loans made by supervised lending institutions, which include banks, life insurance companies, federal savings and loans associations, some state associations, and other institutions where deposits are insured by the Federal Deposit Insurance Corporation. Other lenders included in this group are approved mortgage companies, pension funds, and individuals. All approved mortgages must be serviced in accordance with practices of prudent lending institutions. If the borrower defaults on his or her obligation, the lender can apply to the FHA, which will take over the property and pay the lender in cash or government debentures for any portion of the loan remaining. The individual lender may decide to hold the property and dispose of it through a trustee's sale, or foreclosure by court action, which may be less time-consuming.

FHA-insured loans have the following advantages that other types of conventional financing may not offer:

1. Lower interest rates than conventional loans with PMI.
2. Longer maturity than a conventional mortgage with PMI.
3. A larger L/V ratio.
4. Protection of the lender against default, and protection of the investor who may purchase the mortgage in the secondary mortgage market (discussed in Chapter 19).
5. Improved housing standards through minimum specifications and building standards.
6. Provisions for a single monthly payment, which includes principal, interest, insurance, and taxes.

FHA has developed a system to reduce the risks in loaning money on real property by careful evaluation of the individual borrower and by establishment of standards for the appraisal of the property involved. A rating is based on an investigation of an individual's credit characteristics, property buying motives, ratio of effective income to total obligations owed, adequacy of other available assets, and the stability of effective income. Generally an individual can afford to pay a maximum of two and one-half times annual income for a home.

The property appraisal is based on livability and the estimated economic life of property with appropriate adjustments for economic and social deterioration.

Two types of commitments can be made by the FHA. A *firm loan commitment* is requested when the mortgagor desires a definite commitment on a specific property with a definite borrower. When the borrower or mortgagor is not known, a *conditional loan commitment* is requested. A conditional commitment is usually good for six months and is contingent upon a mortgagor qualifying for such a loan.

Basically, the National Housing Act permits FHA to insure loans for the purpose of (1) improvements, repair, and alterations to the property, and (2) purchasing one- to four-family dwellings and large rental developments. Under Title II of the National Housing Act, individual mortgage loans can be insured. Title II contains several sections; Section 203b covers loans for construction or purchase of single-family dwellings. Insurance on approved existing or proposed construction was 97 percent of the first $25,000 and 95 percent thereafter up to a maximum mortgage amount of $67,500 (1985 figures). Loan cost to the borrower includes current interest plus 0.5 percent mortgage insurance premium based on the average outstanding balance of the principal for any twelve-month period. The borrower also is required to place in a loan trust fund a proportionate amount for taxes, special assessments, and hazard insurance. These items are included in the monthly payments. Other expenses include an FHA application fee, initial service charge, recording fees, credit reports, and a survey of title and title insurance.

Loan insurance examples[8] The method used by FHA to calculate the amount of insurance and down payment for a loan application can be seen in several selected examples:

Sales price or offer	$40,000
Repairs	1,000
Closing costs (Cc)	1,000
Prepaids (hazard insurance, property tax, mortgage interest under an assumption)	500

(a) Buyer and seller pay their own Cc; seller pays the repairs:

Actual sales price = Sales price = $40,000

$40,000 actual sales price
+1,000 Cc

$41,000 total acquisition cost

$41,000 − $25,000 = $16,000 × 0.95 = $15,200
+ first $25,000 × 0.97 = +24,250

$39,450 Maximum mortgage

Down payment = Total acquisition cost − Maximum mortgage
= $41,000 − $39,450
= $1,550

(b) Seller pays buyer's Cc and prepaids; seller pays repairs:

Actual sales price = Sales price − Cc − prepaids
= $40,000 − $1,000 − $500 = $38,500

$38,500 Actual sales price
+1,000 Cc

$39,500 Acquisition cost $39,500 − $25,000 = $14,500 × 0.95 = $13,775
+ first $25,000 × 0.97 = +24,250

$38,000 Maximum mortgage ←—(rounded)——————————————— $38,025

Down payment = Total acquisition cost − Mortgage
= $39,500 − $38,000 (rounded) = $1,500

(c) Seller pays buyer's Cc; buyer pays prepaids:

Actual sales price = Sales price − Cc = $40,000 − $1,000 = $39,000

$39,000 Actual sales price
+1,000 Cc

$40,000 Acquisition cost $40,000 − $25,000 = $15,000 × 0.95 = $14,250
+ first $25,000 × 0.97 = +24,250

$38,500 Maximum mortgage ←————————————————————— $38,500

Down payment = Total acquisition cost − Mortgage
= $40,000 − $38,500 = $1,500

(d) Seller pays buyer's Cc and gives rent-free occupancy for 4 months. HUD estimates rental value of $250 per month in this area; buyer pays prepaids; seller pays repairs:

THE DECISION TO FINANCE THE TRANSACTION

Actual sales price = Sales price − Cc − Rent-free value
                   = \$40,000 − \$1000 − \$1000 = \$38,000

\$38,000 Actual sales price
+1,000 Cc
―――――――――
\$39,000 Total acquisition cost   \$39,000 − \$25,000 = \$14,000 × 0.95 =   \$13,300
                                              + first \$25,000 × 0.97 = +24,250

\$37,550 Maximum mortgage ⟵―――――――――――――――――――――――――― \$37,550
Down payment = Total acquisition cost − Mortgage
             = \$39,000 − \$37,550 = \$1,450

(e) Buyer and seller pay their own Cc; sales agreement is silent on who pays
the repairs:

Actual sales price = Sales price = \$40,000

\$40,000 Actual sales price
  1,000 Repairs
+1,000 Cc
―――――――――
\$42,000 Total acquisition cost   \$42,000 − \$25,000 = \$17,000 × 0.95 =   \$16,150
                                              + first \$25,000 × 0.97 = +24,250

\$40,400 Maximum mortgage ⟵―――――――――――――――――――――――――― \$40,400
Down payment = Total acquisition cost − Mortgage
             = \$42,000 − \$40,400 = \$1,600

(f) Seller pays \$750 of buyer's Cc; seller and buyer to split the cost of
repairs equally:

Actual sales price = Sales price − Cc paid by seller for buyer
                   = \$40,000 − \$750 = \$39,250

\$39,250 Actual sales price
    500 Repairs
+1,000 Cc
―――――――――
\$40,750 Total acquisition cost   \$40,750 − \$25,000 = \$15,750 × 0.95 =   \$14,963
                                              + first \$25,000 × 0.97 = +24,250

\$39,200 Maximum mortgage ⟵―(rounded)―――――――――――――――― \$39,213
Down payment = Total acquisition cost − Mortgage
             = \$40,750 − \$39,200 = \$1,500

Veterans Administration (VA)

To show its appreciation to servicemen and servicewomen returning from World
War II, Congress in 1944 passed far-reaching legislation to aid veterans in education,
hospitalization, employment training, and housing. In the area of housing, the popu-
larly named G.I. Bill of Rights empowered the comptroller general of the United
States to guarantee the repayment of a portion of first mortgage real estate loans
made to veterans. For this guarantee, no fee would be charged to the veteran, and the
government would stand the losses. The original 1944 law provided that lenders
would be guaranteed against losses up to 50 percent of the amount of the loan. The
objective was to enable a veteran to buy a home with no cash down payment. Due to
the increasing cost of homes, the guarantee has been increased several times and in
1985 stood at \$27,500 or 60 percent of the loan amount, whichever is less. Generally,

a $27,500 guarantee means a veteran can purchase up to a $110,000 home with no down payment, provided that the veteran has enough income to support the monthly payments. Whether or not a lender will make a no-down-payment VA loan is entirely up to the lender. Some lenders believe the borrower should make at least a token down payment to acquire a sense of ownership. However, the majority of lenders, if they have the funds available, require none. The amount the veteran borrows above the $27,500 must be based on personal credit and typically must be covered by PMI.

In the original G.I. Bill of 1944, eligibility was limited to World War II veterans. However, subsequent legislation has changed the requirements to 181 days for those serving during peacetime, and 91 days for those serving during World War II, the Korean conflict, and the Vietnam conflict. The veteran's discharge must be on conditions other than dishonorable and the guarantee entitlement is good until used.

The Veterans Administration works diligently to reduce its exposure to foreclosure losses. When a veteran applies for a VA guarantee, the property is appraised and the VA issues a certificate of reasonable value (CRV), which informs the lender of the property's value defined as the lower of the selling price or the appraised value. Also, the VA issues a *certificate of eligibility,* which tells the lender the amount of the $27,500 that can be applied to the loan. The VA has established income guidelines to make certain the veteran can comfortably meet the proposed loan payments. It makes no sense, for either the veteran or the VA, to approve a loan that the veteran will have trouble repaying.

The VA guarantees loans for periods of up to thirty years on homes, and there is no prepayment penalty if the borrower wishes to pay sooner. A veteran wishing to refinance a currently owned home can also obtain a VA guaranteed loan.

No matter what loan guarantee program is elected, the veteran should know that in the event of default and subsequent foreclosure he or she is required to make good losses the VA incurs on the loan. This is not true with FHA-insured loans where the borrower pays for protection against possible foreclosure losses. Even if the veteran sells the property and the buyer assumes the VA loan, the veteran is still financially responsible if the buyer later defaults. To avoid this situation, the veteran must arrange with the VA to be released from liability when the property is sold.

Several points regarding the VA guarantee program should be covered since they answer frequently asked questions. First, the programs are designed to be used for owner-occupied housing only. Second, a veteran can qualify for up to a "fourplex" loan if he or she lives in one unit. Third, a veteran who takes out a loan with a "high" interest rate can refinance at a lower rate when the rates drop sufficiently. Fourth, a veteran who has a loan under the VA programs can have all or part of the $27,500 eligibility restored by (a) selling the house to a buyer who obtains a new loan and pays off the old VA commitment, or (b) selling the house to another veteran who will replace $27,500 with all or part of the buyer's $27,500 entitlement. Fifth, not all of the $27,500 has to be used for one property. Sixth, the $27,500 never expires. It can be used and restored with subsequent transactions. Seventh, the $27,500 guarantee is not a loan to the veteran from the lender. It is assurance that the lender will not suffer a loss in this amount should the veteran default in the monthly payments.

As Congress frequently changes eligibility and benefits, a person contemplating a VA or FHA loan should inquire at the field offices of these agencies and to mortgage lenders to ascertain the current status and details of the law as well as the availability of state veteran benefits. Several states offer special advantages, including mortgage loan assistance, to residents who have served in the armed forces.

Farmers Home Administration

The Farmers Home Administration (FmHA) is an agency of the U.S. Department of Agriculture that was created to distribute credit to rural residents, farmers, and communities. It provides counseling and technical assistance in addition to credit to ensure that participants are given maximum assistance.

The FmHA has loan programs to provide additional employment, operate farms, purchase homes, increase the standard of living, and enhance business opportunities for rural areas. Some loan programs are designed for individuals and their families and others are for groups of individuals and communities.

The purposes of the FmHA rural credit program are: To expand businesses and industries that increase employment and income and reduce air pollution, to assist in building the family-farm system, to provide modest homes at prices that families of moderate and low incomes can afford, and to establish waste and water systems.

The FmHA operates two programs for credit. One is the guaranteed loan program in which the loan is made by the local lender and the FmHA guarantees a percentage of the debt against borrower default. The second is the direct insured loan program in which the loan is made and serviced directly from the FmHA.

POINTS

An applicant for a new loan may be quoted "points" or a "loan origination fee" by the lender during the application process. One point is defined as one percent of the mortgage amount and used to give the lender an additional return on the mortgage. An old rule of thumb is that one point of the mortgage amount is equivalent to one-eighth of one percent in the interest rate or yield to the lender.

Points are charged by the lender to make up additional interest earnings that it will lose on this loan from one of three reasons. First, the loan involves either VA, or FmHA, and their mortgage interest rates, which may be lower than the prevailing rate that could be earned on a conventional loan, are set in Washington. The reader should remember that in November 1983 the President signed legislation that allowed the local lender to set the FHA interest rate. Second, the lender may want to sell this loan to an investor, and the investor will not pay the face amount of the mortgage. The lender charges the points to make up the difference. Third, the state usury law may not allow the lender to charge a competitive rate. Providing that the state courts have not prohibited the additional assessment of points, the lender may charge the points to make up the interest lost on this loan.

Points are caused not by the lender but by the conditions of supply and demand for credit in the residential mortgage market. Consequently, their discussion is in Chapter 19, "Lenders and the Secondary Mortgage Market."

ALTERNATIVE MORTGAGE INSTRUMENTS AND AMORTIZATION

An alternative mortgage instrument (AMI)[9] features some alteration of the basic characteristics of the typical conventional mortgage—fixed interest rate, fixed maturity date, fixed monthly payments, and full amortization by maturity. Various plans have been proposed either to allow the lender to increase the profitability of mortgages or to induce new homebuyers into the housing market by providing payments tailored to their income patterns.

Increasing Mortgage Profitability

Variable rate mortgage   One of the first new residential mortgages introduced in the United States by mortgage lenders was the *variable rate mortgage* (VRM). Although several varieties are used in other countries, a typical VRM in the United States includes (1) an interest rate that can be increased or decreased by the lender in relation to movements in a financial market index beyond the control of the lender, (2) a fixed maturity date, (3) monthly interest payments that change with the interest rate, and (4) a maximum limit on the amount of any individual and overall change in the interest rate.

An example is helpful in comparing properties of the typical mortgage used in the United States for more than forty years and the features of a variable rate mortgage. Consider Mike and Ann Kincaid who contract with a local savings and loan for a $40,000 fixed-rate conventional mortgage at 13.0 percent interest for thirty years. Their payments to the principal and interest are $442.48 per month, an amount that remains constant throughout the term of the mortgage. The **debiting factor** for their mortgage, found by dividing the interest rate by twelve months (0.13/12), is 0.010833. Each time the Kincaids make a monthly payment, the amount paid to the principal is subtracted first and the debiting factor is multiplied by the remaining mortgage balance to determine the amount of the interest owed.

Ending mortgage balance—first month	$40,000.00
minus principal payment	
$40,000 mortgage × 0.010833 debiting factor = $433.32 interest	
$442.48 total payment − $433.32 interest = $9.16 principal payment	− 9.16
Mortgage balance beginning the second month	$39,990.84
minus principal payment	
$39,990.84 mortgage × 0.010833 debiting factor = $433.22 interest	
$442.48 total payment − $433.22 interest = $9.26 principal payment	− 9.26
Mortgage balance beginning the third month	$39,981.58

The features of a fixed interest rate, fixed monthly payments, fixed maturity date, and full amortization imply several other characteristics. First, the debiting factor remains constant over the term of the loan. Second, the interest component of the monthly payment is large at first and gradually declines over the term of the loan as the remaining mortgage balance each month gradually declines. The principal component is small at first and gradually increases. Third, as the example shows, the debiting factor is applied to the declining mortgage balance.

The remaining mortgage balance to be paid and the interest payments are shown graphically in the four charts in Exhibit 16-6. Chart 1 shows that the remaining mortgage debt to be paid declines at an increasing rate as the mortgage approaches maturity. Chart 2 shows that the total payments to the debt accumulate at an increasing rate toward the mortgage maturity date, when the owner's equity from the debt is equal to the original mortgage amount. Chart 3 shows that in the first mortgage payment of $442.48 only a small sum of $9.16 is paid toward the debt, but this amount increases steadily. Chart 4 shows that $433.32 of the first payment goes toward the interest payment, but this amount declines at an increasing rate. The monthly payment of $442.48 remains constant throughout the term of the mortgage.

What is not shown is the total accumulation of interest over the term of the mortgage, which could equal two to three times the amount of the mortgage. Chart 4 shows that the lender receives the major part of the interest payment during the first few years of the mortgage when the mortgage balance is the highest. For this reason, a lender may not want the borrower to repay or refinance the loan during the first years because the interest lost could be significant, depending on local market conditions. A borrower, however, should always insist on the prepayment privilege because he or she may wish to sell the property and refinancing of the debt may be a necessity for the new buyer.

The same example can be used to illustrate the features of a variable rate mortgage. The Kincaids contract for a $40,000 loan for thirty years with an initial interest rate of 12.5 percent. The slightly lower interest rate usually given is an incentive to take the VRM. The interest rate can be altered in 0.5 percent changes within any six-month period. The maximum increase over the term of the loan is 2.5 percent, and no minimum is imposed on the decreases. The Kincaids will be given a thirty-day notice of an impending interest rate change. Once they receive the notice, they have the option of accepting it or refinancing into a conventional fixed-rate mortgage at the prevailing interest rate. The following figures describe the loan for the first month:

Ending mortgage balance—first month	$40,000.00
minus principal payment	
$40,000 $\times$ 0.0104166 = $416.66	
$426.90 total payment $-$ 416.66	
= $10.24 principal payment	$-$ 10.24
Beginning mortgage balance for the second month	$39,989.76

The characteristics are the same as those of a traditional mortgage except that the debiting factor is lower.

EXHIBIT 16-6 Payments to the debt, interest, and remaining balance for a fixed-interest rate, level-payment mortgage

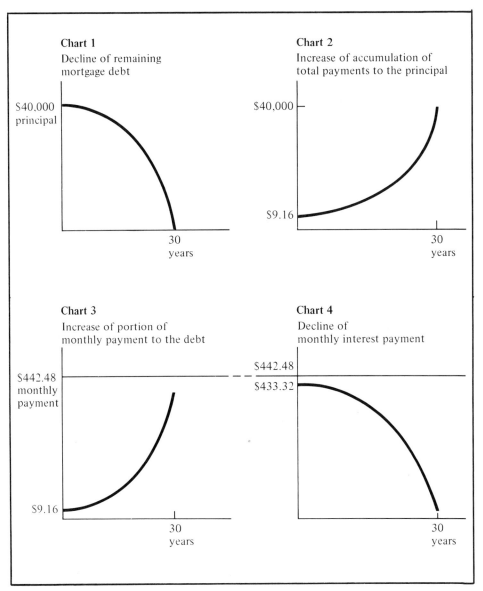

Chart 1
Decline of remaining mortgage debt

$40,000 principal

30 years

Chart 2
Increase of accumulation of total payments to the principal

$40,000

$9.16

30 years

Chart 3
Increase of portion of monthly payment to the debt

$442.48 monthly payment

$9.16

30 years

Chart 4
Decline of monthly interest payment

$442.48

$433.32

30 years

In the eleventh month, the Kincaids receive a notice that the interest rate will be raised to 13 percent. They decide to accept the change rather than refinance into a conventional fixed rate loan. Their payments rise to $442.48 from $426.90, and the debiting factor rises from .0104166 to .010833. From this point on, the new debiting factor is applied and the payments are the new amount.

Renegotiable rate mortgage (RRM)[10] Any federally chartered savings and loan may make, purchase, or participate in an RRM for a one- to four-family home. Sometimes called a "rollover" mortgage, the interest rate and the resultant monthly payment are held constant for only three, four, or five years. At that time, the lender has the option of changing the interest rate in the mortgage to the current market level in the FHLBB's most recent monthly national average. If this rate has fallen from the original contract interest rate, the lender must lower the mortgage rate.

The RRM is viewed as a series of short-term loans ranging from three to five years that have been secured by a long-term mortgage of up to thirty years. The maximum rate increase or decrease per year is 0.5 percent. The maximum increase or decrease over the life of the mortgage is five percentage points. The borrower pays no fees to renew the loan. The loan payments are adjusted with the interest rate to amortize the balance to zero by maturity.

This mortgage has been introduced to allow the lenders to capture additional interest when interest rates have increased. In addition, it is much easier for the potential homeowner to understand, since the characteristics are very similar to the current conventional mortgage.

Alternative mortgage loan (AML) and the adjustable rate mortgage (ARM) In 1981, the Federal Home Loan Bank Board approved a set of regulations that allowed all federally chartered savings and loans to issue AMLs on one- to four-family dwellings. Also, the Controller of the Currency approved regulations that allowed all federally chartered commercial banks to issue AMIs. Most conventional residential mortgages issued by these two groups of lenders after this date will be issued under these new regulations and will be labeled an AML or an ARM.

Essentially, the lender is allowed within limits to design the terms of the loan to fit the needs of the lender and the borrower. A summary of the regulations follows:[11]

☐ *Variable interest rate*
   The heart of these new adjustable rate mortgages is an interest rate that may change several times over the life of the mortgage. In addition, the monthly payment may change, and they may not occur at the same time. For example, the rate may change annually for a five-year period while the monthly payment changes only in five-year cycles. A "cap" or maximum may or may not exist.

☐ *Mortgage interest rate index*
   Changes in the interest rate must be tied to an index. The lender is given the choice from a variety of alternatives. A typical index used

recently is the Federal Home Loan Bank Board survey of rates on new mortgages issued within the past six months.

☐ *Monthly payment changes*

The monthly payment can be designed to change in longer intervals than the interest rate, which will produce a fixed, level payment. Once the payment period ends, the payment is adjusted to reflect changes in the interest rate. A "cap" or maximum may or may not exist.

☐ *Initial interest and payment rates*

The initial interest rate should be determined by adding the level of the interest rate index selected for judging movements to an initial profit spread for the lender. The AML payment must be set initially using this interest rate. The ARM rate does not have to amortize the loan for the first five years.

☐ *Negative amortization*

Negative amortization occurs when the payment does not cover the total amount owed to the lender. The additional amount is added to the total debt. One type of loan sets a limit on negative amortization while another allows the lender to establish the limit.

☐ *Servicing*

Taxes are owed on the interest when they are actually paid to the lender. Prepayment and due-on-sale clauses are permitted. Commercial banks must transmit a disclosure notice to the customer when the rate changes, while savings and loans must send the notice when the payment changes.

☐ *Major risks*

Several risks exist with an adjustable mortgage. First, considerable misunderstanding can occur between the lender and the borrower over the terms. Second, the payment changes can be large if no cap exists. Third, negative amortization can cause the borrower to owe more at the end of the year than at the beginning.

Adjustable rate mortgage note   The ARM note is signed in place of the note shown earlier in Exhibit 16-2. Parts 3 and 4 of this note, shown in Exhibit 16-7, give the lender the right to change the interest rate and the payment relative to movements in the weekly average yield on U.S. Treasury securities. This change may occur once per year, and may cause the interest rate to change by one percent.

Making the Mortgage Affordable

The Housing and Community Development Act of 1977 made permanent the graduated payment mortgage (GPM), which was created to allow younger couples to enter the home-buying market with lower initial mortgage payments.[12] Under the GPM, the lender loans additional funds in the early years, which are applied to the early

EXHIBIT 16-7

ADJUSTABLE RATE NOTE

THIS NOTE CONTAINS A PROVISION ALLOWING FOR CHANGES IN MY INTEREST RATE. IF MY INTEREST RATE INCREASES, MY MONTHLY PAYMENTS WILL BE HIGHER. IF MY INTEREST RATE DECREASES, MY MONTHLY PAYMENTS WILL BE LOWER.

February   1, 19 86   Little Rock   , Arkansas
                                        City   *State*

#16 Hidden Valley

Property Address

1. BORROWER'S PROMISE TO PAY

In return for a loan that I have received, I promise to pay U.S. $ 68,000 (this amount is called "principal"), plus interest, to the order of the Lender. The Lender is Fourth Federal Savings and Loan

I understand that the Lender may transfer this Note. The Lender or anyone who takes this Note by transfer and who is entitled to receive payments under this Note is called the "Note Holder."

2. INTEREST

Interest will be charged on that part of principal which has not been paid beginning on the date I receive principal and continuing until the full amount of principal has been paid.

Beginning on the date I receive principal, I will pay interest at a yearly rate of 12.5 %. The interest rate that I will pay will change in accordance with Section 4 of this Note. The interest rate required by this Section and Section 4 of this Note is the rate I will pay both before and after any default described in Section 7(B) of this Note.

3. PAYMENTS

(A) Time and Place of Payments

I will pay principal and interest by making payments every month.

I will make my monthly payments on the first day of each month beginning on March 1, 19 86. I will make these payments every month until I have paid all of the principal and interest and any other charges described below that I may owe under this Note. My monthly payments will be applied to interest before principal. If on February 1, 2211, I still owe amounts under this Note, I will pay those amounts in full on that date, which is called the "maturity date."

I will make my monthly payments at Fourth Federal Savings and Loan or at a different place if required by the Note Holder.

(B) Amount of My Initial Monthly Payments

My initial monthly payments will be in the amount of U.S.$ 741.44 This amount may change to reflect changes in the interest rate that I must pay. The Note Holder will determine my monthly payment in accordance with Section 4 of this Note.

4. INTEREST RATE AND MONTHLY PAYMENT CHANGES

(A) Change Dates

The interest rate I will pay may change on the 1st day of February 19 87, and on that day of the month every 12 months thereafter. Each date on which my interest rate could change is called a "Change Date."

(B) The Index

Beginning with the first Change Date, my interest rate will be based on an "Index." The Index is the weekly average yield on United States Treasury securities adjusted to a constant maturity of 2 years, as made available by the Federal Reserve Board. The most recent Index figure available as of 45 days before each Change Date is called the "Current Index."

If the Index is no longer available, the Note Holder will choose a new index which is based upon comparable information. The Note Holder will give me notice of its choice.

ARKANSAS—FHLMC UNIFORM ADJUSTABLE RATE LOAN—(TREASURY INDEX)—3/83

EXHIBIT 16-7 (continued)

(C) Calculation of Changes

Before each Change Date, the Note Holder will calculate my new interest rate by adding ....
.... percentage points (........1..0.............%) to the Current Index. The sum will be my new interest rate.

The Note Holder will then determine the amount of the monthly payment that would be sufficient to repay in full the principal I am expected to owe on the Change Date in substantially equal payments by the maturity date at my new interest rate. The result of this calculation will be the new amount of my monthly payment.

(D) Effective Date of Changes

My new interest rate will become effective on each Change Date. I will pay the amount of my new monthly payment beginning on the first monthly payment date after the Change Date until the amount of my monthly payment changes again.

(E) Notice of Changes

The Note Holder will mail or deliver to me a notice before each Change Date. The notice will advise me of:

(i) the new interest rate on my loan as of the Change Date;

(ii) the amount of my monthly payment following the Change Date;

(iii) any additional matters which the Note Holder is required to disclose; and

(iv) the title and telephone number of a person who will answer any question I may have regarding the notice.

5. BORROWER'S RIGHT TO PREPAY

I have the right to make payments of principal at any time before they are due. A payment of principal only is known as a "prepayment." When I make a prepayment, I will tell the Note Holder in writing that I am doing so.

I may make a full prepayment or a partial prepayment without paying any penalty. The Note Holder will use all of my prepayments to reduce the amount of principal that I owe under this Note. If I make a partial prepayment, there will be no delays in the due dates of my monthly payments unless the Note Holder agrees in writing to those delays. My partial prepayment will reduce the amount of my monthly payments after the first Change Date following my partial prepayment. However, any reduction due to my partial prepayment may be offset by an interest rate increase.

6. LOAN CHARGES

If a law which applies to this loan and which sets maximum loan charges is finally interpreted so that the interest or other loan charges collected or to be collected in connection with this loan exceed the permitted limits, then: (i) any such loan charge shall be reduced by the amount necessary to reduce the charge to the permitted limit; and (ii) any sums already collected from me which exceeded permitted limits will be refunded to me. The Note Holder may choose to make this refund by reducing the principal I owe under this Note or by making a direct payment to me. If a refund reduces principal, the reduction will be treated as a partial prepayment.

7. BORROWER'S FAILURE TO PAY AS REQUIRED

(A) Late Charge for Overdue Payments

If the Note Holder has not received the full amount of any of my monthly payments by the end of ....30........... calendar days after the date it is due, I will pay a late charge to the Note Holder. The amount of the charge will be ...12..5..............% of my overdue payment of principal and interest. I will pay this late charge promptly but only once on any late payment.

(B) Default

If I do not pay the full amount of each monthly payment on the date it is due, I will be in default.

(C) Notice of Default

If I am in default, the Note Holder may send me a written notice telling me that if I do not pay the overdue amount by a certain date the Note Holder may require me to pay immediately the full amount of principal which has not been paid and all the interest that I owe on that amount. That date must be at least 30 days after the date on which the notice is mailed or delivered to me.

(D) No Waiver by Note Holder

Even if, at a time when I am in default, the Note Holder does not require me to pay immediately in full as described above, the Note Holder will still have the right to do so if I am in default at a later time.

(E) Payment of Note Holder's Costs and Expenses

If the Note Holder has required me to pay immediately in full as described above, the Note Holder will have the right to be paid back by me for all its reasonable costs and expenses to the extent not prohibited by applicable law. Those expenses may include, for example, reasonable attorneys' fees.

EXHIBIT 16-7 (continued)

8. GIVING OF NOTICES

Unless applicable law requires a different method, any notice that must be given to me under this Note will be given by mailing it by first class mail or by delivering it to me at the Property Address above or at a different address if I give the Note Holder a notice of my different address.

Any notice that must be given to the Note Holder under this Note will be given by mailing it by first class mail to the Note Holder at the address stated in Section 3(A) above or at a different address if I am given a notice of that different address.

9. OBLIGATIONS OF PERSONS UNDER THIS NOTE

If more than one person signs this Note, each person is fully and personally obligated to keep all of the promises made in this Note, including the promise to pay the full amount owed. Any person who is a guarantor, surety, or endorser of this Note is also obligated to do these things. Any person who takes over these obligations, including the obligations of a guarantor, surety, or endorser of this Note, is also obligated to keep all of the promises made in this Note. The Note Holder may enforce its rights under this Note against each person individually or against all of us together. This means that any one of us may be required to pay all of the amounts owed under this Note.

10. WAIVERS

I and any other person who has obligations under this Note waive the rights of presentment and notice of dishonor. "Presentment" means the right to require the Note Holder to demand payment of amounts due. "Notice of dishonor" means the right to require the Note Holder to give notice to other persons that amounts due have not been paid.

11. THIS NOTE SECURED BY A SECURITY INSTRUMENT

In addition to the protections given to the Note Holder under this Note, a Mortgage, Deed of Trust or Deed to Secure Debt (the "Security Instrument") with an Adjustable Rate Rider, dated the same day as this Note, protects the Note Holder from possible losses which might result if I do not keep the promises which I make in this Note. That Security Instrument and Rider describe how and under what conditions I may be required to make immediate payment in full of all amounts that I owe under this Note. Some of those conditions are described as follows:

"Transfer of the Property or a Beneficial Interest in Borrower. If all or any part of the Property or an interest therein is sold or transferred (or if a beneficial interest in Borrower is sold or transferred and Borrower is not a natural person) without Lender's prior written consent, Lender may, at Lender's option, declare all the sums secured by this Security Instrument to be immediately due and payable. However, this option shall not be exercised by Lender if exercise is not authorized by Federal law.

"If Lender exercises such option to accelerate, Lender shall mail Borrower notice of acceleration in accordance with paragraph 14 hereof. Such notice shall provide a period of not less than 30 days from the date the notice is mailed within which Borrower may pay the sums declared due. If Borrower fails to pay such sums prior to the expiration of such period, Lender may, without further notice or demand on Borrower, invoke any remedies permitted by paragraph 18 hereof.

"Notwithstanding a sale or transfer, Borrower will continue to be obligated under the Note and this Security Instrument unless Lender has released Borrower in writing."

Witness the hand(s) and seal(s) of the undersigned.

....(Seal)
               Borrower

....(Seal)
               Borrower

....(Seal)
               Borrower
          (Sign Original Only)

mortgage payments. The additional loan is added to the mortgage balance and repaid by higher payments in later years.

The five available GPM plans differ in only two points:

☐ The annual rate of increase in the monthly payments, which can equal 2, 5, or 7½ percent

☐ The number of years over which these payments can increase, which is either five or ten years

For example, consider the different payments shown in Exhibit 16-8 using the following mortgage terms:

Mortgage amount	$50,000.00
Maturity	30 years
Interest	9%
Payment on this loan under a conventional mortgage	$402.50

Any one of these five plans allows lower monthly payments for the first four years than the payment of $402.50, which is required under this mortgage as a conventional loan. However, the borrower should be aware of two characteristics of the GPM plan: (1) The payments will take an increasing proportion of the family income. To accommodate for this, the borrower should be able to project an increasing family income, which will ideally allow the percent going to the mortgage payment to remain constant. (2) Over the life of the loan, the borrower will pay more interest than would be paid on a conventional loan for the same amount and interest.

In sum, the GPM has a constant interest rate over the life of the mortgage with payments that increase on a predetermined schedule in the early years of repayment. The debt will equal zero by maturity, and the maturity date typically does not change. If the loan is not paid before maturity, the total interest paid the lender may be larger than a conventional mortgage.

Graduated equity mortgage (GEM) The graduated (growing) equity mortgage has been offered by lenders as an alternative to a high interest rate conventional mort-

EXHIBIT 16-8 Five GPM payment plans

Source: Federal Housing Administration, *Own . . . with a Graduated Payment Mortgage* (Washington, D.C.: HUD, December 1978).

Year	2½% 5 yr I	5% 5 yr II	7½% 5 yr III	2% 10 yr IV	3% 10 yr V
1	$366.22	$333.53	$303.94	$355.97	$334.47
2	$375.38	$350.21	$326.74	$363.09	$344.51
3	$384.76	$367.72	$351.74	$370.35	$354.84
4	$394.38	$386.11	$377.59	$377.76	$365.49
5	$404.24	$405.41	$405.91	$385.31	$376.45
6	$414.35	$425.68	$436.35	$393.02	$387.75
7	$414.35	$425.68	$436.35	$400.88	$399.38
8	$414.35	$425.68	$436.35	$408.90	$411.36
9	$414.35	$425.68	$436.35	$417.07	$423.70
10	$414.35	$425.68	$436.35	$425.42	$436.41
Remaining payments	$414.35	$425.68	$436.35	$433.92	$449.50

THE DECISION TO FINANCE THE TRANSACTION

gage. One plan issued by a state housing agency[13] requires that the monthly payments increase by 3 percent annually for a period of nine years. The additional 3 percent that is paid each year by the borrower is credited toward reducing the debt. The result of these additional payments is that the loan is paid typically five to ten years sooner. The borrower owns the property sooner, and much less total interest is paid the lender. The interest rate never changes, and the payments change according to a predetermined schedule.

Buydown mortgage   In a typical buydown loan, a party to the transaction, usually the seller, pays part of the interest in advance to give the borrower a lower interest rate during the early years of the loan. Using this technique, the borrower may be able to qualify for a loan if the family income was not sufficient to qualify prior to the buydown.

For example, consider the FNMA 3-2-1 buydown. A party to the transaction prepays interest in an amount equal to 3 percentage points less than the mortgage rate the first year, two points less the second, and one point less the third. The result of this 3-2-1 buydown on a 15 percent mortgage is that the buyer pays an interest rate of 12 percent the first year, 13 percent the second, and 14 percent the third. After the third year, the mortgage rate would be 15 percent until maturity.

Other Types of AMIs

Other types of AMIs have been discussed and in some cases implemented. For example, the Flexible Loan Insurance Plan (FLIP)[14] requires the borrower to give part of the down payment to the seller, and the remainder goes into an interest-bearing savings account held by the lender. The lender can loan approximately 99 percent of the purchase price using the interest-bearing savings account as collateral for part of the loan. The borrower's initial payments are lower than a conventionally financed loan, with the balance of the monthly payment taken from the pledged account. The borrower's monthly payments rise and, eventually, the interest-bearing savings account is gone. At this point, the borrower assumes the full payment.

The variable rate maturity mortgage (VRMM)[15] is very similar to the VRM except the borrower is given an option when the initial changes in the interest rate occur. A change in the rate can be accepted or the maturity date can be altered to keep the monthly payment constant.

Another mortgage plan that has received considerable recent attention is the shared appreciation mortgage (SAM). Under this mortgage, the lender offers the homeowner a lower-than-market rate of interest. The lost interest must be repaid at a predetermined time in the future. At this date, the homeowner either sells the property or refinances into a type of mortgage that has been determined in advance. This arrangement can be negotiated where the buyer accepts a lower initial interest rate in exchange for a specific percent of the equity at a predetermined future date. Thus, the buyer pays a lower rate for the first few years, enabling the purchase to be made, and the lender participates in the increased equity.

Other types will probably be created in the future. They will attempt to either (a) increase the lender's earnings on existing loans, or (b) bring new homebuyers into the market by causing their initial payments to be lower.

A COMPARISON OF MORTGAGE LOANS

A potential borrower can acquire very useful information by comparing the monthly payment, end-of-year totals, and outstanding mortgage balance for several selected types of mortgages. Exhibits 16-9 through 16-14 illustrate these totals for a loan of $100,000 at a contract mortgage rate of 15 percent with a maturity date of thirty years. A veteran may acquire this loan for 13½ percent. The GEM loan is designed to be paid in full in eleven years, five months. The ARM has a cap on the interest rate increases or decreases of 2 percent per year.

An important conclusion in reading these charts is that no one mortgage is "good" or "bad" for all types of borrowers. Each one must fit the needs of the particular lender and borrower. For example, the lowest amount of total payments made over the life of the loan, $225,713, was with the GEM, but the payments escalated annually from $1,264.44 to $2,162.62. The GPM started with the lowest payment of $990.23, but the debt owed did not fall under the original $100,000 until after the fifteenth year. The FNMA 3-2-1 buydown allowed the borrower to pay three years of lower payments which were $1,028.61, $1,106.20, and $1,184.87, respectively. Beginning with the fourth year, the payments resumed to the $1,264.44 level until maturity.

EXHIBIT 16-9   Conventional level payment loan

Copyright for all charts by Medical Economics, Inc., Oradell, NJ 07649. Reprinted by permission.

		End-of-year totals		
Year	Monthly payment	Principal paid	Interest paid	Outstanding mortgage balance
1	$1,264.44	$ 186	$ 14,988	$99,814
2	1,264.44	402	29,946	99,598
3	1,264.44	652	44,870	99,348
4	1,264.44	943	59,753	99,057
5	1,264.44	1,280	74,590	98,720
10	1,264.44	3,975	147,765	96,025
15	1,264.44	9,656	217,954	90,344
20	1,264.44	21,626	281,854	78,374
25	1,264.44	46,850	332,500	53,150
30	1,264.44	100,000	355,220	0

Amount financed: $100,000 — *Term: 30 years / Interest rate: 15%*

Total payments over life of mortgage: $455,220

THE DECISION TO FINANCE THE TRANSACTION

EXHIBIT 16-10   VA loan

Amount financed: $100,000   *Term: 30 years*
                                               Interest rate: 13½%

| Year | Monthly payment | End-of-year totals | | |
		Principal paid	Interest paid	Outstanding mortgage balance
1	$1,145.41	$ 261	$ 13,484	$99,739
2	1,145.41	559	26,931	99,441
3	1,145.41	900	40,335	99,100
4	1,145.41	1,290	53,690	98,710
5	1,145.41	1,736	66,989	98,264
10	1,145.41	5,132	132,318	94,868
15	1,145.41	11,777	194,398	88,223
20	1,145.41	50,221	293,404	49,779
25	1,145.41	50,221	293,404	49,779
30	1,145.41	100,000	312,350	0

Total payments over life of mortgage: $412,350

EXHIBIT 16-11   Graduated payment mortgage

Amount financed: $100,000   *Term: 30 years*
                                               Interest rate: 15%

| Year | Monthly payment | End-of-year totals | | |
		Principal paid	Interest paid*	Outstanding mortgage balance
1	$ 990.23	$− 3,341	$ 15,224	$103,341
2	1,064.50	− 6,263	30,920	106,263
3	1,144.34	− 8,629	47,018	108,629
4	1,230.16	−10,271	63,422	110,271
5	1,322.43	−10,991	80,119	110,991
10	1,421.61	− 7,960	162,275	107,960
15	1,421.61	− 1,574	241,184	101,574
20	1,421.61	11,885	313,020	88,115
25	1,421.61	40,243	369,957	59,757
30	1,421.61	100,000	395,495	0

Total payments over life of mortgage: $495,495

*When the annual interest due exceeds the annual payment, there is negative amortization. But the mortgagor (home buyer) can deduct for tax purposes no more than his actual annual payment.

THE RESIDENTIAL MORTGAGE AND THE APPLICATION PROCESS

EXHIBIT 16-12   Graduated equity mortgage

Amount financed: $100,000   *Term: 11 years, 5 months*
                                                                      Interest rate: 15%

Year	Monthly payment	End-of-year totals		
		Principal paid	Interest paid	Outstanding mortgage balance
1	$1,264.44	$ 186	$ 14,988	$99,814
2	1,327.66	1,214	29,892	98,786
3	1,394.04	3,262	44,572	96,738
4	1,463.74	6,535	58,864	93,465
5	1,536.93	11,276	72,566	88,724
6	1,613.78	17,767	85,440	82,233
7	1,694.47	26,340	97,201	73,660
8	1,779.19	37,380	107,511	62,620
9	1,868.15	51,338	115,971	48,662
10	1,961.56	68,742	122,106	31,258
11	2,059.64	90,205	125,359	9,795
12	2,162.62*	100,000	125,713	0

Total payments over life of mortgage: $225,713

*For four months with a final payment of $1,498.30.

EXHIBIT 16-13   Adjustable-rate mortgage (2% interest rate cap)

Amount financed: $100,000   *Term: 30 years*
                                                              Interest rate: adjusted annually*

Year	Index	Effective rate to borrower	Monthly payment	End-of-year totals		
				Principal paid	Interest paid	Outstanding mortgage balance
1	14.50%	15.00%	$1,264.44	$ 186	$ 14,988	$99,814
2	16.80	17.00	1,425.68	324	31,958	99,676
3	16.25	16.50	1,385.15	507	48,397	99,493
4	13.50	14.50	1,224.56	828	62,771	99,172
5	14.00	14.25	1,204.69	1,216	76,839	98,784
6–10	13.50	13.75	1,165.11	4,499	143,460	95,501
11–15	16.00	15.75	1,324.62	9,682	217,752	90,318
16–20	14.00	14.25	1,204.69	22,307	277,408	77,693
21–25	12.50	13.00	1,106.20	49,016	317,069	50,984
26–30	12.00	12.50	1,067.26	100,000	330,120	0

Total payments over life of mortgage: $495,495

*No rate increase or decrease can exceed 2% per year.
Note: For illustrative purposes, interest-rate movements were assumed.

THE DECISION TO FINANCE THE TRANSACTION

EXHIBIT 16-14 FNMA 3-2-1 buydown

Amount financed: $100,000

Term: 30 years
Interest rate: 15%
Seller/builder payment: $5,687

Year	Monthly payment	End-of-year totals		
		Principal paid	Interest paid	Outstanding mortgage balance
1	$1,028.61	$ 186	$ 12,157	$99,814
2	1,106.20	402	25,215	99,598
3	1,184.87	652	39,183	99,348
4	1,264.44	943	54,066	99,057
5	1,264.44	1,280	68,903	98,720
10	1,264.44	3,975	142,078	96,025
15	1,264.44	9,656	212,267	90,344
20	1,264.44	21,626	276,167	78,374
25	1,264.44	46,850	326,813	53,150
30	1,264.44	100,000	349,533	0

Total payments over life of mortgage: $449,533

OTHER MORTGAGES AND CONTRACTS

Other types of mortgages and contracts can be used in a residential real estate transaction.

Blanket Mortgage

A blanket mortgage is one loan covering several parcels of real property. The borrower does not have to negotiate each mortgage separately. This type of mortgage is used primarily in subdivision development. It typically contains a release clause that releases the mortgagor from a portion of the original debt as each parcel is sold.

Package Mortgage

A package mortgage is one mortgage covering real property and certain pieces of personal property used with it. The borrower does not have to negotiate a separate mortgage for the property and other items such as the oven, air conditioning, and carpets. This mortgage is common in the financing of hotel, motel, and apartment projects.

Open-end Mortgage

An open-end mortgage is one mortgage document providing for future advances of additional funds. The advance can be automatic or optional with lender evaluation before more funds are extended.

Leasehold Mortgage

A leasehold mortgage, used primarily with commercial ventures, enables the borrower to own the rights to develop and/or manage property in the form of a lease. The developer wants a mortgage that will be repaid from the sale of a product from the property or just the rental of space.

Estoppel Certificate

An **estoppel certificate** provided by the mortgagor-debtor states the precise amount of debt owed and any other outstanding claims on the property. By requiring this certificate, the buyer and future lender are aware of the precise dollar amounts owed.

Assignment

An assignment is a document that transfers the rights to the property or specific rights to another party. For example, an assignment can be written and recorded to show that a mortgage has been transferred to another owner. Also, an assignment can be written and recorded to provide proof that the right to collect rents on a parcel has been transferred. This document is used to provide proof of a legitimate transfer without fraud.

Subordination

A subordination contract is filed in the county courthouse when a previous claimant to the property value, such as a lender or lienholder, agrees to take a lower position. Filing this contract gives constructive notice and changes the ranking of the claim involved.

THREE FEDERAL ACTS

The Depository Institutions Deregulation and Monetary Control Act (DIDMCA)

The DIDMCA, signed by the President in March 1980, is viewed by some analysts to be one of the most important financial acts since the 1930s. Its content is discussed in this chapter and later chapters.

Two parts of the act may be viewed as influencing the residential mortgage and the application process. Each is discussed briefly:

New real estate lending authority   Federal savings and loans will be permitted to make second mortgage loans, make residential mortgage loans without any geographical restrictions, ignore previous statutory limitations on home loans and home improvement loans, and invest in home mortgage loans of up to 90 percent of the appraised value of a property that includes a building. (On unimproved lots, the mortgage may be 65 percent of the appraised value. It may be 75 percent of the appraised value of an improved lot without a building.)

Permanent federal override of state usury ceilings   This provision applies to mortgages and a three-year preemption for business and agriculture loans over $25,000.

The first part should make the lending institutions much more competitive for the borrower's business. If the mortgage lending part of the real estate transaction does become more competitive, the borrowers should receive additional benefits in the form of lower financing costs wherever possible. The second part should reduce the credit outflows from some states with low usury ceilings and help to reduce the points paid because of low usury ceilings.

Garn-St. Germain Act of 1982

This act covered a wide range of new authority that was given to lenders. Savings and loans now have the authority to create a savings account that is equivalent to and competitive with money market mutual funds. This account has no minimum balance, no minimum maturity, no interest rate ceiling, and is not subject to the reserve requirement. This act authorized federally chartered savings and loans to issue commercial loans up to 10 percent of their assets and to expand nonresidential lending and consumer loans.

Housing and Urban Recovery Act of 1983

The HURRA included several new authorizations for FHA discussed earlier in this chapter. Briefly, these gave the FHA new authority to issue an indexed mortgage, an adjustable rate mortgage, and a shared appreciation mortgage. It also allowed the local lender to determine the level of the interest rate, and thus minimized the amount of points that could be paid by any party to the transaction.

CHAPTER SUMMARY

In a typical residential real estate transaction, the borrower uses equity funds from personal assets and debt funds from the assets of a lender. Lenders are a necessary part of the transaction because the purchase price of the property greatly exceeds the amount of cash an individual typically can pay.

All potential borrowers should assess their available cash carefully because all lenders require a down payment. Possible sources of additional equity funds are the cash value in a life insurance policy, relatives, sale of other assets, and an advance on future wages.

The borrower must find a lender whose down payment and economic terms suit the borrower's needs. The borrower should allocate sufficient time to shop among the lenders and compare terms.

The lender can give the borrower a mortgage with a promissory note or a deed of trust with a promissory note. The latter provides for a speedy foreclosure in the event of buyer default.

The lender may ask that the borrower purchase default insurance on a portion of the loan, or the buyer can request insurance from FHA or FmHA or a guarantee from the VA if qualified. The borrower's credit history is evaluated by criteria that indicate the price the individual can afford to pay for a house in relation to anticipated income and other debt.

By using new types of mortgages, such as the alternative rate mortgage, lenders are able to collect additional interest through time on mortgages. Using the graduated payment mortgage, the borrower can tailor the debt service payments to anticipated income. The result is typically a lower than usual payment for the first few years.

Several important federal acts influence the lender and the potential borrower. Their content should be known by both parties. These include the Real Estate Settlement Procedures Act, the Equal Credit Opportunity Act, the Truth-in-Lending Act, the Depository Institutions Deregulation and Monetary Control Act, and the Garn-St. Germain Act.

Review Questions

1. What is the difference between equity and debt funds? Why is a prospective homebuyer interested in both?
2. Identify several sources of equity funds that a potential buyer should investigage if additional equity funds are needed.
3. What is the difference between refinancing and financing? Is there a difference between a buyer's reasons for refinancing and an owner's reasons for refinancing?
4. What is meant by "taking out the equity"?
5. What is seller financing? Why is it important to the homebuyer?
6. Does a lender use the loan-to-value ratio in making a residential loan? How?
7. The typical conventional mortgage that has been used in the United States since the 1930s has several basic characteristics. Describe them briefly.
8. A typical residential mortgage written on a mortgage form supplied by the Mortgage Corporation has seventeen uniform covenants that are identical in all states. Identify and summarize those covenants.
9. Additional covenants that are unique to an individual state may be added to the mortgage. Identify several of these covenants.
10. What is the purpose of a promissory note? Identify several of the clauses found in this document.
11. What is the difference between a mortgage and a deed of trust?
12. What is the application procedure for a conventional loan? Is it different for FHA? VA? FmHA? If so, identify the differences.
13. How is a lender influenced by the Equal Credit Opportunity Act? RESPA? Truth-in-Lending?

14. Does Regulation Z cover a broker's ad in a newspaper? How?

15. How is a residential loan application typically evaluated?

16. Describe the differences among the agencies that typically issue default insurance for most of the loan. Describe the one that issues a guarantee for a portion of the loan.

17. How does the default insurance issued by a government agency differ from private mortgage insurance?

18. What are the characteristics of an alternative rate mortgage? A variable rate mortgage? A graduated payment mortgage? Why has each been proposed?

19. For what purpose is a debiting factor used? Give an example.

20. How does the DIDMCA influence the residential mortgage and the application process? What is the effect of the Garn-St. Germain Act on residential lending?

21. Describe each of the following: blanket mortgage, package mortgage, second mortgage, purchase-money mortgage, leasehold mortgage, open-end mortgage.

22. When would an assignment and an estoppel certificate be used?

Discussion Questions

1. Compile a list of the questions that a typical residential borrower should ask a prospective lender.

2. Would you prefer a conventional mortgage with fixed monthly payments or a variable rate mortgage with a possibility of changing monthly payments?

3. Does the lender have an obligation to arrange the best terms to fit the potential borrower's situation?

4. What is your opinion about the future relationship between equity and debt funds in a real estate transaction? Will one tend to grow in proportion more than the other?

5. Assume that a prospective homebuyer examines all available sources for equity funds and discovers that the total is less than the amount required by the lender. What are the options?

6. How can an agent help a buyer or seller in arranging financing?

7. Under what conditions would a prospective buyer prefer to purchase equity rather than refinance the loan?

Notes

1. Benjamin H. Henszey and Ronald Friedman, *Real Estate Law* (Boston: Warren, Gorham, and Lamont, 1979), p. 198.

2. Ibid., p. 199.

3. Editorial Staff, "Nondiscrimination in Lending, Applications, and Advertising," *Federal Home Loan Bank Board Journal,* Vol. 12 (December 1979), p. 26; Armin Guggenheim, "Do You Offer Equal Services to All Prospects?" *Real Estate Today,* Vol. 13 (April 1980), p. 21.

4. Board of Governors, *Truth-in-Lending* (Washington, D.C.: Federal Reserve System), p. 1.

5. Ibid.

6. Ibid., pp. 9, 100.

7. For a good discussion of these points covered under Regulation Z, see L. Randolph McGee and Carl Stich, Jr., "Truth in Lending in Advertised Real Estate," *Real Estate Review,* Vol. 8 (Fall 1978), pp. 85–89.

8. These examples were provided by the Mortgage Credit Department, FHA District Office, Little Rock, AR.

9. For an excellent discussion of the various alternative mortgage instruments, see Federal Home Loan Bank Board, *Alternative Mortgage Instruments Research Study,* Vol. I–III (Washington, D.C.: FHLBB, November 1977).

10. Editorial Staff, "FHLBB Authorizes Use of Renegotiable Rate Mortgages for Thrifts," *Federal Home Loan Bank Board Journal,* Vol. 13 (May 1980), pp. 52–54, 59–60; Editorial Staff, "RRMs: New Flexibility for Mortgage Lending," *M.G.I.C. Newsletter* (May–June 1980), p. 4.

11. Executive Summary, *Adjustable Rate Mortgages,* Republic Mortgage Insurance Co., June 1981.

12. Emma McFarlin, "The Graduated Payment Mortgage," *Federal Home Loan Bank Board Journal,* Vol. 13 (January 1980), pp. 14–17; William Dan Helpbringer, "Graduated Payment Mortgages," *Federal Home Loan Bank Board Journal,* Vol. 12 (November 1979), pp. 16–18.

13. Arkansas Housing Development Office, Little Rock, AR, 1983.

14. *Wall Street Journal,* June 23, 1977, p. 13.

15. Donald R. Epley and James A. Millar, *Basic Real Estate Finance and Investments* (New York: John Wiley & Sons, Inc., 1984), pp. 272–74.

Additional Readings

AGARWAL, VINOD. "Mortgage Rate Buydowns: Further Evidence." *Housing Finance Review* 3 (April 1984): 191–98.

ANDERSEN, JON LEE and HAROLD BOWMAN, "Does Your Advertising Pass the Trust-in-Lending Test?" *Real Estate Review* 13 (Spring 1983): 92–97.

DEL DONNO, RUDY. "Arranging Financing." Lectures delivered to the Arkansas REALTORS Association Graduate Institute I and II, April 1976.

DRAPER, DANIEL, "Alternative Mortgage Instruments," *Real Estate Review* 11 (Fall 1981): 32–38.

EPLEY, DONALD R., and JAMES A. MILLAR. *Basic Real Estate Finance and Investments.* New York: John Wiley & Sons, Inc., 1984. Chapters 7, 8, 9, and 11.

Federal National Mortgage Association. *A Guide to Fannie Mae.* Washington, D.C.: FNMA, May 1975.

GRIER, MARCIA. "Keeping on Top of the Money Market." *Real Estate Today* 9 (August 1976): 20–23.

HARRIS, CLAVIN J. "Making the Most of Financing." *Real Estate Today* 9 (May–June 1976): 48–52.

Federal Home Loan Mortgage Co., *Home Mortgages Underwriting Guidelines.* March 1976.

JONES, OLIVER. "VA Finds Borrowers Prefer to Pay Tax and Insurance Bills Monthly." *The Mortgage Banker* 34 (March 1974): 30–32.

KRATOVIL, ROBERT. *Modern Mortgage Law and Practice.* Englewood Cliffs, N.J.: Prentice-Hall, Inc., 1972. Chapter 8.

———. *Real Estate Law, Sixth Edition.* Englewood Cliffs, N.J.: Prentice-Hall, Inc., 1974. Chapter 20.

MARCIS, RICHARD, "The Shakeout in Alternative Mortgage Instruments," *Real Estate Review* 13 (Spring 1983): 29–34.

PLANT, T. W. "Proposed Model Residential Real Estate Mortgage Loan Application for Use Under the Equal Credit Opportunity Act." *Circular No. 760164* (November 30, 1976). Federal Reserve Bank of Dallas.

REID, NORMAN. "Mortgage Creditworthiness is Most Important Underwriting Evaluation." *The Mortgage Banker* 35 (January 1975): 35–38.

"Settlement Costs and You." *A HUD Guide for Homebuyers* (June 1976).

WATSON, JEANNE. "Qualifying the Prospect." *Real Estate Today* 6 (January 1973): pp. 18–20.

"What to Do When They Can't Get a Mortgage." *Real Estate Today* 8 (February 1975): 4–13.

17 The Commercial Loan

QUESTIONS TO BE ANSWERED _____

1. Where does a person apply for a commercial loan?
2. What are the requirements for obtaining a commercial loan?

OBJECTIVES _____

When a student finishes the chapter, he or she should be able to

1. Explain the difference between residential and commercial loans.
2. Describe the difference between equity and debt funds.
3. Compare a syndicate to joint ownership of property and explain the advantages of each.
4. Explain the difference between a construction loan and a permanent loan.

5. Illustrate the ideal components of a commercial loan application.

6. Explain the key financial ratios often used to evaluate a commercial loan application.

7. Contrast the types of amortization typically used to repay commercial loans.

8. Explain the purpose of a second mortgage and the subordination and default in prior payment clauses.

9. Explain the assignment contract and the estoppel certificate.

IMPORTANT TERMS

Assignment Contract
Balloon Note
Building Area Ratio
Commercial Financing
Construction (Interim) Loan
Debt Financing
Debt Service Ratio
Default in Prior Payment
   Clause
Default Ratio
Equity Financing
Estoppel Certificate
Financial Ratio
Gap Financing
General Partnership
Holdback (Retainage)
Joint Ownership
Land-Building Ratio

Leverage
Limited Partnership
Loan Per Square Foot
Loan-to-Value Ratio
Overall Cap Rate
Partial Amortization
Participation Loan
Permanent Loan
Real Estate Investment Trust
   (REIT)
Second Mortgage
Stabilized Vacancy Ratio
Subchapter S Corporation
Subordination Clause
Syndicate
Takeout Commitment
Term Amortization

INTRODUCTION

Commercial real estate loans are used in the purchase and development of all types of income-producing property. Many individuals use such loans to purchase property for their own business enterprise or as part of the financing for a real estate investment. The consumer, therefore, needs to understand the nature of the commercial loan, the types of commercial investment organizations, the sources of commercial funds, commercial loan requirements, and the financial ratios used to evaluate commercial loan applications. The consumer will use this knowledge to make a sound decision about buying or investing in commercial property, chosing the most suitable type of investment organization, finding a lender, and preparing a loan application.

THE NATURE OF THE COMMERCIAL LOAN

A commercial loan differs from a residential loan in several respects. A commercial loan is given on property that produces an income stream from the sale of a product. The product can be rental space, the sale of portions of the property such as condominium units, or items such as pizzas, clothing, or chemicals. The income stream to the property is used to make the loan payments, pay expenses, and generate a profit. In addition, part of the owner's return may be generated from an expected increase in property value through time.

The application for a commercial loan is evaluated by the lender on the basis of a combination of factors, such as expected future income from the sale of product(s), the past earnings and credit record of the borrower, the location of the site, and the number of potential buyers in the market. These factors are evaluated jointly and various weights are applied to each to determine potential success or failure. Consequently, a commercial loan application is more difficult to evaluate than a residential loan application. Residential lending is based on a smaller number of factors such as past credit, nature of employment, and expected wage earnings, which are easier to measure.

Commercial loans are usually much larger in amount than a residential loan and may carry a comparable maturity period. In addition, the lender may impose requirements on the borrower as a condition for receiving the loan, such as a restriction limiting expenses.

Need for Commercial Financing

The need for **commercial financing** is similar to the need for residential financing. The economy needs commercial businesses just as it needs residential properties. Commercial businesses produce and/or sell products to satisfy the demands of the public. The flow of income generated from the sale of these products earns the investor a profit that is a return on the investment.

Commercial financing can be viewed as an outlet for investment funds that is comparable to other competing outlets such as the stock market. In both cases, the investor looks for the highest return on his or her money.

Commercial lenders may band together to underwrite a single commercial loan since it may be larger than the amount a local regionalized lender would be able to grant in one loan. A failure and foreclosure of a commercial loan for a large amount could bankrupt a small lender because the amount could represent a large percentage of the institution's assets.

Debt Versus Equity Funds

Commercial financing consists of two components. One is **equity financing,** the amount of a buyer's own assets used to purchase a parcel of property. The other is **debt financing,** the amount of another party's assets used to help purchase the property. Often, a potential buyer raises equity funds from personal assets for the down payment and borrows the mortgage amount from a debt lender(s). For example,

John Kennedy has $100,000 cash which he plans to use as equity for a down payment on a small business. He needs an additional $400,000 for a mortgage (debt funds) to pay the required purchase price of $500,000. John obtains the loan from Long-Life Insurance Company at the current market rate of 13.5 percent.

Equity funds can be raised from an individual's own assets or provided by several investors pooling their assets. Similarly, debt funds can be raised from a lender or a group of lenders.

An investor can be a demander or a supplier of equity and/or debt funds. Which role the investor decides to assume depends on his or her objectives, motives, and expected return on each individual project.

Favorable Leverage

Any commercial investor should be aware of the use of borrowed funds to magnify the amount of return on the equity invested in the project. In general, leverage is considered to be *favorable* when the return on the equity is larger than the cost of the money and *unfavorable* when the opposite holds. In a rising market, the purchase of property with debt funds as opposed to a purchase with all cash will normally result in a larger rate of return on the amount of equity paid by the investor.

For example, consider property that is purchased for $200,000 with all cash, held for one year, and sold for $210,000. The return would be

$$\begin{array}{r} \$210,000 \text{ selling price} \\ -\,200,000 \text{ cost} \\ \hline \$\ 10,000 \text{ gain} \end{array}$$

and

$$\frac{\$\ 10,000 \text{ gain}}{\$200,000 \text{ equity}} 100 = 5\% \text{ return or equity compared to a}$$
$$0 \text{ debt service rate: } \textit{positive leverage}$$

Now consider the purchase where the buyer paid $20,000 down, financed the balance with a $180,000 mortgage at 13 percent for thirty years, and sold the property in one year. The return would be,

$$\begin{array}{r} \$210,000 \text{ selling price} \\ -\,200,000 \text{ cost} \\ \hline \$\ 10,000 \text{ gain} \end{array}$$

and

$$\frac{\$10,000 \text{ gain}}{\$20,000 \text{ equity}} 100 = 50\% \text{ a } 13\% \text{ debt service rate: } \textit{greater}$$
$$\text{a } 13\% \text{ debt service rate: } \textit{greater}$$
$$\textit{positive leverage}$$

An investor can achieve a high rate of return on the equity funds invested in real estate by combining where possible a small down payment with a large mortgage. In this manner, the two combined can be used to purchase high-priced property. Real estate is unique in that the investor can acquire higher-priced property with a small down payment to achieve the maximum leverage.

COMMON FALLACIES ABOUT COMMERCIAL PROPERTIES

Several common fallacies about commercial properties discourage many people from investing in such property, or encourage people to buy it for unsound reasons. Knowledge of these fallacies enables a prospective buyer to evaluate his or her objectives and to make a rational decision about buying commercial property.

Fallacy 1: "All property is valuable and increases in value."

Will Rogers said, "Land is a good buy because they ain't making it no more." Although land is fixed in supply, it has a value only if someone is willing to purchase it. Part II explains the concepts of value in use and value in exchange as the determinants of the demand curve. Together, these factors are interpreted to mean that property must offer a potential value for holding it to generate an income, or it must offer a potential for growth to generate a capital gain. If a potential purchaser can not see either use value or exchange value, the property has no value. Consequently, not all property is valuable because all property does not have a potential use or good prospects for growth.

Fallacy 2: "I should not purchase real estate because my cash would be tied up for a long period of time."

A real estate investment is not like a purchase of stocks or bonds that is carried out in an organized market with continuous quotation of prices. In any real estate transaction, a buyer must seek out a seller, or vice versa. In addition, real estate typically is not purchased for immediate resale unless the investor is a speculator. It is purchased with the intention of holding it for a period of time to generate income and/or a capital gain; it does tie up cash for a period of time. Therefore, any investor who anticipates that the cash to be used for the investment might be needed in the immediate future should not invest in commercial property. A purchaser should remember, however, that a bank will usually give a loan for 60 to 70 percent of the property's equity if the market shows growth and the investor needs cash.

Fallacy 3: "Distressed and problem properties are good buys because the price may be lower than that of comparable structures that do not have the same problems."

Any property can become a good buy if the price is lower than that of comparable properties with the same problem. However, a purchaser should always ask why the price is so low and investigate whether the problems can be remedied. Distressed or problem property should not be purchased unless the buyer is a specialist in such properties. Otherwise, the purchaser may be forced to give someone else a good buy with a lower price at a future date because of a lack in demand.

Fallacy 4: "A good approximation of the value of the property is found by dividing the net operating income by the property's capitalization rate."

Estimating the value by the formula $V = I/R$ involves three basic assumptions:[1] the income flow continues indefinitely, the income in each year remains constant, and the capitalization rate in each year is constant. Because many properties cannot satisfy this set of assumptions, other appraisal methods are presumed to be more accurate (See Chapter 5).

Fallacy 5: "Sellers in areas of high potential demand are charging a higher price because they want to obtain abnormally large profits."

A basic rule of pricing is to charge what the market will bear. The owner cannot be blamed for exercising this option. However, a potential buyer should always buy "where the action is" or purchase in an area of strong current and potential demand even though the purchase price is slightly higher. The reason for this recommendation is that the strong current and potential demand will cause the value in exchange of the property to increase even more than that of a comparable property in an area that does not have such a high growth rate.

COMMERCIAL INVESTMENT ORGANIZATION

Any individual or group contemplating a real estate investment must decide which form of investment organization is most suitable. The type of organization selected should be determined after careful consideration has been given to the *marketability of the properties* that the organization or individual will sell, *liability* of the individual investors, *tax benefits,* and *requirements of the lenders* with whom the group or individual must work. These factors can be used to evaluate the following forms of investment organization.

Syndicates

A **syndicate** is an organization that pools investment funds from investors under the guidance of a professional in the real estate business. The organization can manage, acquire, operate, develop, or market, or perform some combination of these activities. The syndicate can assume any legal form of ownership, but the usual form is a limited partnership.

A syndicate offers several benefits that may not be available to an individual investor, such as a tax shelter, an attractive return for little time involved in the operation of the organization, the knowledge and services of a professional in real estate, and the opportunity to invest in a larger property than would be feasible for an individual. The professional in the real estate business can benefit from acquiring a share of the ownership in exchange for knowledge and time, a fee for selling, buying, managing, or performing services for the group, and additional business by increasing the marketability of properties listed with his or her firm.

Limited partnership   The most popular form of syndicate in the United States is the **limited partnership.**[2] This organization is composed of general partner(s) and a number of limited partners. The general partner typically is the organizer (syndicator) who has the real estate expertise, and the limited partners are the investors who supply the investment funds. Limited partnerships can be organized by a syndicator, managed by a general partner, and joined by limited partners.

This investment vehicle has several advantages: (1) It provides income tax benefits in that profits and deductions from the investment can pass through the partnership to the individuals to be used on their personal tax returns. (2) Each limited partner has limited liability against lawsuits in the amount of his or her investment funds. (3) The limited partners do not participate in the management of the investment; this is left solely to the general partner.

A limited partnership organization must be distinguished from a corporation for taxation purposes. The tests used to differentiate the two are the continuity of the organization, centralization of the management, limited liability, and transferability of the ownership interest. *Continuity of the organization* is a corporate characteristic—the organization persists after the resignation, death, etc., of an officer that would cause a true partnership to be dissolved. If the state law provides for a technical division of the partnership, the organization qualifies as a limited partnership and the partnership agreement can be used to establish its continuity in the event of death, resignation, etc. *Centralization of management* means that management is essentially separated from the ownership. A typical criterion for a corporation is that all management decisions are made and administered by the board of directors. In a partnership, this function is carried out by the general partner. *Limited liability* typically exists for a corporation if the directors do not have substantial assets in the corporation or simply work as agents for the shareholders. In a partnership, the general partner must not own substantial assets or simply work as an agent for the limited partners. *Transferability of interests* means that shares of the corporation can be transferred in the open market. In a partnership, the transferability of interest must not be substantially restricted by the partner agreement.

These four criteria are used by the IRS to determine whether an organization is a corporation or a limited partnership. A ruling that the organization is in essence a corporation means that the limited partnership loses its tax advantages.

Subchapter S corporation   A corporation that qualifies under the tax code as a *subchapter S corporation* offers some of the tax benefits of a partnership. Congress attempted to give the small businessperson the advantages of limited liability and fringe benefits but keep the passthrough deduction of the partnership. It is viewed as a corporation that has the following characteristics:

1. No more than thirty-five eligible shareholders.
2. New subchapter S companies may have an unlimited amount of passive income such as rents, interest, and dividends. The old rules limited passive income to 20 percent of all income.
3. Real estate companies organizing in 1983 or after will have the option of electing to be either a partnership or a corporation.

4. New companies must be organized on a calendar year basis unless a good reason exists for using another business year.

The corporation typically is used for holding property while the owners receive limited liability and deduct the expenses from the operation of the property. Any gain on the sale is passed on to the shareholders.

General partnership A **general partnership** is a group of investors who pool their investment funds to participate in real estate ownership collectively. Each investor is viewed as co-owner. The profits and losses are distributed on a proportional basis according to each partner's share of the ownership.

The general partnership has three characteristics: (1) A test for continuity of the organization requires that the partnership be dissolved if a partner dies, resigns, etc. However, if the state law provides for a technical division upon death, resignation, etc., of a partner, the organization qualifies as a partnership. A contractual agreement can be written to continue the organization. (2) Each partner has unlimited liability for any obligations of the organization. (3) All members of the partnership have equal management rights to contractually commit and bind the whole organization. This principle can hold even though the partnership may centralize its management by an internal agreement.

Real Estate Investment Trust (REIT) An association or a trust that invests primarily in real estate and mortgages may elect special tax treatment as a REIT. The characteristics of a REIT depend on whether it was established before or after passage of the Tax Reform Act of 1976. Selected features of a REIT follow.[3]

A REIT established prior to the Tax Reform Act of 1976 must

- ☐ Be a trust or unincorporated association
- ☐ Derive 95 percent of its income from passive sources such as certain rents (no active participation in the management) and 75 percent of its income from certain real estate sources; thus, another 20 percent could be earned from real estate or other permitted sources
- ☐ Limit short-term capital gains to a maximum of 30 percent
- ☐ Annually distribute 95 percent of its taxable income to the owners
- ☐ Be managed by one trustee
- ☐ Be owned by 100 or more persons who received certificates as proof of ownership
- ☐ Establish a limit of 50 percent on the interest owned by five or fewer people

A REIT established after the Tax Reform Act of 1976 must[4]

- ☐ Be a trust or incorporated if it is neither a financial institution nor insurance company
- ☐ Accept a 100 percent income tax rate on net income from the greater of the amount by which the REIT fails the 95 percent or the 75 percent income test described above

□ Accept a redefinition of income under the 30 percent rule to include income from the sale of property in the ordinary course of business and income from the sale of mortgages held less than four years

REITs provide for a pooling of investment funds under the guidance of a real estate specialist. However, because of limitations placed on a trust or association to qualify as an REIT, this type of organization may not suit the needs of many investors, especially those searching for a tax shelter. A REIT, unlike a limited partnership, does not pass losses through to the individual investor.

Historically, REITs have been identified according to the types of real estate investments they purchase. *Equity REITs* supply equity funds by specializing in equity purchases in property. *Mortgage REITs* supply debt funds by granting long-term mortgages on property. During the last few years, the equity REITs have shown higher rates of return on their investments than the mortgage REITs.

Corporation   A corporation is an organization that exists separately from the shareholders and can own assets.[5] Individual shareholders cannot use corporate property, have liability limited to the amount of their investment, can transfer ownership of their shares by selling them to any willing buyer, and expect continuity of the organization in the event of death of a shareholder.

A corporation does not offer the same advantages as a partnership with respect to income taxes. The corporation is a separate entity and must pay corporate income taxes on its income. However, the corporation does offer several benefits such as diversification of real estate owned. Several different types and amounts of property can be readily purchased. The shares give some degree of liquidity to the owner because they can be resold for cash. The corporation can establish its own credit and potentially raise more capital than a partnership. The corporation may be in a position to extend additional fringe benefits to the person or group organizing the syndication.

Joint Ownership

Joint ownership refers to joint tenancy, tenancy in common, and tenancy by the entirety.[6] (Each of these arrangements is defined in Chapter 1.)

Tenancy ownership provides several advantages. One is the right of survivorship in joint tenancy whereby ownership automatically goes to the surviving tenant(s). Second, under tenants in common, each owner can make his or her own election of accounting methods, depreciation schedules, and so on, without regard to the choices made by other owners. Third, an audit of the tax return of one owner does not necessarily cause an audit of the returns of the other owners as it could in a partnership. Perhaps the greatest single advantage of a joint tenancy ownership is the right of survivorship.

Individual Ownership

Sole ownership (legally referred to as tenancy by severalty) is used when no benefits are to be gained from pooling an individual's funds with those of others. If an individual can independently accomplish his or her objectives, acquire the desired tax benefits, and accumulate all of the financing that is needed, joint ownership or a syndicate may not be advantageous.

SOURCES OF COMMERCIAL FUNDS

Statistics on commercial loans usually are reported as the amount of mortgage debt outstanding by type of lender as shown in Exhibit 17-1. Normally, no attempt is made to divide the loans into the amounts provided by equity lenders and the amounts provided by debt lenders. For example, savings and loans had $50,391 million in commercial mortgage debt outstanding at the end of the first quarter in 1983. However, the statistics do not always indicate what proportion of that debt is equity funds and what proportion is debt funds. Most likely, the lenders have no incentive to accumulate the data in two distinct groups.

Statistics are not generally reported by type of loan per lender. The $50,391 million in commercial loans from the savings and loans is not divided by the purpose of the loan, which could include uses such as hotels and motels, office buildings, shopping centers, warehouses, and retail outlets.

Some lenders are known from their loan history as favoring either debt or equity financing for particular purposes. For example, a savings and loan can be viewed as a debt lender for all residential property and all commercial properties up to a predetermined limit depending on the size of the institution. The REITs have historically consisted of one group that specializes in equity financing and another that specializes in debt financing. An individual or group of investors should approach the commercial lender that provides the type of financing needed for the purpose desired. An individual desiring debt funds in the form of a mortgage to pay the purchase price of an apartment building, for example, could approach a savings and loan, a commercial bank, a mortgage banker, a mutual savings bank, a REIT, a pension fund, a corporation, a life insurance company, a partnership, or an individual.

The largest holders of privately held commercial mortgage debt at the end of the first quarter in 1983 were the commercial banks with $101,575 million, followed by the life insurance companies, savings and loans, individuals and others, and the mutual savings banks. The largest holders of mortgage debt outstanding for multi-family dwellings were the savings and loans with $36,511, followed by individuals and others, life insurance companies, commercial banks, mutual savings banks, and a variety of public agencies. The latter group typically purchases all or a part of the loan that has been originated by the local lender. The main sources of mortgage debt outstanding for farms in 1983 were the Federal Land Banks with $47,485 million and individuals and others with $28,951. As farm lenders, life insurance companies and commercial banks each loaned much less, $12,625 and $8,520 million, respectively. The Farmers Home Administration mortgage pool shared an increase in farm loans to $8,770 million. Savings and loans did not report farm loans of significant magnitude.

EXHIBIT 17-1 Mortgage debt outstanding ($millions, end of period)

Source: Federal Reserve Bulletin.

Type of holder and type of property	1973	1975	1977	1979	1981	1983
All holders	682,321	801,537	1,023,505	1,333,550[r]	1,583,264	1,679,911[r]
Multifamily	93,132	100,601	111,841	130,713[r]	136,354	138,164[r]
Commercial	131,725	159,298	189,274	238,412[r]	279,889	301,703[r]
Farm	41,253	50,877	65,824	92,357[r]	101,727	107,032[r]
Major financial institutions	505,400	581,193	75,401	939,487[r]	1,040,827	1,026,582[r]
Commercial banks[1]	119,068	136,186	178,979	245,998[r]	284,536	305,672
Multifamily	6,932	5,915	9,215	12,546[r]	15,132	16,147
Commercial	38,696	46,882	56,898	77,096[r]	91,026	101,575
Farm	5,442	6,371	7,751	10,381[r]	8,365	8,520
Mutual savings banks	73,320	77,249	88,104	98,908[r]	99,997	93,697
Multifamily	12,343	13,792	15,304	17,180[r]	15,960	14,917
Commercial	12,012	13,373	15,110	16,963[r]	15,810	15,170
Farm	64	59	53	59	40	28
Savings and loan associations	231,733	278,590	381,163	475,797	518,547	484,080[r]
Multifamily	22,779	25,547	32,513	37,588	37,699	36,511[r]
Commercial	21,876	29,140	37,964	43,773	47,706	50,391[r]
Life insurance companies	81,369	89,168	96,765	118,784	137,747	143,133
Multifamily	18,451	19,629	18,807	19,274	19,283	19,054
Commercial	36,496	45,196	54,388	71,137	88,163	94,618
Farm	5,996	6,753	8,843	12,180	13,100	12,625
Federal and related agencies	46,721	66,891	70,006	97,293	126,094	140,023[r]
Government National Mortgage Assn.	4,020	7,438	3,660	3,852	4,765	3,785
Multifamily	2,574	2,710	2,112	3,089	4,072	3,120
Farmers Home Admin.	1,366	1,109	1,353	1,274	2,235	2,077[r]
Multifamily	29	215	275	71	473	380[r]
Commercial	218	190	149	174	506	337[r]
Farm	376	496	303	612	342	653[r]
Federal Housing and Veterans Admin.	3,476	4,970	5,212	5,764	5,999	5,156
Multifamily	1,463	2,980	3,585	3,901	3,710	3,273
Federal National Mortgage Assn.	24,175	31,824	34,369	51,091	61,412	73,666
Multifamily	3,805	6,011	5,865	5,603	5,426	5,296
Federal land banks	11,071	16,563	22,136	31,277	46,446	50,544
Farm	10,948	16,014	21,466	29,725	43,658	47,485
Federal Home Loan Mortgage Corp.	2,604	4,987	3,276	4,035	5,237	4,795
Multifamily	158	399	538	976	56	55

EXHIBIT 17-1 (continued)

Note: Based on data from various institutional and Govt. sources, with some quarters estimated in part by Federal Reserve in conjunction with the Federal Home Loan Bank Board and the Dept. of Commerce. Separation of nonfarm mortgage debt by type of property, if not reported directly, and interpolations and extrapolations where required are estimated mainly by Federal Reserve. Multifamily debt refers to loans on structures of five or more units.

Type of holder and type of property	1973	1975	1977	1979	1981	1983
Mortgage pools or trusts[2]	18,040	34,138	70,289	119,278	163,000	234,596r
Government National Mortgage Assn.	7,890	18,257	44,896	76,401	105,790	127,939r
Multifamily	329	719	1,341	1,855	2,783	3,457
Federal Home Loan Mortgage Corp.	766	1,598	6,610	15,180	19,853	48,008
Multifamily	149	249	989	3,031	352	433
Farmers Home Admin.	9,384	14,283	18,783	27,697	36,640	40,492r
Multifamily	138	295	759	2,163	3,426	4,344r
Commercial	1,124	1,948	2,945	4,328	6,161	7,115r
Farm	2,664	2,846	3,682	6,322	8,675	8,770r
Individuals and others[3]	112,160	119,315	138,199	177,492r	253,343	278,710r
Multifamily	23,982	22,140	20,538	23,436r	27,982	31,177
Commercial	21,303	22,569	21,820	24,941r	30,517	32,497
Farm	15,763	18,338	23,726	33,078r	27,547	28,951

r = revised
[1]Includes loans held by nondeposit trust companies but not bank trust departments.
[2]Outstanding principal balances of mortgages backing securities or guaranteed by the agency indicated.
[3]Other holders include mortgage companies, real estate investment trusts, state and local credit agencies, state and local retirement funds, noninsured pension funds, credit unions, and U.S. agencies for which either amounts are small or separate data are not readily available.

Specialization by the Lender

Certain lenders, such as savings and loans, typically specialize in certain types of commercial loans when they make loans in this area—long-term, permanent mortgages. Other types of lenders, such as commercial banks, typically specialize in certain types of loans—short-term construction loans. Specialization occurs for the following reasons. First, the lender attempts to loan according to the maturities of the funds received. Short-term receipts are loaned with short-term maturities, and long-term receipts are loaned with long-term maturities. Since a commercial bank receives primarily short-term funds, it tends to specialize in short-term construction lending. Savings and loans are associated with long-term funding. Second, the servicing of each type of loan is different. A short-term construction loan can require day-to-day supervision and auditing whereas a long-term loan requires servicing only periodically and in the event of default. A bank supervises other types of short-term loans for consumers and can adapt its established management to construction loans. A savings and loan has established its servicing and management for the long-term mortgages.

TYPES OF COMMERCIAL LOANS

Construction Loan and Gap Financing

A *construction loan* is a short-term loan given for the construction of an improvement on the property. The builder-developer may require *gap financing* if the lender supplying the permanent, first lien mortgage will not pay the full amount of the mortgage until the newly constructed building attains a predetermined occupancy or usage level. This *retainage* or *holdback* described in the following paragraph must be covered by the builder-developer with another loan from another lender, which is called *gap financing.*

Permanent Loan

A *permanent loan* is the first lien mortgage on the property. Permanent lenders give the construction lender a **takeout commitment,** agreeing to pay off the construction loan once the building is complete. No takeout will occur until the building is free of potential liens. In addition, the permanent lender may insist on a **retainage** or **holdback** from the amount of funds paid to the borrower. This amount protects the lender from the risk of a failure to complete the job or bankruptcy of the borrower. Typically, the permanent loan is approved prior to the construction loan to assure the interim lender of the "takeout" once the project is complete. The construction loan is paid out in increments based upon stages of completion.

Evaluating the application for a permanent loan is much more subjective than evaluating a residential application, because so many additional factors are involved and their quantification is difficult. To assist the lender in processing the loan application and to ensure a fair evaluation, the borrower should provide supporting documents. The application can be divided into four basic parts.[7] The applicant should emphasize those parts that reflect the unique aspects of the proposed project. (The need for feasibility studies was explained also in Chapter 9.)

The overall project   The overall project report should contain an overall description of the overall physical features and design elements of the entire project. Although the borrower may be asking for funds to cover only an initial phase of the development, the lender needs a total view of the entire project. This report should include the *feasibility study,* which shows that the proposed project will support itself once constructed. It could be a financial, market, site, or cost study depending on the project and the use of funds. This information assists the lender in evaluating the risk involved in the loan. The overall project cost that the borrower thinks is realistic should be stated.

A typical feasibility study requested by a lender is a composite of the market study and the financial study. The market study typically includes the following components:[8]

☐ A careful identification of the market the product serves

☐ An identification and analysis of the market conditions including a careful review of the population that will possibly use the product and their income levels

- [ ] An identification and analysis of the supply, including an estimate of the competition in the form of existing stock and new construction under way and proposed
- [ ] An examination of possible locations of the structure that will best serve the defined market
- [ ] A marketing recommendation for the product including the best type of project, quality of products, best prices, advertising, and the expected rate of sales

The financial study typically includes the following points:

- [ ] An estimation of potential income under various assumptions about growth and inflation
- [ ] An annual income projection for each year that the investor expects to hold the project
- [ ] An annual expense projection for each year that the project will be held
- [ ] An estimation of the rate of return calculated before and after taxes
- [ ] A thorough discussion and evaluation of the construction costs, if applicable

The borrower and advisors A past record of successes in real estate projects is good evidence that the borrower can interpret the local market trends correctly. All previous projects that the borrower has developed or constructed and the names of the loan officers should be provided. The potential borrower should also supply information to indicate his or her creditworthiness. Figures on net worth and financial condition provide evidence that the borrower can pledge collateral for a loan if it is required. Supporting information about the architect and the contractor should be included. The lender is always interested in the capacity of the contractor to perform quality work and to finish the job. The architect should have experience in designing the type of structure proposed.

The completed project Additional documents describing physical details of the completed project should be presented—a street map serving the site, property survey, aerial photos, present zoning, appraisal, and description of general and special amenities. A set of building plans and a specifications manual should be provided. The lender also would like to have a detailed breakdown of the projected income and expenses. This statement should include a description of income from all sources such as sales, rentals, and maintenance agreements. If the property is rental, copies of the tenants' leases or intent to lease should be provided.

Financing A complete financing plan should be presented to the lender. The amount of equity the borrower is providing, the amount of loan the lender is asked to commit, the payback periods, the amount of amortization, and the suggested interest rate should be stated. The borrower can suggest a system of draws that allows payments to be made as each phase of the building is completed. The borrower tells the lender the manner in which the funds are needed, and the lender agrees or modifies the request.

Participation Loan

Unstable conditions in the money and capital markets have caused lenders to seek additional methods of collecting interest to compensate for the risks of incorrectly judging the future level of interest rates. One method has been a *participation commercial loan.*

Three types of participation loans have been created by the lenders. The first is an income participation where the lender gives the borrower a fixed, lower-than-the-market interest rate in exchange for a future percent of the effective gross income, net operating income, or effective gross income above a specified minimum. The second is a fixed interest rate in exchange for a percent of the future net sales receipts or equity from refinancing. The third is a fixed interest rate plus a percent of the income plus a percent of the future net sales or refinancing proceeds.

AMORTIZATION

Exhibit 17-2 is an amortization schedule for a typical residential mortgage decribed in Chapter 16. It is called a *constant payment* plan. The residential mortgage for $40,000 is for thirty years with a 13 percent interest rate. The monthly payments are $442.48. The first month's interest payment that is part of the $442.48 is figured by first dividing 0.13 by 12, which equals 0.0108333, the *debiting factor,* and then multiplying $40,000 by 0.0108333, which gives $433.33. For the second month, the principal payment of $9.15 is subtracted from $40,000 leaving $39,990.85. The borrower pays another $442.48, which includes a $433.23 interest payment and a $9.25 principal payment. Exhibit 17-2 shows the remaining debt balance, total monthly payment, principal payment, and the interest payment for the first twelve months.

EXHIBIT 17-2 Amortization schedule: Constant payment

End of month	Remaining debt before payment	Total	Principal	Interest
1	$40,000.00	$442.48	$ 9.15	$433.33
2	39,990.85	442.48	9.25	433.23
3	39,981.60	442.48	9.35	433.13
4	39,972.25	442.48	9.45	433.03
5	39,962.70	442.48	9.55	432.93
6	39,953.15	442.48	9.66	432.82
7	39,943.49	442.48	9.76	432.72
8	39,933.73	442.48	9.87	432.61
9	39,923.86	442.48	9.97	432.51
10	39,913.89	442.48	10.08	432.40
11	39,903.81	442.48	10.19	432.29
12	39,893.62	442.48	10.30	432.18

Amortization schedules for typical commercial loans can be negotiated. Exhibit 17-3 shows a partial amortization with a balloon note and Exhibit 17-4 shows a term amortization. **Partial amortization with a balloon note** is a repayment plan whereby the borrower can delay repaying a portion of the debt. In this case, the total loan is for $40,000 at 13 percent for one year. The borrower agrees to pay $2,679.52 per month for twelve months, which will repay the $30,000 with interest. In addition, the borrower agrees to repay $10,000 in one single payment with accumulated interest in the twelfth month. The resultant payment during the twelfth month consists of the following:

Partial amortization of $30,000 ($2,650.81 principal, $28.71 interest)	$2,679.52
Balloon note of $10,000 (with $1,300 interest)	11,300.00
TOTAL	$13,979.52

This repayment arrangement reduces the monthly payments during the first eleven months compared to what they would have been had the borrower agreed to a monthly payment that would amortize the full $40,000.

Term amortization is a repayment plan whereby the borrower pays the debt balance at the end of the loan period. The interest may be paid either at the end or in periodic payments during the life of the loan. Exhibit 17-4 is the schedule for a

EXHIBIT 17-3 Amortization schedule: One-year partial amortization with a one-year separate balloon note

Monthly payments on the $30,000 partial: term payment on the $10,000 balloon with interest

End of month	Remaining debt before payment		Total	Principal	Interest
	Partial	Balloon			
1	$30,000.00	$10,000	$ 2,679.52	$ 2,354.52	$325.00
2	27,645.48	10,000	2,679.52	2,380.03	299.49
3	25,265.45	10,000	2,679.52	2,405.81	273.71
4	22,859.64	10,000	2,679.52	2,431.87	247.65
5	20,427.77	10,000	2,679.52	2,458.22	221.30
6	17,969.55	10,000	2,679.52	2,484.85	194.67
7	15,484.70	10,000	2,679.52	2,511.77	167.75
8	12,972.93	10,000	2,679.52	2,538.98	140.54
9	10,433.95	10,000	2,679.52	2,566.49	113.03
10	7,867.46	10,000	2,679.52	2,594.29	85.23
11	5,273.17	10,000	2,679.52	2,622.39	57.13
12	2,650.78*	10,000	13,979.52	2,650.81*	28.71
				10,000.00	+1,300.00

*These two figures do not equal because of rounding errors.

EXHIBIT 17-4 Amortization schedule: One-year amortization, single payment of principal and interest

End of Month	Remaining Debt before Payment	Total	Principal	Interest
1	40,000	0	0	0
2	40,000	0	0	0
3	40,000	0	0	0
4	40,000	0	0	0
5	40,000	0	0	0
6	40,000	0	0	0
7	40,000	0	0	0
8	40,000	0	0	0
9	40,000	0	0	0
10	40,000	0	0	0
11	40,000	0	0	0
12	40,000	$45,200	$40,000	$5,200

term loan of $40,000 for one year at 13 percent interest. The total $40,000 plus $5,200 interest for the prior year is repaid at the end of the twelfth month.

The most obvious advantage of the term amortization is that the borrower has one year to raise the $40,000 debt balance. Also, the borrower can use the interest payment of $5,200 as a tax deduction. Typically, however, the lender requires partial amortization whereby the borrower repays at least a portion of the balance of the loan before maturity. The financial burden is thus less severe for the borrower when the note is due.

KEY FINANCIAL RATIOS

Several **financial ratios** can be used by the potential borrower or the lender to evaluate the worthiness of the application. Exhibit 17-5 illustrates the magnitude of ratios that one large underwriter has used to evaluate applications for a loan for an office building, apartment building, shopping center, and warehouse. Considered collectively, these ratios provide a "ballpark" estimate of the worthiness of the application. Most of these ratios are defined below and in Chapter 7.

- **Debt service coverage ratio** This is the ratio of the net operating income to the debt service.
- **Loan-to-value ratio** The proportion of the loan to the value of the property.
- **Default ratio** This rate tells the proportion of gross income that is committed to loan payments and expenses.

THE DECISION TO FINANCE THE TRANSACTION

EXHIBIT 17-5 Key financial ratios for evaluating commercial loans

Ratio	Office buildings	Apartments	Shopping centers	Warehouses
Debt service coverage ratio	1.25%–1.3%	1.2%–1.25% minimum	1.25%–1.3%	1.2%–1.3%
Loan-to-value ratio	75% of economic value but not to exceed 90% of cost or purchase price	80% of economic value but not to exceed 90% of replacement costs or purchase price	75% of economic value but not to exceed 90% of cost or purchase price	75% of economic value but not to exceed 90% of cost or purchase price
Default ratio	70%–80%	80%–85%	70%–80%	70%
Stabilized vacancy ratio	10% of gross income	—	5%–10% of gross income	5%–10% of gross income
Land-building ratio	Not to exceed 100%	—	—	—
Building area ratio	85%+	—	—	—
Overall cap rate	1% over interest rate	—	1% over interest rate	1%–2% over interest rate

- ☐ **Stabilized vacancy ratio** — This figure tells the amount of gross income that will be lost because of vacancies.
- ☐ **Land-building ratio** — This ratio gives a figure that can be computed by dividing the square feet of the building's ground floor by the square feet of the site.
- ☐ **Building area ratio** — The amount of the total building that can be leased is given.
- ☐ **Overall cap rate** — Net operating income divided by the sales price or market value.

Consider a mortgage application for an office building that has the following characteristics.

- ☐ **Debt service coverage ratio:** 1.33
- ☐ **Loan-to-value ratio:** 90% of the cost approach figure is $1,050,000 and 75% of the income approach is $825,000

☐ **Default ratio:**	78.4%
☐ **Land-building ratio:**	90%
☐ **Building area ratio:**	88%
☐ **Stabilized vacancy** ratio:	8%
☐ **Overall cap rate:**	11.5%

All of the financial ratios are within acceptable ranges or exceed the minimum. Therefore, the mortgage application for $825,000 would probably be approved if the remainder of the application were satisfactory.

These financial ratios enable the borrower to evaluate the mortgage application before presenting it to the lender. Also, by comparing these figures with figures for similar projects, the borrower can determine whether the proposed project is competitive.

SECOND MORTGAGE

A **second mortgage** is a second loan using the same property as collateral. In a purchase, the buyer may use a second mortgage to raise additional cash to pay the purchase price or the down payment. In addition, an owner may take out a second mortgage from a lender to borrow against the equity in the property without disturbing the original loan.

For example, consider Janet Redling who owns a dress boutique that she opened in 1980 in a new building she owns near a large shopping mall. She borrowed $50,000 at 8.5 percent interest for twenty-nine years on a commercial loan from a local bank that estimated her business and building were valued at $60,000. During 1985, she decides that she needs more capital to expand her dress line and inventory and therefore approaches several lenders about a second mortgage. Her building and business are estimated to be worth approximately $90,000. Since the current mortgage balance is $44,000, her equity is $46,000 ($90,000—$44,000). A new first mortgage would be granted for $70,000 at a prevailing interest rate of 13.5 percent. Two local lenders offer second mortgages for 70 percent of the equity or $32,200 at 13.5 percent interest. Since Janet likes the terms and the lower interest rate on the current first mortgage, she decides to accept the second mortgage loaned against the property's equity.

Subordination Clause

A **subordination clause** within the second mortgage states that the second loan will always remain in a secondary relationship to the first mortgage and to any new first mortgage that may be placed on the property in the future.[9]

Default in Prior Payment Clause

A **default in prior payment clause** within the second mortgage allows the second lender to correct a default in the first mortgage by making the payments, adding the amount to the indebtedness of the second loan, and foreclosing on the second loan. In this manner, the second lender can judge the appropriate time to foreclose to avoid losses in situations such as an interruption of the income flows from rentals that are in turn paid to the lender for mortgage payments.[10]

These two clauses make the second mortgage distinctive from other mortgages.

ASSIGNMENT AND ESTOPPEL

The buyer can protect rights to the income stream by requiring the seller to produce an abstract. This document shows whether the seller legally has the right to sell the income stream. Also, the buyer can require the seller to sign and file in the county courthouse an **assignment contract,** which gives the buyer the legal right to collect the income stream. Third, the buyer can require the seller to produce an **estoppel certificate.** This certificate requires the seller to state the exact balance of the mortgage that the mortgagor is paying and whether the seller has any claims against the income stream that are unknown. This certificate "stops" the seller from changing the balance or making other claims later.

Assume, for example, that the Land Auction Real Estate Company has recently missed three payments on a mortgage for a duplex from which they receive about $550 net income per month. The lender is holding a $30,000 outstanding mortgage on the unit. Exercising the right to claim the income stream in the event of default under a *mortgagee in possession* clause in the mortgage, the lender, First State Bank, requests an abstract and asks Land Auction to pay the costs. An estoppel certificate and an assignment contract are signed by the Land Auction Real Estate Company. The First State Bank knows that it has the legal right to collect the rents by the abstract, gives constructive notice of this right by filing the assignment contract, and stops Land Auction from changing their claim or mortgage balance by the estoppel certificate.

EXAMPLE OF A COMMERCIAL LOAN APPLICATION

This section consists of several pages taken from an actual loan application that was submitted to a large life insurance company for a commercial loan. Several pages have been extracted to illustrate the content. Names have been changed to protect the identity of the properties and the parties. Since certain information is confidential, the whole report could not be presented.

A LOAN APPLICATION FOR
A PROPOSED 208-UNIT APARTMENT COMPLEX
LOCATED ON 1600–2000 NORTH APACHE ROAD
IN HOUSTON, TEXAS

Table of Contents

Section 1   Loan Summary

SMOKEY HILL APARTMENTS

Security:	Proposed 208-unit, two-story, garden apartment complex containing 186,672 sq. ft. of gross building area and 184,480 sq. ft. of net rentable area. The complex will have 22 separate two-story buildings, two swimming pools, two cabanas and a leasing/management office. The complex will be separately wired and metered, with tenants paying electrical bills. The exterior of the complex will be brick, stucco and diagonal wood siding with the brick predominating. 365 parking spaces will be provided for a resultant parking ratio of 1.75 per unit.
Borrower:	Raney & Son Real Estate Developers, Inc.
Net Worth of Borrowers:	$1.2 million shown on attached balance sheet that has been audited by Sam Wright, CPA.
Location:	1600-2000 North Apache Road, Houston, Texas
Zoning:	Multifamily (MF-1)
Land:	382,021 sq. ft. or 8.77 acres with 550' of frontage on dedicated roads.
Land Value:	$590,000 (1.55 per square foot)

THE DECISION TO FINANCE THE TRANSACTION

Cost of Project:	$4,270,000
Income to Project:	$629,782
Competitive Sites and Projects:	$4,360,000
Final Estimate of Value:	$4,270,000
Loan Request:	$3,140,000
Terms:	9½%, 28 years with loan call options by the lender at the end of the 15th, 20th and 25th loan years
Prepayment:	See Application
Loan-to-Value Ratio:	73.5%
Loan per Square Foot (gross building area):	$16.82
Loan per Square Foot (net rental area):	$17.02
Loan per Unit:	$15,096
Funding:	18 months (full, with liability in accordance with enclosed application)
Debt Service Ratio:	1.33
Servicing Fee:	1/8 of 1%

Section 2   Cost of Project

Explanation of Cost Factors

Characteristics of the subject property are described in the Description of Improvements Section of this report. The direct cost estimates of the subject property are based on data obtained from several sources including the Marshall Valuation Service and the Dodge Reports. Indirect costs, including interim financing and closing costs, architectural fees, engineering fees and miscellaneous fees are estimated on the basis of current market conditions.

Explanation of Depreciation

The subject property is proposed and no immediate repairs are assumed to be necessary after completion of the improvements. The project does not have any functional or economic obsolescence and, therefore, no depreciation is considered necessary.

COST APPROACH SUMMARY

Direct Cost

Living Area	184,480 sq. ft. @ $16.50	$3,043,920
Office, Laundry, and Cabanas	2,192 sq. ft. @ $16.50	35,072
Parking and Drives	108,000 sq. ft. @ $ 0.60	64,800
Walkways	11,160 sq. ft. @ $ 0.80	8,928
Pools, Deck, Fencing & Lighting		40,000
Landscaping (including trees to remain on site)		80,000
Total Direct		$3,272,720

Indirect Cost

Interim Financing (18 mos.), Fees and Closing	$280,000	
Architectural & Engineering Fees	125,000	
Total Indirect		$ 405,000
TOTAL IMPROVEMENTS		$3,677,720
Less Depreciation:		-0-
Depreciated Value of Improvements:		3,677,720
Add Land Estimate:		590,000
		4,267,720

ESTIMATE OF VALUE BY COST APPROACH	$4,270,000

Supporting data attached

Section 3   Income to Project

RENTAL UNITS

Description	Type	No. Units	Size S.F.	Unf. Mo. Rent	Rent PSF	Mo. Gross
1BR-1BA	A-1	24	688	$210	$0.305	$ 5,040
1BR-1BA-FP	A-1	40	688	220	0.320	8,800
1BR-1BA-Den-W&D	A-2	16	876	255	0.291	4,080
1BR-1BA-Den-FP-W&D	A-2	24	876	265	0.303	6,360
2BR-2BA-W&D	B-1	30	978	280	0.286	8,400
2BR-2BA-FP-W&D	B-1	46	978	290	0.297	13,340
2BR-2BA-Den-FP-W&D	B-2	28	1,100	320	0.288	8,960
		208	184,480		$0.298	$ 54,980

GROSS ANNUAL RENTAL INCOME	$\times$ 12
	$659,760
Laundry and Vending Income @ $4.00/unit/mo. (66 units)	3,168
GROSS ANNUAL INCOME	$662,928
Less 5% Vacancy Allowance	33,146
EFFECTIVE GROSS INCOME	$629,782

(FP - Fireplace; W&D - Washer and Dryer Connections)

Supporting data attached

Section 4 Competitive Sites and Projects

The Market Approach is the analysis of market transactions of comparable properties, an abstraction of comparable units of measure, and a comparison of various sales transactions. Different units of comparison may be derived and used in the estimation of market value, including sales price per square foot, sales price per unit, and gross rent multiplier. To use the sales price per square foot and sales price per unit, the appraiser must have complete information about the construction, layout, land costs, and so on, for the comparable projects and the proper adjustments must be made on each comparable project to equate the comparable sales to the subject property. A gross rent multiplier adjusts itself within the market as it properly reflects the rentals collected in the various locales and the sales prices in the area. It is the appraiser's opinion that the gross rent multiplier is the best indicator of market value and the indicator most commonly used in the Houston area for comparing one property with another.

Comparable sales for apartment projects are listed on the following pages. It is felt that an investor of apartment complexes uses the same criteria to determine value from one locale to another. Three of the sale comparables are in Houston and the fourth is in a suburb. These sales are shown along with an analysis of the transaction and pertinent data on the property. An analysis of these comparables was made to determine the market value of the subject property via the Market Approach.

Analysis of sale comparables As pointed out above, greater emphasis is placed by the appraiser on the gross rent multiplier than the sales price per square foot or sale price per unit. As indicated in the comparables' sales, the gross rent multiplier for the various complexes ranges from 5.29 to 6.38. All of the sales have occurred in 1984 or 1985.

The Now World Apartments sold at a Gross Income Multiplier of 6.38. This property, in the appraiser's opinion, sold for slightly more than is typical in the marketplace because of the financing available. This sale therefore would require some downward adjustment in the gross rent multiplier.

The Chateau Apartments has the lowest Gross Income Multiplier of any of the sale comparables. The complex was constructed in the 1970s and the purchaser may have discounted the property somewhat because he felt there was some deferred maintenance.

The Village Apartment was an FHA project and lacks some of the amenities of the subject property. The sale is included because it is felt that this sale typifies what an apartment purchaser is paying in the marketplace.

The North Hill Terrace Apartments is a complex of above average quality and is situated in a popular area. Although the units are smaller than those in the subject property, this sale is considered a good indicator of value for the subject property.

The gross annual income for the subject property is estimated to be $662,928 with the tenants paying for electricity. The gross income of the comparable sales is based on the landlord paying all utilities. Thus, an upward adjustment of the subject's gross income is required before using the Gross Income Multiplier. On the basis of surveys made by various utility companies and governmental agencies, as well as operating statements on comparable apartment complexes, it is estimated that the gross rental income would require an upward adjustment of 35 cents per square foot annually to compensate for the differential. Thus, our adjustment factor is 35 cents per square foot $\times$ 184,480 square feet, or $64,568 annually. Our potential gross income figure is $662,928. Adding $662,928 to $64,568 equals $727,496, which is the adjusted potential gross income for the subject.

After review of the sale comparables it is estimated that the Gross Income Multiplier for the subject property would be 6.00. By multiplying 6.00 $\times$ $727,496 we have an indication of the market value by the Gross Income Multiplier. This is equivalent to the value of $4,364,976, say $4,360,000.

Section 5   Dun and Bradstreet Report on Raney & Son Real Estate
             Developers, Inc. (confidential)

Section 6   Financial Statements (confidential)

Section 7   Preliminary Plans and Specifications (confidential because
             the proposed building was unique)

CHAPTER SUMMARY

Commercial financing involves equity and/or debt funds. Typically, a financial institution assumes the role of a debt lender.

Many potential purchasers of a commercial property hold misconceptions that discourage them from buying such property or lead them to buy it for unsound reasons. A prospective buyer who is aware of the fallacies is able to evaluate his or her objectives and to make a rational decision about buying commercial property.

The investor(s) should select in advance of the investment the proper type of organization to achieve their objectives. A group of investors can pool their money with a professional in real estate to purchase property, or they can rely on some form of joint ownership. The maximum tax benefits for each individual are obtained in the limited partnership and the subchapter S corporation. The advantages of pooling funds, although with few tax benefits, can be obtained in one of the tenancies of joint ownership.

In searching for a commercial loan, the potential investor should find a lender that has a history of providing the type of funds (debt or equity) needed. In addition, the investor should examine the type of loans typically granted by the lender as a guide to current approval of the loan application.

No standardized loan application procedure is used by all commercial lenders. However, several components of an ideal application can be identified. It should thoroughly describe the overall project, the borrower and advisors, the completed project, and the financing.

Several key financial ratios can be used to develop an overall indication of the worthiness of the project: the debt service ratio, loan-to-value ratio, loan per square foot, default ratio, stabilized vacancy ratio, land-building ratio, building area ratio, and the overall cap rate. These ratios should be considered as a group rather than individually to make judgments on specific aspects of the project.

The amortization schedule of a commercial loan can be negotiable. The repayment of a commercial loan and the interest typically is a constant level payment, partial payment with a balloon note, or term payment. The first requires a fixed periodic payment, usually monthly, where the interest owed is computed on the declining balance. By maturity, the remaining debt is equal to zero. Under partial payment, a periodic repayment is required and interest is computed on the declining balance. By maturity, the repayments have not reduced the balance to zero so a single large payment is required with interest. Under term payment, the whole loan plus interest is repaid in one payment when the loan matures.

A second mortgage is a junior loan on the property. Typically, it is placed on the property by the owner to raise additional cash. This mortgage can contain a subordination clause or a default in prior payment clause that defines the second lender's responsibility in the event of default.

Review Questions

1. Should an investor avoid real estate investments because the equity is committed for long periods? Why?
2. Describe and evaluate several common fallacies about the purchase of commercial property.
3. What type of organization gives the maximum tax benefits to the individual?
4. When is ownership under a tenancy advantageous to the investor?
5. Where does a borrower receive a commercial loan? A farm loan? A multifamily loan?

6. What are the risks to a lender in loaning money for a commercial project, and how does the lender evaluate these risks?

7. What is favorable leverage? Does a buyer want favorable leverage? Why or why not?

8. Why would a lender want a participation loan?

9. Explain the meaning of the terms *takeout* and *holdback.*

10. State the components or steps of a commercial loan application. Be sure to identify the reasons for including each part.

11. Describe several of the financial or operation ratios that a lender can use to evaluate the mortgage application.

12. Contrast partial amortization with a balloon note to term amortization. How do these two differ from the payment schedule contained within a residential mortgage?

13. What is the purpose of a second mortgage? What is the purpose of a subordination clause and a default in prior payment clause?

14. When is an assignment contract used? Why?

15. When is an estoppel certificate used? Why?

Discussion Questions

1. Are there any circumstances in which an individual would want to invest in property as an individual? Identify them.

2. Explain the difference between the application process for a residential loan and the process for a commercial loan.

3. Can you identify any additional financial ratios that might be used to evaluate a commercial loan application for a specific use?

4. What are the most likely sources for a commercial loan? Farm loan? Multifamily loan?

5. *Should* a commercial borrower ask for an amortization schedule that is not at a constant level like the residential mortgage? Is it not actually more efficient management to repay the debt on a regular basis, which reduces the balance to zero by maturity?

6. Explain the market conditions that would create an incentive for a borrower to request a second mortgage rather than refinancing.

Notes

1. Austin J. Jaffe and C. F. Sirmans, "Some Myths About Real Estate," *Real Estate Review,* Vol. 8 (Spring 1978), p. 40.

2. Stephen D. Messner; Irving Schreiber; and Victor L. Lyon, *Marketing Investment Real Estate: Finance, Taxation, Techniques* (Chicago: REALTORS National Marketing Institute, 1975), Chapter 8.

3. Ted D. Englebrecht and John L. Kramer, "Tax Breaks for REITs Under the Tax Reform Act," *Real Estate Review,* Vol. 7 (Spring 1977), pp. 33–39.

4. Ibid.

5. David G. McGrady and William C. Weaver, "Why Set Up a Corporation to Own Real Estate?" *Real Estate Review,* Vol. 10 (Fall 1980), pp. 89–93.

6. Messner, Schreiber, and Lyon, *Marketing Investment Real Estate,* Chapter 8.

7. For a discussion of commercial lending, see Marshall Dennis, *Fundamentals of Mortgage Lending* (Reston, Virginia: Reston Publishing Co., 1978), Chapter 8.

8. John B. Bailey; Peter F. Spies; and Marilyn Weitzman, "Market Study + Financial Analysis = Feasibility Study," *Appraisal Journal,* Vol. 45 (October 1977), pp. 550–76.

9. Milton R. Friedman, *Contracts and Conveyance of Real Property* (New York: Practicing Law Institute, 1975), pp. 616–19.

10. Ibid.

Additional Readings

EPLEY, DONALD R., and JAMES A. MILLAR. *Basic Real Estate Finance and Investments.* New York: John Wiley & Sons, Inc., 1980. Chapters 12–13.

FARRELL, MICHAEL and GAYLON GREER, "Financial Leverage: A New Look at an Old Concept," *Real Estate Review* 11 (Winter 1982): 83–85.

GAINES, JAMES P., and FORREST E. HUFFMAN, "Negotiating the Terms of Participation Mortgages," *Real Estate Review* 12 (Fall 1982): 38–46.

GRAASKAMP, JAMES. "Rational Approach to Feasibility Analysis." *Appraisal Journal* 40 (October 1972): 513–521.

GRAYBEAL, RONALD. "Condominium Computerized Feasibility Analysis." *Appraisal Journal* 41 (October 1973): 526–34.

HALSTEAD, CLARK. "Financing the Project." *Real Estate Today* 8 (April 1975): 48–50.

HANDORF, WILLIAM, and EUGENE DUNHAM. "Land Development Acceptability: A Capital Budgeting Analysis." *Federal Home Loan Bank Board Journal* 9 (June 1976): 9–12.

HANFORD, LLOYD. *Feasibility Study Guidelines.* Chicago: Institute of Real Estate Management.

"How to Finance Commercial Properties." *Real Estate Today* 8 (February 1975): 20–22.

IRWIN, ROBERT. "Financing the Commercial Project." *Real Estate Today* 7 (August 1974): 28–30.

KIRBY, JIM. "Proper Submission Speeds REIT Loan Approvals," *Mortgage Banker* 34 (May 1974): 68–72.

LUM, TAN TEK. "Feasibility Analysis of Condominiums," *Appraisal Journal* 40 (April 1972): 246–52.

MCCRARY, DENNIE. "Standby Permanent Financing for Condominium Development." *Real Estate Review* 4 (Spring 1974): 74–77.

REPPE, ROD. "Winning Over the Condominium Lender." *Real Estate Review* 5 (Summer 1985): 104–9.

ROSENTHAL, S. A. "Checklist Helpful in Avoiding Loan Submission Turndowns." *Mortgage Banker* 36 (July 1976): 40–41.

ROSS, THURSTON. "The Counselor and Investment Feasibility." *Appraisal Journal* 44 (January 1976): 44–45.

ROWLSON, JOHN. "The Feasibility and Appraisal of Garden-Type Condominiums." *Appraisal Journal* 41 (July 1973): 338–49.

STEGELAUB, HAROLD. "The Mortgage Applications: Sophisticated Approach to Borrowing Money." *Journal of Property Management* 41 (March/April 1976): 57–63.

TRAPASSO, VICTOR G., "Investment Success Through Ratio Preference Analysis," *Real Estate Review* 12 (Winter 1983): 60–66.

WILBUR, ROBERT, and JAMES SHORT, "The Desirability of Leverage: Expanding the Concept," *Real Estate Review* 13 (Summer 1983): 41–46.

WOODARD, F. O., and D. R. EPLEY. "Feasibility Study of Richmond Coliseum: A Comment." *Appraisal Journal* 39 (April 1971): 285–92.

18 | Creative Financing

1. What alternative methods of financing are available?

2. What additional financial documents may be used in a real estate transaction?

OBJECTIVES _____

When a student finishes the chapter, he or she should be able to

1. Explain various market conditions that can cause either the buyer or the seller to desire a financing arrangement other than a typical mortgage or deed of trust.

2. Explain the common types of financing arrangements that can be used under each market condition.

3. Identify the important components of each financing arrangement.
4. Give illustrations of each type of financing that can be used for residential and commercial property.

IMPORTANT TERMS

Assumption (Equity Buy)	Participation Loan
Balloon Note	Piggyback Loan (Split Loan, Joint Loan)
Blanket Mortgage	
Bond for Title	Purchase-Money Mortgage
Contract for Deed (Title)	Rent With Option to Buy
Delayed Closing Date	Sale-leaseback
Exchange	Sandwiched Lease
Junior Lien	Second (Junior) Mortgage
Land Contract	Standby Permanent Financing
Open-end Mortgage	Subordinated Ground Lease
Package Mortgage	Wraparound Mortgage

INTRODUCTION

Knowledge of methods of real estate financing is important to buyers, sellers, and agents because a particular real estate transaction may require financial arrangements other than a conventional mortgage (discussed in Chapter 16). The type of financial arrangement may need to be tailored to fit the specific needs of the buyer/seller. Also, current economic conditions may motivate the parties involved to seek funds through special arrangements. Thus, the choice of an appropriate financing technique is based on the special circumstances of the transaction.

This chapter describes common situations in real estate transactions that require creative financing arrangements.

SITUATIONS REQUIRING SPECIAL FINANCING

Buyer Does Not Have Enough Cash and Lacks Assets

Commonly a buyer does not have enough cash to purchase a property at the agreed price. The lack of sufficient funds can be due to several factors: (1) The buyer may be shopping in a market that is priced beyond personal income and current assets; (2) The local economy may be in a tight money phase when mortgage funds are extremely difficult to obtain from local lenders. To purchase (sell) property, the parties to the transaction must be innovative in their financial arrangements; (3) The buyer may have the income to make a mortgage payment but does not have the current cash or assets to make the down payment or purchase the equity.

Solution 1: Second mortgage   The borrower may obtain a **second** or **junior mortgage** as described in Chapter 17. The same property is used as collateral. The lender providing the second mortgage can be a third party, such as a second financial institution or even the seller, subject to possible restrictions within the first mortgage. The mortgage document contains many of the same terms as a first mortgage, but with several differences. A second mortgage typically carries an interest rate that is higher than the rates charged on first mortgages. The lender wants compensation for the additional risk of being second in line in case of borrower default. The maturity is shorter than that of the first mortgage. Also, the second mortgage may contain a subordination clause or a default on prior mortgage clause (as explained in Chapter 17).

Example Bill Brown wants to purchase a parcel of property in Denver that has an appraised value of $50,000. He has submitted a loan application to First Federal Savings and Loan, and it has been approved provided that he pay 13 percent of the appraised value as a down payment. Bill has examined his available resources and can raise only $2,500. He needs to find another $4,000.

Bill has no other property that he can use for collateral to secure another mortgage. He is a midlevel engineer for a local food processing plant and has good income-earning potential for the near future. His past credit is good. Bill applies to a local commercial bank for a second mortgage and receives the $4,000 at 13.5 percent over eight years, with the property pledged as collateral.

Example Janette Worley is attempting to purchase a commercial office building on East Huntsville Street in Springdale, Georgia. Jack Hugley, the owner, is asking $100,000 for the building and Miss Worley has agreed to the price provided that she can obtain the necessary financing. The office building has a good income and would easily pay for itself. However, Miss Worley only has $2,000 cash. Miss Worley and the agent handling the transaction apply to the First Mortgage Company in Savannah for a commercial loan in the amount of $80,000 for twenty years at 13 percent. Also, they ask the First National Bank of Springdale for a second mortgage on the building in the amount of $18,000 for ten years at 13.5 percent. First Mortgage accepts the venture because of Miss Worley's good financial statement. Her employment and income potential are good, and the First National Bank approved the second mortgage. The property was well located causing the value of the collateral to grow with time.

Solution 2: Sale-leaseback   A sale-leaseback is explained in Chapter 15. The use of a **sale-leaseback** is based primarily on financing motives. For example, an owner-potential lessee may select the alternative of selling the property to an investor and simultaneously leasing it back rather than applying for a new mortgage.[1] The funding for a new mortgage may not be available, the terms of new mortgages may not be favorable (for example, a prohibitively high interest rate), or the terms of the loan may be incompatible with the owner's objectives. For the owner of the property, a sale-leaseback provides immediate cash that can be used for development under terms that are compatible with the proposed project. In addition, this type of financing can be used to alter the owner's tax position. Rental payments are deductible as a business expense and thus can lower the lessee's tax liability.

This type of financing can be an acceptable solution for an owner who possesses property but has no additional assets that can be used to raise the funds to develop it. Consequently, the owner looks for a potential investor who will supply cash for the purchase of the property and is willing to lease it back. The new investor can receive a depreciation deduction and a steady taxable income through the rental payments.

An owner who becomes a lessee can in turn sell the new lease to a second investor, sublease from that person, and continue to operate the property. The second lease is called a **sandwiched lease** and gives a fixed return to the second investor, its owner. The sublessee pays rent to the second investor who in turn pays rent to the first investor, the fee owner. The second investor keeps the difference between the rental payment owed on the main lease and the sublease payment received.

The second investor carries a risk that a default could occur on the sublease and the payments on the main lease would still be owed. To compensate for this risk, the second investor may require a percentage of the income over and above the rental payment in the sublease. This arrangement is called a participation loan and is discussed later in the chapter.

A **subordinated ground lease** can be created whereby the owner sells the land to another party and leases it back on the condition that the owner's claim to ownership will be subordinated to any interim and permanent financing that can be arranged.[2] Subordination allows a greater amount of additional financing to be obtained at a low interest rate. In effect the subordination combined with interim and permanent financing reduces the amount of equity that the developer must raise. He or she may have to pay the landowner-lessor a higher than normal ground rent for the subordination, but the saving in the financing usually justifies the additional payment.

Example Don Anderson owns a twenty-acre plot on a north bypass in Los Angeles that has good potential for commercial development. Don has no cash for construction so he approaches a local real estate department of a large life insurance company that maintains a central office nearby. After considerable discussion, the company expresses interest in purchasing the property site on a sale-leaseback arrangement.

The life insurance company agrees to purchase the property site when a 50,000 square foot shopping center has been constructed. Don must lease the building for forty years and become the manager. Don uses this permanent commitment to obtain an interim construction loan from a local bank. Don receives the cash needed for construction, develops the property, and gains employment for the forty years. The insurance company improves its ground site by requiring construction and is guaranteed a steady rate of return on its investment through the lease requirements.

Example The president of a construction company in St. Louis wants to convert the sizable equity in his real estate holdings into cash. He owns a three-acre industrial site on which he has built a 9,600-square-foot office building with a construction loan at 14 percent interest but has not been able to obtain permanent financing. In addition to the office building, the loan is further secured by a five-acre industrial tract consisting of land and a shop-warehouse. This information is presented by a broker at a meeting of the St. Louis Real Estate Exchange. A client is found, and the following proposal is made. The seller (construction company) will build a crane-supporting facility and warehouse at an estimated cost of $125,000. The sale price of the land and the office building will be $415,000. The seller will lease both properties on a twenty-year net lease (11 percent return) with monthly payments of $4,953.33. The lease will provide an option to repurchase the property after twelve years.

A lender is found who will loan the buyer $375,000 on a first mortgage. The seller carries a $30,000 second mortgage at 10 percent with monthly payments of interest only, and the total principal is due at the end of ten years. Also, the seller carries a $10,000 third mortgage with the same terms as the second. At closing, plans for a shop-warehouse are filed with the escrow agent, and an escrow account is established from which funds will be drawn to pay for the material and construction of the building. The sale-leaseback provides the construction company with the necessary funds to pay off the construction loan and to release the five-acre industrial tract and the shop-warehouse that were held as additional security.[3]

Solution 3: Purchase-money mortgage   A **purchase-money mortgage** is a mortgage commitment offered by the buyer to the seller as a part of the selling price. It is a financing technique whereby the seller extends credit to the buyer. The buyer is telling the seller within the offer that he or she does not wish to pay the full purchase price in cash. The buyer signs a purchase-money mortgage and a promissory note that cover the entire price. If the mortgage contract contains no subordination clause and is filed with the deed, it is a lien against the property that has priority over dower and homestead rights.

The current first mortgage on the property can be either refinanced or assumed by the new buyer. If it is assumed, the purchase-money mortgage is viewed by the parties as a second mortgage to the current first mortgage. The purchase-money mortgage can be a first mortgage if the current mortgage is refinanced.

Example Anita House wants to purchase from Jacquelyn Smith a parcel in Phoenix that has an appraised value of $40,000. Anita is going to pay cash but has only $35,000. In the contract of sale given to Jacquelyn, Anita asks Jacquelyn to extend credit for the additional $5,000 which will be amortized over twenty-five years at 13 percent. Jacquelyn accepts Anita's offer but wants the $5,000 to be repaid over ten years. Anita signs a purchase-money mortgage contract and promissory note and gives them to Jacquelyn at closing.

Example Bill Norvel is negotiating to buy a commercial office building from Norma Denham in Reno, Nevada. He offers her $100,000 for the property under the following terms: he must find a $70,000 first mortgage, $10,000 is to be paid to Norma in cash, and a purchase-money mortgage in the amount of $20,000 payable over ten years at 13 percent is to be carried by Norma. She accepts the arrangements.

Solution 4: Wraparound mortgage   The buyer wants to purchase a specific property by assuming the current mortgage, but lacks the additional cash to cover the entire selling price. He or she can obtain a second mortgage from an institutional lender, offer a purchase-money mortgage to the seller, or attempt to find a wraparound lender. A wraparound lender loans the buyer all of the equity if no down payment is paid by the buyer, or part of the equity if a down payment is paid. One mortgage is written on the total, which is a second mortgage on the property. The buyer makes one payment to the wraparound lender who in turn pays the debt service to the first lender on the current mortgage. The wraparound lender can be the seller or another financial institution.

The wraparound requires the buyer to make both the payments on the assumed mortgage *and* the payments on the additional amount to the wraparound lender.[4] Because this lender makes the payment to the first mortgage lender, default cannot occur on the first mortgage without the wraparound lender's knowledge. Foreclosure typically is rapid in the event of payment default by the buyer. These conditions are outlined within the mortgage contract.

A **wraparound mortgage** is basically an assumption of a first mortgage and normally is used in market conditions where the buyer has an incentive to assume the mortgage.[5] For example, it may be used if the interest rate on the first mortgage is significantly lower than the market rate, if the terms of the first mortgage such as a prepayment penalty do not encourage paying off the balance, or if the terms of a second mortgage are not attractive to the buyer or seller.

A financial institution would have an incentive to become a wraparound lender if it could charge an interest rate on the newly loaned funds that is very competitive in the market. If the underlying equity in the property is substantial, the local market where the property is located appears to indicate strong growth, and the new buyer has good credit and income, the loan would be relatively risk-free.

Example Sally Ho wants to buy a parcel in Tampa that is appraised for $40,000. It has a first mortgage in the amount of $20,000 at $7^3/4$ percent interest for another fifteen years. Sally can raise $4,000 in cash for a down payment. The current interest rate on new first mortgages is 13 percent with $4,000 as a down payment. The seller, Al High, has indicated his willingness to have the mortgage assumed, and the lender will not raise the interest rate upon assumption.

Sally finds a local finance company that is willing to loan $16,000 ($40,000 − $20,000 − $4,000) for fifteen years and become the wraparound lender for an interest rate of 11 percent. They will write a wraparound mortgage for $36,000 at 11 percent. Al is not interested in becoming a wraparound lender because he needs the $20,000 cash to replace the property for his personal use. Sally signs a $36,000 wraparound mortgage with the finance company, assumes the first mortgage that formerly belonged to Al, and pays Al $20,000 cash ($16,000 + $4,000). Sally makes payments to the finance company, which can foreclose on the mortgage if she defaults on payments.

Example An apartment complex in beautiful Columbus, Ohio, has a market value of $3,000,000, an $8^1/4$ percent mortgage interest rate, and a current unpaid balance of $700,000. The owner/mortgagor of this property wants to borrow an additional $1,500,000 using this property as collateral for another part of the development. The wraparound lender receives a promissory note in the amount of $2,200,000 bearing 10.5 percent interest secured by the mortgage, disburses only $1,500,000, and assumes the obligation of making the payments on the first mortgage loan of $700,000.

Solution 5: Land contract   A **land contract**, sometimes called a land installment contract, is a financing arrangement between the seller and the buyer to satisfy two objectives individually or together.[6] First, it can benefit a buyer who does not have enough cash and needs additional time to raise the money. Second, it enables the owner (seller) of the property to defer a capital gains tax. Thus, the land contract is an arrangement whereby the seller becomes the lender and extends credit at a competitive interest rate.

A buyer who is acceptable to the seller may need additional time to convert assets to cash or to process a loan application form for the type of financing desired. The land contract gives the buyer a claim to ownership and allows the necessary time.

The buyer makes a cash payment to the owner and signs an installment note for the balance. The note carries a competitive rate of interest on the balance and is amortized according to a predetermined schedule. Normally, the installment note does not allow the deed to pass from the owner to the buyer until the final payment is made and consequently the deed is not recorded. Foreclosure and possession of the property as stipulated within the note occur upon default in the payments by the buyer. A new deed could be passed and recorded at the option of the parties involved, but this would cause difficulties for the seller if foreclosure became necessary. In addition, the seller can require the buyer to sign a purchase-money mortgage and promissory note in lieu of the installment contract.

A second use of a land contract is to defer and minimize the capital gains tax for the seller. The capital gain received at the closing must be reported for taxation purposes in the year that the gain is realized.

By electing an installment sale at closing, a seller is able to defer payment of the tax until he or she actually receives the additional cash owed from the buyer. The tax is due as these payments are received. The result is that the percentage of the total capital gain reported in any taxable year is not greater than the percentage of the total price paid in cash in that same year. Thus, the benefit of this type of sale depends on the ability of the seller to accept only a portion of the sales price at closing.

To qualify as an installment sale, the transaction must satisfy two conditions:

1. A maximum of 30 percent of the total sales price can be received in the year of the sale. However, as of the printing date of this book, the specific details of the installment sales method were being reconsidered by Congress (See Chapter 10).
2. The seller must elect the installment method on his or her tax return.

The total cost to the buyer or the total sales price must include the following items:

1. The amount by which any mortgage assumed is greater than the seller's adjusted basis of the real estate
2. Cash

3. Appraised value of other items given as part of the price

4. The seller's debts paid by the buyer.

Any of the seller's expenses incurred in the sale are not included.

Both parties to the transaction should remember that all payments received through the end of the year in which the sale occurs count as payments in the year of sale. They include deposits, payments in a prior year, and amortization payments made before the end of the year. The seller cannot receive more than 30 percent of the total sales price in the year of the sale.

The taxpayer selects the installment sale option by explaining the terms of the transaction in a rider attached to the tax form. The rider should show total gain over the life of the installment contract, the gain to be taxed in any single year, and all other pertinent facts relating to the case. Once declared, the election is binding. An election is normally not allowed in an amended return unless the facts demonstrate that the sale was treated in a manner consistent with the installment sale election.

In an installment sales transaction, the seller may ask the buyer to sign a purchase-money mortgage for the balance of the price not paid in the first year. The distinction between the interest payment and sales price within the buyer's subsequent payments is important. Section 483 of the IRS code states that when no interest is charged, or when the interest on deferred payments is unreasonably low or zero, the payments will be treated as including interest at 7 percent compounded semiannually for transactions after July 23, 1975. Thus, deferred payments cannot be treated as 100 percent principal.

Example Mr. Ross wants to buy a commercial office building in Lubbock, Texas, from Mr. Parker by using a purchase-money mortgage, but his offer is refused. Mr. Parker, however, makes a counteroffer: total sales price of $162,500, 29 percent down ($47,125), assume a current mortgage in the amount of $55,000 at 8 percent with $630 monthly payments, and amortize the balance ($60,375) over fifteen years at 13 percent. The building has a monthly income of $1,275. Taxes and insurance on the building total $1,400. Mr. Parker wants to make use of an installment land contract in helping Mr. Ross purchase the building. However, Mr. Ross refuses the offer as he does not have the necessary cash for the down payment nor does he believe the building is worth $162,500. In this case, the legal technicalities between a purchase-money mortgage and a land contract are not as important as the economic terms.

Comment on solutions 1 through 5   Mortgages that are seconds, purchase-money, subordinated sale-leasebacks, and wraparounds are called **junior liens.** However, purchase-money mortgages can be first mortgages if there is no existing first lender in the transaction. They are second in priority as a claim to the value of the property in the event of borrower default. Each can be used to increase the user's leverage and give the following advantages, some of which are shown in the preceding examples:[7]

1. Provide an alternative to refinancing the entire purchase price

2. Provide an alternative to reorganizing an investment venture into a partnership

3. Provide lease payments that serve as a tax deduction and tax shelter

4. Avoid unattractive features of the first mortgage, such as prepayment penalties

5. Make possible a larger total loan than might be obtained under one mortgage only

6. Make it possible to extract equity dollars from the transaction that might not be taxable

Solution 6: Contract for deed   A **contract for deed** (title), sometimes called a *contract of sale in escrow* and a *deed in escrow,* is a purchase arrangement whereby the buyer and seller sign an escrow agreement prior to closing. A third party such as a commercial bank serves as the escrow agent. Typically, the seller gives the escrow agent the abstract, the new deed, and the old first mortgage. The buyer typically gives the seller a cash payment and agrees to assume the payments on the current first mortgage balance. In addition, the buyer agrees to pay the seller periodic payments at a competitive interest rate on any additional sum that has not been paid by the buyer. The escrow agreement contains a provision that allows foreclosure in the event that the buyer defaults on the payments. Usually the deed is not recorded until the buyer makes the last payment. This arrangement is similar to the equity buy (assumption) except that it involves a third party who serves as the escrow agent. Also, the deed may not be recorded until the escrow agreement is satisfied.

The contract for deed is useful when the buyer cannot obtain mortgage money, when the seller wants to extend credit to collect the interest, or when the interest on the current mortgage is lower than the market rate of interest and the buyer desires an assumption.

Example Larry Kemp wants to purchase a parcel in Buffalo from Chet Jones. It is appraised at $50,000. The balance on the current first mortgage is $25,000 and the interest rate is 8 percent. Because the current market rate is 13 percent, Larry wants to assume the first mortgage but he has only $10,000 cash. Chet agrees to a contract for deed, and they contact an attorney to write the escrow agreement.

Larry gives Chet the $10,000 at closing. He agrees to pay Chet a rate of 13 percent interest on the remaining $15,000 ($50,000 − 25,000 − 10,000) over the next seventeen years. He also agrees to assume the current first mortgage debt of $25,000 and to make the monthly payments until maturity or refinancing, whichever comes first. Chet gives the escrow agreement to the escrow officer at the Second National Bank and has the new abstract, the new deed, and the first mortgage contract sent to the escrow officer before the closing. The escrow agreement states that Larry may not record the deed until both debts are satisfied. Also, the escrow agent may foreclose on the property and return the deed to Chet if Larry defaults on the payments.

Solution 7: Standby permanent financing   Most new construction is supported by financing from two loans—a construction (interim) loan to pay the costs of construction and a permanent loan, which pays the construction lender and requires the owner to make periodic payments that amortize the loan. Generally the permanent loan must be approved first. With this commitment, the developer can usually acquire a construction loan.[8]

Sometimes the permanent financing is not available because of unfavorable market conditions or competitive projects that are more attractive. In these cases, **standby permanent financing** can be offered as a permanent financing commitment given to the developer/contractor through which another lender can make the construction loan. The lender usually includes additional charges that serve as an incentive for the developer to replace the loan with another permanent commitment. The additional charges may include a commitment fee to hold the line of credit and another commitment fee to be paid at closing. This fee may take the form of a percentage of the profit to compensate the lender for risk. In addition, the mortgage interest rate may be slightly higher than competitive rates on similar mortgages.

Example Kay Beaver wants to construct an eight-unit apartment building on a lot given to her by her father. Kay has not done a good job of surveying the market to determine the rental potential. Also, mortgage money is restricted in the area because of high market rates and a low state usury limit that reduces lender profits. After much searching, Kay finds a life insurance company that is willing to give her a standby permanent financing commitment. The analyst believes that the market is not saturated with apartment units of the type Kay wants to build.

The commitment offered is for $150,000 on a line of credit for which Kay would pay 1 percent upon acceptance. In addition, the company wants a mortgage rate of 13.5 percent over twenty years which is 0.5 higher than competitive lenders' rates. The company also requires 2 percent annually of the units' net income. The loan would give the lender the right to review and restrict property expenditures over $250.

This permanent commitment would enable Kay to obtain an interim construction loan from a local bank. Also, it would give her time to find another permanent lender that might offer better terms. Kay is unsure, and decides to postpone construction.

Example Marianne Reed is planning to build a home for herself and her children on an acre of land she purchased on New Hope Road just south of Wichita. She has been unable to obtain a permanent commitment from any of the lending institutions because of the uncertainty of the money market. Mrs. Reed had planned to obtain interim financing from Second National Bank of Wichita, but without the permanent loan commitment, she is unable to do so. Finally, a local lending institution, First Federal, tells Mrs. Reed that they would probably be able to take over the loan once the house is built. In essence, they offer Mrs. Reed a standby commitment that would enable her to obtain construction funds. Mrs. Reed does not accept the proposal as she feels there is too much uncertainty involved. The appraised value of the house is $82,500 and the loan offered is $66,000 for thirty years at 13 percent. The Second National Bank would provide the construction financing at 13 percent. Although First Federal is offering Mrs. Reed reasonable terms, she is disturbed by the fact that they do not guarantee that they will take over the loan.

Solution 8: Bond for title A **bond for title** is used when the buyer and seller agree to a closing date in the future. The buyer pays rent for the property in the interim period, and a portion of the rent may apply to the purchase price. The seller offers a bond that he or she will deliver a deed upon closing. The buyer takes a risk that the seller will not perform.

Solution 9: Delayed closing date   A variation of the bond for title agreement is called a **delayed closing date.** The buyer agrees to purchase the property and close at a date in the future, say one year. The buyer pays rent at a higher level than is normal until closing. The additional rent compensates the seller for the risk that the buyer will not perform.

Bond for title and delayed closing date are two techniques of creative financing in that they allow the transaction to take place when the buyer is short of cash. Both are arrangements whereby the buyer is given possession of the property with the understanding that a sale will take place at a predetermined future date. The buyer is given time to raise the necessary cash. Thus, the arrangements are tailored to fit the needs of individuals at a particular time for a specific property.

Example In June 1980, Mr. and Mrs. Henry Myers contracted to purchase a house and lot in Santa Fe from Mr. and Mrs. John Graham. The sales price was $69,900 and Mr. Myers expected to pay with a 100 percent VA loan. The contract stipulated that the transaction was contingent upon obtaining the VA loan. The closing date was delayed approximately six weeks; however, the Myers were allowed to move into the house and to pay rent at a rate of $550 per month. The Myers were turned down for their loan request because of poor credit and were forced to move from the property after one month.

Solution 10: Rent with option to buy   **A rent with option** to buy is an arrangement whereby the buyer signs a lease for a period of time, say one year, and agrees to purchase the property at a predetermined date. The purchase price is negotiated when the lease is signed. In addition, the buyer may be asked by the seller to give a nonrefundable deposit as earnest money guaranteeing that the buyer will close on the sale.

Buyer Does Not Have Enough Cash but Owns Assets

In this situation, the buyer does not have enough cash for the down payment on the desired property but does have other assets that can be pledged as collateral. Thus, the buyer can obtain the necessary funds by using a financial arrangement involving other property.

Although various types of loans can be arranged, perhaps the most popular types are the second mortgage and the exchange.

Solution 1: Second mortgage or loan on another asset   A potential buyer who owns another asset may seek a second mortgage or a loan on the asset that can be used as a down payment on the property desired.

Example Meredith Jones contracts with Jeff Rogers to buy a new house that Mr. Rogers constructed in Eugene, Oregon. The purchase price is $46,250. Ms. Jones can obtain a 90 percent loan at 13 percent for thirty years from First National Service Corporation, which would require a down payment of $4,625. However, she has only

$2,000 in cash. She obtains a short-term loan in the amount of $4,000 from the First National Bank of Eugene by pledging her Mercury as security. Ms. Jones has a good job and will not have problems making the payments—the problem was the need for additional cash for the down payment. The loan is made and Ms. Jones moves into the house.

Solution 2: Exchange   Section 1031 of the IRS code allows property to be exchanged for like property, and no capital gains or losses are taxable if the property is held for productive use in a business or for an investment. Qualification under this section of the law is *mandatory,* not elective. Consequently, investors desiring to defer a capital gain or loss should plan the **exchange** transaction well in advance. There is no limit to the number of tax-deferred exchanges or the amount of taxes postponed. Personal residences are excluded.[9] In addition to providing a tax deferral, the exchange makes a transaction possible when the buyer does not have enough cash for a normal purchase or the seller does not receive enough cash in a normal sale to reenter the market and purchase another property.

The most important criteria to be satisfied in qualifying a transaction as an exchange are that the property transferred by an owner *and* the property received must qualify as either an income-producing asset or an investment in the owner's portfolio. Income-producing properties must be *like* or similar in character. The fact that the basis of the previously owned property transfers to the property newly received is the justification for the taxation postponement. The basis of property is its original cost, which may be adjusted for capital improvement, miscellaneous costs, and allowable depreciation. Further adjustments are made for unlike property traded in the exchange.[10,11]

Example An investor holds several acres of land that were purchased for $100,000. The land shows no prospects for increased growth and has decreased in value to $80,000. The owner decides to exchange into an $80,000 apartment unit. The $100,000 basis transfers to the rental unit, which gives depreciation plus some income.[12]

Example A farmer holds thirty acres on the edge of a city. He purchased the land thirty years ago for $500 per acre and it is currently worth $30,000 per acre. Instead of realizing the capital gain by selling, he can exchange the property for a commercial or industrial investment valued at $900,000. The new property has no mortgage and the new $900,000 investment will generate a retirement income.

Example A widow owns a small chicken ranch in the rural area. She wants to return to the city where she can be near friends, family, and social activities. The property is unencumbered and valued at $45,000. The widow needs additional income and would like to trade her property for apartment units. Broker A, the widow's broker, advertises the ranch in the exchange section of the local newspaper and sends out a bulletin to his cooperating brokers.

Broker A receives a call from Broker B saying that he has a client with a fine large home in the city valued at $50,000 who would like the ten-acre ranch. But the widow with the ranch does not want a large home. Broker A suggests that if the owner of the city house is interested in the ranch and will wait a few weeks, he will endeavor to find a "third leg" to the exchange. Broker B asks his client, the city homeowner, to sign an exchange agreement to trade the city house for the ranch.

Among the replies to the original advertisement of Broker A is one from Broker C who has a client with an eight-unit apartment house valued at $85,000 on which there is a $35,000 mortgage. This apartment owner is not interested in a ranch but would take a good city home in exchange for his apartment house. Broker A arranges to show the widow the apartment house belonging to Broker C's client and has the widow sign an exchange agreement to trade her ranch for the income property. Because the ranch is worth $45,000 and the equity in the apartment house is $50,000 ($85,000 − $35,000), Broker A asks the apartment house seller to carry a second mortgage on the apartment house for $5,000 ($50,000 − $45,000). Broker C's client signs an exchange agreement to exchange his apartment house for the city home. Meanwhile, Broker B has shown the ranch to his client, the owner of the city home, and has him sign an exchange agreement to give the city house in exchange for the ranch, contingent upon consummation of the rest of the exchange. Now all that remains to make the three-way exchange is to have Broker C show the apartment house to B's client with the city house and have him sign an exchange agreement to trade his city house for the ranch. The result of the exchange is that A's client, owner of the ranch, receives the apartment house in exchange. B's client, owner of the city home, receives the ranch in exchange. C's client, owner of the apartment house, receives the city home in exchange.[13]

The Buyer is Negotiating with a Seller Who Wants to Become the Lender and Extend Credit on All or Part of the Sale

Often a seller wants to carry part or all of the selling price of the property to earn a competitive return on the money loaned. In addition, the seller may want to defer the capital gains tax and pay it over time or defer it by exchanging the property.

Solutions   The seller can use several types of financing arrangements—for example, a second mortgage, a purchase-money mortgage, a wraparound mortgage, a land contract, or an exchange. It is conceivable that the seller can be the lender by issuing a standard mortgage or deed of trust. The following examples illustrate several possible solutions.

Solution 1: Exchange   The owner could seek an exchange of like property to defer the capital gain. Examples of this solution are given in the section on the buyer who lacks cash but owns asssets.

Solution 2: Land contract   Bill Harp is negotiating with Jim Goheen to buy a lot in Omaha. Mr. Goheen does not want the full purchase price. They agree on a selling price of $20,000 subject to the terms of a $4,500 down payment and the remainder, $15,500, to be carried by the seller at 13 percent interest with $181.60 per month for twenty years. The seller is interested in drawing interest. The mortgage and the deed are escrowed at the bank.

Solution 3: Purchase-money mortgage   Tom Harvey is negotiating with Jane Ross to buy a house and lot in Springdale, Arkansas. A sales price of $62,500 is agreed upon between the parties; however, the seller does not want the full purchase price in cash. The terms agreed upon are a $5,000 down payment and a $9,500 second mortgage on the buyer's property until sold, with a purchase-money first mortgage in the amount of $48,000 at 12.5 percent for fifteen years. The buyer could not obtain a new loan and the seller wants an interest payment so the contract is acceptable to both parties. The mortgage and deed are filed in the county courthouse.

Example Mr. Phil Taylor is trying to obtain construction funds for building a house. The lot that Phil would like to build on is owned by Mrs. Louise Sullivan. The lot price is $14,000. Mr. Taylor has only $3,550 to put down, and Mrs. Sullivan does not want the full purchase price. She offers to take the down payment of $3,550 and accept a purchase-money mortgage for $10,450 with interest only payable for the first six months at 13 percent. The $10,450 must be paid over eight years in monthly payments at 13 percent interest. Mr. Taylor is in favor of the proposition. However, he is unable to obtain construction funds and therefore does not need the lot.

Solution 4: Second mortgage   Sometimes the seller of the property will "take back" a second or even third mortgage to facilitate the sale or because he or she does not want the cash. *Taking back* a mortgage means that the seller holds a mortgage. For example, a buyer pays $200,000 for property with $30,000 down, and the seller takes back a mortgage for $170,000. Also, the seller may take back a second mortgage if there is a first loan on the property. For example, a buyer purchases a parcel for $200,000 with a $120,000 loan and pays $30,000 to the seller. The seller could take back or carry a $50,000 second mortgage.

The Buyer Is Negotiating with a Lender Who Wants a Return on the Profit Potential of the Property

A buyer may be negotiating with a lender who wants a return from the property in addition to the mortgage interest rate. The justification is that the lender does not want to bear all the risk and none of the gain. If the property is extremely profitable, the lender wants to receive part of the equity in the property or the income in addition to the mortgage interest rate.

Solution 1: Participation loan   A **participation loan** is an arrangement between the borrower and lender whereby the lender joins the borrower in assuming part of the risk and resultant profits of the investment.[14] Traditionally, a fixed interest rate, fixed amortization schedule, and fixed monthly payments were committed by a borrower to obtain the needed funds. During periods of tight money and inflation, however, the fixed interest rate return may not compensate lenders adequately for their risk. They are repaid with "cheaper" dollars and the yields on competing investments became increasingly attractive through time. Further, lenders argue that under a fixed interest rate return arrangement, they assume the same risk and supply the same amount of funds on successful projects as on unsuccessful projects. On successful projects, the borrower reaps maximum returns, but the lender's return is restricted. Consequently, participation loans have become the borrower's alternative to accepting a higher fixed interest rate.

Most participation loans are made by life insurance companies as a result of regulatory restrictions on other financial institutions and partially because of scale. The participation instrument is complex, requiring considerable time to negotiate and administer. Consequently, participations usually are restricted to large projects.

Participation loans are of two types, equity and income. An *equity participation* is created when the lender takes a position of partial ownership of the investment as a condition of extending funds. If the borrower is a corporation with public stock, the lender may require a number of shares. Alternatively, the lender may receive a percentage of any resale or refinancing proceeds. This type of loan may involve a commitment to the lender beyond the term of the loan. Thus, the borrower can owe the mortgage plus a share of the equity.

The most common participation arrangement is an *income participation* whereby the lender can request a portion of the project's income before or after the debt service. The borrower can be committed to repaying a mortgage and a percentage of the income.

Percentage of gross income Because this arrangement is beneficial only to the lender, the borrower will not be satisfied. The lender assumes no risk, makes no allowance for increasing costs, offers no advantage to the borrower over a standard fixed rate mortgage, and creates an expense restriction to the borrower that cannot be minimized. Further, this arrangement may violate state usury law because the percentage payment may be interpreted as interest.

Percentage of gross income over a definite dollar amount This arrangement is a variation of the preceding one. The lender benefits only if the gross income rises above a stipulated amount.

Percentage of defined net operating income A percentage of the net operating income from the project is promised for a leasehold mortgage on the improvements.

Another type of participation loan involves a sale-leaseback where the lender buys the site from the borrower who leases it back. The borrower signs a mortgage which includes a commitment to pay the lender a percentage of defined net operating income (which is described in Chapter 9). This arrangement has the following advantages to the borrower:

1. The need for immediate cash is reduced.
2. The borrower can deduct lease payments for tax purposes.
3. Under the leasehold financing on the improvements, the borrower retains the right to deduct the depreciation on the improvements.
4. This arrangement for net operating income participation does not decrease the market value of the project since an appraisal may be based on net operating income.
5. The arrangement places controls on the borrower's expenses because the lender defines and limits certain expenses to retain partial control over the size of net operating income.

The lender's participation does not begin unless net operating income is larger than debt service and expense. The lender assumes more risk that is determined by market conditions and consequently has a higher expected return.

Example Carl Smith sells his apartment house in Minneapolis for $150,000. He receives $50,000 in cash and takes back a purchase-money first mortgage of $100,000. He finds that he is unable to sell the purchase-money mortgage but is able to interest a mortgage banker in lending $75,000 on the security of the apartment house. He thereupon subordinates his purchase-money mortgage and sells a $75,000 senior interest. In the event of foreclosure of the mortgage and sale of the property, the senior interest would be paid out of the proceeds first and if any balance were left, it would go to the holder of the purchase-money mortgage.

Example Hugh Kincaid wanted a $120,000 mortgage at 12 percent for twenty years on income property valued at $160,000. Second Federal Savings and Loan would make the loan only if they would receive 15 percent of the net operating income and 15 percent of the proceeds of resale twenty years hence when the mortgage is fully paid off.

Solution 2: Piggyback loan   A **piggyback loan,** sometimes called a *split loan* or a *joint loan,* is a financing arrangement between two lenders to advance the borrower a loan for a high percentage of the selling price. Essentially it is one mortgage on one property that is secured by two promissory notes. The first mortgage, say for 95 percent of the property value, is originated by the local lender who provides 75 to 80 percent of the mortgage funds. The remaining amount is supplied by a second party, normally another lender. The second lender asks the borrower to provide private mortgage insurance on its funds, and its note becomes subordinated to that of the original lender, who is the first mortgage lender.

Example Cheryl Ache wants to purchase residential property with a $70,000 appraised value. She has $7,000 to put down on the property. She goes to a local lending institution and finds that they can lend only $50,000 on the property but that they might be able to find a joint lender for the additional $13,000. The senior lender is able to find a junior lender who will loan the additional funds. Therefore, a 90 percent loan in the amount of $63,000 is made to Cheryl.

The Buyer Wants to Preserve the Terms of the First Mortgage

A buyer may want to preserve the terms of a first mortgage for several reasons. First, the first mortgage may have a lower interest rate than is obtainable in the current market. Second, the first mortgage may have a high prepayment penalty and therefore an assumption would involve less cost than refinancing. Third, mortgage money may not be available, and the interest rates may be so high that they are prohibitive.

A wraparound and a purchase-money mortgage can be used to preserve the terms of the first mortgage. In addition, a contract for deed is popular especially when tight money conditions prevail in the market and mortgage money is not plentiful.

Solution 1: Assumption   An **assumption** (equity buy) is described in Chapter 16. The buyer pays the seller for the financial interest in the property and agrees to pay the remaining debt. The first mortgage remains intact but two promissory notes are in effect, one signed by the first mortgagor and one signed by the second mortgagor.

Example Jimmy and Jane Williams were negotiating with Johnny Mallard to buy his house in Rogers, Ohio. Mr. Mallard was asking $75,000 for the property, which had a current loan balance of $30,247.52. The loan was with First Federal Savings and Loan and originally was for thirty years at 9 percent interest. It had been in effect for five years. Principal, interest, taxes, and insurance payment totaled $465 per month. Current interest rates in the market were 13.5 percent. Mr. and Mrs. Williams wanted to assume the current mortgage because the interest rate was lower than that currently available in the market. They offered Mr. Mallard $74,000 for the property, and the offer was accepted. The Williamses were approved by the lending institution for the assumption. They paid Mallard $43,752.48 and assumed the current mortgage. Mallard requested that the lender release him from any further debt liability. This release and the new deed were recorded.

Solution 2: Wraparound mortgage

Example F & M Cabinet Shop is negotiating with Pat Carty to buy an industrial building on three acres. They agreed upon a price of $125,000 subject to the following terms. The property has a current mortgage of $60,000 at 10 percent interest with seven years of payments remaining. F & M Cabinet Shop wants to assume the current mortgage because the interest rate is low in comparison with the current market rate. They want to make a payment of $15,000 and obtain a wraparound mortgage from Mr. Carty in the amount of $125,000 at 11 percent interest amortized over twenty years with a ten-year **balloon note.** Mr. Carty's agreement to become the wraparound lender (at a competitive interest rate), enables F & M Cabinet Shop to preserve the terms of the current mortgage.

Solution 3: Purchase-money mortgage   The seller can extend credit to the buyer through a purchase-money mortgage. The arrangements are similar to those described for the situation in which the buyer lacks both cash and assets.

DISADVANTAGES

The financing arrangements outlined above may be needed in certain stages of the business cycle since mortgage money may not be readily available. In this type of market, the buyer, seller, or agent must be more innovative in the financing arrangements to allow the purchase (sale) to be completed. Several disadvantages can exist and should be remembered in using any one or several of these techniques:

☐ These financing solutions require special knowledge about real estate finance. The buyer and the seller are not involved in a typical transaction where an application is submitted to a financial institution. Gaining knowledge of these instruments and their advantages and disadvantages requires extra time, study, and experience.

☐ The buyer, seller, or agent could be easily involved in a property management responsibility to assure that the financial arrangements negotiated endure. A financing plan may look good at the outset and turn sour because of the failure of one party to perform the agreed responsibilities.

☐ A recessionary market can eliminate the incentives for entering into some of the financing techniques discussed above. A wraparound mortgage, for example, typically is used when the existing mortgage has a lower rate than the market rate of interest.

☐ A buyer, seller, or agent who negotiates a significant number of these transactions could receive a reputation of being a "wheeler-dealer" that can hurt future business.

Regardless of these disadvantages, a successful buyer, seller, or agent must be able to arrange financing for the transaction in all stages of the business cycle to complete the transaction. This extra knowledge and skill with financing separates the successful transactions from those that are not successful.

COMPREHENSIVE EXAMPLE

The following example illustrates how the financing tools can be used in combination to solve the needs of the parties involved. The owners of an income-producing property want to improve its marketability by refinancing the mortgage and making the equity requirement less for a potential buyer. This solution would be helpful to a buyer who is short of cash.

Example Jim and Janet Smith own a small eight-unit apartment building that they have placed on the market for sale. They are asking $250,000 but no buyers have expressed an interest within the past three months. The property is well located in an area with good growth potential. The local market indicates a strong potential for the continuation of the rental income stream. The apartments are approximately six years old and the maintenance has been good. Jim and Janet decide to examine their financing structure to determine whether the financing arrangements might be beyond the reach of the local market, thus driving away interested buyers.

The Smiths are advertising the property with the following financing arrangements:

First mortgage	$160,000
Second mortgage	$ 20,000
Cash required from the buyer	$ 70,000
	$250,000

Both mortgages can be assumed by an interested buyer. The second mortgage matures in 15 months. Jim learns by examining data on comparable properties that the $70,000 cash required is too much for the local market. Similar units have sold recently for less cash down payment.

First Federal Savings and Loan informs Jim in response to his questions that they would refinance the first mortgage from $160,000 to $180,000, which would create $20,000 in tax-free cash to Jim. The new mortgage would carry an interest rate $\frac{1}{4}$ percentage point higher and would have a new maturity that is six years longer. Jim could use the $20,000 to pay off the second mortgage. However, this alternative still requires the buyer to produce $70,000 to buy the property.

Jim talks to the lender of the second mortgage and discovers that the lender would refinance the second loan at the same time the first mortgage is refinanced to $180,000. The second lender would agree to lowering the mortgage amount by $10,000 with no prepayment penalty provided that Jim would pay another $10,000 on the principal. The lender wants a new mortgage of $12,500 that would carry an interest rate that is $2\frac{1}{4}$ percentage points higher with a maturity date of six years. Thus, Jim would pay $10,000 in cash and receive a new mortgage for $12,500 that would carry a higher interest rate for the next six years.

In addition, Jim and Janet examine all recent sales of comparable properties and conclude that the selling price of their property is similar to the comparable properties, but the cash required by the buyer is about $12,000 to $15,000 too much.

After reexamining their financial needs and surveying the market, Jim and Janet decide on the following steps:

1. Refinance the second mortgage to $12,500 with an interest rate $2\frac{1}{4}$ percentage points higher than that of the current mortgage and a maturity date that is six years in the future.
2. Refinance the first mortgage to $180,000 with an interest rate that is $\frac{1}{4}$ percentage point higher and a maturity date that is six years longer.
3. Take the $20,000 cash from refinancing and use $10,000 of it to pay on refinancing the second mortgage.
4. Attempt to sell the property under the restructured financial arrangements for $250,000.

Thus, the new arrangements are

New refinanced first mortgage to be assumed by the buyer	$180,000
New refinanced second mortgage to be assumed by the buyer	12,500
Cash required by the buyer	57,500
	$250,000

Jim and Janet have lowered the amount that a potential buyer would need to raise by $12,500 ($70,000 − $57,500) to fit within the norm observed in the market for similar properties. When the property is sold, the Smiths will receive $57,500 from the new buyer and $10,000 from refinancing the two mortgages ($20,000 from the first minus $10,000 paid on the second) for a total of $67,500.

LOANS FOR THE CONVENIENCE OF THE LENDER OR THE BORROWER

Some loans are tailored for the convenience of the lender or the borrower. For example, a mortgagor wants to purchase property and furnish it with items that are usually thought to become fixtures, such as a stove, carpet, hot water heater, and air conditioning. The buyer who has good credit could obtain a separate loan for each item from the store where it is purchased.

Solution 1: Package mortgage   Instead of requiring the mortgagor to negotiate separate mortgages for the property and everything within it, the lender can give one mortgage, called a **package mortgage,** to cover real and personal property.

Example Paulene Bakker bought a restaurant in Dallas, Texas, for $100,000. She obtained a mortgage from a local investor in the amount of $60,000. This mortgage was a package mortgage in that it covered land, building, and equipment. The mortgage specified that it covered real and personal property.

Solution 2: Blanket mortgage   A lender may give the mortgagor one mortgage to cover several purchases of real property at one time. This is called a **blanket mortgage.**

Example Ruth Ryan needed money to purchase four lots in different locations. To obtain the funds, she placed a blanket mortgage in the amount of $45,000 on all four with terms of ten years at 13 percent with a five-year balloon note. As each lot is developed and sold, Ruth will request a release for that lot in order that the property may be transferred to the buyer without the lien created by the blanket mortgage.

Solution 3: Open end mortgage   The lender can approve a fixed line of credit under one mortgage contract with an **open end mortgage.** The mortgagor receives only the amount needed at one time. Interest is paid and amortization begins automatically. Future advances can be made automatically or by lender review under the same mortgage. The borrower saves the time and expense of reapplying and paying closing costs each time funds are needed.

Example Laura Scott owns a house and two acres in Jackson, Mississippi, on which she has an original mortgage of $40,000. She subdivides the tract and with the sale of the lots reduces her original indebtedness to $15,000. She needs capital for other investments and, because she has an open end mortgage, she is able to go back to the original mortgage and obtain an additional $25,000 without new documents being drawn or a new appraisal being made.

CHAPTER SUMMARY

Real estate financing can be arranged to fit the needs of the parties involved so they are able to complete the transaction. Special financing arrangements are commonly used when certain market conditions motivate the buyer or the seller to search for alternatives. For instance, a buyer may not have enough cash, a seller may not want all of the cash at once, or the seller may want to defer any anticipated capital gain. Also, creative financing arrangements can be used in combinations to satisfy the needs of both the buyer and seller.

Review Questions

1. What are the various market situations that create the need for alternative types of financing?
2. Describe the following financial arrangements and explain the circumstances in which each would be used:
   (a) second mortgage
   (b) purchase-money mortgage
   (c) wraparound mortgage
   (d) exchange
   (e) standby permanent financing
   (f) sale-leaseback
   (g) sandwich lease
   (h) participation loan
3. Create a situation that would cause a buyer or seller to desire a combination of financing alternatives.

Discussion Questions

1. Can you name any additional "creative" financing arrangements to fit the situations indentified in the chapter?
2. Why must the buyer, seller, and the agent be aware of these methods of financing property?
3. Will a state usury limit influence the use of these financing arrangements? How?
4. Who bears the final responsibility for proposing a financing arrangement to fit the needs of the buyer (seller)? Does the agent have a motive to acquire this information?
5. Do you think that the use of these financing tools will follow cycles? Why? Give examples.
6. Can you think of any financing needs of the buyer (seller) at some point in the market that cannot be satisfied by these mortgages and financial arrangements? Give examples.

Notes

1. William Hondorf and Gordon May, "Making Fixed Assets Work: Sell Your Building and Lease It Back? It's a Possible Source of Investable Funds," *Federal Home Loan Bank Board Journal,* Vol. 9 (October 1976), pp. 16–21.

2. "Using the Subordinated Land Lease," *The Mortgage and Real Estate Executives Report,* Vol. 9 (February 1, 1977), pp. 3–4.

3. Weldon J. Zoellner, "Sale Leaseback Helps Close Deal," *Farm and Land REALTOR,* Vol. 10, No. 6 (June 1978), pp. 8–9.

4. Francis Gunning, "The Wraparound Mortgage . . . Friend or U.F.O.?" *Real Estate Review,* Vol. 2 (Summer 1972), pp. 35–48.

5. Charles Trowbridge, "What is a Wraparound Mortgage?" *Real Estate Today,* Vol. 8 (December 1975), pp. 44–53.

6. Robert Feinschreiber, "The Taxwise Real Estate Installment Sale," *Real Estate Review,* Vol. 4 (Summer 1974), pp. 109–114.

7. Subcommittee on Junior Lien Financing, MBA Income Property Committee, "Junior Lien Financing—Five Varieties and the Advantages They Offer," *The Mortgage Banker,* Vol. 38, No. 8 (May 1978), pp. 41–46.

8. Dennis McCrary, "Standby Permanent Financing for Condominium Development," *Real Estate Review,* Vol. 4 (Spring 1974), pp. 70–77.

9. Stefan Tucker, "Don't Sell Your Real Estate—Exchange It," *Real Estate Review,* Vol. 5 (Winter 1976), pp. 94–101.

10. Irene Tolbert, "Why Exchange?" *Real Estate Review,* Vol. 9 (March 1976), pp. 42–43.

11. Ralph Righton, "Pyramiding Your Way to Wealth with the Real Estate Exchange," *Real Estate Review,* Vol. 1 (Fall 1971), pp. 89–97.

12. Robert Petermann, "Exchange: Duplexes for Apartments," *Real Estate Today,* Vol. 8 (October 1975), pp. 52–54.

13. Stanley Sotcher, "Exchange of Real Estate," contained in *Real Estate Encyclopedia,* edited by Edith J. Friedman (Englewood Cliffs, N.J.: Prentice-Hall, Inc., 1963), pp. 291–92.

14. Lowell Chesborough, "Do Participation Loans Pay Off?" *Real Estate Review,* Vol. 4 (Summer 1974), pp. 95–100.

Additional Readings

ALDRICH, ELBERT. "Nobody Wanted Cash." *Farm and Land REALTOR* 30, 6 (June 1978): 11.

DENNIS, MARCHALL. *Fundamentals of Mortgage Lending.* Reston, Va.: Reston Publishing Co., Inc., 1978. Chapters 13–14.

EPLEY, DONALD F., and JAMES A. MILLAR. *Basic Real Estate Finance and Investments.* New York: John Wiley & Sons, Inc., 1984. Chapter 10.

KATZ, NEIL J., and ROBERT A. PRIORI. *Real Estate Exchanges and How to Make Them.* Boston, Mass.: Warren, Gorham, & Lamont, 1977.

ROULAC, STEPHEN. *Case Studies in Property Development.* Menlo Park, Calif.: Property Press, 1973. Part II.

STRATHMAN, JAMES G., ET AL. "Creative Financing Concessions in Real Estate Sales: Effects and Implications." *Housing Finance Review* 3 (April, 1984): 149–69.

TURNER, CARL. "Creative Financing Nets Million Dollar Purchase." *Farm and Land REALTOR* 30, 6 (June 1978): 9–10.

WILEY, ROBERT J. *Real Estate Investment.* New York: Ronald Press Co., 1977. Chapter 9.

19 | The Lenders and the Secondary Mortgage Market

QUESTIONS TO BE ANSWERED _____

1. Where does a person go to obtain a mortgage?
2. Where does the lender obtain the funds to loan?
3. What is the secondary mortgage market?

OBJECTIVES _____

When a student finishes the chapter, he or she should be able to

1. Identify and describe the sources of residential and commercial loans.
2. Explain the purpose of the secondary mortgage market.
3. Identify and contrast the institutions that operate in the secondary mortgage market.

4. Define and explain the purpose of points and a discount.

5. Explain the purpose of recent innovations in the secondary mortgage market such as mortgage-backed certificates, money market certificates of deposit, and the futures market.

6. Describe the impact that the federal and state governments have had on real estate financing.

7. Explain the nature and purpose of an advance.

8. Discuss the importance of recognizing the level of credit demand and supply in the local market.

IMPORTANT TERMS

Advance
Credit Union
Demand for Credit
Depository Institutions Dereg-
    ulation and Monetary Con-
    trol Act
Depository Institutions Dereg-
    ulation Committee
Discount
Disintermediation
Farmers Home Administration
    Insured (Direct) Loan
Federal Home Loan Bank
    Board
Federal Home Loan Mortgage
    Corporation (The Mortgage
    Corporation)

Federal Land Bank
Federal National Mortgage
    Association (FNMA)
Futures Market
Government National Mort-
    gage Association (GNMA)
Hedge
Intermediation
Mortgage-Backed Bonds
Mortgage Backed Certificates
Mortgage Banker
Mutual Savings Bank
Pass-Through Certificates
Point(s)
Savings and Loan Association
Secondary Mortgage Market
Supply of Credit

INTRODUCTION

The purpose of this chapter is to describe the sources of mortgage loans for the public and one source of mortgage money for lenders, the secondary mortgage market. In addition, recent innovations in the secondary mortgage market and the role of the federal and state governments are explained.

SOURCES OF RESIDENTIAL AND COMMERCIAL LOANS

Any prospective mortgagor can visit a number of *mortgage originators* to find a lender who will grant a loan on the property desired. A mortgage originator is a lender who makes residential and commercial loans directly to the public. Several types of organizations, as well as individuals, are mortgage originators.

Savings And Loan

As a group, the nation's 5,500 **savings and loan associations** are the single most important source of loan money for residential real estate. Exhibit 19-1 shows that savings and loans provided $475,797 million or 35.7 percent of the mortgage debt outstanding in 1979. Savings and loan associations are now found in all fifty states (in Louisiana they are called Homestead Associations and in Massachusetts Cooperative Banks). Most savings and loans are locally oriented, collecting their deposits and making loans within 100 miles of their offices. Specialization in limited geographic areas has been a major factor in their excellent record of making sound loans.

A savings and loan association can be either state or federally chartered. In the latter case, the word *Federal* appears in its name. A charter is an association's permit to operate. Federal charters are issued by the **Federal Home Loan Bank Board,** the savings and loan regulatory agency in Washington. A federally chartered association must be mutually owned (owned by its depositors), be a member of the Federal Home Loan Bank System (FHLBS), and carry Federal Savings and Loan Insurance Corporation (FSLIC) insurance.

An outgrowth of the 1930s, the FSLIC is an agency of the federal government that insures savers' deposits against the possibility that the funds will not be available whenever demanded. For this insurance, a savings and loan (S&L) association pays an insurance premium of 1/12 of one percent per year times its savings deposits.

EXHIBIT 19-1   Mortgage debt outstanding, 1983
Source: Federal Reserve Bulletin, Table A37.

Holder	Total of all property types (millions)	Percent distribution
All sources	$1,826,344^{r}	100.0
Commercial banks[1]	328,878^{r}	18.0
Manual savings banks	136,054^{r}	7.4
Savings and loan associations	493,432	27.0
Life insurance companies	151,599	8.3
Federal and related agencies	147,371	8.1
Mortgage pools or trusts[2]	285,021	15.6
Individual and others[3]	283,989	15.5

r = revised

[1]Includes loans held by nondeposit trust companies but not bank trust departments.

[2]Outstanding principal balances of mortgages backing securities insured or guaranteed by the agency indicated.

[3]Other holders include mortgage companies, real estate investment trusts, state and local credit agencies, state and local retirement funds, noninsured pension funds, credit unions, and U.S. agencies for which amounts are small or separate data not readily available.

The FHLBS was created during the Depression to strengthen weak laws regulating savings institutions. Today the FHLBS regulates the geographic loan area of a federally chartered S&L, sets maximum loan-to-value ratios, and limits the ratio of home loans to other types of loans. The FHLBS helps an individual S&L reach the nation's capital markets through its support of a secondary mortgage market (explained later in this chapter).

State-chartered associations can be mutually owned by depositors or can be corporations owned by stockholders. FHLB membership and FSLIC insurance are optional. Whether operating under a federal or a state charter, an association must be financially sound, have a sound lending policy, and maintain adequate amounts of cash and other liquid assets to meet depositors' withdrawal demands. The FHLBS and the FSLIC periodically audit the accounting books of members to ensure compliance with regulations and sound lending practices. State-chartered associations are subject to audit by state banking boards.

Mortgage Bankers

Mortgage bankers, also known as mortgage companies, operate under the laws of the state in which they are located. They act primarily as loan originators for various lending institutions including insurance companies, savings and loan associations, commercial banks, mutual savings banks, and sometimes individual investors. In many cases they have funds of their own.

A **mortgage banker** typically accumulates a number of mortgages and sells the package to an investor. The process begins by finding borrowers, qualifying them, preparing the necessary loan papers, and making the loans. Once the loans are packaged, they are sold for cash to a life insurance company, pension or trust fund, savings institution, or government agency. The mortgage banker is usually retained by the mortgage purchaser to service the loan by collecting the monthly payments and handling the insurance and property tax escrow, delinquencies, early payoffs, and mortgage releases.

Each potential investor sets the criteria that the mortgage banker must follow in compiling the package of loans. For example, an investor may seek diversity in the loan-to-value ratios by requiring that one third of the package be residential loans for more than 90 percent of the value, one third be loans for 90 percent of the value, and one-third be loans for 80 percent of the value. In addition, the investor may want all maturities to be similar and the dollar amount of each third to be approximately equal. A minimum dollar amount may be imposed on the whole package.

Mortgage bankers often take the form of mortgage companies that are locally oriented, originating loans within twenty-five or fifty miles of their offices. This orientation gives them a thorough understanding of their market, greatly aids in identifying sound loans, and facilitates loan servicing. For their efforts, mortgage bankers can receive one percent of the outstanding balance each year thereafter for servicing. On larger loans, the fee drops to 1/10 of one percent.

Mortgage banking is not limited to mortgage companies. Commercial banks, savings and loan associations, and mutual savings banks in active real estate areas often originate more real estate loans than they can hold themselves and sell them to other investors. Thus, they behave in a manner that is similar to a mortgage banker.

Mortgage Broker

A mortgage broker is an individual or firm who takes a mortgage application and attempts to find an investor who will purchase it. The broker is paid a commission by the investor for locating an acceptable investment. The mortgage application will contain pertinent facts about the applicant and his or her credit history. Typically, it includes a description of the property and the mortgage terms that the prospective borrower is offering.

Commercial Banks

The nation's 14,200 commercial banks handle much more of the country's money than the S&Ls. However, only one dollar in six goes to real estate lending. As a result, in total number of dollars, commercial banks rank second behind S&Ls in importance in real estate lending. By 1983, mortgage debt outstanding held by commercial banks amounted to $328,878 million, which was 18 percent of the total.

Commercial banks tend to emphasize short-term maturities because most of a bank's loan money comes from demand deposits (checking accounts) and a much smaller portion from savings and time deposits. Consequently, banks are particularly active in making loans to finance real estate construction because these loans have maturities of six months to three years. They are less inclined to hold long-term real estate loans; usually they offer maturities of five to fifteen years on such loans, rather than twenty-five to thirty years. There are exceptions to this general practice. In rural areas where longer term savings deposits make up a larger portion of a bank's funds, the town bank is a major source of long-term real estate loans. The other exception is the bank that makes twenty- and thirty-year loans but sells them rather than keeping them in its own investment portfolio, much like a mortgage banker.

Mutual Savings Banks

Important contributors to real estate credit in several states are the **mutual savings banks.** Mutual savings banks are found primarily in the northeastern part of the United States where they compete aggressively for the savings dollar. The states of Massachusetts, New York, and Connecticut account for 75 percent of the nation's total number of these banks.

As the word *mutual* implies, the depositors are the owners, and the "interest" they receive depends on the bank's success or failure in lending. To protect depositors, laws require mutual savings banks to place deposits in high-quality investments including sound real estate mortgage loans. Loan-to-value ratios can be 70 to 80 percent (higher for FHA and VA loans), maturities are of twenty to thirty years, and as a rule loans are made within a 100-mile radius of the bank. Real estate loans currently account for three of every four loan dollars at mutual savings banks. In 1983, mortgage debt outstanding at mutual savings banks amounted to $136,054

THE DECISION TO FINANCE THE TRANSACTION

million or 7.4 percent of the total. Mutual savings banks are chartered and controlled by state regulatory agencies.

Credit Unions

A **credit union** is a state or federally chartered organization of people with a common bond who pool their savings and make loans to members. Credit unions typically are established at a place of employment where the members are employees. A federally chartered credit union with assets of $2,000,000 or more, or any other federal credit union with prior written consent of the administration, can originate loans secured by first liens on residential real property, with maturities in excess of twelve years and not exceeding thirty years within the limitations of written policies adopted by the board of directors, provided that specific guidelines are followed. These may vary with time.

Pension Funds

Pension fund assets represent a large potential source of funds for real estate investments. Historically, these assets have not been placed in real estate because of the risk, but this trend is changing. The newer Government National Mortgage Association (GNMA) pass-through securities (discussed later in this chapter) provide an excellent outlet for pension funds, since they have two characteristics that a pension fund investment must possess: (1) safety of the principal and (2) predictability of the return. In future years, as pension fund managers are able to better discriminate among types of risks among various uses of property, they will most likely move more funds into real estate investments. One recent source suggests that commercial mortgages and sale-leaseback arrangements could be attractive investments for funds.[1] Another points out the advantages of a pension fund manager using a wraparound mortgage.[2]

Individuals

Individuals are sometimes a source of cash loans on residential real estate. Generally, maturities on loans made by individuals are shorter than those obtainable from institutional lenders and interest rates are competitive. Individuals are particularly helpful in granting short-term loans extending up to five years. In some cities, persons can be found who specialize in making or buying second and third mortgage loans with a maximum of ten-year maturities.

Direct Loans from a Quasi-Public Agency or a Public Agency

A borrower can request a direct loan from the Farmers Home Administration or the Federal Land Bank.

Farmers Home Administration insured (direct) loan   The FmHA has two programs to benefit potential borrowers. The first is the guaranteed loan that is made and serviced by a private lender and guaranteed by the FmHA up to a maximum percentage. The second is the insured loan that is made and serviced directly by the FmHA. Typically, these loans are made to lower-income families in the rural areas, who may not be eligible for credit from any other source.

The FmHA approves loans for a variety of purposes, including farm ownership, and gives technical management assistance to applicants who will operate family farms. Loans can be used to finance structures or farming enterprises that are consistent with local antipollution or environmental quality standards and regulations.

Each farm ownership loan is tailored to the individual borrower's needs. The lender or the Farmers Home Administration county supervisor helps the borrower analyze his or her situation, determine available resources, and plan how these resources plus those obtained by the loan can best be used. Technical assistance is provided to help the borrower solve problems that arise in making major adjustments in operations and in adopting improved business practices.

The maximum term is forty years and the interest rate is computed on the unpaid balance. A borrower can make large payments in years of high income to build up a reserve to keep the loan in good standing during years of low income. Each borrower is expected to refinance the unpaid balance of the loan when it becomes financially feasible to rely solely on commercial sources. Farm ownership borrowers are required to maintain their property and to pay taxes and property insurance premiums when due.

Federal Land Bank

The Farm Credit System was established by the Farm Credit Act to provide credit designed to satisfy the highly specialized needs of farmers and their marketing, supply, and business service operations. The system is composed of twelve Farm Credit Districts, each of which has a Federal Land Bank, Federal Intermediate Credit Bank, and Bank for Cooperatives located in the same city. The **Federal Land Banks** offer long-term mortgages on farm real estate. The Intermediate Credit Banks provide financing for the local production credit associations. The Banks for Cooperatives make loans to local farmers' cooperatives.

The operations of the Federal Land Banks (FLB) were expanded in the revision of the Farm Credit Act of 1971 and an FLB now can make nonfarm rural housing loans, finance rural business, grant a loan up to 85 percent of the appraised value, and make more decisions locally. Loans cannot be made in cities or villages of more than 2,500 population. In addition, the mortgages are variable rate loans.

Life Insurance Companies

Life insurance companies were making loans for real estate purchases as long ago as the 1800s. Such loans are advantageous to life insurance companies for several reasons: (1) The loans purchased from various sections of the country allow a company to take advantage of different growth rates; (2) The rates of return on real estate investments are attractive in comparison with those of competing investments; (3) The real estate loans give diversification to the company's portfolio.

Life insurance companies provide both residential and commercial funds to borrowers. They enter the secondary market directly and purchase and sell mortgages, and they negotiate loans directly with the borrower through their district offices.

A life insurance company is one of the best sources for commercial loans. A prospective borrower should contact the company directly to obtain a copy of its application guidelines.

Real Estate Investment Trusts and Syndicates

REITs and syndicates are sources of funds for loans. Both are discussed in Chapter 17.

CYCLES IN THE REAL ESTATE LOAN MARKET

The real estate loan market is characterized by cycles of activity. The most evident cause of these cycles since World War II has been a relationship among short-term interest rates, the availability of money for mortgages, and new construction. This relationship has been inverse, that is, rising short-term interest rates cause the availability of money for mortgages to decrease, which decreases the amount of new construction in the form of housing starts, and vice versa.

Restricted Interest Rates

Money for real estate loans has been scarce during certain periods of the business cycle because the lenders who accept deposits and convert them into loans have been restricted on the maximum interest rates they can pay on savings deposits. Regulation Q, administered by the Federal Reserve Board, controlled the maximum interest rates that commercial banks could pay on savings deposits and certificates of deposit. The maximum rate the savings and loans could pay was controlled by a committee that derived its authority from the Stephens Act of 1966. Control over rates of interest on savings deposits was given in 1980 to the Depository Institutions Deregulation Committee (discussed later). This Committee phased out this interest rate control.

At various stages of the business cycle, the interest rates paid on competing investments rose above the maximum interest rates that the savings institutions could pay. Consequently, the savers transferred their deposits into competing investments. When the business cycle caused interest rates on other investments to decline, the interest rate set on the thrift institutions again became competitive and the inflow of deposits provided funds for real estate loans.

Disintermediation and intermediation An *inflow of deposits* caused by deposit interest rates that are competitive with rates paid on competing investments is called **interme-**

diation. An *outflow of deposits* caused by deposit interest rates that are lower than rates paid on competing investments is called **disintermediation.**[3]

During the 1970s, disintermediation became so severe that many savings and loans were experiencing small or negative profits and were forced to reduce their lending activities. To provide relief, the Congress passed a series of acts. New federal laws and new regulations were attempting to accomplish the following objectives:

1. *Elimination of the maximum ceilings placed on interest rates that the lenders could pay to attract deposits.* Giving the lenders the authority to pay a variable rate reduced the depositor's incentive to withdraw the deposits and transfer them to a competing investment.

2. *Creation of a set of new mortgages that would allow the lender to vary the interest charge to the homeowner to reflect changing interest rates in the economy.* Collecting additional interest creates additional profits for the lender.

3. *Creation of new mortgages that have monthly payment plans more closely related to the borrower's income.* The purpose is to qualify more new first-time homebuyers, which causes an increase in the number of new potential mortgages.

4. *Creation of new securities backed by pools of home loans which can be sold to large investors such as the pension funds.* These sales by lenders attract additional capital into the home finance industry.

5. *Establishing new types of liabilities such as NOW (negotiable order of withdrawl) accounts,* similar to checking accounts, *and new types of assets such as trust accounts to allow lenders to attract additional deposits and earn additional profits.*

Several of these federal acts include individual statute authority and sweeping legislation such as the DIDMCA of 1980, the Garn-St. Germain Act of 1982, and the Housing and Urban Recovery Act of 1983.

Sources of Loans and the Market Cycle

At various stages of the loan market cycle, changes occur in (1) the best source for obtaining a particular loan and (2) the types of loans in which the lenders have traditionally placed their funds. For example, the savings and loans have always ranked residential loans as first priority and commercial loans as second priority. When disintermediation occurs and loan money becomes scarce, these lenders will reduce the number of commercial loans made and tighten the criteria for awarding residential loans. Thus, savings and loans are sources of residential and commercial loans at one stage of the cycle but offer only residential loans during periods of disintermediation.

The same situation applies to the other lenders. Commercial banks are good sources of short-term loans such as construction loans and short-term commercial loans. However, during scarce-money stages of the cycle, they also reduce significantly the amount of funds channeled into commercial loans.

Mortgage bankers package residential loans for potential investors and attempt to place commercial money into worthwhile projects for any investor, but primarily for life insurance companies. During periods of rising interest rates, the investors may not be as willing to purchase commercial projects.

The lender's priority in placing loan funds might be residential first and commercial second, but the loans available in the second category can be reduced to zero during certain periods of the market cycle. During these stages of restrictive lending, a potential borrower should examine all sources of loans to determine which potential lenders are making the type of loan desired.

THE INSTITUTIONS IN THE SECONDARY MORTGAGE MARKET

Any real estate lender who accepts savings deposits, such as a savings and loan, commercial bank, or mutual savings bank, can acquire funds to loan from both savings deposits and the secondary mortgage market. A savings and loan has a third option of borrowing from its Federal Home Loan Bank. Also, a mortgage banker can acquire loan funds from the secondary mortgage market, life insurance companies, or individuals.

The Uncertain Level of Savings Deposits

The real estate loan business is directly influenced by the flow of savings deposits to and from the lending institutions that make real estate loans. Historically, savings and loans have relied heavily on depositors' funds as the major source of money for residential loans. If deposits increase in a particular year, a higher volume of loans can be made and/or higher L/V loans can be made. When deposits decrease in a given year, the volume of loans tends to decrease. Thus, S&Ls need to attract savings depositors to increase the availability of residential loan money. In addition, these institutions need a guarantee that the deposits will not be withdrawn within the near future.

The level of interest rates on competing investments has greatly influenced the volume of deposits in the savings and loans through time. During periods when rates on competing investments are greater than the rates the S&Ls can pay, deposits have been withdrawn, the number of home loans has declined, and new construction has decreased. The opposite pattern has occurred when the competing rates declined.

To attract deposits at all stages of the market cycle and to hold these deposits, heavy penalties can be placed on savings withdrawn early. Second, the S&Ls have started issuing a special certificate of deposit that pays a rate of interest tied to the most recent U.S. Treasury Bill rate. Third, the lenders issue mortgage-backed securities to attract cash that can be converted into new loans.

The Secondary Mortgage Market

The housing sector of the economy is able to compete for funds with other investment outlets through the **secondary mortgage market.** The institutions that participate in the secondary mortgage market sell bonds, and in some cases stocks, to attract money that they can use to purchase the loan originated by the local lenders. By paying competitive rates of return on the bonds, these institutions compete for money and channel it into housing, thus stimulating the housing market.

In addition, the secondary mortgage market provides mortgage money to economically deprived regions where housing credit may not be available. One institution, the Government National Mortgage Association, has a program designed for these types of loans.

The secondary mortgage market is composed of two groups of investors—the buyers and the sellers. The buyers purchase mortgages and financial securities to hold for the yield on the investment. The sellers offer the mortgages and securities for sale to obtain cash. The buyers are primarily federal and quasi-public agencies that supply funds to the lenders at the local level. The sellers are primarily local lenders who have originated the loans. This section describes the buyers, whose objective is to provide an orderly supply of credit for use in mortgages through all stages of the market cycle.

The secondary mortgage market is used by local lenders to acquire new funds to loan to new customers. For example, consider a savings and loan that conducts a campaign to attract new depositors and receives $0.5 million in new funds. Within the following month, the institution receives twenty new loan applications in the amount of $50,000 each. The lender can accept the first ten loan applications received and turn down the others, or it can accept the first ten, sell the mortgages in the secondary mortgage market, and recover funds that can be reloaned to most of the second ten applicants. Thus, the secondary mortgage market enables the local lender to service its customers, regain loanable funds, and stimulate the local housing market.

The buying side of the secondary mortgage market supplies the cash to purchase the loans offered for sale by the local lenders. The institutions that participate in this market frequently and influence its direction significantly are described hereafter.

Federal National Mortgage Association (FNMA)   The **Federal National Mortgage Association** (FNMA) was incorporated in 1938 under the National Housing Act to provide a secondary mortgage market for originators of residential loans. FNMA borrowed funds entirely from the U.S. Treasury and used them to puchase loans made by approved lenders. In 1954, "Fannie Mae" was reorganized and charged with three major functions:

1. The Special Assistance Function of designing special programs to assist the housing market where unfavorable economic conditions prevail
2. The Management and Liquidation Function for servicing and disposing of the mortgage portfolio
3. The Secondary Mortgage Market Function of purchasing and reselling home mortgages originated by its approved lenders

In addition, the FNMA issued nonvoting preferred stock that was purchased by the U.S. Treasury and nonvoting common stock that was purchased by its approved lenders. This transaction made the FNMA a quasi-public agency that is privately owned by stock ownership and publicly controlled by Congress. In 1968, the first two functions were transferred to the new Government National Mortgage Association created within the Department of Housing and Urban Development, and the third function was left with the FNMA. The FNMA can raise capital funds by marketing its own bonds.

The primary purpose of the secondary mortgage market is to provide an even flow of credit to residential borrowers during all stages of the market cycle. FNMA attempts to accomplish this objective by requesting that its approved lenders participate in its Free Market System auction. An approved lender can submit a competitive bid for mortgage funds or a noncompetitive bid. The competitive bid requests a predetermined dollar amount at a yield that must compete with those yields submitted by other approved lenders. A noncompetitive bid requests an amount of funds at a yield that is the weighted average of all the yields in competitive bids. This option is useful to a lender that wants to sell part or all of its mortgages regardless of the yield. Minimum and maximum amounts are set for each type of bid. A typical commitment given by the FNMA to honor an acceptable bid is four months although commitments can be larger for condominiums, planned unit developments, and approved subdivisions. The lender must deliver the mortgages within this time period to obtain the required funds. The FNMA charges a fee of 0.5 percent of the amount requested as a charge for its obligation to purchase.

Government National Mortgage Association (GNMA)   "Ginnie Mae" was created as an agency within the Department of Housing and Urban Affairs in 1968 and was assigned the two functions described heretofore. The **Government National Mortgage Association** actively purchases mortgages at yields below the market rates and resells them through competitive bidding to investors at a discount, which enables the investors to obtain a reasonable yield. The difference is paid by the federal government, which supports selected types of housing and markets. In 1974, the GNMA was given authority to buy and sell certain conventionally financed mortgages. This agency obtains its funds from the U.S. Treasury by selling its own securities in the market.

The GNMA has conducted two recent programs to expand the available supply of residential mortgage credit. First, various *tandem programs* have been conducted in cooperation with the FNMA. The GNMA makes commitments to buy mortgages at less than the market yields and sells them later to FNMA or another investor at market yields. Any loss that may occur is borne by the GNMA. These programs are an attempt by the government to stimulate rehabilitation or construction of housing for low-income and moderate-income families.

A second program is the promotion of *mortgage-backed securities*. A lender can pool residential mortgages with similar characteristics and ask the GNMA for its guarantee to be placed on the pool. This guarantee assures the buyer that the principal and interest will be paid. One type of security is called the *pass-through*, because the issuing lender passes through to the investor its proportionate share of principal and interest from the pooled mortgages. Delinquencies are made up by the issuing lender and collected later when the payments are brought up to date. Also, a *bond-*

type security (mortgage-backed bond) can be issued whereby only the interest is paid in periodic payments and the principal is paid at maturity. (Additional details of these securities are given in the next section.)

Both types of securities are designed to attract funds from the capital markets. Historically, a mortgage has been an unattractive investment for an individual, a corporation, and the pension funds. Now a local lender can package these illiquid assets, ask for a GNMA guarantee, and sell a financial security backed by the pool. Thus, the illiquid mortgage asset is turned into cash through the GNMA security.

Federal Home Loan Mortgage Corporation (FHLMC) The **Federal Home Loan Mortgage Corporation,** sometimes called "Freddie Mac," was created by Congress in 1970 to serve as a secondary mortgage market corporation controlled by the Federal Home Loan Bank Board. The Mortgage Corporation purchases mortgages from federally insured institutions and qualified mortgage bankers through a competitive and noncompetitive bidding system. An approved lender can submit a competitive bid soliciting a certain amount of funds at a yield that is competitive with those of other bidders. Alternatively, a lender can bid noncompetitively, requesting that a specific amount of funds be provided at a yield that is equal to the weighted average yield in the competitive auction. Lenders can ask for funds to purchase mortgages that they will deliver immediately or those with a forward commitment that will give the lender time to originate the loan.

The FHLMC obtains its operating funds from the sale of its bonds and participation certificates, which are undivided interests in pools of mortgages.

Life insurance companies, savings and loans, real estate investment trusts, mortgage bankers, commercial banks, credit unions All of these groups can purchase a mortgage from a lender and hold it or resell it to another investor.

Future role Exhibit 19-2 shows the mortgage debt outstanding in one- to four-family units at the end of 1977 and 1983. The largest growth has been in the FHLMC and GNMA debt because of the popularity of the mortgage-backed security.

The use of the GNMA guarantee to provide backing for the new pass-through security will continue to increase. The lenders want to attract additional loan funds, and this security is a relatively risk-free method. In addition, the institutions in the secondary market will be essential in times of disintermediation when the lenders have an outflow of deposits.

RECENT INNOVATIONS IN THE SECONDARY MORTGAGE MARKET

Several recent innovations within the secondary mortgage market are important to the lender, the borrower, and the investor.

Mortgage-backed Certificates

Mortgage-backed certificates are obligations sold by an issuer to an investor which are backed by a pool of similar mortgages. The certificates may be *bonds* or *passthroughs.*

EXHIBIT 19-2   Mortgage debt outstanding, 1-4 family units
Source: Federal Reserve Bulletin, Table A37.

Holder	1977 total (millions)	1983 total (millions)	% Change
GNMA	$ 1,548	−630	−60.6
FNMA	28,504	−78,256	+174.5
FHLMC	2,738	−7,576	+176.7
Individuals & Others[1]	72,115	−185,270	+156.9
Mortgage Pools or Trusts[2]			
GNMA	43,555	−155,801	+257.7
FHCMC	5,621	−57,206	+917.7
FNMA	11,397	−25,121	+120.9

r = revised

[1]Other holders include mortgage companies, real estate investment trusts, state and local credit agencies, state and local retirement funds, noninsured pension funds, credit unions, and U.S. agencies for which either amounts are small or separate data are not readily available.

[2]Outstanding principal balances of mortgages backing securities insured or guaranteed by the agency indicated.

Bonds   **Mortgage-backed bonds** are the direct obligation of the issuer secured by the pool of similar mortgages.[4] The bond carries a maturity of usually five to twelve years, and the issuer guarantees the principal and interest payments to the purchaser. It is a method whereby a lender can use home loans with low interest rates to attract new funds that can be invested at higher rates. For example, a lender can pool a large number of home loans that are paying an interest rate of, say, 7 percent, issue a bond that pays 8.5 percent, and reloan the new funds at 9.5 percent in home loans.

Two points must be remembered with respect to the bonds: (1) They are direct obligations of the issuer whose commitment to the investor is that the interest payments will be paid on time and the principal will be returned; (2) The issuer typically must have a large number of home loans that can be used to satisfy the bond rating services that give the bonds an investment rating.

Pass-throughs   Pass-throughs are certificates whereby the issuer simply serves as a conduit to pass through to the investor any interest and principal payments made by the mortgagor.[5] Each purchaser of a **pass-through certificate** is issued a certificate that entitles the holder to a share of the principal and interest payments made by the underlying pool of mortgages. The lender makes no guarantee for these payments.

The most popular type of pass-through certificate in recent years has been the GNMA pass-through created by the Housing and Development Act. The GNMA was given the authority to issue a guarantee on a pool of federally insured or guaranteed mortgages issued by a private lender. The investor benefits in two ways: (1) The underlying pool of mortgages is insured or guaranteed against borrower default by the FHA, VA, or FmHA. (2) The GNMA guarantee placed on the pool guarantees the interest and principal payments to the investor in the case of default.

Futures Market[6]

In 1976, the FHLB Board allowed all federally chartered savings and loans to participate in the GNMA **futures market** that was created in 1975. The regulations allow these lenders to make fixed-rate forward commitments to builders and hedge them for a maximum of eighteen months to protect the commitment against adverse changes in the market rate of interest. Also, these lenders are allowed to estimate future cash transactions and commit favorable current interest rates in the futures market to protect operating margins against adverse interest rate fluctuations.

Savings and loans can **hedge** in the market but not speculate. *Hedging* is taking a position in the futures market that is equal to but opposite the position taken in the cash market so that any interest losses are exactly offset by capital gains and vice versa. A speculative transaction, in contrast, has no offsetting current cash transaction.

Consider the situation where Thrifty Savings and Loan commits to loan a builder a predetermined amount at 12.0 percent in twelve months. But assume that in the next twelve months the interest rate increases to 12.5 percent. The lender is losing interest in the intervening year that it could have earned had the commitment not been given. To protect itself from losses due to unexpected fluctuations in the interest rate during the period between commitment and the granting of the loan, the association enters the futures market when it gives the loan commitment to the builder and commits to sell GNMA future contract(s) in one year at a predetermined price. The association expects the prices of these contract(s) to fall if interest rates rise and they can be purchased in the future at a lower price than the commitment price to sell. Thus, the lender earns a capital gain on the future contract(s) that can offset all or part of the interest loss. If the lender suspected that the market interest rates would decrease and the builder would not use this loan commitment, an opposite transaction would have been used.

Relevance to the Homebuyer

The purpose of the recent innovations in the secondary mortgage market is to enable the institutions granting home mortgages, primarily the savings and loans, to (1) attract new deposits by competing with other investment outlets, and (2) protect interest earnings. They have had a major effect on the condition of the housing sector of the economy and the ability of the potential homebuyer to acquire a mortgage.

One recent report issued by the GNMA states that more than 75 percent of all FHA insured loans being closed used funds raised by the GNMA guaranteed obligations. In addition, the *Wall Street Journal*[7] has reported that the money market certificates of deposit have contributed significantly to decreasing the outflow of deposits from the savings and loans during periods typically characterized by disintermediation. Furthermore, the option of the savings and loans to hedge enables the institutions to make long-term commitments that might not have been made without the futures market. The ultimate effect of these three innovations has been to assist the homebuyer in acquiring mortgage money.

THE DECISION TO FINANCE THE TRANSACTION

POINTS AND DISCOUNT

A local lender or an institution in the secondary mortgage market may occasionally charge a seller of property or a new borrower points as a requirement for approving and/or purchasing the loan. One **point** is defined as one percent of the mortgage balance. The purpose of this charge is to increase the return to the lender on the mortgage. Points are discussed in this chapter since they are caused by demand and supply conditions in the mortgage market.

Administered Interest Rates

The VA and FmHA announce the interest rate that a lender can charge on loans they insure or guarantee. But the prevailing interest rate on a conventional loan, which is determined by the forces of supply and demand, may be higher than the interest rate allowed by one of these agencies. Therefore, to make up the interest lost by giving the funds to a customer under these programs, the lender assesses the seller an extra interest charge at closing in the form of points.

Typically, the lender determines the interest lost over a twelve-year period, expecting this period to be the appoximate length of the loan before it is refinanced. This amount is divided by the mortgage amount required, and the result is the total number of points to be assessed.

The National Housing Act of 1954 requires that these points be paid by the *seller* on loans carrying a guarantee or insurance given by the VA or the FmHA. In a conventional loan, they can be paid by anyone.

Usury Laws

A state usury law can cause lenders to assess points. For example, the usury law in Arkansas in 1980 was 10 percent with a severe penalty for violators. However, the market rate on mortgage loans rose to a range of 12.0 to 13.0 percent. To make a loan to a customer, the lender would be required to charge an interest rate of less than 10 percent and would need to assess one of the parties the necessary points to make up the interest lost. Even the assessment of points may not be allowed in states that have ruled that points are interest and must be entered into the calculation of the total interest paid on the loan. In recent years, various state legislatures have either established higher usury rates for loans by type of loan or indexed the usury rate to a financial market rate.

Discount

The **discount** is the difference between the mortgage amount and the amount the lender actually pays or loans. For example, consider a customer who requests a $40,000 loan that the lender agrees to grant if 5 points are paid at the closing. The lender is actually loaning only $38,000 because the seller or borrower is paying $2,000, which is given back at the closing to make up the full $40,000. If the lender is reselling this loan into the secondary mortgage market, the market may have determined the points necessary to make this purchase competitive. The secondary mortgage market purchaser may have offered the loan originator $38,000 for the $40,000 mortgage. Thus, the lender had to make up the $2,000 by charging the points.

Causes of Points

The basic cause of the lender's need to charge points is the *interaction of credit demand and supply in the economy.* The basic *cause* is the level of demand and supply, and the *effect* is the level of administered interest in comparison with the interest rate set by the market. For example, the level of **supply of credit** and **demand for credit** might determine an interest rate of 10 percent. The responsible authorities react to this rate by establishing a rate on VA and FmHA loans at 9.5, which causes the lenders to charge points. Points might not be needed if the lender were allowed to charge the borrower the interest rate determined by the market.

Influence on the Transaction

Points are often the single largest cost for closing a transaction. They can become so high at times when the market interest rate is high that they cause the transaction to fail. Buyers commonly view points as prohibitive and not worth paying because no benefits are received except an income tax deduction. A purchaser may very well postpone a purchase until the shortage of funds and the points decline.

Loan Origination Fee

The lender may assess the mortgagor a mortgage-servicing fee of one to two percent of the mortgage amount to cover necessary expenses in processing the mortgage application. This amount is a one-time charge that is paid when the mortgage is signed and is a tax deduction for the mortgagor.

ADVANCES

Advances are not a part of the secondary mortgage market but should be described in conjunction with the market because they do provide a source of additional funds to some lenders. All federally chartered savings and loans have the option of borrowing funds from their district Federal Home Loan Bank to protect them from cash shortages. This loan, called an **advance,** may take several forms and may be subject to guidelines unique to a particular district bank. Common types of advance include the following arrangements:[8]

> ☐ *Fixed rate and term:* An individual savings and loan can apply for a loan for a maximum term of ten years. The rate charged is the lower of the rate on the date of commitment or the rate on the date of disbursement. Usually there is a prepayment penalty. No amortization may be required for

the first five years. The bank's agreement to the loan must be used within ninety days.

- □ *Line of credit:* A ninty-day line of credit may be approved for a one-year period. The lender can borrow for ninety days at a time, and the total amount of credit remains valid for one year. There is no prepayment penalty and all payments restore the credit, as in the case of a consumer revolving charge account.
- □ *Special:* A ninty-day advance may be approved with an interest rate that is fixed at the level on the date of disbursement. Prepayments are permitted without penalty at any time. Funds must be taken by the individual lender once the commitment is approved.

CREDIT DEMAND AND SUPPLY

Anyone involved in the real estate loan market must remember that it is subject to cycles. The broker, attorney, contractor, builder, appraiser, and loan officer participate in the market at one moment in time when the funds available for a loan may be plentiful or scarce. A real estate transaction becomes impossible if lenders refuse the loan application. The brokers do not sell; the contractors do not buy appliances, carpets, and paint; the attorneys have no abstracts and deeds to prepare; the appraisers receive no requests to estimate value; and the loan officers cannot expand their loans when real estate funds are not available. Consequently, a consumer must be aware of the condition of the local real estate credit market to evaluate accurately a future course of action.

An examination of current and potential demand and supply for credit gives a possible picture of a surplus or shortage and the possible influence upon mortgage interest rates. The essential question is whether the economy will be able to generate enough funds to satisfy private demands for credit.

Projections for the demand and supply of credit have been done by one source, and the results are shown in Exhibits 19-3 and 19-4. Exhibit 19-3 shows the projected demand and credit supply as a percent of GNP. Exhibit 19-4 shows projections in billions of dollars. The underlying figures reveal that total domestic nonfinancial credit as a percent of GNP has remained reasonably constant from the period 1960 through 1980. Using this critical relationship and others necessary to make projections, the results reveal that domestic nonfinancial demand for credit will steadily increase faster than the domestic nonfinancial supply of credit.

The implication is that interest rates for mortgages could remain at reasonably high levels for the next two to three years. This assumes that the basic assumptions remain valid.

Relationship between the interest rate and demand   The relationship between the interest rate paid for the use of credit and the quantity of credit demanded is generally thought to be inverse. The higher the interest rate, the less credit will be demanded.

Relationship between the interest rate and supply   The relationship between the interest received and the quantity of credit supplied is thought to be direct. The higher the

EXHIBIT 19-3 Projected Credit and Demand Relative to GNP

Source: Bernard M. Markstein, "Crowding Out? An Analysis of Credit Supply and Demand," *Mortgage Banker* 44 (June 1984), p. 36.

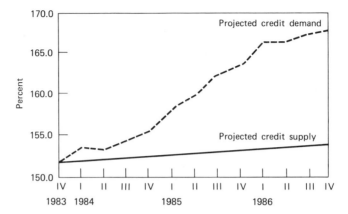

interest received, the greater the amount of credit supplied. Some researchers might argue that credit availability becomes tighter as the interest rate rises, and eventually new loans are restricted at high interest rates. The lenders require larger down payments and better credit terms; these factors combine to ration what credit is available.

CURRENT FACTORS INFLUENCING THE MORTGAGE MARKET

The purpose of this section is to identify briefly several of the factors that are currently influencing the direction of the mortgage market.

EXHIBIT 19-4 Credit Supply and Demand

Source: Bernard M. Markstein, "Crowding Out? An Analysis of Credit Supply and Demand," *Mortgage Banker* 44 (June 1984), p. 37.

Date	Total domestic nonfinancial credit supply	Total domestic nonfinancial credit demand	Supply-demand
1984.1	5348	5397	− 49
1984.2	5469	5510	− 41
1984.3	5602	5675	− 73
1984.4	5731	5835	−104
1985.1	5861	6065	−204
1985.2	5975	6234	−259
1985.3	6093	6457	−364
1985.4	6222	6643	−421
1986.1	6378	6918	−540
1986.2	6555	7105	−550
1986.3	6731	7340	−609
1986.4	6917	7562	−645

THE DECISION TO FINANCE THE TRANSACTION

Fiscal Policy of the Federal Government

The federal government's *overall level of expenditures* influences the demand for credit and goods and affects personal income, consumption, savings, prices, and interest rates. *Taxation policy* and the treatment of interest payments, capital gains, and tax credits influence the consumer's incentive to invest. The impact of this level of government on real estate mortgage markets is enormous and the list of specific actions is lengthy.

Monetary Policy of the Federal Reserve

Of critical importance to the real estate mortgage markets is the decision by the Federal Reserve Board to fight inflation by tightening the money supply and raising interest rates. Rising interest rates in other sectors of the economy can contribute to disintermediation in the thrift industry, which influences the amount of money available to be loaned.

Will the Saver Be Subsidized?

One method of attracting deposits to a savings and loan is to pay the saver a *competitive* interest rate that holds the impact of inflation constant. The saver who receives a competitive rate has no incentive to transfer funds during periods of disintermediation. Important questions to be resolved are, What rate should be paid? and What is the source of this additional funding?

State Usury Limits

Some states have a low usury limit on mortgage loans with a severe penalty for violation. How can this limit be offset to avoid a significant diversion of mortgage money away from these states during periods when the market interest rate is higher than the limit? One solution is to exempt FHA and VA loans from state usury laws. Another is to sue the state for violation of federal antitrust laws to allow the free movement of funds from state to state as interstate commerce. Still another solution is to allow federal banks the right to charge some predetermined percent more than the federal discount rate. Also, the state legislature could peg the usury rate to a financial market index or simply raise the rate.

Depository Institutions Deregulation and Monetary Control Act

On March 31, 1980, President Carter signed this act into law. Viewed by some as one of the most sweeping financial reform acts of federal legislation since the 1930s, it contained several components that directly affected the individual lender and the secondary mortgage market. Chapter 16 contained a discussion on two other components of this act that pertain to (a) new real estate lending authority and (b) a permanent federal override of state usury ceilings. Much of this discussion was taken from Richard G. Marcis and Dale Riordan, "The Savings and Loan Industry in the 1980s," *Federal Home Loan Bank Board Journal,* Vol. 13 (May 1980), pages 2–15. Relevant additional issues in this act are addressed below.

- □ *Nationwide Negotiable Order of Withdrawal (NOW accounts).* By January 1, 1981, thrift institutions were authorized to issue NOW accounts that were similar to checking accounts issued by commercial banks.
- □ *New consumer lending powers.* Savings and loans were allowed to invest up to twenty percent of their assets in consumer loans, corporate debt, bankers acceptances, and commercial paper.
- □ *Increase in FDIC limits to $100,000.* The insurance coverage on each account was raised to $100,000.
- □ *Mutual capital certificates.* Federally chartered savings and loans were allowed to issue a certificate that paid dividends rather than interest so that the certificates would be considered as equity. These could be used to raise funds.
- □ *Increased investment authority in service corporation.* A federally chartered savings and loan was allowed to raise from one percent to three percent the percentage of assets that it placed in a community investment or development service corporation.
- □ *Gradual phaseout of Regulation Q.* Perhaps the most controversial feature of this act was the gradual phaseout of Regulation Q over a period of six years. (Under this regulation, maximums were established on the rates that could be paid on all types of time deposits.)

Evaluation   This act made the lenders who relied upon time deposits for loans much more competitive for the consumer's savings dollar. In addition, the NOW accounts and the new consumer loan authority made the savings and loans much more competitive with the commercial banks for the short-term consumer loan business.

The impact from phasing out Regulation Q has been debated for many years. The prevailing argument appears to be that the lender's bidding for the consumer's savings dollars kept the rates as low as they possibly could while simultaneously allowing the lender to pay whatever market rate was necessary to compete for the deposits. The result was that disintermediation and intermediation were greatly reduced since no artificial controls existed on deposit rates after six years.

CHAPTER SUMMARY

A potential borrower can obtain residential and commercial loans from several sources—the savings and loans, commercial banks, mutual savings banks, mortgage bankers, life insurance companies, real estate investment trusts, syndicates, credit unions, and individuals. Many of these sources should be pursued within the region to determine whether they have funds available, their lending policies are acceptable to the borrower, and their guidelines for applying for the loan can be easily satisfied.

The secondary mortgage market is composed of institutions that purchase mortgages from lenders dealing directly with the public. In addition, they buy and sell mortgages among themselves. Their combined activities serve to channel mortgage funds into the housing sector and enable local lenders to recover their loan funds. Recent innovations such as mortgage-backed certificates, money market certificates of deposit, and the futures market allow the local lenders to remain competitive in attracting deposits and to protect their interest earnings on loans.

A lender may charge points to originate a mortgage. Points are additional interest typically collected at the closing to increase the lender's rate of return or yield on the loan.

If a federally chartered savings and loan does not desire to use the secondary mortgage market, it has the option of seeking an advance from its Federal Home Loan District Bank. This loan can be used for day-to-day operations or loans and is subject to the restrictions imposed by the district bank.

The federal government and the state governments have exercised a tremendous influence on the real estate financing market and will continue to do so as long as the public views the single-family unit as ideal for all families.

All participants in the real estate financing market should be aware of the regional conditions influencing credit demand and supply. Any participant must react and be subject to the local conditions, which may not be the same as conditions at the national level.

Review Questions

1. Describe briefly the role of the following in providing residential and commercial loan funds:
   - (a) savings and loans
   - (b) commercial banks
   - (c) mutual savings banks
   - (d) life insurance companies
   - (e) Veterans Administration
   - (f) mortgage bankers
   - (g) credit unions
   - (h) Federal Land Bank
   - (i) Farmers Home Administration

2. What is the secondary mortgage market? Does it have any relationship to a second mortgage? What?

3. Identify the institutions that operate within the secondary mortgage market and explain their role.

4. Explain the purpose of each of the following:
   - (a) mortgage-backed bond
   - (b) pass-through certificate
   - (c) money market certificate of deposit
   - (d) futures market
   - (e) a hedge

5. What is a point? Why is it charged? Who must pay points on a federally

insured or guaranteed mortgage? On a conventional loan? What is the purpose of a discount?

6. Explain the purpose of an advance.

7. Have the federal and state governments exercised much influence in the real estate financing sector? How? Why?

8. Who are the largest demanders of credit in our economy? The largest suppliers?

9. Why should a participant in the real estate loan market always examine the current conditions of credit demand and supply within the local region? Are national conditions always identical to the local conditions? Why or why not?

Discussion Questions

1. Should a prospective borrower check with all of the sources of credit before submitting an application? If so, isn't this approach extremely time consuming?

2. What do you think would be the state of the housing market in the United States without the secondary mortgage market?

3. Recent innovations in the secondary mortgage market were created in response to a need. What was that need? Were the innovations a treatment of the "symptom" or a "cause"?

4. Should points continue to be paid as a part of the cost of closing or is a better alternative to allow the lender to charge whatever interest rate is necessary in relation to the market?

5. Can you think of any reasons why a federally chartered savings and loan would *never* feel a need to use the secondary mortgage market *or* ask for an advance?

6. Can you think of any reasons why a federally chartered savings and loan would use the secondary mortgage market exclusively? Use advances exclusively?

7. Should the federal and state governments continue to have an active role in the real estate financing sector of the economy?

Notes

1. Peter C. Aldrich and King Upton, "Pension Funds Finally Move into Real Estate," *Real Estate Review,* Vol. 7 (Winter 1978), pp. 30–35.

2. Richard T. Garrigan, "Opportunities for Pension Funds in Wraparound Loans," *Real Estate Review,* Vol. 9 (Winter 1980), pp. 30–38.

3. R. Alton Gilbert and Jean M. Lovati, "Disintermediation: An Old Disorder with a New Remedy," *Federal Reserve Bank of St. Louis* (January 1979), pp. 10–15.

4. Government National Mortgage Association, *How the GNMA Backed Securities Program Works* (Washington, D.C.: GNMA, no date).

5. Mortgage Guaranty Insurance Corporation, *Insured Conventional Mortgage-Backed Certificates* (Milwaukee, Wis.: MGIC, April 1979), pp. 1-3.

6. Kenneth M. Plant, ' 'Using the GNMA," *Federal Home Loan Bank Board Journal,* Vol. 9 (July 1976), pp. 2-7.

7. *Wall Street Journal* (May 22, 1979).

8. *Policy Covering the Extension of Credit to Members* (Little Rock, Ark.: FHLB).

Additional Readings

ALLEN, CHARLES. "The Mortgage-Backed Bond Regulations: How They Work." *Journal of the Federal Home Loan Bank Board* 8 (June 1975): 13-15.

"Board Authorizes MBBs for FSLIC-Insured S&L's," *Journal of the Federal Home Loan Bank Board* 8 (May 1975): 5.

BOMAR, THOMAS R. "FHLMC and the Private Secondary Market." *Journal of the Federal Home Loan Bank Board* 5 (August 1972): 16-17.

BRECKENFELD, GURNEY. "Nobody Pours It Like Fannie Mae." *Fortune* 85 (June 1972): 86-89.

BRIMMER, ANDREW. *Life Insurance Companies in the Capital Market.* East Lansing, Mich.: Michigan State University, 1962.

CLIFTON, RUSSELL. "New Program at FNMA—A Hopeful Source of Mortgage Credit." *The Mortgage Banker* 34 (April 1974): 66-73.

DENNIS, MARSHALL. *Evolution of an Industry.* Washington, D.C.: Mortgage Bankers Association.

DOCKSON, ROBERT. "Marketing Mortgage-Backed Bonds." *Journal of the Federal Home Loan Bank Board* 8 (November 1975): 8-11.

DUBLIN, JACK: *Credit Unions: Theory and Practice.* Detroit, Mich.: Wayne State University, 1966.

Farm Credit Administration. *42nd Annual Report of the Farm Credit Administration and the Cooperative Farm Credit System.* Washington, D.C.: FCA, 1976.

Federal Land Bank Association. *Federal Land Banks: How They Operate.* Washington, D.C.: FLB Association, April 1973.

FERREIRA, EURICO J. "Assumable Loan Value in Creative Financing." *Housing Finance Review* 3 (April 1984): 138-48.

FHA/VA Home Mortgage Programs and How They Work. Washington, D.C.: FNMA.

"FHLMC—Its Financing, Functioning, and Goals." *Journal of the Federal Home Loan Bank Board* 4 (August 1971): 1-6.

GANIS, DAVID. "All About the GNMA Mortgage Backed Securities Market." *Real Estate Review* 4 (Summer 1974): 55-65.

———. "GNMA Futures Market Has Advantages, But Not a Way to Make or Take Delivery." *The Mortgage Banker* 36 (January 1976): 16-23.

HARRINGTON, PHILLIP N. "FREDDIE Mac: Big Man in Mortgages." *Real Estate Review* 3 (Winter 1974): 102-104.

HAVERKAMPF, PETER T. "The Pension Trusts Move into Real Estate—Slowly." *Real Estate Review* 4 (Spring 1974): 126-29.

HENDERSON, JOHN E. "Stock Market Debacle Moves Canada Pension Funds Toward Mortgages." *The Mortgage Banker* 37 (March 1977): 18-26.

HUNTER, OAKLEY. "Fannie Mae Prepared for a New Role in Conventional Mortgage Market." *Banking* 64 (October 1971): 66, 70, 108.

––––––. "Rethinking the Problem of Housing in America." *Real Estate Review* 3 (Winter 1974): 52-60.

JACOBS, STEVEN, and JAMES KOZUCH. "Is There Future for Mortgage Futures Market." *The Mortgage Banker* 34 (June 1974): 5-13.

JACOBS, STEVEN F. "Mortgage Bankers Must Develop Knowledge and Strategy To Use GNMA Futures Market." *The Mortgage Banker* 37 (April 1977): 53-57.

KAPLAN, DONALD. "Mortgage-Backed Bonds: A New Source of Funds for the Savings and Loan Industry." *Journal of the Federal Home Loan Bank Board* 8 (March 1975): 13-24.

KINNEY, JAMES M. "Mortgage Futures Market—A Useful Tool for Reducing Risk." *The Mortgage Banker* 36 (September 1976): 38-44.

LUBCLENCO, MICHAEL, and STEVEN G. WAGNER. "T-Bill Futures Market Possible Buffer to Erratic Short-Term Rates." *The Mortgage Banker* 36 (July 1976): 37-39.

MACK, PAMELA. "GNMA Redesigns Mobile Home Mortgage Security Program." *The Mortgage Banker* 37 (March 1977): 48-50.

MARCIS, RICHARD. "Mortgage Backed Securities: Their Use and Potential for Broadening the Sources of Mortgage Credit." *Journal of Economics and Business* 27 (Winter 1975): 172-76.

MILLER, THOMAS C. "GNMA Options Market—A Proposed New Marketing Tool." *The Mortgage Banker* 37 (April 1977): 58-60.

––––––. "Mortgage Bankers Must Know Basics of Pension Fund Investments." *The Mortgage Banker* 36 (September 1976): 32-37.

MONTE, NICHOLAS. "Those Government Folks." *Real Estate Today* 9 (May–June 1976):10-15.

MOODY, J. CARROLL, and GILBERT FITE. *The Credit Union Movement: Origins and Development 1850-1970.* Lincoln, Neb.: The University of Nebraska Press, 1971.

MORRIS, PETER. *State Housing Finance Agencies.* Lexington, Mass.: D.C. Heath, Lexington Books, 1974.

"Mortgage Backed Bonds Proposed by Board as Aid to S&L Industry." *Journal of the Federal Home Loan Bank Board* 8 (February 1975): 2-7.

MURRAY, JAMES E. "Fannie Mae Goes Shopping for Conventional Mortgages." *Real Estate Review* 1 (Fall 1971): 54-60.

National Association of Mutual Savings Banks. *Mutual Savings Banks Annual Report.* New York: NAMSB, May 1976.

National Association of Mutual Savings Banks. *Mutual Savings Banks: Basic Characteristics and Role in the National Economy.* Englewood Cliffs, N.J.: Prentice-Hall, Inc., 1962.

"Pension Funds Willing, But Hesitant, Enter Mortgage Market." *The Mortgage Banker* 37, 2 (November 1976): 5-22.

PLANT, KENNETH M. "FHLMC and the Capital Markets." *Journal of the Federal Home Loan Bank Board* 4 (September 1971): 27-28.

––––––. "Using the GNMA Futures Market." *Journal of the Federal Home Loan Bank Board* 9 (July 1976): 2-7.

"Questions and Answers with the FHLMC." *Journal of the Federal Home Loan Bank Board* 5 (March 1972): 6–11.

SNIDER, WAYNE. *Life Insurance Investment in Commercial Real Estate.* Homewood, Ill.: Richard D. Irwin, Inc., 1965.

STRUCK, RONALD. "The Mortgage Corporation." *Journal of The Federal Home Loan Bank Board* 9 (March 1976): 17–19.

TECK, ALAN. *Mutual Savings Banks and Savings and Loan Associations: Aspects of Growth.* New York: Columbia University Press, 1968.

"The GNMA Story: Important Facts for Investor and Issuer." Three articles in *The Mortgage Banker* 37 (February 1977): 8–36.

"Two New Secondary Markets Ready to GO." *Banking* 64 (February 1972): 21–22, 64.

"Union Pension Funds Can Add New Dimension to RE Investment." *The Mortgage Banker* 37, 2 (November 1976): 5–22.

WHITE, SHELBY. "The Siren Call of Ginnie Maes." *Institutional Investor* 10 (December 1976): 81–82.

WIGGIN, CHARLES. "Doing Business in the Secondary Mortgage Market." *Real Estate Review* 4 (Spring 1974): 126–29.

20 | Title Insurance, Property Insurance, and the Homeowner's Warranty

QUESTIONS TO BE ANSWERED

1. What is title insurance? Why is it needed?
2. What is covered and omitted in the policy?
3. What is the homeowner's warranty?

OBJECTIVES

When a student finishes the chapter, he or she should be able to

1. Explain the need for title insurance.
2. Explain the defects that are covered and those that are not covered in a standard and extended coverage policy.
3. Describe the types of title insurance policies which are issued in the market.

4. Outline the typical perils covered in a homeowner's insurance policy.

5. Explain the differences among title insurance, property insurance, and a homeowner's warranty.

6. Explain the need for a homeowner's warranty.

7. Describe the typical coverage in the warranty.

IMPORTANT TERMS

Abstractor
Binder
Extended Coverage Policy
Homeowner's Basic Policy
Homeowner's Broad Policy
Homeowner's Comprehensive
    Policy

Homeowner's Warranty
  (HOW)
Perils
Property Insurance
Standard Coverage Policy
Title Company
Title Insurance

TITLE INSURANCE

Definition

The standard title insurance policy insures the new buyer-owner against any loss in value that could possibly result if the property purchased was subject to undisclosed claims by other parties, or if the insured did not actually own the property. The title company agrees to undertake legal action at its own expense to eliminate any subsequent claims upon the title. Title insurance differs from other types of insurance in that it is insurance against actions that have occurred in the *past* as opposed to, say, property insurance, which insures the owner against actions that might occur in the *future*.

Need

Several reasons create a need for title insurance. First, the deed is drafted by the attorney selected by the seller, and can be a different person through several sales of the same property. Different attorneys can insert different language, which can cause confusion or doubt. Second, the parties signing the documents typically are not subject to definite verification of their identity, marital status, and age. Third, the method of indexing and preserving the documents can vary from location to location.

In addition, the title search for an abstract can be conducted by the abstractor first and the results then given to an attorney. Another procedure is for the attorney to examine the public records and then render an opinion on his/her own abstract. Furthermore, the attorneys involved could conceivably disagree in their research of the documents.

The result from the foregoing points is that the seller may issue a deed to the buyer that is given in good faith that the title is good and marketable. However, the deed may be defective, the seller may not own all of the rights that are covered in the deed, the previous owner's title may be in question, missing heirs may exist, or previous common-law spouses may have rights.

Examples. Several short examples illustrate the need for title insurance:[1]

> Joe Roble had lived in his house for two years when he was notified that the abstractor who produced the abstract had missed a sum of old taxes which had to be paid.
>
> Janet Weiss was required to move her carport when her neighbor learned that the surveyor made a mistake. The structure was built partly on the neighbor's property.
>
> Bob and Sue Gree were surprised to learn that the single man from whom they purchased their house was secretly married. They paid legal expenses to defend their title and lost to the wife in court.
>
> The man and woman who sold the McNews their house were actually a man who owned a one-half interest and his mistress. After accepting the money, they disappeared and the man's wife made a claim on the property since she owned the other one-half interest.
>
> Amy Kristen purchased a house from the estate of Sara Beth. Sara had a daughter who was born after her will was drawn, which omitted her. This daughter made a claim on the property after Amy had purchased it.

Types of Title Insurance

Several types of title insurance policies are issued in the marketplace. Each attempts to cover and defend the particular rights in question. For example, the most common is the *owner's standard policy,* which insures the rights of the new owner up to the value stated in the policy. A *mortgagee's title insurance policy* insures the rights of the new owner up to the amount of the existing debt, but the beneficiary of any loss and subsequent payment is the lender. A *leasehold title insurance policy* insures the lessee that he or she possesses a valid lease. A *certificate of sale title insurance policy* insures the rights in property that has been purchased from a court sale.

Coverage

This section will discuss the coverage in a homeowner's standard title insurance policy that is the most common. A person desiring title insurance coverage makes an application to the abstractor who is typically employed by the title insurance company. The applicant pays a fee, based upon the value of the property, which covers the search through the public records and the insurance. This fee is paid once, typically by the seller of the property, and covers the insurance that is written to include the period of the new owner's possession and the heirs. If the new owner ever resells the property, a new policy is required.

The applicant for title insurance may purchase the standard coverage policy, which usually insures against defects in the public documents and specific items such as forgeries, incorrect marital statements, and incorrect grantors. The applicant may purchase an extended policy that includes the standard coverage and additional insurance against defects that may be uncovered only by physically inspecting the property, interviewing the people who actually possess the property, or reexamining an accurate survey.

Typical Defects.   The following examples are common defects typically covered in a title insurance policy:

- Duress in the execution of the instruments.
- Marital rights of the spouse reported incorrectly
- An undisclosed divorce
- False representation of the true owner
- Forged documents
- Deeds written by grantors who were minors, aliens, or of unsound mind
- Misinterpretation of wills
- Missing or undisclosed heirs
- Erroneous tax reports
- Deed from a bigamous couple
- Incorrect acknowledgements
- Falsification of records
- Surviving children omitted from a will
- Mistakes in recording legal documents
- Deeds by persons who are reported to be single but are actually secretly married
- Errors in indexing
- Incorrect descriptions that appear to be adequate
- Birth or adoption of children after the date of the will
- Use of an expired or fabricated power of attorney to execute legal instruments
- Deeds delivered after the death of the grantor or grantee, or without the consent of the grantor
- Errors in the tax records such as recording payment under the wrong property
- Claims from creditors against property sold by the heirs or devisees
- Deeds to or from defunct corporations
- Prescriptive easements not discovered by a survey

Items Not Covered.   If the abstractor discovers a serious defect, the title insurance company typically will issue a *binder*. The binder will state the company's desire to insure the property upon the proper actions taken by the parties involved to solve or remove the defect. If this defect is not removed, no insurance is written to cover this one risk although it is probably written to cover the remainder of the known rights.

A potential applicant for title insurance should remember that, basically, the insurance covers only errors in the public documents. Unrecorded documents are not covered. Questions pertaining to the accuracy of the survey are not covered. Verification of the legal rights of the parties actually in possession of the property is not covered. And any defects listed under the binder are not covered.

PROPERTY INSURANCE

Property insurance covers risks to the property value which may occur in the future. These risks, called *perils,* include the following:

1. Riots
2. Explosion
3. Fire, lightning
4. Aircraft damage
5. Windstorm, hail
6. Smoke damage
7. Theft
8. Glass breakage
9. Vandalism
10. Damage to property by vehicles not owned by occupants
11. Objects falling from the sky
12. Leakage, overflow, or steam from plumbing or air conditioning
13. Weight or damage from ice and snow
14. Collapse of building structure
15. Damage from hot water system
16. Freezing damage
17. Damage from short circuits

Types of Policies

The purchaser may select from several types of policies. The basic difference among them is the number of perils covered, the dollar amount of risk that is insured, and, of course, the premium which the purchaser pays for the coverage.

For example, the purchaser may elect to buy the standard *homeowner's basic policy* which typically includes the following coverage:

Perils: 1–10 above

Amount of Insurance on	
trees, shrubs, plants	5% of amount on house
detached structures	12% of amount on house
house and attached structure	minimum of $20,000 but based on value
personal property	½ of the insurance
Personal Liability:	$50,000 liability for persons injured while on your property
Medical Payments:	$1,000 per person for injuries suffered while on your property

The purchaser may elect to cover the property with the *homeowner's broad form* which typically covers perils 1–17, and the insured amounts are higher in all categories. The most complete coverage is the *homeowner's comprehensive form* which will cover the property against every peril except any that are specifically named.

HOMEOWNER'S WARRANTY

Title insurance provides the new owner-buyer with protection against *past* defects in the title records that might create future claims to the title. A *homeowner's warranty policy* gives the owner-buyer protection against *future* defects in the electrical and plumbing features in the property. While a standard homeowner's property insurance policy covers against destruction and loss such as fire, tornado, and hail, the homeowner's warranty is purchased by the seller to give the new buyer protection against the defectiveness of the property's major systems or built-in appliances within the foreseeable future. The exact coverage can vary among states and companies.

The warranty typically is purchased by the seller to assist in the sale of the property since the potential buyer does not have to worry about defective electrical and plumbing features. Sellers hope for a quicker sale, typically don't pay a premium until the property is sold—expect fewer legal problems after the sale—and anticipate easier financing for the buyer. The buyer is assured that large unforeseen repair bills are insured.

Coverage

A typical warranty could include the following:

☐ *Major home systems*
  Hot water heater
  Heating system

Plumbing system
Electrical system

☐ *Appliances (built-in)*
Exhaust fans in the kitchen, attic, and bathroom
Oven, dishwasher, range, trash compactor, garbage disposal, and microwave appliances

☐ *Optional in some states*
Exterior well pump
Central air conditioner or evaporative cooler
Spa and swimming pool equipment

Brief History of Warranty Programs

The first warranty program for homes was contained in the 1954 National Housing Act, which required builders to give the buyer a warranty on homes sold under FHA/VA loans. In the 1970s, the National Association of Homebuilders (NAHB) sponsored the Home Owners Warranty (HOW), and the National Association of Realtors (NAR) developed the Home Protection Program. All three programs are aimed at home fitness, but they are not designed to accomplish the same objectives.

The FHA/VA program was designed to cover new homes for the first twelve months of occupancy. Builders must adhere to the program, but the enforcement was minimal. The NAR program was limited to used homes, ran from twelve to twenty-four months, and was limited to inspected items. The HOW program describes standards of workmanship and quality of materials for a ten-year period.

CHAPTER SUMMARY

The property owner should be aware of two types of insurance that can protect the value of the property. The first is title insurance, which provides liability coverage against errors of title that have occurred in the past. Property insurance provides protection against various perils on the premises that can occur in the future. A third type of coverage is the homeowner's warranty, which is purchased by the seller for the benefit of the new owner. It typically gives the buyer coverage against structural defaults, defective appliances, and a breakdown in the electrical and plumbing systems.

Review Questions

1. Why should a potential property owner consider buying title insurance? What is its purpose? What does it cover?
2. Explain the defects that are covered and those which are not in a standard and extended coverage policy.
3. Describe the types of title insurance policies that are issued in the market.

4. What is the difference in coverage between a title insurance policy and a property insurance policy?
5. What are the typical perils covered in the property insurance policy?
6. Why does a seller need to purchase a homeowner's warranty? A buyer?
7. What is the typical coverage in the warranty?

Discussion Questions

1. Can you think of any reasons why a potential property owner would not want title insurance?
2. In your opinion, is evidence of good title in the form of an abstract and opinion ever as good as title insurance?
3. Is property insurance a necessary expense for the owner? Do any situations exist in the market where it is not needed?
4. Can a seller sell the property without a warranty? If yes, why pay the added expense?
6. What are the advantages and disadvantages of title insurance, property insurance, and the homeowner's warranty?

Notes

1. Guy Adamo, "Title Insurance: Buyer Security," *Real Estate Today,* Vol. 16 (July–August 1983), p. 42; also, "Thirty-Five Title Troubles," *Lawyers Title Insurance Co.,* no date.

Additional Readings

ADAMO, GUY. "Title Insurance: Buyer Security." *Real Estate Today* 16 (July–August 1983): 42–44.

Guaranteed Homes, Inc. *This Home Is Protected.* Lake Saint Louis, Mo.

POLLAY, RICHARD. "What You Should Know About Title Insurance." *Real Estate Today* 16 (July–August 1983): 45–46.

REILLY, JOHN. *The Language of Real Estate.* Chicago: Real Estate Education Co., 1982. 480–82.

ROMANSKI, FREDERICK. "What's Covered in a Title Policy?" *Real Estate Today* 16 (July–August, 1983): 44.

21 | Preparing for the Closing

QUESTION TO BE ANSWERED

What are the steps in preparing for closing?

OBJECTIVES

When a student finishes the chapter, he or she should be able to

1. Describe the nature and purpose of closing, title, and conveyance.
2. Explain the relationship between closing, the listing, and the sales contract.
3. Discuss the importance of good title.
4. Specify the components of a valid deed.
5. Contrast a deed that contains a warranty to one that does not.

6. State the responsibility of the seller, buyer, and the closing agent in enforcing the contract terms.

7. Discuss the importance of distributing escrowed funds to the proper party.

8. Explain the importance of the Real Estate Settlement Procedures Act and the Truth-in-Lending Act to the closing.

9. Discuss the importance of a responsible party supervising the closing.

10. Give recommendations to an average buyer, prudent seller, and agent to ensure that the closing will progress smoothly.

IMPORTANT TERMS

Abstract and Attorney's Opinion
Abstractor
Annual Percentage Rate (APR)
Bargain and Sale Deed
Certificate of Title
Closing
Closing by a Deed in Escrow
Consideration
Conveyance
Covenant of Further Assurance
Covenant of Quiet Enjoyment
Covenant of Seizin
Deed
Escrow Account
Evidence of Good Title
Good Faith Estimate of Settlement Costs
Grant Deed
Grantee
Granting Clause (Words of Conveyance)

Grantor
Habendum Clause
Lien Waiver
Merchantable or Marketable Title
Quitclaim Deed
Real Estate Settlement Procedures Act (RESPA)
Settlement Agent
Sheriff's Deed
Special Warranty Deed
Termite Bond
Termite Inspection
Termite Inspection Receipt
Title
Title Insurance
Torrens Certificate
Truth-in-Lending Act
Warranty
Warranty Deed

INTRODUCTION

This chapter describes the responsibilities of the buyer, seller, and agent from the time the sales contract is accepted to the time the property is exchanged. It includes a discussion of the relationship between the listing and sales contract and the settlement.

THE NEED FOR PREPARATION

The actual closing is the last step in the real estate transaction. It will progress smoothly only if all the conditions in the listing contract and the contract of sale are fulfilled prior to the closing. For example, if the seller agreed in the listing to provide an abstract or title insurance, the abstract (chain of title) must be ordered and examined and a decision reached about the need for title insurance. In addition, if an agent has agreed in the listing contract to find a buyer who is ready, willing, and able to purchase the property, the agent wants to be sure the buyer applies for a mortgage and raises the necessary cash because the commission most likely will not be paid until closing.

Setting the Closing Date

Closing is the exchange of the deed for the agreed-upon price. It takes place at a date, time, and location agreed upon by the buyer and seller in the sales contract. If an agent is involved in the transaction, he or she will set the closing at a convenient time when all documents will have been prepared and all parties can appear.

Title and Conveyance

A **title** means the *proof of ownership*. A **conveyance** is any legal document that transfers the title. For example, a deed is the conveyance used to transfer the title in most transactions. The term *title* can be used separately from the term *conveyance*. A buyer can write in a contract of sale that he or she wants "free and clear title," which is interpreted to mean that the buyer expects to receive a deed that conveys this type of title. Once the deed has been passed from the owner to the new buyer, the terms *title* and *conveyance* lose their distinction. The new owner possesses both the title *and* the deed, which is the document that can be used to transfer that title again. Thus, the two terms often are used interchangeably.

In many states, the last legal step in a title transfer is the delivery and acceptance of the deed by the new owner. The buyer must have the deed in his or her possession. This explains why the buyer and seller may both be present at closing.

Relationship to the Listing Contract

By means of the listing contract, the seller employs an agent to represent the property at a price. Within the listing contract, the seller has agreed to pay the agent a commission for the services of locating a buyer who is ready, willing, and able to buy the property. Legally, the agent's right to the commission can be thought to be earned when the seller accepts the buyer's offer, but a commission is usually not paid until closing for two reasons: (1) The seller may not have the funds prior to the closing; (2) No one knows that the buyer is actually "ready, willing, and able" until the money is presented at closing.

In some states, the agent of the seller is expected to supervise the closing. In other states, an escrow agent handles the closing. In either case, the closing agent typically gives constant encouragement to the seller to satisfy the conditions of the sale that are the responsibility of the seller, such as ordering and paying for the abstract and the deed. Further, the closing agent should constantly check with the buyer to be sure the buyer has obtained the necessary funds and is informed of the progress toward closing. The closing agent also is expected to prepare the settlement statements for the buyer and the seller and to supervise the exchange of funds and title transfer at closing. The latter two points can be part of the real estate broker's responsibilities specified in the state licensing law.

Relationships to the Contract of Sale

The contract of sale requires that a date be determined for closing that is agreeable to the buyer and the seller. By affixing their names to this contract, both parties are stating their intention to appear at closing.

The date should be set to allow sufficient time for all conditions outlined in the contract to be satisfied by all parties. For example, several weeks may pass before the title company can provide the abstract. The buyer may need several days to obtain an attorney's opinion to determine whether the title is fee simple. A termite inspection may take several days to schedule. The buyer could request that a survey to identify the property lines be performed by a professional surveyor.

All of the conditions within the contract of sale are considered to be prerequisites to closing. They must be fully satisfied prior to the title transfer. A seller should not accept an offer if the conditions cannot be met. The buyer usually is responsible for determining that his or her conditions are satisfied prior to the closing, even if a real estate agent is involved.

The proper role of the real estate agent is to make certain that all conditions placed within the contract of sale are fulfilled so that closing can progress smoothly. The agent is a catalyst who encourages the parties involved to perform their obligations. Sometimes the agent may actually take care of the contract provisions as a service to either party. The agent best represents the seller by ensuring that closing involves no misunderstanding or ill will.

GOOD TITLE

A seller can sell any combination of rights to the property that he or she actually owns but can sell no rights that he or she does not own. The buyer must assume the responsibility of determining whether the seller actually owns all of the legal rights to the property that he or she purports to own. This section explains how the buyer can confirm that the seller owns the rights and that there are no outstanding claims on the property value. **Evidence of good title** or ownership that is free of known claims to the value can be shown by an abstract and attorney's opinion, a certificate of title, and a Torrens certificate.[1] If the parties to the transaction choose, one may purchase a title insurance policy that protects the new owner against a possible loss of the title from a future claim to the value. The type used is determined by state law and local custom.

Abstract and Attorney's Opinion

An **abstract** is a chronological list of previous transfers of ownership and claims of value upon the property and the removal of these claims. It usually starts with a land description and summarizes all of the succeeding deeds, mortgages, judgments, liens, and other claims to the value. The abstractor's certificate identifies the records that have and have not been examined.

Abstractor The **abstractor** prepares the abstract. Typically, abstractors are attorneys, title companies, and public officials. In some regions, the abstractor may be required to post a bond against careless workmanship. The abstractor is liable for any records stipulated to be included in the abstract that are omitted. The abstractor is not liable for an opinion of the title.

Attorney's opinion An attorney is typically employed by the buyer to render an opinion on the condition of the title. The attorney reviews the abstract to determine whether any previous transfers were incomplete or whether any claims to the value remain outstanding. This **attorney's opinion** tells the seller that a warranty, quitclaim, or special warranty deed may be issued. It also tells the seller whether title insurance must be purchased.

Certificate of Title

An abstract may be disregarded, and legally a **certificate of title** may be issued by an abstractor, usually an attorney, who simply examines the public records.

Torrens Certificate

The Torrens system is a procedure for land registration that originated in Australia and is used in some metropolitan areas in the United States. A landowner brings the deed and abstract to a public office to apply for a registration of the title in his or her name. Any person identified in the abstract and application is given a length of time to contest the application. If the application is not successfully contested, the owner receives a certificate of title attesting to his or her ownership. The **Torrens certificate** lists all of the claims to the value of the property.

No subsequent transaction is valid until a new registration is received. Thus, the owner may not simply pass a deed to a buyer but must submit the new deed and the appropriate documents to the public office again and wait for a new registration in the name of the new owner. The defense of the claims of ownership is assumed by the previous owner rather than the public official who issues the registration.

Title Insurance

Title **insurance** is sold by a title insurance agent to protect the new owner against any loss from undiscovered title defects within the records examined. The premium is a one-time charge usually paid by the seller. The policy is nontransferable.

The seller makes an application to the title company for the insurance. The company examines the title records and renders a decision. Generally, a policy will not be issued unless the title appears to be good. The insurance will cover only items that are listed, and exceptions are noted. A standard policy usually insures against defects that may be discovered later in the public records such as forgery, minor or insane parties who have contracted, or incorrect marital status. The seller may request an extended policy covering those items plus additional items that can be uncovered only by inspection of the property, such as survey lines, and by interviews with the parties involved.

If the title company elects to issue the policy, it covers only the public records on file at the date of the policy. It protects the new owner from defects within those records that are discovered later. It does *not* protect the new owner from instruments not identified when the policy is issued, such as a new document presented by an unknown heir. Typically, the policy is an owner's policy rather than one requested by the mortgagee (the lender). It contains a list of the items not covered, such as unrecorded documents, later survey questions in boundary disputes, encroachments, and other factors affecting the right of possession.

Abstract or title insurance   A buyer can request an abstract with opinion, title insurance, or both, depending on the custom within the region. An abstract with an opinion may require more time to prepare, especially if the buyer requests an abstract that traces the history of the property over forty years instead of twenty-five. Further, for title insurance without an abstract, the title company prepares a *title record* covering the same records as an abstract but not typed in final form. The title insurance agent must examine these records to determine the extent of the coverage. Also, the title record may not extend more than twenty-five years into the past.

For maximum protection, the buyer could request an abstract for forty years with an opinion *and* title insurance. The abstract gives a detailed history of all transactions with respect to the property, and the legal opinion indicates the validity of the transfers. The title insurance gives liability coverage over any mistakes contained within records that were examined.

The seller's decision to provide both depends on the local custom of providing evidence of good title. The seller may have an option of providing an abstract *or* title insurance within the sales contract.

Merchantable Title (Marketable Title)   *Insurable Title*

The contract of sale may require the seller to provide a deed that is merchantable. If the seller accepts the buyer's offer with this statement in the contract, the seller agrees to provide a deed that is free from any clouds or defects. Specifically, it is " . . . free of defect, such as mortgages, tax liens, and other liens and encumbrances. It is a title under which the buyer may have quiet and peaceful enjoyment on the property, and one which could be sold to a reasonable and prudent purchaser familiar with all the facts relative to the title of the property."[2] A **merchantable title** may also be defined as one that a court of law would require a new owner to accept in the transaction.

THE DEED

The seller has agreed in the listing contract to provide a merchantable title, and the buyer has reinforced this point by requesting this type of title in the sales contract. Also, the seller has agreed in the listing contract to provide either an abstract acceptable to the buyer's attorney or a policy of title insurance.

The seller requests that his or her attorney write a new deed. The two contracts state that it must be merchantable, and the evidence in the form of an abstract plus the opinion assures all parties that it is a marketable title.

The Document

A **deed** is a written instrument used to convey some right, interest, or title in real estate from the owner (**grantor**) to the buyer (**grantee**). The precise form and the language used in deeds varies in individual states. A deed typically will be considered valid if it contains the following components.

Document must be in writing   The statute of frauds enacted by all states requires that documents for the exchange or sale of real property be in writing.

Parties must be capable of contracting   The parties to the contract must be able to contract; this is called *contractual capacity*.

Parties to the contract must be named   Two points are important. First, the name of the grantors on the new deed must be identical to the names of the grantees on the current deed to establish a correct chain of title. Second, the grantee must be clearly named.

Consideration is identified   The deed typically identifies the **consideration.** Usually, the omission of this part does not invalidate the deed with the exception of a bargain and sale deed (explained hereafter). Consideration can be written in any of three ways:

The actual cash and debt, if applicable: "$_____ in cash and a first mortgage for $_____."
Other valuable consideration: "$1 and other good and valuable consideration."
Love and affection: "The sum of $10 and love and affection."

The phrase "other good and valuable consideration" is used to disguise the amount paid because deeds are public records. The "love and affection" phrase disguises the amount also in a sale or gift between family members.

Description   Because the deed is conveying the title and will be used to give constructive notice of ownership by being recorded in the courthouse, it must contain a very accurate description of the premises purchased. This description must be legal such as metes and bounds, government rectangular survey, plat map (lot and block), or an appropriate combination as described in Chapter 3.

Granting clause (words of conveyance) The **granting clause** does not consist of any specific set of words but describes the intention of the owner to transfer interests, rights, or the property at the present time. Typical wording includes "grant, bargain, and sell," "convey and quitclaim," and "convey and warrant."

When it is used, the ***habendum clause*** typically follows the granting clause and describes the extent of the estate granted but is not essential to the deed. It starts with the words, "To have and to hold. . . ."

Delivery of the deed to the grantee The deed must be delivered and accepted by the grantee before the transfer of title is complete. Because the deed is a conveyance of the title, it must be held by the grantee to give evidence that the title has been transferred and accepted.

Warranty

Deeds used in the United States can be classified into two categories on the basis of whether or not the grantor gives a **warranty.** Common examples of each type are explained hereafter.

Deeds not giving a warranty

Quitclaim deed The **quitclaim deed** has that name printed across the top to identify it. This type of deed does not convey the property. The grantor gives up the right to claim the rights, interests, and title held at the time of the transfer. A quitclaim deed is typically used to correct a defect in the title or when the grantor does not desire to make any claims about the ownership. It is important to remember that this deed contains no warranty by the grantor.[3]

Bargain and sale deed A **bargain and sale deed** has two principal components: it conveys the property to the grantee, and it contains the consideration. A true bargain and sale deed conveys no warranties. Some states have legislated a warranty by state law.[4]

Sheriff's deed A **sheriff's deed** is given to the new owner after a sale of property to recover past-due taxes. The deed contains no warranty.

Grant deed A **grant deed** does not contain any stated warranties from the grantor, but state law typically requires the grantor to imply a warranty by using the word *grant.* The warranty typically includes the grantor's covenant that (a) the property has not already been conveyed to another party, and (b) the property has no encumbrances made during his or her possession only.

Deeds containing a warranty

Warranty deed In a **warranty deed,**[5] the grantor gives all (full) covenants. These covenants differ among regions depending upon their breadth, but typically include the following:

Seizin:	The grantor (seller) possesses good title and can give possession and the inherent rights to the property. Typically, a grantor who gives this **covenant of seizin** is also giving a covenant covering the *right to convey*. Essentially, this covenant states that the grantor owns the right to transfer the title.
Quiet enjoyment:	The **covenant of quiet enjoyment** states that the grantee (buyer) will not be bothered by subsequent claims of ownership from superior title(s) that can be used later to interfere with the ownership and use of the property by the new grantee. Some states identify separately the **covenant of further assurance.**[6] By adding it to the deed, the grantor assures the grantee that additional action will be taken by the grantor to correct a problem or mistake discovered at a later date.
Against encumbrances:	No additional encumbrances exist other than the ones that are known and stated. This covenant is often interpreted by the courts to be identical to a *covenant of warranty.*[7]

In general, the warranty deed carries the grantor's covenant that he or she will take legal action to defend his or her claim to the title during his or her period of ownership and any other period. This deed conveys the property.

Special warranty: The only difference between a general warranty deed and a **special warranty deed** is that the warranty given here covers only the period *after* the grantor assumed the ownership. This deed conveys the property.

A Warranty Deed

Exhibit 21-1 is a warranty deed. The relevant components are described hereafter:

- □ *Document in writing.* The transaction is contained in a written document. The type of deed is printed at the top of the page to prevent confusion.
- □ *Parties must be capable of contracting.* To the best of everyone's knowledge, all parties are capable of contracting. In addition, the abstract has shown no reason why any of these parties should not enter this contract.
- □ *Parties to the contract are named.* The names of the grantor and the grantee are specifically stated.
- □ *Consideration.* The consideration is stated to be $50,000.
- □ *Description.* The description is by lot and subdivision.
- □ *Granting clause.* The words *"hereby grant, bargain, and sell"* are the granting clause. It is followed by the *habendum* identifying the rights that are passed. The warranty is contained in several sentences that transfer title, state that the grantor is lawfully seized of the premises, that the same is

THE DECISION TO TRANSFER THE TITLE

EXHIBIT 21-1

Courtesy of McRoy and McNair, Inc., Fayetteville, Arkansas.

STATE OF GEORGIA, County of..**.**

This INDENTURE, Made this.....................day of ....in the

Year of Our Lord One Thousand Nine Hundred and... between

....

of the State of.........................and County of................................of the first part, and

....

of the State of.........................and County of ....of the second part,

WITNESSETH: That the said part........of the first part, for and in consideration of the sum of

....Dollars,

in hand paid, at and before the sealing and delivery of these presents, the receipt of which

is hereby acknowledged, ha........ granted, bargained, sold and conveyed, and by these presents

do........ grant, bargain, sell and convey unto the said part........... of the second part,....................

heirs and assigns, all that tract or parcel of land lying and being in

TO HAVE AND TO HOLD the said tract or parcel of land, with all and singular the rights,

members and appurtenances thereof, to the same being, belonging, or in anywise appertaining,

to the only proper use, benefit and behoof of the said part...........of the second part,....................

heirs and assigns, forever, in Fee Simple.

AND THE SAID part.............of the first part, for .... heirs,

executors and administrators, will warrant and forever defend the right and title to the above

described property, unto the said part.............of the second part,.................... heirs and assigns,

against the claims of all persons whomsoever.

IN WITNESS WHEREOF, the said part............. of the first part ha........ hereunto set...........

hand and seal..........., the day and year above written.

Signed, sealed and delivered in presence of:

....(Seal)

....(Seal)

....(Seal) unencumbered, and that the grantor will warrant and defend forever the title against all claims.

☐ *Signatures of the grantors.* The grantors have signed the deed, and a notary public has witnessed the signatures.

Legal Versus Equity Title

Legal title belongs to the party who has possession of the deed and is named in the document as the grantee. *Equity title* is claimed by the party who has a financial obligation to repay funds used for the purchase of the property. The two can be separated in a transaction whereby a deed is transferred to the new owner giving legal title, but the current mortgage is untouched. For example, the deed can be exchanged for money, but the commitment to repay the outstanding mortgage debt can still remain with the previous owner. One party holds the deed, and another party holds the obligation to repay the debt. This situation can arise in an equity buy when no assumption statement is filed with the lender to release the previous mortgagor from the debt and commit the new mortgagor. The lender has no way of knowing that the property has been sold. The new owner typically must make some arrangement with the previous owner to make the payments on the debt.

Separation of the two types of title is unwise unless the parties are attempting to accomplish a specific purpose which requires such a transaction. A buyer should always request that legal title and equity title be transferred in the sale.

Recording and Revenue Stamps

In most states, all conveyances of title are taxed. In some states, the seller is required by law to purchase revenue (transfer, documentary) stamps from the State Revenue Department, which will be affixed in the second box in the upper right corner. (These stamps are explained in Chapter 22.)

Recording is best for the new owner. If recording is desired, the deed must have the revenue stamps affixed or evidence of payment of the transfer tax must be obtained before the deed is presented to the proper government office. The new owner pays a filing fee set by the state. The time, date, and place of recording are printed in the box in the upper right corner. These facts establish a priority to the claim of the property value and represent *constructive notice of ownership.*

ENFORCEMENT OF THE TERMS OF THE CONTRACT

A common question is, Who has the ultimate responsibility for ensuring that all conditions contained within the sales contract are satisfied prior to the title being transferred? For example, the buyer could have included minor repairs within the offer, such as, agreeing to replace the window glass in the storm door, at his or her own expense, prior to the closing. Who is responsible for making certain the glass is actually replaced by a reputable, qualified person subject to the buyer's satisfaction?

Such responsibilities typically rest with the buyer. Since the buyer has imposed the conditions, he or she must determine that they have been fulfilled. The seller can satisfy these conditions in a haphazard manner or can perform them very conscientiously.

Typically, no real estate agent will take responsibility for evaluating the degree to which the conditions have been satisfied. The agent would not risk a possible lawsuit in the event that the buyer is not satisfied after closing. In addition, if the property is offered by sale under a listing contract, the agent is responsible primarily to the seller as the principal.[8]

Several general rules should be observed by the buyer, seller, and agent:

1. The seller should agree to no conditions within the sales contract that he or she cannot satisfy or fulfill in a satisfactory and responsible manner. If the buyer asks for a termite bond and the seller cannot provide a bond without a tremendous expense, the seller should not accept the offer with that condition.

2. The buyer should allow enough time to solicit evidence that the conditions have been satisfied prior to closing.

3. The real estate agent best represents the seller by ensuring that the seller agrees to no conditions that he or she cannot satisfy. In addition, the agent best represents the seller by seeing that there are no problems such as unsatisfied conditions at the closing. The agent therefore should inform the buyer of all actions that have been taken to satisfy the buyer's demands within the offer.

4. The agent should not assume the liability of judging the degree of satisfaction. Competent, qualified workers, such as pest control personnel, should perform the task.

Inspection of the Premises by the Buyer before Closing

How can the buyer be certain that all the conditions outlined within the sales contract have been carried out satisfactorily? A general recommendation for the protection of the buyer's interests is that the buyer must allow sufficient time to determine that all of the conditions within the contract of sale have been met in a satisfactory manner. The buyer should demand a key from the seller or agent and personally inspect the premises. Any painting, carpentry work, masonry work, finish work, or cleaning that is in the contract as a condition of the sale should have been completed to the buyer's satisfaction by the time of the inspection.

The buyer should ask for receipts for work required within the contract. The seller should be expected to provide evidence that the carpentry work has been completed as required, the termite bond renewed, or that the carpets and drapes have been professionally cleaned.

Termite Inspection Receipt

The requirements for termite control within the contract are critical in some states. Compliance can take several different forms:

1. The buyer can ask the seller to provide a receipt from a competent pest control agent showing that the property has been inspected and is free of termites.

2. The buyer can ask for a **termite inspection receipt** that states the property is free of termites and gives an estimate of any damage from termites that infested the property previously.

3. The buyer can ask for a **termite inspection,** with the provision that any damage be repaired prior to the closing at the seller's expense. The seller would present receipts showing that the damage had been corrected.

4. The buyer can ask the seller to place a **termite bond** on the property if one is not already in effect. A chemical treatment is applied to the ground and foundation to repel termites and protect the property for a period of time, say 5 years. An insurance policy sold with the treatment covers the property against damage should the treatment not be effective. The owner pays a onetime charge for the treatment and policy, and another annual nominal fee for an annual inspection by the company. If the seller agrees to this provision in the contract, he or she must bear the expense of the bond prior to closing.

5. The buyer can request that a current bond be updated. The seller must present evidence that the annual inspection has taken place and the annual fee has been paid.

All five alternatives assure the buyer that the property does not have termites at the time ownership is assumed. It does not assure the buyer that termites will not infest the premises the day after closing. This risk must be borne by the buyer.

Which type of requirement the buyer should impose on the seller depends on the property and the region. For example, property in the cold regions of the North may need only a statement from a termite company that no termites are present. In contrast, property with a wood structure located in the deep South should not be built or bought without a permanent termite bond. Cedar and redwood houses supposedly repel termites and may not need a permanent bond depending on their location.

The best recommendation to the buyer is to require an updated termite bond. The protection is relatively permanent and eases the worry about future infestations. This recommendation must be tempered by the convention of the locality and the resistance from the seller. The convention within the region could be to impose on the seller an inspection only. Responsibility about future infestations would be borne by the buyer. If the seller strongly objects to purchasing a permanent

THE DECISION TO TRANSFER THE TITLE

bond because of the cost, the buyer can have the property inspected and take out the bond after the closing.

The seller should be prepared to provide receipts and cancelled checks covering termite treatment, inspection, and damage repair. An agent can obtain these receipts before closing and give copies to the buyer prior to the title transfer.

Utility Receipts

A contract of sale may require that all utility bills be paid on the date of closing. The buyer should request receipts and the seller should be expected to provide them. The buyer does not want to move in and find the water shut off because of an unpaid bill.

Buyer Alternatives if the Conditions Are Not Satisfied

If the buyer discovers that the conditions imposed on the seller within the sales contract have not been satisfactorily fulfilled before the closing, two practical options are available. First, the buyer can inform the seller that the conditions have not been satisfied, the contract has not been properly performed because there has been a breach by the seller, and the buyer will not appear at closing to pay the funds. This impasse will persist until one party takes some positive action to break it—the seller can satisfy the conditions, the buyer can agree to the seller's performance on the conditions, and the agent can attempt to negotiate an agreement between the two parties. The second alternative is for the buyer to accept a cash settlement from the seller. For example, if the buyer wanted the bedrooms painted before the closing but the seller did not have the painting done, the buyer could obtain an estimate from a painter and deduct that amount from the funds to be paid at closing.

It is important to all parties involved that the conditions, problems, and misunderstandings be resolved prior to the closing. Otherwise, ill will is created and a lawsuit for breach of contract or misrepresentation may result. Moreover, because an agent's future business depends on referrals, he or she wants all parties to be satisfied.

Death of Either Party

The buyer or the seller could die after the acceptance but prior to the closing. Therefore a statement is sometimes placed in the contract of sale that "the contract will be executed through the estate of either party in the event of the death of either the buyer or the seller." This statement requires the surviving spouse (if there is one) of either party to proceed with the transaction. If no such statement exists, the contract of sale typically is considered to be a voidable contract.

Renting Property to the Seller after Closing

Often the seller needs the money from the sale to purchase replacement property. If the replacement property is not available at the time of closing, the seller may want to remain in the first property for several days.

The buyer can decide to let the seller stay. However, the buyer should remember that after closing he or she is the new owner and must bear the expense of any additional damage or wear and tear to the property. The collection of funds to compensate for these expenses can be very difficult.

A good recommendation is to set the closing date at a time when the buyer can take possession immediately after the title transfer. If the seller wants to remain longer, the closing should simply be delayed until the seller can vacate the premises. Asking the buyer to close early and to allow the seller to remain on the premises after closing is asking the buyer to provide equity funds for the seller's convenience. The buyer is often well advised to resist these requests and ask the seller to make arrangements for needed cash at the bank.

If the buyer is willing to rent the property to the seller after closing, the buyer should require a bond or deposit and a daily rent compatible with local market rents. The property is technically rental property and the rent must be counted as taxable income by the buyer. Therefore, the conditions of the rental should be similar to those in the local market.

RESPONSIBILITIES OF THE CLOSING AGENT

The steps to be followed by the closing agent are universal. Some steps may be omitted depending on who is selected to perform the closing. However, for property transfer financed by a conventional loan, the responsibilities of the closing agent generally include the following items (in some instances, the roles between the real estate agent and the closing agent overlap):

If a new loan is involved

☐ Make sure the buyer makes an application for a new loan within a reasonable period after the acceptance. The sales contract should specify the time period, for example, within one week. Thus the buyer cannot avoid the sales contract by simply not filing an application for new financing.

☐ Ask the buyer to sign the mortgage and record it on the day of the closing to ensure that it is the first lien.

If there is an assumption of the seller's loan

☐ Make sure the buyer orders an assumption statement from an attorney and files it with the lender. This gives the lender notice that the legal responsibility for the debt has been transferred to the buyer. Also, it gives the lender notice that a closing is pending, and the lender should investigate the credit of the buyer if he or she desires.

If the seller will pay off any old loans

☐ Obtain a payoff balance for the day of closing that can be used in the seller's settlement statement.

☐ Ask the lender to prepare a release document that can be recorded with the new deed after the closing.

If the seller is to provide an abstract

☐ The agent orders an abstract on the seller's behalf. It should be sent to the attorney designated by the buyer.

☐ A title insurance policy can be purchased by the agent for the seller if necessary.

☐ All requirements suggested by the attorney pertaining to the title should be resolved.

☐ The agent can request a credit check on the buyer from the local credit bureau.

If a termite inspection is required

☐ The seller contacts the pest agent of his or her choice to schedule the inspection. Any infestations or damage can be discussed at that time with the pest personnel and the seller. A termite bond is provided after the inspection if the homeowner wants to purchase it and if it is required in the contract of sale. The seller should be instructed to keep proof of payment.

Order a new deed

☐ The agent orders a new deed on the seller's behalf. If the seller agrees, it can be ordered from the same person or company that prepares the abstract.

If a survey is required

☐ The agent orders a survey from a professional surveyor on behalf of the seller.

Check of the property taxes and special assessments

☐ The agent asks the seller for property tax receipts. In addition, he or she should check with the tax collector to determine that past property taxes have been paid. If these funds are being deposited to an escrow account, the lender would be called to determine whether past taxes have been paid and that the escrow account has a sufficient amount to cover the payment period.

Insurance

☐ The buyer has either assumed the seller's old policy or purchased a new one. If the buyer has assumed the policy, the agent informs the insurance carrier so that the liability for the policy can be transferred. If a new policy has been presented, the agent must obtain a copy of the front page for the protection of the seller and the buyer.

Utility receipts

☐ The agent asks the seller to provide the receipts or copies of them prior to the closing to show that all utilities have been paid.

Special contract conditions

☐ The agent asks the seller for evidence that special contract provisions have been satisfied, for example, cancelled checks to an appliance repair service or to a painter.

☐ Other documents may be needed relative to the terms within the sales contract.

Settlement statements

☐ The agent prepares a settlement statement for the buyer and one for the seller. To avoid misunderstandings at the closing, the agent shows the respective statement to each party prior to the closing.

☐ When the settlement statement is shown to the buyer, the agent should be careful to explain that payment can be accepted in certified check, cashier's check, or money order.

If possession is given to the buyer at the closing

☐ The agent can minimize potential ill feelings due to the condition of the property by asking the buyer to inspect it before the closing.

Final check prior to the closing

☐ The agent should verify that all or most of the foregoing points have been satisfied one day prior to the closing.

Checklist of Responsibilities

The following checklist can help the closing agent remember all items for which he or she is responsible. It also can be used by the seller and the buyer to make sure all of the requirements for the closing have been satisfied:

☐ *Termite clearance.* No infestation is present and any damage has been repaired by the seller prior to the closing. The buyer can reasonably expect the property to be free of termites and any termite damage on the day of closing.

☐ *Title work.* An *abstract* may be required, a *survey* may be needed for the boundaries, all *property taxes* that can be paid should be paid, and all *requirements given by the attorney* in the opinion on the title should be satisfied prior to the closing. The seller typically agrees to provide a warranty deed and the closing agent needs to assure the buyer that this type will be provided.

☐ *Hazard insurance.* Hazard insurance should be purchased by the buyer to protect his or her investment. The buyer can purchase a new one-year policy or assume the seller's current policy. If a mortgage is involved, the lender will require that an acceptable policy be purchased prior to the closing.

☐ *Lender's approval.* The lender typically will want to examine and approve all documents. The lender has the largest financial stake in the property and wants to know that the transaction involves no problems that might affect the property value.

- [ ] *Truth-in-lending statement.* If a new loan is involved, the full interest cost must be disclosed by the lender and the borrower must sign a form to declare that the cost is known. Typically, signing this form is a part of the lender's standard office procedure prior to giving the borrower the mortgage funds.

- [ ] *Good faith estimate of settlement costs.* If a new loan is involved, the Real Estate Settlement Procedures Act requires the lender to disclose the closing costs for the loan when the borrower applies for a loan. Typically, a lender will require the borrower to sign a **Good Faith Estimate of Settlement Costs** form as part of standard office procedure prior to giving the borrower any funds.

- [ ] *Photographs.* A photograph is evidence confirming that the seller is selling the desired property and the buyer is purchasing the property wanted.

- [ ] *Appraisal.* Typically, the lender will acquire an appraisal to estimate the property value. Was an appraisal conducted, and did the buyer pay for it?

- [ ] *Recording.* Suggest very strongly to the new buyer that all loan releases, the new deed, and any mortgages be recorded immediately following the disbursement of funds by the agent. Early recording protects the interests of the parties involved by ensuring that first priority to the property value is established for these items.

- [ ] *Escrow account.* If the lender requires all borrowers to escrow tax and insurance premiums, make sure that the buyer has opened this account.

- [ ] *Real estate commission.* The real estate agent should inform the seller in advance of the amount of the commission.

- [ ] *Payoff statement.* The closing agent can calculate the settlement statement much more easily if the lender provides a payoff statement. This statement contains the exact amount owed by the seller on the day of closing.

- [ ] *Settlement statements.* The closing agent is responsible for preparing the closing statements for the buyer and the seller. *Closing statements should be shown in advance to the respective party* so that both are aware of the amount of funds involved.

- [ ] *Lien waivers.* If new construction is involved, the settlement agent can ask all of the subcontractors to sign a **lien waiver** to assure the new owner that no future claims to the property value will arise. In addition, the new owner could sign a lien waiver to show that no charge accounts remain unpaid.

ESCROW ACCOUNTS

The standard first mortgage contract recommended for use by The Mortgage Corporation (Chapter 16) requires the borrower to accumulate payments for property taxes and insurance with the lender unless the borrower has obtained a written waiver prior to signing the mortgage. These funds are placed into *escrow,* which is an account held by a neutral party for the borrower with predetermined instructions covering the use of the funds.

The amount of the monthly payment to the **escrow account** is found by dividing the annual payment by 12. For example, an annual property tax bill of $720 would require a monthly payment of $60. The premium for the property insurance is processed in the same manner. The homeowner selects the company (subject to approval of the lender) and the type of policy that he or she desires. The lender divides the total premium by 12 and this amount is added to the monthly payment.

Responsibility for the Payment

The actual payments for property taxes and insurance are made by the lender from the borrower's escrow account. However, the borrower is ultimately responsible for the payment. Thus, the borrower should make a note in his or her payment book to check with the lender on the dates that the property taxes and insurance premiums are due to make sure the payments have been sent.

The bills for the taxes and the insurance premiums are sent from the county tax collector and the insurance company to the party responsible, either the borrower or the holder of the escrow account. If no escrow account has been created, the borrower receives and pays the bills. If an escrow account has been established, the bills generally are mailed directly to the holder of the escrow account, who pays them and mails a receipt to the borrower.

Reasons for an Escrow Account

The lender has two reasons for asking the borrower to escrow property tax and insurance payments. First, a tax lien filed by the collector for unpaid property taxes has priority over other claims on the property value. This lien reduces the lender's claim to second place. In addition, if the property is sold by the county to collect unpaid taxes, the lender may incur significant expenses and a potential loss in loan value. Second, the lender wants to be certain the insurance premium is paid to protect the property from loss in case of such disasters as fire. Consequently, the lender requires that the funds be escrowed, makes the payments when they are due, and keeps the tax payment and the insurance premium receipts.

Interest Payments on the Escrowed Funds

The payment of interest to the borrower by the lender on the escrowed funds is determined by state statute. Some states do not require the lender to pay interest on these funds. Others require interest to be paid. Others consider the additional escrow funds to be prepayments on the mortgage debt. No separate account is kept. When the insurance and taxes are due, the amount is loaned and added back to the mortgage debt.

Relationship to the Sales Contract

The contract of sale usually includes a provision that the escrow account be prorated and distributed to the rightful owner on the date of closing. Failure to follow this provision is a breach of the contract.

A *rule of reason* that can be applied in the proration is that the property tax payments in the escrow account awaiting disbursement on the tax payment date shall remain with the property. They become the property of the new owner. Insurance premium payments paid to the account remain with the seller.

Even though the contract of sale may include a provision that requires these funds be prorated on the closing date, their disposition is still negotiable. The buyer is free to state within the special conditions section of the contract of sale that the total amount is to be retained within the escrow account. Conversely, the seller can accept the contract with the provision that all the escrow account be returned. The buyer, the seller, and the agent should be aware of the fact that the disposition of the escrow account needs to be decided in the sales contract. (The concepts and mechanics of prorating are shown in Chapter 22.)

Responsibility of the Seller

The escrow account at the lending institution is in the name of the seller. The seller has the responsibility of closing the account and disposing of the funds in the manner specified within the sales contract. This procedure is normally accomplished by informing the lender in writing that the account should be closed and indicating the manner in which the funds are to be distributed.

If the property taxes and insurance payments are not escrowed with the lender, the seller must provide the funds at closing in the manner identified in the sales contract. The seller could be required to make a cash payment to the lender for the creation of a property tax escrow account in the name of the buyer.

Responsibility of the Buyer

The buyer's responsibility is to follow the conditions within the contract of sale. If the buyer is given a check from the seller for property tax payments escrowed to date, he or she will deposit the check into the newly opened escrow account with the lender.

A buyer typically follows the rule of reason. At closing, the buyer should expect to receive and should ask for payment of all funds deposited to the seller's account that cover property tax payments to date. The buyer normally should not expect to receive the monies escrowed for insurance premium payments.

Responsibility of the Agent

The real estate agent's role is to make certain that the provisions of the contract of sale are satisfied prior to the closing. The agent should be sure that the seller notifies the lender in writing about the disposition of the account. Any funds to be paid by the seller to the buyer or to another lender can be supervised or paid by the closing agent for the seller at the closing.

REAL ESTATE SETTLEMENT PROCEDURES ACT REQUIREMENTS

The **Real Estate Settlement Procedures Act (RESPA)** was passed in 1974 (amended in 1975) to protect the potential homebuyer from harmful practices (such as kickbacks), to provide the homebuyer with relevant cost information before the closing, and to gather national statistics on closing costs and procedures. The Department of Housing and Urban Development has the authority for administering the requirements.

Coverage

RESPA applies to any loan secured by a first lien on residential real property designed for the occupancy of one to four families. All lenders who are regulated by or whose deposits are insured by the federal government are covered. Loans guaranteed by the Secretary of HUD or intended to be sold to the Federal National Mortgage Association are included. Under Section 103(f) of the Truth-in-Lending Act, any creditor who originates more than $1 million must comply.[9]

Exemptions[10]

The following loans are exempt:

- ☐ Home improvement loans
- ☐ Refinancing home loans
- ☐ Loans for the purchase of vacant lots, provided that a one- to four-family unit is not constructed
- ☐ Loans for the purchase of more than twenty-five acres
- ☐ Assumptions or an equity buy on an existing mortgage
- ☐ Loans for the construction of one- to four-family units, provided that the lot is owned by the borrower
- ☐ Land sales where the title has not passed
- ☐ Loans to pay for property that will be resold

Lender Requirements

RESPA imposes four requirements on lenders and loans that qualify.[11]

1. *Good faith estimate of settlement costs.* The lender must provide within three business days of the receipt of the application a good faith estimate of the range of the costs that the borrower will be expected to pay. These estimates must be reasonable ranges for the costs.

2. *HUD information booklet.* The lender must provide the prospective borrower with a copy of the HUD information booklet within three business days of receipt of the application. It explains the nature of settlement costs, how to select an attorney, how to select a lender, and how to select a settlement agent.

3. *Completion of HUD Form 1.* The settlement agent must complete this form, which itemizes all settlement costs, and must make it available *one business day prior to the closing.* It must be given to the buyer and the seller prior to or during the closing.

4. *Retaining a copy of HUD Form 1 for two years.* The lender must retain a copy of the form for at least two years or can dispose of the form earlier if the lender has no further interest in the property.

Special Provisions

Certain acts are specifically prohibited under the *RESPA* regulations:[12]

☐ *Kickbacks:*	No special payment for the referral of settlement business is allowed.
☐ *Fees:*	The lender may not charge for the preparation of HUD Form 1 or the Truth-in-Lending statement.
☐ *Title company:*	The seller may not require that a specific title company be used.
☐ *Escrow account:*	The lender may not require more funds to be placed into escrow than would be required for a full payment after one year.

TRUTH-IN-LENDING

Truth-in-lending (Regulation Z) was described in Chapter 16 since the lender must disclose the *finance charge* and the **annual percentage rate (APR)** to the potential borrower. Whenever the funds are received for the transaction, the borrower will sign a statement certifying that he or she has been given the appropriate information concerning these two. This signed document becomes the lender's evidence that the requirements of the act have been met.

SUPERVISION OF THE CLOSING

An agent retained by the seller is responsible for the closing. This agent can be the real estate broker, an attorney, an abstract company, a lender, or some other party who is allowed by state law to supervise the closing. The **settlement agent** accepts the payments from the buyer, pays the necessary expenses, and gives the remaining sum to the seller. The real estate broker's responsibility to the closing is outlined by the state license law in certain states.

In certain states, the seller's broker can give the closing responsibility to another party such as the lender. If there is a fee for conducting the closing, the broker is expected to pay it from his or her commission. If no agent is involved, the buyer's lender may require that the closing be held in its office to ensure that all forms are properly completed to protect its loan. Also, a title company can conduct the closing, or an attorney can perform this function.

Closing by the Seller's Agent

The listing broker who represents the seller may have the responsibility of conducting the closing. The broker makes sure that all conditions within the contract of sale are satisfied prior to closing and all expenses are paid immediately after the closing. The closing agent prepares the settlement statements.

The buyer is given a copy of the settlement statement before the closing showing the precise amount of funds to bring to the closing. The buyer should be informed that the funds must be in the form of a cashier's check, certified check, or money order. A personal check is not acceptable.

In addition, before the closing, the seller and the buyer are given a copy of all documents that they are expected to sign at the closing. Any misunderstandings and additional questions can be resolved prior to the actual closing. The state licensing law may impose additional requirements on the closing agent. For example, he or she may be required to keep a copy of the settlement statements for several years after the closing.

Closing by Another Party

Closing can be conducted by the lender, title company, an attorney, or an escrow agent. One of these parties, such as the lender, may insist on the right to supervise the closing to ensure that all documents are properly completed. In this manner, the lender minimizes the risk in granting the loan. The others may conduct the closing for a fee. They can pay the necessary expenses, see that the necessary legal documents are prepared, and prepare the settlement statements.

THE DECISION TO TRANSFER THE TITLE

Some real estate agents may prefer to allow the lender to conduct the closing. However, the agent still has a responsibility to represent the seller's interest and must comply with the state licensing law requirements.

Closing by a Deed in Escrow

Closing by a deed in escrow is the same as a contract for deed. This transaction is actually an assumption whereby the buyer agrees to take over the seller's mortgage. The assumption agreement, abstract, old mortgage, and the new deed are given to an escrow agent. The agent agrees to follow the terms of an escrow agreement that is drawn up between the two parties outlining the terms, such as the amortization schedule, right to foreclosure in the event of nonpayment, and passing of the deed. The deed does not normally pass to the buyer until the last payment of the loan is made. The escrow agent in this arrangement can only perform those duties assigned by the escrow agreement.

This type of closing is useful if one party wants to preserve the terms of the first mortgage, if current interest rates are high and the buyer does not want a new loan, or if the seller is reluctant to pass the title for some reason.

The actual closing is conducted by a real estate agent, lender, title company, or attorney, and all the documents are placed with the escrow agent during closing. The escrow agent also may conduct the closing.

RECOMMENDATIONS TO THE BUYER, SELLER, AND AGENT

The preceding description of the preparation for closing includes numerous recommendations for the buyer, seller, and agent. The suggestions are summarized hereafter for each of these participants in the transaction.

The Buyer

The buyer's principal interest is to be certain that the conditions he or she placed within the sales contract are satisfied.

1. The buyer should make sure that these conditions are satisfied *prior* to the closing. The buyer does not have to appear at the closing if the conditions are not honored because the contract has been breached. Relying on the seller's word to rectify an unsatisfied condition is risky because the buyer has little recourse but to sue for breach of contract once the closing has occurred. This legal action can be costly and certainly will create ill will. If an agent is involved, the buyer can rely on the agent's goodwill and reputation to rectify a breach, but this remedy is beyond the buyer's control.

2. If conditions within the contract of sale have not been fulfilled and the buyer still wants to close immediately, the buyer can ask the seller for a cash settlement to be paid prior to the closing.

3. The buyer normally should not rent the property to the seller after the closing, unless the seller puts up a bond for damage and the rent is competitive with rental levels in the area. Preferably the buyer should take possession upon closing. The closing date should be set to coincide with the date the seller is to vacate the property.

4. The buyer normally should ask to have the closing late in the day so a daylight inspection can be made of the exterior and interior of the property prior to the closing. The buyer should acquire the keys prior to the closing and personally inspect the property to determine whether all of the conditions have been met. The buyer should switch on all of the appliances to be sure everything is in working order. An appliance that does not work properly should be examined by a serviceperson, brought to the attention of the seller, and repaired before closing. A cash settlement from the seller to the buyer can be used in place of actual repair.

5. The buyer should request an abstract with an opinion *or* title insurance on any property purchased. Either will provide a basis for providing good title to the buyer.

6. The buyer should not purchase any property without employing an attorney to examine the abstract and give an opinion on the title. This opinion gives the parties involved information that can be used to prepare the deed and to purchase title insurance that may be necessary to cover clouds on the title.

7. The buyer should ask the seller or the agent, if one is involved, for permission to read all the documents that he or she will be required to sign at closing at least one day before the closing. The buyer should resolve any misunderstandings prior to the closing and should not sign any document at closing that he or she has not read in advance.

8. The buyer should be prepared to pay the funds at closing in the form of a cashier's check, certified check, or money order. A personal check should not be presented.

9. The buyer should protect the new title after the closing by recording the deed and having the county tax assessor enter the property on the tax rolls in the buyer's name. Recording the title gives constructive notice of ownership. Placing the property on the tax rolls shows the new owner's intent of paying property taxes.

The Seller

The seller's primary interests are to ensure that the buyer appears at closing and to receive the money.

1. The seller should not agree to any terms within the contract of sale that he or she cannot or does not intend to satisfy. Noncompliance with accepted terms is a breach of the contract.

2. The seller should check on the location of the last abstract on the property to determine the length of time needed to produce it and the approximate expense. This information can be used in setting a date for the closing and in setting the final selling price. In addition, it gives the seller an indication of the type of deed that can be provided and the possibility of needing to provide title insurance.

3. The seller should ask the agent, if one is involved, or the closing agent for a copy of all documents that he or she is requested to sign at the closing. The seller should read them and resolve any misunderstandings prior to the closing, and should sign no additional forms at the closing that were not read earlier.

4. The seller should expect to give possession of the property on the day of the closing. If the seller should negotiate a longer period of possession with the buyer, he or she should be prepared to pay a bond for damage and a rent that is competitive with local trends.

5. The seller should allow enough time for preparation of the proper documents before the closing. These include the new deed, the abstract, perhaps a survey, and perhaps a title insurance policy.

6. The seller should tell the buyer, through the agent if one is involved, that he or she will accept no payment at the closing other than a cashier's check, certified check, or money order. The deed passes for these funds at the closing and the funds must be good.

7. The seller should check with his or her attorney to be sure that the type of deed requested in the sales contract and verified by the abstract can be provided. Additional legal action by the seller may be necessary, for example, if the abstract indicates that a special or quitclaim deed is the only legitimate type that can be used and the seller agreed to provide a warranty deed.

8. The seller should gather all receipts showing current payment for utility bills and property taxes. In addition, a termite control receipt should be ready for the buyer if it is required in the contract of sale.

The Real Estate and Closing Agent(s)

The agent is interested in facilitating the closing and collecting his or her commission. The agent earns the commission by representing the interests of the seller and ensuring that the buyer is able, willing, and ready to pay the seller.

1. The agent should make sure no conditions are placed into the sales contract that the seller cannot satisfy. He or she should counsel the buyer to make sure that any requests are reasonable to the seller.

2. The agent should check on the progress of the transaction as it proceeds toward the closing. In some states the agent can assume the responsibility of ordering the abstract, deed, and title opinion for the parties involved. Other steps such as the purchase of revenue stamps and recording of the deed can be done by the closing agent.

3. The agent should give the buyer and seller copies of all documents to be presented at the closing for reading prior to closing.

4. The seller's settlement statement should be confidential between the agent and the seller. The buyer's settlement statement should be confidential between the agent and the buyer.

5. Some agents prefer that the buyer and the seller do not actually meet at the closing. Such a meeting is acceptable if the agent has resolved all the differences beforehand.

6. The agent should provide the seller with copies of checks written on his or her trust account to pay the expenses charged to the seller, such as fees for the abstract, deed, title insurance, loan points, a survey, revenue stamps, and the old loan balance.

7. The agent should inform the buyer prior to the closing that he or she must pay all funds with a cashier's check, certified check, or money order.

8. The agent should ask the seller for copies of the receipts for paid taxes and utility bills. If the sales contract calls for termite control, the receipt should be given to the agent. The agent can show the receipts to the buyer or give copies.

CHAPTER SUMMARY

Closing is the exchange of funds for the deed, which takes place at a date, time, and place agreed upon by the buyer and seller. The closing agent supervises the closing and reminds the buyer and the seller of the conditions within the listing contract and the sales contract that must be satisfied before the closing.

One of the most important points in a real estate transaction is evidence of good title. The seller must be able to present a title acceptable to the buyer's attorney. No buyer wants to purchase property subject to title defects or later claims that can adversely affect its value.

Several types of deeds can be used in the transaction depending on the information uncovered in the abstract. The buyer should always insist upon a warranty deed unless special circumstances suggest that another type is acceptable. The warranty deed, in general, states that the grantor will take legal action to defend his or her claim of ownership during his or her period of ownership and any earlier or later periods. This type gives the new owner the maximum amount of ownership protection.

The buyer and seller need to be aware of the special requirements imposed on the lender and other participants in the settlement process. The Real Estate Settlement Procedures Act and the Truth-in-Lending Act require the lender to provide information to the borrower, give estimates of settlement costs, and allow a choice of persons to perform part of the settlement work. Truth-in-lending requires the lender to disclose the interest rate paid.

Preparation for the closing is as important as the closing. Assuring that the terms within the listing and sales contracts are satisfied is essential to all parties involved.

Review Questions

1. What is the closing, and what is the role of a *title, deed,* and *conveyance* in the closing?
2. Is the closing related to a listing contract? How?
3. Is the closing related to a contract of sale? How?
4. What is evidence of good title?
5. Why should a buyer be interested in good title?
6. Outline the components of a valid deed.
7. What are the three types of consideration? Give examples.
8. Describe accurately the meaning of a warranty.
9. Contrast a warranty, quitclaim, special, bargain and sale, and grant deed.
10. Who has the responsibility of enforcing the terms within the sales contract?
11. Should the buyer insist on a termite inspection? Are any other alternatives available?
12. What is the purpose of an escrow account? How is it typically distributed at closing?
13. How does the Real Estate Settlement Procedures Act influence the closing?
14. How does the Truth-in-Lending Act influence the closing?
15. Give several requirements that a closing agent must satisfy in supervising the closing.
16. What recommendations would you give to the buyer, seller, and the agent for ensuring that the closing progresses smoothly?

Discussion Questions

1. Why must a seller be prepared to present evidence of good title? Why should a buyer always request this evidence?
2. Why must a buyer take steps to protect his or her rights of ownership when purchasing property? Why won't the agent perform these steps?
3. Why should the buyer always require the seller to eliminate existing liens prior to the closing. Should the buyer ever rely on the seller's promise to pay the liens after the closing?

4. Describe a situation in which the new owner would be satisfied with a quitclaim deed.

5. What is the advantage of describing the consideration as "$1 and other good and valuable consideration"?

6. If the buyer takes an active role in protecting his or her own rights during a real estate transaction, what role does the agent perform? Why is an agent needed?

7. Explain why an agent who is involved in a closing that does not proceed smoothly should be concerned, even though the transaction did conclude and both parties did receive what they wanted—a sale and purchase.

8. Describe the circumstances in which the buyer would willingly purchase property without any of the following: abstract, attorney's opinion, title insurance, survey, termite inspection.

Notes

1. Robert Kratovil, *Real Estate Law,* 6th ed. (Englewood Cliffs, N.J.: Prentice-Hall, Inc., 1974), Chapter 4.

2. Harold Lusk and William French, *Law of the Real Estate Business* (Homewood, Ill.: Richard D. Irwin, Inc., 1975), p. 312.

3. Ibid., Chapter 5.

4. State of California Department of Real Estate, *Real Estate License Examination Study Manual* (Sacramento, Calif.: 1974), p. 44.

5. Lusk and French, *Law of the Real Estate Business,* Chapter 5.

6. Philip B. Bergfield, *Principles of Real Estate Law* (New York: McGraw-Hill Book Co., 1979), pp. 136–37.

7. Ibid.

8. John M. Payne, "Who Pays Damages When a Buyer Defaults on a Real Estate Contract?" *Real Estate Law Journal,* Vol. 7 (Summer 1978), pp. 46–51.

9. D. Edwin Schmelzer, "New Developments in Truth in Lending and RESPA," printed in *The Thrift Industry 1978: Legal and Business Problems of Savings Banks and Savings and Loan Institutions* (New York: Practicing Law Institute, 1978), pp. 249–72.

10. Morton Fisher, Jr., and Gregory L. Reed, "The Amended Real Estate Settlement Procedures Act—Part I," *The Practical Lawyer,* Vol. 22, No. 7 (October 15, 1976), pp. 45–56.

11. Ibid., Part II, Vol. 22, No. 8 (December 1, 1976), pp. 23–36.

12. Schmelzer, "New Developments in Truth in Lending and RESPA."

Additional Readings

ATTEBERRY, WILLIAM; KARL PEARSON; and MICHAEL LITKA. *Real Estate Law.* Columbus, Ohio: Grid, Inc., 1974. Chapters 5, 11, 14.

BERGFIELD, PHILLIP B. *Principles of Real Estate Law.* New York: McGraw-Hill Book Co., 1979). Chapters 13–14, 17, 22.

KRATOVIL, ROBERT. *Real Estate Law,* 6th ed. Englewood Cliffs, N.J.: Prentice-Hall, Inc., 1974. Chapter 4.

HENSZEY, BENJAMIN N., and RONALD M. FRIEDMAN. *Real Estate Law.* New York: Warren, Gorham, and Lamont, 1979. Chapters 10, 13.

LUSK, HAROLD, and WILLIAM FRENCH. *Law of the Real Estate Business.* Homewood, Ill.: Richard D. Irwin, Inc., 1975. Chapters 7–8, 11.

SEMENOW, ROBERT. *Questions and Answers on Real Estate.* Englewood Cliffs, N.J.: Prentice-Hall, Inc., 1976. Chapters 2, 6.

22 | The Closing

How are the funds distributed to the seller and the buyer?

OBJECTIVES _____

When a student finishes the chapter, he or she should be able to

1. Explain the relationship of the listing contract and the sales contract to the closing.
2. Describe the documents that must be prepared for the closing under various types of financing arrangements.
3. Explain and illustrate the purpose of prorating.
4. Name the accounts that are typically prorated and those that are typically listed as expenses.

5. Explain and illustrate the debits and credits that are used in the two-column settlement statement.

6. Explain and illustrate a typical settlement statement for the buyer, seller, and the broker.

7. Make recommendations to the buyer, the seller, and the closing agent that will ensure a successful and smooth closing.

8. Explain the final step of title transfer.

9. State the alternatives available when the buyer or the seller defaults at the closing.

10. Explain the relationship between the settlement statement provided by the lender under RESPA and the settlement statement provided by the closing agent.

11. Discuss the regulations covering closing that are imposed upon the broker by the state license law.

IMPORTANT TERMS

Assessed Value	Payment in Arrears
Credits	Prorating
Date of Assessment	Real Property Taxes
Debits	Settlement Statement
Default by the Buyer	Special Assessments
Default by the Seller	Tax Bill
Payment in Advance	

INTRODUCTION

The purpose of this chapter is to describe the supervision of the closing and the disposition of the funds to the appropriate parties. This information is essential to any person placed in charge of the closing and is useful to the buyer and seller as participants in the transaction. The state licensing law in some states imposes the responsibility of supervising the closing on the listing broker regardless of whether he or she actually conducts the closing. A seller can employ a lawyer, a title company, lender, or escrow agent to assume the responsibility of closing and ensuring that all documents are properly prepared, signed, and recorded.

RELATIONSHIP OF CLOSING TO THE LISTING CONTRACT AND THE SALES CONTRACT

Closing is the exchange of funds for the deed at a date, time, and place agreed upon by the buyer and seller. Both the buyer and the seller indicate by the transfer that they are satisfied with the conditions and terms of sale. The closing implies that all the conditions of the listing and the contract of sale have been satisfied in the opinion of the parties involved.

Relationship to the Listing Contract

The seller agrees in the listing contract to provide a warranty deed, abstract or title insurance, and evidence that all delinquent and current taxes on the property have been paid. The person supervising the closing takes the initiative in determining whether the documents have been prepared and can be presented at the closing. Because the listing agreement and the sales contract are valid contracts, the buyer can refuse to appear at the closing until all of its conditions are satisfied.

Relationship to the Sales Contract

The buyer The buyer agrees in the contract of sale to apply for a loan. In addition, the buyer has the option of hiring an attorney to render an opinion on the abstract if the seller chooses to give it in lieu of title insurance. In addition, the buyer agrees to take possession of the property without imposing liability on another person for information or statements about its condition. The closing agent should make certain the buyer applies for a mortgage loan, seeks an attorney's opinion, and inspects the premises before the closing.

The seller In addition to the conditions contained within the listing contract, the seller agrees in the contract of sale shown in Chapter 15 to provide a statement from a pest control company that the property is free from infestations and has no damage from termites. Also, the seller agrees to give possession on the day of closing and should make arrangements for vacating the property at that time.

    The closing agent should make sure an abstract or title insurance is ordered. Either item may require several weeks to prepare and the closing should be scheduled accordingly.

    The buyer may have placed other conditions within the offer that the seller accepted. Such a condition could have been repainting a bedroom, repairing the kitchen sink, or reinstalling a garage door that has been removed. The seller must fulfill these conditions because they are contained within a valid contract.

Responsibility of the Agent

The real estate agent or other closing agent typically does not judge whether the terms in the listing agreement and contract of sale have been satisfied. The agent acts as a catalyst in encouraging the buyer to agree that the seller has attempted to meet all of the conditions, and vice versa. The agent could be legally liable for his or her decisions if the closing proceeds on the assumption that the buyer and seller are satisfied. The real estate agent should ensure that all parties are satisfied by maintaining communication with them, reminding each of the conditions in the contract, and gathering as much written verification as possible that conditions have been met.

DOCUMENTS REQUIRED AT CLOSING

The documents required at closing depend on the terms and conditions in the contract of sale and the type of loan. Exhibit 22-1 shows the documents that can be required in a typical transaction.

The items listed in the table are discussed in other chapters. All new loans typically require default insurance, an abstract with an opinion, title insurance if necessary, a termite inspection, a homeowner's insurance policy, a real property tax receipt, a new deed, and lien waivers to show that all contractors have been paid if construction was involved. A mortgage and a note will be required by a lender if the property has been financed. A truth-in-lending document and a Good Faith Estimate of Settlement Costs will be signed to satisfy federal requirements. The mortgage, note, and the latter two documents can be signed prior to the closing and given to the lender.

PRORATING

Certain bills against the property, such as property taxes and insurance payments, are paid under different payment systems. General property taxes are said to be a **payment in arrears,** because they are paid in the year after they are assessed. For example, a property owner will pay taxes in 1986 on property owned and assessed in 1985. Insurance premiums are a **payment in advance** because the property owner must pay the premium before the policy is issued. Another bill that is normally paid in arrears is mortgage interest. The borrower pays interest on the mortgage balance that has already been used for the previous period.

Special property taxes levied for special improvements are usually paid *in advance,* that is, they are paid within the same year that the property is owned and assessed. Some streams of income from the property, such as rental payments, also are commonly received in advance.

Purpose of Prorating

Because certain payments on the property are classified as payments in advance while others are payments in arrears, someone must decide who owes what to whom on the day of closing. Determining this amount and informing the proper person that it is owed or will be received is part of the process of **prorating.** Proration also includes the calculation to determine the amount that is paid in advance or in arrears and the amount of income that is received in advance or in arrears.

Prorating is typically applied to general property taxes and special property taxes, mortgage interest, insurance, and income generated from the property. Other items may need prorating such as utility bills, accrued salaries that are unpaid by the closing, or special unpaid bills. The following sections explain how the items appearing in a typical transaction are prorated. The same principles apply to those items that may be in need of prorating in a transaction but not explained here.

EXHIBIT 22-1 Documents typically required for closing

Note: Documents required on individual loans may change through time.
This table is indicative of documents required to close.

Document	Residential					
	Conventional with PMI	Assumption (equity buy)	Contract for deed	FHA	VA	FmHA
PMI Approval	X				X	
Abstract	X	X	X	X	X	X
Abstract Opinion	X	X	X	X	X	X
Title Insurance, if required	X	X	X	X	X	X
Termite Inspection	X	X	X	X	X	X
Homeowner's insurance policy	X	X	X	X	X	X
Real Property Taxes Receipt	X	X	X	X	X	X
Deed	X	X	X	X	X	X
Lien Waivers (if construction)	X	X	X	X	X	X
Survey				X	X	X
Financing (could be signed prior to the closing)						
Mortgage or Trust Deed	X			X	X	X
Promissory Note	X	X		X	X	X
Assumption Statement		X	X			
Promissory Note	X	X		X	X	X
Installment Note		X	X			
Escrow Agreement			X			
Truth-in-Lending	X			X	X	X
RESPA	X			X	X	X

Property Taxes

Tax bill   In many states, real property taxes are determined by multiplying the mill levy by the assessed valuation on the tax rolls. For example, a property placed on the tax rolls at $8,000 by the tax assessor in a region where the government has imposed a mill levy of $0.007 (dollars per $1,000 of assessed value) would have a **tax bill** of $0.007 × $8,000, or $56.00. The yearly tax bill covers general public services benefiting all land parcels in the taxing district such as police protection, sanitary services, water, and fire protection.

Assessed value   The **assessed value** is the property value that is placed on the tax rolls by the county tax assessor. State statutes and/or the state constitution tell the assessor what criteria to use in determining this value. Some states may require that the assessed value be a predetermined fraction of the market value. For example, in 1986, Arkansas requires that property be placed on the tax rolls at 20 percent of its market value. The Arkansas legislature requires that market value be measured according to a manual prepared by its Assessment Coordination Division.

EXHIBIT 22-1 (continued)

	Special Financing Techniques		
Wraparound mortgage	Purchase money mortgage	Land installment contract	Construction loan
	X		
X	X	X	
X	X	X	
X	X	X	
X	X	X	
X	X	X	
X	X	X	
X	X	X	
X	X	X	X
X	X		
X	X		
X	X	X	
X	X		X
X	X		

Mill levy   In some states, the governments that have been given tax-levying authority by the legislature can impose a mill levy on property within their jurisdiction. One mill equals $0.001, and the mill levy is usually quoted as "____ mills per $1,000 of assessed value." The exact number of mills is determined by the governments in their budgetary process. If a mill levy is not used, the property owner typically is billed for "____ dollars per $100 of (type) value."

Date of assessment   States require that the property owner declare all property owned on a certain date, typically January 1. The tax bill on the property is calculated and paid in the *following* fiscal year on payment dates determined by the state. Thus, property taxes are said to be paid in arrears.

Prorating real property taxes   Prorating of **real property taxes** must be related to the conditions contained within the contract of sale. The property tax funds set aside to accumulate until the date of payment are usually transferred with the property. The seller gives them to the new owner. Thus, the seller owes the buyer the amount of tax funds that will have accumulated from the assessment date, say January 1, through the day of closing.

For example, assume that the contract of sale requires the property taxes to be prorated, the listing contract shows that the property taxes are $630 for the current tax year of 1985, and the **date of assessment** is January 1. These 1985 taxes assessed on January 1 will be paid in 1986. The person supervising the closing must be sure the money for the taxes remains with the property. The seller owes the buyer property taxes for the period from January 1 through the closing date of February 10. The year is considered to contain 360 days in this region. Thus,

Days
January 1 through February 10 = 40 days

Rate per day
$$\frac{\$630 \text{ tax bill}}{360 \text{ days}} = \$1.75 \text{ per day}$$

Amount
40 days $\times$ $1.75 = $70.00 taxes

The seller is expected to pay this amount to the buyer at the closing.

Special Assessments

Special assessments are special levies for special improvements. Such improvements are usually initiated and requested by local residents, and the taxes are self-imposed. Examples include installation of curb and gutter, paving, and special projects for flood and irrigation control. The total tax bill is usually divided by the number of years that the government officials will allow for payment, and that amount is imposed on the taxpayer each year. The principal difference between the real property tax payment and the special property tax payment is that states require the special property taxes to be paid on the payment dates within the *same* year as they are imposed. Thus, they are said to be paid in advance.

Prorating special assessments   The seller pays special assessments in advance. If the buyer and seller agree to prorate a special assessment that has been paid prior to the closing, the buyer must reimburse the seller for an amount covering the period from the day after closing to the last day of the tax year.

For example, assume that the contract of sale requires special assessments to be prorated, the listing contract shows a special assessment of $225 on the property, and the date of the assessment and the payment dates are identical to those for the real property tax. The state requires special assessments to be paid within the year of the assessment, in this case 1985. The closing agent must make sure the seller is reimbursed for the period from the day after closing to the last day of the tax year. Thus,

Days
February 11 through December 30 = 320 days

$$\frac{\overset{\textit{Rate per day}}{\$225 \text{ special assessment taxes}}}{360 \text{ days}} = \$0.625 \text{ per day}$$

Amount
320 days × \$0.625 per day = \$200.00

The buyer is expected to reimburse the seller for this special assessment at the closing.

Taxes for the Previous Year

The taxes for the previous year should have been paid or may need to be paid soon, depending on the payment dates. The closing agent can call the county tax collector to find out whether the taxes for the previous year have been paid, and if they have not been paid, the amount that is due is delinquent. The buyer or the agent should ask the seller to pay these taxes before closing if they can be paid according to the state's payment date. If the closing occurs at a time when the previous year's taxes cannot be paid, the buyer or the agent should require the seller to compensate the buyer for the amount needed to pay them on the first payment date. Taxes for a previous year are *not* prorated. Typically, the amount is added to the prorated amount for the current year and the total is expressed as a single figure that the seller owes.

For example, assume that the closing agent has called the county tax collector and discovered that the taxes for the tax years of 1983 and 1984 have been paid. Thus, the buyer will not discover any delinquencies at a later date. The 1985 tax bill of \$630 was due on February 4, but has not been paid. The agent will ask the seller to pay the \$630 to the buyer at closing or present a paid receipt. The buyer pays the money to the tax collector within the payment dates set by state law. Thus, the seller pays the buyer for the amount that has been prorated plus the taxes that are due.

Mortgage Interest

If the buyer assumes the seller's current mortgage debt at the closing, the seller pays the buyer a prorated amount of mortgage interest, which is shown on both settlement statements. If the buyer obtains a new first mortgage and the seller pays the lender the remaining mortgage balance, the seller pays a prorated amount of mortgage interest to the lender. The amount is entered on the seller's statement only.

The interest paid covers the use of the mortgage balance during the previous period, usually a month. The amount for one month can be approximated by multiplying the outstanding balance at the beginning of the year by the interest rate and dividing by 12. For example, a mortgage with an outstanding balance of \$30,000 carrying an interest rate of 9 percent would require an interest payment of \$2,700, or roughly \$225 per month. The exact amount would be determined by a debiting factor (0.09/12) to compute the interest on the mortgage balance owed immediately after the last payment. This total can be computed or taken from a book of amortization tables. The seller owes the amount of interest from the date of the last payment through the date of closing because interest typically is paid in arrears. The seller owes the mortgage during this period and is not released from it until it is satisfied at the closing. For example, if the payment was made on February 1 and closing is on February 10, the seller would owe interest for 10 days.

Assume that the listing contract shows that the last mortgage payment of $241.39 was made on February I. Interest through February 10 is owed by the seller because the mortgage is still the seller's liability until closing. This amount can be approximated by the following calculation.

Days
February 1 through February 10 = 10 days

Rate per day
$30,000 \times 0.09 = $2,700 per year

$$\frac{$2,700}{360 \text{ days}} = $7.50 \text{ per day}$$

Amount
$7.50 \times 10 days = $75.00

The seller would be expected to pay this amount at the closing.

Technically, the precise amount of interest would be calculated on the mortgage balance remaining after the February 1 payment was made. According to the listing, the mortgage was originated exactly two years ago. The remaining balance would be $29,520. The precise interest would be

$$29,520 \times 0.09/12 \text{ months} = $221.40$$
$$221.40 \times 0.333 \text{ month} = $73.73$$

The individual conducting the closing should verify the prorated amount for mortgage interest with the lender.

Insurance

In some states, the buyer is responsible for insurance on the property through the day of closing, and in others, the seller is responsible. The contract of sale in Chapter 15 gave this responsibility to the seller.

The buyer has two options in purchasing insurance. One is to buy a new policy, in which case the seller cancels the current policy at midnight on the day of closing. The new policy goes into effect the day after the title transfer. This type of transaction does not involve proration and does not enter the closing at all except that the buyer must present evidence that an insurance policy has been purchased. The seller notifies his or her insurance company of the cancellation and receives a refund directly from the company.

The buyer's second option is to assume the seller's policy. This procedure requires a prorating. The seller has paid the policy premium in advance and expects to be reimbursed by the buyer from the day after closing to the date of the next premium payment.

For example, assume the contract of sale shows that the insurance annual premium of $720 was paid on December 1. Because the buyer is going to assume the coverage, he or she owes the seller an amount equal to the premium covering the period from the day after the closing to December 1 of the next year.

Days
February 11 through December 1 = 290 days

Rate per day
$$\frac{\$720 \text{ premium}}{360 \text{ days}} = \$2.00 \text{ per day}$$

Amount
$2.00 × 290 = $580

The buyer is expected to reimburse the seller for this amount at the closing.

The closing agent should examine the sales contract to determine whether the buyer is taking out a new policy or assuming the seller's policy and must calculate the appropriate proration.

Income Generated from the Property

Income from the property is determined from a rental agreement that typically requires rental payment in advance of usage. A payment required in advance can be considered to be in arrears if it is delinquent.

The seller has the right to receive the income from the date it is due through the closing. Thus, if the rent has been paid prior to the closing, the seller has the right to keep the amount covering the time period from the date it was due through the date of closing. The remaining amount is paid by the seller to the buyer.

For example, assume the listing contract shows that the property includes a rental unit above the detached garage. The rent is $175 per month payable on the first of each month. The rent was paid on February 1. The seller retains the portion for February 1 through 10. The remainder of the payment is given to the buyer at the closing. Thus,

Days
February 11 through February 30 (30 days in a month) = 20 days

Rate per day
$$\frac{\$175 \text{ rent}}{30 \text{ days}} = \$5.833$$

Amount
20 days × $5.833 = $116.66

The seller is expected to give this amount to the buyer at the closing.

Payments due at the end of the time period are prorated the same way. The seller can retain the portion of the payment covering the period through the day of closing. The remainder is given to the buyer.

Number of Days

A year with 360 days should be used unless local custom dictates otherwise. Standard accounting procedure uses an equal number of days in each month. In addition, the financial institutions typically use 360 days as a year.

EXPENSES

Other expenses must be paid prior to or at closing. These items and the person paying them are identified within the sales contract. The expenses are typically divided between the seller and the buyer as follows.

Typical seller expenses

- □ *Abstract.* The seller may have agreed in the contract of sale to provide an updated abstract, which is commonly prepared by a title company.
- □ *Title insurance.* The seller may have agreed to provide title insurance if it was requested by the buyer.
- □ *New deed.* The seller will need to have a new deed prepared to transfer title to the buyer.
- □ *Survey.* The seller may have agreed to provide a recertification of the property boundaries by a professional surveyor.
- □ *Termite protection.* The seller may have agreed to pay for an inspection, correction of damage, or a permanent bond.
- □ *Revenue stamps.* If revenue stamps are required on the title transfers, the seller usually purchases them.
- □ *New mortgage fees.* The seller may have agreed to pay for a portion or all of the mortgage fees imposed on the buyer; a prepayment penalty may be included.
- □ *Agent's commission.* The seller may have agreed to pay an agent a commission.
- □ *Loan points.* The seller may have paid loan points on a VA, FHA, and FmHA loan received by the buyer.

Typical buyer expenses

- □ *Abstract examination.* A buyer should always have an attorney examine the abstract to ensure that the title is fee simple; the attorney can determine whether title insurance is necessary.
- □ *Appraisal.* The buyer may want the property appraised to be sure the offering price is appropriate; the lender may require an appraisal as a part of the loan application.

- □ *Assumption statement.* An assumption statement needs to be prepared by an attorney if the seller's mortgage is assumed.
- □ *Processing fee.* The lender will typically charge a fee to record the assumption statement.
- □ *Credit report.* The lender may require a credit report if a new mortgage is involved.
- □ *Origination fee.* The lender may charge a fee to process a new loan application amounting to one to two percent of the mortgage amount.
- □ *Loan points.* The borrower may need to pay points to receive the loan.
- □ *Recording fee.* The buyer should have the new deed recorded.

SETTLEMENT STATEMENT

A **settlement statement** shows the money owed and money to be received at closing. Separate statements are prepared for the buyer and for the seller. An additional statement is prepared for the closing agent if one is involved. The closing agent sees all three. A seller sees only his or her own. The same is true for the buyer.

The statements are prepared by the party who is employed by the seller and responsible for conducting the closing. If the buyer is applying for a new mortgage, the lender may request that closing be conducted on its premises.

As a matter of procedure, settlement is always conducted with the buyer first. If the buyer does not have the necessary funds, the transaction stops.

Debits and Credits

Each settlement statement includes a list of prorated items, expenses paid by the individual, and the amount of money owed or to be collected. The amounts corresponding to these items are shown as **debits** and **credits.** Rather than memorizing certain items as debits and others as credits, it is better to learn the concepts as they apply to the people in the closing so that each item can be shown under the appropriate heading.

The buyer's settlement statement shows the following debits and credits.

Debits equal all figures that the buyer *owes* at the closing from the view of the closing agent's trust account. Prorated amounts, receipts, and expenses can be included.

Examples

purchase price	assumption statement filing fee
abstract examination fee	recording fee
special assessments	insurance proration if policy was
assumption statement fee	assumed

Appraisal fees, loan points, and credit report fees owed by the buyer may not enter the trust account; they may be paid directly to the lender.

Credits equal the following figures from the view of the closing agent's trust account. Prorated amounts, receipts, and expenses can be included.

- ☐ Accounts the buyer agrees to pay in the future because they fall due after the closing.
  Examples include all first and second mortgage balances.
- ☐ Accounts that the buyer has already paid.
  One example includes the earnest money attached to the contract of sale.
- ☐ Accounts that the seller owes to the buyer.
  Examples include property taxes, mortgage interest, and rental payments that are paid in advance.

The seller's statement shows the following debits and credits.

Debits equal all figures that the seller *owes* at the closing from the view of the closing agent's trust account. Prorated amounts, receipts, and expenses can be included.

Examples

remaining balances on all mortgages	loan points, if applicable
mortgage interest	a survey expense
property taxes	rent for the balance of the month after closing
abstract preparation	agent's commission, if one was employed
termite control fees	

Credits equal all figures that are *owed to the seller* at the closing from the view of the closing agent's trust account. Prorated amounts, receipts, and expenses can be included.

Examples

purchase price
balance of the insurance premium, if one was assumed
balance of the special assessment if it was paid prior to the closing

The closing agent's statement shows the following debits and credits.

Debits equal all figures *actually deposited* to the closing agent's trust account. Prorated amounts are excluded.

Examples

earnest money
purchase price

Credits equal all disbursements *actually paid* from the closing agent's trust account. Prorated amounts are excluded.

Examples

fees for the abstract	deed preparation
title insurance	recording
abstract opinion	payoff of a mortgage
termite inspection	

The person in charge of the closing is responsible for the funds that are transferred among the buyer, seller, and outside parties. If a real estate agent is involved, the settlement statements can be viewed as a balancing of the trust account that holds money belonging to other parties. If a title company, a lender, or other closing agent is in charge, the statements still involve a balancing of the real estate trust account, because the agent will be directed to disburse the funds.

The closing agent may prepare three separate statements. One is given to the buyer to show the expenses that he or she is expected to pay at the closing and the total amount of money to bring to the closing. The second statement shows the net amount of money that the closing agent owes the seller after the agent has paid the seller's expenses. The third statement is the closing agent's own summary showing the funds paid from the trust account. If the closing has been conducted by the real estate agent, the only amount remaining in the acount should be the commission.

Master Worksheet for Settlement Statements

The closing agent must provide a settlement statement first to the buyer that shows the money the buyer owes. No funds are shown on the settlement statement unless they enter the agent's trust account. The financing fees paid to obtain the mortgage, such as points, appraisal, and the credit report charge, may be omitted if they have been paid in advance directly to the lender.

The master worksheet shown in Exhibit 22-2 is a convenient method for compiling the necessary figures. Using this format, the agent can prepare both the buyer's and the seller's settlement statements at once. The agent's secretary can type the relevant figures to be given to the seller because each party does not normally see the statement of the other party. The figures are taken from the listing contract and the contract of sale. The calculations for the prorated amounts are shown in other places in the chapter.

EXHIBIT 22-2

Master Worksheet for Settlement with the Buyer and Seller

Name: Jody Marie and
      Jay Robert Dutton

Name: James D. and
      Mary R. Dunn
      2232 Smokey Hills

Date of Closing: Feb. 10, 1986

Settlement with the buyer			Settlement with the seller	
Debit	Credit	Item	Debit	Credit
		Prorated		
	$ 70.00	Real property taxes payable the next year	$ 70.00	
$ 580.00		Insurance, property and liability		$ 580.00
200.00		Special assessments		200.00
		Mortgage interest owed to lender	73.73	
	116.66	Rental payments	116.66	
		Expenses and Receipts		
	45,000.00	First mortgage		
		Abstract	95.00	
85.00		Abstract opinion		
		Title insurance*	none	
		Termite inspection	30.00	
		Deed preparation	45.00	
		Revenue stamps	55.00	
3.00		Recording fee		
	630.00	Real property taxes payable the current year	630.00	
	none	Real property taxes that are delinquent	none	
	2,500.00	Earnest money		
50,000.00		Purchase price		50,000.00
		First mortgage payoff at closing	29,520.00	
	2,551.34	Balance due from buyer		
$50,868.00	$50,868.00			
		Commission owed real estate agent	3,500.00	
		Net amount owed seller	16,644.61	
			$50,780.00	$50,780.00

*No title insurance was purchased in this transaction.

Settlement with the Buyer

The left side of the master worksheet shows the expenses and prorated amounts for the buyer. They include the following items, which are shown in Exhibit 22-3.

Prorated items *Real property taxes payable the next year* The $70 is the prorated amount from January 1 through the day of closing. The agent is collecting this money from the seller and giving it to the buyer to be held until the next payment date. This amount is *credited* to the buyer because it is considered money owed by the seller.

Insurance The buyer assumed the insurance coverage and payments from the seller. Thus, the buyer owes the seller for the premium that the seller has already paid. The $580 is *debited* to the buyer because he or she owes it at closing to reimburse the seller for time covering the day after closing through the day the next payment is owed on December 1.

EXHIBIT 22-3

Note: No title insurance was purchased in this transaction.

Settlement with the Buyer		Feb. 10, 1986
Name: Jody Marie and Jay Robert Dutton		Name: James D. and Mary R. Dunn 2232 Smokey Hills

Date of Closing: Feb. 10, 1986

Settlement with the buyer		Item
Debit	**Credit**	
		Prorated
	$ 70.00	Real property taxes payable the next year
$ 580.00		Insurance, property and liability
200.00		Special assessments
	116.66	Rental payments
		Expenses and Receipts
	45,000.00	First mortgage
85.00		Abstract opinion
3.00		Recording fee
	630.00	Real property taxes payable the current year
	none	Real property taxes that are delinquent
	2,500.00	Earnest money
50,000.00		Purchase price
	2,551.34	Balance due from buyer
$50,868.00	$50,868.00	

Special assessments This assessment has already been paid and the buyer and seller agree to prorate the $225. The buyer must reimburse the seller for the time period covering February 11 through December 30, an amount which is $200. This amount is *debited* to the buyer since it is owed at closing.

Rental payments The rent has been paid to the seller for the entire month, but he or she owns the property for only ten days. Thus, the seller is expected to reimburse the buyer for the remaining twenty days at the closing. This amount of $116.66 is *credited* because it is money owed to the buyer.

Expenses and receipts *First mortgage* The buyer has agreed to raise $45,000 of the $50,000 purchase price by applying for a first mortgage. This amount is *credited* to the buyer because it represents a sum that he or she agrees to pay in the future.

Abstract opinion The seller has elected to pay for an abstract and the buyer must pay for an attorney's opinion on the title. This $85 is money that the buyer owes at closing and is *debited*.

Recording fee The recording fee of $3 is paid by the buyer. It is shown as a *debit* because the buyer owes it to the broker at closing.

Real property taxes payable the current year Property taxes for the 1985 year were due on February 4, 1986, and have not been paid. The agent needs to collect the $630 owed. Thus, the agent collects it from the seller and gives it to the buyer as a *credit* on the buyer's statement.

Earnest money The sum of $2,500 is money that the buyer has already paid and is *credited*.

Purchase price The price of $50,000 is owed by the buyer at closing and is *debited*.

Balance due from buyer This sum is defined as the difference between the debits and credits. The difference of $2,551.34 is always shown as a *credit*. This figure is the amount that the buyer should bring to the closing in the form of cashier's check, certified check, or money order.

The buyer is given the settlement statement just before the closing or at the closing. Usually the buyer's statement is not shown to the seller.

Settlement with the Seller

The seller's settlement statement, taken from the right side of the master worksheet, is shown in Exhibit 22-4. It accounts for all monies received into the agent's trust account and disbursed from it to pay expenses in behalf of the seller. The following items appear on the statement shown in Exhibit 22-4.

Prorated items *Real property taxes payable the next year* The sum of $70 is *debited* to the seller because he or she owes property taxes from the date of assessment of January 1 through closing. This money is given to the buyer to be held until the next payment date.

EXHIBIT 22-4
Note: No title insurance was purchased in this transaction.

	Settlement with the Seller	

Name: Jody Marie and
        Jay Robert Dutton
	Feb. 10, 1986
	
	Name: James D. and
	         Mary R. Dunn
	         2232 Smokey Hills	

Date of Closing: Feb. 10, 1986

	Settlement with the seller	
Item	**Debit**	**Credit**
Prorated		
Real property taxes payable the next year	$ 70.00	
Insurance, property and liability		$ 580.00
Special assessments		200.00
Mortgage interest owed the lender	73.73	
Rental payments	116.66	
Expenses and Receipts		
Abstract	95.00	
Termite inspection	30.00	
Deed preparation	45.00	
Revenue stamps	55.00	
Real property taxes payable the current year	630.00	
Purchase price		50,000.00
First mortgage payoff at closing	29,520.00	
Commission owed real estate agent	3,500.00	
Net amount owed seller	16,644.61	
	$50,780.00	$50,780.00

Insurance The figure of $580 is *credited* because the buyer owes this amount to the seller at closing. It represents the remaining portion of the insurance premium from the day after closing to December 1. The seller has already paid this amount, and the buyer is assuming the policy.

Special assessments The seller has already paid for special assessments. The buyer is reimbursing the seller from the period extending from February 11 to December 30. This amount is *credited* because it is money owed to the seller.

Mortgage interest The seller owns the mortgage through the day of closing. He or she should pay the lender for accrued interest from the last payment date of February 1 through the day of closing. This amount of $73.73 is *debited* because the seller owes it to the lender.

Rental payments Rent was paid to the seller on February 1 for the entire month. Because the seller owns the property for only 10 days, he or she should reimburse the buyer for the remaining 20 days. This amount, $116.66, is *debited* because the seller owes it to the buyer.

Expenses and receipts   *Abstract*   The seller has decided to provide an abstract, and a local title company will charge $95 to prepare it. This amount is *debited* because it is an expense.

Termite inspection The termite company has charged $30 for an inspection. This figure is *debited* because it is an expense.

Deed preparation The attorney has charged $45 to prepare a new general warranty deed. This figure is *debited* because it is owed at closing.

Revenue stamps The state in this transaction requires the seller to purchase revenue stamps for the amount of $1.10 per $1,000 of sales price or fraction thereof which equals $55 ($1.10 $\times$ 50). This figure is a sales tax on the conveyance, and is shown as a *debit* because it is owed at the closing.

Real property taxes payable in the current year Property taxes for the 1985 tax year were payable on February 4, 1986. The seller should reimburse the buyer for the $630 that the buyer needs to make the payment. The seller owes this amount at closing, and it is shown as a *debit.*

Real property taxes that are delinquent No property taxes are delinquent for past years.

Purchase price The seller is owed the $50,000 purchase price, which is shown as a *credit.*

First mortgage payoff The seller owes the lender a balance of $29,520 on the existing mortgage, which will be paid at the closing.

Commission The seller owes the broker a commission of $3,500, which is shown as a *debit.*

Net amount due seller This amount is defined as the difference between the debits and credits and is always shown as a *debit.* The closing agent will present the seller with a check on the trust account for this amount at the closing.

This settlement statement is given to the seller just before closing or during closing. Usually it is not shown to the buyer.

Closing Agent's Settlement Statement

Exhibit 22-5 is the closing agent's settlement statement. Arthur Sinet, the real estate broker for the sellers and the closing agent, is attempting to account for all *cash* deposited into and spent from the trust account. Because the settlement is with the trust account, Arthur views debits as assets and credits as liabilities. In the transaction, Arthur receives three cash payments: earnest money from the buyer, balance due from the buyer at closing, and the first mortgage total from the lender. Arthur's trust account would show receipts of $50,051.34.

THE DECISION TO TRANSFER THE TITLE

EXHIBIT 22-5

| Settlement Statement (Broker's) | | | Feb. 10, 1986 |

Name: Jody Marie and
　　　Jay Robert Dutton

Name: James D. and
　　　Mary R. Dunn
　　　2232 Smokey Hills

Date of Closing: Feb. 10, 1986

Item	Debit	Credit
Deposits		
Earnest money	$ 2,500.00	
Balance due from buyer	2,551.34	
First mortgage	45,000.00	
Checks		
Mortgage interest owned lender		$　　73.73
Abstract		95.00
Abstract opinion		85.00
Termite inspection		30.00
Deed preparation		45.00
Revenue stamps		55.00
Recording fee		3.00
First mortgage		29,520.00
Net owed the seller		16,644.61
	$50,051.34	$46,551.34
Balance remaining (commission)	$ 3,500.00	
Share of commission to Pete Boot (45%) (selling broker)		$ 1,575.00
Share of commission to Janet Watson (50% of $1,925) (independent contractor)		$　962.50
Balance for Arthur Sinet	$　962.50	

From this account, Arthur will write checks to pay for the expenses incurred in the transaction. For example, he will write a check to the title company for $95 to pay for the abstract, another check to the buyer's attorney for $85 to pay for the opinion, another check to the pest company for $30 to pay for the termite inspection, and so on down the list of credits shown in Exhibit 22-5. Once all of the checks have been written, the balance remaining should be the commission.

Because the property was sold by another broker, Pete Boot, Arthur must immediately pay Pete his share of the commission. The check for $1,575 represents the 45 percent that a selling broker receives when the property is listed and sold through the multiple listing service. Pete, in turn, will pay his salesperson, Alice Jones, from his trust account when he receives the money. Arthur pays Janet Watson, a salesperson working as an independent contractor from his office, her agreed-upon share of 50 percent amounting to $962.50. The remaining total of $962.50 can then be transferred from Arthur's trust account to his personal account for his own use.

No prorated amounts enter this settlement statement. This account receives *cash* deposits and disbursements only. Prorated amounts are used to determine the Balance Due from the Buyer and Net Balance Owed the Seller. These may be considered *adjustment* totals and not cash totals.

Settlement with an Assumption (Equity Buy)

Exhibits 22-2 through 22-5 show the calculations and the resultant totals when the buyer obtains a new first mortgage. When the buyer assumes the seller's mortgage by paying for the equity and agreeing to assume the payments on the remaining debt, the master worksheet would contain the following adjustments:

Buyer		Item	Seller	
Debit	Credit		Debit	Credit
		Mortgage interest owed to lender	$73.73	
		(is replaced by)		
	$73.73	Mortgage interest owed to buyer	$73.73	
	$45,000.00	First mortgage (is replaced by)		
	$29,520.00	Mortgage assumption		
$65		Assumption statement		
$75		Assumption statement processing fee		

In the first adjustment, the seller owes the mortgage interest from the last date of payment, February 1, through the closing date of February 10 to the buyer, since the buyer is responsible for the next interest payment to the lender. In the second adjustment, the buyer is agreeing to pay in the future the remaining mortgage balance of $29,520 rather than $45,000 on a new mortgage. In the third adjustment, the buyer pays $65 to an attorney for preparing the assumption statement, and $75 to the lender for processing this document. The remaining prorated amounts and expenses remain the same. The balance due from buyer, the net owed the seller, and the column totals reflect these changes.

Recommendations for Conducting the Closing

The actual closing should occur when all the documents have been prepared and the required financing has been arranged.

Satisfaction of terms before the closing   All terms and conditions contained within the contract of sale should be satisfied before the closing. The responsibility of enforcing the terms lies with the buyer. The recommendations given in Chapter 21 should be followed by the buyer, seller, and agent in preparing for the closing.

THE DECISION TO TRANSFER THE TITLE

Buyer and seller meeting If all the contract terms and conditions have been satisfied, the buyer and seller can meet at closing to sign the necessary documents concurrently. If some disagreement has arisen during contract negotiation, the agent may not want the buyer and seller to meet during the closing process, because a meeting would enable the buyer and seller to rediscuss controversial matters. The closing agent could settle first with the buyer on the day of closing. The agent could acquire the new signed deed from the seller and keep it until the funds are received from the buyer. The agent can then record the deed for the buyer after settlement with the seller.

Confidentiality of the settlement statement The settlement statements for the buyer and the seller are usually regarded as confidential. Each party sees only his or her own statement.

COMPLETION OF THE TITLE TRANSFER

The title transfer is completed when the deed is accepted voluntarily by the new owner. It must be physically in the new owner's possession.

Recording

Recording of the deed is usually optional for the new owner. *All deeds should be recorded immediately to provide constructive notice of ownership.* In cases such as an installment sale, the seller may prefer not to record the deed, in order to facilitate foreclosure in the event of default by the buyer.

Property Tax Assessment

The new owner should have the property assessed in his or her name at the tax assessor's office. This action establishes the owner's intention of paying property taxes. It is not part of the title transfer but helps protect the new title against fraud once the new owner receives it.

DEFAULT OF CLOSING

What happens if one of the parties fails to complete the closing and indicates a desire not to exchange the deed for money?

Default by the Buyer

The listing contract states that if the buyer defaults on an accepted contract, the agent and the seller will divide the earnest money deposit. The terms of this division in case of **default by the buyer** usually are printed on the contract. If not, the agent generally requests that his or her expenses be reimbursed and the remainder is divided evenly.

The purpose of the earnest money deposit is to serve as liquidated damages and to compensate the damaged parties in the event of the buyer's default. If the seller suffers damages from the default that exceed the amount of the earnest money deposit, he or she can take legal action to sue the buyer for damages or to sue for the buyer to perform on the contract.

Legal action is time-consuming and can be costly in attorney's fees. The best alternative is to be certain that the earnest money deposit is large enough to pay for the inconvenience to the damaged parties in the case of a buyer default.

Default by the Seller

If the seller decides not to complete the closing, resulting in a **default by the seller,** the buyer has three alternatives; (1) The buyer can simply forget the transaction and destroy the offer; (2) The buyer can take legal action to sue the seller for damages if there are damages; (3) The buyer can sue the seller for specific performance of the contract.

The agent should keep abreast of the seller's wishes to prevent a breach from occurring. The seller should be aware that a commission may need to be paid to the agent if the seller refuses to complete the sale. Consider the case in which the agent finds a buyer (who is ready, willing, and able to purchase the property) and writes a contract of sale covering the conditions exactly as specified in the listing contract. The agent presents the offer to the seller and the seller rejects it. Because the agent has accomplished the objective set forth within the listing contract, he or she may ask the seller for the commission. (This situation is described in Chapter 9.)

REAL ESTATE SETTLEMENT PROCEDURES ACT

The Real Estate Settlement Procedures Act (RESPA) requires that the lender give the new mortgagor a settlement statement one day prior to the closing if the mortgagor requests it. If he or she does not request the statement in advance, it will be provided usually when the mortgage is signed. The lender's settlement statement shows all the charges necessary to obtain the loan—the credit report, appraisal, and loan origination fees; points and prepayment penalty if applicable. These amounts may not enter the closing agent's trust account because the buyer or seller pays them directly to the lender. In fact, they may have been paid *prior* to the closing conducted by the closing agent.

LICENSE LAW AND RULES AND REGULATIONS

A typical state license law requires the broker to establish a trust account to hold all funds coming into his or her possession that belong to other parties. The broker is always responsible for the funds in the trust account and may be responsible for the closing, even though he or she may not actually conduct it. The lender or the title company may actually conduct the closing, but the listing broker is responsible for the distribution of funds from the firm's trust account.

A typical state requirement in the rules and regulations is that the broker maintain all records pertaining to the transaction for a minimum period of time, such as three years. These records must be available for commission investigators in case a complaint arises.

CHAPTER SUMMARY

All terms and conditions that have been agreed upon in the listing contract and the contract of sale should be satisfied before the closing.

Prorating is used to allocate accounts such as taxes, insurance, rents, and mortgage interest between the buyer and seller. It is necessary because the payment dates on these accounts are not consistent with the closing date. The seller has already paid taxes or insurance and the buyer refunds the unused premium or payment. These amounts are not actual cash expenses but represent adjustments to the totals paid by the buyer to the closing agent and by the agent in turn to the seller.

The prorated amounts and cash expenses are shown in the settlement statements for the buyer and seller as debits and credits, defined in relation to the agent's trust account.

The title transfer is completed when the new owner voluntarily accepts the new deed. If the buyer should default at the closing and refuse to pay the funds in exchange for the deed, the seller and agent can divide the earnest money as outlined within the listing contract. Other alternatives are to sue for nonperformance of the contract, or to sell the property and sue the buyer for any damages. If the seller fails to perform by not delivering the deed, the buyer can sue for nonperformance.

Review Questions

1. John Smith is selling his house for $65,000 and the closing is set for February 1, 1986. Answer each of the following questions.
   a) The property taxes for 1984 have been paid in the amount of $720. The taxes for 1985 are the same amount and may be paid anytime between the third Monday in February and October 10, 1986. What is the prorated amount to be collected from the seller on the date of closing? What is the total amount entered into the seller's settlement statement? Are property taxes shown as a debit or a credit?
   b) The buyer is assuming John's insurance policy on the property. The annual premium of $640 was paid on December 15, 1985. What is the prorated amount that the buyer owes the seller? How is it shown in the seller's and buyer's settlement statements? What amount is shown in the settlement statements if the buyer presents his own policy at the closing?

c) John's house was part of a special improvement district, which built curb and gutters for the neighborhood. John owed $300 for the year 1986 in special property taxes. Does this figure enter the seller's settlement statement? How and in what amount? Does it enter the buyer's settlement state? How and in what amount?

d) John's house has an apartment in the basement, which John had rented to a student for $95.00 per month due on the first of the month. The rent has not been paid for February 1, 1986. Does this figure or the prorated amount enter the seller's or the buyer's settlement statement? How, and by what amount?

2. What is the relationship of the listing contract and contract of sale to the settlement statements?

3. Identify several accounts that are typically prorated.

4. Define a debit and a credit in the buyer's, seller's, and closing agent's settlement statement.

5. Which accounts are typically paid in arrears? Why?

6. Which accounts are typically paid in advance? Why?

7. What recommendations should be given to the buyer, seller, and agent for ensuring an uneventful closing?

8. Explain the difference between determining whether property taxes are paid and prorating taxes.

9. What is the difference between the settlement statement provided by the lender to satisfy RESPA requirements and the one provided by the closing agent?

10. What alternatives are available to the buyer if the seller defaults prior to the closing? What alternatives are available to the seller if the buyer defaults?

Discussion Questions

1. Under the typical requirements of state real estate licensing law, who has the responsibility of conducting the closing? Why? Does this responsibility still apply if another party, such as the lender, conducts the closing?

2. Should the agent take an active role in resolving any disputes that might arise prior to the closing?

3. Are prorated amounts actual cash totals? State in a brief sentence how these amounts influence the amount the buyer owes at closing and the amount the agent owes to the seller.

4. This chapter recommends a 360-day year for prorating unless local custom dictates a 365-day year. Are there any circumstances in which a 360-day year could violate a state usury limit?

5. A real property tax bill that is delinquent is sometimes shown by an agent as a prorated amount. Why?

6. How does an agent handle the real property tax bill if the closing occurs on a date when the taxes cannot be paid by state law?

7. Mortgage interest typically is paid by the seller from the date of the last payment to the date of closing. Are there any circumstances in which the buyer would pay this amount?

8. How would rental income be shown in a settlement statement if the rent were owed but late?

9. This chapter illustrates the two-column, debit-and-credit approach for preparing settlement statements. Can you think of any other methods that can be used in these statements?

10. What steps can an agent take to ensure that the buyer or seller does not default prior to the closing?

Additional Readings

EPLEY, DONALD F., and JAMES A. MILLAR. *Basic Real Estate Finance and Investments.* New York: John Wiley and Sons, Inc., 1984. Chapters 7, 12.

FISHER, MORTON P., and GREGORY REED. "The Amended Real Estate Settlement Procedures Act" (RESPA)—Part I. *The Practical Lawyer* 22, 7 (October 15, 1976): 45–56.

——. "The Amended Real Estate Settlement Procedures Act" (RESPA)—Part II. *The Practical Lawyer* 22, 8 (December 1, 1976): 27–36.

KRATOVIL, ROBERT. *Real Estate Law.* Englewood Cliffs, N.J.: Prentice-Hall, Inc., 1974. Chapter 12.

RABIN, EDWARD. *Fundamentals of Modern Real Property Law.* Mineola, N.Y.: The Foundation Press, Inc., 1974. Chapter 5.

Glossary

absorption analysis An examination of the changes in the economic and demographic factors on the demand side of the market to ascertain the length of time required for the vacant units in the market to be purchased or rented.

abstract and attorney's opinion A chronological history of previous transfers of ownership and claims of value that is reviewed by an attorney who renders an opinion on the rights in the estate.

abstractor The person compiling information from the public records for use as evidence of good title.

accelerated cost recovery system (ACRS) The system initiated by the IRS in 1981 that identifies the years during which different kinds of property (real and personal) can be depreciated.

accelerated depreciation Mathematical expressions used to represent a situation in which the value declines in the early years of the useful life period are greater than the value declines in the latter years of the useful life period.

acceleration Moving the maturity date to the current date as the first step toward foreclosure.

acceptance A statement made by the seller to accept the buyer's offer unconditionally and without change.

accrued depreciation The value decline attributed to a structure as a result of physical deterioration, functional obsolescence, and economic obsolescence.

active market A market in which changes in the economic and demographic factors produce rising prices, an increased number of sales, or a combination of these two increases.

actual gross income The total income received by an income-earning property and based on the fact that each unit of rentable space receives the contract rent specified in the lease that the landlord and the tenant signed.

additional (excess) depreciation The difference between the straight-line depreciation charge and the accelerated depreciation charge that is actually taken by the investor.

adjusted basis The value of real property for income tax purposes.

advance A loan given by the district Federal Home Loan Bank to a federally chartered savings and loan.

affirmative marketing agreement An agreement between members of the local board of REALTORS and the Department of Housing and Urban Development to support equal opportunity in housing.

after-tax cash flow The numerical value of net operating income minus mortgage debt service, income taxes, and selling expenses, if a sale is involved.

air rights The legal claim to use of the air space above the land.

amortization Periodic repayments of the debt.

annual percentage rate (APR) An interest rate that can be found by dividing the finance charge for one billing period by the median balance for that period and multiplying the result by the number of periods in one year.

appraisal An estimate of the value of real property.

appraisal process An orderly, logical, and concise step-by-step process for estimating the value of a parcel of real property.

appraiser An individual who estimates the value of property.

area analysis The use of general data about the nation, the region, and the local community to determine the factors that can affect the market value of the subject property.

area regulations Section of a zoning ordinance that specifies how a site can be used. It covers setback and side yard requirements.

assessed value The value of the property estimated by the tax assessor for property tax purposes.

assignment A document that transfers the rights of ownership to another party. In a lease, it transfers the rights of ownership held by the original tenant to a new tenant who becomes responsible to the landlord for all of the provisions and obligations specified in the lease issued to the original owner: in a commercial loan, it transfers the right to collect income from the propety from the mortgagor to the mortgagee in the event of default.

assumption (equity buy)   A sale wherein the buyer agrees to purchase the owner's equity in the property and take over the debt payments.

assumption contract   A document given to the lender by the buyer that states the buyer is assuming the liability for the remaining debt in an equity buy.

attorney's opinion and abstract   A chronological history of previous transfers of ownership and claims of value that is reviewed by an attorney who renders an opinion of the rights in the estate.

attribute analysis   Analysis of the intrinsic geological features of the land, the structural and design features of the improvement, and the relationship of these features to the environment.

balloon note   An amortized loan schedule whereby the last payment is larger than the preceding payments.

band-of-investment technique   A technique used by an appraiser to generate the basic rate of interest.

bargain and sale deed   A type of deed that conveys the property to the grantee and contains the consideration; it conveys no warranties.

basic rate of interest   An interest rate that reflects conditions in the money market and represents a rate of return on the investment.

before-tax cash flow   The funds remaining after debt service is subtracted from net operating income.

bilateral contract   A contract in which the two parties make a promise or extend an offer and simultaneously receive a promise or an offer from the other party.

blanket mortgage   One mortgage that covers several parcels of real property.

bond for title   A situation in which closing is set for a future date, the buyer rents the property, and the seller posts bond that a deed will be delivered upon closing.

breach of contract   The failure to perform the acts or promises stipulated as terms of the contract.

breakeven or default ratio   Total operating expenses plus debt service divided by gross income.

building area ratio   Net leasehold area divided by gross building area.

building code   A police power designed to establish minimum acceptable standards for construction of improvements within the local jurisdiction (same as *construction code*).

business or income risk   The risk that future levels of actual gross income will be less than their forecasted or anticipated levels.

buyer's market   A dull market.

capital gain   The gain derived by a property owner when the sales price is greater than the adjusted basis of the property.

capital improvement expenditures   An expense incurred by the owner to improve the property and thereby increase its rent-earning potential and/or lengthen its economic life.

capital recovery rate A rate that reflects the loss in value of an improvement over its economic life and represents a rate of return of the investment.

capitalization rate A discounting rate used to generate the value estimate; it is composed of two interest rates known as the basic rate of interest and the capital recovery rate.

certificate of eligibility A document given by the VA, to the lender, that certifies the veteran is eligible for the loan and gives the amount of the $27,500 guarantee (1986 figures) that can be applied to the loan.

certificate of occupancy A certificate that permits a building to be used after it is inspected for compliance to all zoning construction codes, and health department codes.

certificate of reasonable value A document given by the VA, to the lender, that contains the selling price or the appraised value, whichever is lower.

certificate of title A document issued by an abstractor, after reviewing the public records to determine the rights in the estate.

circular flow of income model An economic model of an economy that identifies the major sectors of an economy and the real and money flows that link those-sectors.

close on the buyer Any technique used to obtain an offer from the buyer.

closing The exchange of the deed for the price at a date, time, and place agreed upon by the buyer and the seller.

closing by a deed in escrow Another name for a *contract for deed* whereby the deed is placed in escrow and not given to the buyer until predetermined terms are met.

cohort survival technique A population updating technique based on the use of age cohorts in the population, death (survival) rates, birth (fertility) and migration.

commercial financing Funds used to purchase property that generates an income flow.

commission split The sharing of a total commission between the listing agent and the selling agent when they are not the same firm.

community property A situation, descending from Spanish rule, in which property owned by a couple is either *separate* or *community*. Community property refers to all assets received after the marriage excluding inheritance: each spouse is considered to have a separate and equal ownership in the real estate.

comparable property Residential units that have recently been sold and are very similar to the subject property in physical features, neighborhood location, terms of the sale, ownership rights, and time of sale.

comparative method A method for estimating reproduction costs based on the use of published data on construction costs for standard residential units.

concentric zone (ring) model A model of urban development that postulates the urban area as a series of concentric zones with different land uses in each zone or ring.

consideration The value exchanged for the title.

construction code A police power designed to establish minimum acceptable standards for construction of improvements within the local jurisdiction (same as *building code*).

construction cost study   A type of feasibility study that focuses on the cost of building a new structure or rehabilitating an existing structure to meet the needs of a user.

construction eviction   An intentional and permanent action or default on the part of the landlord that renders the property uninhabitable or unusable by the tenant.

construction (interim) loan   A loan for a short term to allow construction.

consumer research   The process of obtaining information about consumers, especially data about habits, preferences, taste, usage levels, etc.

contract for deed (title)   A purchase arrangement whereby the present mortgage is assumed, the assumption statement and the new deed are placed in escrow, and the seller may carry some financing; the deed is passed when predetermined conditions are satisfied such as the final payment.

contract rent   The rental income generated as a result of the contractual commitments in the lease.

conventional loan   A mortgage without any government insurance or guarantee against default.

conveyance   A document that transfers the title, such as a deed.

cost approach   An appraisal technique in which construction data and the concept of accrued depreciation are used to estimate the current market value of the subject property.

cost of capital   The rate of return or the interest payment that must be paid in order to borrow money.

covenant of further assurance   A clause within the warranty wherein the grantor states that he/she will take legal action to defend his/her ownership rights.

covenant of quiet enjoyment   The grantor's statement in a deed that no better title or lien exists that can be used later to interfere with the ownership and use of the property by the new grantee.

covenant of seizin   A clause within the warranty whereby the grantor states that he/she has full possession of the property and the rights—grantor guarantees good title.

credits   One column in the settlement statement: *buyer*—all totals that the buyer agrees to pay in the future because they fall due after the closing, or that have been paid, or are owed by the seller; *seller*-all totals that are owed to the seller; *agent*—all totals that are owed (and paid) from the trust account.

credit union   An association of people joined by a common bond, such as employment, who pool their savings.

cumulative use zoning   A zoning system that allows less restricted uses (residential) in more restricted land use areas (commercial).

date of assessment   The date on which the owner must declare all real property owned for property tax purposes.

debiting factor   A constant found by dividing the mortgage interest rate by the period of the payment, usually twelve.

debits   One column in the settlement statement: *buyer*—all totals owed in the transaction; *seller*—all totals owed in the transaction; *agent*—all totals owed (and deposited) to the trust account.

debt financing The use of assets belonging to other parties to purchase property.

debt funds Assets belonging to other parties that are used to purchase property.

debt service Interest and amortization payments made by the owner of property to repay the mortgage loan.

debt service coverage ratio Net operating income divided by debt service.

declining balance depreciation methods Accelerated depreciation methods based on the use of some multiple of the straight-line depreciation rate, which is applied to the undepreciated balance of the value of the improvement.

deed A document that conveys the title and represents proof of ownership.

deed of trust An instrument used in lieu of a mortgage in some states because it provides faster foreclosure.

default by the buyer A situation in which the seller accepts the buyer's offer in the contract of sale and the buyer later does not fulfill the commitment to appear at closing with the required funds.

default by the seller A situation in which the seller accepts the buyer's offer in a contract of sale and later does not fulfill the commitment to appear at closing with a new deed.

default in prior payment clause A clause within the second mortgage that allows the second lender to correct a default on the first mortgage by making the payment, adding this amount to the indebtedness of the second loan, and then foreclosing on its loan.

default ratio Loan payments plus operating expenses divided by potential or effective gross income.

delayed closing date A situation in which the buyer agrees to purchase the property and close at a future date and to rent the property until that date.

demand The inverse relationship between price and quantity that represents the ability and willingness of consumers to purchase a commodity.

demand for credit The total level of credit desired by all users at a given interest rate.

Depository Institutions Deregulation and Monetary Control Act (DIDMCA) A federal act (1980) that contains sweeping financial reform ranging from giving new real estate lending authority to savings and loans (e.g., the expansion of loans into short-term consumer loans) to the gradual phaseout of depository controls on interest rates (Regulation Q).

depreciation recapture The process by which the Internal Revenue Code requires the equity investor to calculate excess depreciation claimed and to add this figure to personal income in the year of sale.

design study A type of feasibility study that examines the impact on revenues and operating costs of different building characteristics such as floor plans, height, etc.

direct prospecting Soliciting potential buyers by contacting specific individuals.

direct regulations Local government regulations that affect development in a direct manner (i.e., zoning, subdivision regulation, construction codes).

discharge of contract   The complete performance by both parties of the obligations that each incurred under the contractual agreement.

discount   The amount subtracted from the mortgage; the balance is loaned by the lender or purchased by an institution in the secondary mortgage market.

disintermediation   An outflow of deposits caused by deposit interest rates that are lower than rates paid on competing investments.

disposable income   The amount of current (nominal) income remaining after federal, state, and city income taxes are paid.

dispossession proceedings   The legal process by which the landlord petitions the courts in the local jurisdiction to regain possession of property that is currently in the possession of a tenant who is in default of the lease agreement.

division of twos   A question that asks a person to choose between two alternatives.

dual agency   A situation in which one agent has contracted with a seller and a buyer concurrently; typically, the contract with the seller authorizes the agent to sell and the contract with the buyer authorizes the agent to buy.

due on sale clause   One part of the uniform covenants in a mortgage that allows the lender to call the loan due or adjust the interest rate on the remaining debt to market rates under certain conditions.

dull market   A market in which changes in the economic and demographic factors produce a decline in price, a reduction in number of sales, or a combination of the two.

easement   The right of one person to use the real estate of another for a specified purpose and under certain conditions.

easement appurtenant   An easement that exists where there are at least two parcels of real estate and one of these parcels (the dominant estate) receives benefits that derive from the use of the other parcel of real estate (the servient estate).

easement in gross   An easement involving only one parcel of property where an individual, other than the owner, has the right to use that parcel for a specified purpose in a specified manner.

economic base model   A descriptive model of a local economy that identifies the major economic sectors, the interrelationships among these sectors, and the nature of the sectors and interrelationships.

economic life   The number of years over which an income-earning property will generate a competitive level of net operating income.

economic obsolescence   A reduction in value caused by economic, physical, social, and governmental factors that are external to the subject property.

effective gross income   The income earned by the subject property after vacancy and collection losses are subtracted from potential gross income.

Ellwood method   A sophisticated version of a band-of-investment technique to generate a capitalization rate.

eminent domain   The right vested in the state government and given to local government, and at times even to private agencies, to acquire possession of private property for public purposes after paying fair or just compensation and allowing the owner the right of appeal.

employee   An agent who works for a firm wherein someone has the right to control his or her actions.

environment   The social, physical, political, and economic characteristics of the area surrounding a property that affect its value.

Equal Credit Opportunity Act   A federal act that prohibits the lender from denying credit on the basis of sex, marital status, age, race, religion, national origin, and color.

equity   Personal assets of the buyer used to purchase the property: the current market value of the property less the unpaid mortgage.

equity dividend rate   Periodic cash flow (before-tax cash flow) divided by the investor's equity in the property.

equity financing   The use of one's own assets to purchase property.

equity funds: Personal assets that are used to purchase property.

equity yield rate   The current value of periodic cash flows over the holding period plus the equity increases over the holding period divided by the investor's equity in the property.

escalated lease   A lease in which the rent repayment is established as a fixed or flat amount plus a predetermined yearly change based on some specific price index or component of the property's operating expenses (same as *index lease).*

escheat   The right of a state government to claim ownership of land if its current owner dies without leaving a will and if legal heirs cannot be found.

escrow account   A fund kept by the lender that includes monthly payments by the mortgagor for property taxes and property insurance premium.

estate building   The practice of utilizing one property to obtain, by purchase or trade, a second property that is more valuable or more profitable.

estate for years   A leasehold that continues for a definite period of time, such as one year.

estate from year to year   A leasehold that comes into effect after an estate for years expires and the landlord agrees to the tenant's continued possession of the property.

estate pur autre vie   A freehold estate not-of-inheritance that lasts for the lifetime of a third party.

estoppel certificate   A document prepared and signed by the mortgagor-debtor that states the precise amount of the remaining debt owed and any outstanding claims on the property.

eviction   A term commonly used as a synonym for dispossession proceedings.

evidence of good title   Proof that the seller possesses those rights requested by the buyer.

exchange   A trade between sellers where "likes" are exchanged for "likes."

exclusive agency listing contract   A contractual relationship between the agent and the client whereby no other real estate agency can be used by the owner, but no commission is paid if the owner sells the property.

exclusive right-to-sell listing contract A contractual relationship between the client and the agent whereby the agent is paid a commission regardless of who sells the property.

exclusive use zoning A zoning system that does not permit very restricted uses (industry) in the next less restricted land use area (commercial).

export base theory An economic theory that links the growth of a local economy to its ability to sell exports to non-local buyers.

express contract A written or oral contract in which there is an explicit agreement between the two individuals.

farm A term used by real estate agents to describe a range of property prices, a particular location of properties, or a particular location of people from which listings frequently are obtained.

Farmers Home Administration (FmHA) Any agency under the USDA that sells default insurance to a lender or loans directly to the borrower.

Farmers Home Administration Direct Loan A mortgage given directly by the FmHA to an eligible applicant.

feasibility analysis A technique used to examine all of the pertinent facts and variables affecting an equity investment in order to decide whether that proposed investment enables the investor to accomplish or achieve investment objectives.

Federal Home Loan Bank The regulatory agency for all federally chartered savings and loans; the federal Home Loan Bank Board determines policy that is carried out by the twelve district banks.

Federal Home Loan Mortgage Corporation (The Mortgage Corporation) An institution controlled by the Federal Home Loan Bank Board that participates in the secondary mortgage market.

Federal Housing Administration (FHA) A quasi-public agency that sells default insurance.

Federal Land Bank An institution created as part of the Farm Credit System to provide credit for the highly specialized needs of farmers and their marketing, supply, and business service operations.

Federal National Mortgage Association (Fannie Mae) An association that is publicly controlled and privately owned that participates in the secondary mortgage market.

fee simple title Full rights of ownership, which may be limited by known conditions.

fiduciary relationship The agent's responsibility to be loyal to, and to act in, the best interests of the principal.

financial ratio Calculations that illustrate levels of performance that collectively indicate success or failure.

financial risk The risk that future levels of net operating income (generated by the property) will not be sufficient to allow the owner to repay the mortgage loan.

financial study A type of feasibility study that investigates whether the rate of return on a project is large enough to attract capital to the project or meet an investor's needs.

fixture An item of personal property that is legally considered to be real estate because it is attached either to the land or to an improvement that is itself permanently attached to the land.

fraud A misrepresentation of a material fact, made either with knowledge of its falsity (intentional) or in reckless ignorance of the truth (unintentional) that results in injury to the other party who relies on the fact.

freehold estate The rights of ownership in real estate that last for the duration of a lifetime.

freehold estate of inheritance A freehold estate in which the owner has the right to dispose of the property in addition to the rights of use, possession, and exclusion.

freehold estate not-of-inheritance A freehold estate in which the current owner cannot dispose of the property through a sale or gift but can lease the property to a third party. The owner of this estate has only the rights of use, possession, and exclusion.

functional obsolescence A reduction in value caused either by inherent defects in the design of the structure or by its inability to satisfy current consumer needs.

futures market The buying and selling of future contracts; a savings and loan may buy or sell future contracts that will exactly offset a current decision to protect interest earnings.

general agent A licensed firm or individual who is authorized by a client to accomplish a given objective for compensation; the agent has the right to make decisions about the best methods to employ in accomplishing the objective; real estate listing contracts are typically viewed as special agency contracts.

general contractor An individual who enters into a contract with a client to build a structure by supervising all of the individual suppliers of products and services.

general data Economic, physical, social, and governmental factors in the local economy, its region, and the national economy.

general lien A lien that affects the asset holdings or the wealth of an individual without specific reference to certain pieces of property.

general partnership A business owned by any number of partners that does not have the same tax treatment as a limited partnership.

Good Faith Estimate of Closing Costs A document prepared by the lender and required under RESPA, stating estimates of the range of all closing costs.

Government National Mortgage Association (GNMA) A department within the Department of Housing and Urban Development that participates in the secondary mortgage market.

government survey A legal description based on lines of latitude (baselines) and lines of longitude (principal meridians), as well as distances and directions away from these baselines and meridians, used to specify the dimensions of a parcel of land.

graduated payment lease A lease in which the rent payment level increases in a predetermined manner as time passes.

Graduated Payment Mortgage (GPM) A loan for which the initial monthly payments are lower than those required for a conventional loan and that increase annually from 2 to 7.5 percent over a period of five to ten years.

grant deed A deed that contains no stated warranties from the grantor but, as typically required by state laws, implies a warranty—no encumbrances have been placed on the property during the grantor's ownership and the property has not already been conveyed.

granting clause (words of conveyance) A phraseology within the deed whereby the owner expresses his/her current intent to pass the title.

grantor The owner transferring title.

gross income multiplier A technique that can be used to convert either monthly or annual gross income into an estimate of current market value for an income-producing property.

gross lease A lease in which the rent payment is established as a fixed or flat payment.

gross rate of return The before-tax cash flow plus the equity increase due to mortgage repayment divided by gross income.

ground lease A lease agreement that is made for vacant land.

habendum **clause** A clause in the deed that explains the extent of the rights transferred; contains the warranty.

hedge A position taken in the futures market that will exactly offset a decision in the current market; hedging is done to protect interest earnings on a loan.

height restriction Section of zoning ordinance specifying maximum building height.

highest and best use The legally permissible use of real estate that yields the highest return to the owner over a reasonable period of time.

holdback (retainage) An amount of the permanent loan that is withheld by the permanent lender to cover risk of early default by the borrower.

holding period The length of time that the investor retains ownership of the real estate equity investment.

housing code A police power designed to establish socially acceptable minimum standards for safety and health both in existing and newly constructed buildings (same as *occupancy code*).

housing inventory method A population updating technique that relies on building permit data and household size.

improvements Man-made additions or changes to the land that make it usable for some economic purpose.

improvements-on-the-land Permanently erected man-made structures that are placed on the land.

improvements-to-the-land Man-made additions or changes to the shape, slope, or substance of the land.

income approach An appraisal technique in which the potential revenue and the operating expenses of the subject property and an appropriate capitalization rate are used to estimate current market value.

income tax depreciation techniques Mathematical techniques established to represent value decline of a physical asset for income tax purposes.

independent contractor   An agent who works for a firm wherein no one can control his/her actions.

indexed lease   A lease in which the rent repayment is established as a fixed or flat amount plus a predetermined yearly change based on some specified price index or component of the property's operating expenses (same as *escalated lease)*.

indirect prospecting   Soliciting potential buyers by advertising the property in anticipation that interested parties will identify themselves.

indirect regulations   Local government actions and programs that are designed to provide public services but, in so doing, also affect development (i.e., provision of waste and sewer services, road construction, etc.).

interest or money market risk   The risk that future value of the investment will be less than forecasted because the capitalization rate in the future will be higher than it was at the time of the initial appraisal and investment decision.

intermediate theory   A concept applied in some states whereby the mortgage is interpreted as being under title or lien theory and the courts have interpreted the opposite.

intermediation   An inflow of deposits caused by deposit rates that are competitive with rates paid on competing investments.

internal rate of return   A rate of return that makes the initial equity investment equal to the present value of a stream of future benefits or cash flows.

investment   The purchase of an income-earning asset.

joint ownership   Ownership of property as joint tenants, tenants in common, and tenancy by the entirety.

joint tenancy   A form of co-ownership in which each joint owner has an equal and undivided interest in the real property and upon the death of one joint owner the rights of ownership pass to the surviving joint owners.

junior lien   A claim to the value of the property that is second in priority in the event of buyer default.

land   The surface of the earth plus mineral rights and air rights.

land-building ratio   Square feet of the site divided by gross building area.

land contract   A transaction whereby the seller extends credit to the purchaser for part of the selling price; typically, the buyer receives possession and its benefits but does not receive the deed until the last payment is made.

leasehold   A synonym for less-than-freehold estate.

legal description   Legally accepted method for stating the physical dimensions of a parcel of land.

less-than-freehold estate   The rights of ownership in real estate that are possessed for less than a lifetime.

leverage (positive)   The use of borrowed money to purchase an asset (whose rate of return should be greater than the interest rate on the borrowed funds).

lien   The right of a creditor to petition to the courts to force the sale of a debtor's property in order to obtain payment.

lien theory A concept applied in some states whereby the mortgage is viewed as leaving the deed and possession with the mortgagor while giving the mortgagee a lien on the property.

lien waiver A statement signed by laborers and suppliers of materials that no bills owed by the owner are unpaid.

life estate A freehold estate not-of-inheritance that lasts for the duration of the current owner's lifetime.

limited partnership A pooling of investment funds characterized by a general partner and one or more limited partners that is given special tax treatment.

liquidated damages A sum of money, mutually determined at the time of the making of the contract by the parties to the contract, that will be paid to the injured party in case of nonperformance or breach of contract.

liquidity The ability to convert an asset into cash within a relatively short time without a loss of value in the transaction.

listing A term used to describe the contractual relationship between the agent and the client.

listing agent The firm representing the principal.

loan per square foot Mortgage loan divided by gross leasable area.

loan-to-value ratio Mortgage loan divided by property value.

local board The community association of REALTORS and REALTOR-ASSO-CIATES that is part of the State Association and the National Association of REAL-TORS.

location study A type of feasibility study that identifies sites that will satisfy the needs of a project or use.

lot and block system A legal description based on the use of maps and showing the dimensions of a site and its relationship to adjoining sites.

management by objectives Establishing definite goals and developing a day-to-day plan to accomplish those goals.

market The economic environment in which property is exchanged.

marketability analysis (study) Examination of the economic, legal, and physical factors that affect a specific property.

market analysis (study) Examination of the market for a specific type of real estate. It examines demand and supply factors that affect the disaggregated real estate.

market data approach An appraisal technique in which the sales prices of comparable properties that have been sold in the very recent past are used to estimate the market value of the subject property.

market disaggregation The process of subdividing real estate into standardized groupings based on physical characteristics and locational attributes

market price The price of the product established in the market by the interaction of demand and supply.

market rent The rental income that a unit of space would most probably command in the open market as indicated by the current rents being negotiated for comparable space.

market segmentation The process of subdividing consumers into homogeneous groupings based on their demographic, economic, and/or psychographic characteristics (tastes, preferences, habits, etc).

market value The market price established in a market that is characterized by several necessary conditions, such as rational, well-informed, and typically motivated buyers and sellers; reasonable time of exposure of the product on the market; normal circumstances surrounding financing of the purchase; and freedom from undue bargaining power by one of the parties in the transaction.

material fact A piece of information or evidence that a reasonable person would consider important when determining a course of action or reaching a decision.

mechanic's lien A state right given to laborers and suppliers of materials to attach a claim upon the value of property for the nonpayment of labor or supplies.

merchantable or marketable title A title that a court of law would require the buyer to accept; one that is free from clouds or defects.

metes-and-bounds system A legal description whereby distances, directions, and angles of change in direction are used to specify the dimensions of a parcel of land.

mineral rights The legal claim to the minerals below the surface of the land.

misrepresentation An unintentional incorrect or improper statement about a fact.

mistake of fact A mistake that occurs when a certain piece of information or conditions are not true.

mistake of law A mistake that arises when a person who has full knowledge of the facts makes an erroneous conclusion about the legal effect of those facts.

mortgage-backed bonds A bond that is issued by a lender and backed by a pool of residential mortgages; the lender guarantees the principal and interest payment.

mortgage-backed certificates Securities that are issued by a lender and backed by a pool of residential mortgages.

mortgage banker A private company that attempts to find borrowers for money obtained from the secondary mortgage market or private investors.

most probable selling price The market price established under somewhat less rigid requirements than market value. Buyers and sellers need not be completely informed; their abilities to obtain financing and the time period for exposure of the property in the market need only approximate normal circumstances.

multiple listing service (MLS) An organization of local real estate firms that agree to share listings to give the property maximum exposure.

multiple nuclei model A model of urban development that postulates the urban area having several, not just one, focal points or cores.

mutual savings bank A private company that accepts savings deposits and reinvests them wherever the highest return can be received.

National Association of REALTORS A national trade association that provides education, supports a code of ethics, and represents the members' interest politically.

natural increase and migration method A population updating technique that uses birth (fertility), death (mortality), and migration data to adjust existing population figures.

neighborhood   A portion of a larger community characterized by homogeneity, or at least a complementary grouping, of inhabitants, buildings, and land uses.

neighborhood analysis   The use of general data about the immediate surroundings of the subject property to determine the factors that can affect the market value of the subject property.

net household formation   The change in the number of households brought about by the formation of new households, the dissolution of existing households and net migration in the local market.

net lease   A lease in which the rent payment is established as a fixed or flat amount plus one or more of the operating expenses associated with the property.

net listing   A contractual relationship between the client and the agent whereby the client specifies a minimum price for the property; the agent keeps as the commission any amount obtained over the minimum.

net operating income (NOI)   Effective gross income minus operating expenses.

nominal income   The income of a consuming unit, or a household, measured by the number of dollars actually received in the form of wages, salaries, dividends, interest payments, etc.

nonconforming use   A use of land that existed before the existing zoning ordinance was imposed, which does not conform to the existing, permissible use of land.

occupancy code   A police power designed to establish socially acceptable minimum standards for safety and health both in existing and newly constructed buildings (same as *housing code*).

offer   A conditional promise made by the potential buyer to the seller of property.

open end mortgage   One mortgage that covers a commitment by the lender to advance additional funds in the future; the advances can be automatic or reevaluated upon each request.

open listing contract   A contractual relationship enabling the owner to use as many agents as he or she desires; a commission is paid to the agent who presents the first acceptable offer to the owner.

operating cost study   A type of feasibility study that examines whether operating costs can be reduced.

operating expense ratio   Total operating expenses divided by effective gross income.

operating expenses   The total of all expenses incurred by the landlord and directly associated with providing the services and space that generate the rent revenue.

option   A legal instrument that allows a potential buyer to control a piece of property while a contingency (zoning change, financing, etc) is being investigated and removed. The right to control is purchased.

overall cap rate   Net operating income divided by the sale price or market value.

ownership costs   The expenses that must be incurred by the owner of property to generate the benefits from the property and to maintain the property in the condition required to perpetuate the benefits.

package mortgage   One debt that covers both real and personal property on a particular parcel.

partial amortization   Periodic repayment of the debt that does not reduce the debt to zero by the maturity date.

participation loan   The lender claims a portion either of the equity in the property or of the future income in addition to an interest rate.

pass through certificates   A certificate that is issued by a lender and backed by a pool of residential mortgages; the lender serves as a conduit and transmits principal and interest payments from the underlying loans to the investors.

payment in advance   A liability on the real property that is paid the same year as the date of assessment and billing, such as special property taxes.

payment in arrears   A liability on the real property that is paid the year following the date of assessment and billing, such as real property taxes.

percentage lease   A lease in which the rent payment is established as a percentage of the commercial tenant's gross sales.

periodic cash flow   The funds that are derived from an investment and received on some definite, periodic basis.

permanent loan   The long-term, first mortgage secured by the property.

physical deterioration   Structural disintegration or the wear-and-tear inherent in a structure.

piggyback loan (split loan, joint loan)   A financing arrangement between lenders to advance the borrower jointly a high percentage of the selling price.

plat map system   A legal description based on the use of maps showing the dimensions of a site and its relationship to adjoining sites.

point   One point is an amount equal to one percent of the mortgage balance. Points are charged by the lender to increase the return on the mortgage and typically are paid at the closing.

police powers of the state   The powers granted to federal and state governments in their constitutions to protect the public by regulating factors that can affect the health, morals, safety, and general welfare of the community.

potential gross income   The total income generated by an income-earning property based on the assumption that the property receives market rent.

present-value technique   A method used to calculate the present value of a stream of benefits or cash flows that will be received in the future.

price appreciation   An increase in the sales price of real property.

principal   The client, typically the seller.

principal risk   The risk that the future sales price of the property will be less than anticipated.

priority of liens   The order in which liens are honored in the case of actual sale; liens that are recorded first are given first priority.

procuring cause   Successful effort by an agent that leads to the buyer's purchase of a property. Proof of the agent's involvement is required if the agent is to collect a commission.

property manager   An individual who specializes in the full-time administration of property for a fee.

proprietary power A government's power to accept or refuse development action and plans under subdivision regulations and possible government problems and regulations.

prorating The process of dividing income and debits between the owner and the buyer.

purchase money mortgage A mortgage commitment offered by the buyer to the seller in the purchase price whereby the seller extends credit for a portion of the total purchase price.

purchasing power risk The risk that the money an investor receives in the future will have less purchasing power than anticipated.

pyramiding The practice of utilizing one property to obtain funds, or to collateralize the purchase of a second property.

pyramid zoning See cumulative use zoning.

qualifying the buyer Part of the counseling process whereby the agent attempts to determine the buyer's financial assets to ensure that the property in question can be purchased using financing available to the buyer.

quantity survey method A method to calculate reproduction costs based on establishing an inventory of all materials and labor required to reproduce the subject property.

quitclaim deed A deed that contains no warranties.

ratio technique A population updating technique, which uses a known, current value for a large region to derive an unknown, current value for a subarea of that region.

real estate A physical entity that consists of land and the man-made improvements permanently attached to it.

real estate agent An individual licensed by the state to represent a client in a real estate transaction for compensation. A firm that may be represented by licensed salespeople.

real estate business All individuals and organizations receiving compensation for providing services.

real estate commission A state board authorized to enforce the state license law by granting, revoking, and suspending licenses, and by enacting rules and regulations that govern the conduct of the business; in some states, a commissioner serves in lieu of a commission.

real estate counselor Any individual who offers advice about real estate for a fee.

real estate developer Any person or firm that transforms property from one stage of use to another.

real estate equity investment The use of accumulated savings to purchase income-earning real property.

Real Estate Investment Trust (REIT) A trust or association that has invested primarily in real estate and has applied for special tax treatment.

real estate lender An individual or institution that loans funds for the purchase of real estate.

Real Estate Settlement Procedures Act (RESPA)   A federal act designed to protect the buyer from harmful loan practices, to provide relevant cost information prior to the closing, and to gather information statistics on closing costs and procedures.

real income   The income of the household measured in terms of the goods and services that the actual or nominal income can purchase—purchasing power.

real property   The rights of ownership that are inherent (real estate).

real property taxes   Annual tax bill paid by the property owner for the general public services that benefit all land parcels in the taxing district, such as police protection, sanitary services, water, and fire protection.

REALTOR   A principal, partner, or officer who is actively engaged in the real estate business and a member of the local real estate board, State Association, and National Association of REALTORS.

REALTOR-ASSOCIATE   A salesperson, independent contractor, or certain affiliate members who are affiliated with a member firm of which the principal, partner, or officer is a REALTOR.

refinancing   The act of replacing the current first mortgage by a new first mortgage.

Renegotiable Rate Mortgage (RRM)   A loan issued for a term of three, four, or five years that is secured by a long-term mortgage of up to 30 years.

rent with option to buy   A situation in which the renter agrees to rent the property for a specified period of time with the right to purchase the property at a predetermined date.

replacement cost   The current cost incurred to construct a substitute property that is not necessarily similar to the subject property but provides the owner with the same level of benefits and satisfaction.

reproduction cost   The current cost that would be incurred to construct an exact replica or a perfect substitute for the subject property.

restrictive covenant   A statement placed in the deed by the seller that limits the buyer's use of the property.

rights of ownership   The right to use, to possess, to exclude other people from, and to dispose of real estate.

role playing   Simulating an actual situation in which the agent is asked to respond as on the job to enable outsiders to view the technique and provide constructive criticism.

sale and leaseback agreement   A lease agreement in which the current owner offers to sell the property to a prospective buyer under the condition that a lease is executed at the time of sale giving the current owner the leasehold estate after the freehold estate is sold.

salvage value   The value of the improvement on the property at the end of the useful life.

sandwich lease   The lease signed by the second investor in a situation wherein an owner becomes a lessee by selling the new lease to a second investor, subleases from that person, and continues to operate the property.

savings and loan association A private company that accepts savings deposits and loans them in real estate mortgages.

secondary mortgage market A group of quasi-public, public, and private institutions who buy mortgages from originators; they also buy and sell among themselves.

second (junior) mortgage A debt on real property that has a claim to the value of the property that is second in priority to the first mortgage.

sector model A model of urban development that postulates the urban area as being composed of sections containing different land uses.

security deposit Funds paid by the tenant to the landlord at the time the lease is executed as security against undue wear and tear or damage to the property.

seller financing A process whereby the seller becomes a lender for all, or a portion, of the sales price.

seller's market An active market.

sensitivity analysis A technique used to determine the impact of changes in revenues, operating, financing, and tax expenses and other factors (holding period, etc.) on the present value or on the internal rate of return.

settlement agent The person responsible for the closing and the preparation of the settlement (closing) statements.

settlement statement A listing of income, expenses, and prorated amounts (if applicable) prepared typically by the settlement agent to account for all monies in the transaction; separate statements are prepared for the seller, the buyer, and the agent.

sheriff's deed A type of deed given to the new owner after a sale of property to recover past-due taxes; it contains no warranty.

sinking fund The amount per period that will grow to $1 at a given rate in a given period of time.

site-development standards Sections of a zoning ordinance that affect the manner in which a site can be developed by setting minimum standards for square footage of the lot; setback; frontage and width; and maximum standards for height or the structure and land coverage. (See also area regulations and height restrictions.)

special agency with the buyer A contractual relationship between the firm and the principal (the buyer) whereby the agent is given instructions to accomplish a certain task, such as locating and purchasing a special type of property.

special agency with the seller A contractual relationship between the firm and the principal (the seller) whereby the agent is given authority to "find a buyer who is ready, willing, and able to purchase the property."

special agent A licensed firm or individual authorized by a client to accomplish a given objective for compensation; typically, the special agent's right to make decisions about methods to accomplish the objective is limited. Listing contracts are typically viewed as special agency contracts.

special assessments A separate tax bill paid by the owner of real property for special improvements that the neighborhood has requested from the taxing government, such as curb and gutter, paving, and irrigation controls.

special warranty deed A deed containing a warranty that covers only the grantor's period of ownership.

specific data Physical and legal factors that characterize the site, the improvements, and the rights of ownership inherent in a particular piece of real property.

specific performance A legal remedy for breach of contract whereby the courts grant the injured party a court order requiring that the defaulting party perform the contract according to the specific terms of the contract entered into by the parties.

spending power Use of a government's spending to affect development. Examples are land purchases for roads, schools, parks, utilities, etc.

stabilized vacancy ratio A percentage of gross income.

standby permanent financing A commitment for a first mortgage that allows a developer to seek construction financing to initiate construction.

stock of housing The number of housing units of a certain type in existence at a given point in time.

straight-line depreciation A mathematical relationship stating that the value of property declines by an equal percentage in each year of its useful life.

subchapter S corporation A corporation that may qualify for some of the same tax benefits as a limited partnership.

subject property The property that is being considered or appraised.

subletting The process by which the original tenant enters into a separate and distinct lease with a new tenant to transfer a portion, but not all, of the original tenant's rights in the leased property.

subordinated ground lease The owner sells the land to a third party and leases it back on the condition that the owner's claim to ownership will be second in priority to any financing offered by a future lender.

subordination clause A clause within the second mortgage that places the second lender in second priority to the first lender.

sum of the years' digits An accelerated depreciation technique in which the depreciation rate is established as the number of years of useful life remaining divided by the sum of all the digits in the useful life.

supply The direct relationship between price and quantity that represents the sellers' or producers' ability and willingness to produce and offer for sale units of commodity during a given period of time.

supply of credit The total level of credit provided at a particular interest rate.

survey of the competition A component of a marketability study that investigates the competition faced by the subject property.

syndicate A pooling of investors and their investment funds with a real estate professional to purchase property.

takeout commitment A promise by the permanent lender to pay off the construction (interim) lender when the construction is complete.

taxable income The numerical value of net operating income minus mortgage interest payments and depreciation charges.

tax bill   The amount owed on the property for real property taxes.

tax deferral techniques   Procedures whereby the Internal Revenue Code allows the investor to defer the payment of capital gains and depreciation recapture until some point in the future.

taxing power   Use of a government's ability to collect taxes in order to affect development; examples are the *ACRS,* investment credits by the federal government and property tax exemptions, differential tax rates and assessments by a local government.

tax shelter   A means by which some portion of an individual investor's gross income can be protected from tax liability under the Internal Revenue Code.

tenancy at will   A leasehold for which the duration is not definitely specified; the duration continues as long as both the landlord and the tenant agree to its continuation.

tenancy by sufferance   A leasehold that comes into existence when a tenant's rights under one of the other leaseholds expires and the tenant retains possession against the landlord's wishes.

tenancy by the entirety   A type of ownership for married couples where they own property as a sole owner if married. at the time of accepting a deed.

tenancy in common   A form of co-ownership in which each owner owns a separate and identifiable interest in the property.

term amortization   A type of loan repayment where the debt is repaid in one final payment at maturity.

termite bond   An insurance policy against future termite damage issued to the property owner after an inspection of the premises by a reputable pest control company, elimination of any infestation, and application of permanent chemicals around the foundation.

termite inspection   An inspection of the premises by a reputable pest control company and a verbal statement concerning infestation and damage.

termite inspection receipt   A document from a reputable pest control company stating that the property has no infestation and is free of damage.

that's right—that leaves . . .   A response that enables the user to progress to the alternative response desired.

tie-down   A reflexive statement ending with a question that provides a response to the client without giving information and solicits additional information.

title   The proof of ownership.

title company   A private company that prepares real estate title abstracts and usually sells title insurance.

title insurance   Protection sold to the new owner by an insurance company to cover any loss from undiscovered title defects within the records.

title theory   A concept applied in some states whereby the mortgage is viewed as leaving the deed with the mortgagee and possession with the mortgagor.

Torrens certificate   A certificate of title issued by a public official who reviews the deed and other appropriate documents to determine proper ownership; part of a system of land registration.

trustee   The escrow agent for a deed of trust.

Truth-in-Lending (Regulation Z)   A federal law that requires the lender to disclose the finance charge and the annual percentage rate to the borrower in order that the cost of credit is known by the borrower in advance.

unenforceable contract   A valid contract that is not recognized by the courts in the event that any legal action is brought before the court to enforce it.

unilateral contract   A contract in which one person makes a promise or extends an offer and the other person receives the benefit of that promise or offer contingent upon the performance of some act.

unit-in-place method   A method for calculating reproduction cost based on the cost of assembling major components of the subject property.

useful life   The time period over which real property may be useful to the investor in the operation of a business or the production of income.

use regulation   Section of a zoning ordinance that specifies the extent to which land can be put to good use. (Also the land use regulation).

vacancy analysis   An examination of the number of vacant housing units in the market at the prevailing price in the market; consideration is given to the economic and demographic factors on both the demand and supply sides of the market.

VA guaranteed loan   A loan obtained through a local lender that carries a Veterans Administration (VA) commitment to guarantee a predetermined amount of the loan in the event of default.

valid contract   A contract that fulfills all the legal requirements imposed by the body of law known as contract law.

value-in-exchange   The ability of one product to be exchanged for other products or commodities.

value-in-use   The satisfaction derived by the owner from use or consumption of a product or real estate.

variable rate mortgage   A mortgage wherein the borrower allows the lender to change the interest rate and monthly payments under certain conditions.

verification of deposit   A form that the lender may ask the loan applicant to complete to allow the lender to verify the source of the necessary funds for the downpayment.

verification of employment   A form that the lender may ask the loan applicant to complete to identify the employer, the type of work, and the length of service.

Veterans Administration (VA)   A government agency that administers benefits to qualified veterans under the G.I. Bill of Rights.

voidable contract   A contract in which one party can exercise the right to avoid, or to rescind, the contractual obligations incurred.

void agreement   An agreement that does not fulfill the legal requirements imposed by contract law; a contract that is not valid.

warranty   In general terms, the grantor's (owner's) statement that he or she will take legal action to defend his or her claims to the ownership during his or her period of ownership and possibly earlier or later periods.

waste   An act that does permanent injury to real estate that is owned as a life estate.

wraparound mortgage   A situation in which a lender loans funds to a buyer who uses the money to purchase property by assuming an existing mortgage; the new lender writes the wraparound mortgage for the total of the assumption plus the amount loaned and charges the interest rate on this amount.

"yes" response question   Any question or comment that requires a "yes" response from the client; it attempts to generate a positive attitude.

zoning ordinance   A local ordinance whereby the local jurisdiction regulates the use of individual parcels of property.

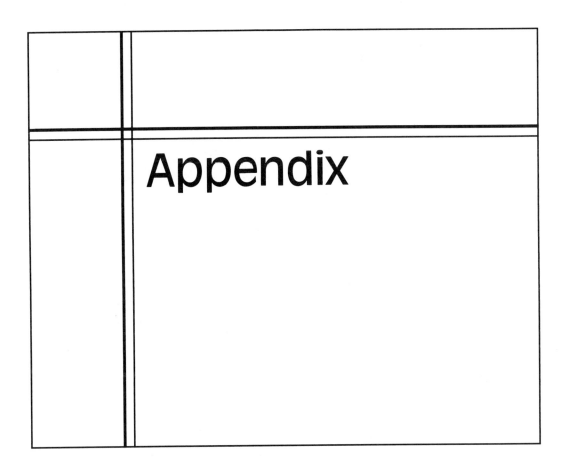

Appendix

Source for all tables: Austin J. Jaffe, C.F. Sirmans, Real Estate Investment Decision Making, © 1982, pp. 536, 540, 541, 543. Reprinted by permission of Prentice-Hall, Inc., Englewood Cliffs, N.J.

Monthly compound interest tables (10%)

Year	Month	Amount of one	Amount of one per period	Sinking fund factor	Present worth of one	Present worth of one per period	Partial payment
	1	1.00833	1.00000	1.00000	.99174	.99174	1.00833
	2	1.01674	2.00833	.49793	.98354	1.97527	.50626
	3	1.02521	3.02507	.33057	.97541	2.95069	.33890
	4	1.03375	4.05028	.24690	.96735	3.91804	.25523
	5	1.04237	5.08403	.19669	.95936	4.87739	.20503
	6	1.05105	6.12640	.16323	.95143	5.82882	.17156
	7	1.05981	7.17745	.13933	.94356	6.77238	.14766
	8	1.06864	8.23726	.12140	.93577	7.70815	.12973
	9	1.07755	9.30591	.10746	.92803	8.63618	.11579
	10	1.08653	10.38346	.09631	.92036	9.55654	.10464
	11	1.09558	11.46998	.08718	.91276	10.46930	.09552
1	12	1.10471	12.56557	.07958	.90521	11.37451	.08792
2	24	1.22039	26.44692	.03781	.81941	21.67085	.04614
3	36	1.34818	41.78182	.02393	.74174	30.99124	.03227
4	48	1.48935	58.72249	.01703	.67143	39.42816	.02536
5	60	1.64531	77.43707	.01291	.60779	47.06537	.02125
6	72	1.81759	98.11131	.01019	.55018	53.97867	.01853
7	84	2.00792	120.95042	.00827	.49803	60.23667	.01660
8	96	2.21818	146.18108	.00684	.45082	65.90149	.01517
9	108	2.45045	174.05371	.00575	.40809	71.02936	.01408
10	120	2.70704	204.84498	.00488	.36941	75.67116	.01322
11	132	2.99050	238.86049	.00419	.33439	79.87299	.01252
12	144	3.30364	276.43788	.00362	.30270	83.67653	.01195
13	156	3.64958	317.95010	.00315	.27400	87.11954	.01148
14	168	4.03174	363.80920	.00275	.24803	90.23620	.01108
15	180	4.45392	414.47034	.00241	.22452	93.05744	.01075
16	192	4.92030	470.43637	.00213	.20324	95.61126	.01046
17	204	5.43552	532.26278	.00188	.18397	97.92301	.01021
18	216	6.00469	600.56321	.00166	.16654	100.01563	.01000
19	228	6.63346	676.01560	.00148	.15075	101.90990	.00981
20	240	7.32807	759.36883	.00132	.13646	103.62462	.00965
21	252	8.09542	851.45024	.00117	.12353	105.17680	.00951
22	264	8.94311	953.17377	.00105	.11182	106.58186	.00938
23	276	9.87958	1065.54909	.00094	.10122	107.85373	.00927
24	288	10.91410	1189.69157	.00084	.09162	109.00505	.00917
25	300	12.05694	1326.83339	.00075	.08294	110.04723	.00909
26	312	13.31946	1478.33575	.00068	.07508	110.99063	.00901
27	324	14.71419	1645.70239	.00061	.06796	111.84461	.00894
28	336	16.25495	1830.59451	.00055	.06152	112.61764	.00888
29	348	17.95706	2034.84724	.00049	.05569	113.31739	.00882
30	360	19.83740	2260.48790	.00044	.05041	113.95082	.00878
35	420	32.63865	3796.63800	.00026	.03064	116.32338	.00860
40	480	53.70066	6324.07948	.00016	.01862	117.76539	.00849

674

Monthly compound interest tables (12%)

Year	Month	Amount of one	Amount of one per period	Sinking fund factor	Present worth of one	Present worth of one per period	Partial payment
	1	1.01000	1.00000	1.00000	.99010	.99010	1.01000
	2	1.02010	2.01000	.49751	.98030	1.97040	.50751
	3	1.03030	3.03010	.33002	.97059	2.94099	.34002
	4	1.04060	4.06040	.24628	.96098	3.90197	.25628
	5	1.05101	5.10101	.19604	.95147	4.85343	.20604
	6	1.06152	6.15202	.16255	.94205	5.79548	.17255
	7	1.07214	7.21354	.13863	.93272	6.72819	.14863
	8	1.08286	8.28567	.12069	.92348	7.65168	.13069
	9	1.09369	9.36853	.10674	.91434	8.56602	.11674
	10	1.10462	10.46221	.09558	.90529	9.47130	.10558
	11	1.11567	11.56683	.08645	.89632	10.36763	.09645
1	12	1.12683	12.68250	.07885	.88745	11.25508	.08885
2	24	1.26973	26.97346	.03707	.78757	21.24339	.04707
3	36	1.43077	43.07688	.02321	.69892	30.10751	.03321
4	48	1.61223	61.22261	.01633	.62026	37.97396	.02633
5	60	1.81670	81.66967	.01224	.55045	44.95504	.02224
6	72	2.04710	104.70993	.00955	.48850	51.15039	.01955
7	84	2.30672	130.67227	.00765	.43352	56.64845	.01765
8	96	2.59927	159.92729	.00625	.38472	61.52770	.01625
9	108	2.92893	192.89258	.00518	.34142	65.85779	.01518
10	120	3.30039	230.03869	.00435	.30299	69.70052	.01435
11	132	3.71896	271.89586	.00368	.26889	73.11075	.01368
12	144	4.19062	319.06156	.00313	.23863	76.13716	.01313
13	156	4.72209	372.20905	.00269	.21177	78.82294	.01269
14	168	5.32097	432.09698	.00231	.18794	81.20643	.01231
15	180	5.99580	499.58020	.00200	.16678	83.32166	.01200
16	192	6.75622	575.62197	.00174	.14801	85.19882	.01179
17	204	7.61308	661.30775	.00151	.13135	86.86471	.01151
18	216	8.57861	757.86063	.00132	.11657	88.34310	.01132
19	228	9.66659	866.65883	.00115	.10345	89.65509	.01115
20	240	10.89255	989.25536	.00101	.09181	90.81942	.01101
21	252	12.27400	1127.40021	.00089	.08147	91.85270	.01089
22	264	13.83065	1283.06528	.00078	.07230	92.76968	.01078
23	276	15.58473	1458.47257	.00069	.06417	93.58346	.01069
24	288	17.56126	1656.12590	.00060	.05694	94.30565	.01060
25	300	19.78847	1878.84662	.00053	.05053	94.94655	.01053
26	312	22.29814	2129.81391	.00047	.04485	95.51532	.01047
27	324	25.12610	2412.61012	.00041	.03980	96.02007	.01041
28	336	28.31272	2731.27198	.00037	.03532	96.46802	.01037
29	348	31.90348	3090.34813	.00032	.03134	96.86555	.01032
30	360	35.94964	3494.96413	.00029	.02782	97.21833	.01029
35	420	65.30959	6430.95946	.00016	.01531	98.46883	.01016
40	480	118.64772	11764.77249	.00008	.00843	99.15717	.01008

Monthly compound interest tables (13%)

Year	Month	Amount of one	Amount of one per period	Sinking fund factor	Present worth of one	Present worth of one per period	Partial payment
	1	1.01083	1.00000	1.00000	0.98928	0.98928	0.01083
	2	1.02178	2.01083	0.49731	0.97868	1.96796	0.50814
	3	1.03285	3.03262	0.32975	0.96819	2.93616	0.34058
	4	1.04404	4.06547	0.24597	0.95782	3.89397	0.25681
	5	1.05535	5.10951	0.19571	0.94755	4.84152	0.20655
	6	1.06679	6.16487	0.16221	0.93740	5.77892	0.17304
	7	1.07834	7.23165	0.13828	0.92735	6.70626	0.14911
	8	1.09003	8.31000	0.12034	0.91741	7.62367	0.13117
	9	1.10183	9.40002	0.10638	0.90758	8.53125	0.11722
	10	1.11377	10.50185	0.09522	0.89785	9.42910	0.10606
	11	1.12584	11.61562	0.08609	0.88823	10.31733	0.09692
1	12	1.13803	12.74146	0.07848	0.87871	11.19604	0.08932
2	24	1.29512	27.24166	0.03671	0.77213	21.03411	0.04754
3	36	1.47389	43.74335	0.02286	0.67848	29.67892	0.03369
4	48	1.67733	62.52281	0.01599	0.59619	37.27519	0.02683
5	60	1.90886	83.89445	0.01192	0.52387	43.95011	0.02275
6	72	2.17234	108.21607	0.00924	0.46033	49.81542	0.02007
7	84	2.47219	135.89486	0.00736	0.40450	54.96933	0.01819
8	96	2.81344	167.39423	0.00597	0.35544	59.49812	0.01681
9	108	3.20178	203.24153	0.00492	0.31233	63.47760	0.01575
10	120	3.64373	244.03692	0.00410	0.27444	66.97442	0.01493
11	132	4.14669	290.46340	0.00344	0.24116	70.04710	0.01428
12	144	4.71906	343.29824	0.00291	0.21191	72.74710	0.01375
13	156	5.37045	403.42601	0.00248	0.18620	75.11961	0.01331
14	168	6.11175	471.85336	0.00212	0.16362	77.20436	0.01295
15	180	6.95536	549.72591	0.00182	0.14377	79.03625	0.01265
16	192	7.91543	638.34741	0.00157	0.12634	80.64595	0.01240
17	204	9.00802	739.20154	0.00135	0.11101	82.06041	0.01219
18	216	10.25142	853.97683	0.00117	0.09755	83.30331	0.01200
19	228	11.66644	984.59483	0.00102	0.08572	84.39545	0.01185
20	240	13.27679	1133.24235	0.00088	0.07532	85.35513	0.01172
21	252	15.10942	1302.40807	0.00077	0.06618	86.19841	0.01160
22	264	17.19501	1494.92414	0.00067	0.05816	86.93941	0.01150
23	276	19.56848	1714.01369	0.00058	0.05110	87.59053	0.01142
24	288	22.26957	1963.34472	0.00051	0.04490	88.16268	0.01134
25	300	25.34349	2247.09152	0.00045	0.03946	88.66543	0.01128
26	312	28.84172	2570.00460	0.00039	0.03467	89.10720	0.01122
27	324	32.82281	2937.49017	0.00034	0.03047	89.49539	0.01117
28	336	37.35342	3355.70069	0.00030	0.02677	89.83650	0.01113
29	348	42.50941	3831.63784	0.00026	0.02352	90.13623	0.01109
30	360	48.37709	4373.26978	0.00023	0.02067	90.39961	0.01106
35	420	92.34492	8431.83906	0.00012	0.01083	91.30810	0.01095
40	480	176.27321	16179.06553	0.00006	0.00567	91.78403	0.01090

Monthly compound interest tables (15%)

Year	Month	Amount of one	Amount of one per period	Sinking fund factor	Present worth of one	Present worth of one per period	Partial payment
	1	1.01250	1.00000	1.00000	0.98765	0.98765	1.01250
	2	1.02516	2.01250	0.49689	0.97546	1.96312	0.50939
	3	1.03797	3.03766	0.32920	0.96342	2.92653	0.34170
	4	1.05095	4.07563	0.24536	0.95152	3.87806	0.25786
	5	1.06408	5.12657	0.19506	0.93978	4.81784	0.20756
	6	1.07738	6.19065	0.16153	0.92818	5.74601	0.17403
	7	1.09085	7.26804	0.13759	0.91672	6.66273	0.15009
	8	1.10449	8.35889	0.11963	0.90540	7.56812	0.13213
	9	1.11829	9.46337	0.10567	0.89422	8.46234	0.11817
	10	1.13227	10.58167	0.09450	0.88318	9.34553	0.10700
	11	1.14642	11.71394	0.08537	0.87228	10.21780	0.09787
1	12	1.16076	12.86036	0.07776	0.86151	11.07931	0.09026
2	24	1.34735	27.78808	0.03599	0.74220	20.62424	0.04849
3	36	1.56394	45.11551	0.02217	0.63941	28.84727	0.03467
4	48	1.81536	65.22839	0.01533	0.55086	35.93148	0.02783
5	60	2.10718	88.57451	0.01129	0.47457	42.03459	0.02379
6	72	2.44592	115.67362	0.00865	0.40884	47.29247	0.02115
7	84	2.83911	147.12904	0.00680	0.35222	51.82219	0.01930
8	96	3.29551	183.64106	0.00545	0.30344	55.72457	0.01795
9	108	3.82528	226.02255	0.00442	0.26142	59.08651	0.01692
10	120	4.44021	275.21706	0.00363	0.22521	61.98285	0.01613
11	132	5.15400	332.31981	0.00301	0.19402	64.47807	0.01551
12	144	5.98253	398.60208	0.00251	0.16715	66.62772	0.01501
13	156	6.94424	475.53952	0.00210	0.14400	68.47967	0.01460
14	168	8.06056	564.84501	0.00177	0.12406	70.07513	0.01427
15	180	9.35633	668.50676	0.00150	0.10688	71.44964	0.01400
16	192	10.86041	788.83260	0.00127	0.09208	72.63379	0.01377
17	204	12.60627	928.50137	0.00108	0.07933	73.65395	0.01358
18	216	14.63278	1090.62252	0.00092	0.06834	74.53282	0.01342
19	228	16.98507	1278.80538	0.00078	0.05888	75.28998	0.01328
20	240	19.71549	1497.23948	0.00067	0.05072	75.94228	0.01317
21	252	22.88485	1750.78785	0.00057	0.04370	76.50424	0.01307
22	264	26.56369	2045.09527	0.00049	0.03765	76.98837	0.01299
23	276	30.83392	2386.71394	0.00042	0.03243	77.40546	0.01292
24	288	35.79062	2783.24935	0.00036	0.02794	77.76478	0.01286
25	300	41.54412	3243.52962	0.00031	0.02407	78.07434	0.01281
26	312	48.22253	3777.80202	0.00027	0.02074	78.34102	0.01277
27	324	55.97451	4397.96112	0.00023	0.01787	78.57078	0.01273
28	336	64.97267	5117.81360	0.00020	0.01539	78.76871	0.01270
29	348	75.41732	5953.38562	0.00017	0.01326	78.93924	0.01267
30	360	87.54100	6923.27961	0.00014	0.01142	79.08614	0.01264
35	420	184.46475	14677.18016	0.00007	0.00542	79.56631	0.01257
40	480	388.70069	31016.05477	0.00003	0.00257	79.79419	0.01253

Index

Appraisal, 85
Appraisal form, 133-36
Appraisal process, 77, 86-91
Appraisal techniques:
   cost, 89, 126-33
   income, 90, 140-71
   sales comparison, 89, 116-26
Appraiser, 25
Appreciation, 235
Area analysis, 91, 95
Area regulation, 42
Asking price, 295
Assessed value, 628
Assessment, 47, 630
Assignment, 401, 502
Assumption (equity buy), 468, 538
Assumption contract, 468, 470, 527
Attachment (to define a fixture), 8
Attachment, landlord's, 416
Attorney's opinion, 598
Attribute analysis, 56

B

Balloon note, 523, 538
Band-of-investment technique, 160-64
Bargain and sale deed, 601
Basic rate of interest, 159, 160
Before-tax cash flow, 243-45, 250
Binder, 589
Blanket mortgage, 501, 556
Blockbusting, 335
Bond:
   termite, 606
   for title, 546-47
   mortgage-backed, 571, 572
Breach, 295
   of lease covenants, 412-13
   of listing agreement, 295
   of sales contract, 374-76
Breakeven ratio, 247
Building area ratio, 525
Building (construction) code, 41, 44, 71
Bundle of rights, 15, 119
Business risk, 238
Buydown mortgage, 497, 500, 501
Buyer's market, 193

C

Capital:
   gain (loss), 267, 283
   gain deferral, 268
   gain exclusion, 268
   gains tax, 267, 283

improvement expenditure, 152
   recovery, 159
   recovery rate, 159, 165
Capitalization, 159-69
Capitalization rate:
   definition, 141, 159
   derivation, 159-69
Cash flow:
   after-tax, 280
   before-tax, 234
Certificate:
   of eligibility, 474, 486
   estoppel, 502, 527
   mortgage-backed, 571, 572
   of occupancy, 71
   pass through, 571, 573
   of reasonable value (CRV), 471
   of title, 598
   torrens, 598
Circular flow of income model, 213
Civil Rights Act (1968), 334
Clauses, in commercial lease:
   abandonment,
   agreement on competitive space, 428
   assignment, 435
   breakdown, 431
   condemnation, 435, 444-45
   damage and destruction, 435
   fixtures, 430, 435
   holding over, 436
   hours-of-business, 431-32
   improvements by tenant, 430
   landlord's right to mortgage the property,
     436, 439
   landlord's right to relet the space, 436
   landlord's right to relocate tenant, 430-31
   maintenance and repair, 434, 435
   merchandise-inventory, 431-32
   nondisturbance, 441
   option to purchase, 442-44
   recapture, 426
   rent payment schemes, 425-29, 434
   repairs by landlord, 434
   repairs by tenant, 435
   right of redemption, 445
   signs, 432, 436
   subletting, 435
   subordination of future mortgage, 440
   tenant's right to mortgage leasehold, 442
   term, 429, 434, 436
   utilities, 432, 434
Clauses, in deed:
   granting clause, 601, 602
   habendum, 601
   warranty convenants, 601
Clauses, in deed of trust (*see also* Clauses, in
     mortgage):
   power of sale, 463
Clauses, in mortgage and deed of trust:
   acceleration, 458, 460
   application of payment, 455, 457

Contract: *(cont.)*
  net listing, 312
  nonperformance of, 372
  open listing, 311
  performance of, 370-74
  real estate sales, 348-82
  subordination, 502
  unenforceable, 349
  unilateral, 350
  valid, 349
  void, 349
  voidable, 349
Contract rent, 142
Conventional level (constant) payment, 498
Conventional loan, 471
Conveyance, 596, 601
Co-ownership, 12
Corporation, 516
Cost approach, 89, 126-33
Cost of capital, 250
Costs:
  replacement, 127
  reproduction, 127
Counselor, real estate, 29
Courtesy, 11
Covenants (in the deed):
  against encumbrances, 602
  of further assurance, 602
  in a mortgage, 455
  nonuniform in a mortgage, 458-59, 460-61
  of quiet enjoyment, 602
  of seizin, 601, 602
  uniform in a mortgage, 455, 457-58, 460
  of warranty, 602
Credit:
  conditions, 185, 222
  demand for, 573, 577
  supply of, 573, 577-78
  tax, 266
  union, 565
Credits (settlement), 635
Cumulative use zoning, 70

D

Damages:
  compensatory, 375
  liquidated, 365, 375
  nominal, 365, 375
Data:
  general, 91-100
  site specific, 100-112
Date of assessment, 629-30
Debiting factor, 488, 522
Debits (settlement statement), 635
Debt:
  funds, 451

service, 151, 220, 452
service coverage ratio, 246, 524
Declining balance depreciation methods, 272-78
Deductions (annual itemized), 264-65
Deed:
  bargain and sale, 601
  definition, 600
  grant, 601
  quitclaim, 601
  reconveyance, 463
  sheriff's, 601
  special warranty, 601, 602
  of trust, 461, 464-67
  warranty, 601
Default, 480
  by the buyer, 645
  insurance, 480
  on the mortgage, 458, 527
  in prior payment clause, 527
  by the seller, 646
  by tenant, 416
Default ratio, 247, 524
Deficiency judgments, 463
Delayed closing date, 547
Delivery of possession, 396-97
Demand:
  for credit, 576
  definition, 60, 178
  economic and demographic factors, 178-86
Depository Institutions Deregulation and
        Monetary Control Act (DIDMCA), 502,
        568, 579
Depreciation:
  accelerated, 271-78
  component, 275-76
  declining balance, 272
  guidelines, 258-59, 276-77
  methods, 271
  recapture, 283-84
  straight-line, 271-72
  techniques, 269
Design study, 210-11
Developer, 31
Direct prospecting, 327
Direct regulations, 67
Disaggregation, housing market, 175-76
Discharge of contract, 370-72
Discount, 575-76
Discrimination, 310
Disintermediation, 567-68
Disposable income, 184
Dispossession proceedings, 412
Distraint, 416
Distress, 416
Division of twos, 341
Dower, 11
Downpayment, 452
Dual agency, 294
Due on sale clause, 459, 460, 467, 471, 475
Dull market, 191, 192
Durability, 17

G

GAP Financing, 520
GARN-St. Germain Act (1982), 503, 568
General contractor, 34
General data, 88, 91-100
General partnership, 515-16
Geographic features of the site, 95, 105-9
Geological features of the site, 95, 105-9
Good Faith Estimate of Closing Costs, 474, 477, 611
Good title, 597
Governmental factors and features:
  in area analysis, 93-94, 99
  in neighborhood analysis, 99
  in site analysis, 101
Governmental survey, 102
Graduated equity mortgage (GEM), 496
Graduated payment mortgage (GPM),.492, 499
Grantee, 600, 601
Grantor, 600
Gross income multiplier technique, 169-71
Gross profit, 286
Gross rate of return, 248
Ground lease, 433, 540

H

Habendum clause, 601
Habitability, implied warranty, 398-400
Hedge, 574
Hedge against inflation, 213, 237
Height restriction, 42
Highest and best use, 54, 111
Holdback (retainage), 520
Holding period, 256
Holding period analysis, 256-57
Homeowner's:
  basic property insurance, 590
  broad form, 591
  comprehensive form, 591
  warranty (HOW), 591
Housing and Community Development Act (1977), 492
Housing and Urban Recovery Act (HURRA) of 1983, 475, 503
Housing (occupancy) code, 41, 45, 72
Housing inventory method, 208, 216-17

I

Impossibility of performing, 372-74
Improvement:
  analysis, 109

definition, 6
on-site, 7
on-the-land, 6
to-the-land, 6
valuation techniques, 127
Improvement expenditures, 266, 282
Income:
  actual gross, 141
  current, 184-85
  disposable, 184-85
  effective gross, 148
  household, 184-85
  nominal, 184-85
  net operating (NOI), 153
  potential gross, 141
  real, 184-85
  real disposable, 180
  taxable, 278
Income analysis, 141-49
Income appraisal:
  analysis, 140-71
  compared to investment analysis, 240-42
Income approach, 90, 140-71
Income participation loan, 551
Income risk, 238, 249-55
Income tax concepts:
  adjusted basis, 267, 271, 282
  capital gain, 267, 283
  capital gains tax, 283
  depreciation guidelines, 276-77
  depreciation recapture, 282, 283
  depreciation techniques (methods), 269, 271
  effective tax rate, 279
  exchange, 85-86, 548
  installment sale, 286, 543-44
  marginal tax rate, 279, 280
  minimum tax, 266, 284-85
  salvage value, 270
  tax deferral techniques, 285-87, 548
  taxable income, 278
  useful life, 269
Independent contractor, 325
Indirect prospection, 328
Indirect regulations, 67
Installment note, 454
Installment sales, 286, 543-44
Insurance:
  default, 480
  hazard, 151, 590
  liability, 393-94
  mortgage, 481
  property, 151, 590
  title, 588, 598-99
Interest rate risk, 239
Intermediate theory of the mortgage, 455
Intermediation, 567-68
Internal rate of return, 255-56
Investment:
  analysis, 231-62
  compared to income appraisal, 240-42
  decision (after tax), 281

Property management agreement or contract, 390
Property manager:
  characteristics, 388
  definition, 29
  professional designations, 389
  services, offered, 29
Proprietary power, 67-68, 73
Prorating, 627
Proration clause, 365
Psychological factors affecting investment, 238
Purchase money mortgage, 454, 541
Purchasing power, 60, 184, 223
Purchasing power risk, 229
Pyramiding, 237
Pyramid zoning, 70

Q

Qualifying the buyer, 328
Quantity survey method, 128
Quitclaim deed, 601

R

Racial steering, 335
Rates of performance:
  disadvantages, 248
  future period ratios, 249
  initial period ratios, 245
Ratios:
  building area, 525
  debt service, 524
  default, 524
  financial, 524, 525
  land-building, 525
  loan-to-value, 524
  stabilized vacancy, 525
  technique, 218
Real disposable income, 184
Real estate:
  agent, 21, 294
  business, 18
  commission, 21, 296
  components, 5
  counselor, 29
  definition, 5
  developer, 31
  equity investment, 232
  lender, 24, 469, 517, 561
Real estate investment trust (REIT), 515
Real Estate Settlement Procedures Act (RESPA), 477, 614
Real income, 184
Reality of consent, 356-59
Real property, 9
Real property taxes, 628
Realtor, 21

Realtor-associate, 21
Recission, 374-77
Refinancing, 452
Reflexive statement, 333
Remedies for breach, 374-77
Renegotiable rate mortgage (RRM), 491
Rent payment by tenant, 395
Rent payment schemes, 425-30
Rent with option to buy, 547
Repair expenditures, 265
Replacement costs, 127
Reproduction costs, 127
Reserves for replacement, 152
Restrictive covenants, 51
Retainage (holdback), 520
Return of the investment, 159, 272
Return on the investment, 159, 272
Revenue characteristics, 144-49
Revenue sources, 142-44
Right of entry, 403
Right of redemption, 445, 461
Rights of ownership, 5, 41
Risk, 238-39
Role playing, 324

S

Sale-leaseback, 437, 539
Sales comparison approach, 89, 116
Salvage value, 270
Sandwich lease, 540
Satisfaction, 371
Savings and loan association, 562
Secondary mortgage market, 569
Second mortgage, 526, 538
Second (junior) mortgage, 544
Sector model, 79
Security deposits, 404
Seller financing, 453
Seller's market, 193
Selling agent, 297
Sensitivity analysis, 256
Settlement agent, 608
Settlement statement, 637
Shared appreciation mortgage, 497
Sheriff's deed, 601
Sinking fund factor, 253
Site:
  analysis, 100
  data, 100
  development standards, 70
  specific determinant of value, 100 (*see also* Specific data)
  valuation, 126
Situs, 18
Size of household, 183
Social factors or features:
  in area analysis, 92
  in neighborhood analysis, 94